Captain Sam Grant

BY LLOYD LEWIS

Myths After Lincoln

Chicago — the History of Its Reputation
   (*with Henry Justin Smith*)

Sherman, Fighting Prophet

Jayhawker
   (*with Sinclair Lewis*)

Oscar Wilde Discovers America
   (*with Henry Justin Smith*)

John S. Wright, Prophet of the Prairies

It Takes All Kinds

Granger Country: a Pictorial Social History of the Burlington
   Railroad
   (*Edited with Stanley Pargellis*)

Captain Sam Grant

—

U. S. Grant, 1843, as Brevet Second Lieutenant,
Fourth Infantry — His First Commission

CAPTAIN
SAM GRANT

by Lloyd Lewis

LITTLE, BROWN AND COMPANY

Boston   Toronto   London

FIRST PAPERBACK EDITION

Material from Horace Porter's *Campaigning with Grant* is used by permission of Appleton-Century-Crofts, Inc.; from John Eaton Grant's *Lincoln and the Freedman* by permission of Longmans Green & Co., Inc.; from Charles Winslow Elliott's *Winfield Scott, the Soldier and the Man* (Copyright 1937) by permission of The Macmillan Company; from Hamilton Basso's *Beauregard the Great Creole* and from D. H. Maury's *Recollections of a Virginian in the Mexican, Indian and Civil Wars* by permission of Charles Scribner's Sons.

LIBRARY OF CONGRESS CATALOGING-IN-PUBLICATION DATA

Lewis, Lloyd, 1891–1949.
  Captain Sam Grant / by Lloyd Lewis. — 1st pbk. ed.
    p. cm.
  Originally published in 1950.
  Includes bibliographical references and index.
  ISBN 0-316-52348-8
  1. Grant, Ulysses S. (Ulysses Simpson), 1822–1885. 2. United States — History — War with Mexico, 1845–1848. 3. Generals — United States — Biography. 4. United States. Army — Biography. I. Title.
E672.L48 1991
973.6'092 — dc20
[B]   90-27738

10 9 8 7 6 5 4 3 2 1

MV-PA

Published simultaneously in Canada by Little, Brown & Company (Canada) Limited

PRINTED IN THE UNITED STATES OF AMERICA

To Kathryn

Contents

Captain Sam Grant

CHAPTER ONE

"Somewhere, Where There Are Girls"

J ESSE GRANT AWOKE.
It was his twenty-fifth birthday. Through the window of the
inn where he roomed he could see the village stirring after
the long winter night. Axes were ringing in back yards where firewood was being split for the day. Cabin doors slammed as shivering
boys dashed out and ran back with kindling.

Chimney smoke rose in wavering spirals that were white against
the dark forest that ringed the Ohio frontier village. Small windows
in the log cabins or the little frame houses began to glow as
women, inside, raked ashes off chunks that had smouldered in the
fireplace all night, and threw on enough chips to start a blaze. In
houses too poor to afford candles, the women, holding shawls
around their shoulders with one hand, touched long splinters to the
fire and carried the little flame to the kitchen table where rags,
floating in dishes of oil, began to burn.

Powder horns clanked against rifle barrels as men, belting bear-
skin coats about them, clumped off down the village road toward the deer trails in the woods. From barns came the voices of
loggers, talking to horses while they threw hay and corn into
troughs.

Jesse Grant got out of bed and said to the man who had slept
beside him that he wouldn't be working in the tannery today. Today was Saturday, the twenty-third of January, 1819 — Jesse's
twenty-fifth birthday — the day he had set aside, ten years before,
as a milestone in the schedule of his life.

Jesse had to explain this, for his bedfellow was his employee and,
as such, accustomed to the tremendous pace Jesse had set ever
since he had come to this village of Ravenna, two years before:

"I always promised myself a wife at twenty-five, if I should have
the means to support her. Now I have the property, but I don't

know where to look. However, before going to bed, I'll make a start in some direction." [1]

He had been figuring up his property — a half interest in the tannery and the leather which he and his partner, John F. Wells, had curing in the sheds. He was worth $1500, which probably made him the richest man in the village, richer than any of the store-keepers or lawyers or blacksmiths in this, the seat of Portage County.

His bedfellow saw that he meant what he said when, instead of putting on his rough clothes, he crawled into his Sunday suit. De-termination was all over him — in the thin lips that slit his pink face, in the forward thrust of his high, stooping shoulders, in the sharpness of his small, nearsighted eyes peering out through spec-tacles from between his heavy brows and his high cheekbones.

Jesse went out of the inn across to the tannery, gave orders for the day and then came back. He was walking up and down in the main room of the inn, thinking deeply, when his landlady saw him. She stopped. The young man was usually bending his six feet for-ward, talking voluminously to someone. Here he was, silent, not at work, and in his Sunday suit, too!

"What are you thinking about so seriously?" she asked.

"About looking for a wife."

"Where are you going to look?"

"Well — I don't know — somewhere, where there are girls." [2]

Then he went on walking and studying. His life had been too hard for him ever to have been a beau. Raised in the wilderness, he had been earning his own living ever since he had been eleven. He had taught himself to read and write and cipher long before he had had his first and only schooling, two winter terms of three months each. What he needed was grammar so that he could write better articles for the newspapers. He had sharp, pointed opinions on local and national politics, gained from devouring every news-paper and book that came his way, and from talking spiritedly with people. He wanted to get into politics.

He must get ahead and, now that he was ready for marriage, he understood better than ever before what a good wife could mean to a man. It had been his mother who had held their family to-gether; when she died he and his six brothers and sisters had been forced to make their own way or to find homes with neighbors or relatives.

Up to that tragic day, April 10, 1805, when she had died in their cabin at Deerfield, the next township to the east, Jesse had, like most small boys, taken his mother for granted. Then when she was gone, he had been old enough to begin realizing that it had been she, the Irish girl, and not his father, the man of Scotch descent, who had managed things. Her shrewdness and industry had stretched the money her husband earned cobbling shoes and raising crops as they moved from frontier to frontier, ever westward. So long as she had lived, everything had seemed comfortable, but without her it became apparent how shiftless and bibulous his father, Captain Noah Grant, had been. What had seemed adventurous and romantic was revealed as restlessness and improvidence.[3]

For the first five years of Jesse's life they had lived in a clearing on the wooded banks of the Monongahela River in Westmoreland County, Pennsylvania, twenty miles above the trading post of Pittsburgh. A short, dark-haired man who talked picturesquely, Captain Noah told stories about the Revolutionary War, in which he had served more than six years. He had not told enough history, however, to give Jesse any idea, at the age of five, who George Washington had been. At least, in December 1799, when Jesse had seen his mother weeping one day, and had asked why, she had explained, "George Washington is dead."

"Was he any relation of yours?" the little boy had asked.[4]

Captain Noah told how his own father, also named Noah, and his uncle, Solomon, had been killed fighting the French and the Indians in an earlier war, and how his ancestors, for five generations back, had been sturdy farmers, town officials and church people in Connecticut. They had all stemmed from Matthew Grant, who had arrived in Massachusetts on a ship from England in 1630.[5]

Captain Noah had come out of the Revolutionary War with a captaincy, an appetite for liquor and a wife, Anna Buell Richardson, a widow whom he had married while on furlough. He had tried to settle down to farming and cobbling in the Connecticut Valley and to close his ears to the drum-drum-drumming of emigrant feet — particularly his old comrades' feet — on the trails that led over the mountains to new lands, more adventure and a wild, free life again. Little by little he had lost the property his Uncle Solomon's will had left him — real estate that should have fixed him for life.[6]

For seven or eight years he had held out against the westward urge; then his wife died. He broke up the home, sent the elder of his two sons, Solomon, aged eleven, to live with his Buell grandparents, and, with his second son, Peter, aged nine, struck out for the Monongahela, sometime between 1789 and 1791. There he had married again, March 4, 1792, a settler's daughter, Miss Rachel Kelly and, bringing her to his cabin, began adding babies more rapidly than acres. Nine months and three days after the wedding Rachel bore him a daughter, Susan, and thirteen months later, a son, Jesse Root, named for an admired Chief Justice of the Connecticut Supreme Court; fourteen months after that, another daughter, Margaret; twenty-six months later, a boy, Noah B.; then, in nineteen months, a boy, John Kelly; in another nineteen months a boy, Roswell, and then in eighteen months, on September 10, 1802, the last child, Rachel. How many more she would have borne was a question never to be answered, for in nineteen months she was dead.[7]

In eleven years she had produced seven babies, while managing her household and moving twice with her "do-less" husband and her flock to new cabins on the rough frontier. Wherever they had lived, the story was always the same — Indians trading skins with her husband and drinking with him. Everybody liked Captain Noah; he was well educated yet apparently untroubled that he should be bringing up children in the wilderness where there were no schools.[8]

Jesse's lack of education had not troubled him in his younger boyhood. His first five years had been along the Monongahela where adventure was constant — friendly Indians bringing down from the mountains hides and tales of big hunts, the river alive with canoes or with keelboats and flatboats carrying the settlers' potatoes, venison or distilled whiskey down to Pittsburgh, white hunters coming into the Grant home to have shoes made.

It had also been fun for Jesse, at five, to find his father, at the age of fifty-one, romantic enough to load the whole family, their horse, two cows, skillets, spinning wheel and all, onto a flatboat for a westward move. They drifted down to Pittsburgh, out into the

Ohio River and on down 45 miles to Fawcettstown, Ohio. For another five years they had squatted there, where a half dozen log houses huddled. Captain Noah was waiting for certain lands that had been ceded by Connecticut to be opened up in the new State of Ohio.[9]

Baby brothers and sisters had kept coming so fast that in 1802 Jesse's half brother, Peter, announced that, since he was so soon to be twenty-one, he thought the time had come for him to make his own career. The family saw him off down the Ohio, and, in time, heard that he had set up a tannery of his own at Maysville, Kentucky, not far from the metropolis of Cincinnati, where as many as 500 people were said to live. By the autumn of 1804, Peter had progressed to the point where he was taking apprentices "to learn the mystery of shoe and boot maker." Word came to Captain Noah, too, about his first-born, Solomon. He learned that the boy had, at twenty, sailed to British Guiana to be an overseer on a sugar plantation, but his grandparents in the East had not heard from him since 1798, and supposed him to be dead.[10]

Jesse had been ten when his father, hearing that the new lands, called the Western Reserve, were now open to settlement, moved his family forty miles west through the woods to Deerfield Township in Portage County. Another cabin, another struggle, another year of it and Jesse's mother died. Captain Noah, at fifty-seven, behaved as he had at forty when his first wife had died: he broke up his home. The two oldest children, Susan and Jesse, thirteen and eleven, set out to make their own way in the world; the next three in age, Margaret, Noah B. and John Kelly, found homes with neighbors and relatives, while the captain with the two youngest, Roswell and Rachel, found refuge with Peter, who was getting rich at Maysville operating a tannery and selling salt.[11]

For three years Jesse, working for his board and keep among farmers in the general vicinity of his broken home, had, at fourteen, been lucky on the farm of George Tod, near Youngstown, twenty-five miles west of Deerfield: he met, in Mrs. Tod, an angel. In years to come he could not speak of her without a quaver in his voice. "She was the most admirable woman I ever knew." Although he had lived with the Tods only two years — from 1808 to 1810 — it was long enough to give purpose and direction to his life. Here were people who cared about his future. With George Tod away from home much of the time, serving as a judge of the Ohio Supreme Court, the strong Grant boy worked the farm; but in the evenings Mrs. Tod saw that he had books to read and encouraged him to learn a trade that would be more profitable than farming. There was money in tanning. She wanted her own son, David, to grow up to learn a trade too — blacksmithing perhaps.[12]

The Tods arranged for Jesse to enter his first school and to have clothes that he would not be ashamed to wear. They fitted onto him a suit that the Judge no longer needed, and they paid him wages that enabled him, for the second winter term, to blossom out in "store clothes" of his own. So marked was Mrs. Tod's influence on him that in after years it was said that she "had brought him up." [13] In her home he had his first vision of what wealth might mean. Not rich themselves, having come West to seek their fortunes, the Tods nevertheless had dishes of china and spoons of silver, whereas Jesse had only seen those of pewter and wood.

Sitting down by the fireplace to eat mush and milk on his first night in this new home, Jesse had stared at the dish and spoon.

"What are the spoons made of?" he had asked little David, the three-year-old who had come up to sit beside him.

"Silver."

"What are the bowls made of?"

"China."

"What did they cost?"

"I don't know, I'll go and ask Mother," and David ran into the other room, returning with the word, "Eighteen dollars." The enormity of the sum had not stumped Jesse; he had promised himself that he would have spoons and bowls like that someday.[14]

As a new world opened to him, Jesse drew up a program — one that would reverse his father's course. Where his father had started with property and lost it, Jesse, starting with nothing, would, he swore, be rich enough to retire at sixty. He would marry when he became twenty-five and support a wife in a way his father had not.[15]

At sixteen his mind was made up; he was ready to learn the tanner's trade and, telling the Tods farewell, struck off, working briefly in a Deerfield tannery before deciding that he would do better by apprenticing himself to Peter in Maysville. Peter's wife, Pamelia, might sign legal documents with her mark instead of her signature, but she was a helpmate in Peter's march toward wealth and would, in time, bear him ten children. For five years Jesse worked for Peter, toiling by day, reading at night.[16]

Kentucky was already an old state with a culture more mature than that of the Western Reserve. Life in the port of Maysville grew more varied after the first steamboats came in 1812. When the War of 1812 crashed down, Jesse did not go whooping off to kill British as did so many of Kentucky's young men; Jesse stayed with the hides. Whether this was because he blamed army life for his father's faults, or because he would let nothing interfere with his own success program, he did not say in later years when talking of his apprentice days. Nevertheless, by 1815 he had all of Kentucky's enthusiasm for the hero of the Battle of New Orleans, General Andrew Jackson, from neighboring Tennessee, and it was as a champion of blunt, brusque, forthright "Old Hickory" that Jesse returned to northeastern Ohio when, at the age of twenty-one, his obligation to Peter was paid. Later Jesse would say that he had made the move because "I would not own slaves and I would not live where there were slaves and not own them." [17]

The first tannery at which he worked after his return to Ohio was owned by an abolitionist, Owen Brown, who, like the Grants, had emigrated from Connecticut, and who made Jesse one of his large family. While Owen Brown was quietly antislavery, his oldest son, John, a strapping boy of fifteen when Jesse Grant arrived, was outspoken on the subject. Always given to odd and original thoughts, young John had been spurred to this new curiosity by an incident that had happened in 1812.

His father, who had become a beef contractor for the Army during the war, sent John with cattle to various forts, and on one of these trips the landlord at an inn made much over the boy, toasting him to the other guests as a remarkable youth to be, at the age of twelve, driving wild steers a hundred miles and more from home singlehanded through the forests. Pondering these compliments, John began to compare himself with a Negro slave boy of his own age whom this same landlord beat with an iron shovel and housed in an unheated hovel in the coldest weather. What hope was there for slave children who had no fathers and mothers to protect them?

Could it be that God Himself was not the father of Negro children too? [18] Living with the Browns for a year or more, Jesse Grant remembered them best of the few tanner families for whom he worked in the region while preparing to go into business for himself.

This chance had come in 1817, when John F. Wells, a tanner at Ravenna, made him a partner.[19] He had poured all his energy into the new job, had prospered, and now, upon his appointed twenty-fifth birthday, stood ready for a wife. But where was the girl? He strode up and down, searching his mind. The clock ticked. Down at the tanyard his men were not wasting time; they were making money. They were working in their leather aprons, not standing around in their Sunday suits.

At last he thought of a girl he might try, one here in Ravenna — Miss Clara Hall. He had met her but once, and that fifteen months ago. It would be a shot in the dark, but the morning was already gone, and by the time he had finished his noon meal he decided to risk it and soon barged in upon the girl. According to the tales told years later, Jesse attempted to conceal from Clara what was on his mind, but was so transparent of manner that she quickly began talking up her first cousin, Prudence, at a great rate. Prudence lived nearby, the daughter of Clara's Uncle Timothy. Jesse must stay to tea and Clara would have Prudence over. Prudence came. Things went well. Jesse escorted her home, found her willing to see him again and thereupon launched a courtship which, within a few months, pledged Prudence to wed him come next October.[20]

His success schedule was running on time, and it stood out in all the greater relief that February of 1819 when he heard from Peter that their father had, on the fourteenth, laid down for the last time the pathetic cobbler's tools with which he had, for so many years, made shoes for his children and grandchildren. Captain Noah, at seventy-one, had died knowing that all of his children were on the road to wealth or "comfortable competency." Susan had been married four years before to Bailey Hudson, a prosperous Ohioan; Margaret had married a Virginia emigrant, John G. Marshall, and was doing well on a farm near the old home in Deerfield Township. The four younger children were in Kentucky or Virginia, guided by the affluent Peter in the paths of prosperity.[21]

That Jesse grieved for his father was not to be doubted, for "family" was always a word full of meaning to him; but it was spring, and the summer of his betrothal, and happiness seemed just ahead. Then, in August, came a calamity — an epidemic of malaria called "ague" swept Ravenna, took him down, and for a year he could not lift a hand to earn a cent. His cash vanished; creditors took his share of the business. Debts began to pile up. His engagement to Prudence Hall was broken off. In January of 1820 he was able to drag himself to Peter's home where he slowly wore out the alternating chills and fevers. By summer he felt strong enough to work. Hearing that a tannery was to be opened at Point Pleasant, a little nest of some dozen houses across the river on the Ohio shore and some thirty miles downstream, he went there in June. Thomas Page, who had built the third house in the hamlet, five years before, was planning to add a tannery to the store and warehouse which he was operating.[22]

Jesse got the job, some neighbors recalling, later on, that he had received a share of the business in exchange for teaching Page's son the arts of the tanyard.[23] Whatever his financial interest might have been, it was only temporary, a step in his march toward a tannery of his own and a girl as good or better than the one he had lost at Ravenna.

As he scraped leather, Jesse kept his ears open for talk of marriageable girls. Thomas Page knew where there were two, back on the farm ten miles inland which he had sold in 1817, when he had moved[24] to Point Pleasant — daughters of the man who had bought it, John Simpson, an immigrant from Pennsylvania — fine family — substantial people — one son besides the two girls — lived on good land near the little crossroads post office at Bantam — back over there away from these steep and gully-cut hills along the river.

Each trip that Jesse Grant made inland, buying hides, he could see how the region was settling up. A rider would come up through the woods to where the road went over one of the gently rolling hills and he would stop and see new islands of brown that had not been there in the green ocean of foliage the last time he had come this way. Axmen had deadened trees, chopping off rings of bark wide enough to make the leaves wither and let the sun in on the patches of corn and tobacco. On some days, especially in winter, a rider would always be within sound of axes popping on the deadened trees like rhythmic woodpeckers, the crash of falling timber, the shouts of ox drivers hauling and rolling the logs into piles for burning, the whoops of children as they threw onto the fires armloads of underbrush that had been grubbed from around the new cabins.

From the hills a rider could see smoke hanging over whole areas where last autumn there had been only haze, and at night a dozen "deadenings" would glow red on the sky. Summer, winter, spring and fall, the fragrance of smoke always hung in the air, newcomers from the East saying that out here it smelled all year round like it did in the fall back home, when leaves were burning in the village streets.

Here and there in the larger clearings were extensive farms and houses of brick instead of logs — establishments like the 600-acre Simpson place. This substantial brick house had been built thirteen years before by Thomas Page, soon after he had emigrated from New Jersey.

The wife-hunting Jesse Grant soon learned that the Simpsons "were very highly respected; people of veracity and integrity," although as a man of inveterate "push" he could not help but observe that they were "not of any particular ambition beyond that of living as independent farmers." Having an endless zeal for genealogy, he must have been disappointed to discover that the head of the family, John Simpson, could not name his ancestors beyond his paternal grandfather. He was surer about his father, also named John, who had been born in the North of Ireland around 1738, shipped to Philadelphia, where on November 25, 1762, he had married Hannah Roberts, presumably Welsh, and the following year gone to farming in Montgomery County near the city. He had fought the British during the Revolution, and had died in 1804. His son, the John Simpson whom Jesse Grant was meeting, had been born on his father's farm in 1767, had married Rebecca Weir of Philadelphia in 1793, and buried her in 1801. A widower with four children, Mary aged seven, Samuel five, Hannah three, and Sarah only a few months old, he had continued on the farm, but four years later had married Miss Sarah Hare of Philadelphia, a woman of thirty-two, whom the neighbors said "became a true mother to his young children." How long the baby, youngest of Sarah's stepchildren, lived was not recorded. Jesse Grant, a great man to be pursuing relationships, never mentioned her as having lived. Her place was taken on December 7, 1805, when Sarah gave birth to Anne.[25]

On the rolling countryside of Horsham Township, north of Norristown, Pennsylvania, the Simpson children grew up with apparently few, if any, thoughts of steprelationships. Under Sarah's management her people, the Hares, were regarded as "cousins" by the children. One of her relatives, Elizabeth Hare, said later that she and Hannah Simpson had been, in and out of school, "like sisters." Elizabeth thought Hannah "an unusually bright woman" with a strong mind "but even-tempered and kindly." Members of the Presbyterian Church of the neighborhood recalled, long afterward, how pretty Mary Simpson had been and how "handsome" her sister Hannah.

The pattern of life became settled for John Simpson. On the death of his father in 1804 he acquired the old homestead and moved in. On a corner of the farm, James Griffith, a blacksmith who married Mary in 1812, set up a shop and, in 1815, made John Simpson a grandfather. But in 1817 "The Ohio Fever," the contagion for emigration, took James and Mary Griffith westward to Bethel in Clermont County, and later that summer John Simpson caught it, too. He sold the old farm, moved his family into a temporary residence and went to Bethel. After a survey of the region he bought the Thomas Page place (600 acres for $6 an acre), went home, and in the autumn, came rolling westward in a Conestoga wagon. His son Samuel in aftertimes liked to recall that journey, 450 miles to the Ohio River — five weeks and three days — camping out — then the transfer to a flatboat at Wheeling, Virginia, and the gliding voyage 200 miles downstream to Point Pleasant, where they landed and moved by wagon across to Bantam.

In the Simpson family the story ran that it had been the removal of his daughter and son-in-law that had prompted John Simpson at fifty years of age to uproot himself and follow on. Probably his wife, Sarah, was in great part responsible, for people who knew her, a little later, remarked her brightness, her imagination and energy.

It was Mrs. Simpson who next to Hannah impressed Jesse Grant when, in 1820 or early 1821, he came calling. Hannah meant romance to him, but Mrs. Simpson could talk to him about the books he read. She had his own eagerness for reading, and was, he later said, "a great student of history." Neighborhood gossip later had it that John Simpson was somewhat less ready than his wife to accept Jesse Grant as the ideal catch for Hannah. The neighbors were themselves surprised that one of the Simpson girls, heirs to a 600-acre farm, should be receiving the attention of a young man hardly yet established in business. But such talk, as Jesse put it, "did me no harm."

Everything about Hannah made her, in Jesse's eyes, the girl for whom he had been searching. He described her later as having been at the time, "a plain unpretending country girl, handsome but not vain." He saw what others in the neighborhood or in Bethel saw — she was a good worker, steady, gentle, patient, immaculately neat and cleanly, "remarkable for good sense, attention to her domestic duties, and serious Christian character, blended with easy manners." "Graceful in manner" one neighbor thought her. And what was even more attractive to so talkative a man as Jesse — amazingly silent. Another relative, in after years, thought her sense of duty "strict" and that "she thought nothing you could do would entitle you to praise . . . you ought to praise the Lord for giving you an opportunity to do it." Her slim figure, above medium height, was always erect, her delicately chiseled brunette face forever composed. Mrs. Simpson told Jesse that, having brought Hannah up, she could say that the little girl "at seven years of age had as much the deportment of a woman as most girls at twenty."

Hannah's devotion to Methodism pleased Jesse, for he had the common desire of males in the West, that their women folks should belong to a church even if they themselves did not. Back in Pennsylvania Hannah had been a Presbyterian but, as her cousin Elizabeth Hare understood, when she settled in Ohio, "there being no churches, only circuit-riding Methodists," she finally took to that church.

However blunt and direct Jesse's suit might be, Hannah listened to it. She was on the brink of becoming an "old maid" — twenty-three her next birthday, November 23, 1821. If Mr. Grant was eccentric, odd-looking, noisy, he was also kind, affectionate and likely to become a good provider. He was doing well at the tannery, his debts vanishing.

Jesse noted how quickly the disapproval of the neighbors was vanishing, too: "As soon as it was seen how I was getting along, I heard no more about it." And in telling, later, the story of his courtship he added dryly, "I suppose there could hardly be a marriage at which somebody would not be surprised." [26]

So, in time, the girl who said only "yes" and "no" to people, said "yes" to Jesse Grant, and they were married in her father's home on June 24, 1821, and went to live in the one-story frame house which Jesse had rented from Lee Thompson, next door to the tannery in Point Pleasant.[27]

As Jesse said, he had not one dollar to his name, but his credit was good.

The house was one of the best in the village, built by Thompson in 1817, a two-room frame building, 16 by 19½ feet in size, its roof steep, its exterior boarded in Allegheny pine, a large chimney rising at the north end. A spacious fireplace in which Hannah cooked dominated the living room; the bedroom at the south was tiny.

One hundred yards down the slope the wide Ohio made a bend so that the bride, looking far up the blue expanse, could see the ships coming and going, and could realize that she was living on one of the great highways of her time.

Her thoughts she kept to herself as she went about her work, so neat, so cleanly a housekeeper, moving more quietly that autumn as she felt a baby growing underneath her apron.

CHAPTER TWO

"He'll Take Care of Himself"

FOR THE FIRST FOUR WEEKS of his honeymoon Jesse
Grant took lessons in grammar.

It was not enough that he, the best writer in the village,
should be called upon to serve as secretary at many of the public
meetings. He must improve the political articles which he kept
firing at the newspapers of the vicinity.[1]

In the evenings he rehearsed speeches for the debating societies
which discussed national affairs in general and, in particular, just
then, the Missouri Compromise, by which statesmen had attempted
in the past year to heal the growing breach between the Slave and
the Free States. Jesse's idol, Andy Jackson, was becoming an issue,
too, and although President James Monroe had been re-elected
almost unanimously that autumn of 1820, the party of Thomas Jefferson was breaking into factions.

Jesse's intensity, coming out brusquely in argument, sometimes
wounded the feelings of his neighbors, but it only served to heighten,
by contrast, their regard for the silent Hannah. Toward her, Jesse
was as kind as he knew how to be, and joined the Methodist Church.

If the smell of dried blood, wet leather and decaying shreds of
flesh followed her bridegroom when he came home from the tanyard, it was less than Hannah might have found in another tanner-
husband. Jesse was a man of self-respect and would have washed
long and hard at the pump before coming back into the house.

Hannah accepted a husband, cooking, scrubbing — and a baby —
as they came.

The dogwood blossoms were gone, the oak leaves were larger
than a squirrel's ear, the corn had been planted between the stumps
and the 1822 season for emigrant flatboats was in full tide when
Hannah took to her bed and Jesse sent for the neighborhood doctor.
It was April 27 when the baby was born — a boy weighing 10¾
pounds.[2]

As Jesse described the event, several of Hannah's family were present and at their suggestion that the baby be named, he had said, "When the mother is well enough we will pay you a visit and on that occasion will name him." His memory, later, was that "in about a month" he had driven Hannah and the baby to Bantam for the ceremony. All the family but Hannah's brother Samuel were present and the discussion commenced. Hannah spoke for "Albert," in honor of Albert Gallatin, the Pennsylvanian whose reputation in national statesmanship, finance, philanthropy and scholarship was so high that it had become fashionable, particularly in the West, to name boys for him. Hannah's sister, Mary Griffith, agreed with her. The other sister, Anne, at seventeen, chose "Theodore" for some romantic reason. Grandfather Simpson said, "Hiram, because it is a handsome name," but Grandmother Simpson, more romantic than any of them, said, "Ulysses" and argued her case strongly, with Jesse proving an ardent second.

Persons familiar with Jesse's shrewdness wondered if he had used diplomacy in bringing his mother-in-law to her choice. At some previous time he had loaned her one of his favorite books, Fénelon's *Telemachus*, in which Jesse had formed admiration, as he said, for "Ulysses, the great Grecian general who defeated the Trojans by the strategy of the wooden horse." He admitted that Mrs. Simpson, in reading the book, had also "taken a great fancy to Ulysses." In his written accounts of the naming, Jesse would merely state that the family council had finally selected "Hiram Ulysses" to please both grandparents, but in conversation he would be understood to say that there had been first a decision to leave the matter to chance. Each relative wrote a name on a slip of paper and deposited it in a hat. Anne, the youngest, did the drawing; it read "Ulysses." Thereupon as Jesse said, he stopped the ceremony and announced "to gratify his father-in-law" that the name would be "Hiram Ulysses." The story in the neighborhood was that a check of the ballots showed Hiram 1, Theodore 1, Albert 2 and Ulysses 2.

With Grandfather Simpson honored, irrespective of the drawing, the father and grandmother calmly proceeded to have their way — the baby was thereafter called by his middle name. "My Ulysses," was Jesse's word for the infant, "a most beautiful child." It's coloring was his — hair reddish-brown, eyes blue, skin pink and white.[3]

All that now remained in Jesse's schedule for success was to have a tannery of his own. He wanted wealth but valued independence still more, and when a regional dignitary, General William Lytle, offered to back him in a tannery at Cincinnati, twenty-five miles downstream, he refused on the grounds that his policy was "a sure thing rather than a large one." [4]

The place for a tannery was back from the river, among the oak forests whose bark supplied the tannic acid which gave the business and craft its name. Leather would be in ever greater demand, for immigrants were pouring down the Ohio and poling flatboats up creeks to find homes inland. The newcomers, mainly from New England and Pennsylvania, were bringing a new jargon, a new talk of money and industry, into counties that had been settled long before by more leisurely Kentuckians, Marylanders and Virginians.

The beauty of the Ohio River and the old Kentucky shore was not for Jesse's eyes as he looked down from Point Pleasant's hill. Poetry was not in his soul, the verse that he wrote for newspapers never going beyond humorous doggerel. It was not the white breasts of steamers gliding against the sunlit current that he saw, nor the long, shivering reflections of the campfires on the rafts that came in at dusk to tie up at the riverbank. He did not warm to the songs keelboatmen sent echoing up the walnut hills as they floated across the pale path of the water-moon. His eyes were straining to see what cargoes passed and how rapidly immigration and trade were mounting. Leather for shoes, boots, harness would be in ever-growing demand.

He had been in Maysville when the first stern-wheeler had passed down the river in 1811, and now steamers raced from Pittsburgh clear to New Orleans in ten days — and came back against the current in only thirty-five. Prosperity for Ohio was only beginning.

Jesse saved his money and looked for a tannery site as sharply as he had looked for a wife. By the spring of 1823 he was ready. For having been, as he said, "not worth a dollar, when I married," he had in two years paid off his debts and saved up $1100, all but $100 of it in silver. In the condition of frontier finances, this made his coin worth at least $1300 in paper money.[5]

Twenty-five miles to the east in the valley of White Oak Creek, a stream that in New England would have been called a river, lay the village of Georgetown which Jesse had been watching with interest since it had been laid out, four years before, as the seat of Brown County. Although it still held scarcely more than the fifteen families that made up the village of Point Pleasant, it would grow faster. Jesse could stand on its hill by the courthouse and gloat over a sea of tanbark rolling in all directions.

If there was a question how he, a Yankee, would get on with the Southerners who dominated the village, he brushed it off. The buildings around the courthouse square were grouped in what was called "the Kentucky style." Tobacco was the main crop of the region. The Georgetowners were probably more Southern than even the people of Maysville, Kentucky, since that port, like others on the Ohio, had become somewhat cosmopolitan in the rush of traffic and emigration from all parts of the East. But if Jesse was a Yankee in ancestry and habit, his idolatry of Andy Jackson showed that he was not narrowly sectional. And if he was an abstemious man moving into a heavily drinking community, he was not bigoted. Jugs of corn whiskey, taken from charred oak casks in cellars, waited at the end of each corn row in fence corners for hoers and huskers. Barrels of it, bearing party labels, stood near polling places on election day. Casks of it were in grocery stores where customers were expected to refresh themselves, tin cups dangling on long strings. It gurgled in glasses and mugs at the American Hotel, a small brick building that had gone up in Georgetown two years before. Wine bottles popped in homes across Brown County, which had become one of the leading grape-producing regions of the state. "Jackson suppers," "Clay suppers" and "Adams suppers" were the excuse for roaring sprees. Every man was expected to do his share of drinking, and unless he got drunk at least three times a year — Washington's Birthday, the Fourth of July and the Anniversary of the Battle of New Orleans — it was said he "could hardly maintain his standing in the community, or in the local churches." [6]

What was reassuring to a Yankee newcomer was that the most popular man in the village was an Easterner too, Thomas L. Hamer, the justice of the peace before whom Jesse appeared on August 23, 1823, to pay fifty dollars for Lot No. 18 on the Georgetown plat.

At twenty-four years of age, Hamer was the coming man of the region; everybody said so; and it was not only to Jesse's advantage, but a compliment to him, that the two should become warm friends. Both were Democrats, Masons, inexhaustible talkers, excited about politics, admirers of Jackson, and fond of writing controversial articles for the newspapers. Hamer would within a year take over the Georgetown *Benefactor* and edit it for some twelve months. But where Hamer's arguments usually captivated, Jesse's often seemed overbearing.

Red-haired Hamer was a natural spellbinder whether on the stump or on a bench by the fireplace. From him poured eloquence, vivacity and a vast friendliness that made listeners forget his homely face. Born in 1800 on a Pennsylvania farm, he had been raised on Lake Champlain where, at the age of fourteen, listening to the thunders of Commander Thomas Macdonough's victory over the British fleet, he had decided to be a warrior some day. The war had ended, however, before he was old enough to get into it, and he had kept on farming, for his family was poor. When his people had moved to Ohio, in 1817, he had left them en route to make his own way and had wound up, a schoolteacher with only one suit of homespun clothes, in Clermont County. Studying law at Bethel, one of the county's older villages, he had moved to Georgetown in 1821. Friendship with Hamer brought Jesse Grant intimacy with the most powerful politician of the region, Thomas Morris, a Pennsylvania emigrant who had been in the Ohio State Legislature almost continuously since coming to Bethel in 1804. It was in Morris's office that Hamer had studied law, and Morris was sponsoring the younger man's career, with only one difference, and that not yet serious, to be seen in their political thinking. Morris was gravitating toward the antislavery cause, while Hamer was not.[7]

Jesse Grant's arrival meant the addition of an industry employing several hands to the growing town. The tanyard rose, three hundred feet east of the town square, at the intersection of Water and Main Cross streets, with its brick currier shop, where the hides were finished and sold, occupying the corner. Behind it lay the more malodorous paraphernalia, the lime vats, called "bates," where hair was loosened on bloody hides, the beam house where experts, laying the wet hides across beams, cut off the loosened hair and adhering flesh, more vats where sulphuric acid soaked out the lime, and still more vats where oak-bark liquor gave "the cure."

Here the hides lay for months, with workmen frequently sprinkling ground oak bark between them. Next they were rinsed, the bark scrubbed off and so to the currier shop to be treated with tallow and fish oil, a process called "dubbing," and at last rubbed soft by hand. In the center of the yard stood a roofless shed, one hundred feet long, where oak bark was corded and, as needed, ground in a mill which any boy could feed so long as he was alert enough to keep his fingers out of the iron grinders in the hopper and duck his head out of the way of the pole which a horse drew in endless circles around the mill.

Through the summer Jesse built a small two-story brick dwelling on Lot No. 264, across the road from his currier shop, and in the autumn of that year, 1823, moved Hannah and the baby over from Point Pleasant.[8]

The baby was Jesse's endless wonderment. Whether it would "take after" him or its mother was the question. Its reddish coloring was his, but its regular features and shyness were hers. In structure it was short and fat, like neither of them. In the spring of 1824, when the baby was nearing its second birthday, an incident indicated that this shyness could disappear under the pressure of a great interest.

A traveling one-ring circus and menagerie came to town. Little Ulysses attended in petticoats. The splendor of the performance came to a climax when a trained pony was put through its paces. Suddenly the ringmaster cried:

"Who will ride the pony?"

Ulysses begged so hard that he was "held on the steed's back, and rode two or three times around the ring, manifesting more glee than he had ever shown before." [9]

A few weeks later there was a sign that the baby might be developing its mother's poise and, perhaps, an unusual nervous system. He was in his father's arms on the village square one day at a public gathering when a town boy, fooling with a pistol, began speculating what the baby would do if the weapon were to be discharged close to its head.

Jesse told the boy to go ahead and try it. "The child has never seen a pistol or gun fired in his life."

Older hands slowly pressed the baby's fingers down on the trigger. The explosion came, but Ulysses did not jump, twitch or start; even his eyelids did not quiver.

"He neither winked nor dodged," said a nervous bystander.

The one funny story the family told about the baby had as much to do with this chronic composure as it did with humor. At three Ulysses, ill with a fever, heard the doctor prescribe a powder for him, and immediately responded by sobbing and wailing, "No, no, no! I can't take powder; it will blow me up." [10]

The baby's trust in horses appalled the neighbors. It was bad enough to see him playing alone in the stall under the bellies of his father's horses, but it was downright frightening to see him crawling among the feet of strange teams which stamped at flies as they stood in the road by the tannery gate, or to see him swinging on their tails so close to iron-shod heels. Yet when the neighbors would rush indoors to warn Hannah she would listen patiently, then quietly say, "Horses seem to understand Ulysses."

Horses fascinated Ulysses and he loved nothing so much as to hold the teams of drivers who halted at the tannery. He would stand there, alone with the horses, not listening when other children called to him to come and play. The minutes would pass. From inside the currier shop would come the excited voices of men arguing. From the little creek would rise the shouts of young bathers or of valiant warriors slaying imaginary Indians, but little Ulysses would be hearing nothing as he stood there with the dust of the road on his petticoats and bare feet, looking up into the patient faces of the horses.

Horses were silent. His mother was silent. Everything would be all right.

The neighbors said that when Ulysses was ill Hannah dosed him with castor oil, "put him to bed and went calmly about her work, trusting in the Lord and the boy's constitution." [11]

Jesse allowed the infant to ride the work horses down to the creek for water at noon and night and glowed with pride to see him, at five years of age, standing on the backs of the trotting animals, balancing himself with the reins.

Confidence was all over the home. The mother had confidence in the Lord, the father had confidence in the son and the son had confidence in horses.

The family was growing. A second boy, named Samuel Simpson

Grant for Hannah's brother at Bantam, was born September 23, 1825, and Jesse added to the home a kitchen lean-to. Money was coming in. The cost of the house had been paid off within a year after it had been built, and Jesse felt able not only to subscribe to newspapers but to assemble a library of some thirty-five volumes. To a neighbor boy, a few years older than Ulysses, it looked "like a mighty big book collection." [12]

With Jesse so interested in education and so convinced that his eldest was a remarkable child, Ulysses found himself in school almost before he was out of petticoats. Jesse would recall the boy as having started when he had been "about four" and Ulysses afterward thought he had been "five or six."

The only school in the village was private — a subscription school supported by those parents who wanted it for their children. Teachers, mainly from the East, started these institutions by passing papers through communities, asking parents to subscribe on the bases of $1.50 to $2 per pupil for a term of thirteen weeks. Equivalent amounts of corn, wheat, flax and tobacco were acceptable if coin was not available. When subscriptions reached a total of $8 or $10 a month and a building was provided, a school would be born.

Jesse Grant was dismayed to find the Georgetown school no better than the one he had attended so briefly, thirty years before. The same single room crowded with pupils ranging all the way from infants to strapping axmen of twenty-one, and buxom girls of eighteen — all reciting the three R's and little else. The teacher, an old gentleman named Barney, was a graduate of a college back East, but Jesse saw that he had "no stamina."

So far as school work went, Ulysses did it as obediently and cheerfully as the chores at home, where he brought in chips for the stove and ran errands. But the enormous amount of whipping that went on astonished him. His parents had never switched him nor, as far as he could ever remember, even given him a scolding, yet here the dust seemed always to be spurting out of boys' coats, and pieces of broken switches flying about the schoolroom. It was all very new and strange; you didn't handle colts that way. And when a firmer teacher, John D. White, replaced Mr. Barney, the number of lickings grew. The switch was in White's hand all day long. "It was not always the same one either," Ulysses would later recall. "Switches were brought in bundles from a beech wood near the schoolhouse, by the boys for whose benefit they were intended. Often a whole bundle would be used up in a single day." [13]

With masculine pride Ulysses would later recall that he had not been "exempt" from the rod, but most of his classmates disagreed. One girl said, "He never whispered like the other boys and the teachers were never obliged to whip or correct him." Another schoolmate recalled that Lyss had been punished once, but the fault was the master's. "Some of the boys attempted to take his knife away from him and the teacher, suddenly coming upon the fracas, ordered Lyss to hand it over." He refused and although the teacher switched him, "he neither flinched, begged nor surrendered, and kept the knife." Some of the pupils remembered him as bashfully sitting on a stump most of the time at recess, watching the others play. He would, however, shoot marbles and take part in snowball fights. George Lyons, who was in school with Ulysses one term, always remembered him as "a bad boy to play teeter with, for when he would be down and the other boy up, Grant would get off to see the other fellow 'caplunk!' " [14]

Skating and sledding fascinated Ulysses and once he came home with feet frozen; he had strapped his skates too tightly. His mother thawed them out in smouldering hay, then bound them in bacon.

Jesse consoled himself with reports that the boy studied well in school, but Ulysses never remembered it so. "I was not studious in habit." A girl schoolmate thought him "not particularly bright, just like the rest of us." [15]

Coaching the boy at home, Jesse was delighted to see him, at six, able to read a life of Washington. That same year Jesse added a two-story front to the house. A daughter, Clara, was born December 11, 1828. The tanyard expanded. Jesse was buying town lots, farm lands near town and a fifty-acre oak forest a mile away to supply his own tanbark. To assure a constant supply of hides, he set up a butchering business as a side line, and to make money out of his horses when there was no wood to haul or corn to plow, he took on general teaming, and, a little later, a casual livery business, driving passengers to nearby towns or from the stage station on the village square to their homes. [16]

It was enough to make the average boy's chest swell with pride to see how the circuit-riding Methodist preachers singled out his father's house when they rode into town seeking fried chicken and a feather bed. A brick house was usually, in Ohio, the home of a well-fixed family, and moreover, the horseback clergy kept posted on which homes, in any community, would best understand their poverty and the honor that was due them.

Little Ulysses' eyes twinkled as, taking the visiting ministers' saddlebags at the door, he heard them order "plenty of oats" for their horses. He noted that they all rode "good horses," too.

When Jesse Grant had embraced his wife's religion he had gone into it as into everything else, "whole hog," a Methodist clergyman later declaring him to have been "a ruling spirit in church affairs . . . serving as Trustee, Steward and class leader." [17] A leader in the church, in Masonry, succeeding Tom Hamer as master of Georgetown Lodge No. 72, and in business, Jesse was keeping up to his success schedule, and to cap the climax his six-and-a-half-year-old son was turning out to be a genius! With his characteristic enthusiasm, Jesse discovered this, all in a flash one autumn day in 1829:

"I had gone away from home, to Ripley, twelve miles off. I went in the morning and did not get back until night. I owned at the time a three-year-old colt, which had been ridden under a saddle to carry the mail, but had never had a collar on. While I was gone, Ulysses got the colt and put a collar and a harness on him, and hitched him up to a sled. Then he put a single line on to him and drove off, and loaded up the sled with brush and came back again. He kept at it, hauling successive loads, all day, and when I came home at night, he had a pile of brush as big as a cabin. He used to harness horses when he had to get up in the manger to put the bridle and collar on, and then turn the half-bushel over and stand on that, to throw the harness on."

To the neighbors little Ulysses was no genius, for all his talents with horses. He was a boy "who never put himself forward," was endlessly generous and painfully honest. Mrs. George B. Bailey, who with her doctor-druggist husband was the nearest neighbor and most intimate friend of the Grants, was very fond of little Ulysses, noting how "exceedingly kind and amiable" he was, and so honest that one day, while playing with her sons, having knocked a ball through her window, he followed it right into the house to assure her that he was already on his way uptown for another pane of glass and would be back in a minute to put it in.[18]

A woman of large heart, Mrs. Bailey did not blame Ulysses when he became innocently involved in the death of one of her sons. For some time her boys had come home asking if their horses were really as thin and slow as Lyss said. They would tell how, when galloping horses down to water, Lyss would plague them about the poorness of their animals. Flashing ahead and balancing himself on one foot, he would laugh back at them. Although they kept astride of their horses and did not imitate his circus technique, they did try to keep up, with the result that one of them was killed when his horse shied, fell and rolled on him.[19]

Another of Ulysses' playmates, Dan Ammen, could have been pardoned for not sharing Hannah's faith that the Lord would always protect her boy. Dan felt that upon at least one occasion he himself had been a better watchman. The two boys had been intimate since Ulysses was seven and Dan nine, fishing, swimming and riding together, striking off bareback on their horses to course the country.

"We were so young," said Dan in later years, "that when the streams were swollen we thought that the fish would be more plentiful." One day they dismounted to examine a stream that rains had turned into a swirling torrent. "A large poplar log that had lodged on the bank, and at an incline extended partly over the water, seemed to offer my young companion a favorable seat from which to throw his line. . . . In a moment his heels were in the air and he plunged head downward into the rapidly flowing muddy water."

Dan raced downstream, "with the celerity of an active boy nine years of age," to a point where willows overhung a narrowing stretch of the river. "As good luck would have it, when my companion came within reach, he was above the surface; I grabbed him and drew him out." What fixed the incident so vividly in Dan's memory was the shirt Lyss was wearing. He had become accustomed to Mrs. Grant dressing her children "with a neatness unusual in the community," but this garment was "a waist of Marseilles cloth" striped gorgeously with red, and buttoned onto the trousers, and it seemed to Dan that it "must be irretrievably ruined from its drenching in muddy water."

Boys of Dan's and Ulysses' age wore full-length pantaloons and tough cowhide boots that were copper-tipped for those whose fathers could afford it, and by fashion so tight-fitting that bootjacks were always kept at the front door. Some of the neighbors said in after years that the home was better furnished than most of the others. Whether Hannah cooked at the fireplace or at a cookstove they did not recall. It would be ten years before cookstoves became common and five years before matches would reach general use. Ohio boys sat in the evenings rolling newspaper strips into long, tight spills with which fire could be carried from the fireplace to the candles or sperm-oil lamps. In the morning when the fire was found dead on the hearth, a boy scurried over to the neighbors' and raced back with blazing splinters.

Hannah's reputation for neatness and cleanliness was won in a house where flies abounded, what with the tannery and the barn just across the street breeding insects furiously. Flies and odors could be checked with lime in the privy behind the house, but not even a man of Jesse's cleanly habits could lime the horse manure in all the barns, the yards and the street where teams stopped at the currier-room door. The dirty street would be a river of mud after a rain or a thaw, with small boys tracking it into the house. But Dan Ammen in later life looked upon Hannah as "a cheerful woman, always kind and gracious to children and, in my eyes was handsome."

He would never forget how Ulysses once told him, in after years, "I never saw my mother cry."

Ulysses and Dan were all the more intimate because their fathers were friends. Both Jesse Grant and David Ammen had quit the South on account of slavery. With his wife, David Ammen had left Virginia and come to Brown County, Ohio, so that their four children would not be brought up in a slaveholder's civilization. On Free Soil he had come closer than Jesse Grant to joining those radical abolitionists who cried for the extinction of slavery all through the nation. It had been to Ripley, the largest town and chief river port of Brown County, that David Ammen had migrated around 1822, and with his family had moved into half of the house occupied by the most famous abolitionist of the region, the Presbyterian preacher, John Rankin, who also had left Virginia because of slavery.

Little Dan Ammen, youngest of the children, had been old enough to see and hear dramatic things in that house, for it stood on a high hill above the town and in its windows candles could be seen from the Kentucky shore, beacon lights for fugitive slaves crossing in boats, or by swimming, or on the ice. One Negro husband and wife had crossed on floating cakes of ice, the woman carrying a baby, while the baffled bloodhounds howled behind them.

The Reverend Rankin's sons said that no runaway slave who reached their home was ever recaptured. Their father religiously refused to entice slaves to quit Kentucky, and merely received and sheltered them, leaving it to his nine sons, armed with revolvers, to spirit the fugitives north over the Underground Railroad toward Canada. The town of Ripley was a hotbed of antislavery workers, very different from Georgetown.

Little Dan's father was a newspaper editor who had brought with him, when he moved from Ripley to Georgetown in 1826, the *Castigator*, which he had started four years before — the first paper published in the county. Jesse Grant wrote political articles and rambling doggerel humor for the *Castigator* and loved to sit in Ammen's office devouring the exchange newspapers as they came in. For a year after the Ammens came to town, Ulysses would look at Dan's idolized brother Jake, twelve years older than Dan, working in the printing office. Then Jake disappeared — gone to West Point to learn soldiering.

In the *Castigator* office, in his own home, and on numerous trips to Ripley, the trading metropolis, Ulysses heard the evils of slavery, but from some of the other Georgetown boys came a different story. The Negroes were better off under slavery. Slaveowners were kind. For example, there was the tale told by the grandchildren of the town's most famous old man, Colonel Robert Higgins, who had died when Ulysses was three. Before the Revolutionary War, Grandpa Higgins, as a planter and cattle drover of Virginia, had once seen a gigantic and oddly tattooed Guinea Negro, "Jack," chained to a pillar of a hotel with his owner standing nearby offering to sell him for forty dollars because he was "vicious." Higgins had asked Jack if he'd be willing to come along and drive cattle. The Negro had looked Higgins over from head to toe, and finally said, "Yes." With that Higgins had bought him, and struck off the chains and led him away. Ever after Jack was faithful, and when

Higgins shouldered a musket and went off to fight the redcoats he told Jack to take care of Mrs. Higgins and the children and the whole plantation. Soon after, Higgins had been captured by the British, and had lain three years in prison at New York, hearing nothing from home. When at length he was released, he hurried back to Virginia. The plantation was prosperous, but his wife had died and Jack had not only managed the place but had cared for the motherless children.[20]

Among Grant's playmates, Carr and Chilton White, two and four years younger than he, leaned to this view of slavery, for their father, the schoolmaster, was a strong Democrat from Virginia.

The White boys, in later years, delighted to tell a great joke on Ulysses, one that everyone in town laughed about. There were two versions of the story, the Whites' and that told by the Walker boys, also playmates of Ulysses.

The rival versions agreed up to a certain point. Ulysses, at eight, coveted mightily a colt owned by a farmer, Robert Ralston, and one day when Ralston appeared at the tannery offering to sell it for twenty-five dollars the boy pressed his father to make the purchase.

Jesse refused, saying the animal was worth no more than twenty dollars. After Ralston had gone, Ulysses had begged so hard that the father had relented, telling the boy to go on and buy it, but to use strategy; maybe it wouldn't be necessary to give the full twenty-five.

According to the White boys, Ulysses had ridden up to Ralston and blurted, "Papa says I may offer you twenty dollars for the colt, but if you won't take that I am to offer you twenty-two fifty, and if you won't take that, to give you twenty-five." Ralston took the twenty-five. Ulysses took the colt and the story was soon tickling the town.

The Walkers' version was that Ulysses, knowing the colt better than did his father, had said "Mr. Ralston, father told me to offer so much for the colt, but he is worth more and I'll give you so much," naming the price he knew the colt was worth. The Walkers said that the whole thing illustrated the boy's good eye and honesty, not his folly, and of the Whites' version, "It makes him stupid, which he wasn't."

Ulysses, telling the story in later years as a comic one, would give it as the Whites told it, adding that this was "nearly true" and that "I certainly showed very plainly that I had come for the colt and meant to have him." Nevertheless, he would point out, the colt had actually been worth much more than twenty-five dollars, as was evidenced by the fact that he had worked it for several years, then sold it for twenty dollars even though it had gone blind. And there might have been a hint of explanation when, in reciting how the story had been preserved by the Whites, he would point out that the Whites had been violent Democrats, whereas his own father, not long after the incident, had deserted the party.

The fact that the story had got out among the boys caused Ulysses, as he liked to recall in later years, "great heart-burning" and "it was a long time before I heard the last of it." However much he in after years stressed his mortification at becoming the town butt at eight years of age, he had been apparently able to bear up at the time without too much difficulty. That same year his father gave him his fondest wish, the regular job of wagon driver, hauling wood day after day, a post which put him far in advance of other boys of his age.[21]

"There would be a man in the woods to load, and another at the house to unload," Jesse boasted, "but Ulysses would drive the team. I never knew a team to balk with him." Moreover, Ulysses' father allowed him the free use of the team for bobsled rides and his popularity rose, as he sat amid screaming bevies of girls coursing the snows, sleigh bells jingling under the horses' bellies and the moon dancing overhead. Girls liked him; he did not use tobacco nor "bad words" as did so many boys. One of them later said, "he was a real nice boy who never had anything to say and when he said anything, he always said it short." [22]

One of Ulysses' intimates, Jimmy Sanderson, three years his senior, said in after years, "He usually went with boys older than himself because he passed for a boy three or four years older than he really was." Below the average of his playmates in general athletic ability, Ulysses nevertheless excelled in those sports which interested him — sports that, in general, demanded no large groups or teams, for his intimates were relatively few. In crowds he was still shy and would fall silent, while in a small circle he was talkative. "In swimming he was quite an expert," Jimmy Sanderson remembered, "and many a time outswam boys larger and stronger than he."

He was growing up fat and strong, even though the fever and "ague" (chills) that haunted the West struck him severely for long spells now and again.[23] By the time he was nine Ulysses had developed what his father described as "the most wonderful faculty for breaking horses to pace," and for taming fractious colts. Always within a few hours — and Jesse saw him do it upon occasion in one hour — the boy could turn a colt into a pacer. So many farmers of the region brought him their animals to train that he grew bashful. People would soon be regarding him, so small a boy, as a professional jockey — a calling held in low regard. Still, he wanted to do what friendly people asked of him, and he kept on at the work, which was itself sheer sport, until a piece of deception gave him a chance to end it. A neighbor came to him one day with a colt, asking in apparent innocence if for two dollars he would ride the horse to Decatur, thirteen miles away, and deliver a letter. Ulysses agreed and, as he started off, heard the owner say, as if it had just occurred to him:

"Oh! I wish you would teach that pony to pace."

In the evening when Ulysses returned, the horse was pacing beautifully, but when he discovered that the letter was only a ruse, he announced that he was done, for good and all, with this thing of training other people's horses.

To break the fractious animals which farmers brought him was, however, a different matter. Here was something far above the hostler's or jockey's role. For all his sedateness and all his modesty, he seemed to the townsfolk to love to break fiery colts on the village square with crowds looking on. He had improvised his own technique for the struggle. Whenever the horse suddenly stopped its plungings and reared, pawing at the sky, the little fat boy dug his bare heels into its flanks and hung on. When it reversed its violence, "swallowed its head" and flailed its hind hoofs at the treetops, he gripped its neck with his short arms and burrowed his toes in behind its shoulder blades.

Jimmy Sanderson saw him "sometimes ride at a breakneck speed, with only a bridle on the horse's head, . . . dashing through the village at a speed that frightened nearly every female, old and young, in the place." It seemed funny to Jimmy to see this done by "one

of the quietest boys I ever knew." Nor did Ulysses shrink when
owners of horses suffering from distemper brought them for him
to cure by the favorite method — a prolonged run at top speed until the heat had burned out the disease.[24]

Basking in the equestrian fame of his small son, Jesse allowed him
to use the teams, now and then, to make money for himself. Rumor
had it in town that the boy, at nine, had bought a horse of his own
with seventeen dollars he had accumulated, and at ten, when his
father had added the livery business to their enterprises, Ulysses
drove passengers to points as distant as Cincinnati.[25]

Jesse was so delighted with his boy's precocity that he seemed
reconciled to the artfulness with which Ulysses evaded work in the
tannery. Jesse had thriftily looked forward to the time when his
elder son could take a hand at the bark mill, yet when that day
arrived and things turned out differently, he felt actually boastful:

"When I said to him, 'We shall have to go to grinding bark,'
he would get right up without saying a word and start straight for
the village and get a load to haul, or passengers to carry, or something or other to do, and hire a boy to come and grind the bark."

Townspeople said that Lyss would cajole other boys into feeding
the hopper for him at a wage of twelve or fifteen cents a day while
he made a dollar or a dollar and a half for himself. He was not above
inveigling girls into substituting for him at the mill. "I detested
the trade," said Ulysses in later years, "preferring almost any other
labor, but I was fond of agriculture, and of all employment in which
horses were used."

He noted that everybody worked, more or less, and that the
people with the most money were those who worked hardest: "It
was only the very poor who were exempt." [26]

Passengers, engaging transportation to distant points, often objected to being entrusted to the hands of so small a boy, and even
when convinced that the youngster was a master of horses, argued
that it was dangerous to have him come back alone through strange
deep forests. Jesse always laughed:

"Oh, no, he'll take care of himself." [27]

The distances which the little fellow drove passengers became
legends in the community and grew to incredible lengths, making
Jesse's accounts seem tame by comparison. One story was that

Ulysses drove two lawyers across the state, more than two hundred and fifty miles by winding roads, to Toledo. Another described how he had hauled a preacher's family with household furniture 200 miles, the preacher reporting to Jesse that he had "never had such a good and silent driver." [28]

It was natural for a boy so curious about travel, new sights and fresh scenery to return from trips by new roads. When, in hunting a destination, he "got past the place without knowing it" he would, as he later said, not turn back but "go on until a road was found turning in the right direction, take that, and come in by the other side." This habit was, he later concluded, a superstition, a strange dread of retracing his way. [29]

No thought of danger apparently troubled him in the far country where highwaymen on dark wilderness roads were not unknown; nor did he have the average country boy's timidity in large cities. When delivering passengers in Cincinnati, he put up at the best hotel, the Dennison House, where he became friendly with the landlord's son, William Dennison, seven years older than himself. Before starting home, Ulysses would search around town for passengers — a resolute businessman of ten. [30]

On the Fourth of July, when all the other boys of Georgetown were wild with excitement all day long, little Ulysses went through the shooting with them cool as a cucumber. "He was up to any lark with us," said Jimmy Sanderson, "but went about everything in such a peculiarly businesslike way." Jimmy noted that Lyss "always seemed to be thinking, and to take things that excited us — so easy. I don't remember that I ever saw him excited."

The whole town grew accustomed to seeing Ulysses ride trick horses with complete gravity when circuses came to town. His father said that it was a regular practice for Lyss to emerge from the audience when the ringmaster would call out:

"Will any boy come forward and ride this pony?"

The ponies were trained to unseat their riders with sudden stops and starts, artful bucks and abrupt wheelings, but the townsfolk grew accustomed to Ulysses' victories. Jesse, one day, saw him defeat all such maneuvers of a horse, then manage equally well the added distraction of a large monkey which the ringmaster tossed onto the boy's shoulders. With the horse pitching between his legs, the monkey pulling his hair and scratching his neck, the crowd whooping, "not a muscle of Ulysses' face moved." A few more rounds and the ringmaster gave up.

Jimmy Marshall, Ulysses' cousin from Deerfield, saw Ulysses at a circus refuse to be drawn into the pursuit of a kangaroo, because he "was a plump boy, and not a good runner," but bide his time for the appearance of the trick pony. The boy who would ride this horse would win five dollars. Jimmy saw Lyss sit back, studying the pony's technique as it threw candidate after candidate. It was exceedingly fat and round, "slick as an apple," as Lyss said; but eventually he told Jimmy that he saw how the thing could be done and, leaping aboard, locked his arms around its neck and held on till the clown said All right, all right, here was the five dollars.[31]

Cousin Jimmy was a novelty. He came from "farther off" than Ulysses' cousins on "the Simpson side" who would in time total more than a dozen, distributed among Uncle John and Aunt Elizabeth Griffith Simpson, on the home place at Bantam, and his two aunts and uncles in Bethel. Aunt Anne had married a Pennsylvania farm immigrant, John Ross, and Aunt Mary's husband, Uncle James Griffith, was Bethel's blacksmith.

There was always much talk in Ulysses' ears about his first cousins on "the Grant side," for Jesse had a tremendous interest in his nephews and nieces, a swarm which, in the general fecundity of the Grants, would in time total thirty-nine. As letters came in chronicling births, Ulysses could eventually count thirteen first cousins in Ohio, five at Aunt Margaret and Uncle John Marshall's house and eight more at Aunt Susan's, six by her first husband, Bailey Hudson, two more by her second mate, Henry Grimes. But in the South, across Kentucky and Virginia, he could count twenty-six — ten of Uncle Peter's, five left by Uncle Noah when he died, three of Uncle Roswell's; and Aunt Rachel Tompkins at Charleston, Virginia was producing youngsters at a rate that would soon bring her score to eight.

Although all of these Southern nieces and nephews were in comfortable, if not wealthy, circumstances, Jesse watched over the children of his dead brothers, once, in 1832 or 1833, traveling to Connecticut to recover for them an inheritance that had been lost through a legal error. He retrieved some $3000 for the heirs and could have made it more if he had not taken pity on some poor widows who lived on the property in question and were unable to pay the judgments against them.

What worried him about his young Southern relatives was the life they led, and he probably told them at this period, as he did later on, "that they had depended too much on slave labor to be trained in self-reliance, whereas his children had to wait upon themselves even so far as to black their own shoes." [32]

Family troubles took Jesse to the opposite end of the country in 1832, when word came that the most traveled of his brothers, John Kelly, had died in Texas at the age of thirty-three, possessed of much property. This was the second brother to die young of consumption, Noah having been taken off at twenty-four. Concluding that the disease ran in the family, Jesse worried over the severe spells of fever and ague that occasionally struck Ulysses. In the home of a man as much traveled and widely read as Jesse, it was likely Ulysses received the standard medical treatment, doses of calomel and sassafras tea and quinine when that rare powder could be brought from Cincinnati, and that he escaped the "cures" common among the more ignorant settlers, spoonfuls of human urine, or the wearing of spiders on strings around the patient's neck. Georgetownians like Jesse Grant or Dr. Bailey would have looked with disgust upon the brews of "sheep-turd tea" with which various diseases were fought in some backwoods cabins.

Ulysses was plump and sturdy, and his life in the open air by day would, it was hoped, counteract any weakness in the lungs; but the night air was worrisome, being always damp and cool in so heavily forested a country. Immigrants from the older states always remarked how cool it got when the sun went down. The thick trees shut out the rays from so much of the soil, swamps were so common and water stood so long after a rain.[33]

Ulysses had not accompanied his father on the trip to Texas, a sorry fact indeed, since it had cost him the clear title of the traveling championship among boys of the village. There was no disputing his claim to the title on the basis of number and length of journeys around Ohio and Kentucky, but the Walker boys had been privileged to travel clear to Texas. It was true that their trip to this strange land had been something of a fiasco. Their father, John, had moved his family there, only to turn around and scuttle home as soon as enough money could be raised. Still, the Walker boys had been all that tremendous distance and distance was what counted.[34]

To make matters worse, Ulysses' father had written for a local newspaper so lengthy and enthusiastic an account of his own trip that some townsfolk had laughed behind their hands and the boys had taken to calling Ulysses "Texas." [35]

"Texas Grant! There goes Tex Grant."

True, it was not so uncomfortable a nickname as "Lyssus" or "Useless" and it soon died out. Ulysses shrank from all nicknames. What he wanted to be called was "Hiram." He wrote his name "Hiram U. Grant" all over the flyleaves of his books.[36]

Whatever chagrin lingered from his failure to visit Texas must have been practically wiped out the following year, 1833, in the pleasure that followed, an indirect result of the death of his uncle, John Marshall, at Deerfield. Jesse, hurrying off to settle the estate for his widowed sister Margaret and her five children, took Ulysses along — a great trip up the wonderful Ohio. While his father closed out Uncle John's affairs, Ulysses played with his cousins, John and Jimmy, who were near his own age. And when all the Marshalls came home to Georgetown with him and his father to live, it was exciting indeed.

When their steamer, the *Lady Byron,* halted at Wheeling, Virginia for repairs, Ulysses had a chance to introduce Cousin Jimmy to the ways of the business world. While examining the town the boys were asked by a stranger at a hotel what they would charge to carry his trunk to the wharf, a mile away.

"A fi'-penny bit," announced Jesse's son, and the two boys tugged the trunk, which proved to be surprisingly heavy, the whole distance for the reward of twelve and one half cents.

As if to balance business with recreation, the boys fell to considering what sport could be extracted from a company of odd-looking, funny-talking German immigrants who were on the *Lady Byron* en route to Cincinnati or Louisville. The cousins concluded that the maximum of fun was to be expected from a careful rearrangement of the planks which ran from the boat to the wharf, so they laid their trap and stood back to see which German would be the first to go through into the Ohio River. Their victim, however, turned out to be a three-year-old Teuton in a red flannel dress. Before they could stop him he was in the water and hubbub in the air. Reaching hands caught the baby by the hair as it came up the second time and quiet was restored without the criminals being caught. But their fright was a sharp one and might have prompted the special protectorship Ulysses, as he grew older, would give the younger children of Georgetown.

Jesse could not remember how young Ulysses had been when he "rescued an inoffensive boy, who worked for us, from a trick that a large number of his companions were about to perpetrate upon him." He knew Ulysses had been "quite small" and it had been stirring to see him go to the house and take a gun for self-defense when the angry crowd of baffled pranksters had turned on him.

Cousin Johnny Marshall, who from the age of nine worked in Uncle Jesse's tannery, had his reservations, too, about the unbroken sedateness of Cousin Ulysses. One day Ulysses offered to bet him a half-dozen marbles that he could clear twenty-five feet at one jump if privileged to select his own ground. Cousin Johnny took the bet and was led to a high bluff near the creek where Cousin Ulysses leaped off, winning the wager, but sinking to his waist in soft mud.

What Cousin Johnny remembered more happily were the alcoholic nips to which Cousin Lyss introduced him. These juvenile debauches probably began that summer of 1833, when the Asiatic cholera paralyzed Cincinnati. Fearful that it would spread to Georgetown, the villagers asked Uncle Jesse, as the most widely traveled and experienced man available, to go to Maysville and discover and bring back the most likely preventatives. Cousin John had seen Uncle Jesse return with two bottled cures. One a jug of "Number Six," reputedly the best mixture of drugs, and the other a jug of blackberry cordial, a remedy for diarrhea which accompanied cholera. Side by side in the cellar these demijohns were standing on a subsequent Sunday morning when, with his parents away at church, Ulysses hospitably invited a group of playmates, thirsty from hot acrobatics on the tanbark, to repair to his residence with him and partake of the cholera medicine. Ulysses passed the jug of "Number Six." The boys spat out the sample. He then took down the second antidote, the jug of blackberry cordial, which the boys quickly came to regard with enthusiasm.

"Thereafter," said Cousin Johnny, "we often went down cellar to have a pull at the cholera medicine. I don't know whether we took it right or not, but certain it is that we did not take the cholera." [37]

The year that the Marshalls came to Georgetown, Ulysses was, at eleven, still small for his age, but strong. A schoolmate saw him, in a fight with a larger boy named Mount, receive a brisk scratching on the face for a time, then suddenly twist away and land a resounding kick upon young Mount's buttocks. "That ended the matter," said an onlooker; "Mount gave a tremendous yell, and started for his house, and Ulysses also scampered home at the top of his speed, perhaps afraid of Mount's father." [38]

Ulysses fed the animals, milked the cows and took over all the farm work that could be done with horses.[39] He was falling in love with farming at a time when inventors were hitching horsepower to machinery to make the work lighter. Well-read men like his father used the lighter cast-iron plow which had come into Ohio eight years before, and machinists, within four years, would have a still better one, made of steel. In the last three years, the cradle, a big scythe with long wooden fingers, had made wheat cutting swifter, but it was already shadowed by the talk of a reaper drawn by horses, which an ex-sailor, Obed Hussey, was demonstrating in nearby Hamilton County that August of 1833.

CHAPTER THREE

"No Very Common Head"

WHEN ULYSSES reached the age of twelve, his father believed his precocity was accepted in the region. A series of incidents pointed up the boy's capacities.

First, the performance at the ford.

Ulysses had driven two horses and a two-seated buggy to Augusta, Kentucky, twelve miles away, and, coming home, had picked up two fares, a brace of young ladies who became greatly agitated when they saw looming ahead the White River ford in a roaring flood. Their small driver hunched on the front seat drove straight in. White River came over the spokes until it embraced the passengers' waists. The horses were swimming. The young ladies began shrieking at the top of their lungs. Drowning was upon them.

Ulysses glanced around and, as Jesse told it, merely said "with an air perfectly undisturbed":

"Don't speak! I will take you through safe."[1]

Next, there was the performance with "Dave."

That spring of 1834 Jesse took the contract to build a new Clermont County jail on the Georgetown square, a job that would take seven months, since huge logs must be cut and hauled two miles or more. Ulysses told his father he would do all the hauling if they could buy from a neighbor a certain big, powerful horse, "Dave," which he had long wanted.

"I agreed to do it," Jesse later said, "but without any idea that he could possibly hold out for over a week — he was such a little bit of a fellow. I even hired another man to work the team, and told him to go along with Ulysses, but not to let him know, until the boy was tired out, what he was hired for. The man accompanied him for a number of days, when he came to me and said, 'There is no use in my going with that boy any longer; he understands the team and can manage it as well as I can, and better, too!' "

One noontime Ulysses came home with the team, saying there was no use in going back for another load; the woodchoppers weren't working and he could keep up with their hewing the next day. Jesse asked him how, if there were no men in the forest, he had managed.

"Oh, Dave and I loaded."

"What do you mean?" asked Jesse, thinking how impossible it was for him to have lifted such immense logs onto the wagon.

"Yes," Ulysses answered, "Dave and I loaded. I took a chain and hitched it to the end of the logs and we managed to get them in." He then explained that he had found a tree half felled and lying at a slant up which the logs could be dragged, then slipped off onto the wagon which he had backed underneath.

"This was much talked of in the neighborhood," said Jesse, "as it was considered a great achievement for a boy of his size." The father was especially proud since he, at the age of six, had done practically the same thing on a smaller scale. Riding home from the mill astride a bag of meal, he had fallen asleep and awakened to find himself and the bag on the ground beside the horse. Rolling the sack up a sloping tree he had slid it off onto the horse's back and then, hopping aboard, had "jogged home in triumph."

It would embarrass Ulysses, later on, when his boyhood friend, Isaac N. Morris, son of Jesse's friend, Thomas Morris, publicly recited the "Dave" story and others like it, and told how celebrated they had been in the community. Isaac would proclaim them as evidence that little Ulysses had "an original and uncommon power of adapting measures to conditions" and was "as serious as one mature in years." He thought Ulysses had "a faculty for business, never without some particular purpose in hand, requiring responsibility, perseverance and zeal." When pressed in after times, Ulysses would shyly admit that Isaac's stories of his boyhood were "substantially correct," although "flattering." [2]

All that summer and autumn of 1834, Ulysses hauled logs for the jail, taking only one week off to go to Louisville on legal business for his father. Jesse was waging a lawsuit, back in Connecticut, over the property left by Uncle Solomon, and had been vainly trying to get his lawyers to secure a certain deposition in Louisville.

"I can do it," Ulysses said; so Jesse sent him off alone, equipping him, however, with a letter informing all who might be concerned that the boy had permission to travel. Runaway boys lured by the romantic life on the river kept steamboat captains on their guard. On the return trip, Ulysses found the steamer's captain refusing to let him come aboard until he produced his credentials; then the officer became so intrigued with the self-reliant boy that he gave him his homeward passage free.[3]

Most wonderful of all the demonstrations given by Ulysses that year was, in Jesse's eyes, the encounter with the phrenologist.

This pseudo scientist, the first of his kind to reach Georgetown, had been in the village several days, lecturing and feeling the heads of subjects, and delivering profound predictions as to their futures. As Jesse told it:

"One Dr. Buckner, who was rather inclined to be officious on most occasions, in order to test the accuracy of the phrenologist, asked him if he would be blindfolded and examine a head. This was at one of his public lectures. The phrenologist replied that he would. So they blindfolded him, and brought Ulysses forward to have his head examined. He felt it all over for some time, saying, apparently to himself: 'It is no common head! It is an extraordinary head!' At length Dr. Buckner broke in to ask whether the boy would be likely to distinguish himself in mathematics.

" 'Yes,' said the phrenologist; 'in mathematics or anything else. It would not be strange if we should see him President of the United States.' "

There were townsfolk who reported that the whole thing had been prearranged between Dr. Buckner and the quack as a joke upon Jesse Grant, a burlesque of his fatuous pride in the boy, and that the crowd had guffawed and applauded loudly during the "reading." This version had Jesse beaming with delight over the crowd's ratification of his own belief in his son's talent.[4]

Other versions of the incident, however, made Jesse less ridiculous. It was standard routine for phrenologists to predict the presidency for boys. And it would have been easy for this quack, skilled in collecting information in advance of "readings," to have discovered that the Grant boy had a reputation in arithmetic. Ulysses' schoolmates had always remarked this and, according to one of them, Jimmy Sanderson, his proficiency in "mental arithmetic" had been hard for some of his companions to endure. It was bad enough to have him beat them in figuring problems on his slate, but when the teacher introduced the system of calling out problems and requiring pupils to work out the answers "in their heads," he had shown his superiority even more.

"The teacher used to give us a lot of them, one after another, every other day during the term," said Jimmy in after times. "Most of us hated them and would make all kinds of excuses to get out of the exercises, while young Grant was anxious to have the teacher fire them at him. His mind seemed exactly fitted for solving such problems on a moment's notice. While the majority of us pupils would be just getting the problem settled in our minds Ulysses would shout an answer. That would make the older pupils feel ashamed that such a little fellow was smarter than they were."

Thomas Upham, who taught the village school for two winters when Ulysses was eleven and twelve, recalled later that his "standing in arithmetic was unusually good, but that he had no taste for grammar, geography, and spelling, although he was not noticeably dull in any of these studies." [5]

It was inevitable that some Georgetownians should become eager to hear anything that might show Ulysses to be not so precocious as Jesse Grant was forever insisting. Parents of boys less talked about could take comfort in the thought that Ulysses was stupid except when reciting mental arithmetic or handling horses. His silence, except when with intimates, was so pronounced that some persons who saw him casually felt sure he was backward.

Also, it was hard for other boys not to be jealous when they saw him indulged in his choice of jobs, or starting off in his carriage for distant cities. He was more neatly dressed than most boys, and in his home there was no dancing, no card playing, no wine drinking. He did not swear and in time to come would explain that his reason was that swearing started fights: "When a man flies into a passion his adversary, who keeps cool, always gets the better of him," and furthermore, "it is a great waste of time." [6]

The town boys were loosely divided into two camps, one experimenting with profanity, tobacco, liquor and the bolder forms of mischief, while the other, being older and more industrious, was generally more sedate. Ulysses belonged to the more sedate of the two groups.

To many of the boys it seemed squeamish in Lyss not to hunt. Everybody hunted. Why didn't he? Was his heart or his stomach to blame? A friend of Ulysses' said in later years, "He was unusually sensitive to pain, and his aversion to taking any form of life was so great that he would not hunt." Another man who ate with Ulysses almost daily for years noted, "If blood appeared in any meat which came on the table, the sight of it seemed entirely to destroy his appetite. . . . Fowl and game he abhorred." Ulysses himself would say later on, "I never could eat anything that goes on two legs." [7]

Jimmy Sanderson knew of only one time that Ulysses had gone with his friends on a long hunt, and he had come home from that one on the morning of the second day, "tired of the excursion." Yet Ulysses, he said, "loved to shoot at a mark, and when about fifteen years of age was a good marksman. I think he won a badge for the best shooting among the boys of his age at a Fourth of July celebration. He always had some kind of a firearm for shooting in those days. A pistol was his favorite, while we had shotguns."

While some boys disliked the way Ulysses' father always "knew it all" and went around quoting newspapers and books, Jimmy Sanderson was eager to get into that Grant library, and one day broached the matter to Ulysses — who said, "I don't care to read books myself," but he'd see what could be done. Finally he announced that he would be able to bring Jimmy the books, one at a time, on two conditions. Jimmy must return each volume before he received another, and he must also arrange for Ulysses to ride that fancy four-year-old colt in the Sanderson pasture. Jimmy said he'd see about it. Ulysses delivered the books and, as Jimmy later declared, "His eyes fairly stood out with delight when I told him one day, after I had found that my father had gone several miles away from home, that he could put a bridle on the favorite animal and ride him up and down the road for half an hour."

The only curb Jimmy put upon Ulysses was to refuse to let him jump the colt over fences — it might get hurt and the surreptitious riding be discovered.

Jimmy knew from the inside of the first book loaned to him, Irving's *Sketch Book*, that it had never been read, although "Hiram U. Grant" was scrawled possessively all over the flyleaf. One of the other books, a collection of articles on American Methodism, was too much for even Jimmy's hunger for reading. Ulysses "laughed a little when I opened the book and showed how dry it was." [8]

Whatever his joys in Georgetown, Ulysses was thought by certain villagers to have grown more bashful after his twelfth year. Some guessed that this was due to chagrin over his father's increased boasting about him.[9] Others who watched his development guessed that the boy was at this age merely what he had always been — his mother's son. The village now noticed it more — that was all. Still others concluded that if there was any increase in his shyness the cause lay in the approach of puberty with its added burden of self-consciousness. While it would be true in after years that he never mentioned the embarrassing phrenologist, he would recite with relish many other laughable defeats and predicaments of his boyhood.

The frequency with which he would refer to his Georgetown days as happy ones made it plain that, for all his extreme sensitiveness, they had left no scar whatever of shame and silence upon his mind. He had never been outwardly vain about his feats in the circus ring — feats which would have turned a lighter-headed boy into a pillar of conceit — and he now gave them up altogether, saying that he was too big for ponies.

He was terrorized when Teacher Upham introduced "speaking pieces" into the school. It had been bad enough when Upham had required pupils of his age to compose 150-word essays. Upham said Ulysses tried hard to avoid these essays, "although he wrote two or three of merit for a boy of 11 or 12 years." But when the teacher extended this work to include declamations every two weeks, he saw that this "was unbearable to young Grant. He spoke only once or twice, and then by the greatest exertion." Upham noted that Ulysses simply "could not bear to get up and face a whole room full of boys and girls." A recitation of Washington's "Farewell Address" finished him. "He made fearful work of it," said Upham, "and after school said he would 'never speak there again, no matter what happened.' " [10]

Ulysses, who hated arguments, found in his twelfth year a horrible one shaking his home — and for that matter, the whole town. Jesse had quarreled with Tom Hamer! The two men had quit speaking when they passed on the street. The trouble was politics, the one field where they had worked together virtually as partners. For the Democracy they had stumped the region side by side, filled Hamer's *Benefactor* with propaganda, and written keynote statements for conventions. No one had worked harder than Jesse for Tom's three elections to the State Legislature and for his elevation to Speaker of Ohio's House of Representatives in 1829. In the 1832 campaign, when Hamer had been elected to Congress and President Jackson had carried Brown County almost two to one, the two friends had prepared the official address for the county convention. They had teamed to build up the Georgetown debating society, usually taking opposite sides to make the programs livelier.

But in the fall of 1833 they differed over President Jackson's withdrawal of funds from the United States Bank. Like so many businessmen, Jesse thought this a reckless risking of the nation's financial structure. Hamer stood with his idol, Jackson. The difference grew into a quarrel and then into haughty mutual scorn.

Ulysses knew that "both of them felt badly over this estrangement, and would have been glad at any time to come to a reconciliation, but neither would make the advance." What helped keep the breach unhealed was Jesse's drift away from the Democratic party toward the newly organized Whig party, and his growing admiration for the Whig leader, the magnetic senator from Kentucky, Henry Clay. In the home he taught Ulysses to follow Clay. Jesse's progress toward the Whigs was slow, and when Clay was not their nominee in 1836, he would stay away from the polls entirely, unwilling as yet to vote against the Democracy but too distrustful of Jackson's choice, Martin Van Buren, to support him.

The break with Hamer made new enemies for Jesse. Tom's popularity was so firmly established that the backwoodsmen in his district even forgave him when they heard that when he was in Washington he shaved every day. And it enabled him, in his race for Congress, to defeat the great man in the region, Thomas Morris. His split with his former patron had been over national finance, although the slavery issue, rising so bitterly in the early 1830's, had hastened it. Morris was more drastically antislavery than was Jesse, and his bold speeches against "the character of the slave power as an aristocracy" were converting young men across the state, notably one in Cincinnati, Salmon P. Chase.[11]

As abolition sentiment increased, it was rumored in Georgetown that Jesse had helped found an antislavery society in Kentucky ten years before, a charge that Jesse would partially explain: "I was never what was technically known as an abolitionist." But to hot-headed Southerners there was small difference between a man merely opposing the spread of slavery into new territory and men demanding that it be abolished where it existed. And in George-town these criticisms of Jesse were often translated by town boys into jeers at Ulysses.[12]

Jesse Grant's temper could be violent, as the village saw one day when he cornered one of his thieving employees in the tavern and ordered him to leave town. The fellow, a journeyman tanner who had stolen six calfskins to trade for whiskey, drew a knife on Jesse. Quickly Jesse's powerful arms tore away the weapon and he shouted to little Ulysses to run get the cowhide. When the boy brought it, Jesse laid it on the rogue with vigor.[13]

It was probably in this summer of 1836 that Jesse's plans for Ulysses' education began to center on the United States Military Academy in New York. The boy's talents warranted sending him to college, and West Point was the cheapest of all colleges, with the Government paying all expenses. Fourteen now, he would be ready for admission in three years, perhaps two, since some cadets were admitted at sixteen. Talk of West Point was common in Georgetown. "Old Irish Jimmy" Allen, a citizen, was talking about his son, Robert, who would graduate there in July. Dave Ammen was sending Ulysses' closest friend, Dan, to the Academy in the fall, not as a cadet, but as a student to prepare himself, oddly enough, for service as a midshipman in the United States Navy. Tom Hamer had secured the naval appointment for Dan and, when the boy's education was pronounced deficient, arranged to have him accepted at the Military Academy for three months so that his older brother Jake, a lieutenant on the faculty, could tutor him. Relatives of Jesse claimed in later years that he said "he had determined to use all the influence he could bear when his son was old enough, to get him into West Point." [14]

In the meantime Ulysses must have better preparatory education than Georgetown provided. The school Jesse selected was Richeson's and Rand's at Maysville, where Peter Grant's widow, Aunt Pamelia, could keep an eye on him. So far as relatives went, it might be better to place him with his Aunt Rachel, whom he resembled more than any of the Grants, but Aunt Rachel lived far away at Charlestown, Virginia, where she was the wife of a money-gathering man, William Tompkins. [15]

Jesse was worrying about finances in the fall of 1836, for there were signs of a collapse of prices here and there in the nation, and his home expenses were increasing. Another girl, Virginia, had been born, February 20, 1832, and a third boy, Orvil, on May 15, 1835. Simpson, at nine, was working when not in school as a printer's devil on Dave Ammen's *Castigator*. [16]

But whatever the cost, Ulysses entered Richeson's and Rand's that autumn and the father was soon gratified to learn that the boy was "studious." Ulysses later denied this, saying that he probably had not made "progress enough to compensate for the outlay for board and tuition." However, he was finding it possible to overcome some of his terror of public speaking. In the Philomathean Debating Society a fellow member, A. H. Markland, thought him "a good debater for one of his years" and as an executive officer of that society "he was firm and steady." The boys debated such questions as the abolition of slavery, the respective horrors of war and intemperance, the superiority of writers over orators, and the wisdom of the Texans in freeing the Mexican General, Santa Anna. As one of the Society assigned to defend the Texans, Ulysses was perhaps pleased. Boys across the whole nation had enjoyed prolonged thrills during the last year reading the exploits of the dauntless Texans in their War of Independence against Mexico and their magnanimity in refusing to wreak vengeance upon Santa Anna for his treacherous butchery of captives.

Young Markland liked Ulysses, thought him "exceedingly kind, popular, even-tempered and generous," and was sorry to learn that he would not be back next year. Ulysses was apparently not sorry. He did not blame Professor Richeson, who had turned out many bright scholars, but here in what purported to be a higher sphere of education he was going over the same old textbooks he had known at Georgetown and was being given such familiar injunctions as "A noun is the name of a thing." Later he drolly observed that he had already been taught this fact for so many years prior to the Maysville experience that he "had come to believe it." [17]

The national panic was reaching its peak in the spring of 1837 as Ulysses returned from Maysville and, with economy in the air, found he would attend the village subscription school next winter.

The economies of a West Point education came with redoubled force to Jesse Grant that April as he learned that his next-door neighbor, Dr. Bailey, had placed his son Bartlett at the Academy. Congressman Hamer had begun pushing the appointment the previous December and now on April 13 Dr. Bailey was signing and sending to the Secretary of War his written consent. Bart, who was sixteen, would leave in May for the examination which came around June first. Among the boys who discussed this dazzling news, Carr White was the one to note that it had agitated Jesse Grant exceedingly. Carr understood that there had always been a spirit of rivalry between Jesse Grant and Dr. Bailey as to the future of Ulysses and Bart, and that when Jesse heard of Bart's appointment "he had sworn to get even" and had promptly discussed an appointment for Ulysses with his friend Thomas Morris who, after his defeat for Congress, had been elected United States Senator. Jesse himself remembered long afterward that his appeal to Morris had not come until 1839.[18] Although his two favorite playmates, Dan and Bart, were away among stirring sights, Ulysses found the year 1837 far from dull at home. His father was elected Mayor for a two-year term, proving that a vehement Whig could, if respected enough, be elected in a Democratic town. Dave Ammen sold the *Castigator* to some Whigs who soon moved it to the larger and less Democratic town of Ripley on the river. Dr. Bailey and Tom Hamer got religion during a protracted meeting which for weeks tore the nights with wild cries, bellowing exhortations and ecstatic songs as Ulysses lay in his bed across the street from the little Methodist church. A full hundred and fifty sinners went to the mourners' bench during the revival, but the greatest shouting of all came when Tom Hamer's red head bent in surrender. He had contributed heavily when the church had been built ten years before, but until now had never given his soul to Jesus.[19]

Such frenzies, which were part of an evangelistic fire that had been burning across Ohio in recent years, had no charm for the Grants. Jesse was hardheaded. Hannah shrank from crowds and excitement, and in her inordinate modesty could only have been repelled by the sight, at the wildest of the revivals, of young men and women ostensibly wrestling with the Devil up and down the aisles, but in reality rolling and pitching in each other's arms, and of rows of women jerking and twitching in the straw of the "penitents' pen," howling like wolves or giving off that famous "holy laugh" which was believed to signal the moment when the struggling heart tore itself free at last from Satan's icy fingernails. The neighbors would remember Hannah as having been "very tolerant" in religious as in other matters, and there would always remain a question of how consistently Ulysses had accompanied his parents to church. For some reason he did not join the church or receive baptism as did his brothers and sisters. Later on, persons familiar with his life wondered if his parents could have excused him from constant church attendance because of his peculiar nervous revulsion against music. Not only was he growing up incapable of "telling one tune from another," but as he would in time explain to a clergyman, "all music seemed to affect him as discord would a sensitive and cultivated ear," and "in church he always experienced a feeling of relief as each stanza of the hymn was sung and so disposed of." The boy whose nerves would tolerate sudden pistol shots without a twitch "would go a mile out of his way rather than listen to the playing of a band," — those brass bands and squealing fife and drum corps which played at muster days for the militia and at political or patriotic gatherings.[20]

Then there was the excitement that summer of 1837 when Jake Ammen came home from West Point on vacation and, upon invitation, drilled the militia company. As one who had spent four of the six years since his graduation from the Academy teaching either mathematics or philosophy to the cadets, Jake was, in Jesse's mind, just the man to talk to about Ulysses' future. One of the *Castigator's* printers saw Jesse step out of a crowd of spectators as Jake brought the militia drill to an end, and heard him question the lieutenant-professor most earnestly about the Academy. Ammen answered in detail, and eventually Jesse broke off the conversation with, "I am determined that Ulysses shall go to West Point." [21]

Since Jake Ammen was resigning from the Army that autumn to become a professor of mathematics in a Kentucky college, it would have been natural for him to give Jesse the average officer's view of the Academy — a place where a boy could secure a college education at no cost and then, within a few years, quit the Army for a better paying post in civil life. For example, when Jake would hand in his resignation in November, he would be the twenty-third of his graduating class to have abandoned the uniform, leaving only nine still in service. Three of the twenty-three were already college professors and ten civil engineers. West Point-trained men were in great demand for civil engineering jobs on the canals, river and harbor improvements, railroads, new towns, new counties, new states which must be surveyed and built. Only one other college in the nation, Rensselaer Polytechnic Institute at Troy, New York, was turning out civil engineers, and its graduates had only begun to appear in 1836.

With the public excited over trade, transportation and industry, the church colleges, which had been turning out only lawyers, preachers, doctors, gentlemen, were feeling the need to produce businessmen, and as a result were increasing their mathematics departments and hiring West Point graduates as instructors. West Point produced men trained in mathematics, system, precision, discipline.

It was no disgrace for an Academy graduate to resign from the Army to take a better position. Low pay and slowness of promotion alone justified the change. Many officers whom Jake Ammen had known in West Point or who had graduated shortly before his entrance in 1827, had resigned after years of service — Albert Sydney Johnston after twelve, Horace Bliss after fourteen, Daniel Tyler after fifteen, Jefferson Davis after eight, Joseph E. Johnston after eight. It was also after eight years that a Virginian who had made distinguished marks at West Point, Robert E. Lee, gave intimate friends the impression he would throw up his commission in the Engineers if one of those private corporations dealing in internal improvements were to offer him a job.

Nor was it a sin for a graduate to resign as soon as his original five-year term of enlistment, four years in the Academy and one in the Army, ran out. Lieutenants George A. Meade, Jubal Early and a promising soldier of Ammen's own class, Samuel R. Curtis, had done this. Some boys, especially those with influential connections, had been able to resign without serving the required year in the Army after graduation: Leonidas Polk, son of a Southern banker, had gotten away in five months, Lloyd Tilghman, a high-toned Marylander, in two months and Senator Henry Clay's son and namesake, who had finished second in Jake Ammen's class, had resigned within four months.

Officers were resigning at a rate which by the end of the decade would leave in service only 395 of the 1058 men who had graduated from the Academy. In the twenty years which would end in 1838, practically 45 per cent of the 445 men graduating in that period would have left the Army, more than half quitting within two years after completing Academy work.

With the Army so small — 6000 officers and men — and with professional soldiers generally unpopular with Americans, West Pointers were apt to see no future in the uniform. Periodically state legislatures denounced the Academy as "aristocratical" or "inconsistent with the spirit and genius of our liberal institutions." Congress in that year, 1837, was considering abolishing it altogether. Stump speakers in political campaigns asked uneducated voters why they should be taxed to turn out pampered snobs and loafers when, as everybody knew, the great American farmer would rise overnight and handle any possible enemy, redskin or redcoat.

To a father and businessman like Jesse Grant, in the panic year of 1837, West Point had its appeal. That Ulysses obviously had no leaning toward the life military evidently was not important. Neither was the memory of the bibulous habits Jesse's own father had learned in the Army. Both objections would have meant nothing if Jesse expected his boy to get the free education, then resign.

Whatever Jesse might be thinking about West Point, he kept it from Ulysses for a year — a year which the boy spent happily with horses, working them through the summer and after school in autumn, winter and spring. Of all his journeys with customers, the most enjoyable came that summer of 1837 — a 140-mile round trip to Flat Rock, Kentucky, with a timorous adult male passenger.

The fun really began when, preparing for the return trip, he had traded one of his carriage horses for an unbroken colt. There had been the customary pleasure in convincing the colt's owner that he, a boy, was always permitted to make legal transactions, that he could manage a wild animal, and, last of all, that he should have ten dollars to boot in the trade. Finally, when he had won and was off for home, the team took fright at a bad dog and ran away, the new horse kicking at every jump. This frightened the passenger, a Mr. Payne of Georgetown, but Ulysses finally quieted them and started up once more. Instantly the colt went into a fit of kicking, and the runaway started all over again. This time the boy halted the team on the edge of a twenty-foot embankment; the new horse "trembled like an aspen," as Ulysses told it, "but he was not half so badly frightened as my companion."

Mr. Payne had had enough and, crawling out, caught a ride to Maysville in a fine, slow freight wagon, leaving the small driver to the fruits of his own overconfidence. Ulysses was, as he admitted, "in quite a dilemma," for every time he shook a rein the new horse answered with both heels. Finally the boy's readiness at improvisation rescued him; blindfolding the animal with his big bandanna handkerchief, he was able to trot off peacefully and to arrive at Maysville next day, much to the surprise of Mr. Payne. Borrowing a horse at the home of his Uncle Roswell Grant, he persuaded Mr. Payne to return to his original seat and together they drove placidly to Georgetown.[22]

Everything went well until the summer of 1838, when his father suddenly told him one day that he was needed in the beam room. There was a shortage of workers. It was a crisis, for Jesse, knowing the boy's horror of the place, had never made the suggestion before. As Jesse later described the event, Ulysses had agreed to go but had frankly added:

"Father, this tanning is not the kind of work I like. I'll work at it though, if you wish me to, until I am twenty-and-one; but you may depend upon it, I'll never work a day at it after that."

"No, I don't want you to work at it, now, if you don't like it and mean to stick to it," Jesse replied. "I want you to work at whatever you like and intend to follow. Now, what do you think you would like?"

Ulysses guessed that he would like to be a farmer, or a trader down the river or get an education. He had seen the flatboats, which were called "broadhorns," leaving Ripley for the sugar and cotton plantations of Louisiana and Mississippi, each boat carrying 1000 to 1200 barrels of pork that had been packed in the town. The owners would have money in their pockets when they returned on steamboats.

Jesse disapproved of the brawling, gambling life on the river. He had insufficient acreage to set up the boy as a farmer and Hannah's portion of the Simpson place at Bantam, which she had inherited upon her father's death in January 1837, was rented. Jesse also said that with hard times still on the country, he did not feel justified in withdrawing money from his business to send Ulysses to college.

"How would you like West Point?" he ventured. "You know the education is free there, and the Government supports the cadets."

According to the father, Ulysses replied, "First rate." [23]

Ulysses himself recalled that the subject of West Point was not brought up until several months later. All he remembered about the plans for his education in the summer and fall of 1838 was that he prepared to enter the Presbyterian Academy at Ripley, of which great things were expected. The Reverend John Rankin as its president was working to have it turned into a college and would, indeed, achieve his goal in 1840. Perhaps he might have succeeded in 1838 if his lectures across the nation for the Antislavery Society had not been taking so much of his time the past two years. He brought home to Ripley tales of the mobs that frequently threatened him during his tours. Abolitionist excitement was particularly violent in Ripley as school began, in '38, for one of Rankin's young lieutenants on the Underground Railroad. The Reverend John B. Mahan had been indicted in Kentucky for stealing a slave and harboring it in the temperance tavern he kept in Brown County. In September Ohio's Governor had permitted Mahan to be extradited. Tom Hamer had refused to represent Mahan in legal arguments against extradition. Abolitionist mass meetings were adopting resolutions condemning both the Governor and Hamer. News of the trial came across the river to Ripley. Mahan was contending that all he had done was to give the slave free room and board in his tavern. The jury freed him, but protests against the "outrage" continued. In a year the excitement was even greater, for Preacher Mahan was jailed again, this time in Georgetown for inciting a mob to rescue another slave from a constable in the county. Senator Morris defended him, and Tom Hamer helped with the prosecution. Hamer won, but the Ohio Supreme Court reversed the verdict — fifty dollars fine and ten days on bread and water.[24]

While the town and the proprietors of the Academy shook with these excitements, Ulysses was finding that a noun was still the name of a thing. In his hands were the same kind of readers, spellers, grammars, geographies, arithmetics he had always known. And, as before, reports that went to Jesse marked him "studious," a verdict which his schoolmates supported, saying later that while he played ball, skated and wrestled with them, he was too busy with his studies to go to student parties. "He was there for business," one of them remembered. He got into no mischief, was never punished and was known as silent except in class, where he fired questions at the teachers as if determined to get his money's worth. Outside class he whittled and did most of the listening while the other boys talked. Girls of the town thought him countrified and slow. His homemade clothes, which had made him more neatly dressed than most boys in Georgetown, now spoke of the backwoods.[25]

In after times Ulysses told friends in Ripley that he had been happy at the Presbyterian Academy, but there was no question that its lack of new subjects disappointed him. More to his taste was the busy life on the river front — two shipyards building steamers, Negro roustabouts rolling barrels of pork and wine and hogsheads of tobacco up gangplanks, droves of cattle and hogs arriving at the packing houses. He could remember when farmers had driven cattle and hogs clear to Baltimore and Philadelphia, a footsore journey of four to six weeks. Wagonloads of wheat now came in to Ripley's wharf. He could remember when it had been cut with little hand sickles, before the wooden-fingered cradle had appeared on the scene.[26]

On the steamers he saw cabin boys whose fathers, somewhere inland, were wondering where they were — lordly youngsters who disdained to notice spineless shore-bound oafs who went to school

— lucky cabin boys leaving for Memphis, for Vicksburg, Natchez, St. Louis, New Orleans, the far-off cities of the South, where sights were to be seen and money to be made.

Back home, Jesse Grant was working hard to keep his boy from the life of a down-the-river trader. He was talking and writing, that autumn of 1838, to his friend Senator Morris about West Point. Perhaps the Senator would have an appointment to bestow. No, the Senator discovered, he did not. He had had one but since there was no application at the time, he had given it to a Congressman from Pennsylvania. But he suggested that Jesse write direct to the War Department, for there was a vacancy in Jesse's own congressional district.[27]

Leaping at the chance, Jesse wrote to the War Department, applying for his son's appointment. From Senator Morris he discovered why the vacancy had suddenly appeared. Bart Bailey had left the Academy, or was soon to do so. The whole thing had been, up to now, a tremendous secret.

As Jesse got the story, Bart had failed to pass his examinations in the middle of his first year and had resigned; but his father "who was a proud-spirited man" kept it a secret and did not let him return home, placing him instead in the private military school of a Captain Partridge in the East to be tutored for a second try at the Academy. Jesse believed that Bart's failure to pass the examination a second time had come not from "a want of talent" but from unwillingness "to apply himself to study." Insofar as Bart's first year was concerned, Jesse's explanation seemed approximately correct when, in time, the Academy records and Hamer's letters were examined. Bart had been admitted to the Academy on July 7, 1837, had passed his first examinations, but had quit before the January examinations. Hamer, who was summoned by Dr. Bailey to look into the matter, gathered that Bart had "resigned in December" and had remained "at West Point under a private tutor expecting a reappointment." All of which indicated that the Academy authorities were friendly. On February 13, 1838, Hamer nominated him again and on March 23 Dr. Bailey knew that the War Department would make the appointment. On April 29 Bart accepted it and, entering again in July with the new class, had run into trouble, handing in his resignation which was marked on the Academy books as accepted on November 13 to take effect February 3, 1839, "at which time he will be considered as discharged from the service of the United States." Two arrests for making "false reports and representations" were apparently behind his resignation and references to a court-martial were found on the "conduct" reports of the Academy.[28]

Ulysses' first inkling of his friend's fate came during the Christmas vacation in 1838. Arriving home from Ripley, he saw his father open a letter from Senator Morris, read it, then say, "Ulysses, I believe you are going to receive the appointment."

"What appointment?"

"To West Point. I have applied for it."

"But I won't go!"

Then, as Ulysses later recalled the scene, "He said he thought I would, *and I thought so too, if he did.*"

The trip to West Point on the Hudson would be a fine one, giving him clear title to the travel championship among the boys. Where would the Walkers be with their Texas when he came home with Philadelphia and New York? But could he hope to pass those examinations that had defeated Bart? He had never seen an algebra. "I could not bear the idea of failing," he remembered years later.[29]

One comfort attended him as he returned to Ripley at the holidays' end — the appointment might not come through, and hope brightened as January and February passed and March began with no news. Then the dark word came. He had been appointed and would leave in May. His father was jubilant.

On February 19, Jesse had done the one thing he hated to do, yet for Ulysses' sake would do — ask Tom Hamer for a favor. With his pride in his pocket and his pen in his hand he had written:

GEORGETOWN, February 19, 1839

To HON. THOMAS L. HAMER — DEAR SIR:

In consequence of a remark from Mr. Morris (while here last fall), I was induced to apply to the War Department, through him, for a cadet appointment for my son, H. Ulysses.

A letter this morning received from the department informs me that your consent will be necessary to enable him to obtain the appointment. I have thought it advisable to consult you on the subject, and if you have no other person in view for the appointment, and feel willing to consent to the appointment of Ulysses, you will please signify that consent to the department.

When I last wrote to Mr. Morris I referred him to you to recommend the young man, if that were necessary.

Respectfully yours,

JESSE R. GRANT [30]

Slowly the letter had gone East by boat and stage and reached Hamer's desk on March 3, when he was clearing it out for his return to Georgetown. He had declined renomination last autumn because, as Dan Ammen understood, "he could not afford to neglect longer the interests of his family." Tomorrow, March 4, his term would be ended. He must move fast. This appointment of Jesse Grant's boy was the chance to end the old quarrel. Hurriedly he filled out the proper papers and, without looking again at Jesse's letter, forgot entirely about H. Ulysses Grant and wrote in "Ulysses S. Grant." Knowing that Hannah's maiden name was Simpson, he carelessly assumed that to be the middle name. Hurrying the application to the Secretary of War, he wrote Jesse, "I received your letter and have asked for the appointment of your son, which will doubtless be made. Why didn't you apply to me sooner?" [31]

The mails West were as slow as the mails East. Hamer arrived in Georgetown ahead of the letter and spent several days waiting for Jesse to thank him. Jesse spent those days ignoring Hamer on the street. Then the letter arrived, the two iron faces relaxed, and their friendship was restored for life. [32]

In town there were people who congratulated Jesse and people who told each other they were surprised that the Government should try to turn so silent, awkward and bashful a boy into a bold commander of soldiers. Of course, Lyss could do wonderful things with horses, but the Army had only one lone regiment of dragoons. One villager angered Jesse by asking incredulously if the report could be true, and when assured that it was, added, "I'm astonished that Hamer did not appoint someone with intellect enough to do credit to the district." But, in time, Jesse could laugh it off as merely the spleen of a farmer who had disliked Ulysses ever since the boy, with quiet humor, had once named a horse after him. [33]

Carr White was sure his father had been the first to suggest West Point to Jesse.[34]

Returning home with the end of school, Ulysses was uncommunicative when the boys who envied him tried to talk about his appointment. It was sad to look at Mrs. Bailey. He knew she loved him, but was he always to be mixed up one way or another with the tragedies which came to her sons? Dr. Bailey had sent Bart word never to come home, and Bart, going out to Illinois to hide his shame, had passed down the river, not ten miles away, without getting off to see his mother.[35]

If Ulysses should fail as Bart had done, his own father certainly wouldn't behave like Dr. Bailey, but his anger would be terrible enough. Were he to escape failure and get through the whole four-year course at West Point, he could resign faster than had Jake Hamer. Ulysses was going into the thing without the faintest idea of staying in the Army. Due at the Academy June 1, he did what he could to prepare for those entrance examinations. On a trip to Cincinnati he bought an algebra, could not understand B plus X, and then discovered that he could solve the problems by arithmetic. He figured his coming expenses: the fare would be $75; new clothes, $25; the Academy demanded a deposit of $60, against the possibility that he would need a ticket home. Against this he had $100 of his own money. His father would make up the difference.[36]

Jesse's confidence in the boy was complete. Physically Ulysses would just make it: he stood five feet one inch, and the minimum requirement was five feet; he weighed 117 pounds, which was enough. His sieges of fever and ague would probably end on the heights of West Point, away from the swamps of the West. That matter of the boy's name, which had been twisted on the record, could be straightened out when he got there.[37]

The days rushed past Ulysses. The middle of May was on him. He paid a last visit to his grandmother and the rest of the relatives. Uncle Samuel Simpson and Cousin Jimmy Marshall helped him tack his initials, H.U.G., in large brass tacks on his trunk. Jimmy heard him say this would never do; the cadets would nickname him "Hug." Uncle Samuel said later that the tacks were taken out at the last moment and rearranged to read U.H.G. without any mention of the alteration being made to Jesse or Hannah. The boy would present himself at the Academy as Ulysses Hiram Grant.[38]

May 15, 1839, dawned. He must be off for Ripley to catch the Pittsburgh steamer. He told the family good-by. It was close to the fifth birthday of the youngest, little Orvil. Hannah was as silent and grave as she had been fifteen years before when Ulysses had crawled among the horses' feet. He would be all right. Beneath her apron another baby was growing — in six weeks it would be due.

Ulysses went out the door. He turned in at the Baileys' gate. Mrs. Bailey kissed him good-by — kissed him and wept. He was touched and astonished.

"Why, Mrs. Bailey," he said. "They didn't cry at our house." [39]

What made it easier for him, as he saw Georgetown disappear behind the trees on the road down to the river, was the hope that he could someway contrive with honor to be back.

He didn't really expect to be gone long.

CHAPTER FOUR

Unwillingly to School

ULYSSES was two boys as, by steamer, canalboat and railroad he journeyed to West Point — he was the confirmed traveler delighting in strange scenes and he was the little boy with the satchel creeping unwillingly to school.

Every mile, except the first leg of the steamer trip up the river, was a new one, and the whole trip was fascinating; but all the way, as he drolly recalled in later years, he kept hoping for a collision, a wreck, any kind of an accident that might injure him just enough to make him ineligible for the Academy without maiming him permanently.[1]

His best hope for this was the railroad — the first he had ever seen. It careened him eastward from Harrisburg to Philadelphia at the average speed of twelve breathless miles an hour, but it had, disappointingly, landed him safe and sound. The ride on the canalboat from Pittsburgh to Harrisburg had been the most enjoyable; he had chosen it rather than the more direct and speedy stagecoach because it brought him so much more slowly toward his dread terminus, West Point, and because it wound through grander sections of western Pennsylvania's mountains — also, possibly, because it added more to the mileage he was rolling up on those Walker boys.[2] Having been born farsighted, he loved distance — the roll of it and the sweep.[3]

Philadelphia, his first big city, excited him; he walked its streets, saw its shrines and theaters and stayed in it for five days, drawing a reprimand from his father, when the news reached Georgetown, for "dallying by the way so long."[4] He stopped with the Hares, those cousins of his mother's. They found him "a very good talker," telling "stories of his life in the West." Elizabeth Hare, who had been like a sister to Hannah in their girlhood, thought Ulysses "a rather awkward country lad, wearing plain clothes and large, coarse shoes as broad at the toes as at the widest part of the soles." Her brother Silas, at whose hat store on Chestnut Street, below Fifth, Ulysses made his daytime headquarters, was amused by the funny things this western cousin said about "the queer Quaker houses" seen on his rambles around town.[5]

New York followed, and although Ulysses stayed long enough to see its sights, there hung over it the shadow of West Point, the next stop just up the Hudson. The sight-seeing trip was almost over.

On May 29, Ulysses landed from the Hudson River steamer at West Point, climbed the stairs to Roe's Hotel on the edge of the military reservation, signed himself "Ulysses H. Grant" in the guest book and then proceeded to the Adjutant's office.[6]

Now was the time to get his self-chosen name officially registered. He could explain later to his father why he had switched from the "H. Ulysses" Jesse had wanted. He wrote firmly in the Adjutant's register, "Ulysses Hiram Grant." [7]

The official at the desk, either Adjutant George Waggaman or his clerk, looked at the signature, compared it with the official list that had been supplied by the War Department, and announced that there was no appointment here for him. There was one for a Ulysses S. Grant of Ohio and one for an Elihu Grant from New York.[8] The boy explained that he was the Ohio Grant; his Congressman had merely got the initials wrong on the appointment papers. It had been figured that the error could be straightened out when the candidate reported for duty.

No, Ulysses was informed, the name couldn't be changed; he could only enter under the exact name shown on the official paper. Any alteration must come from the War Department. Face to face for the first time with military red tape, Ulysses surrendered without, apparently, much of a struggle.[9] Having so recently shuffled his first two names of his own accord, he could take no strong position in the matter. Also he was his mother's son, patient and obedient in the presence of higher powers — man proposed and God disposed.[10] Among the student body it was understood that he made his protest, then told the Adjutant, "The change of an initial makes no particular difference to me; my object is to enter the Academy as a cadet." [11] The other boys learned of the incident quickly, since the authorities, in posting the names of the newcomers on the bulletin board in North Barracks, had abbreviated "Ulysses S." into "U.S." Gleefully the crowd around the board began inventing witticisms: "United States Grant!" "Uncle Sam Grant!" . . . "Uncle Sam!" [12]

It was funnier than ever when they found the new boy, so small, so round-faced, almost a caricature of the tall, lank, lantern-jawed Uncle Sam who was the cartoonists' symbol for shrewd, cunning, aggressive America!

"A more unpromising boy never entered the Military Academy" was the way one cadet later remembered Grant.[13] This cadet, a slim, tall, mischievous red-haired Ohioan, had heard his own middle name, "Tecumseh," ridiculed when he had entered three years before. He had become accustomed to the abbreviation "Cump" or the nickname "Bill," but would always sign himself "W. T. Sherman" rather than "William Tecumseh Sherman."

Ulysses quietly explained the facts about his name to inquiring cadets, but it was an unfortunate beginning for so bashful a boy; he had changed his name once to avoid ridicule only to become saddled with another. "Uncle Sam" was, however, not so bad as "Hug" and perhaps better than "Lyss" or "Texas." And as time went on the situation eased, for he became known as plain "Sam." [14] That he would never refer publicly to this change in his name probably meant that in adulthood he did not remember it as one of those boyhood defeats comic enough for retelling. So far as cadet life was concerned, he quietly continued to sign himself "U. H. Grant" on everything but official Academy papers.

In the barracks the greenhorn candidates bunched like sheep, surrounded by wolves in gray clothing who barked and snarled, reminding them that they would never make soldiers, nor even men, so low were they — mere "Things," wretched, primeval "Things." [15]

For the month of June they were to live in a kind of purgatory, expiating the sins of civilianism and preparing themselves for the Judgment Day which would come around July 1, when the entrance examinations were to be held. Until then they were to wear the clothes in which they had arrived; they weren't worth measuring for uniforms until it was certain they were deserving. They must, however, learn the ways of the cadet corps, learn to march, drill, obey and carry themselves like soldiers during those hours when they were not studying and reciting for the coming examination. Sophomore cadets, selected for excellence in studies, were their instructors, receiving ten dollars a month extra for the pleasurable duty of visiting upon the newcomers their own sufferings of a year ago.[16]

When the candidates were alone, they frolicked in their own way and within a few days after arriving were quick to put on the airs of seasoned veterans and jeer almost as loudly as the older cadets at the belated applicants who straggled up from the steamboat landing, escorted by brisk sophomore orderlies.[17]

Ulysses, the boy who had never been scolded at home, now moved in a world of punishments — "crimes" they were called: seven grades of crimes; if a cadet committed too many of them he was sent home in disgrace. He must learn these taboos, little by little, in a confusing whirl of sounds, the chief which was the drum — the drum beating with tom-tom remorselessness.

From five o'clock in the morning until ten o'clock at night the drums were rolling, drumming Ulysses awake, drumming him to bed, to roll call, to inspection, to drill, to meals, to class, to study and to the sunset parade. And the drums were hard for Ulysses' feet to follow — his small feet — small like his hands. Having no ear whatever for rhythm or music, he had trouble keeping step either with marching men or with companions on a sidewalk.[18] Having spent so much of his life since the age of five on a horse's back, he now walked, at seventeen, with the awkwardness of a veteran horseman. "A clumsy, slow gaited, heavy footed lad, whom some of his associates had nicknamed 'Country Sam.' "[19]

Wherever the diminutive, open-faced boy went in his big-toed shoes and in the Georgetown clothes, which seemed so rustic now alongside the sprucely dressed Eastern and Southern boys, a storm of savage derision washed around his head and those of his fellow neophytes — bullying sounds in the halls as he went to class — ridicule floating down from barrack windows as he pitched along the walks, his shoulders stooped — cutting reprimands on the parade ground — a day-long storm of belittlement:

Salute, salute, stand up straight there, MISter Grant — you're an animal — throw out your chest — say "Sir" — shut your trap — can't you hear the drum — salute — eyes front — who's your tailor — keep step, MISter Grant — put out that light — you're a hell of an Uncle

Sam — pull your chin down, MISter Grant — you're a beast — send him home — salute — pull that belly in, MISter Grant — does your mother know you're out — you're a beast — who in God's name sent that THING here — left, right, left, right, now you've got it, can't you keep it — whose calf is that — salute — you're an animal — salute — salute, salute. . . .

Now and then rifts would come for a moment in the wordy typhoon and summer would be lying on the roofs of the quiet old buildings of stone and brick, on the green sweep of the parade ground, on the fringing groves, on the cedar-swathed mountains beyond, and on the noble Hudson at the foot of the bluffs, a river flowing narrower but bluer than the Ohio back home.

Apparently Ulysses sent home no complaining letters as did so many of the boys. The food which cadets unremittingly denounced, he endured. A plebe, as the newcomers were called, could not lift his voice in a derisive "baa" as did those princely upperclassmen when mutton was banged down before them in mess hall. Not yet could a candidate own one of those big, flat morocco caps — gig-tops — into which a cadet could slip food from the table and carry it out for those forbidden "cadet hashes" cooked late at night in the little fireplaces which warmed the rooms.

For the practical jokes that cadets heaped upon the plebes Ulysses had come prepared. He had brought with him a letter of introduction to an upperclassman and this kindly fellow had, on the first day, warned Grant what to expect. That very night when Ulysses and a fellow "animal" slept, a figure wearing an officer's uniform burst into their room with the command that they have twenty pages of this textbook committed to memory by morning.

"All right, all right," Grant said, and as soon as the martinet slammed out, he rolled back into bed and fell sound asleep again; but his companion, unaware that the officer was only an impostor, sat up all night memorizing.[20]

Sam Grant's classmates saw that while he was "pure-minded and even-tempered," "entirely unselfish," "quiet without diffidence," talkative enough with intimate friends but generally marked "for quietness," he had self-reliance and courage. The plebes saw little Sam one day knock down big, hulking Jack Lindsay who had not heeded an earlier warning to quit shoving Sam out of his allotted place in the line at squad drill. Jack, as the son of an army colonel, had been petted by his father's friends on the Academy staff until he had become swollen with conceit. From this incident apparently there would develop the legend — one that Jesse Grant branded as fiction — that Ulysses had stepped out of the ranks one day to thrash a cadet officer who had humiliated him. Not only that, Ulysses was supposed to have followed up with an offer to whip the second in command and, indeed, anybody else who thought they could put upon him.[21]

Whatever he felt inwardly during this troublesome June, he was still the same boy who would never turn back on a road. A little later, he would tell Elizabeth Hare in Philadelphia that if he had known, before coming to the Academy, how strict the life would be, he would never have come at all, but "as I have started, I am bound to go through." [22]

Examination Day approached. He would do his best with it, stay at the Academy as long as he could but, as he afterward recalled, "A military life had no charms for me, and I had not the faintest idea of staying in the army even if I should be graduated, which I did not expect." [23]

He had good reason for these doubts. In the first place, failures at the first examination sometimes ranged up to 60 per cent.[24] And in the second place, a majority of those who did pass that test failed in later ones — 55 per cent in the past twenty years. To make matters worse, the odds were two to one that any boy from the West would fail to graduate after having gained admittance. In those past twenty years, for example, 65 per cent of cadets entering from Ohio, Indiana, Illinois, Michigan and Wisconsin had not completed the course. Scarcely better off were boys admitted from the South — the Slave States and the District of Columbia — 60 per cent of them had failed. By contrast, only 40 per cent of the boys from the East — New York, New England, New Jersey and Pennsylvania — had failed.

Better preparatory schools in the East was the commonest explanation for this sectional superiority. Richard S. Ewell, who was a member of the senior class as Grant entered the Academy, had written his brother that the Yankees as a rule arrived more adequately equipped for the work, particularly in mathematics.[25] Since a cadet's final standing at the end of each year was determined by relating his classroom marks to those given him for conduct, some Southerners might argue that their schools alone were not on trial — their sons were more hotheaded than the biddable Yankees and quicker to get into disciplinary trouble. And Westerners might contend that their boys were rougher, less conventional than the Easterners and so, certain to receive more bad marks for breaches of military etiquette. But to offset these excuses were the arguments that Southerners arrived more anxious than the Yankees to qualify as officers and gentlemen and find a career in the Army, and that Westerners came with a greater thirst for self-advancement — they were poorer in purse and had more to gain from a four-year course.[26]

But when all the arguments pro and con were made there remained the unquestioned fact that schools in the East, all the way from primary grades through college, were not only more numerous in proportion to population but averaged higher in standards than did those of the South or West.

In the twenty years that ended as Ulysses arrived at West Point, the East had supplied 45 per cent of the boys gaining admission, the South 50 per cent and the West 5, yet an Easterner had graduated first in his class 65 per cent of the time, a Southerner 30 per cent and a Westerner 5. Among the cadets graduating among the honored "first five" in each class 56 per cent had come from the East, 39 per cent from the South, 5 from the West.

The chief prize of all, grades which entitled a graduate to join the Corps of Engineers, cream of the Army, had gone 76 per cent to Easterners, 24 per cent to Slave Staters and had never been won at all by a boy from the West. Southerners might, as it was generally said, set the social tone of the Academy, just as for the Army into which the cadets graduated. General Winfield Scott, head of the Army, might be charged, as he was, with favoring Southern-born officers in Army promotions, but it was apparent in the character of the Academy that neither he nor his predecessors nor the War Department itself had let any such prejudices color the nature of the national Military Academy.

Instead, the West Point which Ulysses was entering in 1839 was, in effect, a New England educational institution in its administration almost as much as in its location. To the east of its ramparts stood those intellectual centers of "Yankeeism," Connecticut and Massachusetts. Twenty-five of the thirty-three men who were operating the Academy were Easterners, eight Southerners. Easterners were at the head of all eight departments, tactics, mathematics, drawing, French, civil and military engineering, natural and experimental philosophy, geography and history and ethics, and chemistry, mineralogy and geology. One of these, Berard, head teacher in French, had been born in France but had come to the faculty after years as an instructor in New York and Pennsylvania. Another, Dennis H. Mahan, professor of engineering, had spent part of his boyhood in Norfolk, Virginia, but he had been born in New York and, as the son of an Irish immigrant workman, was no representative of a Southern viewpoint. When sectional differences would arise he would be instinctively Northern.

Of the nineteen assistant professors and instructors, twelve were Eastern, seven Southern. The system by which the Academy recruited these assistants — bringing back graduates with special talents — had placed on the faculty in the past twenty years a series of officers of whom 68 per cent were Easterners, 27 per cent Southerners, and 5 per cent Westerners.

As Sam Grant listened to older cadets discuss the faculty, he heard much talk about an especially brilliant lieutenant who had just joined the engineering faculty after graduating last June — Henry Wager Halleck, a tall, solemn man of twenty-five, who viewed the world with wide-eyed, staring abstraction.

Halleck had found at the Academy a security and content he had not known at home. Born the eldest of thirteen children on an impoverished farm in the Mohawk Valley, he had been a shy, sensitive boy suffering under the drudgery and the scant schooling a harsh father provided. At fifteen he had run away from home, but his maternal grandfather, Henry Wager, and his uncle, David Wager, had tracked him down and, as enlightened men, had taken him for their own, giving him the education he craved — Hudson Academy, Union College, then West Point. He had finished in third place in the Class of '39, marked by his professors and classmates for a brainy career.[27]

West Point was, by and large, Eastern enough to favor boys from its own section most, Westerners next and Southerners least of all

Sam Grant from Ohio found, to his great surprise, that the entrance examination was easy enough, it seemed, for any Westerner or Southerner to pass it — nothing but reading, spelling, writing and arithmetic through decimal fractions.

At the examination you stood up, as one cadet, George Derby, put it, "between *two* boards, the black board and the board of thirteen army officers!"; you worked out a given problem, turned around, explained it until the chief examining professor said, "That's sufficient, sir," then you went back to your seat.

Sam French, a New Jersey Quaker boy who entered with Sam Grant, found the examination so trivial that, in later years, he had difficulty in recalling it: "I only remember Capt. W. W. S. Bliss (principal assistant professor in mathematics) asking us some questions in a polite manner, and then dismissing us." [28]

Nevertheless the examination, plus the physical tests and other official scrutinies, did manage to reject over 30 per cent of the applicants; 60 of the applicants were admitted.[29]

Sam Grant had made it! He could now be measured for his uniform — a coat of sheep's gray, costing $10.88, swallow-tailed and with a quilted collar so high in the back that, as Sam French commented, "one could not throw his head back and well enjoy a merry laugh." The gigtop cap cost $2.44, and the white pantaloons, which came to $10.50 per dozen, were — as Ulysses wrote his relatives — "as tight to my skin as the bark to tree, and if I do not walk military, — that is, if I bend over quickly or run, — they are very apt to crack with a report as loud as a pistol." [30]

The newcomers were equipped as the whole Cadet Corps moved out, early in July, for the annual summer encampment on the nearby plains. Now came Ulysses' first impressions of what a soldier's life would be — endless drilling, incessant maneuvers, cruel marches — all, as he said, "very wearisome and uninteresting." To the duties of a warrior were added those of a servant. The plebes put up tents for their betters, carried water, ran errands — then in tent at night, just when a weary boy sat down to write a dutiful letter home by candlelight, he would be rewarded with a broom from the outside whacking the tent hard enough to blow the candle out and spill ink every which way.[31]

As a relief to Sam Grant in the two months' encampment came

the sight of two awesome personalities, Captain Charles F. Smith, Commandant of Cadets, and General Scott — "the two men most to be envied in the nation" he thought them. Smith, Pennsylvania-born, tall, straight as a pine, grandly mustachioed, the portrait of Mars, scion of a long and distinguished line of Presbyterian clergy-men and college presidents, famed for the exact justice of his admin-istration, was the idol of the Cadet Corps. Scott, hero of the War of 1812, a six-foot-four colossus, moved in such majesty of manner and splendor of uniform that he was called "Old Fuss and Feathers." Sam Grant would smile in later years remembering how he had stood there, that day, thinking that Scott was the finest specimen of man-hood he had ever seen and that, while he himself could never cut so showy a figure, he just might some day stand where Scott was, reviewing the Cadet Corps. This "presentiment," as Grant dryly called it, was a secret one, since he feared it would make him a laughingstock if he whispered it even to his closest friend. He didn't want to be ridiculed now as he had been at home for the Ralston horse trade.[32] The idea of inheriting Scott's place, probably common to every cadet in the review, was but momentary with Ulysses if, indeed, it was ever a serious one at all. Very quickly he would be remembering that he had no intention of remaining a soldier after his eight years were up.

From afar Grant watched the First Classmen, as the seniors were called. Bill Sherman and George H. Thomas were inseparable friends — Sherman, slender, volatile, always doing or saying funny things; Thomas, statuesque, built like a rock, eternally grave, nick-named "General Washington" by the exuberant and brilliant sopho-more from Ohio, William S. "Rosey" Rosecrans. "Old Tom," as Sherman always called his friend, was, at twenty-four, a man among boys, too kind to torment plebes and much given to easing their homesickness with fatherly advice. He had broken not only tradition but the law as a boy in Virginia, surreptitiously teaching his father's slaves to read and write. He had come to West Point with determination on his face because his Congressman, John Y. Mason, had told him, "No cadet appointed from our district has ever graduated from the Military Academy and if you do not, I never want to see you again." Thomas had worked so hard that he was winning twelfth place in his class of forty-two.

Where Old Tom rode a horse slowly, carefully, his classmate and fellow-Virginian, Dick Ewell, whipped his mounts to breakneck speed, and although he had an impediment in his speech, talked with swift intelligence and, too often, with a "rasping, biting tongue." Dick was one senior underclassmen talked about — twenty-three years old, with thinning hair and piercing eyes — an eagle with a lisp.[33]

The personality of the Academy's Superintendent, Major Richard Delafield, was not a stirring one. A pudgy man with heavy, sandy eyebrows, thick hair and a large nose, he was always bustling about the grounds instituting changes, and his habit of making sarcastic puns had earned him the nickname, "Dicky the Punster." [34]

With the end of August, the boresome field life ended, and back at the Academy again, Sam Grant found the hazing of plebes abating. Also, he drew for his roommate short, bright, energetic Rufus Ingalls, two years older than himself and far more sophisticated. "There always was mirth when Ingalls was present," a classmate said; Rufe was "ever cheerful, never selfish, full of quaint humor," given to playing illegal card games until the lawless hour of 4 A.M.[35] Sam and Rufe had to climb long stairs in the North Barracks to reach their fourth-floor nest up under the eaves, and it was from this lofty window and in the new mood of escape from the encampment that Ulysses, on September 22, wrote to his cousin, McKinstry Griffith in Bethel — a letter beginning with a rhapsody on the vistas that stretched away on all sides:

"This prettiest of places . . . the most beautiful place I have ever seen." Underneath the window was the Hudson "with its bosom studded with hundreds of snowy sails." Look another way and "here is the house Washington used to live in — there Kosisuscko [sic] is used to walk and think of HIS country and of OURS." Across the river stood the home of Benedict Arnold, "that BASE and HEARTLESS traitor to his country and his God. I do love the PLACE — it seems as though I could live here forever, if my friends would only come to. . . . Now this sounds romantic, and you may think it very easy; but I tell you what, Coz, it is tremendous hard."

For two months he had slept upon one single pair of blankets. "Our pay is nominally about twenty-eight dollars a month, but we

never see one cent of it." Everything from a shoestring to a coat had
to come out of this.

The boy who had had his own spending money at nine years of
age, was now suddenly confronted by a system which another
cadet, Decatur M. H. Carpenter of Vermont, more fully described:
"Occasionally a cadet was allowed to purchase what he pleased under
the head of 'sundries' not exceeding one dollar in amount, and that
only on the order of an officer in charge. . . . The regulations not
only prohibited any cadet from receiving money from his parents
and friends, but no place existed . . . on the limits, where cadets
could expend money." [36]

Ulysses went on to tell his cousin about the studies: "We have
tremendous long and hard lessons to get, in both French and algebra." He was studying for the next examination in January — a
"hard one, they say; but I am not frightened yet." Still, with all the
drawbacks, "I would not go away on any account," since "if a man
graduates here, he is safe for life, let him go where he will." He
would stick if he could, "if I cannot . . . the world is wide." He
hadn't seen a familiar face in almost four months now, "or spoken
to a single lady." He wasn't homesick, he declared bravely enough,
although he wouldn't get a chance to come home on a visit, "if I
live," until the end of his second year — the one traditional furlough for a cadet. But, he added, "I wish some of the pretty girls
of Bethel were here, just so I might look at them. But fudge! con-
found the girls. I have seen great men, plenty of them." He named
Scott first, then President Martin Van Buren, then the Secretaries
of War and the Navy, Washington Irving "and lots of other big
bugs."

Then suddenly: "I came near forgetting to tell you about our demerit or 'black marks.' They give a man one of these 'black marks'
for almost nothing, and if he gets two hundred a year they dismiss
him. To show how easy one can get these, a man by the name of
Grant, of this State, got eight of these 'marks' for not going to
church. He was also put under arrest so he cannot leave his room
perhaps for a month; all this for not going to church. We are not
only obliged to go to church, but must march there by companies.
This is not republican. It is an Episcopal church."

He sent his "very best love" to all his friends, especially Grandmother Simpson. "I think often of her . . . I want you to show her this letter and all others that I may write to you . . . write me very soon, for I want to hear much." He signed it "U. H. Grant," clinging to the name he had picked for himself.[37]

A week after he sent the letter the monthly consolidation of the weekly class reports, as made up in the Academy office, showed that Cadet Grant of Ohio was faring better than the majority of the class. Since June 29, he had received only 7 "bad marks." Two New Yorkers, Ed Howe and Jim Hardie had none, Frank Gardner, another New Yorker and a prankish soul, had already rolled up 68, while a freakish North Carolinian, M. L. Caldwell, led the class in errors with 107. September brought enough late-comers to raise the class to 77, among whom Ulysses made friends slowly and without regard for sectionalism — or scholastic preparation — William B. Franklin from Pennsylvania, George Deshon, nicknamed "Dragon," from Connecticut, Joseph J. Reynolds from Indiana and Isaac F. Quinby, called "Nykins," from New Jersey, were high-ranking scholars. Indeed, the boys soon labeled Quinby the most profound intellect in the class. Two others of Grant's friends, Sam French, from a Quaker family in New Jersey, and Christopher Colon Augur from Michigan, stood consistently in the upper fourth. Rufus Ingalls, who was from Maine, and Fred Dent, nicknamed "Jerry," a Missourian, would always be near the bottom. A New Yorker, Fred Steele, nicknamed "Doctor," held to the upper fifth his first year, but would settle thereafter toward the class's tail. Of these nine whom Sam Grant came to know most intimately, Ingalls, Deshon and Steele were each marked for humor and mischief, and Steele, who was the oldest in the class — past twenty — was quick at repartee, a wiry, shrill-voiced wag whose friends could tell by an odd snapping of his eyelids when he was preparing to tell a joke.[38]

Moving quietly, cautiously, in his new surroundings, Grant received no additional demerits during October while Hardie, escaping from perfection, won three, and the rampaging Caldwell ran his total up to 178. By the end of November, Grant had committed enough petty errors to bring his total to 28, below the class average, Hardie had climbed to six; but Caldwell, continuing his wild career, had broken through the Academy deadline, 200, and had reached the soaring total of 293 before the officials could catch up with him, rush him out through the gates, and point him toward North Carolina.

Sam Grant was adapting himself to discipline without difficulty. If he was failing to get his name listed among those cadets who each month were reported as "distinguished for correct deportment," he was also escaping the list actually punished for offenses, as separate from those who were merely given bad marks for small mistakes in punctilio. The usual punishment was one or more extra tours of duty for such deliberate offenses as sitting down on post, deserting sentry post, not being in bed after taps blew at night, lights on after taps, visiting after taps, absence from class parade, playing on musical instrument in study hours, allowing use of tobacco in headquarters, failure to answer to name properly, provisions in quarters, kicking at a horse, throwing bread in mess hall, bottle of liquor in possession, profane language in barracks, concealing self in fireplace to evade Officer of the Day.[39]

For visiting Benny Havens' Tavern outside the limits of the Post the punishment might be arrest and confinement to quarters for seven days or, as Quinby came near to discovering, expulsion. Striking a horse with a saber meant arrest for seven days. Habitual loud talk or tripping a cadet in ranks could earn a cadet two extra tours of duty, as Longstreet found out.

These punishments carried with them more serious demerits than the minor offenses, such as appearing with a torn glove, a soiled belt, an imperfectly shaved face, hair too long, boots insufficiently shined, awkwardly dropping a musket at drill, or blunderingly stepping on the feet of neighbors at drill. Arranged in seven different grades, the demerits ranged from one, for a trivial blunder, to ten for such offenses as disobedience or sitting down when weary of standing guard.

One thing was hard to learn — a willing report on erring comrades to the commandant of cadets. Grant did it when ordered, as in the case of *Taylor* vs. *Hammond*. For Captain C. F. Smith he wrote out what he had seen: During maneuvers Hammond had ordered Taylor to "dress up" and when Taylor "did not appear to obey," had repeated the command "in a very loud and harsh manner," provoking Taylor to call Hammond "by several bad names such as d——d little b——d and other names quite as vulgar and said that if he caught Cadet Hammond out of ranks and if Cadet Hammond spoke to him in such a manner out of ranks — I do not remember which — he would kick him."

Lamely, Grant concluded his report:

> These are the principal circumstances that I remember not expecting to have been called upon to make a statement of them.   *Signed*, CADET U. H. GRANT

No longer fearful of his classes or of discipline, Grant found Academy life boresome. The outside world was far away, and when snow and ice halted river traffic the mails came only at intervals of two or three days. On Saturdays Sam scrubbed the floor of his room and wished that he was coursing the woodland roads, his horse stretching out beneath him, the wind in his face.

In December there came a ray of hope. Congress was debating with unusual fervor another of those bills calling for the abolishment of the Academy. Grant devoured every reference to the question in the newspaper and later said: "I saw in this an honorable way to obtain a discharge, and read the debates with much interest, but with impatience at the delay." When the bill failed he had one more proof that a practical man could never expect an ironic Fate to fulfill his hopes. Inside him was forming another superstition, one stemming from his mother's religious resignation, and phrased by him, later on, "Circumstances always did shape my course different from my plans." [40]

In January came the crucial examination which was harder this year, thanks to Superintendent Delafield's zeal for tightening up the lax administration of his predecessor, Major René De Russy. But Sam Grant passed it. His six months probationary period was ended; he was now a bona fide West Pointer. In his studies nothing but French bothered him. Mathematics was ridiculously easy. The algebra which had been Greek to him last May proved to be nothing at all, now that his teachers had given him the key. Geometry and trigonometry, in their turn, were easy. Although some cadets employed extracurricular aids, books of illustrations giving short cuts to puzzling questions, Sam never bothered with them and, in later years, could not remember ever having heard of them. Mathematics, he said, "was so easy . . . as to come almost by intuition." [41]

Still, as he confessed later on, without reserve, "I did not take hold of my studies with avidity, in fact I rarely ever read over a lesson the second time." Whether he knew it or not, his father was receiving monthly reports of his work and bombarding the authorities when the paper failed to arrive. Rufe Ingalls in later years summed up Sam Grant as a cadet:

> In his studies he was lazy and careless. Instead of studying a lesson, he would merely read it over once or twice; but he was so quick in his perceptions that he usually made very fair recitations even with so little preparation. His memory was not at all good in an attempt to learn anything by heart accurately, and this made his grade low in those branches of study which required a special effort of the memory. In scientific subjects he was very bright, and if he had labored hard he would have stood very high in them.[42]

Indulging that lazy, dreamy streak which was growing inside him, Grant sat in his room reading novels when he should have been declining French verbs — romantic novels borrowed from the Academy's library, Scott, Cooper, Bulwer, Irving, Marryat and Lever. Presumably he read slowly as he did in later years. Only once did he make the forbidden trip to Benny Havens' Tavern, the traditional trip for the adventurous cadets. The time he went "he was beguiled by Rufe Ingalls, a staunch patron of that renowned establishment."[43]

February brought Grant his first listing as "distinguished for correct Deportment" — one of a hundred. And when the spring had gone and summer come and the school year ended, he had still not been punished for an offense. He stood 137th among 233 cadets on the Conduct Roll — and his 59 demerits had come, as Rufe Ingalls noted, not for disobedience but for slouchiness.[44]

More anxiously awaited was the posting of class standings. Up in the administrative offices, the Superintendent and his assistants were working on the record, setting down opposite each cadet's name his numerical grades in each subject, then adding to their total the figure awarded for Conduct, the total establishing his General Merit. "Any special excellence in study would be affected by the manner in which he tied his shoes," Grant sardonically commented in later years.[45] Eventually this list went up and the cadets crowded around the bulletin board. Sam Grant stood number 27 among the 60 boys who had survived from the original 73. In mathematics he was number 16, in French 49. As at home, he had done well the things he liked to do. Rufe Ingalls was number 25, Franklin number 1, Joe Reynolds 4, Deshon 9, Augur 11, Quinby 14, Steele 16, French 19.

The disadvantages of the demerit system bore more heavily upon the graduating class than any other — for example Bill Sherman. He was posted number 6, yet everybody said that without that average of 150 "bad marks" a year, his standing would have allowed him something better than the Artillery, which he was entering. The whole class had turned out a disappointment in that only one man, Hebert, had been deemed worthy of entering the Corps of Engineers. A year ago the Class of '39 had produced five for that Corps.[46]

Authorities listed the graduates according to their records, the exceptional ones being given their choice of any branch, Corps of Engineers, Topographical Engineers, Ordnance, Artillery, Dragoons or Infantry. The men with the next best ratings could usually choose anything but the Corps of Engineers, the third group anything but the Corps of Engineers, Topographical Engineers, Ordnance, and Artillery. The lower half of the class usually had to content itself with Infantry which offered the largest number of jobs, or with the Dragoons if an opening existed in the one regiment of cavalry which the Army maintained. Few graduates willingly took the Infantry, a plodding, footsore assignment with enlisted men who were generally hardened immigrant veterans of European armies with a smattering of tough, wayward or lazy native Americans. The Dragoons, who were almost all American-born, were considered more pleasant to command.

Dick Ewell was picking the Dragoons because that branch would take him to the Far West where, as he told his family, he would have a better opportunity of finding "some more independent way of getting my living" when he resigned as he planned soon to do.[47]

A future in the Army was a dismal prospect to Grant as his plebe year ended. Still, he was more resigned to continuing at the Academy than he had been in December. For one thing, Dickey the

Punster in his reform of the curriculum had introduced a course in horsemanship with a sergeant to act as riding master, four dragoons to assist and forty-two horses for the cadets to ride. Cavalry drill was to be added formally in the coming year.[48]

As a sophomore Grant would be freer to do the one thing of all that he did best.

CHAPTER FIVE

Decision for the Future

T
HE RICH ODORS of a turkey roasting filled the room. The bird hung in the little fireplace at the end of a string, turning and spinning as Sam Grant and Dragon Deshon wound it up and then let it unwind. They were as quiet as cadets always were during these lawless midnight feasts.

Grant had found at the start of this, his second year, that George Deshon was not only a very agreeable boy to room with, but that he was a most enterprising forager. George was so straight-faced a Connecticut Yankee, so remarkable in his studies and so impeccable in conduct that the authorities never suspected that he was as Grant knew him to be, an expert and stealthy raider who "carried off Old Delafield's apples and an occasional turkey or chicken." [1]

Superintendent Delafield had for two years now been trying to stamp out the cadets' ancient custom of stealing food from the mess hall or buying it from neighboring farmers for their forbidden feasts. He had tried improving the regulation fare, hoping to fill the boys up, and had issued so many warnings to farmers that, as Dick Ewell had written home earlier that year, "none of the old women will make pies for the cadets within five miles around." [2]

All these edicts by Dickey the Punster had apparently done nothing more than make boys like Deshon steal fowls instead of buying them. This one — this turkey — was particularly fine —

The door of the room swung open, and there stood the Officer of the Day, Lieutenant William N. Grier, newly returned from fighting Choctaw Indians in the West to serve as instructor in cavalry tactics!

Sam and the Dragon sprang to attention, standing elbow to elbow in front of the fireplace, and as Grier moved this way and that, they shifted like automatons, keeping between him and the turkey. Finally he departed, having inspected everything but the fireplace. [3]

The boys breathed again. Sometimes you got an officer of the day like that. Grier was a good fellow. Sam had already heard of the funny thing Grier had said to the French teacher, Claudius Berard, back in 1832–1835, when Grier had been a cadet. As Grant told it, Berard, meeting Grier for the first time and noting that he came from Western Pennsylvania, had said:

"Grier? Grier? I used to know a Judge Grier from your part of the country. Are you related to him?"

"Yes, distantly."

"Ah, second coosen, perhaps?" Grant emphasized the "coosen" pronunciation; he always disliked the French language.

"No," the cadet had answered, "he is the oldest of twelve children, and I'm the youngest. That's the distance of our relationship." [4]

There was fun, too, that fall of 1840 when word went around that old Delafield was ordering new-style pantaloons. "Divinity pants" the boys had always called the old style — pants of clerical whiteness and Puritanic discomforts, one of which was that they opened at the side and thus consumed much time when you had to dress in haste, as you usually did. It was this buttoned flap that Delafield was eliminating.

The reform had had its birth that September when the new juniors had returned from the summer furlough. One of them, John Pope, whose father had been a big man in the territorial days of Illinois and was now the United States District Judge of the State, had come swaggering up in pantaloons which buttoned down the front — "flies," the innovation would later be called — the first ever seen at the Academy . . . and the Academy was supposed to set fashion for the Army. When the officers' women-folk heard of this style which so boldly recognized male anatomy, there was horror and consternation, and Mrs. Delafield, learning that her husband was praising it on the grounds of economy and practical utility — his two pet hobbies — was reported as saying that "cadets thus dressed should not come in person to the house." But the Superintendent was master of the Academy, if not his own house, and he told the tailors to make cadet pants, henceforth, open in the front.[5]

Sam Grant was finding the start of his sophomore year livelier in many ways. Although some of his classmates, years later, could never remember him attending any of the dances for which girls arrived elaborately chaperoned from New England and New York, Sam wrote in his account book that September, "Dancing master, $2; cotillion parties, $2.26."

He started the term as a first section man in mathematics, each class being divided into groups of fifteen according to their ability to cover ground in the course. To be at the top was a distinction, and especially this year, for sophomore mathematics was recognized as the hardest of all — analytical geometry, calculus and surveying. Some twenty-five years later a relative of Sam's discovered in a descriptive geometry class that the standard solution for a certain problem was one Grant had made.[6]

Sam noted the plebes — Simon Bolivar Buckner of Kentucky, Winfield Scott Hancock of Pennsylvania, Daniel M. Frost of New York, Alfred Pleasanton, District of Columbia, Alexander Hays, Pennsylvania. A small class, and unimpressive; but then, plebes always were.

With his own plebe stigma removed, Grant was free to establish friendships with three from the class ahead, now august juniors — Pete Longstreet, Calvin Benjamin from Indiana, Lafayette McLaws from Georgia and in the senior class, one who was "something of a wag," Alfred Sully, the twenty-year-old son of Thomas Sully, the famous portrait painter, attracted him.[7]

Both Longstreet and McLaws would later say that they were "on terms of the closest intimacy" with Sam Grant in Academy days, Longstreet remembering that this intimacy had begun in 1839, and that he and Grant had become "fast friends at their first meeting." Sam and Longstreet shared a certain air of steadfastness and common sense and a love of horses, although athletic Longstreet enjoyed football, military field maneuvers and sword exercises — slicing at dummy heads from horseback — all of which Grant disliked.[8]

Big, hulking Longstreet thought that it was Grant's "fragile," "delicate frame" that kept him out of sports and that his "distinguishing trait as a cadet was a girlish modesty; a hesitancy in presenting his own claims; a taciturnity born of his modesty; but a thoroughness in the accomplishment of whatever task was assigned him." Longstreet was particularly impressed with Sam's "sense of honor" which "was so perfect . . . that in the numerous cabals which were often formed his name was never mentioned." [9]

The isolation of their life knit the cadets together. Although they were permitted to visit the quarters of their officers and professors on Saturday afternoons, they seldom did so, for the staff and faculty were painfully reserved.[10]

The sophomores gossiped about the upper classmen, guessing as to who would remain in the Army, who would resign, who would make good soldiers. Among the juniors, Longstreet had militarism written all over him. So had Earl Van Dorn, a Mississippian who was almost as small as Sam Grant, a boy with wavy, flaxen hair, ruddy face, finely chiseled features, imperious blue eyes, a way with the girls, and a fiery spirit that was always pulling down demerits upon him.[11] No soldier, apparently, could be fashioned out of Daniel H. Hill from South Carolina, short, slender, intellectual, coldly polite, even morose, his mind centering on mathematics and religion, shaping toward the day when he would be writing textbooks on algebra and the crucifixion of Christ.[12] John Pope, the boy with the flies, was loud, confident, aggressive; he could be a leader. Abner Doubleday from New York was energetic and would probably climb. Rosey Rosecrans should go the farthest, for he was good at everything — his studies, his military duties, his deportment, and talked interestingly, gaily and fast, his imagination racing.

Nobody in school, so the old-timers said, would ever equal the "good boy" record set by a Virginian, Robert E. Lee, between 1825 and 1829, when he had gone all four years without getting a single black mark. Lee was already a captain, superintendent engineer on improvements in the Missouri and Mississippi Rivers.

The juniors — the Class of 1842? Don Carlos Buell had a brilliant mind although his testy temper brought him floods of demerits; in June of '39 he had been confined to his room for assaulting a waiter in mess hall.[13] Schuyler Hamilton should do well; he was the grandson of the immortal Alexander. But it was Nathaniel Lyon who ought to be the soldier of the lot.

Red-haired Lyon of Connecticut was one of the few complete Puritans in the Academy, a slave to duty, a born martinet and an intense student always near the top of his class. Grant always would remember him as "a fellow who was never caught in any scrapes," and a few years after graduation, if not in college, "a fanatic on religious questions." A homely fellow in a school where among the cadets "personal beauty is as much prized as among girls," Lyon was solitary and brooding, giving signs of the reformer's zeal which would set him to scorching orthodox churches for their defense of slavery and their assaults upon Lamarck's theories of evolution — two causes which were, to him, crusades.[14]

Grant would never remember Lyon as an antislavery agitator in college. As one cadet, Truman Seymour, put it, "The discussion of slavery was unknown," although if any had taken place the Northern view would have been the one to be inculcated, since the prejudices of that section dominated the faculty and the staff.[15]

Episcopalianism, the religion preached in the Academy Chapel, frowned upon antislavery agitation. All of the Academy's chaplains, from the first, had been of this faith which was regarded as the ideal one for officers and gentlemen, and the Reverend Martin P. Parks, who was taking over the pulpit in 1840 for a period that would last six years, had been recently converted from low-church Methodism to Episcopalianism. The zeal of the convert was carrying him so rapidly along the high-church path that he was edging toward Roman Catholicism. Deshon and James A. Hardie of Grant's class were among the cadets who absorbed Parks's teachings, but the mass of boys regarded chapel as a chore; indeed some were disrespectful toward it, causing occasional warnings such as, "It has been brought to the notice of the Commandant that some cadets are in the habit of spitting tobacco spittle on the floor of the church on Sunday morning to such a degree as to render part of it unfit for use in the afternoon." [16]

Since the use of tobacco was against the regulations, many cadets chewed tobacco secretly and smoked in private. Sam Grant tried smoking, became very sick and gave it up. His classmate Franklin always remembered how Sam was "a good fellow" with "a sense of humor" and was always ready for a frolic. Grant drank with the boys at times, but when several members of the class swore off in an attempt to remove temptation from a weak member of the class, he joined the rescue movement.[17]

It was his horsemanship that made him a marked man even among those cadets who, knowing him only casually, suspected that he was dull. Longstreet regarded him as "the most daring horseman in the Academy," and others, in later years, remembered him as the "tiny-looking" but resolute figure dressed in old clothes — cadets wore no uniforms in the sweat and dust of the riding hall during ordinary exercises — striding to the stables with his spurs clanging "and his great cavalry sword dangling by his side." [18]

In November and again in December, he was on the list as "distinguished for correct deportment," but, on January 20, 1841, he committed, at last, an offense which brought punishment — visiting after taps — and was given one extra tour of duty. He was beginning to feel at home at the Academy, and through December and January not only quit hoping that Congress would abolish the place, but actually started fearing that it might. His success in mathematics had worked this complete reversal. He planned now to finish the course, graduate, secure an appointment on the faculty as an instructor of mathematics, stay if possible for the four remaining years of his enlistment, then resign and take a professorship of mathematics at "some respectable college." Here lay security, and after a term of years as a professor he could retire, go back to Georgetown and spend his old age driving along those beloved roads that ran down to the Ohio — back with old friends and new horses in the happy scenes of his boyhood.[19]

His dreams still went back to Georgetown even though his father, in recent months, had sold out and moved to the neighborhood town of Bethel, in Clermont County. Jesse had made the change in order to establish a retail outlet at Galena, the famous lead-mining city in northwestern Illinois. Ever since the end of the Black Hawk War, in 1832, had opened that country to settlers, immigrants had poured in. Towns had sprung up along the rivers and Galena had, within a few years, become the metropolis of the Upper Mississippi region. Visiting the place, Jesse had seen fortunes being made in lead mines, in wholesale commission houses and in the shipping trade which kept steamboats crowding up and down the six miles of the Fevre River, between Galena and the Mississippi. Into town farmers were bringing cowhides, and on steamers buffalo skins were arriving from the prairies to the northwest. Everybody in the booming region needed leather for shoes or harness.

To add this rich market to his regular trade in the Ohio River Valley, Jesse had done away with his own retail business and become a wholesaler exclusively. He formed a partnership with E. A. Collins, a tanner of Bethel. By its terms Jesse moved to Bethel, taking Collins's tannery and expanding it, while Collins had taken the combined stocks of prepared hides to Galena, where he opened a retail store. The venture was prospering. Jesse and Collins got on well, and Jesse's son Simpson, who was now eighteen, spent part of his time at Galena. The Bethel tannery was considerably larger than the old one at Georgetown, with the curing hides overflowing on fences along the intersecting streets, Charity and Water. The firm's wagons rolled to Cincinnati, which was twelve miles nearer than when they had gone from Georgtown.[20]

Ulysses, receiving all this news by letter, could visualize it well, for he had often visited his mother's relatives in Bethel. He knew the house on Plane Street into which the family had moved — a good house opposite the old stage tavern.

In June Ulysses would get to see all these changes, since, by Academy rules, a cadet received his first furlough, one of ten weeks, at the end of his sophomore year. Jesse prepared for his boy's home-coming, buying a beautiful bay colt for him to ride — a colt as yet unbroken to harness, just as Ulysses liked them.[21]

Slowly the springtime passed for Ulysses. There was an incident in April, when his name was posted on the "distinguished" list again, and another in May, when he was punished with two extra tours of duty for "kicking a horse." That same month a cadet named Hall was given the same sentence for merely "kicking at a horse." As the end of the term drew near and thoughts of home came faster, Ulysses' old indifference to dress vanished. He ordered a new uniform, one costing $7.79, in which to walk down the streets of Bethel and Georgetown with everybody, particularly the girls, staring, and perhaps some of the elders admitting that they had been wrong to say Jesse Grant's boy would never make a soldier.

The uniform was ready when, in early June, he set out for home. He was taking no academic honors to show his father, but he had not disgraced himself. In his class he stood number 24, his demerits for the year were 69, 8 more than in his freshman year, and on the Conduct Roll he was number 144 among 219.[22]

Ulysses' journey home was all the happier because he joined, at Harrisburg, his favorite relative, Grandmother Simpson, who was on her way back from a visit in Philadelphia. And with her was a girl of his own age, Kate Lowe, who was going to see her relative,

John Lowe, a lawyer of Bethel, who was also a friend of Grant's. Kate recalled in later years how straight the cadet had stood, how soldierly he was in his blue coat and white trousers, how well he talked about horses and novels, once he got over his reticence. She didn't think him awkward. The thing she liked best about him was his thoughtfulness for his aged grandmother.[23]

Down the river — the familiar sights increasing — the steamer stop at the landing — across to Bethel — in at the front door, back home after two years.

His mother said "Ulysses, you've grown much straighter!"

"Yes, that was the first thing they taught me." [24]

There was a new baby he had never seen before, Mary Frances. She would be two on July 20. Orvil was six, Virginia was nine, Clara thirteen and Simpson sixteen. There was his father beaming with pride — and the colt. There were his cousins and friends in Bethel, his schoolmates in Georgetown, Mrs. Bailey, to whom he was devoted, a round of calls, dinners, parties. There was Mary King, a girl to whom he had sent one of his drawings from West Point. Some of the neighbors thought he was in love with her. Others thought he went riding more with Kate Lowe, still others that his favorite riding companions were the daughters of Thomas Morris who, having retired from the United States Senate in 1839, managed his neighboring farms from his home in Bethel — the big house of the town.[25]

Some years later, a friend, sitting by a campfire with Grant one evening, heard him say that "his cadet days were filled with dreams of a young lady he intended to marry as soon as he graduated, and his one thought at West Point was of her. However, his dreams had not come true. He did not mention the girl's name." [26]

Was she Mary King? Mary, in time, married another man. Was she Miss Lowe? Sam bet her one of his paintings against one of her rings that she would be married before he graduated from the Academy. He won the bet. Was she one of the Morris girls? [27]

Whoever the girl was, if indeed she were an actuality, girls as an institution helped make this the happiest summer of his life. Visits to the homes of his relatives — the lush and lazy summer of careless rides along roads that seemed new now that farmers' axes had cut down the forests that had walled in the paths when he had, as a little boy, coursed them standing on his horse's back — new clearings, new houses — the road winding past White Oak Creek where Dan Ammen had saved his life — the roads rolling out onto the gully-cut hills at Point Pleasant where the great river lay below — the river far fuller, now, of those smoking stacks and churning paddles. . . .

It was a lazy, lovely summer with no drums — no drums and, in their place, the soft thud of unhurried hoofs in the leaves and the dust.

"This I enjoyed beyond any other period of my life," Ulysses said later, when he was ready to die. He said he had spent most of the ten weeks with his old schoolmates.[28]

In the summer of 1841 he looked forward to nothing so much as making some money in the world and then coming home to live among these friends.

At last his furlough was done, and off he went to the hateful drums again. He wondered if he would be called out as a cadet sergeant as the worthy juniors expected to be; he had not been good enough to become a corporal in his sophomore year. Yes, when he arrived at the Academy, there was his name posted with Deshon and Steele and fifteen others. He accepted, but, as he later pointed out, "The promotion was too much for me." He was dropped and went back into the ranks, never to rise out of the cadet marching mass again, a born private, like Sherman, so far as the drill masters were concerned.[29]

There was a new adjutant, Ohio-born Lieutenant Irvin McDowell, the wealthy and cultured nephew of the famous soldier-statesman of the Northwest, Lewis Cass. Educated at a military school in France, McDowell had found West Point easy, graduating at twenty in the Class of '38. "No one could know him without liking him," Sam Grant would say, yet "McDowell never was what you would call a popular man." This puzzled Grant, as it would other West Point graduates in later years, for Mac was "a fountain of hospitality," entertaining well and talking intelligently about painting, music, architecture and landscape gardening as well as militarism. Yet he had no magnetism and found it difficult to remember names and faces. Never quite a martinet, he was nevertheless so intense in manner when on duty that his inferiors shrank from him and for

all his masculine poise and virility may have had at twenty-three
the irritating trait he had at forty-three, "a voice like a woman's"
— one that "squealed" when he became excited.[30]

Among the plebes was an aristocrat from Phillips Exeter Academy,
proud and ambitious Fitz-John Porter, a relative of the famous
"Navy Porters" — the family of Commodore David Porter, hero of
the War of 1812 who, still alive, had a nephew, three sons and one
foster son, David Glasgow Farragut, at sea. Porter's roommate was
a bright one, too, William Farrar Smith, a Vermonter called "Baldy"
because, at eighteen, his hair was thinning at the front of the skull.[31]

Henry Coppee of Georgia was marked among the plebes for brains.
A six-foot South Carolinian, Bernard E. Bee, was quiet, gentle and
popular, but an indifferent student, as was twenty-year-old Gordon
Granger of New York, an "Odd Dick" who had taught school
before receiving his appointment and whose ungainly body, bellowing voice and hunger for hunting and good living made men remember him.[32]

Sam Grant's junior year passed more tediously than the second
because it contained no mathematics other than a brief whiff of
astronomy in the experimental philosophy course. His best marks
were in that course, which also touched the scientific subjects of
electricity, magnetism and optics. Chemistry and drawing did not
stir him.

Once he obtained leave to go to New York.[33] It was perhaps the
same trip that took him to see the Hares in Philadelphia. The sisters,
Elizabeth and Sarah, were disappointed to see him arrive in civilian
clothes.

"Ulysses, put on your military!" Sarah said.

"No, I will not make a show of myself!" he answered and then
admitted that he had left his uniform in New York and had bought
a citizen's suit for the vacation. It would go hard with him if caught.[34]

Although he escaped detection for this major crime, he was
punished twice for others, receiving an extra tour of duty for
"neglect of duty as a squad marcher" and, later, two weeks' confinement to his quarters "for speaking in a disrespectful manner to a
superior officer." His demerits, by the end of the year in June 1842,
reached 98, placing him number 158 among the 215 cadets. Among
the 41 boys in his class he was number 20, his standing in philosophy

being number 15, in drawing 19 and chemistry 22. Hard up for money for his senior year, he bought the secondhand textbooks, instruments and sash of a graduating cadet, Edward G. Beckwith, paying $40 for what new would have cost him $49.54. It was a brilliant class he saw departing, seven of them finishing high enough to receive appointment into the Corps of Engineers.[35] And the incoming candidates for plebehood were remarkable too, 164, one of the largest mobs to date, and containing the most variegated characters in Grant's time at the Academy.[36]

One of them was only fifteen, too young to qualify; but the authorities were prepared to make an exception in his case, for he had already attended the University of Pennsylvania for two years and was said to be something of a mental prodigy — a boy named George B. McClellan. His body, though small, was strong enough to meet the physical qualifications, and he bore on "his charming countenance," as one of his classmates, Dabney H. Maury of Virginia, put it, every evidence of "gentle nature and high culture." The son of one celebrated and socially prominent Philadelphian and the brother of another, little McClellan was accepted by the Southerners as that rarity of rarities, a Northern aristocrat.[37]

The most unpromising newcomer? Most cadets agreed, right off, that it was nineteen-year-old Thomas J. Jackson, an awkward, shambling constable from the hills of western Virginia. The cadets had screeched when he made his ludicrous arrival in homespun clothes and a coarse wool hat, and a pair of saddlebags stained with horse sweat hanging from his round shoulders. A deadly determination was on his sober face and in his large brown eyes, and Maury, one of the first to notice it, turned to his fellow Virginian, Ambrose P. Hill, and said, "That fellow looks as if he had come to stay." As soon as he learned where Jackson was from, Maury rushed over to give him a Virginia gentleman's welcome, but was back in a minute, red-faced. The hillman had given him a cold, solemn rebuff.

"It is not desirable to have a large number of intimate friends," Jackson wrote in the book where he kept his precepts.

His big clumsy feet trampled the heels and tore the trousers of the men who marched just ahead of him at company drill and he wobbled so perilously in his saddle during the jumps in riding hall, and botched so horribly his attempt to cut dummy heads in sword drill that everybody was afraid he would kill himself. One cadet discovered that "Old Jack," as the strange boy with the odd mannerisms was soon called, "had been to a common school, knew a little grammar, could add up a column of figures, but as to vulgar or decimal fractions, it is doubtful if he had ever heard of them."

But there was something about the uncouth youngster that touched cadets and instructors even before they knew his story — how when he had been three his father had died after gambling away the family funds — how his mother with three young children had lived, for a time, on charity — how little Tom at six had gone to work on his half-uncle's farm and had grown up largely untutored, working beside slaves, and eventually serving as a constable, delivering summons from the sheriff because he thought the long rides across the mountains would cure the dyspepsia which he had, or imagined he had. Older men, noting his desperate hunger for an education, had managed to get him sent to West Point.

The steady mildness of his eye and the patient earnestness of his smile — "a sweet smile" more than one cadet called it — began to silence ridicule. William H. C. Whiting, head of the sophomores assigned to prepare the "Things" for their examination, was so moved by Jackson that he gave him private lessons in fractions and coached him so constantly that Old Jack became known as "Whiting's Plebe." The spectacle of the back-mountain boy at the examination etched itself on the mind of one classmate: "His whole soul was bent upon passing. When he went to the blackboard the perspiration was streaming from his face, and during the whole examination his anxiety was painful to witness. While trying to work out his example in fractions, the cuffs of his coat, first the right and then the left, were brought into requisition to wipe off the perspiration." The onlooking cadet could never forget how pleased Jackson was when he was told that he had passed and could now take his seat, while "every member of the examining board turned away his head to hide the smile which could not be suppressed."

Had he passed?

Any of the faculty answering such a question could have asked, in return, if West Point were nothing but stone and brick.

By September, when the classroom work was on, the cadets saw Jackson sitting at his table, open book before him, eyes fixed on the blank wall, lost to the world. It was the January examination he was seeing. He was still afraid he would be sent home. "Never was there such a boning," a classmate commented. Before ten o'clock when everybody must be in bed, Old Jack would pile the coal high in his fireplace so that, after taps, he could lie on his stomach studying till the small hours of the morning. And if an Officer of the Day peeped in and caught him so, the door would close softly. The fellow's *lamp* had gone out on time, hadn't it? [38]

Sam Grant saw Nathaniel Lyon all over again in Jackson's fierce devotion to duty: "Some of us regarded him as a fanatic," and at times this fanaticism "took strange forms — hypochondria, fancies that an evil spirit had taken possession of him." [39]

Animated when conversing with a small circle of friends, shy and silent in crowds, "roughly dressed, quiet, stoop-shouldered and a good listener," Jackson a few years later would remind some army officers of Sam Grant. [40]

There were other characters almost as curious in this Class of '46; for instance, George H. Derby of Massachusetts — the imp of imps, nicknamed "Squibob," defacing textbooks with caricatures of professors, playing jokes on teachers and cadets alike, yet committing his crimes with such extravagant humor as to escape full punishment. Sam Grant delighted to recall the time Derby heard his professor ask a problem in tactics — "If you commanded 1000 besieged men with such and such equipment what would you do, keeping in mind the military axiom that after forty-five days any fort will surrender?" Derby's waggish hand waved, the reckless professor nodded to him, and out popped the answer, "I'd march out, let the enemy come in, and at the end of forty-five days I'd change places with him." [41] Humorless, courtly young gentlemen like Maury saw Squibob as merely a coarse and tasteless burlesquer, but less priggish cadets would not be surprised in later years when Derby became nationally famous as "John Phoenix," humorist. [42]

Almost as funny was a big-nosed, short-necked, high-shouldered, eighteen-year-old fence rail of a boy from Vermont who signed himself "Decatur Matthew Hale Carpenter," but was content with "Matt" — a stooping Yankee laughing inwardly at the absurdities of militarism. When it was safe to do so, he would raise his finely shaped head and mimic, devastatingly, a perfect soldier on parade, drawling meanwhile, "I don't believe a man can ever become great by learning to walk a crack with a stiff neck and his fingers on the seams of his pantaloons." The discipline seemed childish to him who, at the age of sixteen, had gone into court as a lawyer, won the case for his client and received a five-dollar fee. Within two years he would leave the Academy, off on a sensational career as a lawyer and political leader in distant Wisconsin.[43]

A fiery Virginian, rebellious against some of West Point's sartorial rules, was George E. Pickett, who had been appointed from Illinois where he had gone to seek his fortune with an uncle, John G. Stuart, a former law partner of Abraham Lincoln. Pickett would be forever slow in class and, thanks to his frequent insistence upon wearing a soft collar and tie instead of the prescribed stock, would always be near the bottom of the Conduct Roll.[44]

A remarkable class, one that would turn out the extraordinary number of seven engineers, five of them Easterners.

For his final year, Sam Grant took Fred Dent as roommate. The legend remained at the Academy long afterward that the two boys one day broke the taboo against discussing the sectional politics which was growing hotter in the nation outside. They stripped for a fight but the absurdity of the quarrel finally forced itself upon Grant and he commenced to laugh, ending the strained situation.[45]

Among the cadets Sam was known for an unshakable poise. Not even the ordeal of the blackboard recitation, bugbear of most cadets, could intimidate him. George Thomas, proverbially the most imperturbable cadet of his generation, had been seen by his bosom friend, Cump Sherman, to turn pale with suffering when, at the blackboard, "he didn't know his lesson." [46]

Sam French saw Grant at the blackboard under unusual conditions. As their section in engineering marched toward the recitation hall one day, Frank Gardner brought out a huge heirloom watch, some four inches in diameter, and passed it among his classmates. By chance Sam Grant was holding it as they entered the recitation room and, with a quick motion, stuffed it into the bosom of his coat and buttoned it down. The boys took their seats. Professor Mahan was absent and in his place was his assistant, Lieutenant Zealous B. Tower. Four cadets, Grant among them, were sent to the board to work out problems. When Grant had finished his figuring, he laid down his chalk, turned and began to explain it in detail. Suddenly there cut across his voice the sound of a great bong, bong, bonging. French said it sounded like a Chinese gong. Tower thought the racket was coming from the hall and ordered the door closed which only made the noise louder. Nobody knew the source of the infernal ringing except Frank Gardner, who sat very still, and Sam Grant, who talked straight ahead, missing no syllable in his mathematical explanation. One by one the cadets realized what had happened — Gardner had slyly set the monstrous alarm in the ancient timepiece just before he allowed his friends to handle it, and now it was bonging away, on and on, and Tower was hunting everywhere in bewilderment, with Sam Grant standing there, the Spartan boy with a clamorous wolf in his breast. Eventually Sam outtalked the alarm, wound up his demonstration, and sat down. It was only after the recitation — and recitations lasted from sixty to ninety minutes — that the cadets could let go their laughter as they scampered into the open air.[47]

Dennis H. Mahan, the great professor of the Academy for over forty years, author of standard textbooks, sharpest of "mental drill-masters" with "an almost intuitive perception of the exact amount of information possessed by each [student]," analyzed Sam Grant years later as, indeed, he analyzed all his students. He said he had found Grant to be "a first-section man in all his scientific studies; that is, one who accomplished the full course. He always showed himself a clear thinker and a steady worker. He belonged to the class of compactly strong men who went at their task at once, and kept at it until finished, never being seen, like the slack-twisted class, yawning, lolling on their elbows over their work, and looking as if just ready to sink down from mental insanity." Years afterward, thinking about Grant, Mahan concluded that his "mental machine" was of the "powerful low-pressure class, which condenses its own steam and consumes its own smoke."

The nervous, imaginative, brilliant professor enjoyed studying his boys and predicting their futures; he was prepared, he said, to learn that this one or that one would "accomplish something great" — Sherman, for instance, but not Sam Grant. The professor saw Grant, with his "round, cheery, boyish face," as a man full of "character and quiet manner," but not of genius.[48]

Military engineering, civil engineering, constitutional and international law, science of war and fortifications, mineralogy and geology, military pyrotechnics, review of artillery and infantry tactics — the classes ground along.

Grant was more popular than in other years. He was elected president of the cadet literary society, "The Dialectic," which, rightly or wrongly, was described as difficult "for the plain pupils to enter." He signed the society's documents, "U. H. Grant" above the signature of the secretary, "W. S. Hancock." With eleven others, including Rufe Ingalls and Nykins Quinby, he belonged to a secret society, "T. I. O.," twelve in one, whose members wore rings bearing the mystic initials and swore never to part with them until marriage came — then their wives should have them.[49]

It was his horsemanship that would be the thing the cadets remembered best about Sam Grant. The plebes especially went to the riding hall just to watch him. Egbert Viele, who had arrived in June 1842, said, "It was as good as any circus to see Grant ride. . . . There was a dark bay horse that was so fractious that it was about to be condemned. . . . Grant selected it for his horse. He bridled, mounted, and rode it every day at parade; and how he did ride! He handled the refractory creature as a giant would a child. The whole class would stand around admiring his wonderful command of the beast and his graceful evolutions." [50]

Rufe Ingalls, noting how Sam always broke the bad horses that were added to the Academy stables, explained how he did it - "not by punishing the animal . . . but by patience and tact, and his skill in making the creature know what he wanted to have it do." [51]

Sam's gentleness with horses was proverbial, yet on March 24, 1843 there went down on a page in the Post Order Books, Special Order 42 — "Cadet Grant, for maltreating his horse, is hereby placed in arrest, limits his room." And on April 1, a hand entered, "Cadet Grant is released from arrest." [52]

Sam Grant was never known to mention this most ironic event of his four years at the Academy — evidently something more serious than "kicking a horse." Had some officer, knowing far less about horses than Grant, jumped to a wrong conclusion while the boy was handling his mount? Or had Sam lost his temper for once? Men who knew him in later years agreed that the only time they had ever seen him lose his self-control was when he saw other men abusing horses.

James B. Fry, a greenhorn plebe from Illinois, saw Grant ride that June of 1843, a sight that stayed with him always. Fry had been wandering around the strange new grounds while awaiting his entrance examination and had stumbled upon an event! The graduating exercises of the Senior Class! The riding hall was full of spectators, professors, official visitors. Superintendent Delafield was there. It was a dashing scene as the horsemen wheeled, flashed their swords, maneuvered, put their horses over the bar. At last it was done, and the riders drew their horses into line down the middle of the long tanbark floor. They waited. Something special, something not on the program was coming!

Sergeant Herschberger, the riding master, strode to the jumping bar, lifted it higher than his head, fixed it in place, then, facing the class, barked, "Cadet Grant!"

Fry saw a slender little cadet dash from the ranks on a big sorrel, wheel and gallop down toward the far end of the hall.

West Pointers were saying to their guests, "He's on York."

York was the great horse of the stables, a powerful long-legged animal whom no one but Sam Grant and his classmate, Cave Couts, could ride — and Cave didn't pretend to ride him as well. Another classmate, Charles S. Hamilton, had once told Sam, "That horse will kill you some day," and had been answered lightly, "Well, I can't die but once." [53]

Now, at the extreme end of the hall, Grant turned York, and then the two of them came thundering down toward the bar, faster, faster — then into the air and over. To Fry it seemed "as if man and beast had been welded together."

Fry heard the old sergeant cut the breathless silence with, "Very well done, sir! Class dismissed."

Years later, when Fry told Grant that he had been present "when you made the great jump in the riding exercises of your graduation," Ulysses said, "Yes, I remember that very well. York was a wonderful horse. I could feel him gathering under me for the effort as he approached the bar."

Army men in after times could not recall whether it was on this or an earlier occasion that Grant and York had set the Academy high-jump record which stood for at least twenty-five years. And there would be arguments as to whether the mark itself had been five feet six inches or "more than six feet." [54]

In the rush of the graduation exercises Grant had no time to notice the plebes who were being harried around the grounds. If he had, he would have found a reminder of his own entrance, four years before, in the troubles a tall, bright-faced, nineteen-year-old boy from Indiana was having with the authorities over his name. They insisted it must stand, as sent, "Ambrose Everett Burnside," no matter how much he insisted that his middle name was "Everts." He explained why it was "Everts": He had been born apparently dead, but the family doctor, Sylvanus Everts, had tickled his nose with a feather, he had breathed, and his mother had given him the doctor's name. Interesting, said the authorities, but the name was still "Everett." [55]

Sam Grant, as one of his friends later said, made one last effort at graduation to have his own name rightfully entered, but the Adjutant General at Washington paid no attention to his request, so he called himself U. S. Grant thereafter.[56] As late as April 8, when Grant had written to New York to buy two of Lever's novels, *Charles O'Malley* and *Harry Lorrequer*, he had still been signing himself "Ulysses H.," but now that he was officially on the rolls as "Ulysses S.," he gave up.[57]

He was taking home a report card that was neither good nor bad — number 21 among 39 in class standing. His fourth-year marks placed him number 16 in engineering, 28 in ethics, 25 in artillery tactics, 28 in infantry tactics, 17 in mineralogy and geology. On the Conduct Roll he stood number 156 in a corps of 233. His final year's demerits, 66, brought his four-year total of bad marks to 290, which meant that he was going out as he had come in, a middle man. Rufe Ingalls noted that Sam had "gone through the four years with ease and probably might have graduated higher in the list if there had been anything to call out exertion on his part." [58]

He viewed the final class standings with less concern than did most of his fellow graduates, for he expected to spend relatively little time in whatever corps he was to join. He hoped to return soon to the faculty, as an assistant in the mathematics department. Until that appointment came, he would content himself in either of the two branches open to a cadet of his standing, the Dragoons or the Infantry. To the authorities he handed his preference, Dragoons first, Fourth Infantry second, but it really was of small importance.[59]

All around him his classmates were discussing their futures. Not one of them had shown enough scholarship to be recommended to the Corps of Engineers, a sad commentary on the class as a whole. The top six, Franklin, Deshon, Brereton, Grelaud, Reynolds and Quinby, could choose anything below the Corps of Engineers. Numbers 7 to 16 might apply for anything but the Engineers and the Topographical Engineers, the rest, numbers 17 to 39, could not enter those two corps nor Ordnance and Artillery.

It would be weeks before the graduates would know the corps and the regiments they were to join. Their rank could be expected to be merely that of brevet second lieutenant for several years, since advancement was at a snail's pace in most regiments. The trouble lay in the reluctance of older officers to resign; the Army had no retired list into which they could step when old, and the War Department was too soft-hearted to kick them out into poverty. As a result, younger officers did the work of superiors who had been absent from their regiments for years, drawing pay in comfortable cities.

Grant left his measurements at the post tailors for two uniforms, one Dragoon, one Infantry, with an order to make up the one he would specify, by letter, when he learned his assignment. His accounts were square. The $54.60 credited to him every two months had exactly paid for his clothes, textbooks, magazine subscriptions, novels, and petty indulgences. As a business man he would not have to apologize to his father so long as he did not bring up the fact that Rufe Ingalls had saved $150 in four years. Rufe was probably leaving with more than that, considering the skill with which he had played cards so many nights.[60]

The classmates shook hands in farewell. Few of them could expect to meet in the same regiments. Most of them were to spend their three months' vacation in travel. Sam Grant was to spend his among his boyhood friends in Ohio. Also he needed rest, since he had been coughing hard the last four months — "Tyler's Grip" the doctors called it. He was painfully thin, his weight down to 117 pounds, just what it had been when he had entered the Academy, although he had grown six inches in the four years. He wondered if he were going to die of consumption as had Uncle Noah and Uncle John.[61] Had he lost his boyhood fever and ague on the heights of West Point only to go home with something more deadly?

Time and fate would tell. Meanwhile, he would go through the motions of being a soldier until he started teaching mathematics.

From the steamer going down the Hudson he saw the tops of the stone buildings on the hill disappear behind the trees. He was not saying good-by. He didn't expect to be gone long.

CHAPTER SIX

Emmy Dent's Enchantment

IT WAS July 28 of that summer of 1843 when Ulysses learned that his second choice, the Fourth Infantry, had been granted him and that he was to join it on September 20 at Jefferson Barracks on the outskirts of St. Louis. Quickly he filled in the standard oath of a commissioned officer, brevet second lieutenant, before John Quinlan, Justice of the Peace in Bethel, mailed it to the War Department and three days later wrote his letter of acceptance to the Adjutant General's office, a letter spotted with a reckless spelling:

> SIR — General Orders No. 42 had been rec'd and this is to notify you that I accept the appointment therein confered [*sic*]. My berth [*sic*] place is Point Pleasant, Clermont Co. Ohio and I was appointed from Ohio.
>   I have the honor to be, etc.
>   U. S. GRANT,
>   *4th Inf.*[1]

To the tailor at West Point he sent the information about the uniform, and then commenced "a time of great suspense." It would take a week for the letter to reach the tailor "and two more to make the clothes and have them sent to me. . . . I was impatient to get on my uniform and see how it looked." More than anything else he wanted his old schoolmates, "particularly the girls, to see me in it." [2] With it he would receive his sword, producing an ensemble far grander than that of a cadet, which, though impressive to his playmates, was still that of a schoolboy.

His father was pleased with him, and in his visits to Georgetown he found Tom Hamer showing him marked "partiality." Retirement from Congress had enabled Hamer to build his law practice into state-wide proportions, and, called upon for Democratic speeches far and wide, he was acquiring such prominence that Ulysses thought him destined, some day, to be President of the United States.[3]

Although Hamer and Jesse were now farther apart than ever politically, they allowed nothing to melt the bonds of their friendship a second time.

The Republic of Texas was the issue now. Ever since it had been established in 1836, pressure to have it annexed to the United States had been growing. The Slave States needed its votes to offset the greater population growth in the Free States. Ex-President Jackson was warning disciples that unless Texas was annexed his old foe, Great Britain, might use it as a base for an armed invasion of New Orleans, stir the Negroes to insurrection and seize the Mississippi Valley. Hamer was standing with Old Hickory, while Jesse was preaching the opposing Whig gospel as spread over the country by Horace Greeley's *New York Tribune*.

The sudden change from the Academy, where politics had been taboo, gave Ulysses his first definite political convictions and these were, as he later said, the principles laid down by Greeley — a protective tariff and opposition to the "conspiracy" by the Slave States to annex Texas for purely sectional advantage. Ulysses absorbed the belief that the slave power had originally planted colonists in the Mexican province of Texas, encouraged them to revolt and sent them sufficient riflemen to wring from the captured Mexican general Santa Anna their formal independence. Greeley held that the agreement, having been signed by Santa Anna when he was "in imminent and well-grounded fear of massacre," could not bind Mexico.[4]

What incensed the Whigs even more was their belief that President John Tyler, who had originally been of their faith, was now preparing to desert to the Democrats, using his support of annexation as bait.

But politics faded from Ulysses' mind in late August when his uniform and sword arrived. As he recited humorously in later years, a wave of conceit now flooded him and, climbing into his new regimentals and with sword dangling, he spurred away to Cincinnati to exhibit himself to friends and a metropolitan audience.

His giddy head started to clear in the big city as a mocking voice from the curb shouted, "Soldier, will you work? No sire-ee; I'll sell my shirt first! Oh, hain't I a big Injun!" And when he returned to

Bethel a bibulous stableman in the stage station paraded the streets in a homemade burlesque of Grant's uniform setting the whole town a-roar. "That put an end to the show business with me," Grant said.

The two humiliations gave him "a distaste for military uniform that I never recovered from." Henceforth he would go to all possible lengths to avoid wearing the full uniform and the sword.

In less jocular moments in time to come, he would admit that another reason for not wearing a sword was that "it hurt my hip when riding." And men who knew him well thought that his dislike of uniformed splendor came from an innate love of comfort and a congenital, rather than temporary, dread of "showing off." Also within a year after he received his uniform he would fall under the spell of a general — his first — who was famous for ignoring military finery, Zachary Taylor.[5]

At any rate, Grant's mortification at the hands of ragamuffins was not staggering enough to prevent him from enjoying the remainder of his vacation in visits over the countryside.

With the end of September he said his farewells and with his favorite saddle horse took the boat for St. Louis. Nine miles before the city was reached, he saw Jefferson Barracks on the Missouri shore — a group of whitewashed buildings on the hills which, in layers, rolled back to end in a forest which stood against the sky. The post had grown in the seventeen years which had passed since the Government had established it. Soldier laborers had built most of the limestone quarters for officers and enlisted men which faced the large parade ground on three sides. Nearby were the brick hospital, stables and barn, while at a safe distance, in natural sinks, were the powder magazines. A magnificent estate of seventeen hundred acres, it had miles of bridle paths running through the meadows and groves from which the underbrush had been cleared. In a garden of almost ten acres officers and soldiers raised vegetables and flowers, and in a hall officers held balls to return the hospitality which the first families of St. Louis showered upon them.

When he arrived on September 20 Grant found eight companies of the Fourth and eight of the Third Infantry at the Barracks. One of his classmates, Bob Hazlitt, was in the Fourth, and another, Charley Jarvis, in the Third. Longstreet was here with the Fourth, and George Sykes and Don Carlos Buell with the Third. Buell was in trouble again — had set the Barracks in an uproar by striking an enlisted man with his saber and been set free by a court-martial only to have General Scott in Washington throw out the decision as contrary to the evidence. The members of the court had refused to try Buell again, Scott had stormed, and President Tyler was ordering the whole thing dropped. Buell was safe and the independence of the court established. There had been a tremendous to-do about liquor in the post. A captain had been court-martialed and dismissed for drunkenness. The commander of the Third, Major Ethan Allen Hitchcock, a Vermonter who was the most scholarly officer at the Barracks, wrote in his diary that this captain "is the last of a set of men who were all drunkards." Temperance orators had been brought in and nearly four hundred men, including several officers, had signed the pledge.[6]

Colonel Stephen Kearny, post commandant, was all right in the opinion of the young officers, permitting them to leave when work was done. The Fourth's Colonel, Josiah H. Vose, was a fine old gentleman but too inactive for drill. The regiment was run by Lieutenant Colonel John Garland, a fifty-year-old Virginian, and the Adjutant, Lieutenant Charles Hoskins, Class of '36. Of the captains only one, Robert C. Buchanan, was unpopular. The young officers said Old Buch was brave enough, as his record against the Indians proved, but he was a gruff martinet. They told how he had once ordered a lieutenant who reported to him to go away and not return until properly dressed. Outside the door, the youngster had found no error in his uniform and had re-entered, only to be sent away once more. Eventually he discovered that his collar was slightly unhooked. The commander of Grant's company, Company I, First Lieutenant Benjamin Alvord, was a Vermonter, Class of '33, who had served two years at the Academy before fighting the Indians and now enjoyed working out difficult mathematical theories and problems when off duty.

The Fourth, like all infantry regiments, was small, its officers numbering 21 and its private soldiers 36 to a company, although the total number of men below the commissioned ranks totaled 449 when all the musicians, blacksmiths, clerks, sergeants and corporals were counted. Company commanders shifted constantly in the ebb and flow of leaves and absences on special duties. The fledgling, Sam Grant, showed sufficient ability to be assigned, five weeks after arrival, to the command of Company F for a term of two months.

Since most of the officers in the Fourth and Third were fresh from Florida or the Western plains, the Barracks roared with tales of adventure — tales of officers competing with religious missionaries for the favor of Seminole or Cherokee mistresses. Dick Ewell brought in a stock joke from the West: "Whenever you ask a red man, 'Indian, is that a white child?' you get the answer, 'Part missionary, part Indian.' " Strident voices in quarters described exploits in the taverns, brothels and gambling houses of St. Louis. Rough voices declared that with army pay so poor — sixty-four dollars a month for a second lieutenant — an officer was a fool to try to support a wife in a frontier post or anywhere, for that matter, unless he could marry a rich girl. Yet romances were always in the air, for the officers were popular with the belles of St. Louis. Dick Ewell wrote home that Longstreet was going to marry Garland's second daughter, Louise, "as soon as she is old enough," and that the elder sister, Bessie, was soon to wed Adjutant George Deas, the handsomest man in the Fifth Infantry. The Garland girls came often from the family home at Detroit to visit their father in St. Louis.[7]

So far as the officers would later remember, Sam Grant showed no interest, these first autumn months after his arrival, in either the social belles or the fleshpots of St. Louis. He was, for the first time in his life, turning student. Correspondence with William Church, his professor of mathematics at West Point, assured him that he would be called back to a faculty position as soon as a vacancy occurred. This might come within a year, certainly within two. "Accordingly," as he later said, "I laid out for myself a course of studies to be pursued in garrison, with regularity, if not persistency. I reviewed my West Point course of mathematics . . . and read many valuable historical works, besides an occasional novel." Diligently he set down in a notebook a digest of everything he read.[8]

When not studying or on duty he rode, and one day set out to find the home of Fred Dent's parents five miles away. Fred, before departing for a Post on the plains, had made him promise to call. The home was called White Haven. Grant saw it in the center of a long valley between wooded hills, a rambling two-story farm house whose white paint showed through the thick branches of honeysuckle vines. Behind it were barns, stables and slave quarters. He reined in his horse at a low turnstile from which a path ran fifty yards between locust trees to the veranda and its small, tall pillars.

As he sat there a group of children came up to stand staring — a white girl of probably six and four pickaninnies.

"How do you do, little girl. Does Mr. Dent live here?" he asked the white child. She was holding in her arms birds' nests which she and the little slaves had been collecting in the woods. She made no answer, and afterward admitted that she had stood there tongue-tied because she thought him "the handsomest person" she had ever seen. She could only stare. Behind her four pairs of eyeballs rolled up at him too.

He repeated the question, and finally she stammered, "Yes," and let the birds' nests fall to the ground. He laughed, dismounted, tied his horse, and went over the stile and up the path, the five children following him like puppies. As the procession advanced he talked to the white girl, and at the door he told the slave who answered that he was Lieutenant Grant who had been Fred Dent's roommate.

Out came a woman in her late forties, short, slender, with smiling gray eyes, and a girl of fifteen — Fred Dent's mother and sister Ellen. They welcomed him and as they stood talking to him, noticed the children staring at him.

"Go away, Emmy, and play," they said. Emmy, they explained, was the youngest of the family, Fred's baby sister.

Little Emmy went away but came back quickly to take up her staring again. While the three adults talked, she kept saying to herself, "He's as pretty as a doll." His cheeks, she noted, were round and plump and rosy. His hair was "fine and brown, very thick and wavy; his eyes were a clear blue and full of light." His features were regular. He was "slender and well-formed" and whenever he moved Emmy thought he was graceful. Yes, he was, in his uniform, like a doll. "He enchanted me," she said afterward. "He was my first sweetheart." [9]

Ulysses met Frederick, Fred's father, a medium-sized, smooth-shaven, white-haired man of fifty-six, who wore a long, black coat and high stock, and loved to sit on the front porch in a rocking chair, smoking a long pipe and quoting the *St. Louis Republican* on politics. Anyone who was an enemy of his personal friend, Senator Thomas Hart Benton of Missouri, or of the Old Democracy of Andy Jackson was his enemy — especially the Whigs and the incendiary abolitionists.

Dent was a Southern gentleman, called "Colonel" by courtesy — one of the Maryland aristocracy by birth, as was Mrs. Dent. She had been Ellen Bray Quenshall; Lieutenant Longstreet's mother was his kinswoman. It had been as a trained lawyer and businessman that he had come to St. Louis, more than thirty years before, with enough money to buy these 925 acres, just twelve miles from the city. When he and his wife had left Maryland, they had gone first to Pittsburgh, where their eldest child, John C., had been born. John was now twenty-four. Dent had done well in Pittsburgh as a merchant, but the life of a planter near St. Louis had been more attractive.

He had named this house "White Haven" after his ancestral home back in Maryland, which had been in the family since the days of King Charles. Here his wife had borne him seven more children — George, now twenty-two, Frederick, twenty-three, Louis, twenty, Julia, seventeen, Ellen, called "Nellie," fifteen, Mary, who had died, and little Emma.

George and Julia were away, George married and Julia spending the winter with Colonel Dent's kinfolk, the O'Fallons. John and Louis and the two younger girls were at home. Colonel Dent was active in promoting schools, and saw to it that his own children had the best education available in the neighborhood, or, as they grew older, in St. Louis.

On the premises were eighteen slaves, six men, five women and seven pickaninnies. Mary Robinson, the young slave woman, was the chief help around the house — a smart, quick girl. The Dents enjoyed company and exchanged visits with the best families in St. Louis. Army officers were more than welcome, especially Fred's roommate.

Little Emmy saw her idol, Lieutenant Grant, come twice a week after that first visit, and "generally stay through the afternoon and sometimes to supper." She remembered afterward how soon "Nellie and I began to wrangle as to which one of us would have him." He would ride Emmy on his shoulder and occasionally kiss her although

she thought she was too big a girl for such babylike treatment —
she would be seven next June! It would incense her greatly when
the Lieutenant and Nellie took to their horses and rode off to get
away from her and her train of pickaninnies, Henrietta, Sue, Ann
and Jeff.

Emmy saw her mother's initial liking of the Lieutenant ripen
into admiration. "She especially enjoyed hearing him discuss politics with my father. I think the rare common sense he displayed,
his quiet, even tones, free from gestures and without affectation,
especially attracted her." By contrast her husband was choleric,
opinionated, dogmatic. Emmy said later, "On many and many occasions after he [Grant] had ridden away, I've heard her say, 'That
young man will be heard from some day. He has a good deal in
him. He'll make his mark.'"

Mrs. Dent would often say to Mary Robinson, "I like that young
man. There is something noble about him. His air and the expression of his face convince me that he has a noble heart." Mary herself thought him "an exceedingly fine-looking young man."

The Lieutenant heard much talk of Julia. Emmy said that their
father gave Julia anything she wanted — anything at all. Julia was
her father's favorite. He had given her a slave of her very own,
"Black Julia." Julia was "as dainty a little creature as one would
care to see, plump, neither tall nor short, with beautifully rounded
arms, brown hair and brown eyes, and blonde and rosy complexion.
She had a beautiful figure." Julia was the belle of the family and
already had had several affairs of the heart. Julia was very attractive,
except for one thing, Emmy said, and that wasn't serious enough to
keep beaux away — one of Julia's eyes squinted slightly — it had got
that way when Julia was a baby — they had taken her out of a hot
bath into a cold room and that had done it. Julia was full of fun
and the Lieutenant would like her when she came home, which
would be in February. The social season in the city always came to
a pause at that time. Julia had finished her work at Professor Moreau's
fashionable finishing school and was staying with Colonel John and
Cousin Caroline O'Fallon, who were among the society leaders of
St. Louis.[10]

The Lieutenant must hear the family tell about the time years ago
when Colonel O'Fallon, a rich widower of thirty-five, had married

Colonel Dent's cousin, Caroline Schutz, the twenty-three-year-old belle from Baltimore. There must have been a thousand men and boys in the charivari on their wedding night, blowing horns, firing guns, beating tin pans, howling around the house. He had sent out word that they were to go wherever they wanted, eat and drink what they liked and send the bill to him. Next day innkeepers and grocers paraded up with bills that totaled over $1000 for goods consumed and property destroyed. He had laughed and paid.

An Indian fighter from Kentucky, he had originally come to St. Louis as a trader and Army contractor, had grown rich in banking and real estate, had turned down the Secretaryship of War in 1841 rather than leave the city he loved, and now with his wife gave "unparalleled charities" to the poor, and endless funds to churches, schools and civic improvements. People said he and his wife sat up all night thinking of ways to help young people. He kept track of his friends' children, one of whom, Mary, daughter of Robert S. Todd in Lexington, Kentucky, had in November 1842 married at Springfield, Illinois, a rising lawyer, Abraham Lincoln. Cousin Caroline had done so much for Julia Dent that Julia in later years called her "the beautiful angel of my childhood."[11]

When Julia returned to White Haven she accepted Lieutenant Grant as another of Fred's friends while he accepted her as another of Fred's sisters. Often Longstreet and Bob Hazlitt from the Barracks accompanied him. Emmy thought Hazlitt very dashing but she was still loyal to her first love.

For a time Emmy saw that her Lieutenant took rides with Julia no more often than with Nellie or John or Louis and that he was taken along as merely a family friend when visits were paid. But as the spring came on, Emmy discovered a shadow creeping over her romance. Lieutenant Grant was coming over from the Barracks four times instead of twice a week, and was yielding more often to Mrs. Dent's insistence that he stay for supper and the night, and was riding more often with Sister Julia alone. Emmy's nose slowly slipped out of joint, and she blamed horses for it. Neither she nor Nellie could ride like Julia. Julia was a wonderful horsewoman and her Kentucky mare, Missouri Belle, was the only one that could keep up with Lieutenant Grant's blooded animal. Emmy from the veranda saw the Lieutenant and Julia dash off for "many a fine ride

before breakfast or through the sunset and twilight after supper."
The slaves, looking on, admired the wonderful way the Lieutenant
mounted his horse — he didn't strain or spring — "neber ben' his
back or neck; he jis' put one foot in stirrup an' rise up easy an'
straight." [12]

Emmy also began to discover that fishing trips were not what
they had been. Aided by her troupe of pickaninnies, she had enjoyed the role of aide to the Lieutenant on family picnics on the
creek banks, securing bait for his hook; but too often now when
they returned with aprons full of grasshoppers, laboriously captured
in the grass, they found that the Lieutenant and Julia had disappeared.

Bitterly Emmy faced the truth: Julia's return meant that "Nell
and I were just children again."

Emmy was perceiving what both the Lieutenant and Julia later
admitted they had not seen — they were in love. Even when Emmy
in a fit of temper let the cat out of the bag, the Lieutenant did not
recognize it. Emmy was walking to school one morning, tending
to her own business and thinking her own thoughts, when the Lieutenant and Julia, out for a ride, overtook her on the road. The Lieutenant insisted upon taking her up on his lap. Emmy said no, she
was too big for that. Finally they compromised by seating her
behind him with her arms clutching his waist. As they approached
the schoolhouse Emmy saw that she was late; school had taken up
and faces were at the window.

"They're looking at us, Emmy," the Lieutenant said. "They're
saying, 'Look at Emmy Dent! Here comes Emmy Dent and her
beau!'"

Outraged, Emmy flared back, "You're more like my sister Julia's
beau, you old black nigger devil." [13]

Down at the Barracks, Longstreet was hoping that Sam Grant's
regular attendance upon Julia meant that "he had gotten over his
diffidence." He saw Sam bring her so often to the military balls
that one night when she came without him Lieutenant Charley Hoskins went up to her and asked, with a pitiful expression on his face,
"Where is that small man with the large epaulets?" [14]

Emmy was apparently not displeased one morning to wake up
and find that her Lieutenant and a lot of other gay young people

had met a pretty ridiculous fate during the night while out on a party to which she had been too young to be invited. Her brother John, Julia, Nellie, Longstreet, Hazlitt and a lot of older girls, had gone in a wagon to a campmeeting, had stayed till the last hymn had been sung and, coming home, had been caught in a thunderstorm. There was no house along the road, "the girls were afraid to get under the trees while the lightning played," and while there was a tarpaulin in the wagon, there were no bows to stretch it on, so they turned to Hazlitt who was quite tall and thin, and as Emmy said, "they used him as a tent pole," — with the girls crouching dry around his feet and the other young men outside soaking.[15]

As the spring of 1844 progressed, the officers noted how often Grant was being excused from the sundown parade so that he might ride over to White Haven, and how frequently he returned late for dinner. By the rules of the regimental mess any officer arriving after soup was fined a bottle of wine, and one evening as Grant slipped tardily into his chair Captain Buchanan, President of the Mess, snapped:

"Grant, you're late as usual; another bottle of wine, sir."

Quietly Grant rose and with an effort at pleasantry said, "Mr. President, I've been fined three bottles of wine within the last ten days and if I'm to be fined again, I shall be obliged to repudiate."

Hotly, Buchanan flared back, "Grant, young people should be seen and not heard, sir!" Some of the officers, recalling the incident in later years, said that neither Buchanan nor Grant ever forgot it.[16]

The spring went into the April of Grant's twenty-second birthday, finding him once more in his idyll — exchanging the garrison drums for the soft thud of two horses' feet on winding woodland roads. Julia knew the names of trees and plants; he was fond of flowers.

One day when they were riding, cries of "Help" brought them to a Negro who had cut his foot with an ax. Grant stopped the flow of blood with his handkerchief, asked Julia to hold it and told the old darkey to press both thumbs against arteries. With the ax Grant cut bark from an oak tree, bruised it on top of a stump and poulticed the gashed flesh. The Negro's wife and two little girls came up wailing. The wife objected when Grant tore out the back of her husband's vest to bind up the poultice. Grant calmed her with a promise to get her husband a new one. Lifting the man onto his horse, Grant took the Negroes to their cabin and left, saying he would be back tomorrow at four in the afternoon.

At the appointed hour he was there, and a surgeon with him — and a new army vest. The injured man's eyes shone. Julia with her slave and a basket of food happened to arrive at the same time, and the surgeon, dressing the wound, told her, in mock seriousness, that the Lieutenant should be a doctor rather than a soldier.[17]

April dreamed on — like the April in which he had been born, twenty-two years before. The dogwood blossoms were gone, the oak leaves were larger than a squirrel's ear, the corn had been planted in Missouri's fields, and the 1844 season for the smoking, puffing steamers was in full tide on the Mississippi below the bluffs, when on the tenth of the month a bugle, sharper, more arrogant than any Grant had ever heard, cut across the springtime of his content.

The Third Regiment must leave, on April 20, for Fort Jesup in western Louisiana "to prevent filibustering into Texas," an explanation that struck Grant as pure "hypocrisy," since everybody knew that the move was a grim warning to Mexico to submit peacefully if and when Texas was annexed. Bitterly opposing the whole train of events, Grant noted the indifference of his brother officers to the issue. Unknown to him, other men of strict conscience — and New England prejudices — were privately declaring themselves in even stronger terms. Hitchcock, in Jefferson Barracks, was calling the whole scheme of annexation "monstrous and infamous" and leading to "a military occupancy" of Texas. Redhaired Nathaniel Lyon, with the Second Infantry at Madison Barracks in Sacketts Harbor, New York, was hoping that President Tyler, as author of these "high-handed" steps toward eventual war, would somehow "receive a suitable reward for his madness and folly." [18]

At White Haven, Colonel Dent talked the Democratic gospel as the newspapers told how President Tyler, on April 22, asked the Senate to approve annexation. The Senate refused, but it was felt the Democrats would have votes enough to jam the measure through at the next session. The country seethed, proslavery and antislavery fires boiling the kettle. Lieutenant Grant evidently joined in the front-porch discussions at White Haven, for Mrs. Dent told Julia, "That young man explains politics so clearly I can understand the situation perfectly." If Mrs. Dent believed the little lieutenant with the big epaulets, she saw annexation to be a "conspiracy" and not, as many others did, the inexorable progress of American civilization westward across undeveloped lands. Grant, like Hitchcock and Lyon, had no ear for thoughtful Southern spokesmen who declared that while certain of their lose-tongued fire-eaters did demand Texas as a political aid to the slave power, the true motive for expansion was national, and basically nonsectional in character. With arguments flying, Grant saw that if he were to visit his home before the Fourth moved South, it had better be done quickly. Securing on May 1 a twenty days' leave, he boarded the first steamer for Cincinnati. Hardly had the ship's smoke died on the horizon before a messenger clattered up to the wharf to call him back — orders had come for the regiment to move on May 7.

By the next boat went a letter from Sam's friend, Jarvis, telling him what had happened and warning him not to open any other letter from headquarters until his leave was up. Jarvis was taking all of Sam's belongings with him. His friendly word, when it reached Bethel, spoiled what had been expected to be another of those blissful rounds of rides and visits. All at once Grant knew why he had been so happy at White Haven — it was Julia — it was love! As he later described that moment in his life, "I now discovered that I was exceedingly anxious to get back to Jefferson Barracks, and I understood the reason without explanation from any one." [19] Back by steamer he rushed, and on May 15 or 16 came hurrying into the office of the Barracks' commandant, Lieutenant Dick Ewell, who sat clearing up matters left undone by the departed regiments. Grant explained the situation: He was not to report here until May 20, but he needed to do something that might take a little longer. Would Ewell give him a few days' extension of the leave? Ewell, understandingly, wrote out the order.

On the wings of love, Grant threw himself on a horse and spurred toward White Haven. It was to be one of his best rides. Not far from his goal, Gravois Creek, which he had always seen as a puny stream, hardly able "to run a coffee mill," loomed before him a roaring torrent. The ford was perilous. Grant sat debating; then, obeying his old rule about never turning back from a destination, he spurred into the rapid current. It swept them well downstream, but the horse was strong and Grant came up on the opposite bank safe though sopping wet.

Little Emmy saw him arrive at White Haven "his clothes flopping like rags." The family broke into roars of laughter, Julia's as hearty as the rest. The Lieutenant took it all good-humoredly, Emmy said, but she saw "a seriousness in his usually twinkling eye." She noted that the teasing didn't last long. Her brother John carried him off to find some dry clothes and when he came back into the room another spasm of laughter rose, for John was so much taller and larger that his clothes "didn't fit the Lieutenant soon enough." Emmy saw her hero's rosy cheeks get rosier.

During the first days he said nothing about love. Julia kept from him the fact that she herself had felt a strange sinking of the heart when she had heard that the Fourth was to leave. Just why she should have been so depressed, she had not known. But now, she knew. Belatedly she had come to share Emmy's view that he was "a beautiful young man."

But it took heaven and high water to manage things for the young pair—she eighteen, he twenty-two. It was a morning of May's best. "We were going to a morning wedding," Julia said in later years, "and Lieutenant Grant was also invited. He came for us on horseback and asked my brother's permission to drive me in exchange for his saddle. . . . The day was beautiful, the roads were a little heavy from previous rain, but the sun shone in splendor.

"We had to cross a little bridge that spanned a ravine and when we reached it I was surprised and a little concerned to find the gulch swollen . . . the water reaching to the bridge. I noticed, too, that Lieutenant Grant was very quiet and that and the high water bothered me. I asked several times if he thought the water dangerous to breast, and told him I would go back rather than take any risk. He assured me, in his brief way, that it was perfectly safe, and in my heart I relied upon him.

"Just as we reached the old bridge, I said, 'Now, if anything happens, remember I shall cling to you, no matter what you say to the contrary.'

"He simply said, 'All right,' and we were over the planks in less than a minute. Then his mood changed, he became more social and in asking me to be his wife, used my threat as a theme.

"After dinner that afternoon, Lieutenant Grant asked me to set the day. I wanted to be engaged, and told him it would be much nicer than getting married — a sentiment he did not approve. We were very quiet at the house that evening and neither said a word of the secret. . . . He was too shy to ask father."

Mary Robinson thought the Lieutenant's shyness justified. "Old Man Dent was opposed to him when he found him courting his daughter, and did everything he could to prevent the match. But Mrs. Dent took a great fancy to Grant and encouraged him in his venture."

Emmy was sure she knew why her father opposed the marriage. He liked Grant well enough but had made up his mind Julia must never marry a soldier. "Her health had never been very strong," at least not strong enough to stand the "arduous, pinched and restless army life." [20]

Also Colonel Dent had seen the folly of delicately bred girls marrying poorly paid officers. Jessie, the daughter of his friend Senator Benton, had secretly married a half-French adventurer, John C. Frémont of the Topographical Engineers, who was always away somewhere in the West. The Colonel knew the details of this because Julia and Jessie were intimates. Senator Benton had forbidden the match, and still thought it an unfortunate one even though his son-in-law's explorations in the Rocky Mountains had been praised by Congress last winter. [21] The neighbors could have warned Lieutenant Grant against Old Man Dent. They knew him as a quick and testy filer of lawsuits and, as one of them said, he was "masterful in his ways, of persistent combativeness, of the grim, set purpose peculiar to the Southerners of the old generation, and was, where foiled, inclined to be vindictive." [22]

Ulysses' own version of his proposal was laconic: "I mustered up courage to make known, in the most awkward manner imaginable, the discovery I had made on learning that the 4th Infantry had been ordered away from Jefferson Barracks." [23]

Blissful though the love days were, Grant could not keep duty from his mind; and before the contrived extension of his leave was up, he was on the steamer plowing downstream, with the engagement still a secret from Colonel Dent and perhaps all the rest of Julia's family except that one who had been the first to detect Cupid on the bridle paths, Little Emmy.[24]

"Curious, Important, Surprising"

THE WONDER of his engagement and the stumbling awkwardness of his proposal were still uppermost in his mind when, three days after catching up with his regiment, he sat down to write to Mrs. Bailey, the woman who with one kiss five years before had revealed to him a new way of demonstrating motherly love:

CAMP SALUBRITY
NEAR NATCHITOCHES LOUISIANA
June 6th, 1844

MRS. BAILEY:

My journey fortunately is at an end, and agreeably to your request, and my own pleasure, I hasten to notify you of my safe arrival here. It always affords me pleasure to write to old acquaintances, and much more hear from them, so I would be pleased if the correspondence would not stop here. As long as my letters are answered, if agreeable to you I will continue to write.

He said that his trip, since telling her good-by in Georgetown, had been —

Marked with no incident, save one worth relating and that one is *laughable, curious, important, surprising,* &c, &c, but I can't tell it now. It is for the present a secret but, I will tell it to you some time. You must not guess what it is for you will go wrong. On my route I called around by the way of St. Louis and Jefferson Barracks, where I spent four or five days very pleasantly among my newly made acquaintances.

He had had a pleasant boat trip down to New Orleans and then back up the Mississippi to the Red River and up that stream to Natchitoches, the oldest town in Louisiana, near which his regiment had been stationed to prevent overcrowding at Fort Jesup, twenty miles to the southwest.

From Natchitoches, he wrote:

> I had to walk (or pay an extravagant price for a conveyance) three miles through the hotest [*sic*] sun I think I ever felt. I found my regiment camping out in small linen tents on the top of a high sandy ridge and in the midst of a pine forest. The great elevation of our situation and the fact that one of the best springs of water in the State puts out here are the only recommendations the place has. We are about three miles from any place, there is no conveyance to take us from on [*sic*] place to another, and everything is so high that we can't afford to keep a horse or other conveyance of our own. I could walk myself but for the intensity of the heat. As for lodgings I have a small tent that the rain runs through as it would through a sieve. For a bedstead I have four short pine sticks set upright and plank running from the two at one end to the other. For chairs I use my trunk and bed, and as to a floor we have no such luxury yet. Our meals are cooked in the woods by servants that know no more about culinary matters than I do myself. But with all these disadvantages my appetite is becoming extravigant [*sic*]. I would like to have our old West Point board again that you may have heard so much about.
>
> As for the troublesome insects of creation they abound here. The swamps are full of Aligators [*sic*] and the woods full of Red bugs and ticks. . . . They crawl entirely under the skin when they git [*sic*] on a person and it is impossible to keep them off. — So much for Camp Salubrity.

As to the war issue which was agitating the nation, he held his tongue, as became an officer. He might be ordered soon to New Orleans! "It is now contemplated that my regiment will go in that neighborhood in case Texas should not be annexed to the U States, but in case of the annexation we will probably have to go much farther West than we are now." He thought this penetration would go as far as the Colorado, a Texas stream 150 miles from Louisiana.

Ulysses told Mrs. Bailey he would be happy to have an answer to his letter "as early as possible" and if nothing more "a Post-Script from the young ladies. Ladies are always so much better at giving the news than others, and then there is nothing doing or said about Georgetown that I would not like to hear."

Then he brought his homesick letter to a close. He could not keep his pen from touching, in carefully guarded terms, the curious, important, surprising thing that had happened to him:

> They could tell me of all the weddings, &c, &c, that are talked of. Give my love to every body in Georgetown.
>
> Lt. U. S. Grant
4th Infantry
>
> P.S. I give my title in signing this not because I wish people to know what it is, but because I want to get an answer to this and put it there that a letter may be directed so as to get to me
>
> USG [1]

Writing steadily to Julia, Ulysses nevertheless kept the secret of the engagement from his comrades. With Bob Hazlitt he shared a Negro body servant, Valere, at a combined cost of eight dollars a month. Valere, who spoke a French-English patois, enjoyed repeating later on stories of how "dat leety man wa't dey call M'sieu Grant" would threaten to "leek Valere good" for minor misdemeanors but would always abandon the idea when Valere would demonstrate his innocence.[2]

Soon after arriving at Camp Salubrity, Sam borrowed a small pony and rode over to Fort Jesup to see his friends, especially Rufe Ingalls. When they saw him, the conqueror of big vicious mounts, jog up on a sorry little beast, they roared with laughter.[3]

Among the officers conversation was buzzing about the new commander who was due to arrive to command both camps in "the army of observation," Colonel Zachary Taylor, Brevet Brigadier General. This indicated action, for the only thing Taylor could do was fight. He had battled stoutly against the British in the War of 1812, and against the Indians all the way from northern Illinois to Florida, but he had learned so little about drill and maneuvers that the War Department could not be sending him, now, for peacetime instruction.

Where Grant, as a cadet, had seen and admired Old Fuss and Feathers Scott from a distance, he now was in camp with a born leader who, so far as dress and manners were concerned, belittled everything that Scott stood for. Taylor had never given a snap of fingers for finery, military etiquette or the punctilios of an officer and a gentleman. There was in him nothing whatever of the martinet, yet Grant saw how he was respected by every officer and man. "Old Zach" would saunter around army posts in blue jeans and a big palmetto hat, chewing tobacco and talking about the crops on his Louisiana plantation. He would sit sideways in the saddle on his famous horse Old Whitey, his trousers showing an expanse of bare leg, his loose linen coat flapping, his feet in common soldiers' shoes instead of shining boots, talking about the price of cotton. He thought army life ruinous to marriage and had once said he'd be damned if his second daughter, Sarah, should marry a young lieutenant, Jefferson Davis, who was hanging around her: "I know enough of the family life of officers. I scarcely know my own children or they me." [4]

When Sarah died in 1835 after eloping with Davis, he had grown grimmer, although his kindness to young officers still drew their affection — and imitation — as before.

To Grant, here was a successful warrior slouching about the Post as if to say that all those teachings about unspotted gloves and shined buttons might be all right in their way for schoolboys, but not for men of action. Here was the Indian fighter showing leniency in matters of drill and decorum to officers and men who had either fought well or gave promise of doing so. Stories were common about Taylor's forbearance toward the enlisted men, who were regarded by most officers as an ignorant and lazy lot, content with seven dollars a month. Many of them, recent immigrants from foreign lands, had difficulty understanding English, a fact that Taylor kept in mind. Once it was said when a burly private, newly arrived from Europe, failed to obey an order, Taylor had seized him by the ear and shaken him — "wooling" this punishment was called. The fellow's face had gone blank with astonishment, then red with anger and he had knocked Taylor flat on the ground. As other officers rushed toward the offender, Taylor, seeing that the fellow had not understood the original order, called, "Let him alone! He'll make a good soldier." In Taylor's command, now that everything was put in readiness for war, officers could no longer assign soldiers to do their domestic work as they had in peacetime, thus saving the extra allowance given them for servant hire.

The Northerners employed Negroes and the Southerners used slaves. The soldiers liked the change to tent life, especially the soldiers who had previously served in the British Army, because it freed them from the American Army custom of having men in barracks sleep two in a bed, a custom which the British had abolished twenty years before. The enlisted men noted how Taylor had offenders flogged less frequently than did most other generals and this again delighted the British veterans, who complained that the American use of the cow rawhide whip on the bare back was at least six times as agonizing as the cat-o'-nine-tails prescribed by British officers. Immigrant soldiers denounced, in general, "the insolent and impertinent tone assumed by native Americans to all foreigners." [5]

Batches of recruits kept coming into Camp Salubrity as the regiment went on war footing. The number of courts-martial for drunkenness, disobedience and inattention to duty meant, to some observers, that not only the men but some of the younger officers felt that now they were under a general who valued spirit more than decorum. Rufe Ingalls boasted that the officers at Jesup were "splendid fellows," wilder than the dashing Irishmen so celebrated in English fiction of the time and that they had "high old times" whenever their Post Commander, Colonel David E. Twiggs, was absent — Twiggs, the bull-necked Georgian, whose cloud of white hair and whiskers framing his cherry-red face made him "look like Aaron." Grant's fitness to command was recognized in his assignment to take charge of Company A from October until February in the absence of Captain Larnard. [6]

Grant saw his dream of the assistant professorship at West Point vanishing. With war in the wind, the Fourth Regiment had on hand barely enough officers to operate it on a peacetime basis, and no mere brevet lieutenant could hope to be detached now that the regiment was being brought up to wartime strength. Six of the line officers were permanently separated from the outfit, serving in staff jobs with the departments of the quartermaster, the adjutant general or the commissary. [7]

Grant sadly closed his mathematics books, gave up his home study and, for that matter, almost all reading of any kind. Pete Longstreet said later that, situated as they were, "removed from all society without books or papers, we had an excellent opportunity of studying each other." Sam bought a horse, joined in the races, and allowed himself to be introduced by Pete, Ingalls and the others to the mysteries of their favorite card games, brag and five-cent ante.

"He made a poor player," Pete commented. "The man who lost seventy-five cents in one day was esteemed . . . a peculiarly unfortunate person. The games often lasted an entire day." Pete noted how Sam, "the soul of honor himself, . . . never even suspected others either then or years afterward," but could be firm when he discovered dishonesty — "his hatred of guile was pronounced, and his detestation of tale bearers was . . . absolute." [8]

There was little to do, between duties at the army post on the sand hills, except play cards, race horses and take nips of something stronger than cholera medicine. On December 1, 1844, Sam wrote to Bob Hazlitt, who had transferred a few weeks before to the Third Infantry:

> There were five days' races at Natchitoches. I was there every day and bet low, generally lost. Jarvis and a number from Jessup were there. Jarvis was pretty high and tried to be smart all the time. He fell over the back of a bench at the racecourse and tumbled over backward in his chair in front of Thompson's Hotel during his most brilliant day. He undertook to play brag at our camp and soon succeeded in ridding himself of twenty dollars, all in quarters. The game of brag is kept up as lively as ever. I continued to play some after you left and won considerable, but for some time back I have not played and probably will never play again — no resolution, though. [9]

Rufe Ingalls always recalled Sam as having been "a good hand" at the camp sports, although Rufe probably erred in saying that Grant joined in "gander pullings," a cruel sport in which a tough old gander, with head and neck plucked and smeared with goose grease, was hung from a limber branch of a tree while horsemen galloped at him trying to pull off his head. A gantlet of footmen whipped the contestants' horses to prevent any slowing up at the crucial moment, and with frequent renewals of grease some ganders ducked hands for as much as three hours, squeaking loudly, however, when yanked hard. Eventually the strongest and most wily bird would tire, and someone would collect the stake money.[10]

As the officers became acquainted in the homes of the wealthy planters of the Red River Valley, their social life expanded. Lieutenant Grant was regarded as "a youth of only the most ordinary type," yet so superb a horseman as to become "somewhat of a social favorite." Great breeders of fast horses, the planters could appreciate a good rider and judge of horseflesh when they saw one.[11]

Occasionally a buzz of excitement would go through the camps as word from Washington hinted that war seemed nearer. Lieutenant Colonel Hitchcock looked at the situation as did Lieutenant Grant, and privately pronounced "infamous" a letter the War Department sent Taylor ordering him to be ready to move on short notice, since the Mexicans were inflaming Indians to murder Texans. The United States was bound to prevent such outrages. To Hitchcock this meant something more than a coercive move against Mexico — it meant that President Tyler had "determined to embroil this country before going out of office and perhaps . . . to prepare the way for a separation of the Union." [12]

Taylor made ready, but no new orders came. The nation was locked in a bitter presidential campaign, with the Democratic candidate, James K. Polk, promising not only one war but two, unless American rights were respected — a war against Mexico over the Texas issue and another against Great Britain over the issue of the Oregon boundary. Grant followed in the papers the fight his father's idol, Henry Clay, was making as the Whig nominee; saw him oppose the annexation of Texas, then, midway in the campaign, straddle, quibble and lose armies of antislavery voters to a third party, the Abolitionist Liberty party — armies large enough to throw the election to Polk in November. Grant noted that Thomas Morris, from Bethel, was the Liberty candidate for Vice-President.

On December 1, when the election returns had been digested, Grant wrote Hazlitt that the men were greatly excited, expecting daily to be ordered to Texas, either Corpus Christi or San Antonio.[13] But again no orders came. Arguments grew hotter. The annexationists had their mandate now, all agreed to that. But there were two views of Polk's intentions, one that he wanted to wrest Texas, New Mexico and California from the Mexicans so that the slave power could have perpetual control of Congress, the other that slavery had nothing to do with this natural expansion of the nation, since no sensible Southerner expected slavery to thrive in the acquisitions west of Texas.

When on March 1, 1845, Congress voted to annex Texas, expecting to ratify the step on July 4, the fat was in the fire. Texas insisted its lower boundary was the Rio Grande, Mexico replying that even if the rest of Texas were independent, which was not to be conceded, the boundary was not the Rio Grande but the Nueces River, which wound its way to the Gulf on line 35, to 140 miles to the north. Since neither Texas nor Mexico had ever developed this wilderness, an area the size of Massachusetts and Connecticut together, legal claims were shadowy. Polk, taking office, insisted that diplomacy could quiet Mexico, but in the Louisiana camps the officers saw that at any minute the army of observation might become the army of occupation, and on April 1 of that quivering summer, Grant asked for thirty-five days' leave to visit St. Louis. He must get Colonel Dent's permission to marry Julia.[14] Julia remembered that at the time of their engagement Ulysses had been "too shy" to ask for her hand, "so he waited till he was stationed and wrote to him." Her father refused to answer the letter, and told her, "You are too young and the boy is too poor. He hasn't anything to give you."

Whereupon said Julia, "I rose in my wrath and I said I was poor, too, and hadn't anything to give him." [15]

Julia was near the truth for, while Dent had land and slaves, his style of farming in Missouri was not profitable and his tendency to become embroiled in lawsuits was expensive. Like many another slaveholder, he was at a disadvantage when competing with neighbors who employed white workmen. Where he housed, fed and clothed his laborers the year round, supporting the infants and old folks, his competitors could hire free white hands only when needed. However, the illusion of aristocracy, and the notion that he was operating a romantic Southern plantation instead of a Middle Western farm, were too strong for him and others of his kind to be realistic.

The stubborn old man was, by chance, at a disadvantage when Lieutenant Grant arrived at White Haven to ask the great favor.

Julia told about it long afterward: The whole family had been on the front porch seeing Colonel Dent off to Washington on business, kissing him good-by and stuffing into his pockets notes of things he was to buy in the East. Suddenly Julia saw a horseman riding up. It was her Lieutenant in a new uniform — her beautiful young man! He swung off his horse, came up on the porch and, evidently knowing a strategic moment when he saw one, asked Colonel Dent for Julia's hand. "Father being in a hurry to get off, consented."

Emmy, when a grown woman, recalled that the Lieutenant, who was "often slow and hesitating in his efforts to come to a decision," now made his statement to Colonel Dent with the air of a man not to be put aside by anything in the world, and that his frankness had won her father. "But after all," she said, "it was all nonsense for father to be pretending that he had anything to say about it. Julia, having once said Yes, had made his decision for him. When Julia wanted a thing from my father, she always got what she wanted."

However sure the sisters might be, Ulysses understood the Colonel to be merely withdrawing his objections for the time being and to be promising to set forth his final views in a letter which Ulysses would receive within a matter of weeks. At any rate, Ulysses saw that it was useless to suggest, as he had hoped, that the wedding could be held during his five days at White Haven. With sickening swiftness came the last ride together in the April woods, the hoarse cough of the steamer, the farewell screech of the whistle, and Ulysses was gone downstream again — and Julia once more waiting.[16]

Little Emmy turned to more interesting things and only thought of her onetime doll-lieutenant when she heard Julia reading his letters to the family, or when something reminded her that he was off somewhere in the same army with her brother Fred.

Back in camp on May 5, Grant found war nearer. Taylor, on orders, was preparing to move to Texas the minute he heard that the young Republic had ratified annexation. Early in July, the Third and Fourth Regiments sailed to New Orleans and camped outside the city, gathering supplies. Yellow fever was on the town, its streets so empty that the only crowd Grant saw in several weeks was two small groups of men on a dueling ground. So far as he could learn, neither of the duelists had been hurt. He only remembered the scene because it made him realize that he could never fight a duel.

If a man should wrong him to the point where death was demanded, he certainly wouldn't give the fellow the choice of weapons, time and place. And if he had wronged a man to the same extent and saw his error, he would try and settle it with reason. He concluded that he didn't have the courage to fight a duel, but then it was possible that most duelists were lacking in something more important, moral courage.[17]

He was touched, while in New Orleans, by the courage of his venerable commander Colonel Vose. Where many elderly colonels and captains suddenly found reasons for not accompanying their regiments toward the threatened war, Vose was, as Grant said, "not a man to discover infirmity in the presence of danger." In fact, decrepit as he was, Vose forced himself out onto the parade ground and took command at battalion drill. He gave two or three orders, grew faint, turned, and fell dead.[18]

To take Vose's place came another ancient who was tipsy much of the time — sixty-five-year-old Colonel William Whistler, son of the Captain John Whistler who had built Fort Dearborn on Lake Michigan's shore, where the town of Chicago had later risen. The Whistlers were a family of soldiers and engineers, although the Colonel's nephew, James Abbott McNeill Whistler, an eleven-year-old in Lowell, Massachusetts, was showing a talent for nonmechanical drawing. Colonel Whistler had been in the Army for more than forty-five years, trailed wherever he went by legends of his strength, endurance and drinking bouts. Standing over six feet and built like Hercules, he had, in his youth, won a famous foot race from the champion Potawatomi runner of the region around Fort Dearborn — a chieftain as large and powerful as himself.

The race was for five miles, each man betting his horse. The Indian's tribesmen had bet their horses, too, against those of Whistler's brother officers. Whistler had won by sixteen yards and collected his bet. The loss rankled in the Potawatomi and when a few years later he was serving with the British Army in the War of 1812, he sent a challenge through the lines to Whistler. He would bet his life against Whistler's this time, the contest to be with knives, swords and tomahawks, hand to hand. Whistler had accepted, gone out and killed him.

Now, in New Orleans, the old hulk of a man would often wind

up drunk in police courts; and once, as the story was later told, Lieutenant Grant, out hunting for him, found him sitting so, awaiting his hearing. As Sam sat beside him to keep him company in his distress, a command, "Ground arms!" rang through the open door. Musket butts crashed on the street outside. Grant went out, to be told by a corporal of his own company:

"We heard that the colonel had got into an ugly scrape with those rascally police, so I have brought up the squad to prove an alibi!" [19]

To the regiment as it lay at New Orleans came word that President Polk, finding that his diplomatic proffers to Mexico were getting nowhere, and that Yankee warships anchored off Vera Cruz were intimidating no one, began to put new pressure on Mexican nerves. He ordered Taylor to move to some location as near the Nueces as prudence would permit. On July 23, Taylor sailed with the Third Regiment for Corpus Christi, an adobe station used by smugglers at the mouth of the now famous little river, and the first week in September the major part of the Fourth followed in the side-wheeler *Dayton* with Grant, back in Company I again, taking the sailing ship *Suviah* a day or two later.

Grant's boyhood faith that man proposed and God disposed came back to him two days before the voyage ended, when from the deck he saw the wreck of the *Dayton* lying where it had blown up on September 13, killing eight members of the Fourth, two of them lieutenants whom he had known as upperclassmen at the Academy.[20]

His first sea voyage brought adventures. One was the sight of the ship's captain, a nervous, sickly man, waving a sword "nearly as large and as heavy as he was, and crying that his men had mutinied." Since the sailors submitted without question, Grant "doubted if they knew that they had mutinied." He wished he had not seen the spectacle, and rejoiced later to learn that the men had been relieved from injustice.

The other adventure was one he liked to tell in later years, as an example of his overconfidence. It happened during the days that the *Suviah* lay well out from the shore, sending baggage in across the shallow waters to the Corpus Christi camp. Assuming that he "had learned enough of the working of the double and single pulley, by which passengers were let down from the upper deck of the ship" he determined to descend without assistance, and suddenly found himself plunging head first into the water twenty-five feet below. Being a good swimmer "and not having lost my presence of mind," as he said, he swam around until the laughing, jeering sailors rescued him.[21]

Once a camp site had been cleared in the snake-infested thickets, Grant enjoyed Texas life. Violent storms stranded enough green turtles to fill wagons. Oysters, which Grant loved, were raked out of the river mouth in basketfuls. The river itself delighted the eyes, "winding through the prairie like a blue ribbon carelessly thrown on a green robe," as Captain E. Kirby Smith, arriving with Fred Dent and the Fifth Infantry, wrote home. From the prairies officers and men brought in wagonloads of deer, duck, wild turkeys and jacksnipe. The fowl Grant could not eat, nor the venison unless it was cooked to a crisp. Only once did he go hunting with the other officers. His friend Calvin Benjamin, arriving with the Fourth Artillery, persuaded him to go after turkeys, but as Grant afterward told it, he himself had stood admiring the big birds as they flew from a pecan tree just over his head, without ever thinking to take his shotgun off his shoulder until they had flown away. "I came to the conclusion that as a sportsman I was a failure, and went back to the house. Benjamin remained out, and got as many turkeys as he wanted to carry back." [22]

Benjamin's knowledge of wild life on another day taught Grant a lesson that he would later apply to human beings. During one of the horseback journeys which Benjamin, Augur and he eagerly took across the plains escorting supply trains and paymasters' wagons to San Antonio, where Taylor had stationed other troops, Grant heard ". . . the most unearthly howling of wolves, directly in our front. The prairie grass was tall and we could not see the beasts, but the sound indicated that they were near. To my ear it appeared that there must have been enough of them to devour our party, horses and all, at a single meal. The part of Ohio that I hailed from was not thickly settled, but wolves had been driven out long before I left. Benjamin was from Indiana, still less populated, where the wolf yet roamed over the prairies. . . . He kept on towards the noise, unmoved. I followed in his trail, lacking moral courage to turn back." Benjamin finally said, "Grant, how many wolves do you think there are in that pack?"

"Suspecting that he thought I would overestimate the number," Grant said, "I determined to show my acquaintance with the animal by putting the estimate below what possibly could be correct, and answered:

" 'Oh, about twenty,' very indifferently. He smiled and rode on. In a minute we were close upon them, and before they saw us. There were just *two* of them . . . seated upon their haunches, with their mouths close together." [23]

Such rumors of war as came to camp were quickly proven false. Grant was told how in late August the Dragoons had saddled up and gone out when heavy artillery had been heard in the distance. It had turned out to be a thunderstorm.

Reinforcements poured down from the North; the camp stretched farther and farther along the beach to the south and the work of clearing the oyster beds and other obstructions from the path of incoming boats grew heavier.

General Taylor told Lieutenant Lafayette McLaws of the Seventh that he had ridden down to the beach one day and noted Lieutenant Grant trying to get his detail of men to clear away these underwater obstructions. Old Zach saw Grant "failing either by words or signs to make those under him understand him . . . jump into the water, which was up to his waist, and work with his men." From the bank "some dandy officers," as Taylor called them, began making fun of Grant, whereupon the General had announced:

"I wish I had more officers like Grant, who would stand ready to set a personal example when needed." [24]

In from the sea came Pete Longstreet with the Eighth Infantry and Sam French with the Third Artillery. By October 1, almost 4000 men were on hand, a force that seemed to serious officers ridiculously small to be shaking its fists under the noses of 8,000,000 Mexicans. To Grant's pacific mind it was pure folly for President Polk to be insisting that they were on the defense. He thought his Commander in Chief was deliberately trying to provoke the first shot. Until Mexico provided this excuse, Polk's plan for grabbing New Mexico and California was stopped. But let the bull be maddened into charging the red flag, and Polk could run to the country with a cry of wounded innocence and all of Congress's skepticism would disappear in a blaze of patriotism. Such a war, Grant thought, would be as wicked and unjust as any in the history of the world.[25]

Perhaps he ought to resign from the Army. It was wrong to stay, but would it be a greater wrong to go? He had sworn to serve his country eight years. He had accepted free training from his Government. The struggle with his conscience was so sharp and so prolonged that it would stick in his memory the rest of his life. And when he made his decision it was one for which he could never quite forgive himself. His only comfort was that any other decision would have been more unforgivable. "I had a horror of the Mexican War . . . only I had not moral courage enough to resign . . . I considered my supreme duty was to my flag." [26]

In a tent not far from Grant's, Lieutenant Colonel Hitchcock was writing in his diary, on November 2, "If I could by any decent means get a living in retirement, I would abandon a government which I think corrupted by both ambition and avarice to the last degree." He felt sure from weighing newspaper accounts that "Mexico will make no movement, and the government is magnanimously bent on taking advantage of it to insist upon 'our claim' as far as the Rio Grande. I hold this to be monstrous and abominable." In August, Hitchcock had been shocked upon examining this claim to find it unjustified, and had written in his diary, "Our people ought to be damned for their impudent arrogance and domineering presumption! It is enough to make atheists of us all to see such wickedness in the world, whether punished or unpunished." [27]

On horseback journeys, some of which reached 150 miles into the interior, Grant noted that Texas had no settlers in the strip it claimed. And the only Mexicans he saw were a few squatters near San Antonio, and many smugglers and horse traders who came up to Corpus Christi from the Rio Grande.[28]

Pete Longstreet saw Sam pay a record price, twelve dollars, for a particularly furious stallion that had been brought in off the plains. Every other officer in camp had refused to buy it, but Sam took it, telling those around him he would either break its neck or his own. He had it blindfolded, put a heavy-bitted bridle and big Spanish saddle on it, "and when firmly in the saddle he threw off the blind." The wild animal stood trembling for a moment; then launched into a series of leaps, bucks and twists — while the shouts of those who had gathered to see the show brought soldiers running from all directions. Finally, at the exact moment when the stallion's will showed the first hint of weakening, Grant loosed the rein, struck home with his spurs and the two, horse and man, held together like the fabled centaur, streaked across the plain to disappear in a thicket of spiny chaparral.

Three hours passed and Peter wondered if he would ever see Sam again. Then in he came, the stallion's head down, its skin dripping with sweat. "For years afterward," said Longstreet later on, "the story of Grant's ride was related at every campfire in the country." The stallion was docile thereafter and Sam's favorite, although he added three more mounts at a cost of twenty dollars.[29]

In December, shortly before starting on one of the overland wagon trips, Sam received notice that he had been promoted from brevet second lieutenant to full second lieutenant, his commission to date from September 30, the day the regiment had fully assembled at Corpus Christi. He had not asked for the advancement and had a strong feeling against ever doing so under any circumstances. Nor would he allow his friends to ask it for him. "This is one of my superstitions," he later decided, not realizing that his fear might have risen from his own bashfulness and from his mother's belief that it was unbecoming, and, indeed, wrong, to push yourself in this world.[30]

Since the promotion had come unsolicited, there was a modest satisfaction in it. Of his thirty-eight classmates, twenty-eight had not yet received it, five had won it earlier and five were accepting it along with him. What he disliked in the orders was the fact that they transferred him to the Seventh Infantry. He had become attached to the Fourth, and in particular to three of its officers, Jenks Beaman, Class of '42, Alexander Hays, Class of '44, and Sidney Smith, a humorous Virginian who had been appointed from civil life in 1839. Smith was a curiously winning character. Grant's classmate, Henry M. Judah, wrote in his diary, "Lt. Smith is a wild, harum-scarum sort of a fellow, with hair down his back, moustaches that reach his ears, and beard to his breast." Yet for all his piratical adornment, "he dreads of all things being conspicuous." [31]

Grant discovered that he and Frank Gardner, of the Seventh, were merely changing places and that Frank was objecting as strongly as he. So they filed requests for return to their original assignments, and by the time Grant returned from a trip to San Antonio, consent arrived from Washington.[32]

With the continued improvement in his health, Grant escaped the dysentery and catarrhal fever which often downed a third of the army. Taylor ignored camp sanitation and the winter was, as Grant wrote to John Lowe, the severest season the natives had seen in many years. To keep men out of the gambling dens set up by camp followers, the commanders urged Lieutenant John B. Magruder, of the First Artillery, to build a theater. Magruder was the man for it, a social lion from Virginia, whose showy hospitality had earned him the nickname "Prince John." On the Canadian border, the splendor of his regimental mess, with everybody in gay dinner jackets, had so impressed the British that one officer, startled out of his good manners, had asked his host, "What is the pay of an American leftenant?"

"Bless you, my dear fellow," Prince John replied, "I don't remember. My servant always gets it."

The Britisher turned to the servant and bluntly asked, "What is it, Patrick?" Patrick replied, "Your honor must perceive the lieutenant is a gentleman and too ginerous to ask me."

Magruder had an 800-seat theater open by January 8 — erected by the enlisted men, and the scenery painted by officers who also served as actors. Tackling farce and light comedy, crowds, spurred on by the sight of the generals buying tickets, came in such numbers that all costs were soon paid. The actors now felt capable of playing tragedy, sent to New Orleans for costumes and began casting *Othello*. Lieutenant Theodoric Porter, of the famous family of "Navy Porters," was to play the jealous Moor. Longstreet was to be Desdemona. Porter, however, said Longstreet was too tall, especially in crinolines; some shorter, slender officer was needed. They decided Grant looked all right in the costume, but could not in rehearsals show "the proper sentiment." He joined Longstreet in the discard. Deciding, finally, that Desdemona was too much for any male actor, the officers chipped in and imported from New Orleans an actress, Mrs. Hart, and some other supporting professionals. Grant and Longstreet had their innings later when the repertoire turned back to comedy.[33]

The theater continued to thrive, one of the few objections coming from a sour-tempered Pennsylvanian, Lieutenant George G. Meade, who had returned to the Army as a topographical engineer. Meade, who was heartily sick of the crude frontier, the greasy Mexicans, the riffraff camp followers anyway, wrote home his disgust with the theatrical company, which turned "farce into buffoonery." [34]

The theatrical season was in full swing, on February 3, when Taylor heard from Washington that the time had come to move to the Rio Grande as soon as the weather permitted. Taylor told his aides their destination would be a point on the Texas side of the river opposite the Mexican town of Matamoros, 150 miles away. By February 9, Grant and the other officers saw an experimental wagon train test the road for sixty miles in wet weather, and on the sixteenth they heard that the Army itself would start around the first of March. Spirits rose as it was realized that the 3900 men assembled made this the largest American Army since the days of George Washington.

President Polk's excuse for ordering the march was that the Mexican Government had for the third time broken its promise to settle the dispute by negotiation. Polk pointed out that in October 1845, when the Mexicans had given their promise, he had sent his envoy to them with full powers, but that Slidell had been turned back "on the most frivolous pretext." When the Mexican Government changed hands early in January 1846 Polk had sent Slidell back to offer, on March 1, money as well as friendship in return for a peaceful adjustment of boundary matters. Backing up his honeyed words now with a practical threat, Polk ordered the naval squadron off Vera Cruz strengthened and Taylor to start his legions overland for the Rio Grande.

Polk's friends were insisting that he neither wanted nor expected war. His cabinet was telling him that war would not be popular with the country. His enemies were declaring that he was deliberately provoking war.

Observers more neutral in character were saying that Polk had at last discarded the old saying of British diplomats, "A Mexican is like a mule, if you spur him too much he will back off the precipice with you."

CHAPTER EIGHT

The First Red Drops

THERE WAS a great clangor and bustle as the army of occupation prepared to start across the disputed strip, 150 miles to the Rio Grande. Almost a thousand men were to remain at Corpus Christi, guarding the camp, or sick in hospitals. Officers stored possessions they could not carry, or sold them to camp followers or shipped them home. The best horseman in the force lost all his horses.

Valere, taking Lieutenant Grant's three horses to water, had fallen from his mount and let them all escape to the open prairie. Grant did not suspect Valere of scheming to be free from a hostler's duties. Valere knew he would have one of the animals to ride and certainly had no ambition to walk clear to the Rio Grande as he now must do.

It amused Grant to hear Captain W. W. S. Bliss, chief of Taylor's staff, say "Yes, I heard Grant lost five or six dollars' worth of horses the other day." [1] Bliss, as a member of the Fourth Infantry, kept in touch with its officers, although elevated beyond them.

Captain McCall, organizing his company, soon asked Grant if he had bought another horse.

"No," the Lieutenant answered, "I belong to a foot regiment." It was his duty to walk with his men.

"I did not understand the object of his solicitude at the time," Grant later said, "but when we were about to start he said: 'There, Grant, is a horse for you.' I found that he could not bear the idea of his servant riding on a long march while his lieutenant went a-foot."

McCall had quietly discovered an unbroken three-year-old mustang that a Negro servant had bought for three dollars, and arranged for Grant to have it for five dollars. When Grant saw McCall's earnestness, he abandoned his ideas of duty and took the horse. [2]

Grant's mind was still troubled by the "unholy" character of the movement now beginning, but he was pleased by the orders which Taylor posted on March 8, the day the advance of 400 men set out — orders enjoining the 2300 men in the occupation army "to observe with the most serious respect the rights of all the inhabitants who may be found in peaceful prosecution of their respective occupations. Under no pretext nor in any way will any interference be allowed with the civil rights or religious principles of the inhabitants. . . . Whatsoever may be needed for the use of the army will be bought . . . at the highest prices." [3]

Grant read into this the belief that Taylor, like himself, was viewing the Mexicans "as the aggrieved party." As a matter of fact, Taylor was repeating what President Polk had ordered.[4]

The orders for the march sent the occupation army out in four columns with a day's interval between them. Grant was to go with the Third Brigade on the last day, March 11, with the supply train, 307 wagons, 80 of which were drawn by ox teams. Each day Grant saw the other brigades march away — Colonel Twiggs with the Dragoons and Major Samuel Ringgold's battery of horse artillery on the eighth.

Next day the First Brigade left under Brigadier General William J. Worth — who, if anything happened to Taylor, would command the occupation army. "His appearance and bearing were imposing and knightly; his person and gait erect and military . . . his utterance very rapid yet distinct," his manners at times "ostentatious." Worth was dramatically different from Taylor in whose "benevolent face" with its "mahogany complexion" there was "no silly pomp" and who "conversed in a stammering voice." Many officers thought Worth's bravery made him sometimes too quick, too decisive in action. Taylor privately considered him "unprincipled," but valued his gifts of leadership and excused some of his "mortifying" quarrels over rank and recognition by attributing them to "excitement from the effects of wine." Grant's classmate, Charles Hamilton, in the Fifth Infantry, noticed how as time went on Worth "lost caste and the confidence of the government by his personal habits." [5]

Closer to Taylor's heart was Captain James Duncan, an aggressive New Yorker "noted for his contempt for graceful bearing and showy dress" although he kept "his guns as burnished as a mirror." As Duncan rode out with the light battery of the Second Artillery at the rear of the First Brigade, the soldiers said that there was a man the Mexicans would need to watch.[6]

On the tenth, Grant saw the Second Brigade start out with Lieutenant Colonel James S. McIntosh riding ahead — Old Tosh, a rough, unread Georgian, who prayed and swore with equal diligence and who kicked the posteriors of privates who came into camp drunk. The Third Brigade marched away on the eleventh with Colonel Whistler, sober or not, in the lead, and First Lieutenant Braxton Bragg's battery behind.

White hair streamed at the head of each column; Whistler was sixty-six, Taylor sixty-two, McIntosh fifty-nine, Twiggs, fifty-six, Worth fifty-two and Worth's second-in-command, Lieutenant Colonel William G. Belknap, was also fifty-two. None of these commanders had attended West Point, and each was prepared to fight in 1846 as his army had fought in 1812. Back home in Princeton University, Belknap's son, William W., was remembering how, a few years before, when he had been with his father in the Florida wars, he had seen "the disgust of General Worth and other old army officers when the percussion guns and caps were first introduced . . . they feared that the caps would be lost and the men left helpless, forgetting that powder for pouring in the pan of a flintlock gun was attended with greater risk of loss." [7]

Only a few of Taylor's companies carried the new percussion-cap muskets, the rest had the historic flintlock. The officers had left their full-dress uniforms behind and for the campaign wore blue frock coats and light blue trousers. The men were dressed in common jackets and trousers of light blue, with fatigue caps of blue cloth. Sam Grant, later on, would say "a better army, man for man, probably never faced an enemy," and Second Lieutenant John Sedgwick, Class of '37, would write home when he joined Taylor a few weeks later, "There never was so fine an American army." The artillery was daringly modern. Ringgold at forty-six, Duncan at thirty-six, Bragg at twenty-nine, and Randolph Ridgely in his early thirties, all West Pointers, were spoiling to use their new "flying artillery," the light horse-drawn guns which Ringgold, as one of an inventive and intellectual Maryland family, had led in developing.

Ringgold, furthermore, had designed a saddletree which would later be improved by and named for George B. McClellan, that bright boy of the senior class which was hungering for July and assignment at the front.[8]

Up and down the column that first day, Grant rode on his unbroken mustang. "There were frequent disagreements between us as to which way we should go," Grant recalled in later years, "and sometimes whether we should go at all. At no time during the day could I choose exactly the part of the column I would march with; but after that, I had as tractable a horse as any with the army." [9]

It was doubtful if Braxton Bragg, riding with his guns, laughed at the spectacle of Sam Grant breaking another wild horse. Laughter never came easily to the intense North Carolinian. His piercing, big, black eyes, shining under heavy brows, were usually on his men, and his nervous, tremulous voice was forever dressing their ranks. The soldiers loved to watch him at battery drill, where "his horses whirled the guns and caissons over the plain with wonderful rapidity and ease." [10]

Already famous for his brains and industry, Bragg would in time be regarded by officers as "perhaps the best disciplinarian in the . . . Army." Puritan and Spartan combined, Bragg was not, however, all martinet as he rode toward the Rio Grande. He looked away from his gunners long enough to approve a certain six-foot, rawboned washerwoman who rode her pony in the column. "The Great Western" everybody called her. Many soldiers admired her "virtuousness" and bravery, which contrasted with the morals of most women camp followers. But of all who admired her, Bragg would be the one who would speak up publicly to honor her at the end of the campaign.

The wife of an enlisted man in the Seventh Infantry, she had come with him to Corpus Christi and had worked as a laundress for a group of young officers. When word came that her husband was to go to the Rio Grande by ship, escorting Taylor's supplies and siege guns, The Great Western announced that she'd not stay in camp. She'd get a pony, go along, and take care of her young officers, keep them clean and fed. Although each company was permitted to issue rations to three laundresses, only eight or ten of the women had volunteered to leave Corpus Christi. The Great Western was anxious to see "her boys" whip the Mexicans.[11]

The march was painful for foot soldiers, a ten-day tramp across prairies where black ashes from recent fires churned up to make the men "resemble Africans." Surgeons thought the men's thirst "terrible," sending them headlong with their horses and dogs to ponds which occasionally appeared. Sam Grant, writing to John Lowe back in Bethel, said that sometimes "ponds of drinkable water were separated by a whole day's march." His admiration for the private soldier grew as he saw them undergo this suffering "without a murmur." Where so many of his brother officers were looking down upon the enlisted men as "dumb foreigners," Lieutenant Grant was learning to share General Taylor's admiration of them.[12]

At times, when the column halted to let the footmen "blow," Grant would ride out onto high ground to see the wild mustangs covering the plain clear to the horizon in three directions, too many, he estimated, to be corraled in the whole State of Rhode Island. The marching men sometimes forgot their pangs as they saw "grand mirages" in the sky — ships and islands reflected from the Gulf sixty miles or more away. But the sun grew hotter and thirst sharper. Then, after 125 miles had been put behind, there loomed ahead a line of chaparral and, at its base, the preceding brigades. The fourth column rushed forward. The Colorado River was at hand and into it the dusty soldiers plunged their heads only to come out spitting and coughing — the water was salt.

They learned that the column had all halted here because a Mexican cavalry patrol, on the twentieth, had warned Taylor's scouts that any advance across the stream would mean war. On the twenty-first, Taylor had been given the same warning by a Mexican officer who handed him a proclamation by the Mexican commander at Matamoros, General Mejía, denouncing the invasion as "that most degrading depredation . . . of the degenerate sons of Washington." Mejía pointed out that while President Polk had his minister, Slidell, in Mexico City, "endeavoring" to lull us into security by opening diplomatic negotiations, an American army had pushed past the Nueces onto ground which was clearly outside the boundaries of Texas. Communications being what they were, Mejía might not have known that, on March 12, his government had again refused to see Slidell and that the United States envoy had started home.[13]

Taylor, paying no attention to Mejía's proclamation, told the emissary that if a single Mexican was to be seen "after my men enter the river, I will open an artillery fire on him." Behind him as the columns came up, his young cannoneers were itching to show what their guns could do. After that, the Mexicans showed themselves infrequently in the chaparral, but kept up a great blowing of bugles and shouting of commands as if massing a powerful force for battle. Out onto the bank strode The Great Western to say to her "boys" that, "if the General would give her a good pair of *tongs,* she would *wade* that river and whip every scoundrel that dare show himself." [14]

Grant, listening to Mexicans blaring defiance in the thicket, braced himself for his first battle. He saw Taylor put men to cutting a roadway down through the thirty-foot bluffs to the water level and then send four artillery companies splashing across with Grant's idolized Commandant of Cadets, Captain Charles F. Smith, in command, his long mustachios flaring. Ahead of Smith at the finish spurred General Worth. But there were no shots as the wet American horses and riders scrambled out and plunged into the chaparral. The Mexicans who had fled were variously estimated at twenty-five to three hundred. Sam Grant thought of the prairie wolves. First Benjamin, and now Taylor, had taught him that the strength of an enemy was not to be judged by noise.[15]

For two days the army waited till the last of the creeping ox wagons arrived; then on March 23, Taylor started the last thirty miles to the Rio Grande, his columns no longer in single file, but four abreast — a magnificent spectacle on the open prairie. The men's spirits rose; the first Mexican troops had fled at the sight of them, and each mile brought thicker grass, more flowers. The cactus blossomed red and gold and the feather-petaled blossoms of the Turk's-head waved in the wind. The flowering acacia grew thicker and the birds sang in trees. Men laughed to see their dogs race with unwarranted confidence after jack rabbits. Excitement was in the air. The men heard scouts say that a large force of Mexicans had crossed the river and was waiting. Fingers itched on triggers, but Lieutenant Colonel Hitchcock was thinking, "We have outraged the Mexican government and people by an arrogance and presumption that deserve to be punished." Telling his men to continue slowly straight ahead, Taylor rode off with an escort to Point Isabel, a town on the left bank of the Rio Grande's mouth, where he had ordered his supply ships to meet him. On the twenty-fifth, word came from him saying the Mexican customhouse and several other buildings in the town had been burning when he arrived. The population had fled.

"How unjust!" wrote Pennsylvania-born Lieutenant George Deas, adjutant of the Fifth Infantry, and husband of Colonel Garland's elder daughter, Bessie. "The march . . . to the banks of the Rio Grande was, of itself, an act of hostility." No Americans or Texans lived in the disputed territory. "All were Mexicans, acknowledging none but Mexican laws. Yet we . . . drove those poor people away from their farms, and seized their custom-house at Point Isabel." Deas's Government was, "in the most solemn manner," throwing upon the Mexicans "the odium of beginning the war." [16]

The army halted ten miles from Matamoros, awaiting Taylor's return. Rumors came that 10,000 Mexicans were ready for them, an army not well disciplined but having officers trained in European military schools. Hitchcock worried about Taylor's colonels: Whistler, who "cannot give the simplest command," McIntosh who was unable to maneuver a brigade, Garland who "could not possibly dispose the brigade for battle." [17]

On Taylor's return, March 28, the force pushed forward those last few miles, catching glimpses of a deep blue haze ahead — the mists over the Rio Grande — then the gunmetal shine of the river itself. At ten-thirty in the morning the soldiers were staring across the stream at Matamoros whose tiled roofs were packed with Mexicans staring back. Mexican soldiers were marching through the streets behind blaring bands. Red flowers were climbing on white walls. Gardens blazed with color. Word spread that two dragoons had been captured and were prisoners. Lines of sentries faced each other with the water between. In the afternoon a party of Taylor's young officers walked through the Yankee line, stripped and began bathing close to shore. As if in answer, a bevy of Mexican girls laughed their way past their sentries and, stepping out of their bright, flaring skirts, pulled their snowy chemises over their heads and slipped naked into the stream. The two bands of frolickers were edging nearer to midstream when the Mexican guards leveled their muskets. Kissing their hands to the tawny nymphs, the Yankee satyrs swam back to their shore while the girls splashed and laughed.[18]

It was the beginning of a never-ending delight and torment for the young men from the North, many of whom did not understand that the lower-class Indians, having no bathtubs in their homes, regarded nude bathing without shame. Yankee diaries and journals daily recorded the pagan voluptuousness of the daily scene — crowds of naked women and girls "chasing each other, . . . diving into the depths of the stream or swimming along its surface with their long, loose, raven tresses flowing behind them. . . . They laugh, shout, sing, wrestle with each other, and display their graceful forms in a thousand agile movements." [19]

Between thoughts of the women at Matamoros and the men of the Mexican Army, Taylor's soldiers found their first night on the Rio Grande "one of great excitement," as Surgeon Nathan Jarvis observed. Rain fell all night long, but it could not dampen the Yankees' fear that the Mexican soldiers would attack and that the Mexican girls would not. As dawn revealed Mexican earthworks newly risen on the opposite bank, Taylor sent Worth over with a flag of truce to learn that General Mejía was breathing fire and that a higher general, Ampudia, would soon arrive to chase the Yankees back to the Nueces.[20]

The news eased the tension. This was the Mexicans' *mañana* — tomorrow or next day they would fight, but not today.

A little later the Mexicans set the ferry working and peddlers came over with fruits, meat and flowers. The two captured dragoons, whose return Taylor had demanded, were sent back with courteous bows. They promptly spread the word that they had been detained more as guests than prisoners.[21]

Down the riverbank each day came Mexican women to laugh, flirt and beckon. Flowers were in their hair and they wore their thin chemises low and loose across their brown shoulders and thrusting breasts. Their voices tinkled across the water as silvery as the church bells which, the soldiers said, rang from dawn till dusk. Native-born Yankees who had never seen Roman Catholic ceremonies joked about "mummery" as they saw priests scattering holy water on the fortifications the Mexicans were erecting. But to the

Catholic immigrants in Taylor's force the processionals in the streets, the fragments of well-known chants, the church bells singing of marriage and death and sacred rituals, brought thought of the homeland. At evening the vesper bells, the spiced and voluptuous perfumes of Mexico, the music of guitars and of women laughing all mingled in the southwest breeze that floated across the river.

Soon the nights were startled by shots — sentries firing at soldiers who could stand the temptations no longer. On April 4, eight days after the army had arrived, Captain Philip Norbourne Barbour wrote his wife, "We have lost about 30 men from the whole Army by desertion. . . . Several slaves belonging to officers have left their masters and gone over to Matamoras. . . . If we are located on this border we shall have to employ white servants." [22]

It was that day that the Mexican General Pedro de Ampudia scattered in Taylor's camp leaflets calling to the English, Irish, German, French and Poles in the invading force to abandon their barbarous and un-Christian aggression: "Separate yourselves from the Yankees, and do not contribute to defend a robbery and usurpation which, be assured, the civilized nations of Europe look upon with the utmost indignation." [23]

On April 3, Surgeon Jarvis noted in his journal that thirty-six men had deserted the night before, fourteen of them from the First Brigade. On April 7, Lieutenant George Meade wrote home that the stories told by the two dragoons had "induced a great many desertions from our side, and in one night we lost fourteen men, who swam the river." Surgeon Jarvis saw deserters, after a night or two of Mexican life, come down to the riverbank and, calling across to their old comrades, recommend most highly the delights they were enjoying.[24]

Although desertions were growing serious, the feeling of security grew as the days passed. Major Trueman Cross, Assistant Quartermaster General, did not come home the night of April 10 from a pleasure ride into the country, but there was a possibility he had been captured by the rancheros, unorganized bands of Mexican cowboys loosely associated with the Mexican army. Searching parties found no trace of him. On the night of the fifteenth, an eccentric South Carolinian, Lieutenant Edward Deas of the Fourth Artillery, told friends he was going to look for Cross, swam the river and disappeared into Matamoros. Some officers said it wasn't Cross he was looking for, but girls. Next day a Mexican officer, under a flag of truce, brought over a message from Deas saying he was a prisoner, had been put on parole, and would his friends please send over some money and a change of clothes. Taylor, in anger, ordered Deas's name stricken from the rolls.[25]

General Ampudia, on April 12, sent Taylor word that unless he withdrew within twenty-four hours to the far bank of the Nueces, he would have provoked war. Taylor made no move to obey.

Grant's captain, George McCall, wrote in his diary on April 14: "The general impression, however, among our officers is, that they [the Mexicans] do not mean to proceed to extremities." Even when Grant's fellow lieutenant in the Fourth, Theodoric Porter, was ambushed and killed with one of his soldiers on the seventeenth, while searching for Cross, and when three days later Cross's body was found with a bullet hole in the skull, there was no proof that the three deaths were by Mexican Army orders. Guerillas might have killed them or it might have been merely cattlemen who had bumped into the strange gringos and started fighting. It was not clear who had fired first.[26]

Taylor, however, took the precaution of requesting the United States naval officers commanding the warships with his transports off Point Isabel to blockade the mouth of the Rio Grande, so that supplies could not come up the river to Ampudia. The latter protested, insisting that the Americans had now committed an act of unquestioned hostility, since Texas had never laid claim to the whole of the river. Mexico, on April 23, declared a "defensive war."

Next day a general of higher rank, Arista, arrived at Matamoros with reinforcements and the announcement that war had begun. His agents littered Taylor's camps with a proclamation offering 320 acres of Mexican land to any soldier who would desert. Reports came that Arista was sending 2500 horsemen across the river above the town and, on the twenty-fifth, Taylor sent a squadron of dragoons to scout the region. Commanding the dragoons was Captain Seth B. Thornton, a slender, sickly Marylander who was always looking for danger. One of his exploits had been to rescue several women and children from the steamer *Pulaski* when it burned at sea, some years before, and then, when the ship sank, to tie himself to a hencoop from which, days later, he had been picked up "a raving maniac." Recovering, he had returned to the Army and had fought Indians recklessly in Florida. With him rode Captain William J. Hardee, who had graduated from the Academy two years before Sam Grant had entered, and who had risen rapidly in the United States Army, thanks to the seriousness with which he studied drill and tactics.[27]

In reckless fashion, Thornton, while questioning Mexicans, managed to get his whole squadron of sixty-three inside a rancho sixteen miles up the river, giving some Mexican troops, said to be regulars sent across by Arista, the chance — which they promptly took — of shutting corral gates and then shooting the Yankees like fish in a barrel. Sixteen dead, forty-seven captured, including both captains, was the word a lone survivor brought back to Taylor.

"Hostilities may now be considered as commenced," Taylor wrote to the Government at Washington on April 26 of that year, 1846. He sent the fateful message along with requests to the Governor of Texas and Louisiana to rush 4000 to 5000 volunteers to him at top speed.

Although later on these brushes would be called "the first red drops of the long impending storm," officers like Sam Grant found optimism in letters which Thornton and Hardee sent across the river on April 28, describing the courtesy and kindness which Arista and Ampudia were lavishing upon them, Arista paying both men half their regular salaries, and Ampudia insisting that Thornton live and eat with him. Arista punished a soldier who had been rude to Hardee.[28]

The Texas horsemen whom Taylor used as scouts reported that Arista was pouring troops across the river downstream somewhere and Taylor, who was running short of supplies, struck off with 2000 men and 250 wagons for Point Isabel. Everybody felt that the new fort was secure with 500 Seventh Infantrymen — and The Great Western — in it, under the command of the competent Major Jacob Brown. As the march started at 3 P.M., May 1, Grant heard that Taylor was prepared to "cut his way through, no matter how superior their numbers" that might oppose, but Grant told himself there would be no fighting. The march was his hardest so far. "Until 3 o'clock at night we scarcely halted," he wrote home. "Then we lay down in the grass and took a little sleep and marched the balance of the way the next morning. Our march was mostly through grass up to the waist, with a wet and uneven bottom; yet we made thirty miles in much less than a day. I consider my march on that occasion equal to a walk of sixty miles in one day on good roads and unincumbered with troops." There was no sign of an enemy.[29]

Arriving at Point Isabel, the wagons rolled down to the beach where Mexican laborers began loading them with the cannon, ammunition, clothing and food which had been landed from the ships. So stained did the Mexicans become from handling slabs of bacon that a war correspondent, writing a few days or weeks later, referred to them as "The Greaser Brigade." Since the whole Army would soon be calling all Mexicans "greasers," some people would believe that the nickname had thus been coined. But there were officers who insisted the word was a corruption of "grazer"; and the Texans insisted they had been applying it to Mexican rancheros, whose leather coats and trousers, worn in the thorny chaparral, shone "from grease and long usage." Here and there an army man would declare that soldiers had used the word in the Indian country as early as 1831. Another explanation was the Mexican term *los grisos* that had been applied centuries before to the half-white, half-red children of the early Spanish invaders — a term derived from *gris*, meaning a mixture of colors.[30]

With the Mexican workmen notoriously slow, Taylor had his men pitch their tents for a stay of some days. Sam Grant slept with weariness. In the morning, the morning of the third, he heard the low mutter of thunder coming in on the west wind. Was it another storm like the one that had fooled the dragoons? Old soldiers who had been through the Napoleonic Wars said no, this was cannon — Arista had crossed the Rio Grande and was bombarding the fort. Veterans looked curiously at the young lieutenants, watching them hear their first hostile guns.

"I felt sorry that I had enlisted," Sam Grant said afterward. He wondered what Taylor was feeling. What did generals think before battles, anyway? What did they do when the enemy started pounding in the rear? [31] Apparently, from the way Taylor was acting, they didn't stampede. Taylor went on loading the wagons and ignoring the pleas of some of his officers to drop everything and rush to the relief of the fort. Old Zach was sure the fort could stand off any attack. Some scouts whipped in with the news that this was true — the Mexican bombardment was doing small harm.

Calmly the loading of the wagons went on. The spring sun slept hotly on the tents. The waves of the Gulf expired on the beach with a monotonous sighing. Yet constantly those distant guns went on shuddering. The time went by; then on the fifth, Taylor was ready. He ordered officers to reduce their personal baggage in the regimental wagons, so that more ammunition and supplies could be carried. Old Colonel Whistler wheezed over to the Fourth's wagon, looked inside, and pointed to a small case of books. Who owned those? Told that it belonged to First Lieutenant Richard H. Graham, "a young officer of literary tastes," he said:

"That will never do, Mr. Graham. We can't encumber our train with such rubbish as books."

Adjutant Hoskins, removing the case, "remarked in a deprecatory manner that not being quite well and requiring a stimulant, he had taken the liberty of putting a small keg of whiskey in the wagon."

"Oh," grunted the old Colonel, "that's all right, Mr. Hoskins; anything in reason, but Graham wanted to carry a case of books." [32]

The young officers realized that unusual responsibility would fall on them if a fight developed. Several colonels and lieutenant colonels were too old and infirm for battle duty. Many of the senior officers were absent. General Worth had gone North, angry because he felt slighted in the matter of rank. Hitchcock had gone North sick. But the young officers were almost all West Point trained, and nine out of every ten men in the force of 2200 were regulars — well-drilled professionals.

Taylor told his men, as the march began on May 7, that they would likely have to cut their way through to the fort, but that they could easily win any battle. The thing to do was to trust the bayonet. There would be no chance to use the two 18-pounder cannon which he had received from the ships, and little to employ the horse guns. The bayonet would be the thing.[33]

Sam Grant, however, kept telling himself that there would be no fight. The Mexicans, for all their bombast and windy threats, were "good for paper wars alone." Even when scouts spurred up, when Taylor's army was nine miles from Matamoros, and shouted that the enemy was drawn up near some small lakes a mile and a quarter ahead, Grant was not convinced. They would fade away, as at the Colorado.[34]

Even when he saw them, he clung to his expectation. At first they were just a line of metal shining in the sun — a line in front of some timber that rose dramatically out of the prairie — *palo alto*, Spanish for "tall trees." Then, as the Yankee army came on, at the measured step of drill day, without the beat of a drum, Grant made out what the metal was: the lances of horsemen — lances gleaming sharp as the darning-needle tips of the grass which came up to his shoulder as he pushed through it. Then he made out the gleam of bayonets above the tall caps of infantrymen, and the glitter of brass cannon, scattered along the line.

The only sound was the swish of the grass as Yankee feet, horses' feet, oxen's feet, wagon wheels, came on. The tall trees dozed in the tropical sun. In the sky buzzards wheeled their endless patrol, floating lazily, coasting, drifting black against the blue, as they eyed the earth for their immemorial food — a dead jack rabbit here, a dying cow there and, on feast days, a bloating mustang.

Captain McCall guessed the enemy at over 6000 — 1200 cavalry in all, 800 lancers sitting their horses in front of the infantry — 10 cannon visible. Before Taylor came within range of these enemy guns he halted and formed a line of his own with his light artillery and his 18-pounders placed in it at intervals. On the right he stationed the Second Dragoons under Captain Charles A. May who, with long hair and beard, gold-tasseled cap, and handsome face was, at thirty, the most picturesque horseman in the force.[35]

When Taylor saw that all was ready, he suddenly ordered one platoon from each company to stack muskets, collect canteens from other platoons and fill them at a stream nearby. The tension off, the soldiers said that Taylor was the kind of general for them, sitting there like that, sideways on Old Whitey, pushing back on his head that floppy palmetto hat, talking casually to anybody at hand, waiting for his men to get a drink. Other generals would have been spurring up and down the line, waving swords and splendor — "Die for the flag! Give 'em hell!" [36]

Grant saw the last canteen distributed. Then the line marched quietly forward. Fire flashed at the foot of the tall trees, smoke bellied out and although no shot yet reached the Yankees, it was apparent the Mexicans were really going to fight. Grant looked down that line of 3000 men and, as he later said, "thought what a fearful responsibility General Taylor must feel, commanding such a host and so far away from his friends." [37]

"This firing commenced at half past 2 o'clock," Ulysses wrote Julia, "and was nearly constant from that until sundown." At first the solid brass balls came bouncing through the grass slowly enough to be side-stepped but "as we got in range they let us have it right and left. Our guns then rounded on them and so the battle commenced." Taylor did not return the fire until he saw that his canister could reach the Mexicans; then he halted the advance, ran his eight 6-pounders and two 18-pounders out in front and cut loose.

"Every moment we could see the charges from our pieces cut a way through their ranks making a perfect road," Ulysses told Julia, after the battle, "but they would close up the interval without showing signs of retreat. Their officers made an attempt to charge upon us but the havoc had been so great that their soldiers could not be made to advance. Some of the prisoners that we have taken say that their officers cut and slashed among them with their sabres at a dreadful rate to make them advance but it was no use. I did not feel a sensation of fear until nearly the close of the firing. A ball struck close by me killing one man instantly. It knocked Capt. Page's under jaw entirely off and broke the roof of his mouth, and knocked Lt. Wallen and one Sergeant down, but they were not much hurt." [38]

More candidly Grant wrote to his friend John Lowe that Captain John Page had lain there with his under jaw "gone to the windpipe, and the tongue hanging down upon the throat. He never will be able to speak or eat." Ulysses told Lowe, "I scarcely thought of the probability or possibility of being touched myself, (although nine-pound shots were whistling all around). . . . You want to know what my feelings were. . . . I do not know that I felt any peculiar sensation." [39]

In his letter he did not mention a curious interlude that had come in the fight when Duncan's battery, firing seven or eight shots a minute, ignited dry grass and started a fire which raced down between the forces, halting the engagement with clouds of smoke. For an hour and more Taylor rode along his line chatting with the men,

Finally when the smoke lifted a Mexican column of infantry and cavalry was seen marching behind a brass band around the Yankee right wing, aiming at the wagons in the rear. With incredible speed Duncan hitched up his guns, whipped them across to a point of vantage, and wiped out the musicians with one bursting shell that left a triumphant toot hanging in mid-air. A second later canister from his other guns was chasing the rest of the column back toward the chaparral.

Sam Grant's first impression of battle came at the moment when field artillery was making a historic demonstration of its power. After being developed by Napoleon, it had fallen into obscurity among European armies, and only among the young, aggressive artillery officers of the United States Army had it been studied and advanced as a vital arm. Grant was watching it rout cavalry and impress infantry with the futility of advancing under such storms of canister. It kept the Mexican Army at so great a distance that no musket fire, other than some hasty carbine shots from galloping cavalrymen, reached the Yankee ranks. Neither were the American flintlocks called into play. Their range, using a paper cartridge charged with powder, buckshot and ball, was so limited that Grant said: "At the distance of a few hundred yards a man might fire at you all day without your finding it out." [40]

When darkness finally stilled all the guns, it was discovered that Taylor's chief loss had been Major Ringgold, mangled so badly by a cannon ball that tore through his legs just below the crotch that he was not expected to live. Dying three days later, he nevertheless lived long enough to see his great faith in flying artillery justified.

What some of the soldiers remembered as the most memorable thing about the battle was that none of the forty yoke of oxen had been hit.[41]

Grant wrote home that "we then encamped on our own ground, and the enemy on theirs. We supposed that the loss of the enemy had not been much greater than our own, and expected of course that the fight would be renewed in the morning. During the night I believe all slept as soundly on the ground at Palo Alto as if they had been in a palace. For my own part I don't think I even dreamed of battles." [42]

CHAPTER NINE

"Dearest Julia"

TAYLOR'S chief officers did not, presumably, sleep as long nor as soundly as did the lieutenants that night of May 8, 1846. Sometime before dawn Taylor gathered ten of his leaders together and asked their advice about tomorrow. Three voted to attack, seven to wait for reinforcements which would soon be arriving at the mouth of the Rio Grande. Taylor called to Captain Duncan, who was riding past, and put the question to him. Anyone who had fought as Duncan had should be listened to.

"We whipped 'em today and we can whip 'em tomorrow!" snapped the cannoneer.

"That is my opinion, Captain Duncan," said Taylor, adding, "Gentlemen, you will prepare your commands to move forward; the Council is dissolved." [1]

Veterans in the ranks winked when they heard the decision. Old Zach had had his mind made up all along; he knew the military adage, "A council of war never votes to fight."

At dawn on the ninth, Taylor sent his wounded back to Point Isabel and his scouts forward. The Mexican rear guard was found to be disappearing along trails leading into the thorny chaparral. General Arista had discovered that the "North Americans" were not merely good hand-to-hand, rough-and-tumble fighters like the Texans; they were amazingly professional. Today he would change his tactics and fight from cover and keep away from those murderous horse guns.

By two o'clock in the afternoon Taylor was marching toward the thickets five or six miles ahead where his scouts had located Arista behind ravines. The fight when it came was in underbrush, "a pell-mell affair," as Grant described it, "everybody for himself." Under the pressure of rifle fire from the Yankee infantry and canister from Ringgold's battery — now commanded by a remarkable gunner,

Lieutenant Randolph Ridgely, Class of '37 — the Mexicans broke and fled. Taylor had been urged, at one point, to withdraw from the hailstorm of bullets, but had answered, "We'll ride forward a little and the shots will drop behind us." When a spectacular charge of a company of Dragoons under Captain Charles A. May overran a Mexican battery but finally fell back, badly cut up, Taylor shouted to Belknap's Eighth Infantry, "Take those guns, and by God keep them!" — which was done.[2]

The Mexican flight was so wild that soldiers attempting to cross the Rio Grande drowned in shoals. A priest, Father Leary, who had come up from the Mexican town of Reynosa, was calming fear-crazed fugitives on a large flatboat tied to the bank when some frantic lancers spurred their horses aboard, swamping the craft. The priest was holding his crucifix aloft as he disappeared beneath the water.[3]

That evening, May 9, the victorious Yankee army divided, part pushing on to the fort, whose besiegers had fled, and part remaining to collect the booty. Next day Captain E. Kirby Smith of the Fifth Infantry saw the buzzard patrol glide down for such a feast as it had never before known. He watched coyotes "howling and fighting over their dreadful meal" while from their banquet rose an "insupportable" stench.[4]

On May 11 when the heavy work of collecting arms and burying the dead was done, Ulysses sat down with pencil and paper to write Julia, a captured drum serving as desk:

> On the 9th of May about noon we left the field of battle (Palo Alto) and started on our way to Matamoras. When we advanced about six miles we found that the enemy had taken up a new position in the midst of a dense wood, and as we have since learned they had received a reinforcement equal to our whole numbers.
>
> Grape shot and musket balls were let fly from both sides making dreadful havoc. Our men continued to advance and did advance in spite of the shots, to the very mouths of the cannon and killed and took prisoner the Mexicans with them, and drove off with their own teams, taking cannon ammunition and all to our side. In this way nine of their big guns were taken and their own ammunition turned against them.

The Mexicans fought hard for an hour and a half but seeing their means of war fall from their hands in spite of all their efforts they finally commenced to retreat helter skelter. A great many retreated to the banks of the Rio Grande and without looking for means of crossing plunged into the water and no doubt many of them were drowned. Among the prisoners we have taken are 14 officers and I have no idea how many privates. I understand that General Larega [La Vega] who is a prisoner in our camp had said that he has fought against several different nations but ours are the first that he ever saw who would charge up to the very mouths of cannon . . . we had three officers killed and some 8 or ten wounded. . . . The Mexicans were so certain of success that when we took their camp we found their dinners on the fire cooking.

After the battle the woods was strewed with the dead. Waggons have been engaged drawing their bodies to bury. How many waggon loads have already come in and how many are left would be hard to guess. I saw 5 large wagon loads at one time myself. We captured, beside the prisoners, 9 cannon . . . probably 1,000 to 1,500 stand of fire arms, sabres, swords, etc. Two hundred and fifty thousand rounds of ammunitions for them, over four hundred mules and pack saddles or harness. Drums, musical instruments, camp equipage, etc., etc., innumerable.

The victory for us has been a very great one. No doubt you will see accounts enough of it in the papers. There is no great sport in having bullets flying about one in every direction, but I find I have less horror when among them than when in anticipation. Now that the war has commenced with such a vengeance I am in hope my Dear Julia that we will soon be able to end it.

In the thickest of it I thought of Julia. How much I should love to see you now to tell you all that happened. . . . When we have another engagement, if we do have another at all, I will write again, that is if I am not one of the victims. Give my love to all at White Haven and do write soon my dear Julia.

I think you will find that history will count the victory just achieved one of the greatest on record. But I did not want to say too much about it until I see the account given by others. Dont [sic] forget to write soon to your most devoted

ULYSSES.[5]

Years later Grant, looking back on the two battles with a kind of affectionate belittlement, would say that they had seemed "pretty important affairs" at the time, but nothing of the magnitude that was given them in the newspapers back home.

The things he as a mature man would tell about the second fight (Resaca) were a mixture of modesty and humor. He had been with the right wing at the start in command of his company as it worked its way through the thickets:

> At last I got pretty close up without knowing it. The balls commenced to whistle very thick overhead, cutting the limbs of the chaparral right and left. We could not see the enemy, so I ordered my men to lie down, an order that did not have to be enforced. We kept our position until it became evident that the enemy were not firing upon us, and then withdrew to find better ground to advance from.
>
> By this time some progress had been made on our left. . . . The Mexicans were giving way all along the line, and many of them no doubt, left early. . . . There seemed to be a few men in front and I charged upon them with my company. There was no resistance, and we captured a Mexican colonel, who had been wounded, and a few men. Just as I was sending them to the rear with a guard of two or three men, a private came from the front. . . . The ground had been charged over before. My exploit was equal to that of the soldier who boasted that he had cut off the leg of one of the enemy. When asked why he did not cut off his head, he replied, "Some one had done that before."

The discovery that he had captured Mexicans who had already been captured convinced him, he said, "that the battle of Resaca de la Palma would have been won, just as it was, if I had not been there." [6]

As the army settled down opposite Matamoros watching the shattered Mexicans, across the river, making obvious preparations to retire into the interior, Grant and his brother lieutenants hashed over their initiation into the art of war. The smell of death was what impressed them. It hung on so long after the clash and fury had vanished. As the river went down corpses of those fleeing Mexican soldiers appeared, caught in the low bushes and now "dropping

piece-meal into the water below" and "floating along, attacked by
the voracious cat-fish, causing them to twitch and roll about, as if
still in the agonies of death."[7]

A later count showed that Taylor had lost twenty-nine killed
and eighty-two wounded, the Mexicans probably a thousand shot to
death or drowned. The horse guns and infantry charges were the
things that won battles. The Mexicans' trust in horse troops was
ridiculous. Their aristocrats, the pure Spanish and mestizos (mixed
white and red blood) went into the cavalry leaving the infantry
to be filled by the pure-blooded Indian conscripts who were poorly
clothed, badly fed and pitiably underpaid.

Grant's captain, McCall, admired two veteran infantry regiments
which had stood up under the awful cannon fire at Resaca until
"almost annihilated; one regiment retiring from the field with but
twenty-five men." Grant later said, "I do not think a more incompetent set of officers ever existed. . . . With an able general the
Mexicans would make a good fight, for they are a courageous
people. It was a pity to see good troops used as the Mexican soldiers were." Another of Taylor's officers wrote home that the Mexicans admitted their lower officers "are generally young men of corrupt morals, dissipated habits, and with little courage or enterprise.
. . . They never LEAD their men." He learned that Mexican infantry habitually marched thirty miles a day, fifty upon occasion,
while the United States troops averaged, by comparison, fifteen.
Adjutant George Deas, of the Fifth, thought the Mexicans aimed
their muskets badly because their cartridges "contained twice as
much powder as was necessary" and consequently kicked painfully.
"It was difficult," he said, "for them [the Mexicans] to comprehend
how soldiers, dressed in common blue jackets, and their Officers
en negligé, could stand before the great appointments of the Mexican army" — their officers in gold braid and brilliant colors, their
men in corded and belted coats of light blue. They maintained "an
enormous band with each Regiment, beside a horde of trumpeters
and buglers," while the Americans had but little music "over and
above the necessary drums, fifes and bugles."[8]

Taylor's men, having whipped the Mexicans in the open plain and
the chaparral, and stood off with ease the long bombardment of
the fort, felt what Ulysses put into a letter to Julia:

"After two hard fought battles against a force three or four times as numerous as our own, we have chased the enemy from their homes and I have not the least apprehension that they will ever return here to reconquer the place." [9]

During the investment of the fort, Bragg had handled his guns superbly and George H. Thomas had behaved characteristically. Sitting calmly on a parapet Old Tom had been asked what he thought of the way they were serving their cannon.

"Service?" he had repeated. "Excellent; but I'm thinking that we'll need, after a while, the ammunition you're throwing away." [10]

The officers laughed when they heard about Taylor's meeting with Flag Officer Conner of the Navy at Point Isabel on May 11. Grant said that Conner, to put the rough old General at ease, discarded his uniform and appeared in citizen's clothes. Meanwhile Taylor, knowing how naval officers, as Grant put it, "habitually wore all the uniform the law allowed," decided to dress up for the occasion. He dug a brigadier general's uniform out of a trunk, got into it and strode out to meet Conner. The spectacle of the two flustered commanders apologizing and explaining convulsed their representative staffs. There were jibes when Thornton and Hardee were exchanged. Now that the other officers had been in battle, they snickered about the "Battle of Thornton's Field" and Hardee's inability to throw down a fence and escape capture. Thornton demanded a court-martial and was exonerated. [11]

Apparently Grant was not among the minority of officers who muttered because Taylor failed to smash on across the river and whip Ampudia again. The majority agreed that Taylor was right to await reinforcements. All carping, however, was washed out as they read the first newspaper accounts of how the nation, back home, was behaving. On May 11, Polk had sent Congress Taylor's dispatch about the opening of hostilities, and on May 13, the President had signed Congress's act authorizing him to appoint generals and call out a maximum of 50,000 volunteers if need be. Except for New England, where Whig disapproval was dominant, war fervor was generally blazing. Volunteers were clamoring to be accepted.

It amused Grant to read "of the deeds of heroism attributed to officers and soldiers, none of which we ever saw. . . . I do not suppose any war was ever fought with reference to which so many romances were invented." [12]

Captain May, for example. According to the press May, the first romantic hero of the war, had won Resaca de la Palma practically singlehanded! His charge had done the trick! His saber had cut down scores of terrified Mexicans! His gigantic horse had bounded over blazing cannon! He wore his hair and beard long because he was disappointed in love! He was one of five brothers all over six feet and all brave! He could swing down from the saddle and pick up a handkerchief! His one possible imperfection, a stumbling gait when he walked, only emphasized the fact that he had lived in the saddle and was nothing less than a centaur!

Soldiers scoffed when word came that May had been given two brevets, going from captain to brevet lieutenant colonel. General Taylor wrote a friend that it was "an extraordinary proceeding to say the least" and showed how it paid to have friends at court. Officers said the tale of May capturing General La Vega was nonsense; a sergeant of the Fifth Infantry had bagged the Mexican leader, and all that May had done was to bring La Vega into camp while the sergeant remained at the front. The gunners, Duncan, Ridgely and Bragg, who had done much more to win the two fights, were each only receiving one brevet. Resentment against May increased in the camps when it was discovered that the myth of his performance had been launched by his close friend, Captain E. Kirby Smith, who had written the first account of the battles to be published in the States. [13]

In contrast to these heroics, Taylor was modest in the face of news showing that he was now an idol at home, where babies were being named for him, organizations sending him swords, politicians proposing him for President. In a private letter written by a soldier after Resaca, and widely published, there had been a sentence that had taken the nation by storm — "we call him Old Rough and Ready." As the adulation flowed down to his camp, Taylor wrote a friend, "I have a great horror of being made a lion of." To young Lieutenant Grant, this was the way for a great general to act. [14]

On May 18, Taylor decided that, although he had not received all the supplies and munitions he wanted, the approach of the Volunteers down the Gulf made him strong enough to oust the Mexican army from Matamoros.

Ampudia, now in command, had been urging Taylor to let distant diplomats settle the question without further bloodshed, but when he saw that Taylor was to cross the river, he marched away to Monterey, so rapidly that he left his wounded behind.

At a place three miles above Matamoros, where the stream was fordable except for a few feet in its center, Taylor sent his men across in small boats and his wagons and cannon on scows. The army of observation, which had become the army of occupation, now became the army of invasion, but Taylor camped it outside town to mollify the citizens. When officers received permission to stroll into the city, they saw the paroled prisoner, Lieutenant Edward Deas, lying drunk in the shade. They thought him "crazy." However, drinking was so common among officers that Deas was, in time, forgiven, restored to his rank and, nine months later, promoted to captain.[15]

Only habitual drunkenness like Colonel Whistler's demanded decisive action. Taylor, unable to depend upon Whistler in the coming campaign, finally asked the old man to resign. "It is impossible," was the reply. "I have spent all my property, and have no other means to live by. Military life is the only one I am acquainted with, and I am too old to learn any other." Reluctantly, Taylor had Whistler court-martialed and a recommendation for his dismissal sent to Washington. The old Colonel took his papers to President Polk who, out of respect for his long service, reinstated him, refraining, however, from returning him to the front.[16]

Drinking among officers increased as wine flowed in the Mexican homes where they were entertained. "The time was whiled away pleasantly enough at Matamoras while we were waiting for volunteers," Grant wrote. "The most important citizens had fled" but "with those remaining the best of relations apparently existed."[17]

What impressed Jesse Grant's son most in Matamoros was, as he wrote home, the fact that it "is not a place of as much business importance as our little towns of 1,000."[18]

What impressed many other officers and war correspondents was not trade but sex. Many of them, at first blush, seemed to think the

Mexican civilization devoted to Venus. With the upper class Spaniards and mestizos gone south, and the remaining members of the middle class keeping as inconspicuous as possible, greenhorn invaders leaped to the conclusion that the lower class women in this border town were typical of all Mexico. Since so many of Taylor's men spoke of the swarthy Mexicans as "yellow" people, it was natural for Volunteers from Southern states to call them "mulattos" and to summon tawny *señoritas* to bed exactly as if they were Negro slave girls back home.[19]

From the street the invaders could peer in through barred windows and see women in scant attire taking siestas or, seated in their boudoirs, "throwing their luxuriant tresses over their heads as they prepared for the evening listlessness." *Señoritas* in "nothing but low-cut chemises" laughed through window gratings as they talked to Mexican men, laughed, exhaled cigarito smoke, and leaned forward careless of the charms they revealed. They walked the streets, "their bosoms were not compressed in stays . . . but heaved freely under the healthful influences of the genial sun and balmy air." They carelessly threw back their long colored scarves "with which they conceal their full bronze busts when convenient." Yankees went to dance halls to learn the fandango in the cool of the evening and did not return to camp till morning. Among the Volunteers who had been pouring in since May 19 were many still too pure of morals or too prejudiced against dark skins to embrace willing *señoritas*. An Ohio major noted that young soldiers "in whose minds romance and poetry had painted glowing pictures of Spanish beauty and grandeur, suffer a disagreeable disenchantment in the city of Matamoras."

"Gomez," correspondent of the *Missouri Republican*, arriving some months later, wrote that while it was true that the Mexican women were "well-formed," thanks to their freedom from corsets, and that their hands and feet were small, their faces — "Oh, cracky! *They are most awfully ugly!*" He said he understood how the legend of loveliness was spread. "Should an unfledged greenish bachelor, who had not seen an American woman for months, find himself sitting on a cushion beside a dark haired, bright eyed girl, whose delicate hand was playing with his sash and whose fascinating voice, melodiously lisped, in her native language . . . then, why then, I should not be surprised if he actually believed that Mexican girls were decidedly handsome." [20]

Grant was too monogamous by nature and too wrapped in thoughts of Julia to covet in all likelihood any of the *señoritas*. At least Julia would say later on, "Every mail brought me a letter; every one of them full of sweet nothings, love and war, and now and then some pressed leaves and flowers. Some were written on drumheads captured from the Mexicans and others on sheets of foolscap, folded and sealed with red wafers. I read each one every day until the next one came." Her sister Emmy heard Julia usually read them to the whole family. "They were more about the army than himself," she said. [21]

The letter which Ulysses wrote his sweetheart on June 5, from Matamoros, was not perhaps of the kind shown to Emmy:

I received a few days ago My Dearest Julia your sweet letter of the 12th of May. How often I have wished the same thing you there express, namely that we had been united when I was last in Mo. You don't know how proud and how happy it made me feel to hear you say that willingly you would share my tent, or my prison if I were taken prisoner. As yet my Dearest I am unhurt and free, and our troops are occupying a conquered city. . . . No doubt we will follow them up. I believe the general's plan is to march to Monteray [*sic*], a beautiful little city just at the foot of the mountains, and about three hundred miles from this place. That taken and we will have in our possession, or at least in our power, the whole of the Mexican territory east of the mountains and it is to be presumed Mexico will then soon come to terms.

I do not feel my Dear Julia the slightest apprehension as to our success in every large battle that we may have with the enemy no matter how superior they may be to us in numbers . . . believe me my Dear Julia you need not feel any alarm for our welfare. The greatest danger is from exposure in the rain, sun and dew in a very warm climate. But for my part I am never sick, and I think I have become well acclimated to the South.

My Dearest Julia when you write to me again tell me if your Pa ever says any thing about our engagement and if you think he will make any further objections. I think from what he said to me when I was there last Spring he will not; but he has not written to me as he said he would do.

But Julia I hope many months more will not pass over before we will be able to talk over this matter without the use of paper. How much I do want to see you again, but I know you would not recognize me. When you see me as you often do in your dreams, you see me as I was not as I am, for climate has made a change. I mean a change in appearance, but in my love for Julia I am the same, and I know too that she has not changed in that respect for she writes me such sweet letters when she does write. In six weeks I have had four letters from you Dear Julia which is much more than I ever received in the same time before. Won't you continue to write to me often for it gives me so much pleasure to read and to answer your letters.

Julia if the 4th Infy, should be stationed permanently in the conquered part of Mexico would you be willing to come here or would you want me to resign. I think it probable though that I shall resign as soon as this war is over and make Gelena my home. My father is very anxious to have me do so.

Speaking of your coming to Mexico, Dearest I do not intend to hint that it is even probable that the 4th Inf. will remain for I think it will be one of the first to leave the country. Give my love to all at White Haven and write very soon and very often to

ULYSSES

Then after signing the letter, he could not resist writing the word *Julia* just once more, and he repeated it at the bottom of the page apropos of nothing but love.[22]

Years later he could confess to an intimate friend that the only men he had ever hated in his whole life were two fellow officers who had mistreated Mexican women. For the Mexican civilians he had the same sympathy he had felt for their foot soldiers in battle. He wrote John Lowe at Bethel, "The better class are very proud, and tyrannize over the lower . . . as much as a hard master does over his negroes; and they submit as humbly." The poor "suffer from the influence of the Church" which, as represented by the Mexican clergy of Matamoros, was "as bad as bad could be." Lieutenant John Sedgwick of the Second Artillery, writing home about the Catholic clergymen who were serving as chaplains or advisors with Taylor's army, said, "The priests that come from the States say they could not recognize the Catholic religion in the mummeries practiced here. . . . Religion is a mixture of Indian idolatry and superstition with the Catholic." [23]

To add to all the powers which Grant considered oppressors of the Mexican people, now came the gringo invaders, of whom he was one. The shame of taking part in the "unholy war" was growing upon him and, in fact, would remain with him as long as he lived. Whenever, in time to come, he would think of Mexico, he would be seeing a gentle, brave, patient people victimized by his own nation and himself. As long as he would live he would never forgive himself for not having resigned from the Army rather than be a part of this sin. If Mexican women slept with Yankee soldiers, if Mexican men stabbed gringo soldiers in dark streets or strangled them with lassos on lonely roads, the blame lay in a tangle of oppressions, old and new. The caste system, the Church, the large landowners, the succession of ruthless military administrations, the endless civil wars, President Polk — and he himself — were to blame, not the ignorant peons.

In Mexico he was seeing between parents and children a display of affection that had been in general missing in his civilization and, particularly, in his childhood home. Many Yankees around him wrote home about the charm of Mexican family life. The same gringos who raped Mexican women and kicked Mexican men off streets played by the hour with brown infants. Surgeon Albert G. Brackett described a funeral he saw — priests with tall crosses leading the procession toward "an old church, half-hid by cypress and poplar trees," and in an open coffin a dead baby covered with flowers and wearing a small wreath of roses around its brow. He said "the little thing looked happy," and fell to comparing the custom "with our stiff and puritanical forms" in the United States. [24]

Mexico, sleeping in the sun, appealed to the torpor that lay so close under Grant's skin. Where other officers might sneer at Mexican sloth, Sam Grant was silent, remembering perhaps siestas of his own: the canalboat in Pennsylvania's Maytime — the snow-sailed Hudson below his drowsy window — the soft drumming of his horse's hoofs on autumn paths beside the blue Ohio River.

Where some officers disapproved Taylor's failure to halt the "outrages" visited upon the Mexicans by the Volunteers, Grant said, in later years, that the troops "behaved well" in the war "and the wickedness was not in the way our soldiers conducted it, but in the conduct of our government in declaring war." He thought Taylor's orders against pillage or the appropriation of property without fair compensation gave Matamoros more prosperity than it had ever known before.[25] Grant's failure to join in condemnation of the "outrages" stemmed perhaps from his admiration for the fighting qualities of the Volunteers, and from a suspicion, common in the Army, that exposés of Yankee "brutality" were a part of the anti-Polk propaganda waged in Whig newspapers at home. Certain it was that the bitterest and most persistent of these attacks upon the morals of the Volunteers were published in journals eager to discredit the war. Also it was true that for every officer known to rail against Volunteers in letters and diaries there were many more who mentioned no depredations whatsoever. Texans drew the sharpest disapproval, many critics failing to appreciate their bitterness over Mexican barbarities at Goliad and the Alamo. Colonel W. B. Campbell, First Tennessee Volunteers, called the Texans "the wildest and most dissipated set of men I ever saw; they remind me . . . of Russian Cossacks," but he noted how often there were "desperadoes and ruffians and renegades from the States," not chargeable to Texas.[26]

Taylor feared the Texans "were too licentious to do much good," and Major Barbour wrote his wife that the Volunteers "were playing the devil and disgracing the country," but few of the regular officers were apparently as revolted as was Lieutenant George Meade of the Topographical Engineers. Crotchety and faultfinding by nature, Meade not only despised the Volunteers for their lawlessness but, a few months later, would ask to be transferred back to Washington, since the system of promotions favored Volunteer officers to his own disadvantage. His letters from the front complained constantly about the Volunteers who were "always drunk . . . they rob and steal . . . they wantonly killed for their own amusement five or six innocent people of the streets . . . they are full of mutiny." Firing their muskets for fun, they carelessly put bullets through his tent one day — a thing that shortened his already short temper. He concluded that Taylor "has neither the moral or physical force to restrain these men." He told how some Kentuckians cruelly shot a twelve-year-old boy cutting cane in a field, and how when "this poor little fellow, all bleeding and crying, was . . . laid down in front of the General's tent," Taylor had done nothing but order the regiment to the rear and had even rescinded that sentence when the soldiers promised to be more careful.[27]

Charges that the men were raping women and looting churches and that Mexican families begged Regulars to live with them as protection against the Volunteers, went the rounds of anti-Administration newspapers in the States. A New Yorker, enlisting in the Regulars, declared that recruiting agents working in the slums of Manhattan, promised "roast beef, two dollars a day, plenty of whiskey, golden Jesuses and pretty Mexican gals." The regiment subsequently saw little roast beef, the pay was $7 a month, but according to the complaints of the Mexican press, the other promises were kept.[28]

Grant saw Old Zach endure with outward calm the caprices of the Volunteers, a calmness which Taylor, in a confidential letter, explained:

> I will try & get through in the best way I can & with at least all the good feelings & temper I can command even should they drive me out of my tent.[29]

Marylanders took a catfish away from some First Ohio fishermen. The latter bawled for their colonel. He rushed up, sword in hand. The Marylanders ran him into his tent. One moonlit night Colonel Edward D. Baker of the Fourth Illinois, returning from a funeral with a squad of men, went aboard a steamer to halt a fight between two Georgia companies. One of their captains, McMahon, challenged him to a duel and as the two officers danced around the deck, parry and thrust, a Georgia private put a pistol ball through Baker's cheek knocking out his upper front teeth. Baker's boys yelled "Rip up McMahon!" and put a bayonet through his cheek. It took the whole Fourth Illinois, who came running from their tents, to enforce order. Reports varied as to whether the dead numbered one or ten and the wounded eight or thirty. Next day, Colonel James H. Lane, a Hoosier politician commanding the Third Indiana, presided at the court of inquiry and eventually freed everybody on the theory that what had been done had been done in the moonlight where no one could be sure who of the four hundred men involved had done what.[30]

The Volunteers, who were quartered on ships or in camps all the way from Point Isabel to Matamoros, called themselves "Guards," "Killers," "Rifles," "Gunmen," "Grays," or "Greens" according to local notions. The "Volunteers of Kentucky" wore three-cornered hats, full beards and hip boots faced with red morocco. Uniforms were patterned on models handed down from the Revolutionary War, the War of 1812, or adaptations of British, French and German military attire, and ranged in color through gray, blue, green and white with trimmings of red, yellow and pink. When home uniforms wore out many Volunteers objected to wearing the regulation Army issue of light blue. "Let 'em go to hell with their sky blue," cried an Indiana soldier, "I'll be blowed if they make a Regular out of me." Irked at receiving no more pay than the despised Dutch, Irish and English "foreigners" in the Regular ranks, native-born Volunteers cursed themselves for ever having become "a seven-dollar target." [31]

Insubordination ranged from open defiance of officers to the invention of mythical scapegoats for depredations. Officers hunting malefactors in Kentucky camps were told to look for a "fellow, name of Cogle," who could be found a little farther on. Among the Tennesseans this phantom scoundrel's name was Locks. The Tennesseans stole the extra uniforms of their officers and smuggled them into the guardhouse so that imprisoned comrades could change clothes and march out, gravely responding to the salutes of the guards.[32]

Lieutenant Meade was disgusted with Southern slaveholders who, now that they were common soldiers, expected the Regulars to carry water and firewood for them. In the heat which some recruits described in letters as reaching 130 degrees, hundreds of caps were thrown away — tall stovepipe hats surmounted with pompons, bell-crowned caps with plumes, flat and flaring leather caps — and the wearers put on straw sombreros, telling their officers that what Old Zach wore was good enough for them. They sang interminably, especially "The Rose of Alabama" and "Alice Gray." But their failures in deportment did not hide from some officers their fighting qualities. "Our boys always look better in a blaze," one older officer told Major Giddings. "You will soon see what stuff is beneath those blue jackets." [33] How many Volunteers descended upon Taylor that summer of 1846 no one ever knew. The highest estimate for the number arriving in both 1846 and 1847 was 20,000, a large portion of whom were sent home. Accustomed to thinking of war as a brief, impromptu defense made by militia against Indians, state authorities enrolled organizations for three months, six months or a year, some units, indeed, reaching the Rio Grande without having registered for any term in any state. Many three-months men arrived just in time to start home.

On June 10 Taylor guessed that he had around 6000 Volunteers on hand, 1000 more than he had asked for, and from 2000 to 3000 others were on the way. Since the War Department had sent him supplies insufficient for even the 5000 men he had requested, the only thing to do was to retain the twelve-months men, send back the short-termers and have authorities at home discharge companies that were forming. Many of the newcomers were glad to go home; homesickness, disease and the pain of drilling had cooled their ardor. Taylor was said to be discharging "all volunteers who are discontented and wish to return" and to wink at the haste with which political colonels shipped back sons of constituents for "physical disability." Newspapers in the States reprinted widely Lieutenant E. Eastman's letter revealing that from 250 to 300 of the "Nashville Blues" had gone home on surgeons' certificates. The Lieutenant boldly asked if every soldier be not "justified in getting discharged who is attacked by diseases which almost invariably proves fatal. He could be of no service to his country here, and by remaining would sacrifice his own life." [34]

A bawling, as of many calves, filled the air — recruits at the front bawling because they were not disbanded, recruits at home bawling because they were. Volunteers who whooped for joy when ordered to take ship for the States changed their tune when astonished crowds met them in their native neighborhood and asked what had happened. With quickly assumed anger they would explain that the damned Regular Army was discriminating against patriotic Volunteers. In congested camps by the Rio Grande boys from isolated farms caught strange epidemics, mumps, measles, smallpox. Reckless about their drinking water and their latrines, the Volunteers were wracked by diarrhea, inflammation of the bowels, bilious fever and chills. Some companies saw half their men on sickbeds all summer and autumn in pitifully inadequate hospitals. Homesickness alone killed hundreds. Private E. O. Hill of the Fourth Illinois "took a hearty cry once a day." Lieutenant Duncan of the First Tennessee said, "The Dead March was played so often on the Rio Grande that the very birds knew it." Major Giddings of the First Ohio thought "the groans and lamentations of the poor sufferers during those sickly, sultry nights were heart-rending." His regiment, which counted 800 men in June, paraded a scant 700 in July and would be down to 500 in August, 300 in December.[35]

Sam Grant and the other officers saw by the newspapers how avidly anti-Administration editors and orators used these tales of disease to play upon voters' fears as the Congressional elections of 1846 rose on the political horizon. Apparently a steady stream of sallow, skeletonized invalids were creeping home to lie — and die — beside the parental fireplace. In September the anti-Polk newspapers were spreading the observation of an anonymous visitor to Taylor's camps, "that if one-half of the western and northern volunteers . . . are effective men on the 15th of October, it is more than he looks for." Another unnamed visitor was widely quoted as saying that a careful estimate by regimental commanders showed that "not less than fifteen hundred volunteers have made their graves upon the banks of the Rio Grande. Many place the number still greater than this." [36]

Taylor's patience with the volunteer generals whom Polk sent him stirred the admiration of many Regulars. One brigadier general arrived in a light buggy, expecting to use it in the coming campaign. It was, indeed, a task — to fit one major general and seven brigadiers, all "deserving Democrats," into an army whose Regulars sneered at military amateurs and politicians. The major general, William O. Butler, had been one of General Jackson's officers in the War of 1812 and was a natural leader, but the news that he was to command the Volunteers in the campaign was resented by the regular officers. Brigadier General James Shields, Irish immigrant and Illinois politician, was as quick of temper as he was innocent of military matters. He had fought one duel in Ireland and only a last-minute apology by a political rival in Illinois, Abraham Lincoln, had prevented another — one with huge broadswords. Men still laughed about what that droll fellow, Lincoln, had said when he accepted Shield's challenge and was asked to name the weapons: "cow-dung at five paces." [37]

The brigadier who aroused Sam Grant's contempt was Gideon J. Pillow, a Democratic orator from Tennessee and former law partner of the President. "Polk's spy," the camps called him and soon added the opinion that he lacked the bravery of Shields or Butler. Everybody laughed when he threw up entrenchments, by way of practice, with the parapet on the wrong side of the ditch. Colonel Campbell who, with Colonel Baker, was one of the few Whig officers in the Volunteer ranks, said, "General Pillow is of the smallest caliber . . . light as a feather . . . here on a political tour to gain reputation." Captain W. B. Bishop of the Second Illinois thought Pillow was "cursed with an unalloyed selfishness," and Private George M. Conkle of the First Tennessee said he was "selfish, tyrannical, cared nothing for his men and was a coward." On marches Pillow was given to imagining Mexican hordes hard upon him, pushing his men for forty miles in cruel heat and then arresting all officers who assured him there was no danger.[38]

Opposed to Sam Grant's ideas about the justice of the war was Brigadier General John A. Quitman. A rich sugar planter who paid all headquarters expenses from his own pocket, Quitman brought to the front a prestige built up in Mississippi as a lawyer, Democratic leader, crusader for higher education and the elimination of gambling and dueling. A New Yorker who had migrated to Natchez as a young man, Quitman had become a passionate convert to the Southern doctrine of state rights, slavery and territorial expansion. He had fought for Texas's independence and, when Polk made him a brigadier, had been head of Mississippi's militia for twenty years. While Taylor, on the Rio Grande, was trying to quiet the clamor of the Volunteers for an immediate advance against the Mexicans, Quitman was making speeches for just such a move. Where Taylor thought the war, at most, should merely "conquer a peace," as Polk expressed it, Quitman was bellowing for the conquest of the whole of Mexico and its military occupation until immigration could prepare it for annexation to the United States. Mexicans, he said, were "a bastard and robber race, incapable of self-government, and only fit for servitude and military rule." [39]

To Sam Grant the arrival of the Volunteers took on a new aspect when, early in August, there arrived a detachment from Georgetown — Carr White, a captain of Company G., First Ohio Volunteers, and Chilton White, now twenty-one and a private in the same regiment, and Tom Hamer! Hamer was a Brigadier General!

From his old playmates Ulysses heard what had been happening. Chilton White had been studying law in Hamer's office when talk of war had started. Hamer had set off immediately stumping the district for recruits. He had been nominated by the Democrats for Congress again, but had campaigned for the war, not himself.

"If you're so anxious to raise volunteers, why don't *you go?*" the Whigs had taunted. So he had enrolled as a private, taking with him not only Carr White, but his own law partner and his bound boy. It had taken his sternest orders to keep his young son from joining too. When the company he was forming was added to the First Ohio Regiment, Hamer discovered that the regiment was planning to elect him colonel. The Whig newspapers laughed at the idea. What did Tom Hamer know of war? Immediately he laughed louder than they, saying that if the Administration wanted speeches made on the Rio Grande, he was the man, but as to commanding a regiment — that was out of the question. He had persuaded the regiment to elect as colonel a Cincinnati lawyer who had been educated at West Point, Alexander M. Mitchell, and compromised by accepting for himself the post of major. The whole regiment had quickly idolized him. He explained this strange new thing of discipline so kindly and clearly. One of the officers said that never in his life had he "listened to a more witching speech" than the one Hamer gave the regiment on the Fourth of July as their steamer ploughed southward. On July 24, before sailing, he had accepted the brigadier general's commission which Polk was offering. He felt that he could succeed in this new profession, and his men approved. So did the Regulars, as soon as they saw him on the Rio Grande studying his new duties. His modesty in placing Mitchell ahead of himself in the regiment delighted the Regulars, one of them, Captain William S. Henry, pointing out how remarkable it was amid so many politicians clamoring for high command, "to see an instance of the most conspicuous man in Ohio acknowledging the superiority of the West Point graduate." Within three months after Hamer's arrival, General Taylor was calling him, "The balance-wheel of my volunteer army . . . a natural soldier . . . whose conduct and bearing were as they would have been had he been trained and brought up in the army."[40]

Hamer called on Ulysses to help him in his military studies. From his camp near the Fourth Regulars he was soon writing home that he had found Jesse Grant's son . . .

> A most remarkable and valuable young soldier. . . . Young as he is, he has been of great value and service to me. To-day, after being freed from the duty of wrestling with the problem of reducing a train of refractory mules and their drivers to submissive order, we rode into the country several miles, and taking our position upon an elevated mound, he explained to me many army evolutions; and, supposing ourselves to be generals commanding opposing armies, and a battle to be in progress, he explained suppositious maneuvers of the opposing forces in a most instructive way, and when I thought his imaginary force had my army routed, he suddenly suggested a strategic move for my forces which crowned them with triumphant victory, and himself with defeat, and he ended by gracefully offering to surrender his sword! Of course, Lieutenant Grant is too young for command, but his capacity for future military usefulness is undoubted.[41]

Back in Brown and Clermont Counties, certain readers of the letter, if they saw it, could have been depended upon to say, "That's a politician for you!"

CHAPTER TEN

The Bloody Streets of Monterey

LIEUTENANT COLONEL John Garland faced a new problem in organization as he prepared his men for the new campaign which Taylor was planning — the invasion of Mexico as far as its northernmost metropolis, Monterey, and possibly beyond. The first step, which would begin July 31, was not the problem. It would take the force only as far as Camargo, a village 100 miles up the Rio Grande at the head of navigation. But from there the march would be across a terrain new in the movement of United States forces — a 150-mile transport of heavy equipment across a region largely barren and rough, with the prospect of marching into the mountains behind Monterey after that city was taken.

Always before in the Army's history, any movement of that distance had been made either by water or wagon, but now a different means of transportation had been forced upon Taylor. This overland journey could not be made by wagon for his wheeled equipment was down to one hundred and eighty — barely enough for the various regimental and staff headquarters baggage. Even if more wagons could be found ox teams would prove too slow for the rapid marches ahead, and the few large wagons that were on hand in this mustang country must be saved for the artillery. Also Taylor had barely enough horseshoes, horseshoe nails and blacksmith's tools for the artillery, leaving the cavalry, as he wrote Washington, "paralyzed."

With Taylor ordering the Quartermaster's Department to bring in nineteen hundred mules, and as many of those big, wooden packsaddles, each capable of carrying three hundred pounds, and to hire native muleteers at twenty-five dollars a month, commanders must quickly find officers capable of handling the new system. Garland, who was in charge of Whistler's Brigade, and Major William M.

Graham, who under him commanded the Fourth Regiment, were middle-aged veterans. What was needed to handle transportation was some young officer from the regiment, and his rank should be one newly created — Regimental Quartermaster, as distinguished from officers of the Quartermaster's Corps.[1]

Until this new rank could be established, the officer must serve nominally as Commissary. He must have, as Henry Coppée of the Third Artillery observed, "system and patience" and should be "some solid, energetic painstaking officer, not necessarily remarkable for dash and valor," who would be expected properly to remain on guard with the camp equipment and pack trains during battle.[2]

Garland and Graham named Lieutenant Grant for the job. He had known the business of transportation from infancy, and was popular enough with other officers to wangle the regiment's share of those meager governmental supplies which the harassed Chief Quartermaster, Lieutenant Colonel Henry Whiting, was trying to have distributed equally among the various regimental representatives who stormed, wheeled, and scrambled at the depots.

The son of a successful businessman, young Grant should be the one to do the business of the regiment, pay out money, keep the long accounts balanced, find "horse furniture," as the Army called harness, for the animals, and secure clothing for the men. Captured uniforms were numerous but, according to a soldier, Tom Thorpe, were "sizes too small for the average of our American troops." Grant must buy fodder and grain for horses and mules, and see that the men had fruit, vegetables and fresh meat to supplement the regular ration of hard bread, sugar, coffee, salt and "side meat or middlings." He must keep the men supplied with haversacks for food and knapsacks for clothes. If wood for the campfire ran short, he must get coal which arrived on ships from Ohio and Pennsylvania.[3]

Grant objected to the assignment when it came. The boy who with Dave had loaded logs in the forest was not afraid of his new job. His reason was different. He wrote Garland:

> I respectfully protest against being assigned to a duty which removes me from sharing in the dangers and honors of service with my company at the front and respectfully ask to be permitted to resume my place in line.

Back came the answer:

Lieutenant Grant is respectfully informed that his protest can not be considered. Lieutenant Grant was assigned to duty as Quartermaster and Commissary because of his observed ability, skill and persistency in the line of duty. The commanding officer is confident that Lieutenant Grant can best serve his country in present emergencies under this assignment. Lieutenant Grant will continue to perform the assigned duties.

LT. COL. GARLAND, *4th Inft. Comdg. Brigade.*

To his family Ulysses wrote, "I do not mean that you shall ever hear of my shirking my duty in battle. My new post of quartermaster is considered to afford an officer an opportunity to be relieved from fighting, but I do not and cannot see it in that light." [4]

If he felt any envy when two of his classmates, Nykins Quinby and Joe Reynolds, were ordered to leave their regiments and return to the West Point faculty, he kept silent. Everywhere officers were being shifted. McCall, captain of Grant's Company I, took a batch of short-term Louisiana Volunteers back to New Orleans, mustered them out, then returned to serve as chief of staff for General Patterson, whose division must remain on the Rio Grande instead of marching into the interior. Another officer of the Fourth, Major Lorenzo Thomas, came on from Washington where he had been working for ten years at Headquarters, and was assigned chief of staff for General Butler. And Taylor, bolstering all his volunteer generals with exceptional West Pointers, was giving Tom Hamer for his chief of staff Lieutenant Joseph Hooker, Adjutant of the First Artillery.

Around Hamer's tent Sam Grant now had a chance to know this Joe Hooker about whom officers talked so much. Sam had been home on furlough the summer of 1841 when Hooker had served as Adjutant of the Academy. Where the older generation of West Pointers insisted that Captain Robert E. Lee was the handsomest of graduates, the younger men insisted that it was Joe Hooker. They pointed to Joe's blond, wavy hair, shining blue eyes, ruddy complexion — a tall, straight robust fellow whose manners proved that Massachusetts could produce as courtly a gentleman as could Virginia.

The regular officers sped up preparations for the march. President

Polk needed a quick victory and peace. The patriotic fervor which had buoyed the nation in May was cooling before the long summer's delay on the Rio Grande and those reports of how disease was riddling the heroic volunteer regiments. The attacks by the Whigs were culminating in a sensational proviso which one of their Congressmen, David Wilmot, wanted to attach to the Administration bill which appropriated $2,000,000 to settle the Mexican quarrel. His proviso, demanding that slavery be excluded from any lands thus acquired from Mexico, would be defeated, but not before it whipped both Slave States and Free States into a storm of recrimination.

The Fourth, which had assembled at Camargo in early August, marched out on September 5 behind Taylor — whose confidence seemed to some officers unwarranted. No one knew how many Mexicans would meet them. If they should have to besiege Monterey, for instance, they had only one cannon large enough to damage stone walls. The volunteer half of the force had not been tested in battle. Young Sam Grant did not share these doubts as to Taylor's competency. Years later he, in admiration, said Taylor "was not an officer to trouble the Administration much with his demands, but was inclined to do the best he could with the means given him . . . without parading his grievance before the public." [5]

On September 6 from a place postmarked Ponti Agrudo, near the "fine city" of "Ser Albo," which Sam estimated was 200 miles from Matamoros and "within six days march of Monterey," being already restive at the dragging slowness of the war he did not care for, he wrote dearest Julia again:

> I am much in hopes my Dearest Julia after this move our difficulties will be brought to a close, and I be permitted to visit the North again. If ever I get to the States again it will be but a short time till I will be with you Dearest Julia. If these Mexicans were any kind of people they would have given us a chance to whip them enough some time ago and now the difficulty would be over; but I believe they think they will outdo us by keeping us running over the country after them.

Sam had no particular feeling against the Mexicans except for their failure to make a fight to end the war and get him back tc

St. Louis County, Missouri. On the contrary he pitied their poverty, their condition of life:

I have traveled from Matamoras here, by land, a distance of two hundred miles. In this distance there are at least fifteen thousand persons almost every one a farmer and on the whole road there are not, I don't believe, ten thousand acres of land cultivated. On our way we passed through Reynoso, Old Reynoso, Camargo, & Mier, all of them old deserted looking places, that is if you only look at the houses, but if you look at the people you will find that there is scarcely an old wall standing that some family does not live behind.

Almost fretfully he continued:

Julia aren't you getting tired of hearing of war, war, war? I am truly tired of it. Here it is now five months that we have been at war and as yet but two battles. I do wish this would close. If we have to fight I would like to do it all at once and then make friends.

Then with the age-old fears of the lover who cannot believe in his own good fortune he reassures himself of Julia's constancy and the permanence of her affection by closing:

It is now above two years that we have been engaged Julia and in all that time I have seen you but once. I know though you have not changed and when I do go back I will see the same Julia I did more than two years ago. I know I shall never be willing to leave Gravois again until Julia is mine forever! How much I regret that we were not united when I visited you more than a year ago. But your Pa would not have heard to anything of the kind at that time. I hope he will make no objections now! Write to me very often Julia. You know how happy I am to read your letters. Mr. Hazlitt is very well. Give my love to all at White Haven. Have Ellen & Ben Farrer made up yet? The time is now getting pretty well up and I am afraid that I may lose my bet.

"I hope he will make no objections now!" is an exclamation rather than an expression of doubt. Sam Grant, veteran of five months of war and two battles, believes he must have new qualifications as a son-in-law even in the doubtful eye of Colonel Dent.

* * *

As Grant followed his regiment on the march he saw why profanity should not be marked in Heaven against the names of muleteers. Once the regiment had left camp in the morning, Grant stood over the drivers as they tied tents, tent poles, cooking utensils, mess chests, axes, picks, coffee mills, ammunition boxes to the huge wooden pack saddles that surmounted the mules. The packing took hours and, as Grant said, by the time the last mule was ready, the others had scattered their burdens far and wide — running, kicking, rolling and rubbing against trees and rocks. After the job was finally done, there followed the day-long task of catching up to the column and having everything ready, tents and food, for the night's bivouac. Lieutenant Alexander Hays, who saw Sam Grant at these quartermaster duties some months later, if not on this march, said, "there was no road . . . so obstructed . . . but that Grant, in some mysterious way, would work his train through and have it in the camp of his brigade before the campfires were lighted." In camp the quartermaster must examine the mules for sore spots. Whenever saddles rubbed away the hide and brought blood, small green flies would lay eggs and, within twelve hours, the sore would be filled with screw worms, boring their way into the flesh so rapidly that within a few days a man could lay his closed fist in the wound. Mules as well as men died of dysentery. Grant must scour the neighborhood for new animals, and have the train ready next morning.[6]

Always ahead, as the column wound southward, other officers would be seeing the new sights as they unfolded, the distant hills, the red birds in the mesquite, but the rolling dust would hide from the commander of the pack train the vanilla perfume of the flowering acacia and brown its white petals by the time he came to them. Two weeks of it, and then, on September 19, Grant brought his wagons and mules into the camp Taylor had selected, Walnut Springs, where there was "living water" in the grove of San Domingo, two miles from Monterey. Looking out from under the Spanish moss which dripped from the huge trees, the soldiers saw the city lying quietly at the foot of towering mountains. The sun was on the church crosses, on the flags and on the white houses whose courtyards were green with acacia and orange trees — a metropolis of 15,000 people, guarded on the south by a river, on the east by Forts Tenaria and Diablo, on the north by the massive

Citadel, called the "Black Fort" and on the west by the heavily gunned Bishop's Palace and Fort Soldado, which from high hills commanded the road to Saltillo. Earthworks supported all forts and city streets were barricaded.

From a hill, Taylor watched his Texas Rangers go toward the town. They were dressed in rough civilian clothes, each carried a heavy rifle, a powder horn, a bowie knife and one or more Colt revolvers. Except for the five-shooters at their hips they might have come riding out of the Revolutionary War. Spurring forward singly, they swooped at the forts like swallows, circling close under the guns, daring each other to go closer, daring the enemy to come out and fight. Beyond a few scattering shots, Mexico waited, motionless.[7]

The Texans brought back word that every housetop seemed to be mounted with sandbags and musketeers, every fort bristling with cannon, every street crossed with barricades. Wretched though his espionage was, Taylor knew that this fortified town, "one of the strongest naturally in the country," was manned by a force "greatly superior to us in numbers," (discovered later to have approximately 10,000), and by night on the nineteeth he knew he would have to storm it. Mexicans, like Spaniards, were said to fight best behind walls.[8]

If the civilian males went to the barricades, as expected, the defenders would outnumber the *Yanquis* two or three to one — perhaps more. European military maxims warned generals not to attack a fortified place unless they outnumbered defenders three or four to one. Moreover, Taylor was deep in the enemy's country, yet he apparently did not worry. He seemed to feel that it was the enemy's place to worry. Tales of his coolheadedness at Palo Alto proved this to Lieutenant John Sedgwick, who had recently come to the Second Artillery at the front. Short, blond, with curly chestnut hair, steady eyes, a short upper lip and an unbroken classic Grecian line from the top of his high forehead to the end of his long nose, Sedgwick was, at thirty-three, an officer to be relied upon, although he had not received the notice given his Academy classmates Hooker, Bragg, Pemberton and Randolph Ridgely. Lieutenant Leslie Chase told Sedgwick that at Palo Alto he had been sent with a message to Taylor warning him that the Mexicans were threatening his rear. Old Zach, with one leg over his saddle, had listened to the exciting news — "the most unconcerned man in the crowd" — and then had calmly said, "Keep a bright lookout for them!" That was all.[9]

Now in front of Monterey, Taylor assigned more trained officers of particular talent to aid the volunteer generals, notably Colonel Albert Sidney Johnston, whom Old Zach called "the best soldier I ever commanded," as chief of staff to Butler. From his Academy days, Class of '26, Johnston had been marked for the heights, a born leader yet always resigning from leadership. He had quit the Army in 1834 and gone to farming in Texas. He had been a general in Texas's War of Independence and the little Republic's first Secretary of War, yet he had gone back to his farm. Now in 1846, he had organized the First Texas Volunteers and when they had gone home from Matamoros at the end of their enlistment term, he had only agreed to stay on as volunteer aide with Taylor till the fight at Monterey was over; then he would go back to his Texas farm.

The Fourth Regiment drew up with Twiggs's division in line northeast of the city on September 20, watching while Worth's division moved through cornfields around to the right, aiming at the road which ran west from Monterey to Saltillo. When dusk came they saw Worth's campfires glow northwest of the city, just outside the range of its heavy guns. That night while the rest of Twiggs's division slept on beds of Spanish moss in the grove at Walnut Springs, the Fourth Regiment stood watch, out on the plain, closer to the city, guarding the heavy cannon — one of them an ancient mortar which the soldiers said looked "like some old witch's soup-pot" when compared with the shining light cannon which had become the pets of the Regulars. A gentle rain fell through the night, "pattering most melancholy music through our leafy camp" where Volunteers lay wondering what a battle would be like. But in the morning spirits rose, an officer in the First Ohio noted how "a fresh and balmy breeze played in the tree-tops, and the sun sent many a warm and kindly glance through the long aisles of the majestic grove." [10]

Guns broke loose on the opposite side of town with "great fury," as Grant observed. Worth was attacking. Taylor let Twiggs's division finish breakfast and then ordered it into line. Garland was to take the regular infantry, plus a company of Maryland Volunteers and Bragg's battery, charge down the slope and attack the northeast corner of the town hard enough to keep the Mexicans from concentrating against Worth on the west. If Garland could take any Mexican works, well and good, but his main duty was to create a diversion that would help Worth.

Grant watched his brigade march off. As Quartermaster he was ordered to stay behind with the one company assigned to protect the regimental camp. He stood among the idle Regulars, the grazing mules, the lolling muleteers, the curtains of somnolent Spanish moss. Cannon began to roar close at hand. Bragg was crowding up to the forts and the walled houses of the suburbs, blasting away though his shells had little effect.

Grant could stand it no longer. "My curiosity got the better of my judgment," he said, deprecatingly, years later, "and I . . . rode to the front to see what was going on." He galloped up just in time to find Garland ordering a charge and "lacking the moral courage to return to camp — where I had been ordered to stay — I charged with the regiment." [11]

A roar came from the right; the Black Fort was speaking. A roar came from the left; Fort Tenaria, the "Tannery," was at work. Between the forts, redoubts and housetops joined in the fury. Caught in this cross fire, the Yankees were tossed up, down, sideways. Alone of all officers in the Fourth, Grant was on horseback. In a few minutes almost a third of the regiment's officers and men had been hit. The charge slowed down, stopped, and the men scurried off to the left, hunting shelter. When they found it in a little vale, and were counting noses, Lieutenant Charles Hoskins, Adjutant of the Fourth, came up panting and wishing he could have a horse to ride, too. Since Hoskins had been sick for days and was exhausted, Grant got out of the saddle and put him up. A little later Grant found another horse for himself, taking it away from a quartermaster's man who came riding by. As the Marylanders in Garland's brigade fell back, one of their captains, John R. Kenly, saw General Twiggs come onto the field in "very unmilitary garb" explaining why he was so late:

I expected a battle today but didn't think it would come off so soon, and took a dose of medicine last night as I always do before a battle so as to loosen my bowels. A bullet striking the belly when the bowels are loose might pass through the intestines without cutting them. [12]

While the Fourth caught its breath in the vale, word came saying Hoskins had been killed and that Lieutenant Grant was to succeed him as Adjutant of the regiment. Another messenger brought orders to try again. Once more they went forward, but not for long. The Mexicans' guns soon halted them in a field of cane. Taylor turned to his Volunteers. They would have their baptism in an attempt to do what the Regulars had failed to do. Grant, peering through the sugar cane, saw General Quitman bring in his Tennessee and Mississippi regiments by a route that preserved them from enemy fire until the very last of their dash at the Tannery. Grant thought how many lives could have been saved if Garland had advanced with that same skill. There was some comfort left for the Regulars, however, for one hundred of them, led by a Captain Electus Backus, a middle-aged officer of the First Infantry, took a rooftop near the Tannery and were picking off defenders as Quitman's men swarmed down. The Tannery's guns checked this new wave for a time, one solid shot killing seven Tennesseans and wounding others. One of the latter crawled onto a rock and sat there clutching his slit abdomen and holding in his intestines while he sang a psalm. Colonel W. B. Campbell of the First Tennessee was surprised that his regiment "did not run off the field like a gang of wild turkeys." Colonel Jefferson Davis, of the Mississippi Rifles, fumed at the delay. He shouted, "Now is the time! Great God, if I had thirty men with knives I could take the fort!" In the final charge that took the Tannery, his men and Campbell's tumbled in together, and quarreled for years thereafter as to which had been first. Davis's men were sure he had been the second man over the works.[13]

With other brigades drawing enemy fire, Garland sent three companies into the streets on the edge of town. Bragg's battery charged with them and General Butler's division of Volunteers followed. Canister and musket balls blew nearly half of Garland's men off their feet, killing ten officers and wounding ten more. "It was as if bushels of hickory nuts were hurled at us," one officer always remembered. Captain Kenly heard a voice rise above the din, "a voice so clear, so distinct, so encouraging and commanding" that he asked whose it was.

"Colonel Albert Sidney Johnston," someone answered.[14]

Major Giddings, bringing in the First Ohio behind Generals Butler and Hamer and Lieutenant Hooker, saw Bragg's battery wrecked near the Tannery, with some of his men and a dozen of his horses "down in the same spot, making the ground about the guns slippery with their gasped foam and blood." Bragg was deliberately "stripping the harness from the dead and disabled animals, determined that not a buckle or a strap should be lost." Sam French, struggling to get the battery out, saw some of his horses with their entrails dragging, eating grass. As the battery finally withdrew from the city, one of the horse drivers was shot out of his saddle. Bragg ordered a halt, even though still under fire, so that French could alight and salvage the dead man's sword. French handed up the man's pocket-knife, too, but Bragg refused to take the latter, "it was not *public* property." [15]

The Volunteers were making most Regulars forget all the hard things that had been said about them. Butler's division pushed through streets and gardens sometimes seeing the enemy through the rolling smoke. Boys in the First Tennessee, the "Bloody First," heard Ridgely's loud laugh ringing out as he dueled with a Mexican battery 200 yards away. They always remembered that exultant laugh, and said, "War was Ridgely's element." When Butler was wounded and carried to the rear, Hamer led the division through air filled with bullets and jagged pieces of masonry knocked from houses. Hearing that Taylor ordered Garland to stop his costly attack, Hamer pulled out his men too — a decision later commended, along with "his calm unbending courage." Backing out of the town, Hamer saw Mexican lancers spearing gringo wounded and chasing surgeons across the field. His Ohioans fired but what routed the Lancers were Ridgely's guns, which, emerging from the suburbs, loosed a volley that hurled Mexican "riders and horses twenty feet in air." [16]

At dusk, Taylor ordered everybody out except Ridgely's battery, and Garland's brigade, which were to hold the captured Tannery and nearby trenches. Through the smoky twilight all the church bells of Monterey, it seemed, began chiming a pean to victory. Rain began. Men groped "in the moonless gloom hunting up the wounded by their groans." Calvin Benjamin came on three figures, one dead, one wounded, one uninjured. The last was holding the head of the second and, as Benjamin wrote home, "giving him water from a canteen and wiping his face with his moistened hand-kerchief." Benjamin looked closer and saw that the Samaritan was "my dear friend, Lieutenant Grant," who, remembering the region where Hoskins had fallen, had come out "alone in the dark on that awful battle-field," found the corpse, straightened its arms and legs and then discovered a wounded man, close by. As the night went on, wagons lumbered onto the field and lurched back, "loaded with the wounded, who shrieked at every jolt." In one of them lay the long body of Hazlitt, wetter now than it had been the day he had served as tent pole for the Dent girls' party in the thunderstorm. Hazlitt had been killed carrying his wounded captain out of a bloody street. The total loss was a heavy price to pay for a few suburban gains — 394 killed and wounded, 34 of them officers.[17]

Over on the western edge of town Worth had taken Fort Soldado and his men, lying in the rain, grumbling because they had been two days without food and no wine, waited for dawn when they would attack the Bishop's Palace. They had lost but few men, since their main charge, which had been led by Captain C. F. Smith, had been up a hill with Mexican bullets flying over their heads. In the rain that fell on Walnut Springs, Taylor was showing young officers how to handle subordinates. He learned that when the Mexican lancers had ridden onto the plain, General Butler, wounded in his tent, had ordered his men to strike tents and make breastworks of their baggage — a foolish plan, since cavalry could not have pene-trated the thick grove. Instead of reproving Butler for a panicky performance, Taylor explained that Butler had only been nervous because of his wound.[18]

During the day Taylor had gone into the town where the fight-ing was thickest and when urged by his staff to leave a bullet-swept street, had knocked at the door of a house. There was no answer. He said to a soldier, "Bring me an ax, I'll see if these Mexican devils won't open the door when I order them." Raising the ax and his voice, he announced, "Now, if you don't open it, I'll break it down." Immediately the door swung open and he walked in to find a table set with an interrupted meal, ready for him and his hungry staff. Men said Old Zach was always at home wherever he was.[19]

Next day the army buried its dead and rested except for a con-tinuing bombardment and one short, successful rush by Worth's

men taking the Bishop's Palace. Then at daylight on the twenty-
third, Twiggs's division began working along the streets from the
east and Worth's from the west. Worth's advance was faster because
Texans, digging through the soft Mexican houses and yelling "Remember the Alamo!" escaped the death that stormed through the
streets.

Adjutant Grant, riding a gray horse, Nellie, was with his brigade
instead of at his post, back in Walnut Springs. The Fourth lost
steadily. In a parallel street the Third lost still more — five of its
twelve officers were hit. A square away from the city's central
plaza where civilians and soldiers were massed, the Yankee attack
bogged down. Ammunition was running low. If the Mexicans should
discover this and pour over the barricades, Garland's men — only ten
badly reduced companies — would have only their bayonets for defense. Their supporting batteries were in other streets and could
not help. Garland hesitated to name any one man to go back through
that blistering fire for ammunition. Almost every street intersection
promised death. Garland called for a volunteer. Grant said he would
go, hooked one foot around the cantle of his saddle, one arm around
the neck of his horse, and, with his body hanging to the sheltered
side of the animal, Indian-fashion, went away at top speed. As he
told it later, only his horse had been "under fire at the street crossings, but these I crossed at such a flying rate that generally I was
past and under cover of the next block of houses before the enemy
fired." He and his horse were unscratched when he reined in at
headquarters with the message.

Telling the story later, he minimized the danger by pointing out
that the two regiments, which were ordered out before the ammunition could be collected, rushed past these same street crossings on
foot, "with comparatively little loss."

Garland thought the whole fight had been a heroic one and reported the reluctance with which he had ordered "this truly Spartan band to retire." [20]

Although Taylor, during the day, refused Ampudia's plea that
the fighting stop so that women and children could be evacuated
from the city, all bombardment of the town ended at nightfall.
With daylight, a white flag came out and officers discussed terms.
The Texans howled their disappointment. One more hour of fight-

ing this morning would have let them through the last thin houses
that separated them from the corralled Mexicans in the plaza. Loose
in that packed mass they could have at last revenged Goliad and
the Alamo.

The Texans — and many other Volunteers, too, and President
Polk, when he heard the news — protested strongly against the
terms Taylor gave Ampudia. All Mexican soldiers with their arms
and accouterments, also six field guns — and their horses — were to
march out with the honors of war, retire unmolested to a line some
70 miles to the south. Beyond this neither they nor the Yankees were to advance for eight weeks at least.

To Grant the terms were justified because they were magnanimous. Lieutenant Meade, jarred out of his scolding habits, wrote
his wife, "It was no *military necessity* that induced General Taylor
to grant such liberal terms, but a higher and nobler motive." He
said Taylor wanted to avoid the slaughter of civilians that would
be inevitable if his men stormed the plaza. Taylor was anxious to
save Mexican soldiers the disgrace of abject surrender. Taylor had
his eye on peace. Ampudia had told him, during the conference,
that the Mexican Government, which had recently changed its president, would now be in favor of peaceful arbitration. Also, Taylor's
army needed rest and reinforcements. The storming of Monterey
in three days had cost him 448 killed or wounded, 43 of them officers. Since Palo Alto he had had 27 officers killed and of these 23
were Regulars. He must receive batches of new officers, for no
matter how well the Volunteers had fought in the actual fighting,
it was the Regulars upon whom he must rely in a campaign.[21]

While the camp argued about the wisdom of Taylor's terms,
Captain Carr White met Sam Grant and gave him news of the
Ohioans. They had lost considerably but nothing like Grant's regiment. The two boys talked of Georgetown. White grew confidential and said that he was engaged to be married. Ulysses said
that he was engaged, too, although there had been a recent difficulty. His sweetheart had written him that her father "had fallen
into pecuniary difficulties, the result of a lawsuit of twenty years."
On this account Julia had offered to release him, but of course, "he
would accept no such freedom." The two Georgetowners promised
to name their sons for each other, if and when sons should come.[22]

The prospects seemed bright, for surely the Mexicans would not continue the war after three whippings. Not only had Taylor cleared the Rio Grande border of Mexico, but another army under General John E. Wool was moving into Coahuila, on the central border, and two other forces under Captain John C. Frémont and Colonel Kearny were conquering New Mexico and California. Most of the officers felt peace in the air as they stood next day watching Ampudia's army march out of Monterey, while Yankee cannon saluted the Stars and Stripes which were rising over the conquered forts. No one bothered to count, with accuracy, the departing men, nor to check Mexican losses during the fighting. Taylor understood there had been 7200 of their Regulars, 2000 Irregulars and "several thousand" citizens under arms at the start of the battle. Now they were leaving twenty-two brass cannon and "immense" amounts of ammunition behind.

Some soldiers laughed to see the "parrots, poodle dogs and other absurdities" which the Mexican camp women were carrying as they trudged along beside their men in the procession. Others hissed as they recognized deserters wearing Mexican uniforms, notably Thomas Riley, a huge Irishman who had gone over to the Mexicans shortly before the declaration of war. He had originally joined the United States Army after deserting his British regiment in Canada, had been a recruiting agent in New York for some time, and rumor had it, once had been a drill sergeant at West Point. At the hisses of his old comrades "the dastard's cheek blanched." [23]

Lieutenant George Deas of the Fifth Infantry thought the Mexican soldiers "fine looking" men in their light-blue uniforms, white trousers, leathern shakos and sandaled feet. Lieutenant Grant of the Fourth was so touched by the pitiable plight of the departing Mexicans that he remembered, later, nothing of the laughter or hisses. He thought "most of our army" felt about the prisoners as he felt. He noted the lancers' horses were "miserable little half-starved" beasts "that did not look as if they could carry their riders out of town." The Mexican soldiers seemed equally abject and he stood there thinking "how little interest the men before me had in the results of the war, and how little knowledge they had of 'what it was all about.'" [24]

More than ever was this war an "unholy one." Grant was now seeing the faces of the conscripts in all the wars he had read about so carelessly in his drowsy room beside the Hudson.

CHAPTER ELEVEN

Red Ball and the White Mountain

THE FIRST of the new crop of Academy graduates that Sam Grant had seen rode into the camp of the Fourth Infantry outside Monterey on October 23, 1846. He was Brevet Second Lieutenant Cadmus Marcellus Wilcox, a Tennessean who had been a plebe when Grant had been a senior. He was nervous over his new duties and awed by the fact that he was joining a regiment of veterans.

It warmed his heart when three lieutenants, Sam Grant, Jenks Beaman and Sidney Smith, took him into their mess, showed him the battlefield and told him how the West Pointers had fared. None of the three had won promotions. Neither had Grant's friends, Longstreet and Benjamin, although Captain Robert Allen, with whom he talked about their fathers in Georgetown, was being made quartermaster of Twiggs's whole division. George H. Thomas was receiving a brevet captaincy for having done such cool, brave things as reloading his cannon and firing a farewell salute into Mexican faces before obeying an order to pull out of the bloody streets.[1]

Lieutenant John C. Pemberton, a stolid Pennsylvanian, Class of '37, had also won a brevet captaincy for gallantry. One incident on a march showed Grant how stubbornly conscientious Pemberton could be. An order for junior officers to trudge with their men rather than ride horses had been verbally revoked because of jagged roads, but, as Grant said, "Pemberton alone said, no, he would walk, as the order was still extant not to ride, and he did walk, though suffering intensely." [2]

Five of Grant's classmates had been made brevet first lieutenants for what they had done in the battle. Of the thirty-four members of the class now in uniform, twenty-nine were still second lieutenants. To the young officers Old Zach was still the great man, although Sidney Smith told Wilcox that Worth had been the specific hero at Monterey.[3]

With heroes all over the place, Wilcox enjoyed eating and loafing with Sam Grant, who had "no pretention to genius, or, . . . to a high order of talent," but was "quiet, plain and unobtrusive" in manner, "of good common sense . . . and much esteemed among his immediate associates for kindly disposition and many excellent qualities." Grant was still Quartermaster; the commissary's duties had been given to Lieutenant Granville Haller, who had been appointed from civil life in 1831.

Wilcox brought Sam Grant news of the Academy: Dragon Deshon was an instructor there, so were Quinby and Rosecrans; Fred Steele, Dick Ewell, Fred Dent and Alf Sully were in army posts back in the States; Rufe Ingalls, Buckner and Franklin were with the expeditions in New Mexico or California. Cump Sherman and Halleck had sailed around the Horn for California in June. McClellan, that bright boy, was on his way to Matamoros to serve with the Engineers.

Tom Jackson, brevet second lieutenant with the First Artillery, came into camp one day in late September, to deliver to General Taylor a siege gun which he had, with tremendous industry, worked through the mud from Matamoros. It dismayed him to hear the officers predicting that the war would now end, since Mexico had surely had enough fighting.

With Jackson came Dabney H. Maury to join the Third Artillery. Sam Grant took this novice, too, under his wing, Maury recalling later how Grant being free as Quartermaster "to go when and where he pleased" took him on long rides. "We were much together and enjoyed the association. Grant was a thoroughly kind and manly young fellow, with no bad habits, and was respected and liked by his brother officers, especially by those of his own regiment." [4]

As the autumn advanced the Volunteers, calmed somewhat by their bloodletting, became less contemptuous of drill and discipline, although they still enriched the gamblers who ran games in the chaparral, and bought too much pulque from the "striped pig" — Mexicans peddling the native intoxicant in pigskins. Drinking was reputedly commoner among the men camped along the Rio Grande than in Monterey. Private Joshua E. Jackson admitted in his diary that while he had never drunk strong liquor at home in Illinois, he did now, "for it is great to a man's health and also to drown trouble for when a man is half drunk there is nothing on his mind only good things, he imagines every button on his coat is gold." [5]

Back in the States, anti-Polk newspapers tempered their joy over Taylor's victory at Monterey with laments over its cost in blood and the continuing drain on the health and morals of boys forced to remain in a foreign land. The voters whooped for Taylor, but in November went to the polls and gave the Whigs control of the House of Representatives. Caught between the Whigs who wanted the war stopped and the ultraradical Democrats who wanted the army to annex all Northern Mexico, the Administration was in trouble. General Quitman at Monterey was writing home complaints against Taylor for not pushing on into the interior. On November 12, Quitman declared that it was a sinful waste of life and money to keep the troops idle, since among the Volunteers who had gone to the front, "there has been an average loss, from disease and incapacities of various kinds, of about thirty per cent." [6]

Although he had no sympathy with Quitman's purpose, Sam Grant could have seen that the Mississippian had stumbled upon one of the great truths about war — deaths in battle were only a fraction of those in camp. Dysentery, which had been slowly sapping General Hamer's "strength ever since he had landed at Point Isabel," did not clear up. His men stated that on the march from Camargo to Monterey he had been scarcely able to ride his horse, but had said "While I am able I'll go at the head of my brigade." He had been ailing after the battles but had been able, on October 31, to attend the funeral of the great young gunner, Randolph Ridgely, whose horse had fallen fatally with him in the peaceful streets of Monterey. The last week in November Hamer had grown weaker, although Sam Grant, as one of those who nursed him, shared the surgeon's belief, on November 30, that he was in no danger. But next day he was worse and his tent was besieged by his men "with sorrowful faces and anxious inquiries." On December 2, at ten o'clock in the night, he was dead. His funeral came December 3, Grant writing home that it had been held "with the 'honors of war,' and with the flag of his beloved country around him. . . . His death is a loss to me which no words can express." Taylor lamented that he had no one now to pacify the Volunteers as Hamer had done. Major Giddings grieved because he would see no more "one of those men, whose souls appear to be ever beaming through their faces." As the crashing salutes of cannon shook the cemetery in the deep, dark woods of San Domingo, the Ohio Volunteers wondered what Hamer would have done had he lived: he had been elected to Congress in the November elections. Would he have stayed in the Army or gone to take his seat? It would have been more like him to have stayed in uniform.

Grant, later on, thought how different his own life would probably have been had Hamer lived. Hamer would have been the logical Presidential nominee of the Democratic party in 1852. A war hero, leading the dominant party, he would have been elected. Then, as Grant speculated, "his partiality for me was such, there is but little doubt I should have been appointed to one of the staff corps of the army — the Pay Department probably," a life of security practically as good as that of a professorship of mathematics in a quiet college town. This only showed, Grant said, how little men had control over their own destiny.[7]

Although Grant would, in time to come, remember his Monterey days as quiet ones, full of pleasant fraternization with the natives, Lieutenant Benjamin's letters told a livelier story. Accompanying his friend on expeditions into the country gathering supplies, Benjamin revealed that Grant had several skirmishes with rancheros. Upon one occasion when the two friends returned to camp, Grant told Colonel Garland, "I lost one man and had a horse wounded. We captured three of the enemy, three horses and a flag and we had a handsome fight."

"Yes, that speaks well for your bravery," Garland answered, "but remember we are in an enemy's country, that enemy alert and enterprising. Be careful to always temper bravery with prudence and caution. Gentlemen, return to your quarters!"

Benjamin reported, "On our way back, after a silence, Grant said to me, 'Yes, caution I will observe, but when there's not more than two of *him* to one of *me*, we'll have a fight; that's what we are here for.' "[8]

Benjamin also told how Grant carried to excess Taylor's policy of paying for all supplies. Taylor had been warned by the Secretary of War that this conciliation policy had not stopped guerillas from killing our soldiers on lonely roads and that, furthermore, the natives reaped such prosperity from the sale of the produce that they would want the war to continue forever. Better commandeer food and make Mexico seek peace. "The army in the field costs at least $50,000 a day." [9]

Taylor had refused the suggestion and Lieutenant Grant had meticulously paid one farmer for his grain even though the fellow had tried to resist. Grant had been inside a large, red barn looking for supplies when he had heard an uproar outside and, through the door, had seen his own squad of five soldiers running away. Darting out a rear door he had leaped into the saddle, caught up with his men, rallied them and, charging back, had disarmed a half-dozen armed rancheros as they searched for him in the barn. Taking his prisoners into town, he had returned for the grain, and paid for it. [10]

None of these exploits came to his mind when, in after years, he wrote about his days in Monterey; instead he mentioned with pride his feat, as a businessman, in rescuing the regimental fund from poverty. This fund supplied recreation to the enlisted men in garrison, books, magazines, tenpin alleys, extra comforts, and paid a substantial portion of the salaries of the regimental band, the regiment covering the rest at its own expense. The favorite device for keeping up the fund was to bake bread. Instead of taking the bread ration in loaf form, a commissary could take it in flour and, with proper management, effect an economy by hiring it baked either by the men themselves or by outside bakers. Grant rented ovens in Monterey, secured Mexican bakers, bought fuels and sold the bread to other regiments in addition to his own. [11]

For all that he disliked the influence of the Catholic clergy upon the people, Grant was apparently not as outraged as were many other Yankees when priests urged Regulars in Monterey to desert. More than fifty men went over to the enemy to form the "San Patricio Battalion" in the Mexican artillery — a Foreign Legion which in time grew to 250 or 300 and drew wild cheers as it paraded through Mexican cities. The Mexican press hailed them as "Roman Catholics" who "following the impulses of their hearts, have passed over to our army to defend our just cause." [12]

Into the ears of Irish and German immigrants, voices whispered the story that the Yankees were fighting to force slavery upon Mexico and suppress the Holy Church. Yankee newspapers were praising the war as the logical triumph of "pure Saxon blood" over a "mongrel race" and the liberation of a downtrodden people from "the thralldom of religious bigotry." Newly arrived Irish boys who had been reared in special abhorrence of rape and iconoclasm were reminded that the Volunteers who violated Mexican girls and churches were mainly from Southern and Western rural portions of the States, where anti-Catholicism was strongest. Clerical propaganda would be summed up a few months later in a formal address issued by seven priests of San Luis Potosí, excoriating the Volunteers as "Vandals, vomited from Hell" who "worship no God but gold," and who "defile churches, destroy venerated vessels, overthrowing holy sacraments." The seven priests asked Mexicans, "Will you consent . . . to have the holy rites of your church abolished and the sign of your redemption exterminated? . . . Your daughters and your wives will be seized in your sight, and made victims to lascivious passions, even in the streets. . . . Two fates are left open to you: to be vile slaves, or independent Catholics." [13]

If the Irish Regulars could not read Spanish, there were the anti-Polk newspapers coming in from the States with translations of Mexican propaganda, as for example the *Diario del Gobierno's* denunciation of the Volunteers "who have . . . clothed themselves in the ornaments of the altars, who have thrown upon the ground the body of Jesus Christ, and have made themselves drunk in drinking out of the sacred vessels." [14]

Major Giddings, whose First Ohio Volunteers were camped outside Monterey, noted that none of the seventy or eighty Irishmen in his regiment deserted and, moreover, helped catch Mexicans who tried to tempt them. "Not a single volunteer, either among the native or adopted citizens," he said, "went over to the enemy." He explained this difference between Volunteers and Regulars by pointing out that the former, across Northern Mexico, were usually stationed in small towns and villages where the priests were "pious men of unblemished lives," while the Regulars, as the better disciplined were quartered in important cities where they came in contact with "pampered and frantic friars." [15]

Here and there soldiers recorded in their diaries a doubt as to

whether desertion among the Regulars was caused more by religion than by hard treatment "at the hands of young snot-nose and
tyrannical officers" — "ignorant and brutal officers." To immigrants
who had recently left the British Army, it seemed incredible that
"conceited Yankee subalterns should be free to strike enlisted men
at the slightest provocation and inflict painful, humiliating punishments." [16]

Second Lieutenant Gustavus W. Smith, the twenty-four-year-old
Kentucky gentleman who was with the Engineers at Camargo, later
told with pride how he had cured insubordination in a Dutch cook,
by marching him alone three miles into the jungle and threatening
to plunge a drawn sword through his body unless the fellow did
the manual of arms for two hours without taking his eyes off a chip
of wood on the ground. Smith also boasted how, when a sergeant
was hesitating to lead his marching men down a very steep riverbank, Smith had given him a swift and sudden shove from behind.[17]

Within a span of twelve months, two attempts would be made
to kill Major Bragg, the eminent disciplinarian, the second coming
on "a fine, moonlight night" at Walnut Springs, when a noncommissioned officer, craving revenge for punishment, touched off an
8-inch shell in Bragg's tent, close to the cot where the Major was
sleeping. Men rushing to the scene found holes in Bragg's blanket,
none in him.[18]

Busy feeding his regiment, Grant saw the autumn and early
winter pass. On December 10, he moved into the city when his regiment became the garrison of the town, four companies and headquarters staff stationed in the Citadel. Since the war was apparently over, he paid no especial attention to the trips Taylor made
consolidating his forces across Northern Mexico — an expedition
to Victoria, 150 miles away on the road to the seaport which the
Navy had occupied — a visit to General Wool, who had come down
through Chihuahua to Parras, 125 miles southwest of Monterey —
the dispatch of reinforcements to Worth at Saltillo, 50 miles from
Monterey, where Worth was imagining himself menaced by a Mexican Army, which never came.

The officers knew that President Polk, in August, had permitted
one of Mexico's ex-presidents, General Santa Anna, to slip through
the blockade from Cuba into Mexico on the understanding that he

would seize the Government and make peace with the United States. Santa Anna had become ruler of Mexico easily enough, but instead of preaching peace, preached war. Expel the gringo invaders! However, there had been no fighting by the time the new year, 1847, came in. Santa Anna was like the rest. *Mañana*.

Ever since the fall of Monterey, the minds of many Volunteers had been on home. There had been days in the late autumn and early winter when regiments marching footsore miles, sick of Mexico, sick of the parrots in the trees, sick of the strange fruits that drained their bowels, would hear something in the sky and stop, faces lifted. Up there was a quavering wild and lonely music that they knew so well — one well-remembered sound that had come to join them for a flying moment in this strange land — the honking of wild geese on their long journey southward. Maybe yesterday a soldier's mother had been looking up at that same high trembling thread from her dooryard in Tennessee?

Sometimes when the geese swung low, the pang would pass swiftly from the young men's breasts, muskets would begin banging and squawking bodies would thud into the grass while feathers danced away on the wind.[19]

Sam Grant and the other young officers of the Fourth Infantry caught the scent of home one day in the first week of January, when orders came to pack and start for the mouth of the Rio Grande on the tenth. That could mean nothing but that they were going home, back to the States. When they got to Point Isabel they would probably find peace had been declared. Excitement shook the young officers as they packed up. General Worth was marching from Saltillo on the ninth, and would pick them up as he went North. Grant's regiment was under Worth now, Twiggs having gone to Victoria.

Sam Grant wanted to get home, but as he followed Worth toward Camargo, quitting Monterey on January 11, he discovered that the General was as incompetent at marching as he had been proficient at fighting. Worth was nervous, impatient, and drove the men as hard as if rushing to the relief of a beleaguered fort. On his schedule, each day's march was determined by the distance between water holes, yet on one occasion at least, as Grant commented, "after having made the full distance intended for the day, and after the troops were in camp and preparing their food, [he] ordered tents struck and made the march that night which had been intended for the next day." Grant was learning that there was as much generalship in marching men as in leading them into battle. Where one general would "get the maximum distance" out of soldiers, another would "wear them out in a few days without accomplishing so much." [20]

At one point where the bivouac was to be on the edge of a stream, the weary officers and men rushed for a bath. Sid Smith pushed through undergrowth to get to the river and found himself attacked by savage peccaries. He jumped to a limb. It bent, dangling him barely above some twenty pairs of snapping tusks. He yelled for help, yelled loud and long, his piratical mustachios shaking. Sam Grant and Jenks Beaman rescued him.[21]

From Camargo the division shipped on steamers down the river to their new camp at the site of the battle of Palo Alto, where they arrived January 23, to make an astonishing discovery. They weren't going home! General Winfield Scott, head of the whole Army, was on the Rio Grande, had been there for a month, preparing to lead an expedition to Vera Cruz, take it, then march on Mexico City: the war was only beginning. Worth had known it all along. That was why he had driven his men so fast. To Sam Grant, however, Worth was still foolish. It would be weeks before enough shipping could assemble to transport the big army down to Vera Cruz.[22]

In the camps two opposing theories about Scott took shape, depending upon the newspapers that were read and the political beliefs that were held. Democrats believed Scott had been sulking, criticizing Polk, hamstringing the war, all because the President had not, at the very start, allowed him to carry out his plan of attacking Mexico by way of Vera Cruz. Democrats said Scott, who was comically conceited anyway, had been insufferably so with Polk, and had been conniving to use the war as a steppingstone to the Whig nomination for the Presidency. Democrats said that Polk was now letting Scott carry out his Vera Cruz plan because no one else could possibly manage it. Taylor was too incompetent for so large an expedition.

Whigs said Scott was a martyr, a patriot whom Polk had kept on the shelf so that he could not win the Presidency on a battlefield. Whigs said that the only reason Scott was now being given his chance was that his Vera Cruz campaign would kill off Taylor's

Presidential chances without "making sufficient capital himself to secure the prize." [23]

Polk had schemed to put another Democratic politician, United States Senator Benton of Missouri, in command of the expedition, but even his own party feared so wild a move. It insisted that the public expected the head of the Army to command.

Lieutenant Grant believed the Whig version of the situation. Also there was the memory of the day nine years ago when he had first seen the awesome Scott at the West Point review.

Captain Robert Anderson, waiting with the Third Artillery on the sands at the mouth of the Rio Grande, wrote home that the army, he was sorry to say, was prejudiced against Scott, partly because of the way he had in the past decided two court-martial cases, one involving Buell and the other Bragg. Both these officers were talking now against him.[24]

Lieutenant Maury heard officers who were leaving Taylor now to go with Scott sneer at "Old Fuss and Feathers" and say they had more confidence in victorious Taylor. Especially did the Volunteers regret exchanging Old Zach, with whom they felt so comfortable, for Scott whom they had been told was a martinet. As Private Joshua E. Jackson set off from Victoria with the division that was marching overland to Tampico, he wrote in his diary of his first and last sight of Taylor:

> He is a very pleasant old man and very sociable not only to officers but to buck privates also. He is not a proud man at all, when he come to see us he road a mule and looked like an old man a going to mill. He left us and bid us goodby as though he had always been acquainted with us and told us to be good boys and fight like men if needs be and then left.[25]

Many of the Volunteers at Victoria had never seen Taylor before this farewell visit, and mistook him for his own orderly. Old Rough and Ready, wearing his civilian frock coat and his huge straw sombrero, came ambling through the camp mounted on a "large and gentle mule," riding ahead of his orderly Fannin, who was dressed in a handsome uniform and bestrode "a splendid dragoon horse . . . Fannin got about six salutes to Taylor's one." [26]

Although Scott tried to be friendly and considerate in his letters to Taylor, explaining why he was taking so many men from the Rio Grande, Old Zach was cold, and managed to avoid meeting his superior. In time, however, he admitted that with the Volunteer infantry and the Regular batteries — notably Bragg's — that were left, he would be ready for anything the Mexicans might attempt.

An army formalist, valuing ceremony, dress and the niceties of military etiquette, Scott was dismayed by the Volunteers he saw on a trip up the river to Matamoros and Camargo. Also he was impeccable, even frigid, in morals, taking pains to praise virgin spinsters as "the blest of their sex," and he wrote the Secretary of War, on January 16, that he was "agonized" by what respectable soldiers, steamship men, and Mexicans had told him about the behavior of Taylor's Volunteers. "If a tenth of what is said be true," he wrote, then the Volunteers "have committed atrocities — horrors — in Mexico, sufficient to make Heaven weep, & every American of Christian morals *blush* for his country. Murder, robbery & rape on mothers & daughters in the presence of the tied up males of the families, have been common all along the Rio Grande. . . . The respectable volunteers — 7 in 10 — have been as much horrified & disgusted as the regulars, with such barbarian conduct. As far as I can learn, not one of the felons has been punished, & very few rebuked — the officers, generally, being as much afraid of their men as the poor suffering Mexicans themselves are afraid of the miscreants. Most atrocities are always committed in the absence of regulars, but sometimes in the presence of acquiescing, trembling volunteer officers." [27]

Scott was permitted to take with him Worth's and Twiggs's divisions of Regulars, but must also be content with the volunteer division of Major General Robert Patterson, a wealthy fifty-five-year-old manufacturer and Democratic leader who had been brought to Pennsylvania from Ireland in his boyhood. Polk had at one period thought of naming Patterson to head the expedition. Patterson had been head of the Pennsylvania militia for twenty years. Quitman, Shields and Pillow were to come along, too, with their brigades.

Making the best of it, Scott moved cheerfully among the ever-growing camps. Thomas Ewell saw him ride up to the tents of the Second Dragoons one day and compliment Major Edwin Vose Sumner on the "extraordinary vigilance" of the scouts whom he said he had seen "peering at him from behind every bush as he approached the camp." This had convulsed Ewell, who knew that those privates had gone to the bushes not at the call of duty but of nature.

"The water here . . . opens the bowels like a melting tar," Tom Ewell wrote his brother Ben. "When we go to drill, the men have to leave the ranks by dozens, and as the Plain is as bare as a table, make an exposé of the whole affair. The effect is unique as they squat in rows about a hundred yards from the batallion, and when we deploy as skirmishers, we run right over them." [28]

Joining the Fourth Infantry, soon after it moved, on February 8, to a new camp, Camp Page, near the sea, came new officers taking the places of the five who had died since that first gun sounded at Palo Alto. Among them was D. H. Hill, the scholarly South Carolinian whom Sam Grant had known at the Academy, and who was officially to be transferred to the regiment from the Third Artillery in March. Hill, strolling through the camps visiting friends, was introduced to a tall odd-looking youngster, Lieutenant Tom Jackson whose captain told him that Lieutenant Hill had been through the fight at Monterey. Jackson's painful reserve thawed a little. He and Hill took a walk along the beach. Jackson said, "I really envy you men who have been in action; we who have just arrived look upon you as veterans." Then he said, "I should like to be in one battle." [29]

Major Graham, transferred to the Second Infantry, was replaced, as commander of Grant's regiment, by Major Francis Lee, who had done well with the Seventh Infantry at Fort Brown and Monterey. Sam Grant saw officers arrive who had been names to him at the Academy: Jubal Early, the crusty, hard-bitten Virginia lawyer, who was now major of the Virginia Volunteers; Captain Joe Johnston who had, nine years before, come back into the Army to make a name for himself — conducting a masterful retreat with his company during the Indian wars in Florida, and administering the duties of Assistant Adjutant General of the whole Army, in Washington; Captain Robert E. Lee — the cadet who had received no black marks in four Academy years, and who had come to Scott now after having won praise for boldness, coolness and brains in scouting for General Wool in Chihuahua. Both highly rated engineers, Johnston and Lee were resuming their lifelong comradeship and were preparing to bunk together on Scott's flagship — especial favorites of the General — when the expedition should start.

As rapidly as transports arrived from the States, during the last three weeks of February, Scott embarked his men, the Fourth sailing on the thirteenth, arriving the twenty-first. The first rendezvous was the island of Lobos, 50 miles below Tampico, where Shields's brigade was waiting to be picked up. By March 2, Scott sailed with 13,000 men from Lobos for the final rendezvous, the harbor of Anton Lizardo, seventeen miles from Vera Cruz — not a long voyage, 200 miles, and relieved soon after starting by a beautiful sight hanging above the horizon like a pointed white cloud, or, as one soldier put it, "like a great liberty cap suspended in the air — no base, no pedestal." It was the snowy peak of Orizaba, the "Starry Mountain," rising above the heavy air of the lowlands. The men told each other that there, at the foot of that shining cone, they would be going ashore, like Cortez in the sixteenth century, to drive overland to the "Halls of the Montezumas."

On March 6 the ships, bearing Worth's brigade, drew near the anchorage at Anton Lizardo. Some sixty vessels were already in the harbor. The beach, three miles away, was bare except for an occasional Mexican lancer cantering along. In and out of the shipping raced a little dispatch boat. Grant and Sidney Smith stared at it. A smokestack declared it to be a steamer, yet there were no paddles turning at its side. And it was strangely silent.

"Why, the thing looks as if it was propelled by the force of circumstances," Smith declared. Grant laughed. Someone explained to them that this was something new, a steamer driven by a propeller under the water.[30]

From this curious craft or some of the others that carried orders to the armada, Worth's men learned that Scott, on his flagship, had secured a copy of Santa Anna's report of a battle with Taylor at a place called Buena Vista, near Saltillo. Santa Anna was claiming a victory in the two-day fight, February 22 and 23, but Scott's staff were pointing out that since the Mexicans admitted retiring from the field, they must have been badly whipped.

Soon after sunup on March 7, the soldiers crowded the rails to see a small steamer, the *Secretary*, that had been captured from the Mexicans, cut through the water toward Vera Cruz and the city's

chief defense, the huge stone castle of San Juan de Ulloa, which
stood close to shore. Word went around that Scott was on the
Secretary with his generals, Worth, Twiggs, Patterson and his engineers, Colonel Joseph G. Totten, Captains Lee and Johnston,
Lieutenants Meade and Beauregard. They were selecting a beach
upon which to land the army. Some hours later there came the flash
of San Juan's guns and then deep rumbling sounds. It looked ridiculous to expose almost all the leaders to the 128 guns of the fort which
British naval officers had always said could "sink all the ships in the
world." Later in the sun anxious eyes saw the *Secretary* cutting back,
safe and sound, and quickly the army learned that ten shells and
one solid shot had come near it, but no one had been hurt. Reports
had it that the landing would come in a day or so at the Beach of
Collado, just outside the range of Ulloa's guns.

For a year the Yankee gunboats, blockading the port, had kept
well away from Ulloa, and the commodores and the naval officers in
Washington had treated as from a "monomaniac" the pleas of Commander Farragut — that foster brother of Grant's dead comrade Theodoric Porter — that he be allowed to attack it. Give him three ships,
Farragut had insisted, and he would batter the great fort to pieces;
he had been inside it once when acting as an observer with the
French fleet to which the castle had surrendered in 1838. Farragut's
belief was that the Navies of the world were wrong to keep saying
that ships could not fight forts and land batteries. He even offered
to take demotion in rank if permitted to prove his point, but the
Navy had thumbed him down, and for years to come, he would
feel that his career was blighted by prejudice against his inventive-
ness.[31]

Home from his daring reconnaissance, Scott announced that the
landing would be on the beach of Collado, three miles from the
city's waterfront and just beyond the Castle's range.

On the morning of the ninth, Worth's 4500 Regulars, who were
to storm the beach, transferred from their transports to naval steamers and by half past one, saw the Castle and the city. Vera Cruz
spread out before them, white buildings apparently old, a walled
town like the pictures of Spanish cities in histories of the Napoleonic Wars. Along the waterfront and back across the sands, enclos-
ing the whole city, ran a brick wall two feet thick, ranging from

ten to twenty feet high, and pierced every two and a half feet for musketry. From the wall there jutted out a dozen forts, while at the wall's foot stood a tangle of prickly pear extending out to a deep ditch which encircled the town.[32]

The landing party was not to attempt so hopeless a task as storming such a city. They were to try to get a foothold on the beach and make a place for the siege guns which would batter the walls.

During the afternoon, Worth's men went over the side of their steamers and took their places in long surfboats, which Scott had made for just such a landing. They sat in the boats, their bayonets glistening. Beside them sailors fingered the oars. They awaited the signal — the moment when the sun, going down behind the city, would touch the snowy peak of Orizaba, fifty miles away to the west.

At six o'clock the red ball and the white mountain met. From the decks of the gunboats bands broke into "The Star Spangled Banner." The sailors laid to their oars and the sixty-five whaleboats shot across the silken roll of the Gulf. The gunboats began to throw shells into the sand hills beyond the beach. Only a few shells from the city came out to splash aimlessly. Lieutenant Meade, watching from a deck, heard an old salt growl, "Why don't they hit us? If we don't have a big butcher's bill, there's no use in coming here." [33]

Fifty feet from shore the surfboats grated on the sandy bottom. Officers and men began jumping out to wade in, General Worth dashing ahead, as he had at the beginning, back at the Colorado. All other boats held carefully in line so that the vain and intrepid Worth might be the first to reach shore. Gustavus Smith laughed at his captain, Alexander J. Swift, as the Engineers landed. Since Swift had insisted upon rising from a sickbed for the landing, Smith had told two hulking corporals to pick him up and carry him in dry at all costs. Swift screamed like a baby at the corporals, kicked, cursed, struck at them, then when at last they let him down on dry sand, he caught hold of himself, thanked them, then soon fainted in the hot sun and was carried back to his ship. In six weeks he was dead.[34]

With the others, Grant rushed the sand hills, weapons ready. No one had been lost in the landing but each minute now the blast must be coming! Then dawned the realization, the Mexicans were not defending the beach! They had ignored the spot where muskets and canister could have riddled the attackers, floundering through the surf.

Except for a few riders far to the rear, the Mexicans were all there inside the city waiting. It would take the *Yanquis* days to prepare for the next move — days, maybe weeks.

Mañana . . .

CHAPTER TWELVE

"Like Plumes in a Helmet"

IRST LIEUTENANT Gustave Toutant Beauregard stood
on a sand hill, straining his large black eyes through field
glasses as he studied the walls of Vera Cruz. It had been nine
years since the olive-skinned immaculate aristocrat had graduated
from the Academy, yet this siege was his first smell of battle. As a
child in the home of his Creole parents he had had a passion for
guns, and when he had been sent from New Orleans to a semi-
military school in New York, he had thrilled to hear his teacher
tell of helping Napoleon take those famous French cannon across
the Alps into the Italy that lay beyond.[1]

His appetite for the science of war had brought him up to second
place in the class that graduated from the Academy in '38, and since
then he had been on important engineering assignments in coastal
waters for the United States Army. Ambitious, tireless, intelligent,
he was winning recognition from Scott as one of the most important
of the Engineers in the investment of Vera Cruz.

The siege had been on for days and, so far, everything had been
in the hands of the Engineers. They had scouted through the sand
hills, under fire, to place the entrenchments which reached from the
waterfront on the south to the shore on the north. They had cut
the city's water supply and had fixed the gun emplacements to
which the artillerymen were dragging the cannon from the beach
up through the ankle-deep sand. Scott was waiting until the Engineers told him the guns were ready. In the trenches the infantry
lolled, contemptuous of the constant rain of Mexican shells which
threw sand in their eyes but ridiculously little lead into their bodies.
The fragments usually flew upward like geysers, and even when
shells burst on top of the ground, were known to miss men lying
incredibly close to the explosion.[2]

After peering through his glasses for a time, Beauregard said to some other officers beside him on the hill that he was going on to an abandoned adobe house where he could see the enemy better. The other engineers, Robert E. Lee, George B. McClellan and Gustavus W. Smith, remaining on the hill, watched him go. Sam Grant, who had come along to watch the engineers do their work, went forward with the Creole.

Inside the shack, the two lieutenants were peeking through an opening in the wall when a shell slammed through the roof, buried itself in the earth floor and exploded. The other officers, rushing by, found them scrambling out, coughing and sneezing, but unhurt.[3] The incident was nothing, just another of those endless showers of sand.

With supplies brought in from the fleet, Grant had time to spend with the Engineers, or to watch the admirable Captain Joe Johnston of the Topographical Engineers make sketches of the Mexican defenses, or visit in the camps. Fred Dent was here with the Fifth Infantry. Pleasure-loving Gordon Granger, over in the Second, was growling because his horses had been killed in the pitching of their transport in storms, and he must now serve on foot.[4] Through the camps, officers growled about the heat and the sandstorms which temporarily blinded them. They said a fellow would get fairer treatment in the newspapers because the War Department had warned officers against acting as newspaper correspondents in this campaign.[5] Veterans of the Rio Grande complained about Scott's delay in front of Vera Cruz — "Monterey, a stronger place, was taken in three days." The European military experts were right in declaring that trench warfare, such as this, made soldiers timid. Patterson and Worth nagged Scott to let them storm the city. "Ugh," grunted Twiggs, as he looked down his nose at the artillery preparations, "my boys'll have to take it yet with their bayonets." The Regulars enjoyed Twiggs's profanity, his rough friendliness and, pointing to his white hair, called him "Old Orizaba."[6]

Scott was firm against thoughts of a frontal attack — it would cost his men 2000 lives, whereas a bombardment would reduce the city with the loss of no more than 100. "For every one over that number I shall regard myself as his murderer." He must conserve lives if he were to march clear to Mexico City. The reinforcements the Administration had promised him were evidently not coming.

He told his "little cabinet," Totten, Hitchcock, Lee and Lieutenant Henry Scott, that he felt "Mr. Polk's halter around my neck." [7]

His Whig party, back in Washington, where Congress was meeting, was hammering steadily at the injustice of the war, the campaign reaching its peak of invective when the Ohio Senator, Tom Corwin, in February, declared, "If I were a Mexican, I would tell you, 'Have you not room in your own country to bury your dead men? If you come into mine, we will greet you with bloody hands, and welcome you to hospitable graves.' " [8]

Scott was determined that the bombardment of Vera Cruz must be a quick success, for by May 1 there would return to the seacoast lowlands the dread yellow fever which the Mexicans called the *vómito* and the Yankees, the "black vomit." Also spies told him Santa Anna was marching down to raise the siege, a threat that grew less serious on March 15, when Scott received official word of what had really happened at Buena Vista — Taylor's 6000 men had whipped Santa Anna's 17,000 soundly, losing only 600 to the Mexicans' 4000. Old Zach had now won four victories, and would certainly be made a candidate for President. When newspapers spoke of it being premature to talk of such things until national convention time, a backwoods Kentuckian roared, "National convention be damned! I tell ye, General Taylor is going to be elected by spontaneous combustion!" [9]

By March 23, Scott had enough cannon in place to justify an official summons to Vera Cruz to surrender. The Mexican Army, numbering 3300, half militia, refused. Scott's mortars began to lob shells over the city walls, and siege guns suddenly blew away chaparral which had masked them. Gunboats ran in closer to bombard both city and Castle. Heavier guns were landed and, night and day, added fury to the cannonade. Watching the sailors work these guns, Sam Grant and other Army officers could see the Navy's reluctance to change customs. Trained never to dodge at the flash of opponents' cannon — since on shipboard one place was as safe as another — the gunners would not duck behind their sandbags which now shielded them from Vera Cruz's cannon. Army engineers cautioned them to hide, as did the artillerymen nearby, but they insisted upon peering through the embrasures so stalwartly that in one day four had the tops of their skulls blown off. One naval lieutenant, an imaginative Marylander, Raphael Semmes, described what he saw standing beside his battery in the night — the lights of the fleet in a swaying Gulf, "the hoarse and plaintive" murmur of the sea, the multitudinous missiles tracing "beautiful parabolas," in the sky and "chasing each other like playful meteors," the hideous explosions followed by the awful screams of women — "some family circle" wiped out. Soon fires were burning throughout the city, voices could be heard begging the soldiers to surrender, and Scott was bringing up new naval guns to add to the already fearsome bombardment of 180 shells an hour.[10]

At dawn of March 26, a white flag waved and Scott sent Worth, Pillow and Totten to meet Mexican commissioners between the lines. Worth was soon back saying, "General, they're only trying to gain time — they don't mean to surrender. They evidently expect forces from the interior to come to their aid and compel us to raise the siege, or else to keep up dilly-dallying until the yellow fever does it for them. You'll have to assault the town, and I'm ready to do it, with my division."

Patiently Scott got Worth to hand over the Mexican papers which were so "impossible"; then he said it was too late to settle anything tonight; he'd sleep on it. But the minute Worth had strutted out of earshot, Scott's head poked out of his tent and he called for his staff to bring interpreters. When they gathered he announced, "Now, let's hear the English of what these Mexican generals have to say." As he listened, his staff saw him show surprise and annoyance. The commissioners had stupidly failed to see that the "Mexicans were only trying to save appearances while submitting to the inevitable."

Overlooking the likelihood that Worth and Pillow were personally ambitious enough to prefer a grand infantry assault to a peaceful surrender, Scott only said to his staff, "And now I am compelled to override their action or be answerable for the lives of two or three thousand men which would inevitably be sacrificed in an assault of the town." He then dictated new terms which would make surrender sure.[11]

Before midnight of March 27, the articles of capitulation were signed. Scott had been better than his word, losing only 67 men killed and wounded, while the enemy had lost 600 soldiers, 400 or 500 civilians, 400 cannon and unlimited munitions. The Castle surrendered too, falling like a ripe apple at the mere shaking of the tree trunk. A Mexican newspaper moaned, "The sun of this day was but the lamp of a sepulchre." [12]

Sam Grant saw that the terms were lenient. Instead of shipping the prisoners back to the States in empty supply ships, Scott was paroling all of them except forty officers whom he was setting entirely free in the expectation that they would preach peace in the capitol. All officers were to keep their side arms and their horses. There must be no "insulting remarks," no fun made of the Mexicans when, on March 29, the formal surrender was to come. And when the Yankees' turn came to occupy the city, there must be scrupulous protection of all property, especially churches.

Lieutenant Grant and the Fourth Infantry had not far to march to the surrender ceremonials which took place near their camp in the green meadow, the Plain of Cocos, a mile south of the city. The morning was a lovely one, Jacob Oswandel of the Pennsylvania Volunteers noted in his diary, and he could see that the whole army had shined itself, as the soldiers and sailors, at 8 A.M., drew up in two lines, facing each other across an aisle down which, at ten o'clock, the Mexican soldiers came to the beat of their drums and the squeal of their fifes — 4000 of them, 3000 from the garrison, 1000 from the Castle.

"As they marched," Oswandel wrote, "we could see them now and then look back at Vera Cruz, kiss and wave their hands, bidding it good-bye." As the Mexicans stacked their arms, one man tore a flag from its pole and slipped it into his bosom. The Yankee officers saw him do it and, when they made no objection, "he was so rejoiced . . . he cried like a child." Private Oswandel watched the surrendering men and wrote in his diary, "I tell you it was hard to see the poor women with their small children strapped upon their mothers' backs, and with what little clothing they could carry, toddling along with the Mexican soldiers." [13]

As they disappeared, their conquerors marched into Vera Cruz to the tune of "Yankee Doodle." General Worth, assigned by Scott to govern the city, rode proudly ahead. The army saw Scott modestly ride in after the fanfare was over. The officers no longer laughed about Old Fuss and Feathers. Lieutenant Grant thought Scott "a great soldier . . . true, patriotic and upright" and only comic in his use of language. Having admired so highly Old Zach's terse, plain orders which were so easily understood and did not "sacrifice meaning to the construction of high-sounding sentences," Grant was amused when he noted that Scott, in stilted rhetoric, "was not averse to speaking of himself, often in the third person, and he could bestow praise upon the person he was talking about without the least embarrassment." [14]

For two weeks Grant waited with the rest of Worth's men in their tents in the Cocos meadows, talking about the siege. The Class of '46 was exultant at not having missed the war after all. Tom Jackson had been promoted from brevet to second lieutenant for skill with the light guns. Like all quartermasters, Grant was busy with preparations for the next move. To replace the horses lost on shipboard, the mounts of sutlers and of private citizens far and near were commandeered. Unable to receive from Washington the five hundred draft horses he had requested for the job of pulling the heavy siege guns, Scott had the quartermasters bring in Mexican mustangs — a poor substitute but the only one. Regimental wagons were to carry four days' supply of grain for their own teams. Each infantryman was to carry forty rounds of ammunition and "in his haversack hard bread for four days, and bacon or pork (cooked) for two days." After the first four days, horse and man must look to the quartermasters and commissaries who would either buy subsistence along the march or send back empty wagons for it in Vera Cruz.

Grant saw Scott go to great lengths to conciliate citizens. Riding his men on a shorter curb than had Taylor, Scott also went further with proclamations, that of April 11, addressed "To the Good People of Mexico," declaring the "Americans" to be "not your enemies, but the enemies, for a time, of the men who, a year ago, misgoverned you and brought about this unnatural war between two great republics." He and his men were, he said, "the friends of the peaceful inhabitants of the country we occupy, and the friends of your holy religion, its hierarchy and its priesthood." He had done all he could to protect the people and their property from "the few bad men in this army." He had punished all offenders and hanged one man, a free Negro, Isaac Kirk, who had come from the United States years before, and who had, on April 4, raped Mrs. María Antonia

Gallegas on a road outside the city, also stealing her comb and ten dollars. "At the end of the war," Scott's proclamation concluded, "the Americans, having converted enemies into friends, will be happy to take leave of Mexico, and return to their own country." [15]

For another reason. Yankee "outrages" in Vera Cruz were fewer than along the Rio Grande. The seaport contained courtesans of many races to slake the soldier's thirst for girls; prostitutes from the States arrived on ships along with the gamblers, sutlers, speculators, actors, reporters, printers and embalmers, the latter advertising "zinc coffins" as soon as they rented rooms. Scott encouraged trade with the citizens. One of his colonels was said to have bought a parrot because the salesman translated its Spanish jabber as "Great God Almighty, the Americans are coming! Run! Run!" [16] Scott paid formal visits to the great cathedral which Private Joshua E. Jackson described as "some of the splendidest grandeur I ever saw." At a special ceremony on April 4, Scott and his staff in full uniform carried candles in a processional, causing officers to whisper humorous predictions as to how the anti-Catholic voters back home would view Scott's presidential aspirations when they heard of this.[17]

Scott was patient but firm when Worth stormed into his headquarters declaring that he was disgraced because Twiggs was to lead off when the invasion started April 8. Scott explained that he couldn't always be giving Worth the post of honor: "Others shall have it in turn, and I will not do injustice to please my best friend." [18]

Grant always remembered how small had been the force, a scant 10,000, which started the 250-odd-mile march to Mexico City, a metropolis of 100,000 souls. Although Scott was leaving behind a garrison to hold the port and guard 1000 sick soldiers, the venture was risky enough to remind men of Cortez burning his ships behind him when in 1519 he left Vera Cruz on the same march.[19] Somewhere on the causeway which Cortez had built to Jalapa, 70 miles ahead, Santa Anna would be waiting. That one-legged genius had succeeded in convincing his people that he had won, not lost, at Buena Vista and in raising so many new regiments that he was rumored to have anywhere from 13,000 to 18,000 confident patriots massed in the hills.

The hardest work Grant had ever known descended upon him as, with his wagons, he brought up the rear of Worth's column in the first day's march on April 13. Ten miles of scorching sand must be crossed before reaching Cortez's hard road. The unbroken mustangs which he had been forced to use in parts of his teams kicked harness, wagon tongues, and doubletrees to bits. When horses balked or gave out, the Quartermaster had to bring out drag ropes and get already weary infantrymen to pull wagons and horses through the ankle-deep sand. He had to try and find room among the chests and barrels and tents which stuffed his wagons for the soldiers who went down with sunstroke. Soon he could take no more — twenty or thirty of the Fourth toppled over that day, six dying, and all he could do was work with the surgeons to make sufferers as comfortable as possible in roadside clumps of shade, leaving them there with guards to be picked up by empty wagons returning to Vera Cruz from Twiggs's column.

All around him the plodding Fourth, dripping with sweat, listened to stragglers from Pillow's force telling how the sun had already killed six of their comrades and disabled 150 more.[20] The path was littered with the knapsacks, coats, extra shoes which staggering men up ahead had thrown away, and with barrels of hard bread and salt pork which had been tossed out to lighten wagons. Exhausted, the Fourth threw itself on the sand when night brought a halt, and slept deep.

Grant's reward for skill and energy came next day when Garland called him up to tell him that from today, April 14, he was no longer the conditional, but the permanent Regimental Quartermaster. Garland was sending notice of the appointment to the Adjutant General's office.

Soon after the aching, limping, groaning Fourth took up its march in the moist heat again, matters took a turn for the worse. They were met by a squad of Dragoons escorting wagons returning to Vera Cruz for supplies, and from their commander, Captain George Blake, the word spread that Twiggs had run against Santa Anna two days ago and was probably fighting him now. At the time Blake had left, Twiggs had been feeling his way toward the strong fortifications Santa Anna had built at the pass of Cerro Gordo where the road turned up into the mountains. There was excitement in the news but woe, too, since Worth, inflamed at the thought of action, took his column forward relentlessly, pushing it well into the night. Although the wagons rolled on the hard road now, there was small improvement in the Quartermaster's lot, for he must work with the rear guard lifting sleepy men from the roadside, hunting them out from the jungle shadows into which they crept, getting them to their feet, harrying them onward.

Worth's erratic mind played the devil with the troops next day, April 15, too, for after announcing that the march would only be five miles he proceeded to drive them, with only short rest periods, fifteen miles. Expecting the short march many men had not bothered to fill their half-gallon canteens, and suffered piteously thereby. One moment of diversion they had. It came at a pause when Major Graham, walking up and down the line, discovered in it the Dutch wife of Private Clancy. She, as laundress and cook of Company B, had been ordered to remain behind at Vera Cruz, but had managed to accompany her mate this far. "The ugliest of her sex," Lieutenant Judah called her — Dutch to extremity, a huge, misshapen body, round ugly face "and given to whipping her husband every little while."

Graham ordered her into an empty supply wagon that was ready to return to Vera Cruz. Mrs. Clancy refused and when three soldiers, at Graham's command, came to load her, "her huge red fist" knocked the first one sprawling. Then she strode to the wagon with the other two guards following at a respectful distance. In the general laughter that arose her ear caught the sound of her husband's voice and "Such a look as she gave him. It foreboded many a hard thump," Judah wrote in his diary.

The fifteen-mile march ended at midnight, with Worth's men camping on the brow of a hill seeing Twiggs's campfire in the valley below.[21]

From stragglers and wounded men who drifted to the rear came the story of what had been happening: The glory so far was all the Engineers'. When Twiggs, on the twelfth, had discovered Santa Anna entrenched at the Pass, he had halted, for both sides of the road were easily defended, high hills and deep chasms. Up a blind footpath Captain Joe Johnston had climbed and come back with a bullet hole through his right thigh, another through his right arm and the news that Santa Anna's batteries could sweep the road. Joe Johnston was, as usual, a magnet for enemy bullets. Back in

1836 the Florida Indians had put thirty balls through his uniform without scratching him, then one slicing his scalp the time he had saved his men by a desperate and skillful retreat through swamps.[22]

Another Engineer, Lieutenant Zebulon Tower, had been more successful locating Santa Anna's batteries than he had been in locating a watch gong in Cadet Grant's breast three years before. Beauregard had dragged himself up cliffs to mark sites from which cannon could enfilade Mexican batteries. And Captain Lee had gone so far into the enemy rear, locating batteries and roads, that he had been forced to lie most of the day behind a log, enduring insect bites while enemy infantrymen either sat on the log or barely missed stepping on him. On another scouting trip Lee and Squibob Derby made what Scott's staff later described as "the boldest examination of all," one that convinced Scott, who had joined Twiggs, that he must flank Santa Anna rather than attack by the main road.

In Worth's camp, the night of the sixteenth, it was understood that the division was to stand in reserve while Twiggs felt the enemy. In the morning Grant saw the scene which, in his careless spelling, he described in a letter home:

> The difficulties to surmount made the undertaking almost equal to Bonaparte's Crossing the Alps. Cierra Gorda is a long Narrow Pass, the Mountains towering far above the road on either side. Some five of the peaks were fortified and armed with Artillery and Infantry. At the outlett of the Mountain Gorge a strong Breastwork was thrown up and 5 pieces placed in embrasure sweeping the road so that it would have been impossible for any force in the world to have advanced. Immediately behind this is a peak of the Mountains several hundred feet higher than any of the others and commanding them.[23]

Grant saw little parties of engineers working with artillerymen to pull cannon up the heights, let the guns down chasms by ropes, and on up more slopes. He saw a party clear a ridge with a swift charge and learned that Frank Gardner had led it, winning praise from Scott himself. There was little actual fighting, but the panorama was magnificent and the promise of tomorrow stirring.

On the eighteenth the attack came, with Worth's men still onlookers. Grant saw the Mexicans beat off for a time the blue infantry which came scrambling up through the rocks, saw them send Pillow's Volunteers running like mad at one point. But the fire from those Yankee cannon on the incredible peaks of vantage began to tell. Then Twiggs's Regulars made the main effort of the day, climbing up the face of Cerro Gordo mountain, the key of the enemy defenses.

"It was on this hight [sic]," Grant wrote home, "that Gen. Twiggs made his attack. As soon as the Mexicans saw this hight taken they knew the day was up with them. Santa Anna vamoused with a small part of his force leaving about 6000 to be taken prisoners with all their arms, supplies, &c."

Contemptuous of the Mexican Army which he understood to have numbered 12,000, Scott estimated the prisoners at about 3000 and the captured muskets to number 5000. The muskets with 43 captured cannon were pitched into deep ravines. Scott guessed the enemy dead at 1000 to 1200.[24]

In the smallness of the Yankee loss, only 63 killed and 368 wounded out of a force of 6000, there was a lesson for Sam Grant to learn: when you charged straight up a steep hill you were safer than when advancing across a plain, for the enemy cannon on the hilltop could not be depressed enough to hit you, and the sharpness of the angle exaggerated the natural tendency of riflemen to shoot too high anyway.

On the nineteenth and twentieth many soldiers wandered over the battlefield, one of them, the poetic Tennessee Volunteer, John Blount Robertson, noting an Indian woman turning over "the blackened bodies and anxiously scrutinizing the features of each half-putrid corpse." At last she eagerly lifted one "from its bloody bed, and lashing the body upright upon a chair," and then strapping the burden to her back, set out to carry it away. Sympathetic Volunteers talked to her, and although their Spanish was not good enough to understand all that she poured out "in wild Indian accents," they learned that she had come twenty miles to search for her "only child." [25]

Sam Grant learned that two of his classmates, Roswell Ripley and Frank Gardner, had earned brevet captaincies. Frank's promotion might be his if they had not changed places back at Corpus Christi. Lyon had taken three guns. The flaxen little Adonis, Van Dorn, had killed two Mexicans with his own hands. In the house where Squibob Derby lay wounded, he entertained other patients with merriment, although the two injured Virginians, Maury and Joe Johnston, on nearby cots called it "a stream of coarse wit." Never a humorous man nor one to overlook petty deviations from orders, Johnston disliked Derby. His anger grew so intense that one day when he heard Squibob calling to a servant to run and seize a kid from a herd of goats passing the door, he roared, "If you dare to do that, I'll have you court-martialed and cashiered, or shot." [26]

Through the army sped the uproarious word that one of Santa Anna's extra wooden legs had been captured in a carriage which he had packed with belongings, especially cooked chicken and bags of gold, at one of his haciendas not far from the battlefield. Captain Justus McKinstry and Second Infantry soldiers insisted they had captured it, but the quarrels between Privates J. B. Smith and Edward Elliott of the Fourth Illinois as to which of them had snatched it from the carriage were more convincing. At least their regiment held a leg and brought it home with them to Illinois, declaring it to be the only real one among the many "original" peg legs of Santa Anna which shrewd Yankee traders sold through the States. For weeks after the seizure, Scott's men in parody sang "The Leg I Left Behind Me." [27]

At 7 A.M., on the nineteenth, Grant was moving with Worth's division up the highway toward the city of Jalapa some twenty miles ahead, following Twiggs's division and the dragoons. Past the Yankee infantry moved Mexican horsemen, part of the 3000 Scott had paroled. The Yankees in turn passed slower-moving Mexican infantry, scattering to their homes far and wide across the nation. The men were cracking jokes at their own expense, the young *señoritas* frisking along with their lovers' sombreros on their heads, the children who had "followed padre and madre to the wars" were prattling "unconscious of the existence of misery in this world." But the older women grieved one Yankee war correspondent as they "moved at a snail's pace, their heavy burthens almost weigheing them to the earth," sacks of food, kitchen utensils — "the woman of sixty or more years — the mother with her infant wrapped in her rebozo, the wife, far advanced in that state that 'women wish to be who love their lords.'" As Grant and his brigade emerged from a section of the road that was lined with corpses of Mexican soldiers and horses, they saw in an open space an American officer directing blue-coated men as they stacked into neat piles captured carts, knapsacks, packsaddles, muskets, beans, rice, bread and shoes. He was Captain Robert Allen, Grant's friend, winding up a three-day display of organizational genius which would bring him a major's brevet.[28]

As the Yankee neared Jalapa, the fragrance of orange trees floated out to meet them, and as they entered the town peddlers sold them lemons, peaches, cherries, figs, bananas, grapes and — ice cream. They saw in windows boxes of flowers and behind the blossoms bevies of what little Lieutenant George B. McClellan thought "exceedingly beautiful" girls. Having for seven months now grown accustomed to the dark, red faces of Indians on the Rio Grande and in Vera Cruz, twenty-year-old McClellan thought how much lighter of complexion the women seemed to be. Other soldiers revealed the slow evaporation of prejudice in the heat of sex when they recorded the number of white, yellow and light-brown faces that smiled down upon them. Henry Judah wrote in his diary, "such beauty I do never recollect to have seen collected together — it seemed as if you could not find an ugly face . . . their complections were perfectly white, eyes mostly hazel, or brilliantly black. Sometimes blue and in almost every case fringed with long, dark eyelashes." Private Oswandel said, "Their features can't be beat for pleasantness." Robertson was ravished by the "dark-eyed donazellas" in the windows; some of them "were smiling, others laughing downright at our ragamuffin and tatterdemalion appearance, and a few red heads amongst us, provoking successive peals of laughter." [29]

Even the women's clothes seemed whiter too. Jalapa was the Garden of Eden, radiantly clean, its washerwomen pounding garments eternally in streams that splashed through ravines in the heart of town.

As Worth's division moved through the city to camping meadows outside, where Scott had located them to conciliate the Jalapeños, many soldiers fell out, vanished into the crowds and came to their bivouacs later with Rabelaisian boasts of their adventures with *señoritas*. Grant's brigade had only a few hours in the city on the morning of the twentieth, yet he saw enough to write home, "Ialapa is the most beautiful place I ever saw. It is about 4000 feet above Sea and being in the Torrid Zone, they have the everlasting Spring Fruit and vegitables [*sic*] the year around. I saw there a great many handsome ladies and more well dressed men than I had ever seen before in the Republic." [30] On the twenty-first he marched up the National Road which, to his farm boy's eye, was "one of the best in the world." The goal was now the Castle of Perote, forty miles to the west — a huge stone fortress with fifty-four frowning guns, quarters for two thousand men, a great moat and a savage portcullis — like a dream from medieval Spain.

A new and even lovelier Mexico was dawning on the Yankees who had an eye for scenery. Beside the causeway that wound up toward the huge plain beyond, there was an endless flash of bright flowers in the trees, strange flowers in the dark glens, flowers even in the air where the sun, striking through the heavy green leaves, painted rainbows on falling water. The splash of unseen cataracts and waterfalls was in their ears. Up ahead the white covers of the wagons wound in and out along the twisting roads. The lift of high mountain air was in the nostrils and heels of the invaders. In the cool, bright transparency of the atmosphere everything seemed nearer and more beautiful than it was. The cliffs echoed the clank of iron wheels as they had echoed the clank of Cortez's armor three centuries before. The soldiers were happy. Once, while Clarke's brigade was resting in the road, a team hitched to a traveling blacksmith's forge up ahead, became frightened and came down the pike hell-to-split. The bumping of the forge and the laughter of the men as they tumbled over the stone fences awakened old, fat Colonel Newman S. Clarke from a nap he was enjoying. Rubbing his eyes he began bawling "Form Square! Form Square!" which set the men to roaring still louder and to howling to the rest of Worth's division, down the road, "Never mind the square. Over the wall, every one of you." [31]

Perote was a ghost castle as Worth's men edged across its drawbridge and moat on April 22. While the Fourth Regiment was staring at it and thinking how it could have been defended, medieval though it was, against them, who should walk up but Mrs. Clancy, looking for her man. She had come to stay and Major Graham threw up his hands. [32]

Two days later Garland marched his brigade twelve miles farther

and camped in the village of Tepeyahualco, only forty miles from
their next goal, Puebla. Resting there for weeks, the men heard how
Worth, back in Jalapa, was quarreling with Scott, insisting that he
had been wronged by being held in reserve at Cerro Gordo while
Twiggs fought the battle. Worth was pronouncing Scott's official
report of the battle as "a lie from beginning to end" because it
glossed over the panic that had hit Pillow's men, and ignored the
fact that Pillow, when wounded in the arm, had cut for the rear at
a lively trot. Grant's sympathies were with Scott. He observed later
that "there was not a battle of the Mexican War, or any other,
where orders issued before an engagement were nearer being a
correct report of what afterwards took place. Worth was also devil-
ing Scott to let him march on, now, while Mexicans were still reeling,
but the General felt his depots at Vera Cruz and Jalapa needed more
strengthening.[33]

From Tepeyahualco, which Ulysses recklessly wrote down as
"Tiping Ahualco," he sent on May 3 a letter back to the States
describing what he had been seeing:

> Between the thrashing the Mexicans have got at Vuene Vista,
> Vera Cruz and Ceirra Gorda they are so completely broken
> up that if we only had transportation we could go to the City
> of Mexica and where ever else we liked without resistance.
> . . . Orizaba looks from here as if you could almost throw
> a stone to it but it looked the same from Ialapa some fifty
> miles back and was even visable from Vera Cruz. Since we left
> the Sea Coast the improvement in the appearance of the people
> and the stile of building has been very visable over anything
> I had seen in Mexico before. . . . The scenery is beautiful
> and a great deal of magnificent table land spreads out above
> you and below you.[34]

Reports of a quarrel going on between Scott and Polk left Grant
more than ever a Scott adherent. Grant believed Scott's story that
half of the men promised him, and many necessary wagons, guns,
ammunition, and money were being "withheld" by Polk, and that
the President, after assuring him that he would have honest and sincere support, had not only forced politically hostile generals upon
him, in every instance, but had continued the scheme to replace him
with Senator Benton. Lieutenant Grant must have speculated on

what the arrival of Benton as the new generalissimo would mean
to his and Fred Dent's fortunes. Benton was famous for favoring
friends and would probably do something special for Colonel Dent's
son and prospective son-in-law.[35]

Scott, fretting in his quarters at Jalapa through late April and
early May, wrote rash letters, openly charging that Polk was deliberately wrecking the campaign so that Scott's political future would
be ruined. Self-pity blinded the old general to the obvious fact that
Polk was entirely too shrewd to have thus wrecked his own Administration by losing the war. To make matters worse, seven regiments,
almost 40 per cent of his little army, served notice that the twelve
months for which they had volunteered would be up in a few
weeks. It would be useless to urge them to re-enlist. They had been
"fooled and bamboozled" by the Government which had assured
them in January that Scott's army would be 50,000 strong and that
peace would soon be won. Here it was May, and no reinforcements
were in sight. The Government was in no hurry to win the war;
"the contractors have not made enough money." [36]

Petulant and babyish though he was toward the Administration,
Scott generously sent the seven regiments home weeks in advance
of their time so that they might escape exposure to the *vómito*. He
was thoughtful, too, of the Jalapeños, sending officers to carry
lighted candles in a Procession of the Host which priests conducted
to the door of a sick grandee. He ordered troops guarding the town
to kneel with muskets in their left hands, caps in right, when the
chanting prelates and their acolytes, swinging braziers of incense,
should pass. The Regulars obeyed orders but the Volunteers refused
to kneel. No official notice was taken of the insubordination. When
some of the Volunteers rushed women hucksters and stole fruit,
Scott made their officers pay for the damages.[37]

From Tepeyahualco, Perote and Jalapa, Yankee soldiers strayed
of evenings into the countryside to see the full-blown system of
peonage that ruled the fertile regions of Mexico — a system far less
developed in the grazing lands along the Rio Grande. Other soldiers
than Grant were finding sympathy for the peons who were always
in debt to their landlords, the grandees in the haciendas. By law
they could not leave their masters so long as they were in debt for
food, clothing and necessities. Robertson, the Tennessean, saw the

whole Indian race, two thirds of all Mexicans, "oppressed by a system of servitude more odious and degrading" than slavery at home in the States. He thought the spirit of the peons permanently broken by their life of hopeless toil, their backs bent from burdens, their feet deformed — "toes wide apart and curved downward as if for climbing steep ascents . . . their dark, unreadable eyes cower beneath the glance of the stranger." Albert Brackett was touched when he saw the peons after a day of plowing with oxen and a crooked stick, come to the hacienda to sing hymns to the Virgin, unearthly, melancholy, wildly pathetic songs, wafting great distances across the plain, reminding him of ancient chants to barbarous stone idols.[38]

On May 10, the sixteen-day stay at Tepeyahualco ended. Scott, having done all he could to strengthen his depots, ordered Worth to start for Puebla with his 2200 men, Quitman following, a day behind, with as many more. To Grant it was the old story. Worth marched far one day, short the next, one night keeping his men in line till morning because he failed to discover that a disturbance on the picket line was merely some pack mules from a merchant's caravan blundering along the road.[39]

There was, however, magnificent scenery all along — mirages, forests, empty plains, ruined churches, gay towns with splashing fountains, jungles, and in the mountains glimpses of white-clad guerillas "gliding among the green trees in all directions" like "scared water fowl." [40]

Worth's gunners rode with their long, slow matches burning. The farther the brigade moved the harder grew the job of collecting food and keeping wagons in repair. Quartermaster Grant wrote home that his position had become "more responsible and laborious." The country "has in it many wonderful things. . . . Its hillsides are covered with tall palms whose waving leaves present a splendid appearance. They toss to and fro in the wind like plumes in a helmet, their deep green glistening in the sunshine or glittering in the moonbeams in the most beautiful way. . . . I have been much delighted with the Mexican birds. . . . Many have a plumage that is superlatively splendid but the display of their music does not equal that of their colors. . . . They beat ours in show but do not equal them in harmony." He was writing with his sword fastened to his side and "my pistol within reach, not knowing but that the next moment I may be called into battle again." In later years he thought Scott had taken an unnecessary risk in marching on Puebla by the direct road. "It could have been passed, its evacuation insured and possession acquired without danger of encountering the enemy in intricate mountain defiles." But he admitted that Scott, so far from his base, believed it imperative to occupy Puebla as rapidly as possible.[41]

Then there came the marching day, May 12, when the white tip of Popocatepetl rose above the hills. A few miles farther and the "Sleeping Woman," Ixtacihuatl, came up beside Popo, then an isolated peak, Malinche, also snow covered. "With these three mountains in front and Orizaba behind," said Lieutenant Wilcox, "the soldiers marched often in silence, awed by the grandeur of their surroundings." The sight stirred Scott, a few days later, to think how Popo and "his white sister" had been so capped ever "since the first snow fell after the creation." [42]

There was excitement among Garland's men, on May 14, at the village of Amasoque, a few hours' march from Puebla, when, after blacking their boots, shaving their faces and combing their hair in preparation for entrance into the great city, couriers spurred up with the news that Mexican cavalry was approaching. Through mud and rain they marched out, saw the riders in the distance, then saw Duncan's shells send the Lancers flying. Nervously Worth kept the Fourth Regiment in line, ankle-deep in mud, a torrential rain beating upon them all day and all night. Next morning, after Puebla's authorities had ridden out and assured Worth there would be no resistance, the men marched into town, down streets filled by what seemed to be all 80,000 inhabitants.

In the great plaza, Garland's infantry, muddy and dog tired, stacked their arms while their officers went off hunting billets for them and for Quitman's brigade which would arrive later in the day. They yawned as they looked at the crowds on the rooftops and in the windows, and at the throng that was pouring into the great square, edging closer.

A handful of 2200 Yankees wandered away to drink pulque or look for girls, but the rest of them lay down on the hard pavement and, with 10,000 pair of dark eyes wonderingly upon them, put their heads on their arms and went to sleep.[43]

CHAPTER THIRTEEN

Red, Ragged Whiskers

HOUR AFTER HOUR the Fourth Infantry waited, on May 15, in Puebla's plaza, while crowds stared at them as if they were animals in a menagerie, and while the other regiments marched away as billets were found for them. Finally word came that through some error the Fourth had been overlooked and must now take its place in the Church of San Agustín, a block away. Headquarters disliked to infringe on the religious feelings of the natives, but there was nothing else to be done at present. As soon as less provocative room was found the regiment should have it.[1]

The men camped in a huge courtyard. The officers bunked in seven small rooms which the priest cleared for them. They all wandered over the building, marveling at the labyrinthine passages and the endless paintings on the walls. While they were still exploring the place next day, orders came to form in line immediately. Guerillas were about to rise and cut the guards' throats! Out poured the whole army, marching here and there, only to find everything quiet. Later, to their disgust, they discovered that Worth had based his alarm on nothing more than an anonymous letter.[2] Nor did the General's nerves grow any steadier in the subsequent week, for, either out of his own imagination or the reports of mischievous spies, he continually expected Mexican armies to come popping over the city walls. He rushed his troops up and down, past citizens who wondered why the soldiers didn't stop and buy ice cream that was for sale, past pottery workers who looked up in wonder, past the throngs of white-splotched bakers who came to the doors to gape at the mad North Americans. *Los gringos son locos!*

The Fourth, rushing to meet the phantom enemies, changed quarters from the church to an old building, the "Alameda," near the western gate of the town, then to another building at the eastern entrance. Sam Grant, for all his weariness, grew amused. He said later, "On one occasion General Worth had the troops in line, under arms all day, with three days' cooked rations in their haversacks. He galloped from one command to another proclaiming the near proximity of Santa Anna with an army vastly superior to his own." Sometimes it was Worth's serious, solemn aide, Lieutenant Pemberton, who had to cry the alarm. Once Worth issued a printed circular accusing the Mexicans of plotting to poison his whole army.[3]

Worth's nervousness and conceit combined to make him ridiculous, as well as offending and frightening the Pueblans. He seemed to Hitchcock, who was still at Jalapa with Scott, to "have assumed for the time the powers and the airs of a Spanish generalissimo." Not only were his terms to the city contrary to Scott's orders, but he sent none of his official proclamations to his superior — and when reprimanded, howled for a court of inquiry. The court promptly declared his terms of capitulation "improvident and detrimental to the public service," and this poison-plot circular to be "highly improper and extremely objectionable." At this, Worth screamed more loudly than ever for the War Department or the President at Washington to rescue his name and fame, a demand which the Administration patiently ignored.[4]

Worrying over what Worth would do next, Scott dropped his work at Jalapa and hurried to Puebla. When he arrived, composure returned to the army, Grant commenting, "Nothing more was heard of Santa Anna and his myriads." [5] Grant saw no foes when he went out on expeditions into the wheat and corn country buying food. With less than a thousand soldiers escorting the long wagon train as it spread far on two-day, three-day or four-day trips, he "never thought of danger." There were stories of lone Yankee riders cut off by stray guerillas but Santa Anna was at Mexico City, raising an army, raising the spirits of the people amazingly after the despondency of Cerro Gordo.[6]

Between forage trips, Grant worked like the other quartermasters at reclothing the army. Since arriving in Mexico, it had received no uniforms, blankets or shoes to replace those worn out in rough marches or lost in battle. Over a thousand male and female Pueblans were hired to make shoes and pantaloons alone. Blankets were bought.[7] A regimental quartermaster had little time to keep up with the squabbles between Scott and Nicholas P. Trist, a State Department official whom Polk had sent down to deal, directly if possible, with Santa Anna. Since the United States now controlled the whole circumference of Mexico, all of the Rio Grande country, all of the vital seaports on the Gulf and the Pacific, Polk had authorized Trist to offer peace and $15,000,000 cash if Santa Anna would quit claim to everything above the Rio Grande including New Mexico and Upper and Lower California.

Polk, in a letter, hinted to Scott that hostilities be avoided until Trist could see Santa Anna. This offended Old Fuss and Feathers. He wrote wrathful letters home, protesting against the degradation of having been ignored while the whole peace question was entrusted to a mere chief clerk from the State Department. He and Trist exchanged bitter letters which drove Polk to bemoan his fate at having been forced "from the beginning, to conduct the war through the agency of two generals, highest in rank," Taylor and now Scott, "who have not only no sympathy with the Government but are hostile to my administration."

When at last Scott ended the quarrel with Trist by sending him some guava jelly, the peace maneuvers took a new turn. Britishers living in Mexico City brought out the hint that a cash bribe to Santa Anna and certain legislators might buy a peace. Trist leaped at the idea. He had a million dollars to spend for just such a purpose. Scott, bending his conscience, approved, and $10,000 was sent to Santa Anna as the first installment. Soon the British intermediaries were back with the word that Santa Anna couldn't persuade the Mexican Congress to listen to reason. However, he kept the $10,000.

Many of the officers rode out to see the ancient pyramid of Cholula, six miles from the city, Beauregard characteristically taking pleasure in his discovery, with instruments, that its height was a few feet greater than the famous German scientist, Humboldt, had declared it to be.[8]

The social season was the gayest most officers had known in years, but Sam Grant saw little of it. His companions noted how he, in marked contrast to the sartorial elegance of his friend, Fred Steele, who had arrived with the Second Infantry, "was careless about his dress, wearing hair and whiskers long and ragged." His young silky beard was reddish. He "always rose early in the morning, . . .

chewed tobacco, but never drank to excess nor indulged in the other profligacy so common in that country of loose morals." From what Ulysses said later on, he overcame his West Point dislike of tobacco and now smoked light cigars and cigarettes, "but it wasn't a fixed habit." [9] That he gambled casually, as at Natchitoches, was likely but he was never quoted as were other soldiers on the number of white-armed ladies who crowded the gambling tables, alongside Yankee officers, priests and dapper Mexican males all in high excitement and betting large sums. The money was silver and the invaders noted how "the Mexicans love the jingle of it." Puebla might be, as the Yankees were told, more Indian of blood than any of the cities they had seen, the pure whites numbering only "about one to thirty," yet its citizens seemed fairer than any yet seen in Mexico, with "a higher percentage of ladies." Young men from the States talked about the "great, black, swimming eyes of the women" and "loose waists cut very low in the neck," but not about "bronze busts." The officers were delighted to take horseback canters with ladies who wore divided skirts, "riding a-straddle." They talked about how the ladies turned their heads delicately to avoid puffing smoke in an escort's face while listening to Worth's brass bands in the plaza play "The Girl I Left Behind Me," "The Star Spangled Banner" and "Dance, Batman Dance." Dinners in wealthy Mexican homes were elegant with the host asking if they preferred their wine at room temperature or "cooled by snow that had been brought down the mountain-side on donkey-back from the bosom of the White Woman." Lieutenant Brackett thought a Mexican lady "a dangerous object to meet with, and unless a man is very cautious, he is apt to see her walk away in a proud and stately manner, bearing with her his heart." Watching the *señoritas* "coquet with their Spanish fans in a most exquisite manner, peering over them with their large, dark Juno-like eyes, and their raven tresses falling in heavy masses over their noble foreheads," Brackett heard a comrade, Graham, beside him moan, "It makes a fellow feel aguish [*sic*] just to look at them." [10]

The charms of one *señorita*, Josefina, began to play upon the young officers of the Fourth soon after they took up their quarters in a house in Tivoli garden in an outer district of the city. Next door lived the Alcalde, or mayor of the district, "a poor man," as Judah observed, "one of the best of Mexicans and a friend of the Americans." The Alcalde's two daughters, Josefina and Loreto, brought over "tea and other niceties" when Lieutenant Judah was ill with a cold, and soon Judah was spending an hour or two each evening with them playing cards or listening to them sing. The elder, Josefina, was the romantic one, "very white of complection," "very pretty, very graceful and intelligent," as Judah wrote in his diary, while the younger Loreto was "good hearted, agreeable and full of humor but not so pretty." Josefina, the young officers learned, had been adopted at the age of four by the Alcalde after her capture from Comanche Indians who had stolen her in her babyhood from parents unknown.

Less intimate with the sisters but friendly with them were Grant, Lieutenant Abram Lincoln, a New Yorker, Class of '45, who had joined the Fourth the preceding year, and Lieutenant Patrick Farrelly who, having served with the Fourth for a time after graduating from the Academy in '45, came over frequently now from his Fifth Regiment to visit his friends.

The officers' pleasure in the girls' company was short-lived. One day a notice appeared on a neighboring church defaming the morals of the Alcalde and his daughters and threatening them with assassination within three days. The Alcalde promptly packed the girls off to a safe place in the country and prepared to defend himself. Nothing happened and within some two weeks he told Judah that his daughters would be slipping back into town on the following Saturday to purchase some silks and embroidery and would leave again on Monday.

Judah happened to mention this to a Mexican friend, a young man of twenty, Antonio Calderón, whose father, a wealthy aristocrat, owned the house in which the Yankees were quartered. Most of Antonio's days were spent with his father at their hacienda in Toascala, in the distant countryside, but he kept a room at the town house so that he might change his clothes when coming into town to exercise four horses which were stabled on the grounds. Antonio had made much over the officers, was "apparently very fond" of Judah, and of late had been urging Judah and Grant to accompany him to the hacienda for a visit, assuring them "that he knew of a by-path by which we could avoid guerillas, and he was very brave and that when we died he would die with us." They had found no chance to accept his invitation but Judah thought him "a true friend."

Immediately Antonio learned from Judah that the sisters were returning, he handed him a letter for Josefina, asking that it be delivered "without letting her father know." After which, Antonio rode away.

The girls arrived, Judah gave Josefina the letter. She read it, then gave it to her sister, then to her father, and quickly Judah was told that "Antonio was a great scoundrel, a very bad man" who, because he was rich and Josefina poor, had now "addressed her in a most villainous manner." It was a reckless letter, telling Josefina that he preferred her company to that of Loreto and that he hated all the Yankee officers, especially Judah, Grant and Farrelly.

At the end of an exciting week end, the girls set off again on Monday morning for their place of refuge. Tuesday morning, Lieutenant Lincoln, remaining in quarters while the other officers went to regimental drill, heard a commotion and looked out to see the Alcalde, next door, whaling Antonio with a pine stick as big as his arm. Lincoln saw that Antonio had two pistols on his person but that he made no move to use them and, instead, "ran like a coward."

Quiet descended upon the neighborhood. Soon after ten o'clock, Judah came down the street, returning from the drill ground. The Alcalde beckoned to him to come in and once the door was closed explained, with weeping, what had happened: Antonio had not gone to his father's hacienda on Saturday, but had lain outside the city on the road where, on Monday, he had waylaid the two sisters, showering them with insults and threatening to shoot Josefina. At length the girls had escaped the distraught young man and Josefina sent a note back to their father, reciting their wrongs. The Alcalde, seeing Antonio show up this morning, Tuesday, had rushed out and punished him.

Certain now that Antonio had planned all along to assassinate Sam Grant and him, Judah boiled with anger but expected himself to have no chance at the treacherous wretch. To his amazement that same night he came upon Antonio, on a bench in the passageway of the house between the patio and the street, sitting there "looking sheepish."

"I went to my room," Judah told his diary, "calling Grant and Lincoln out and we went to the young man and charged him with what Josefina had written." Antonio said it was all a lie and that the officers were his *muchos amigos*. Judah said: "I shook my fist in his face and told him I was his enemy. He would not resent the insult, so I lifted him off his feet by his collar, seizing him by the nape of his neck and kicked the aristocratic villain through the whole passageway and out of his door into the street," up which he ran at top speed. A few moments later the Alcalde told the officers that Antonio was the one who had written and posted that scurrilous paper on the church door.

In time Calderón, the father, came to town and, at a meeting with Grant, Judah, and the Alcalde, confessed sadly that his son was a scoundrel. "Grant and I told him," said Judah, "that Antonio should never put his foot near the house again and that if seen about the premises he would be tied up and whipped." The two officers put all the facts in the hands of General Worth, but with the nonreturn of Antonio the affair ended. The girls returned and Judah scratched in his diary, "so innocence is triumphant and villany defeated." [11]

As at Jalapa, the orders were for soldiers to kneel as did Mexicans when the Host was carried in religious processionals through the street. But for some reason Sidney Smith had not known of the rule until May 19, when in the midst of a conversation with James Simons, Assistant Regimental Surgeon, he saw the doctor suddenly drop to his knees and motion for him to follow. He had obeyed in a "frightened and worried" fashion, and was further appalled when an acolyte, distributing lighted candles through the crowd, thrust one into his hand. Prodded by Simon's example he had joined in the procession, his face, so white with bashfulness, contrasting ludicrously with the daredevil sweep of his long hair, beard and mustachios. [12]

Sam Grant saw many Protestant officers follow Scott to Mass in the Cathedral, but the fascinations of the great building were not for him — the candles on thirty altars, the strange coils of gold on the walls, the statues dreaming in the shadows, the sonorous chants drifting up to the soaring architecture. He had drawn well at the Academy but beauty, in his country-boy's eye, was a thing of Nature — trees, mountains, flowers, birds and the oceanlike roll of the plains. Inside him there had never been a hunger for religion and, moreover, the Methodism he had known as a boy had been low church, while here everything was high church. His training, his temperament, his Western interpretation of democracy, told him the Catholic clergy was "oppressing" the Mexican people. Realist and mathematician that he was, he could catch no glimpse of the comfort that religious devotion might be bringing these swarthy poor. He was not charmed as were other Yankees by the legend of the Cathedral — how when artisans grew weary of twenty-five years' work upon it in the year 1664, angels came by night and rushed the great structure to completion. Nor would Grant's memory ever be haunted as was Wilcox's by the church bells soothing the natives in their sleep, nor by the cries of the night watch calling the hour and the weather, "*Ave Maria! Son las dos, y ventoro!*" — "Hail Mary! it's two o'clock and stormy." [13]

With all his objections to the war, Grant had the healthy male's eagerness to win. He worked on a map of the region, locating roads by quizzing the teamsters and particularly the native scouts — a large band which Scott had recruited from the Puebla jails — outlaws, bandits and political prisoners who were eager now to get, at one swoop, Yankee gold and revenge upon local authorities. At their head rode "Colonel" Manuel Dominguez, most resourceful of them all.[14]

Little by little, across July and August, there came in from Vera Cruz some of the reinforcements which Scott thought had been denied him. In Washington, Polk believed these now brought Scott up to 20,000 men. With water-borne mails so slow, the War Department had not yet grasped the amount of sickness in the army. Even with the arrival of the final brigade of Volunteers in August, Scott could put on parade barely 11,000 of his 14,000 men. In the Puebla hospitals lay 2500 men, in barracks 600 more. Counting the sick at Vera Cruz, a total of 3200 soldiers were incapacitated, many of them doomed to mope around garrisons all summer, derisively calling themselves "Diarrhoea Rangers" or the "Diarrhoea Blues." [15]

With Brigadier General Franklin Pierce, the New Hampshire Democratic leader, bringing 2429 Volunteers on August 6, Scott was ready to march, and he gave orders to commence next day.

It would be Twiggs's turn to lead off — straight for the Halls of the Montezumas.

When the officers saw the garrison from Jalapa among Pierce's men, they knew what Scott had done. He had abandoned the road to Vera Cruz and was doing what the military textbooks at West Point had said a general must never do, cut loose from his base of supplies. Where Cortez had burned his ships behind him, Scott was burning his bridges. Over in London, when the news of the move reached the Duke of Wellington, the old hero of Waterloo would say, "Scott is lost! He has been carried away by successes. He can't take the city, and he can't fall back upon his base." [16]

Pueblans heard wheels on cobblestones in the dark early hours of August 7, then the tramp, tramp of infantry in their new shoes of Mexican cowhide, then the "sharp clattering of iron-hoofed cavalry." Through gratings, the big eyes of the *donazellas* saw the *heréticos* in the gray dawn lining up in the plaza, and at sunrise the ladies wrapped in mantillas filled the balconies as General Twiggs rode into the square to raise his hat and bellow at his division, "Now a regular Cerro Gordo shout!" From his men and from the men of other divisions who packed the square, came an answering whoop. Twiggs roared, "Forward!" The snare drums rolled. The echoes multiplied from one wall of buildings to the other. The march was on. Speaking of himself as the regal "we," Scott wrote, "We had to throw away the scabbard and to advance with the naked blade in hand." [17]

Sam Grant saw his friend Cadmus Wilcox, who had transferred to Twiggs's division as aide to the munificent Quitman, ride down the street and away. Wilcox was thinking that this was the campaign which must not fail; this one was "either victory or a soldier's grave." Ahead were what Scott's staff guessed to be 7000 Mexican regulars and 15,000 irregulars or National Guards, all of whom, if need be, would fight behind walls where they always fought best, and where they would now be fighting for the historic and beloved capital of their land. It was going to be the supreme test of the invaders, who now totaled 10,738. [18]

Grant, in Worth's division, marched out on the ninth, one day behind Quitman, one day ahead of Pillow, whose slight wound at Cerro Gordo had been salved by a Major Generalship from President Polk. With sublime confidence Scott was leaving behind only nine companies of Volunteers, a total of 493 men, to protect 1800 Yankee soldiers in the hospitals from 70,000 Pueblans. Lieutenant Semmes, riding beside Worth, noted that the crowd was so dense "we could scarcely move." Twiggs and Quitman had had no such send-off. Semmes judged, from this and from the "cordial leave-takings," that the Pueblans' imaginations had been touched "by the insouciant nap" Worth's men had taken in the *Plaza Grande* three months before.[19]

Semmes thought Worth admirable in camp the second night out when he sat his horse for two hours in a cold rain until every horse and man had been cared for; "and this was his constant practice. He could never rest, himself, so long as anything remained to be done for his soldiers." Quartermasters like Grant had no time to break out tents from the wagons; the men slept in blankets around huge fires.

Five miles farther next morning; through the mountain mists came an awesome glimpse of something vast and white and mysterious floating ahead, like a glimpse of "an immense inland sea" — then the fog shut down. The men went on. The wagoneers and artillerymen began braking their wheels. The road was turning down. The mists disappeared and there, before them, lay what Cortez's lieutenants had seen — what one of Quitman's men described as "a great garden, dotted with bright lakes, fields of emerald and the white domes and glittering spires of the villages that environ the capital. A valley fifty miles wide, dotted with six large extinct volcanoes far to the south, gleaming with snow — tiny Mexican lancers moving slowly among olive groves and straggling villages." [20]

Scott, who had come to the mountain rim with Quitman the day before, had seen "the object of all our dreams and hopes — our toils and dangers" break upon "our enchanted view." The lakes to him were "pendant diamonds," and Popocatepetl, "apparently near enough to touch with the hand, filled the mind with religious awe." He said to himself, "That splendid city soon shall be ours." [21]

As Garland's men came down the road they saw the white tents of Twiggs and Quitman by the banks of Lake Chalco, thirteen miles to the southeast of the city, and by night they were camped, their own tents raised against the rain.

For the next three days Garland's brigade sat by the waters of Chalco while Scott, from his headquarters at another lakeside point, sent out engineers and dragoons to discover the best approach to the city — whether it be straight down the National Road that ran between Lake Chalco on the south and Lake Texcoco on the north, a route which would bring him to the city's eastern gates, or by a southern route, skirting Chalco and Lake Xochimilco. Mexican cavalry could be seen now and then in the distance, but on Chalco's waters flower women paddled their canoes up to the banks, crying their wares. Lieutenant Semmes always remembered those "tawny, squat expressionless women among the boatloads of flowers." [22]

On one of the days when the Second Dragoons, under Colonel William S. Harney, set out from Worth's camps to explore roads, Grant asked Colonel Garland if he could go along. His wagons were parked, his duties to the camp all completed. Garland, who had had this experience with Grant before, refused to say "Yes" or "No," merely stating that if the force should not be attacked it "was already large enough, and, if it should be attacked, there were already more than we could afford to have killed." Grant, assuming assent, spurred after Harney and came in at the day's end, marveling that they had not been fired on by the Mexican soldiers whom they had passed so closely. "It was a day full of surprises and dangers," friends later heard him say. "In floundering through lagoons and quagmires there was no place on any horse or rider, from the shoes on our horses' feet to the top of our caps, that was not besmeared with mud." When a friend, listening to him tell the story, suggested that the coating of mud made them unrecognizable to the foe, Grant said that "he could not fathom a Mexican's mind, nor account for his failure to shoot at an enemy when he had so good an opportunity." [23]

Finally on August 15, Worth heard that Scott had made up his mind now that all reports were in — the attack would be made by the southern route, the one Worth had recommended. Scott had decided that the defenses between the lakes could not be taken without costly frontal attacks, while those to the south might be taken at less expenditure of life. The southern path was by causeways laid through alternating swamps and impassable rocks.

Grant, poring over his map, disapproved of both routes. He wondered why Scott did not take the army up around Lake Texcoco and the marshes north of it, then circle to the west and come in on the city from the north, down the road past the shrine of Guadalupe — in short, disappear from the front and then reappear in the capital's rear. He wrote home that this would have "avoided all the fortified positions until we reached the gates of the city at their weakest and most indefensible as well as most approachable points." It seemed plain to him that "we would have been on solid ground instead of floundering through morass and ditches and fighting our way over elevated roads, flanked by water where it is generally impossible to deploy forces."

He said he had given his studies of the terrain to his superiors "but I know not whether General Scott was put in possession of the information." Shyly, he asked that the readers of this letter keep it "entirely confidential" since "I am willing to believe that the opinion of a lieutenant, where it differs from that of a commanding General, *must* be founded on *ignorance* of the situation, and you will consider my criticisms accordingly." Forty years later, Grant still believed, in view of all that he had since learned, that his plan would have been less bloody than Scott's, although he admitted "Scott's successes are an answer to all criticism." [24]

Scott's reasons for ignoring this northern route were never clear. Lieutenant Semmes, acting as Worth's aid, declared later that Scott had "not once entertained" the idea. Semmes said, "It would have required us to march thirty miles and more, to reach Guadalupe Hidalgo," a village three miles north of the city, and "it was not known, accurately, what was the nature of the enemy's defenses, in that quarter. At Guadalupe Hidalgo, we should have been met, too, by another causeway, over which it would have been necessary for us to fight our way into the city." [25]

Through the sixteenth and seventeenth, Worth pushed around the southern edge of Lake Xochimilco, filling ditches which the Mexican Army, commandeering neighboring peons, had cut in the road, removing large rocks which had been rolled down from the steep hillside to the left. On one side Mexican sharpshooters fired down, on the other exotic flowers dreamed on the famous floating islands of Xochimilco. Eventually it was C. F. Smith who led his men up through the rocks and drove off the musketeers. Each morning was a blaze of sunshine, each evening a blanket of rain.

When the road rose out of the mud it became a bed of volcanic slag. cutting the soldiers' feet.[26]

From the sleepy village, the Yankees summoned patient peons to come out and fill the ditches they had dug, and remove the rocks they had rolled together. The natives obeyed. It had been like this for generations — Indian armies, Spanish armies, French armies and now a Yankee army — one after another — revolution after revolution — general after general — all alike. Wars came and wars went, and, between times, the frijoles tasted just the same, the flowers were just as red on the adobe walls and Popo just as calm up there against the blue.

The night of the seventeenth, Garland's men spent at the resort town of San Augustín, and next morning pushed up the road between the sedgy western fringes of Lake Xochimilco on their right while on the left frowned the celebrated Pedregal, fifteen square miles of savagely impassable lava beds lying as if in frozen convulsions.

Worth's orders were to demonstrate up this Acapulco Road while the rest of the army passed around south of the Pedregal, and then swinging north to the Contreras turnpike, made a safer flanking approach to the capital.

Worth's advance was nearing the village of San Antonio, three miles from San Augustín, when cannon roared and Captain Seth Thornton fell off his horse dead. Judah, who sometimes spelled as recklessly as did Sam Grant, wrote in his diary, "The first shot cut poor Thornton into." Thornton had climbed out of a sickbed for this fight, still smarting perhaps from the charges made against him after his fiasco at "Thornton's Field" where, eighteen months before, he had started the war.[27]

It was Santa Anna himself who, divining Scott's shift to the southern route, now blocked the Acapulco Road at San Antonio and the Contreras turnpike at the village of Contreras on the southwest edge of the Pedregal.

For two days Garland's men, with the Eighth Infantry, lay before San Antonio, listening to the rest of the army bombarding the mountain breastworks at Contreras. It was, for Grant, Cerro Gordo all over again — standing in reserve while other men, especially the Engineers, now did the work. From a high rock in the Pedregal he peered through field glasses at the fight four miles away.[28] In the early light of the twentieth, it could be seen that the Yankees had won. The Mexicans were fleeing back along the Contreras turnpike toward the capital. Worth now struck too, sending the Fourth Infantry clambering around through the rocks to flank the breastworks ahead. By noon the Mexicans fled, rushing pell-mell toward the Churubusco River two miles away, where Santa Anna had prepared to make the next stand. Soon in their rush Garland's men were joined by the advance from Contreras, and heard details of the two-day fight.

Captain Robert E. Lee had performed what Scott would later conclude to have been "the greatest feat of physical and moral courage performed by any individual, in my knowledge, pending the campaign." Across two days and two nights, through blistering sun, moonlight and wet inky blackness, Lee had threaded his way back and forth across the wild Pedregal, charting the road by which the infantry had flanked the enemy at Contreras. Lieutenant Semmes, hearing Lee make his reports, thought he had a "peculiar talent for topography . . . he seemed to receive impressions intuitively, which it cost other men much labor to acquire." [29]

In the eyes of the men, however, the hero of Contreras was Colonel Bennett Riley, who had led his brigade of Second and Seventh infantrymen over the entrenchments in the dawn attack that had broken Mexican resistance. Grant had heard his classmates Charles Hamilton and Fred Steele tell stories of Riley, who had commanded them at Buffalo Barracks before the war. To Hamilton, Riley was "the finest specimen of physical manhood I ever looked upon . . . six feet two in his stockings, straight as the undrawn bow string . . . broad shouldered, with every limb in perfect proportion, with an eye like an eagle and a step as lithe and springy as the forest tiger." He was sixty now, with a hint of a belly, but he had gone over the breastworks like a boy of seventeen, his voice ringing in that lisping falsetto which his men thought due to a cleft palate and to long residence among Indians on the frontier. Soldiers affectionately mimicked what he had said when the war began: "A yellow thash or thix feet of Mexican earth." They said after Contreras that he was entitled to the yellow sash of a general.[30]

Riley was a different kind of Virginian than the gentlemen Grant had seen, Magruder, Lee, Scott, Johnston, Thomas. Riley was like Jubal Early and Tom Jackson, Virginians from the plain people, more like Westerners. Riley had been a shoemaker before enlisting as a boy for the War of 1812, and the story went that when a genealogically minded man once suggested to him, when he had become famous, that he ought to have his coat of arms drawn up, Riley's Irish temper and humor flared. He told the fellow to clear out, "Because, sir, I never had a coat of any kind till I was twenty-one years old." [31]

Little Lyon had gone over the breastworks in Riley's charge to help take two guns, 200 prisoners — and a brevet captaincy. Charley Hamilton and Longstreet had done things that would win them the same honor. Calvin Benjamin had snatched the Fourth Artillery's flag from a wounded color bearer and had waved it at the head of a charge. Fred Steele in his first fight had won high praise. John P. Johnstone, who had graduated number nine in Grant's class, had been killed working the guns of Magruder's Battery in the First Artillery, and, as he was carried off, the next in line, Tom Jackson, had kept the fire going at a pace which caught the general's eye. Johnstone's death made Captain Lee weep as he took the news to the dead boy's uncle, Joe Johnston, who shivered with grief when he heard it. Captain Johnston had loved this son of his brother, who spelled the name a little differently — loved the boy and expected to make him his heir.[32]

Tom Jackson was happy now that he had joined Magruder's battery after Cerro Gordo, when a vacancy appeared. Other officers had shunned the assignment, for Magruder had a reputation of always being where the fighting was hottest.

One incredible thing had happened: Fitz-John Porter's company of the Fourth Artillery had, in overrunning a Mexican battery, discovered two of the guns to be the very ones which Santa Anna had captured from a battery of the same regiment at Buena Vista. They wept and caressed the black guns as if they were lost children rescued from redskins.[33]

The newest "political brigadier" to join the army, Franklin Pierce, the Democratic leader from New Hampshire, had been hurt in his very first battle. The big black horse which his friends had given him had reared at the explosion of a shell, ground the pommel of the saddle into the General's groin and had then fallen, wrenching its rider's knee. Pierce had fainted from the pain and lain all night unattended in an ammunition wagon. But the soldiers said, "he was on a horse again today, riding forward with his Volunteers, although his face was white from suffering." [34]

Many of the troops at Contreras had won no more honors than Garland's men inching across the Pedregal. The Ninth Infantry, newly arrived, had marched here and there, just missing crucial action, and disappointing privates like Joseph Anthony Mower, a twenty-year-old ship carpenter from Vermont who, after a boyhood spent in hunting danger at sea, had enlisted to seek it in Mexico.

Scott, following his heroes north along the Contreras turnpike through the forenoon of August 20, stopped in a church at San Angel to honor Mexican officers imprisoned there, and as he rode on thought the thoughts he would later put in his formal report: "I doubt whether a more brilliant or decisive victory — taking into view ground, artificial defenses, batteries and the extreme disparity of numbers, without cavalry or artillery on our side — is to be found on record."

His 4500 men had routed "7,000 on the spot and at least 12,000 more hovering within sight and striking distance." Over 700 Mexicans had been killed, more than 800 captured, including 88 officers and 4 generals. The inspectors had counted 22 cannon, 700 pack mules, unguessed quantities of ammunition, shells and the like. Scott's own losses had not yet been computed but they would not go far beyond 100.[35]

As his troops rushed along the roads toward the convent of Churubusco, the next obstacle on the way to the capital, they cheered when they saw his plumed hat, so high on his high body on his high charger. He beamed. They were all his grandchildren and he was losing blissfully few of them to enemy cannon in a campaign which would, he felt, rank with Cortez's. The doors of Montezuma's Halls were opening.

Where be Polk and his plots now?

And where be the Duke of Wellington with his predictions?

CHAPTER FOURTEEN

The Flag on Grasshoppers Hill

THE LATE morning sun of August 20, 1847, shone hot on the green maguey and cornfields that lined the turnpike as the feet of the Fourth Regiment hurried north from San Antonio toward Mexico City.

If Santa Anna were to make another stand this side of the capital, the other regiments of Worth's division, up ahead, would discover it first. Sam Grant, with the Fourth at the rear of the column, suspected as did the other officers, that trouble if it came would be at the point where the maps showed the causeway crossing the Churubusco River, a drainage canal which ran down to Lake Xochimilco on the east. At the left of the road, in front of the river, stood a convent, San Pablo — and convents made stout forts. But there should be no necessity of hard fighting, for, as Grant understood it, Scott was sending Twiggs's division up a parallel road to the west to flank any possible defenders out of the convent before Worth's advance could reach it.

What the officers of the Fourth did not realize was that Worth and Twiggs, having alternated in the lead, were now racing for the capital, and that for the first time since arriving at Vera Cruz the Engineers were now receiving no chance to scout the ground.

Suddenly, a roar of cannon up ahead told the Fourth that the flanking operation had not succeeded and that a fight was on. Lieutenant E. K. Smith, farther on up the column, heard Yankees screaming and "the awful cry of terrified horses and mules." He saw Worth ordering his men off the turnpike into the heavy cornfields. Word came back that Clarke's brigade, leading the column, had been shot to pieces by a sudden blast from the convent and from earthworks, called the *tête du pont*, beside the road at the bridge, and from rows of gunners and riflemen along the high banks on the opposite side of the river.[1]

"We rushed our heads against Churubusco," Dick Ewell wrote home, "and a bloody field it was." Red-haired Lyon, moving up with Twiggs on the left, noted that Worth, "having no share in the glory of Contreras, was determined to bring his division into action under whatever disadvantages," had "blundered upon the tete du pont" and had brought on a battle that with "consequent loss of life was wholly unnecessary." Lieutenant Semmes, carrying orders for Worth, saw one hundred of Clarke's men down inside an acre of trampled corn. The Sixth Regiment, charging down the turnpike, broke, reformed, charged again, broke; and Lieutenant John Sedgwick, coming over from his battery, helped rally the rattled infantrymen for a third attack. A plea to be recalled or reinforced was carried to the rear by Lieutenant Buckner brushing through corn leaves that softly slit and drooped in the leaden hail.[2]

Garland, ordered up with his brigade on the extreme right, thought the fire the hottest he had ever seen — an incessant cross fire coming out of billowing smoke around the convent and entrenchments along the river. Every thirty yards the cornfields were cut by irrigation ditches too wide to jump and too deep to wade. His men grabbed up cornstalks cut by obliging Mexican bullets and filled the ditches, but they did not advance far. Over them rolled shattered companies from up front, fleeing to the rear.

Over to the left Twiggs, abandoning the flanking movement, threw his men head-on against the southwest face of the convent. "Our advance through the corn was necessarily blind and confused," Lyon wrote home, "so that, when within range of the enemy's guns, we were . . . compelled to stand exposed to a fire from men concealed among the maguey plants, behind breast-works, and in the convent." For an hour or more Twiggs held them there, blazing back, while officers, men, artillery horses tumbled and bled.[3]

In an effort to restore his battle to its original plan, Scott sent Generals Pierce and Shields with their men around to the left to turn Santa Anna's right, but the alert Mexican was ready. As the attack failed there, too, Pierce dismounted from his horse and tried hobbling forward up and down the deep ditches, crying "Forward" as he went. All at once his bad knee twisted under him, pain knocked him unconscious and when he regained consciousness he could do no more than lie on his elbow, crying his men on. But the sleet was too deadly, and they clung cowering in the ditches. By three o'clock, Hitchcock, standing beside Scott, saw through his spyglass that the crisis had come. Scott had put in his last man on the field — 6000 against 18,000 — and four of his generals on the semicircle had been stopped. "We must succeed or the army is lost," Hitchcock said to himself.[4]

Officers were dying fast, as from convent windows and from earthworks beside the river bridge, the San Patricio deserters picked off the Yankee disciplinarians whom they hated so bitterly. They had the advantage, one soldier said, of "knowing our way of drilling."[5]

All at once the stalemate broke. Worth noted that the enemy fire was slackening somewhat — due, as it was afterward learned, to lack of ammunition — borrowed a brigade from Pillow and, adding it to his division, sent everybody forward with a whoop. Major Francis Lee, commanding the Fourth, led it in, followed by companies which, with the exception of Captain Buchanan's, were commanded by lieutenants. All other captains were absent, sick or on assignment, and had been so since Vera Cruz. Grant as usual was in the fight instead of at the rear with his wagons. Buchanan was the first of the regiment to cross the river and to storm up the opposite bank as it struck the Mexican line to the right of the bridge. All along the stream the Mexicans broke. Longstreet was one of the two to plant the flag on earthworks at the left of the Fourth. George Pickett clambered up close behind. Worth's men divided, some gathering in prisoners, some turning captured cannons on the fugitives. Others, splashing back across the river to take the convent in the rear, arrived just as Twiggs's men, reaching the front doors, were met by the San Patricio deserters who swung clubbed muskets. These men "fighting with a halter around their necks" fought hardest against Dominguez's "Spy Company" which was early at the convent doors — two rival bands of deserters, asking no quarter and giving none. In the end some eight of the San Patricio Battalion, including Captain Riley, surrendered and, after officers had saved them from the vengeful bayonets of former brother privates, were hustled off to the prison camp at San Angel.[6]

After the Mexicans, who were fleeing up the road to the city, Colonel Harney sent two companies of Dragoons. Mayne Reid, an

Irish soldier of fortune serving as Second Lieutenant in the First New York Volunteer Infantry, saw the cavalcade sweep past Garland's men at the bridge, all the horses matched iron grays, each horse burying its snorting nostrils in the spreading tail of the animal ahead — each Dragoon with his saber sloping back across his right shoulder, and, riding ahead, the hawk-nosed Captain Philip Kearny, nephew of the famous General Stephen Kearny who had run the Mexicans out of New Mexico.

A rich, imperious, and willful descendant of Irish and Dutch aristocrats of New York and New Jersey, impetuous in everything including love and war, Kearny either ignored or failed to hear the bugle with which Harney soon recalled him. Spurring beside him, Dick Ewell heard no recall and as the party caught up with the fugitives at the gate called San Antonio Garita, he was slashing right and left with his saber when suddenly the crowd opened and he saw a piece of artillery frowning over the works. Looking around, he saw to his horror all the Dragoons except himself, Kearny, four or five officers and a handful of men, retiring down the road.

At that moment the cannon belched and Dick's horse went down. Scrambling away unhurt he leaped upon another horse which was bleeding. Near him Kearny, his left arm shattered, was clinging to his horse as it plunged away through clubbed muskets and snatching hands. Ewell and those who were unharmed helped Kearny and two more wounded officers escape. "Only a miracle saved Captain Kearny and myself," he wrote home.[7]

While surgeons were sawing off Kearny's arm in camp that night, his exploit made more talk than May's the night after Palo Alto. Everywhere officers were saying that if the infantry had followed the retiring Mexicans as diligently as Kearny, or if the whole army had moved directly against the city gates instead of blundering against Churubusco, the capital would have fallen. Kearny and his men had actually been inside the Garita for a few moments.

As the Yankee army rested that night, its officers, adding up reports, found that in the two days' fighting at Contreras and Churubusco, 1052 men had been shot down. Fourteen officers had been killed, 62 wounded, while from the rank and file 123 had been killed, 815 wounded — and 38 were missing.

The soldiers had time to rehash the battles, for on the twenty-first, Scott, wanting to end the war without further bloodshed, began negotiations with Santa Anna which soon developed into an armistice that would last until September 7, so that Trist might talk peace with Mexican delegates.

Grant, in later years, would come to think that Scott's decision to fight at Churubusco had been right — at least he regarded Scott's general strategy as proper — but at the time he was more critical, writing back to the States: "If Santa Anna does not surrender the city, or peace be negotiated, much more hard fighting may be expected. My observations convince me that we have other strong works to reduce before we can enter the city. Our position is such that we cannot avoid these." He felt now, more than ever, that if Scott had moved in by the northern route most of this heavy fighting could have been avoided.[8]

In their tented camps the soldiers wondered what Scott would do next. He had not seized the city, the army was down to a scant 7000, and Santa Anna was rumored to be using the armistice to strengthen the defenses at all the gates. More important to many young officers were the brevet promotions that had been recommended for gallantry in the two-day fight. Word was passed that of Grant's classmates, Fred Dent, Fred Steele and Jarvis were to go up to first lieutenant — but not Sam Grant. Of the thirty-four members of the Class of '43 who were still in uniform, six were now captains, nineteen first lieutenants, nine second lieutenants. Grant had gone into every possible fight — gone in beyond the call of a quartermaster's duty — and yet he was nearer the bottom of his class than at any time since he had entered West Point.

Major Lee was preparing to commend by name every officer in the Fourth and to end the list with "And Lieutenant Grant, regimental quartermaster, who was usefully employed in his appropriate duties."[9]

It was faint praise compared with that which, in other regiments, was making brevet majors out of Buell and Van Dorn, captains of Longstreet, Lyon, Dan Hill, Gustavus Smith, Tom Jackson and first lieutenants out of Grant's juniors such as Hancock, Buckner, McClellan, Foster and Granger. The Fourth rejoiced to hear that Colonel Garland was recommended for a brevet brigadier generalship.

Through the long armistice Grant fed his regiment on food bought from the natives or from the city itself, the agreement with Santa Anna providing for wagonloads to be brought out. No long trips could be made into the country since it was said the cavalry of "The Pinto General," Alvarez, would not recognize the truce. There was much talk in the camps of Alvarez's Pintos whose skin was spotted with a species of leprosy peculiar to the region, Acapulco, from which they came.[10]

By the morning of September 7, Grant knew that it was to be hard fighting rather than peace. Scott, discovering that Santa Anna had never intended the armistice to be anything but a period of recuperation, broke off negotiations and ordered Worth to seize, that very night, the principal Mexican defense still left outside the city, a half-mile chain of entrenchments and batteries that lay at the foot of the city's chief fortress, Chapultepec. "The Hill of the Grasshoppers," the Mexicans called it. This hill — which Scott, and the Mexicans, believed to be the key to the city — rose two hundred feet above the cornfields and villages which lay on the plain. Batteries could be seen, through field glasses, dotting its brow and piercing the building which surmounted it, the Military College, Mexico's West Point.

Scott was undecided where to attack the city, by the two gates on the south, at one of which Kearny had made his famous dash, or by the two gates on the west, the Belén Garita at the southwestern, and the San Cosme Garita at the northwestern corner of the town. Roads to both of these western gates ran from Chapultepec, fine causeways which were in reality double carriage roads, since heavy masonry aqueducts ran down the middle of each, providing Mexico City with water.

Whether he should conclude eventually to attack by the west or the south, in either case Scott wanted those defenses at the foot of Chapultepec. At the right, these entrenchments were anchored in a group of low stone buildings called El Molino del Rey (the King's Mill); at the left, in a single building of solid strength, Casa Mata. Spies had told Scott that in Molino Santa Anna was turning bronze church bells into cannon and that a surprise attack could halt this work.

Grant heard that Scott had ordered Worth to "plan and execute" the raid in his own way. The only stipulations were that the attack should be at night and that Worth must not rush on, as he always wanted to do, and try Chapultepec after swarming over Molino.[11]

Worth's way was to postpone the night attack which Scott had proposed and to say that he would move on the morning of the eighth; there would be no chance in the darkness for the artillery to give the infantry columns proper support.

Grant with the Fourth Regiment moved out at three o'clock in the morning to a position where, from the right, they could support the storming party of 500 men who had been picked from various regiments in Worth's division, and who were to be led by Major George Wright of the Eighth Infantry. Clarke's brigade, under Old Tosh, Major McIntosh (Clarke was sick), was to support from the left. Slowly the tropical blackness faded and at five o'clock Molino's stone buildings glowed white up ahead. The bombardment, for which the attack had been postponed, now began, but it was only two 24-pounders that barked in the dawn. Ten shots apiece — then they stopped — and Wright's men ran forward.

The shelling had been absurdly brief. Had Worth discovered the buildings to be lightly defended, or was he yielding to his old passion for the bayonet? Some men who studied him suspected that he was thinking of glory, planning to take Molino with a rush, then sweep on, overwhelm Chapultepec and thus, at one bound, astound both Santa Anna and Winfield Scott.

Whatever Worth might have planned was quickly proved wrong, for the whole Mexican front blazed with cannon and muskets. Within five minutes Wright lost ten of his thirteen officers and a good half of his men. The survivors came tumbling back, chased by Mexican bayonets. Up galloped Duncan with his guns, wheeled and, as Wright's men rallied behind him, sent enough grapeshot into the enemy to send them scampering back to their breastworks and stone walls.

Worth called McIntosh on the left to charge Casa Mata and in almost as short a time, this brigade came scrambling back too, shot to pieces. Old Tosh was down, badly hit. His second in command, Colonel Martin Scott, had suddenly heaved his heavy body into the air with a grunt as a bullet cut through his heart. The next in line, Major Carlos White, also fell seriously wounded. Scott's Inspector General, Colonel Hitchcock, hurrying to the scene of the disaster, saw Captain William Chapman come out weeping, as he pointed to the pitiful remnant of the regiment and sob, "There's the Fifth." Seven of the regiment's fourteen officers were dead.[12]

To collapse Worth's scheme still further, there now threatened, on the left, clouds of General Alvarez's Pinto cavalry. Again it was Duncan who sent over some of his guns to this new front and blew the Pintos back. But when Major Edwin Vose Sumner led 250 Dragoons into that sector, he came within range of the heavy guns on Chapultepec and had 44 men shot out of their saddles.

It was the bitterest moment any of Scott's men had seen since the war began. But Worth, his haughty face masking whatever chagrin he might be feeling, had his batteries give the Mexican line the kind of bombardment it should have had in the beginning, and when that job had been thoroughly done he put in all the rest of the 3100 men with which he had started the day.

Grant, with the Fourth, of Garland's brigade, was on the right as it moved up. Ahead of it galloped Captain Drum with his horse guns to stop within 200 yards of Molino and unlimber.

Before he could unhitch his horses, Mexican grapeshot did it for him. His men cut the writhing, screaming animals out of their harness, then by hand ran the guns up three hundred feet more to a point where their canister could rip up and down the length of the entrenchment ditches as well as blanket the windows of the Mills.

Under cover of this fusillade, the Fourth Infantry dashed forward but ahead of it flashed four companies of C. F. Smith's battalion, Fred Dent in the lead. Smith, the great leader of charges, was sick today, and Captain E. Kirby Smith, taking command, was at Dent's heels as the force ran over a Mexican battery in front of the Mills and then darted in through a gateway between two of the buildings. With clubbed musket, Fred led a squad in clearing the roof of one building, then charged a nearby gun, seizing a moment when the Mexican cannoneers wavered at the sight of another Yankee regiment, probably the Fourth, which was nearing the gateway. From other building tops, there came such a blast of musket balls that Fred's command — all but a sergeant and one private — quit the charge and sought shelter. But Fred kept on, and with his two companions took the gun. The Mexican gunners who had fled, now turned back upon the three. Fred sent one of his two companions for help and stood his ground, "with one foot on the trail" as he afterward reported it, "determined to hold the gun until my men came up, or die." He felt a musket ball strike his thigh, then hot blood running down his leg. He grew faint. He saw his captain, E. Kirby Smith, with some men bolt past him, routing the enemy, then he crept away to a stone wall, climbed over it and lay there, not knowing till later that Smith had caught a bullet, too, and had been carried away to die.[13]

Meanwhile Sam Grant was seeing men fall all around him as Garland's troops, mixed with the Eleventh Infantry and various artillerymen, fought their way through the earthworks in front of the Mills, Sidney Smith down with a wound that would not prove serious, Captain Robert Anderson, the admired Kentuckian in the Third Artillery, down with a ball through his shoulder, and Grant's former commander, Colonel Graham, down with his tenth successive wound. Graham had kept coming on till that last bullet flicked his life away.

"Look out!" Grant yelled through the smoke as he saw a Mexican about to sink a bayonet in the back of Garland's aide-de-camp, Captain Hermann Thorn. The Captain sprang out of the way and shot his assailant through the head just as a sergeant of the Fourth ran his sword through the "greaser's" body. Then Grant, Thorn and the sergeant ran on in among the buildings, Grant recalling later that he was "one of the earliest to arrive." Seeing that the Mexicans had begun to run away, off toward Chapultepec, he darted around behind the building hoping to cut some of them off. His eye caught a group of them on the roof:

> I took a few soldiers, and had a cart that happened to be standing near brought up, and, placing the shafts against the wall and chocking the wheels so that the cart could not back, used the shafts as a sort of ladder extending to within three or four feet of the top. By this I climbed to the roof of the building, followed by a few men, but found a private soldier had preceded me by some other way. There were still quite a number of Mexicans on the roof, among them a major and five or six officers of lower grades. . . . They still had their arms, while the soldier before mentioned was walking as sentry, guarding the prisoners he had *surrounded*, all by himself. I halted the

sentinel, received the swords from the commissioned officers, and proceeded, with the assistance of the soldiers now with me, to disable the muskets by striking them against the edge of the wall, and throw them to the ground.[14]

It was almost as good a joke on himself as the time he had bagged the already captured Mexicans at Resaca de la Palma.

At some moment in the hurly-burly, probably as the shooting was dying out, Grant came upon Fred Dent lying beside the stone wall. He looked at Fred's wound, decided it was not serious and lifted him up on the flat top of the wall so that the surgeons would not miss him when they came up. Then Grant rushed on. Within a few minutes Fred accidentally rolled off, breaking a bone or two and, as he liked to remind Grant, later on, becoming "much worse injured by the fall than . . . by his wound." According to a story told in after years, Fred had concluded, either before or after Sam had "rescued" him, that he was doomed to die unidentified, and had tried to scratch his name on a dismantled cannon with the point of his sword. He had gotten as far as the first letter of his name when he lost consciousness. Surgeons found him; his wound healed quickly, all the quicker, perhaps, after news came that he had been recommended for a brevet captaincy, his second promotion within twelve days. Grant's letter about the wound "kept Mother from worrying," Emmy Dent observed.[15]

By eight o'clock in the morning an end had come to the battle which many young officers condemned, Charley Hamilton describing it as "utter inbecility," Hitchcock saying that Worth had "made the assault blindly" and Lyon writing home that "a proper use of heavy artillery by Worth," of which there was abundance, "would have obtained all that was desired, without the loss of a single man." By contrast old army officers boasted that their ancient trust in the bayonet had been justified — artillery might help in the open field but when walls were to be stormed, steel was still the thing. The common soldiers agreed with the young officers. John Sedgwick wrote his father that soon after the battle some of the men who had fought most gallantly deserted "so desperate they thought our situation." Chapultepec was still to be taken. Nothing of importance had been gained and 798, 58 of them officers, had been killed or wounded. "A few more such victories and this army would be destroyed," Hitchcock wrote in his diary. Scott tried to relieve the gloom of his infantry by telling them, "I am an idiot to bring artillery so far, and at such an expense, when I have such soldiers." [16]

As complete information was assembled it was seen that if Worth, in his pride, had blundered, Scott had been fooled. There were no cannon in the foundry, and no church bells, either, merely some old cannon molds. As if to mock Scott, there came from the city next morning the caroling of innumerable church bells ringing for victory. The Mexicans believed the whole assault had been aimed at Chapultepec and had been broken on the walls of that outwork, Molino del Rey.

There was mourning for the rough, old illiterate Major Martin Scott. Charley Hamilton, who had been hit in the arm soon after his major fell, thought how strangely the old man behaved last night. Always on the eve of other battles Martin Scott had laughed, saying that the bullet that would kill him had never been molded. But last night he had been curiously sad, saying, "We shall be whipped! We shall be cut to pieces." And he had seemed to be in a daze all morning, too. Now he was dead and the news would be reminding people in his native Vermont what a crack rifleshot he had been as a boy and how a raccoon in a tree had once called to him, "You needn't fire; I'll come down!" [17]

To depress the men still more came the grisly news that the first batch of the San Patricio deserters were being punished at San Angel. At a general court-martial on September 8, eighty of these prisoners had been found guilty, fifty-four being sentenced to death for "desertion to the enemy," while some thirty were let off with lighter sentences because they had deserted under various extenuating circumstances before the declaration of war. Most of the latter had been sentenced to be flogged, branded with letter D on the cheek and imprisoned at hard labor until peace should be declared. [18]

In the camps around Molino the men heard that eighteen were being hanged and thirty flogged at San Angel, four more were to be strung up at Mixcoac tomorrow and the final batch, twenty-eight or thirty, hanged at the same place on the thirteenth. [19]

The eighteen were brought in wagons under the scaffolds that had been set up beside the beautiful church at San Angel. The ropes were adjusted, the dooming words spoken, a drum tapped and the wagons rolled away, leaving the trussed men to dangle and choke. Next had come the lighter punishments. Thomas Riley, stripped to the waist, was given fifty lashes by two Mexicans wielding bull-whips. His comrades received in turn fifty or twenty-five. Next hot irons burned the letter *D* into the right cheeks of the bleeding men. Officers, examining Riley's brand, discovered that the *D* had been put on upside down. The iron was applied again right side up to a new place between the cheek and the nose.[20]

To the Mexican people, who regarded hanging as a blasphemous mockery of "Christ crucified," the executions were one more proof that the North Americans were *paganos*. The Mexican newspaper, *Diario del Gobierno* next day, September 10, told its readers how the wife of the British minister, as well as other foreigners, had pleaded for the lives of those deserters who were British citizens, but that "these Caribs, (cannibals) from an impulse of superstition, and after the manner of savages . . . have hung up these men as a holocaust." It lied wildly in describing how the prisoners had been "strangled by their own weight . . . their horrible agony lasted more than one hour" and how the head of "the brave Captain Reilli" had been stuck on a pike and planted at Churubusco. The myth of Riley's "death" was still circulating in Mexico after the war when the fellow, having been discharged from prison, was vainly suing the United States Government in the District of Columbia for $50,000 damages done him as a British citizen.[21]

Charley Hamilton, nursing his wound in the hospital at San Angel, watched the hangings from his window. Near him lay Colonel McIntosh alternately cursing and praying and one day Charley heard the illiterate, gallant old man praying so loudly that Surgeon Benjamin F. Harney, brother of the famous Dragoon commander, came stamping in to say, "Old Tosh, what in hell are you about? If you're going to die, why don't you die game and not make a damned fool of yourself?" McIntosh quit praying, shook his fist in the doctor's face and bellowed, "Damn your old soul, why didn't you come when I sent for you." [22]

Through September 9, the army rested and buried its dead. Worth, whose division had lost over 25 percent in Molino's fire, stood with his officers while chaplains spoke "ashes to ashes" over graves, and while bugles lamented and cannon tolled, Chapultepec's cliff echoed the salutes. Mexicans crowded the battlements looking down on the *heréticos.*[23]

That night Scott asked his generals and engineers where the final assault should be made. Worth stayed away from the council, growling that all the slaughter had not been his fault — the assignment had been, itself, responsible. Captain Lee argued for the southern approach, although this would mean attacking along causeways flanked by wet marshes. He thought he could plant enough batteries in the fields to silence the enemy fire. The Volunteer generals agreed. Scott, Twiggs and Bennett Riley argued for the western entrance by way of Chapultepec. Joe Hooker, sitting in the conference, heard Scott say that "he would have more elbow room at Chapultepec and that he had reason to believe he would be met by a white flag on taking it." General Riley favored this route because it would require less entrenching and more fighting. Last and youngest of all, Beauregard spoke for Chapultepec. Take it, and one part of the army could sweep down the road that led to the Belén Gate while another part could charge along the second causeway to the San Cosme Gate.

They all listened to Beauregard, and Franklin Pierce, who, as a successful lawyer, knew a good plea when he heard one, changed his vote to Chapultepec. Scott ended the council with "Gentlemen, we shall attack by the western gates." [24]

Through the night of September 11, the Engineers took cannon close to Chapultepec and on the twelfth, bombardment raged. Next morning at five o'clock Worth's men moved up, halted just out of cannon range, and stood waiting while the Volunteer divisions of Pillow and Quitman charged the hill. It was the Volunteers' turn after what the Regulars had gone through at Molino.

With whoops they charged up from the south and west, rushing through a great grove of cypress trees, some of which they noted were fifty feet in circumference and must have been there when Montezuma and his women lolled in their shade of long afternoons, looking at the flowers and birds and slipping in and out of the bathing pools. The grove, the hills, the cornfields were so quickly torn by Chapultepec's guns that Pillow quickly called for reinforcements. He had been hit in the foot and his men had forgotten the ladders with which they were to climb up the cliff. They cowered at its base, waiting. Shields was hit in the arm and his men were also stalled by the enemy fire. Scott sent the light batteries forward to shell the hill at point-blank range. Worth ordered Clarke's brigade to bolster Pillow, and Garland's brigade to circle around north of Chapultepec and block the San Cosme route against reinforcements coming in or Chapultepec's defenders running out.

Grant, with Garland, could see Scott's plan. As soon as Chapultepec fell, the Volunteers were to push down the southwestern causeway to the Belén Gate and hold there, since it was the strongest of the *garitas*, as the Mexicans called their gates, while Worth went northward to strike the main blow at the weakest gate, San Cosme.

Each foot of the way Grant was learning how officers behaved in battle. As he swung with Garland's brigade past the embattled hill and headed north toward the road, there loomed ahead a desperate tableau — one tall boy, an officer, walking up and down in a storm of bullets beside a deserted cannon and shouting something toward the bushes and rocks nearby. Around the lone figure were piled men and horses, dead or kicking.

Coming closer, Garland's men saw that it was Tom Jackson, who had pushed his gun so far up on the north side of Chapultepec that it had run into heavy fire from the north defenses of the hill and from a trench in the road ahead. His gunners, unable to stand their losses, had tumbled into the rocks for shelter. He was calling to them to come back: "There's no danger! See, I'm not hit!"

General Worth, arriving close behind Garland, ordered Jackson out, but the fellow, who had no more sense of humor than of danger, sent back word that it was more perilous to retire than to stay where he was. If someone would send him fifty soldiers he would try and take the barricade on the road ahead.

Instead of resenting this disobedience, Worth put Jackson down in his report as having "continued chivalrously at his post, combating with noble courage." Worth sent Garland's brigade around to the left to flank the troublesome barricade, and as Grant and the others went by, it was seen that Jackson had coaxed a sergeant out of hiding and the two of them had the gun going again. Also Jackson's commander, "Prince John" Magruder, came up with another gun just as the Mexican fire began to slacken.[25]

This meant to Garland's men, on the plain below, that the Volunteers had got their ladders at last and were now up on the hill, over-whelming the defenders. Soon Mexicans came rushing out along the San Cosme route and, across the fields, still more could be seen fall-ing back toward the Belén Gate.

Chapultepec had fallen.

It was now a race for the capital, Worth against Quitman, with Quitman having the shorter route by a good half mile.

Worth, who could be generous when the fury of battle was on him, stopped his own advance to help Quitman when he saw that the Mexicans were forming a line in the fields between the two roads — a line whose left lay strongly on the Belén road. Quickly he sent C. F. Smith's battalion and Duncan's guns to smash the line and free his rival.

On top of the Military College surmounting the Hill of the Grass-hoppers, the soldiers looking back saw the Mexican flag come flut-tering down and two flags go up, one the Stars and Stripes, the other Quitman's. A wild yell broke out and spread as the men turned down the road, toward what they now felt sure would be the final fight of the war. To join Garland came the first of Clarke's brigade, from Chapultepec, to tell what had happened up there.

When the storming party had made its first rush, and Pillow had been wounded, Pillow's adjutant general and chief of staff, Joe Hooker, had led the way up the wall, rushing recklessly across ground known to be thick with Mexican mines. Hooker seemed to glory in a crisis when it came. The mines hadn't exploded, thanks to carelessness of Mexican officers and to the quickness with which Yankee muskets shot down those who did try to touch them off. Pillow was praising Hooker to the skies, praise which he would later formulate in his report of the battle — "Captain Hooker, . . . with a firmness few but himself possessed, dashed rapidly forward, . . . calling upon his company to follow." Pillow said Hooker all day had been "greatly distinguished . . . by his extraordinary activity, energy, and gallantry." Up under the wall Pillow's men had waited for scaling ladders, and when these came the advance had gone up the west face of Grasshopper Hill while Quitman's men had driven in from the south. Not many of the eight hundred Mexicans who held the hill remained for the hand-to-hand struggle. The artillery fire from below had butchered many before the attack had been made. Surgeon McSherry, climbing up after the storming party, saw Mexicans on the hill "gasping in the last agonies, with their dark faces upturned to the sun, like fish thrown on shore by the angler, writhing and struggling in death." [26]

The last resistance had come in the Military College where some hundred of the cadets battled stoutly. Because of their youthfulness, Santa Anna had ordered them away before the battle began, but they had voted to stay alongside the Regulars. Forty were captured, "pretty little fellows from ten to sixteen years of age," one Yankee war correspondent wrote, "and several of them were killed fighting like demons." A closer tally found that six were killed, one aged thirteen, one fifteen, one seventeen, one eighteen and two nineteen. The eighteen-year-old, Agustín Melgar, had retired fighting up one stairway after another, till he reached the top of the college where, as an eloquent United States army officer later put it, "on the highest roof-top, beneath the splintered staff where floated the green, red, and white tricolor, the last of the plucky students . . . still plied his musket, until the blue tide reached even that eyrie and engulfed him, defiant to the end." [27]

Over Melgar's body, when the New York Volunteers had bayoneted him, stepped Lieutenant George E. Pickett to haul down the Mexican flag and run up the Yankee banners.

The New Yorkers cheered, and heard from the plain below their comrades cheering, too. None of them could hear the strange cheer that was coming up from the plaza of Mixcoac, some two miles across the plain to the south. There on army wagons beneath scaffolds the final twenty-nine of the doomed San Patricio deserters had been standing for two hours, their feet tied, their hands tied, ropes around their necks, their eyes fixed on distant Chapultepec. Colonel Harney had told them, when he had brought them to the place of execution, that they would die the moment the flag which they had abandoned broke out on the Hill of the Grasshoppers. Harney, standing there, tall, spare, "red as a fox about the head and face," was known for harshness toward deserters. In one campaign against the Seminoles in Florida he had had the friendly Indians who served as his scouts carry ropes to intimidate any soldiers who might be contemplating desertion.

In the hot September sun the doomed men of San Patricio stood in the wagons watching the ebb and flow of the distant battle measure their lives. On the wagon seats in front of them, the teamsters watched. Around them the guards and the sight-seers watched. All eyes strained as the far-off smoke puffed up, sank down, belched out again, sometimes hiding the hill altogether.

One hour — two hours — then suddenly through the dimming smoke a flash of red, white and blue!

A cheer leaped out from the guards, the wagonmen, but as one soldier saw, the doomed men instinctively cheered louder than all — theirs made the valley ring! Hands tied, feet tied, their voices were still free — Hail and farewell! Through their cheers cut the voice of Colonel Harney, who was showing "as much sangfroid as a military martinet could put on." The wagons rolled from under them and, now, their throats were tied, too.[28]

CHAPTER FIFTEEN

"The Deed Is Done"

THE COMPARATIVE ease with which Garland's brigade came up onto the road to San Cosme led Grant afterwards to say "in later years, if not at the time, the battles of Molino del Rey and Chapultepec have seemed to me to have been wholly unnecessary." It was clear to him that Worth's troops could have detoured so as to come on the aqueduct road out of range of the guns from Chapultepec.[1]

It was a plan Scott had abandoned when his Engineers told him Chapultepec's mortars commanded the whole region, and because such a move would expose his rear to a sally from the western gates.[2] Lieutenant Grant did not share the Engineers' respect for the mortars and moreover had learned under Taylor that if a general kept the enemy busy enough he need not worry overmuch about his rear.

Grant's objections, in later years, to Scott's strategy were probably those which he formed at the time, since his memory of details of the Mexican War was sharp, detailed and voluminous. They centered around his belief that victory could have been won with less bloodshed. Temperamentally he had no appetite for battles and apparently derived from them none of the straining excitement that was evident in such officers as Duncan, Lyon, Jackson, Lee and Hooker. "I never went into a battle willingly or with enthusiasm," he recalled in time to come. "I was always glad when a battle was over." However, once a battle had begun, his temperament demanded incessant action, endless attack, and he was well out ahead of Garland's brigade as it advanced toward San Cosme, down the double carriage road which was divided into the center by an aqueduct. With a handful of men Grant darted in and out of the ten-foot arches of masonry which supported the water sluice above. Like Indians in a forest they dodged bullets of the retreating Mexicans and worked rapidly forward until sheets of canister announced that the foe was making a stand. Up ahead where the city's suburbs began, the road turned to the right on its way to the San Cosme Garita, and at the angle a barricade's cannon and riflemen on housetops were awaiting the *Yanquis*.[3]

Three other officers who had come this far with Grant seemed content to hold the squad here in the grottoes until the main body of the brigade came up. Lieutenant John Gore was nominally in command, since he had been commissioned in 1838, five years ahead of Grant. Henry Judah, who had graduated with Sam Grant, had only been transferred from the Eighth to the Fourth Infantry the previous year. The third officer, Lieutenant Semmes of the Marines, was a guest.

Grant, however, could not wait, and as if deciding to do in miniature what he thought Scott should have done at Chapultepec and Molino, he set off alone to see what could be done to flank the enemy. Watching his chance, he skipped across the road between gusts of grapeshot and stole forward on the left side of the causeway, working past a silent house, stone walls and trees, until he found himself in the very rear of the barricade, unseen by the riflemen and gunners.

When he had seen enough he hurried back to the grottoes, skipped back into the arched shelter and told his story: if a dozen or so of the men would volunteer to follow him, they could rush the barricade from the rear and give Gore, Judah and Semmes a chance to lead the rest of the party in a frontal attack. Volunteers stepped forward and, as Grant later told it, "commanding them to carry their arms at a trail, I watched our opportunity and got them across the road . . . before the enemy had a shot at us." Cautioning them not to fire until he gave the word, he was leading his little band stealthily along the route when he saw a movement in a ditch!

It was a hundred Second Artillerymen, carrying muskets, whom Garland had ordered forward under Captain Horace Brooks. In the shadow of garden walls Grant explained what he had discovered and what he was about to do. Although Brooks had been on the West Point faculty when Grant had taken his entrance examination, he was not one to stand on ceremony and, waiving rank, told Grant to lead on, he would follow.[4]

As Grant's force burst out upon the road in the rear of the barricade, Gore and Judah charged, Gore describing it later as a race between the two parties. "The moment was a very exciting one," he reported, and he could not tell whether Grant, Judah or himself had been "first to reach the center of the work."

The Mexicans legged it wildly for a second barricade which stood down the road, half way to the main defense at San Cosme Garita. Gore admitted that Grant and Judah were ahead of him in the pursuit that followed, but only because he delayed a moment to care for a wounded man. But he said that he caught up and was, himself, in the lead when the Americans went over the second barricade in a "very severe fire of shot and grape." The chase now stopped, for the Mexicans, quitting their breastwork, scattered among the houses and patios, clearing the road for two cannon which opened upon the Yankees from behind a barricade under the arched gate at San Cosme. Gore and fifteen of his men crouched on the safe side of the captured breastwork. Grant, Judah and Brooks, sheltering their men behind houses on either side of the road, peeped around corners at the prospect ahead. It would be suicide to continue the charge, for if they survived the canister blasts they would come under a musket fire of Mexicans on rooftops along the way, and around San Cosme itself the house walls were loopholed as well as fortified on tops of sandbags.

Again Grant stood, waiting for reinforcements. Why didn't Garland come up with the cannon and the heavy force needed to smash onward? The only help that came was Lieutenant John Sedgwick, who in the absence of his superior officers was in command of the whole Fifth Infantry today. But Sedgwick had only his own company with him here and, since leaving Puebla, it had lost half of its fifty-four men.[5]

There was now no chance for Grant to think of more flanking maneuvers, for a runner came up with orders from Major Lee for everybody to fall back to the Angel, where a battalion was being formed around a battery of howitzers for the main attack. As the party slipped off through the gardens they saw the Mexicans swarm back and reoccupy the breastwork.

When the counterattack was ready, the Fourth was in the forefront, fighting its way along the sides of the road till the breastwork was recaptured. "Lieutenant Grant and myself were the two first persons to gain it," Gore reported. This time the Mexicans retired to San Cosme Garita, content to make it their last stand.

Colonel Garland, massing his forces around the retaken breast-work, withdrew the Fourth to help the Second Artillery find locations from which his light guns could play upon the belching Garita. Thousands of Mexicans were gathered there, Santa Anna commanding. Major Buchanan worked one of the howitzers onto a rooftop and other guns fired from between houses.

An hour went by.

Grant slipped off alone again to weave his way past houses, trees, ditches along the right of the causeway, hunting a path to flank the Garita itself. He was the boy in the Ohio woods once more, seeking new roads, improvising, working out problems for himself. As before he found the Mexicans careless of their flanks. Past empty houses he stole, on and on, until he could hear the Garita's guns directly on his left.

In times to come Grant would tell how he led the party "over ditches breast deep in water and grown up with water plants" till he came to the locked church:

> When I knocked for admission a priest came to the door, who, while extremely polite, declined to admit us. With the little Spanish then at my command, I explained to him that he might save property by opening the door, and he certainly would save himself from becoming a prisoner, for a time at least; and besides, I intended to go in whether he consented or not. He began to see his duty in the same light that I did, and opened the door, though he did not look as if it gave him special pleasure to do so. The gun was carried to the belfry and put together. We were not more than two or three hundred yards from San Cosme. The shots from our little gun dropped in upon the enemy and created great confusion. Why they did not send out a small party and capture us, I do not know. We had no infantry or other defences besides our gun.

By this time Worth had come up to the captured barricade and, studying the Garita through his glasses, saw that something was disturbing the Mexicans. It was the gun in the belfry. As friends got the story later from Grant, Worth sent a staff officer to ask

Garland who it was in the church tower. Garland said he didn't know, but staff officers of the artillery said that Lieutenant Grant had a gun, some gunners and ammunition.

"It sounds like our gun," they said. "It must be Grant and our men." Worth sent his aide, Lieutenant John C. Pemberton, to bring Grant to him, but when the solemn Pennsylvanian came clambering up into the smoking belfry, Grant explained that he was busy and would like permission to report a little later. Pemberton, however, insisted, and Grant, telling the gunners to keep on firing, followed down the stairs and across the ditches to the General. As they came up Grant was both indignant at having been interrupted and concerned as to why "he might be under arrest." Wet, muddy, black with smoke, he saluted.

The General congratulated him, saying that "every shot was effective" and ordered him to take along another gun with its officer and crew. "I could not tell the General," said Grant later, "that there was not room enough in the steeple for another gun, because he probably would have looked upon such a statement as a contradiction from a second lieutenant. I took the captain with me, but did not use his gun." [6]

When the afternoon was half gone, General Scott arrived on the field with the news that Quitman had crashed through the Belén Gate at 1:20 and was clinging to this toe hold inside the city under a terrific fire from fortified houses. Worth increased the pressure on San Cosme, adding cannon fire as more guns came up, and sending Clarke's brigade burrowing through houses north of the causeway.[7]

Lieutenant Semmes managed to bring another mountain howitzer to a roof across the road from Grant's roaring belfry and the customhouse in the Garita rocked under the converging fire from three quarters. By five o'clock runners went back to Worth with the news that Clarke's pickaxemen were now burrowing in houses close to the Garita and would be bursting out onto the roofs at any moment. To prepare for this moment, Worth sent a horse gun straight up the road to blow a hole through the barricade so that a frontal attack could be made. Lieutenant Henry J. Hunt, a Detroit-born scion of a long line of army officers, rode forward beside his gun, nine cannoneers astride the teams or clinging to caisson seats. For 150 yards they breasted the Mexican fire, then as the horses crashed to the pavement, fifty yards from the Garita, cut the trace chains, swung the gun around and, standing out there on the naked road, dueled with the batteries behind the barricade. Hunt and four men were still up when Clarke's men erupted onto the nearby roofs and Worth's infantry swept past on the dead run, bayonets gleaming. Worth was stirred by Hunt, and said, "It has never been my fortune to witness a more brilliant exhibition of courage and conduct." [8]

For a time there was hand-to-hand fighting at the barricade, in the battered customhouse, on the roofs and in the flanking houses. One Yankee officer, long afterward, told how he found in one house several of his own men who had deserted a few days before and having no men to guard them, he had them thrown to death on some rocks below.[9]

Slowly the Mexicans were driven back from the Garita and took refuge in houses along the streets of the city itself, Worth pounding them with their own cannon seized at the last barricade. By eight o'clock Worth's heavy guns were up and he threw eight warning shells high over the houses clear to the Grand Plaza of the capital, where the Government buildings and great cathedral stood.

That night part of his men slept in houses several hundred yards inside the city, while others, Grant among them, tunneled on through buildings so that the new barricades on streets stretching toward the plaza could be flanked in the morning.[10]

All this work was in vain, for at one o'clock in the morning of September 14 councilmen came out to ask Worth, at the Garita, for surrender terms. Worth sent them on to Scott at his headquarters in Tacubaya, two miles outside Chapultepec. In their wake rumor had it that Santa Anna had marched the remnant of his army out to Guadalupe, halting only long enough in the capital to throw open all jail doors. Worth, in that dramatic way of his, declared that these loosed convicts numbered 30,000. Scott estimated them at 2000.[11]

With the dawn Worth marched his men to the Alameda, a green park halfway to the plaza, his howitzers now and then throwing a shell ahead. At the park a messenger from Scott ordered him to halt; the offer of surrender had been accepted. An hour later, another rider brought the order to go ahead. Officers around Scott thought he was making one last attempt to heal a broken friendship by arranging for Worth to be first into Mexico City, as at Vera Cruz.

Colonel Garland rode ahead as Worth pushed his division forward. For a few minutes the only sound was the tramp of infantry shoes and the clatter of horseshoes on the streets which Grant saw were deserted. Then a shot rang from a roof. Garland reeled, badly wounded. More shots followed and the Fourth, with Old Buch in the lead, began smashing in doors with musket butts and bayoneting occupants whom they accepted as murderous convicts from the jails. "This was no time for half-way measures," said Worth.

The shooting stopped and as the column marched on, Lieutenant Semmes, riding beside the haughty Worth, saw the streets become so full of quietly staring Mexicans that the advance at times was forced to halt. When it came to the Grand Plaza, the balconies and housetops were full, and to Worth's dismay the plaza itself was full of Yankee soldiers. Quitman, refusing to wait at Belén Gate as Scott had planned, had rushed in to beat Worth, had reached the plaza at 7 A.M., entered the National Palace with Lieutenant Beauregard at his side, and had his division flag floating from the roof. All around the great square his Volunteers and a company of Marines were drawn up, awaiting Worth. The Marines had now added the Halls of Montezuma to the faraway places they had seen.[12]

Scott arrived at eight o'clock, wearing all the feathers that his rank would permit and followed by his staff and cavalry escort in full dress. His bands played, his troops presented arms and whooped joyously. Even Mexican aristocrats at balcony windows waved handkerchiefs, for the old man was a massive and magnificent spectacle.

Grant's eye happened to catch an aged Mexican general, whom he thought was Rincón, at a church window where Quitman had penned the surrendering high officers. "He uncovered his head," Grant wrote home, "and his countenance lighted up, and his eyes sparkled . . . he forgot that *he* was defeated and a prisoner, and for the moment entered into the enthusiasm of the occasion." [13]

Scott's great bulk came down off his horse; he lifted his plumed chapeau and walked into the National Palace. He stopped in the patio and said to his generals and their staffs, "Gentlemen, we must not be too elated at our success." Then Cadmus Wilcox, bending forward, heard him say: "Let me present to you the civil and military Governor of the City of Mexico, Major General John A. Quitman. I appoint him at this instant. He has earned the distinction and shall have it." [14] Since his plans for Worth had not worked out, he would make the best of the situation.

He led the procession up the grand stairway to the elegant rooms above, stationed Marines around the Palace and strode to and fro with satisfaction on his large face. If any officers smiled now behind his back, they left no record of it, for while it was true that he was strutting and posturing, it was also true that here he was standing as Cortez had stood. Here he was, the first general of the United States to capture a foreign capital — the first great Yankee Conquistador — and a humane one. Since his landing in March at Vera Cruz, he had conducted one of the most remarkable invasions that recent military history could show, a truth pointed up by Quartermaster General Thomas S. Jesup's official statement: "With our nearest depots farther from the sources of supply than Algiers is from Toulon or Marseilles, we accomplished more in the first six months . . . than France, the first military power in Europe, has accomplished in Africa in seventeen years."

Grant summarized Scott's feat tersely. Scott had within six months "invaded a populous country, penetrating 260 miles into the interior, with a force at no time equal to one-half of that opposed to him; he was without a base; the enemy was always intrenched, always on the defensive; yet he won every battle, he captured the capital, and conquered the government." [15]

Having landed with scarcely more than 12,000 men, he could now count a scant 6000 sound soldiers around him. A few hundred were in garrisons at Puebla and Vera Cruz, 2703 were dead or wounded, the rest were sick or had died of disease. He estimated that of the 30,000 Mexicans who had gathered to oppose him, more than 7000 had been killed or wounded. He had captured 3730 men of whom one seventh were officers, including 13 generals and 3 ex-presidents, together with 75 field guns, 57 "all pieces" (fixed guns in fortresses), 20,000 small arms and unguessed shot and shell.

"The war is not ended," he warned his officers as they gathered in the National Palace. "The Mexican Army and Government have fled only to watch an opportunity to return upon us with vengeance." Everyone must remain on guard, sober and alert. "The honor of the army and the honor of our country call for the best behavior on the part of all."

As he ended a musket cracked in the distance — then another — and a third. Cadmus Wilcox saw Scott turn to a junior officer and say, "Will you have the kindness to go and say to our volunteer friends that it is unsoldierlike, bad manners, and dangerous to discharge arms in a city, and say to their officers that it must not occur again. None of us desire, I am sure, to hear more musketry." [16]

As the young officer ran out into the plaza he saw that the Volunteers, in spite of all their sins, were not now to blame. It was the Mexicans, running and shooting in the streets. The jailbirds were bringing their mischief down to the heart of the city, and soon bullets were coming from roofs and windows in a mounting rain. Quitman sent his men into houses and onto roofs and ordered companies to escort rumbling batteries over the entire city. The shooting spread, and all day there was fighting in one section or another. Cannon shattered houses which held sharpshooters. Infantry bayoneted "assassins" in homes, churches and even in some hospitals which the convicts had seized. Jailbirds and Yankees alike looted and smashed.

Lieutenant George B. McClellan, searching a house, saw a Mexican kill a sergeant. He seized the dying man's musket and killed the killer. Leading a detachment of Engineers, he could count by night fall between fifteen and twenty enemies whom they had killed on house-tops. And that night, when comparative peace had returned to the city, he grew quiet in the house where the Engineer officers were quartered. Gustavus Smith offered him a penny for his thoughts. Twenty-year-old Little Mac said he was thinking about all that he had seen since he had left West Point, fourteen months ago — Matamoros, "the graveyard of our forces," Victoria, Tampico, Vera Cruz with its "horrid sand," Pillow's whipped men at Cerro Gordo, the long stay in the monastery at Puebla, the march over the mountains, the battles in the Valley, San Cosme Garita and now the Capital — all that — "And here we are, the deed is done. I'm glad no one can say 'poor Mac' over me." [17]

In another house Sam Grant was sorrowing that night for three friends. Sidney Smith was dying, hit by convicts' bullets as he rode down the street. Longstreet was wounded, no one knew how badly. And Calvin Benjamin was dead — dead at the Belén Gate. Lieutenant Fitz-John Porter who had seen him fall told about it. Benjamin, with his captain, Simon Drum, and a sergeant, had pulled a light cannon up to, then inside, the Garita barricade and was firing it "rapidly and effectively" into the throng of screaming, shooting Mexicans when Drum went down, dead. Benjamin had picked up the body, carried it to the gate, then returned to help the lone sergeant work the gun. But a solid shot had knocked them down, both mortally wounded. The three heroes, said Porter, had worked "as if striving alone to finish the work." Drum's company had gone in that morning numbering between forty and fifty, and had lost twenty-seven.

In Grant's twenty-five years Death had never touched him as closely as in the deaths of Tom Hamer and Benjamin, and long afterward he would speak of how those two "sad events clung to his memory." [18]

News of other officers, as it came, was less serious. Joe Johnston, who was always getting hit, had caught three bullets today, but was still on his feet. Beauregard had been bruised by three spent balls and, while reconnoitering at night with Quitman, had fallen into a canal, the General plumping in right behind him. Captain Robert E. Lee had spent so many days and nights without sleep that he had fainted at Scott's headquarters the afternoon San Cosme fell.[19]

Next day, September 15, the guerilla warfare continued. Señor Juan de la Granja, late consul general for Mexico at New York and now working for quiet in Mexico City, said that "perfect anarchy" reigned for three days in all. "I saw two wagon loads of bodies of Americans killed in the streets. The Americans on the 14th broke open stores and got drunk. These people appear more like brigands than soldiers, they stroll the streets without order with their arms and are ragged and dirty. From the knowledge I have of the people of the United States, I had expected the opposite." [20]

Many Yankees were stabbed to death in the streets at night, lured by women or stupefied by revels in the *pulquerías*, but by the sixteenth open resistance was crushed and within a week the city was quiet. Eager to prevent Mexico from turning into a nation of guerillas, Scott soothed talk of revenge, and as a gesture, sent Santa Anna's eighteen-year-old wife, who had been captured, to the sixty-two-year-old chieftain at his headquarters in Guadalupe. Captain Kenly, seeing her pass, sighed over her "beautiful figure, fair skin, hazel eyes, and lovely Anglo-Saxon face." The story spread among the Yankees that Santa Anna had married her because he had been unable to corrupt her virtue by other means and, even so, had tricked her by having the ceremony performed by one of his own followers, disguised as a chaplain.[21]

Santa Anna proved no problem to Scott, for his prestige was gone and he soon marched away with the remnant of his army.

Grant, at regimental headquarters at Tacubaya in the suburbs, received a shower of promotions — a full first lieutenancy, as of September 16, replacing Sidney Smith, and word that he would be awarded two honors, a brevet first lieutenancy, as of September 8, 1847 "for gallant and meritorious conduct in the Battle of Molino del Rey" and a brevet captaincy, as of September 13, "for gallant conduct at Chapultepec." The brevets were compliments and an indication of the position he was entitled to hold when vacancies should occur, but the full promotion was concrete, a fixed rating. In subsequent years Grant would grow humorous about the first lieutenancy, saying:

> I had gone into the Battle of Palo Alto a second lieutenant and I entered the City of Mexico sixteen months later with the same rank, after having been in all the engagements possible for any one man, and in a regiment that lost more officers during the war than it ever had present at any one engagement. My regiment lost four commissioned officers, all senior to me, by steamboat explosions during the Mexican war. The Mexicans were not so discriminating. They sometimes picked off my juniors.[22]

As a matter of record the Mexicans had killed only one and wounded but two of his juniors, while killing seven and wounding one of his seniors.

On October 25 Sam finished a letter to Julia which he had begun sometime in September after his entry with the army into Mexico City. The date he started must have been later than the fourteenth, because the letter mentions the death of "poor Sidney Smith." But it does not mention the brevet promotions to first lieutenant as of September 8, and to captain, as of September 13:

> Because you have not heard from me for so long a time you must not think that I have neglected to write or in the least forgotten one who is so ever dear to me. For several months no mail has gone to Vera Cruz except such as editors of papers sent by some Mexican they hire and these generally fall into the hands of the enemy who infest the whole line from here to the Sea Coast. Since my last letter to you four of the hardest fought battles that the world ever witnessed have taken place, and the most astonishing victories have crowned the American Arms. But dearly have they paid for it! The loss of officers and men killed and wounded is frightful. Among the wounded you will find Fred's name but he is now walking about and in the course of two weeks more will be entirely well. I saw Fred a moment after he received his wound but escaped myself untouched. It is to be hoped that such fights it will not be our misfortune to witness again during the war, and how can it be? The whole Mexican Army is destroyed or dispersed, they have lost nearly all their artillery and other munitions of war. We are occupying the rich and populous valley from which the great part of their revenues are collected and all their seaports are cut off from them. Everything looks as if peace should be established soon; but perhaps my anxiety to get back to see again my Dearest Julia makes me argue thus. The idea of staying longer in this country is to me insupportable. Just think of the three long years that have passed since we met. My health has always been good, but exposure to weather and a Tropical Sun has added ten years to my apparent age. At this rate I will soon be old.

The realization that the fighting was over threw Scott's officers into new excitement. They awaited now the official reports of their superiors. Glory was the legitimate reward of the soldiers, and if they failed to receive it for deeds done on September 13 and 14 their last opportunity was gone. Especially keen was the hunger to be cited as the first to have entered the enemy's works in this or that action, and, according to a story told eighteen years later by Henry J. Hunt, Sam Grant shared it with the rest.

Hunt said that Grant asked him:

"Didn't you see me go first into that work the other day?" referring to the storming of the first barricade on the San Cosme road.

"Why, no," Hunt replied, "it so happened I didn't see you, though I don't doubt you were in first."

"Well, I *was* in first," Grant declared, "and here Colonel Garland has made no mention of me! The war is nearly done; so there goes the last chance I ever shall have of military distinction!" [23]

To men who knew Grant's nature and his insistence, later on, that he had never asked for promotion, it was apparent that Hunt had exaggerated the conversation for dramatic effect. It was Gore, not Grant, who filed an official protest against the exclusion of his name from reports of the capture of the barricades. And even more damaging to Hunt's story, is the fact that Garland's report, when it appeared, mentioned Grant three times — pointing out his work at the second barricade and in the belfry and, in summary, saying that Grant had "acquitted himself most nobly upon several occasions under my own observation." Other than members of his own personal staff, Haller and Grant were the only young officers singled out for praise by Garland. Grant was receiving, for the last two fights of the war, such praise as he had never won before. Major Francis Lee was citing him and Brooks for their "handsome" actions at the barricades, and both Grant and Judah for "distinguished gallantry on the 13th and 14th." General Worth's report mentioned some twenty officers in the Division and "S. Smith, Haller and Grant especially." Longstreet would tell later how Grant had been "always cool, swift, and unhurried in battle . . . as unconcerned as if it were a hailstorm instead of a storm of bullets. I had occasion to observe his superb courage under fire — so remarkable was his bravery that mention was made of it in the official report, and I heard his colonel say, 'There goes a man of fire.' " [24]

As the reports appeared Longstreet himself was praised by his colonel, W. R. Montgomery, as having been "always in front with the colors," winning the applause of all who saw him for "his high and gallant bearing." The only reason Pickett had raised the flag over Chapultepec was that he snatched it from Longstreet when the latter, who had been leading, went down wounded. Fred Steele had to content himself with Quitman's report that he had been "among" the first upon Chapultepec's battlements, and Fred Dent was officially protesting that reports did not show him arriving as early as he had, in the main building at Molino.

Whether or not Grant was caught up in the clamor for recognition at the war's end, he was not, before or after that time, anyone to be thinking of himself as "a man of fire." In his mind there were no heroes. Some men did their work more promptly and thoroughly than others, and had the luck to be seen doing it by their commanding officers at spectacular moments. Grant's cool head saw that honorary citations were common enough here at the finish, giving men titles yet leaving them low in actual rank. He would now be called "Captain," yet, like twenty-five others of his Class of 1843, he was still a first lieutenant. Five were still second lieutenants, among them Franklin and Deshon, the number one and number two men on graduation day. Orders had kept this pair at home on engineering or ordnance work.

He wrote Julia in October:

> No doubt before this the papers are teeming with accounts of the different battles and the courage and science shown by individuals. Even here one hears of individual exploits (which were never performed) sufficient to account for the taking of Mexico throwing out about four-fifths of the Army to do nothing. One bit of credit need not be given to accounts that are given except those taken from the reports of the different commanders.

Where Grant, according to West Point standards, had stood number twenty-one among thirty-nine classmates, he now was in the top fourth, judged by battle honors, since he and eight others of the thirty-one still in uniform had won two brevets for gallantry and merit. Sixteen of his classmates had received one brevet, and fourteen none at all. In rapidity of advancement he and eleven others stood among the first third, having climbed from a brevet second lieutenancy, at the start of the mobilization, to a brevet captaincy.

But always the sobering thought remained: he would be only a first lieutenant in the shrunken peacetime organization in years to come. It might well take years before he could become an actual captain.

*   *   *

As the citations were published, Grant saw that his old idol, Charles F. Smith, was among a group of four — Smith, of Pennsylvania, Robert E. Lee, of Virginia, Joseph Hooker, of Massachusetts, and James Duncan, of New York — who had each won three brevets and risen to a brevet colonelcy, but were still ranked as captains.

The officer whom Grant, either now at the war's end or later, came to admire most, Joseph E. Johnston of Virginia, had received only two brevets but had climbed from the rank of first lieutenant to a full lieutenant colonelcy in less than a year. Up with Taylor on the Rio Grande, Braxton Bragg of North Carolina had received three brevets and climbed from first lieutenant to brevet colonel, yet on the rolls was still the "Captain Bragg" whom Old Zach, at Buena Vista, had requested to give the Mexicans "a little more grape." Fighting alongside Bragg, George H. Thomas of Virginia had won two brevets and become a brevet major, yet at the war's end was the same first lieutenant that he had been before it started.

Among the younger officers, Don Carlos Buell and Roswell Ripley of Ohio, D. H. Hill of South Carolina, Tom Jackson of Virginia and Fitz-John Porter of New Hampshire had each won two brevets and become brevet majors, yet were still first lieutenants. Tom Jackson's rise in the field of honors had been the most spectacular in the army — a West Point graduate in July 1846, a brevet major in September 1847, all within fourteen months. (But Johnston after the war called Hill "the bravest man in the army.") [25]

Buell's name was being mentioned when officers guessed who among them would go furthest. Joe Hooker would say, in after times, that the three young officers "who were foremost in the estimation of the Army" were Buell, Thomas and Bragg. William T. Sherman — who had been breveted a captain for service as a staff officer in the relatively bloodless conquest of California — would later describe Buell as "one of the best, if not the best, practical soldier of our army." [26]

As the officers talked in the evenings about what the war had done for them, someone would fall to wondering if Randolph Ridgely, long moldering in his grave at Monterey, might not by now have outstripped them all.

CHAPTER SIXTEEN

"Spanish Is for Lovers"

THE OFFICERS of the Fourth Regiment saw that Sam Grant was in an awkward position. A young Mexican who had become attached to him since they had settled in Mexico City, some weeks before, wanted desperately to ride the magnificent horse which belonged to Lieutenant Henry Prince, and he expected Grant to arrange it.

"I was afraid he couldn't ride him," Grant said later; the horse was a fiery one and from what Grant had seen of the young Mexican's horsemanship, on many rides, the project was a dangerous one. Yet Grant could not refuse because, as he said, "the suspicious Spanish nature would interpret any suggestion of caution as a mere disguise of ungenerosity." Grant was sensitive about hurting other people's feelings; the boy who had been a peacemaker was becoming a man who couldn't say "No" to his friends.

And not only the young Mexican but the young Mexican's uncle were his personal friends. The uncle was the priest in charge of the Convent of San Isabel where the Fourth's officers were billeted. He had stoutly refused to open the door the first day when they had arrived and they had had to splinter their way through with axes; but once he had got to know them, he had melted. He and the Sisters, who were under his wing, had found the invaders not only agreeable but a definite protection against marauding *léperos* or tipsy Volunteers. First he had taken an especial liking to Lieutenant Grant, then to the other officers, and had introduced them to his nephew, whom they thought bright and engaging.

In the end, Grant solved the situation by weakening, making the arrangement with Prince, who was recuperating from a wound; and after a dinner at the regimental mess, where the officers made much of the nephew, the ride began. Not long after the two riders had clattered away, word came that the Mexican was dead. He had lost his head when the horse ran away, had pulled too hard on one

rein, causing the animal to swerve off the causeway and over a
ditch, throwing his rider against a tree. Grant was carrying the body
to the parents' home. The officers hurried to the scene, Prince saying afterward that the lamentations of the young man's mother
touched him deeply. Most of them accompanied Grant to the
funeral and, like him, knelt, candle in hand, during the long church
service.[1]

Sadness was, however, rare among the officers as they waited
during the autumn of 1847 for peace negotiations to begin. It
amused Grant to note that "it looked doubtful for a time whether
the United States Commissioner, Mr. Trist, could find anybody to
negotiate with." Santa Anna, after a weak attempt to besiege Puebla,
had thrown up the Presidency and was hiding somewhere in the
hills. Mexican leaders at Querétaro were trying to elect an Acting
President. The Yankees knew that the war was over and although
they wanted to get home, "they contented themselves," as Grant
said, "as best they could." Nobody worried when it was discovered
that of the 3000 prisoners who had been captured in the battles
around the city, more than half had escaped. Scott had refrained
from jailing them like convicts, and it was easy to walk off from
the lightly guarded churches and homes in which they were kept.[2]

Sam, like many of his fellow officers, admired Mexico City and
had written Julia shortly after the occupation:

> Mexico is one of the most beautiful cities in the world and
> being the capital no wonder that the Mexicans should have
> fought desperately to save it. But they deserve no credit. They
> fought us with every advantage on their side. They doubled
> us in numbers, doubled us and more in artillery, they behind
> strong breast-works had every advantage and then they were
> fighting for their homes. It is truly a great country. No coun-
> try was ever so blessed by nature. There is no fruit nor no
> grain that can't be raised here, nor no [sic] temperature that
> can't be found at any season. You have only to choose the
> degree of elevation to find perpetual snow or the hottest
> summer. But with all these advantages how anxious I am to
> get out of Mexico. You can readily solve the problem of my
> discontent Julia. If you were but here and I in the United
> States my anxiety would be just as great to come to Mexico
> as it now is to get out.

The Yankee soldiers quartered in the city, or scattered, company by company, across towns within a fifty mile radius, made friends with the natives, particularly with the aristocrats and large owners of property who openly said they wished the Yankees would stay until Mexico could be freed permanently from the chronic series of military despotisms and revolutions.

Two of Grant's friends, Longstreet and Tom Jackson, were being charmed by their hosts. Longstreet was healing his Chapultepec wounds and eating delicacies in the home of the Escandóns, a "refined Mexican family." Jackson, for whose "sincere and manly character" Sam Grant had had a growing respect and of whom he later said "personally we were always good friends," was billeted in a monastery, enjoying coffee in bed for the first time in his hard-bitten life, and learning Spanish from the scholarly monks who sat with him in the flower-hung patio. He developed an interest in religion and had several talks with the Archbishop of Mexico.

In the home of the "old Castilian noblesse" his ungainly feet learned the waltz. He fell in love with the country as a whole and with one *señorita* in particular. He thought of marrying and remaining in this enchanted land forever, but the hard ridges of western Virginia were in his spine, and Puritan austerity was in his blood, so he finally quit seeing the *señorita* and, as his relatives subsequently put it, "escaped capture." But every so often, across the rest of his life, he would say, "Spanish was meant for lovers." [3]

Grant was still known to his comrades as "pure-minded," although sex was freer now in Mexico City than at any time during the invasion. The Yankee-run Bella Unión Hotel was a rendezvous for assignations. Surgeon McSherry noted how the numerous French *modistas* of the city welcomed "*Messieurs les jeunes officiers Americains*," at the dances they gave every Sunday night in a former convent in Belemitas street, and how they "surrendered to them unconditionally, after a very trifling resistance." John Sedgwick, losing his money when his valise was stolen, was one of the many officers plagued by the *léperos*, the worst class of Mexicans, who lived by begging and crime. Early in November 1847 a mob of *léperos* had been sabered by dragoons when they tried to rescue some of their criminal comrades who were being flogged in the *Plaza Grande*, and the *North American* had thundered, "The life of one of our soldiers

is worth more than a thousand of these lousy, blanketed miscreants."
Through the winter and spring of 1848, soldiers and *léperos* died
now and then in knife fights in the low grogshops. Guerillas occasionally harassed the road which Scott had opened to Vera Cruz. A priest,
Father Jarauta, crying "Long live the Religion," coursed the countryside for a time with a rumored 800 men, but he and other guerillas
were no serious obstacle to Army expeditions. General Joseph Lane,
with a combined force of Regulars, including Grant's friend, Alexander Hays, and Texas cavalry, crushed rural opposition promptly, *los
Tejons* leaving behind them an abiding terror of their five- and six-
shooters which the Army was buying from the factory of Samuel
Colt in the States. Lane's men came close to capturing Santa Anna
in one of his haciendas, but had to content themselves with a duck
dinner standing on the table and 122 of Señora Santa Anna's gowns.
Lane gallantly delivered the wardrobe to the Alcalde of neighboring
Tehuacan for delivery to the lady.[4]

Although two Mexican officers had to be shot at Jalapa for breaking their paroles and becoming guerillas, the fairness of the Yankee
Judge Advocate at their trial "called forth praise from all parties," as
the correspondent of the *New Orleans Picayune* wrote his editor.
The Judge Advocate was a youngster freshly arrived from West
Point, Ambrose E. Burnside by name. "His duties were arduous, and
of the most responsible and painful character; but — he has done his
duty kindly, delicately, and faithfully." [5] People had begun praising
Burnside in the little frontier town of Liberty, Indiana, where he had
been an apprentice tailor.

Sam Grant and the other recent Academy graduates heard tales
of Burnside's career at West Point, where the tall, open-faced boy's
frankness, modesty and humor had made him a "universal favorite."
He had been the champion hash maker of his day, "an animated
automaton" in drill, and although "somewhat wild when off duty,"
had won the faculty as well as the cadets with his gay candor and
generosity. He had earned his nickname, "Academy Barber," by pretending to be the official haircutter of the institution so that he could
shear the long locks of a greenhorn plebe, timing his operations so
that they were only half done when the drum called the victim to
evening parade. When the Superintendent had noted the comic appearance of the plebe, and had been told that a mysterious person

called the "Academy Barber" was responsible, Burnside had manfully admitted the guilt.[6]

Living costs in Mexico City were high, Surgeon McSherry paying over twenty dollars a week for room, board and "extras." To give the young officers a social center within their means, General Franklin Pierce, aided by Lieutenants Prince John Magruder, Henry Coppée and Charles P. Stone, Captain Charles F. Smith and Colonel John B. Grayson, organized the Aztec Club on October 13, and soon opened it in the "splendid mansion" on The Street of the Silversmiths, belonging to Señor Bocanegra, former Mexican Minister to the United States. With the initiation fee at $20, the membership, which included Sam Grant, soon rose to 166 with the sale of liquor and cigars averaging $100 a day. General Scott, watching over his officers carefully, took alarm when he discovered that book-hating, liquor-loving Captain Buchanan of the Fourth was planning to widen the Club's conviviality. He said nothing when Old Buch persuaded the members to vote on billiard tables, but when he discovered that the next proposal would be gambling tables, the General sent for his fellow Episcopalian and moralist, Surgeon Tripler.

"These men will get together enough votes to carry their schemes against us," he said, and sent Tripler out to organize righteous officers against Old Buch — which the Doctor did with success.[7]

Either in the Club, unknown to Scott, or in less restricted quarters, Grant and other lieutenants played cards with the democratic Pierce and came to know him more intimately than any other General. The two men had much in common, "I hate war in all its aspects," Pierce had written home while marching his brigade from Vera Cruz to Puebla. "I deem it unworthy of the age in which I live & of the Govt. in which I have borne some part." Also he had an extraordinary hunger for family life, the hunger that was mounting in Grant as he waited for his own wedding. To be with his family Pierce had lately given up one of the most promising of national futures in politics, and had only come to the war because he felt it his duty after having advocated the annexation of Texas. Rising from private to Colonel to Brigadier General in the Volunteers, he had made himself popular with the Regulars, and uniformed men crowded the streets cheering when, that December of 1848, he left Mexico City for home.[8]

*   *   *

As for Sam at Tacubaya, four miles from the City of Mexico, Grant longed for peace and Julia, plotted for a leave and wrote his sweetheart on January 9, 1848:

> It is now however strongly believed that peace will be established before many months. I hope it may be so for it is scarcely suportable for me to be separated from you so long my Dearest Julia. A few weeks ago I went to the Commanding Officer of my Regiment and represented to him that when the 4th Infy. left Jefferson Barracks, three years ago last May, I was engaged, and that I thought it high time that I should have a leave of absence to go back. He told me that he would approve it but I found that it would be impossible to get the Comdg. Gen. to give the leave so I never made the application. I have strong hopes though of going back in a few months. If peace is not made it is at all events about my turn to go on recruiting service. As to getting a sick leave that is out of the question for I am never sick a day. Mexico is a very pleasant place to live because it is never hot nor never cold, but I believe everyone is heartily tired of the war. There is no amusement except the Theatre and as the actors & actresses are Spanish but few of the officers can understand them.

At the same time the lucky Longstreet, wounded at Chapultepec and now well enough for travel, told Sam Grant good-by and started home to marry Louise Garland.

Quartermaster and Commissary Grant stayed on. Food must be collected, and he must snatch from the Chief Quartermaster the Fourth's share of the uniforms which hired seamstresses made to cover the army's nakedness. His regiment must get their share of the horseshoes, spurs and flagstaff spearheads which blacksmiths were fashioning out of 20,000 British-made muskets captured in the city.[9]

To revive the regimental fund, which was so low that the bandsmen were not being paid, Grant organized a bakery as at Monterey, a larger one this time, and fed not only his own regiment but sold much to the chief commissary for the rest of the army. Later he would say, as became the son of Jesse, "In two months I made more money for the fund than my pay amounted to during the entire war."[10] It was as near a boast as he would ever make about himself in the entire conflict.

For newspapers Grant had not only the belated gazettes from home, but two local journals published in English, the *North American* and the *American Star*, issued by enterprising Yankee printers. As autumn passed into winter, most of the news seemed to be printed not so much in ink as in the stain of politics. Scott's Whig friends were crying for his nomination as a hero who had triumphed over both Mexicans and Polk. Taylor's Whig friends were torturing their hero's most innocent statements for hidden meanings. Arriving in New Orleans on December 2, he winced when street crowds bellowed "Old Zach for President," and his famous war horse Old Whitey had winced too when idolaters tweaked souvenir hairs from his tail. At a banquet Taylor "timidly and modestly" said that "How much soever he might forget in the hour of battle, the sad consequences of the strife, they always rushed upon his mind afterwards, making his heart to sink and causing him to feel like a child."

The *New York Sun* was trumpeting Worth as the ideal President, and the Democrats were saying General Butler would be their nominee for Vice President. General Shields, having recovered from his second wound, had announced that he would run for the Senate at the next election in Illinois.[11]

As Whig sentiment for Taylor grew, the party increased its wrath against the injustices of the war. An Illinois Representative, Abraham Lincoln, on December 22, had submitted a series of resolutions asking the President to tell Congress whether the spot where the first blood had been shed "is or is not on the soil of the United States." When the Administration sent new regiments to the front so that veteran Volunteers might come home, Whig Senators said it was merely an attempt to overrun all Mexico and annex it.[12]

In the newspaper that Grant read, the Whigs were shouting: "It is folly to absorb such a country into our own, to exhaust such a nation into the healthy veins of a republic like this." Here were the rabid annexationist orators and editors crying: "Destiny! Destiny!" . . . "The Mexicans are aboriginal Indians and must share the destiny of their race — extinction!" . . . "The war must be continued fifty years if necessary to establish the great principle of religious tolerance in Mexico . . . the priceless boon of civil and religious liberty has been confided to us as trustees." — "The North was always destined to over-run the South; England took over the Indian empire, France

Algeria, Americans Texas." . . . "God ordained that Mexico should be an integral part of the Union." . . . "Protestantism is advancing with lightning speed from one kingdom to another; Mexico cannot shut herself out from the light." . . . "When Mexico's errors are pointed out to her, she brings forward, as an offset, the extreme docility of the Mexican character . . . we can make nothing out of it more or less than the docility of the whore who will kindly consent to anything and everything but a virtuous course of life." . . . "A truly republican form of Government cannot exist where Catholicism is still the religion." . . . "If Monkhood will continue to disregard the Scripture, meddle in politics and excite revolutions, if it will resolve to hold back while the people are struggling forward, that people will turn around one of these days, as they did in France and Spain, and in a fit of just impatience, cut Monkhood's throats." . . . "Look at the gold and silver glittering there in masses that await the pick of the Saxon." . . . "God ordained that Mexico should be an integral part of the Union." "Destiny! Destiny!"

The *American Star* dangled Destiny and Opportunity before the eyes of Scott's men week in, week out — 300,000 immigrants a year were pouring into the United States from Europe; give them free lands in a Mexico ruled by the United States, and Democracy, Riches and Progress, all would flower! Look at Mexico now with its little band of overlords at the top, "living in splendid palaces, eating off gold plates, monopolists taxing the eggs, pulque, lotteries, tobacco and fighting-cocks of the ignorant Indians!" "America's duty was to reform this."

In February, the *North American* was campaigning for free schools that would save the Mexican children from being "grudgingly dragged up to the choir, morning, noon and night to recite a mummery." On February 21st, it reported that a number of "benevolent American officers" were organizing a free school system to be supported by subscriptions from the States — eighty-two had signed up to pay from $1 to $10 a month, Generals Worth, Pillow and Patterson, Colonels Duncan and Clarke among them.[13]

Some soldiers like Surgeon McSherry and the English adventurer with the New York Volunteers, George Ballentine, were genuinely horrified at Mexican beggars exposing deformities and ulcers as they chanted, he said, "Caridad por l'amor de Dios," and by maimed soldiers holding up stumps of arms and legs crying "Cerro Gordo" or "Chapultepec." McSherry heard terrible stories of self-mutilation, of parents' putting out the eyes of their children "to insure their claims on public sympathy." [14]

The soldiers read in the *American Star* of December 3, "A traveler has said that there is no country for which God has done so much and man so little as Mexico."

The outcry for the annexation of all Mexico meant little to the army, although Scott himself believed that "two-fifths of the Mexican population, including more than half of the Congress" favored it. He was convinced of this by the repeated pleas of wealthy Mexicans that he resign his commission in the Army and become the dictator of Mexico for a term of years "as a stepping stone" toward bringing the Republic into the United States. As soon as the war would officially end, two thirds of his enlisted men would be entitled to a discharge and then it would be easy for him to persuade 6000 or 8000 of them to join him with the best of the regular officers in forming a new Mexican Army. It was promised that 8000 or 10,000 regular Mexican soldiers would be added and that with so large a force and his own immense prestige, he could govern Mexico handily. In return he was to receive $1,250,000 down and thenceforth the regular salary of the President of Mexico. Five of the richest men in the country said they would put up $250,000 each to guarantee the deal.

Scott refused. He wanted to go home and face his "enemies," President Polk and the Cabinet, and he was "conscientiously opposed" to annexation.[15]

Emissaries sounded Scott's officers as to the scheme. From talks with Grant after the war, a friend understood that "Grant was invited to several conclaves of officers" to discuss the proffers, "but from the first emphatically declined to enter into the plot . . . he had genuine contempt for any adventure which had any flavor of dishonesty or bad faith about it." [16] Also Julia was waiting for him, and his own opposition to annexation was as strong as ever.

Annexation of the whole of Mexico was a dying cause. Most officers knew that it was not an issue in the peace that Polk was offering the Mexican Temporary Government. Polk had dropped his claim to Lower California and would agree to pay the claims of various

United States citizens against Mexico, but otherwise his proposal was what it had been: $15,000,000 for all the land above the Rio Grande and all of New Mexico and Upper California. Through December and January the negotiations went on, the Mexican authorities bedeviled, as John Sedgwick wrote home, by their military chieftains who opposed peace, and by the working classes who had benefited from the war. He told his father, "Some one said that we ought to continue the war and whip them until they consented to take back all Texas." [17]

On February 2, Scott and Trist had brought the delegates up to the point of signing a peace which gave Polk what he wanted, but eleven days after the document had been sent on its way to Washington, in came a special messenger from Polk, removing Scott from command, replacing him with Butler, and ordering him to return home as soon as a court of inquiry, decreed by Polk, was finished.[18]

The news came like a thunderclap to the army, convincing Grant that this treatment of Scott, so "harsh and unjust," had been prompted by politics. "It is quite possible," he concluded, "that the vanity of the General had led him to say and do things that afforded a plausible pretext to the administration for doing just what it did and what it had wanted to do from the start." Scott had been wrangling with Worth and Pillow and Duncan ever since their mutual enemy, the Mexican Army, had quit fighting. His three opponents, in letters to Washington or to home newspapers, had puffed themselves and each other at Scott's expense. Both Worth and Pillow were claiming to have saved the army upon occasions from Scott's blunders. Scott arrested them for violating regulations in such matters as publicity. Pillow was receiving a court of inquiry. Duncan, always ambitious, was said to be listening to Pillow's whispers that he could persuade his old crony the President to name him Inspector General of the whole Army. Pillow had been caught appropriating some captured cannon as personal souvenirs, but had slipped out of the scandal by persuading an understrapper to take the blame.

The court of inquiry itself was a bore to the young officers, who had great contempt for Pillow. John Sedgwick, looking in upon it one day, saw no "more than a dozen persons present." To the Mexicans the news of Scott's removal was incomprehensible, and certain rich men promptly renewed their offer of a dictatorship. He sternly refused. When Worth had been arrested, the Indians, as Sedgwick understood, "wanted to know if his troops would return to the States or join the Mexicans." And when the army paraded on Washington's Birthday, the Indians swarmed in from neighboring towns "thinking it was a pronunciamento . . . in favor of General Scott." [19]

On April 23, when the Pillow court of inquiry adjourned to resume in the States, the cheering army saw Scott off on his way home, and heard, in time, how the Navy had saluted him at Vera Cruz, how citizens whooped for him in New Orleans and New York, and how after the court of inquiry finally exonerated Pillow, the public had consoled Scott with swords, banquets, resolution and demands that he, instead of Taylor, be the Whig's nominee for President.

Grant noted ironically how Polk's attempts to "kill off politically the two successful generals made them both candidates for the Presidency." [20]

Sam Grant's gift for telling his friends funny things that happened to him entertained his brother officers during the days while they awaited the return of the peace treaty from Washington. "He had a very keen idea of the humorous," said one of the newly arrived second lieutenants, DeLancey Floyd-Jones, a New Yorker, Class of '46. "He frequently regaled us with tales of happenings to him in the discharge of his duty." Floyd-Jones always remembered the one Sam told about the wagon and the burro. Sam had been riding along on a heavy army wagon when a burro, wearied by its tremendous load of stone, decided to lie down in the road and rest. Before Grant could halt or turn out, his wagon wheels had run over it. "The little beast got up," he said, "shook himself, looked around with a sort of disgusted air and passed on as though nothing had happened." [21]

It was an old white mule that Grant remembered best from a week's trip he made, in April 1848, with some fifty officers to Popocatepetl. On the first day's ascent the mule, packing barley straw in huge sacks for the officers' horses, hit its head against a ledge and tumbled down a steep mountain slope, on and on, down and down, till it disappeared in the rocks and bushes hundreds of feet below. "We supposed, of course, the poor animal was dashed to pieces," Grant said. But when they bivouacked that night in came the mule, good as new. The sacks of barley had protected it, and its driver, who knew his business, had stayed behind to hunt for it in the depths of the gorge, had found it unhurt and somehow worked it back to the path so far above.

The whole trip would remain clearer in Grant's mind than any of the battles. A snowstorm had convinced him and half the others at the end of two nights that they "had got all the pleasure there was to be had out of mountain climbing" and had gone off via Cuernavaca, a town of heavenly climate, to some famous caves on the road to Acapulco. The other half of the party, including his friend Buckner, went to the top of Popo, but Grant was satisfied with his choice. He had known, in the ups and downs of the road, many climates, frigid and tropical; he had seen ruins, coffee plantations, enormous stalactites, corn patches, banana trees; but the one thing he liked to talk about best was the white mule that came back.[22]

He helped organize a race track which the officers and Mexicans attended and in his rides on army duty added to his fame as a horseman. One day, riding in from Tacubaya to visit Lieutenant Colonel Joshua Howard of the Fifteenth Infantry, who was in command of Chapultepec, he failed to leave his horse at the high breastworks which surrounded the office and clattered down a long, steep flight of stone steps which led to Howard's door. He hitched the animal and went in. When he and Howard emerged, Howard gasped, "How in the world did you get your horse in here?"

"Rode him in, sir."

"How do you expect to get him out?"

"Ride him up the steps instead of down."

Mounting in that peculiar way of his, Grant put his horse up the stairs like a cat, and with a wave of his hat "disappeared like a flash over the breastworks." [23]

One Sunday he went to a bullfight but left before the show was over, sick at the sight of the blood and suffering of the horses, the brutal tormenting of the bull. A flash of humor came to him as he departed. A matador who had been carried off, apparently dead, earlier in the afternoon, was now sitting in the audience. "He was only dead so far as that performance went," Grant said, "but the corpse was so lively that it could not forego the chance of witnessing the discomfiture of some of his brethren who might not be so fortunate. There was a feeling of disgust manifested by the audience to find that he had come to life again." [24]

Julia learned of life in Mexico City and her fiancé's opinions of Mexico:

The better class of Mexicans dare not visit the Theatre or associate with the Americans lest they should be assassinated by their own people or banished by their Government as soon as we leave. A few weeks ago a Benefit was given to a favorite actress and the Governor of Queretero hearing of it sent secret spies to take the names of such Mexicans as might be caught in indulging in amusements with the Americans for the purpose of banishing them as soon as the magnanimous Mexican Republic should drive away the Barbarians of the North. I pity poor Mexico. With a soil and climate scarcely equaled in the world she has more poor and starving subjects who are willing and able to work than any country in the world. The rich keep down the poor with a hardness of heart that is incredible. Walk through the streets of Mexico for one day and you will see hundreds of beggars, but you never see them ask alms of their own people, it is always from the Americans that they expect to receive. I wish you could be here for one short day then I should be doubly gratified. Gratified at seeing you my Dearest Julia and gratified that you might see too the manners and customs of these people. You would see what you never dreamed of nor can you form a correct idea from reading. All gamble, Priests & civilians, male & female and particularly so on Sundays. But I will tell you all that I know about Mexico and the Mexicans when I see you which I do hope will not be a greatwhile off now. Fred is in the same Brigade with me. I see him every day. He like myself is in excellent health and has no prospect of getting out of the country on the plea of sickness. I have one chance of getting out of Mexico soon besides going on recruiting. Gen. Scott will grant leaves of absence to officers where there are over two to a Company. In my Regt. there are three or four vacancies which will be filled soon and will give an opportunity for one or two now here to go out.

In the spring of 1848 the position of recruiting officer was added to Grant's duties and the tasks of all officers grew heavier as discipline relaxed in the wake of Scott's departure. The new commander,

General Butler, lacked Scott's consideration for the Mexican population, and demanded nothing more than resignations from three officers, one of them a Regular, who in April were involved in the robbery of a bank and the murder of a banker.[25]

Outside the city and its environs a few rebellious Mexican generals tried drumming up resistance to the "infamous peace" but public sentiment was overwhelming against them. On May 30 when the Mexican National Congress ratified the treaty of peace, it could count only 1400 soldiers and 1600 officers — "two-thirds of a man to an officer," the *American Star* commented — yet it was a force sufficient to preserve order.[26]

One thing the Mexican Government noted with anticipation, as the Yankees in June began to move, division by division, down to the sea for passage home — the number of Yankee deserters grew. In each regiment were some men who couldn't say good-by to the city where they had lived now for nine months, nor to the strumming guitars and soft love songs in the twilight gardens, nor to the pale moon lighting up the m. untainsides. Surgeon Brackett would never get over the "heavenly quiet" of those nights. Numbers of soldiers came to their colonels confessing that they had married or become the lovers of *señoritas* and asking that as faithful soldiers all during the war, they be discharged on the spot so that they could remain in Mexico. The orders were "No." Any man who stayed behind would be listed as a deserter.

Tough old Colonel Harney was softened by these pleas, however, and, when he reached Washington, took the matter to President Polk who ordered that the soldiers be relieved and remain with their loves. Before any such benefaction could reach the majority of the regiments, many men had already deserted, some to join the well-paid Legion of Foreigners (who, it was whispered, would have the honor of guarding the Palace as soon as the "*Yanquis* had gone" — a sort of Swiss Guard like that which had protected the French Bourbon kings). At least one officer, Lieutenant Michael O'Sullivan, had resigned from the Third Infantry last October, and was said to be a colonel somewhere in the Mexican Army.[27]

The aristocrats in Mexico City were polite to the end, but they were obviously relieved to have their guests depart. One war correspondent declared "the emotions of the Indians to be quite different." He saw "the whole laboring population exhibit sorrow in the most striking and affecting manner. . . . The sojourn of our army has relieved these poor and interesting people from many oppressions and taxes." They had thought the *Yanquis* the kindest men they had ever seen. "There is one single trait of our countrymen which has aroused the liveliest admiration of the poor Indians — their behavior to females." Accustomed to having the upper- and middle-class Mexicans treat them, and their women, like dogs, "they could scarcely understand, much less express their gratitude . . . when they saw an American soldier turning out of his way to let a Mexican woman pass. . . . As our Army passed out of their towns, crowds of these poor people surrounded our troops and threw bouquets and fruit to the soldiers and many of them wept most piteously, crying out that they had lost their only friends." [28]

Sam Grant, disbursing funds at Tacubaya as his regiment prepared for its departure, became worried about the safety of $1000 in government funds which was in his hands. The lock of his trunk had been broken. As he later reported, "About the 6th of June" he took the money to Captain Gore's room and locked it in a stout chest, since he "deemed it safer to have public money in the room of some officer who did not disburse public funds, because they would be less likely to be suspected of having any considerable amount about them." [29]

The money was still there on June 12, when Worth's division, the last to quit the capital, drew up in the Grand Plaza at six o'clock in the morning. All around them crowded the *léperos* who had come out of their squalid huts to see the *Yanquis* off. The Stars and Stripes fluttered down from the National Palace. A Mexican battery fired a salute. A battery from the Third Artillery fired a salute. There was a pause, and then the Mexican flag slowly twitched upward. Another Mexican battery fired a salute, and as its last blast echoed away, among the cheering crowds in streets and balconies, the most murderous of all the Yankee batteries — Colonel Duncan's — roared out in salutation.

Duncan, the great gunner, was having the last say. But it was General Worth, haughty on his tall horse — Worth who had been the first across the Colorado, first into Monterey, first into Vera Cruz, first into Puebla, first inside the gates of Mexico City —

who was now the last man to pass out the eastern gate as the church bells rang eight o'clock in the morning. As his horse's tail swished past the *garita* the crowd closed in behind, some waving farewell, some merely standing and watching him go.[30]

At either side of him rolled a cannon, mouth pointing backward. Through the city went the word that the *Yanquis* had taken with them as trophies the twenty-five cannon captured at Chapultepec, but a little later *léperos*, ransacking the abandoned camps, found that the guns had been left unharmed. Heads shook in amazement.[31]

Los gringos son locos!

Four nights later, while the Fourth Regiment stopped to camp between Puebla and Perote, persons unknown stole Captain Gore's trunk from the tent where he and Lieutenant John DeRussy, a newcomer, Class of '47, were sleeping. Grant's $1000 was gone, and on June 28, when the regiment was halting in Jalapa, he reported the loss. There was no response: no attempt either to blame or exonerate him. All that happened was that one more paper started winding its way through the Army to the Treasury of the United States, where it would be filed with thousands like it — filed and forgotten.[32]

At Jalapa, where Worth's division waited above the *vómito* belt for orders to march down to the transports at Vera Cruz, Grant saw June run out and July come on. For all its wrongs, the war had made him an Army man. Cannon had blown away all those dreams of a quiet, professional life in a college town. He would not renew his application for appointment to the West Point faculty. He was in a hurry to marry Julia. A first lieutenant's pay, around $1000 a year, including rations for himself and wife and forage for his horses, would now be the best security for a livelihood.[33]

His captaincy had been by brevet only. As he had known it would, peace had made the brevet honor merely a complimentary mark on the record. Officers were reverting to their regular rank. Of his thirty-three classmates still in the service, only one, Rufe Ingalls, had become a full-fledged captain, seven had gone back to the second lieutenant's rank, and twenty-five, Grant among them, to the first lieutenancy.

Grant was coming home alive; thirty-nine of the boys he had known at the Academy were not. Four of his classmates were dead and one, Lieutenant George C. McClelland — not to be confused with George B. McClellan — had been cashiered from the Eleventh Infantry for drunkenness at Puebla last October. Grant had lost close friends all across Mexico — Hamer, Benjamin, Hoskins, Sidney, Jenks, and Beaman, who had just died of disease at Tampico in May. Many others were returning with disease still in them. Of the 1365 Academy graduates, not counting the Class of '48, 594 were still in service. Sixty-eight had been killed and 218 had died of disease or accident; the rest were in civil life.[34]

Grant's mother had been right, when she had looked at him as an infant playing among the horses. Nothing could happen to him. Almost three years at the front — three years come September. What had they taught him of this profession of a soldier which he must now be following — following the drum — in the years ahead?

One thing was truer now than when Quitman had said it back in the days of bloody Monterey: disease, not bullets, was the real killer in war. Six men had died of disease to every one killed by gunfire. If the Surgeon General's books be correct in saying disease had killed 103.8 men per thousand, then 9300 had so perished — 9300 out of the 90,000 officers and men who had been in uniform. Only 1500 had been killed by enemy gunfire. Of the 59,000 Volunteers, 6400 had been lost by disease or accident, 600 in combat, 9200 by discharge for disability and 3900 by desertion. Of the 31,000 Regulars, 4900 had died from disease or accident, 930 from enemy bullets, while 4149 had been sent home for disability, and 2850 had deserted.[35]

No count worth the attention of a mathematician had been kept on Mexican losses; all anybody could believe was they had been many times that of the Yankees.

War was a life of camps and waiting more than of marching and fighting. In the two years since he had first smelled gunpowder on May 8, 1846, Grant had been under fire, at the most, twenty-seven days — really only nine days, since the eighteen spent at the siege of Vera Cruz were of negligible danger. More important than shooting and charging were the long weary days spent in massing supplies, arranging transport, hauling food. Only the quartermasters and commissaries and some of the generals knew how much more victory owed to dull, plodding business organization than to bayonet charges — to the Captain Allens with their books and pencils rather than the Captain Mays with their flying hair.

Grant had learned, as had engineers like Colonel Lee, that cavalry was weak against the new light artillery. Mexico's trust in cavalry had been one of that country's great mistakes. The young American officers, as a whole, were coming out convinced that the Old Army's scorn of entrenchments was right — trench life tended to make men cowardly. Charley Hamilton believed that "our victories were nearly all won by charging the enemy with the bayonet." Grant's classmate, Major Riley, poring over reports, studying tactics and strategy, was convinced that disciplined men with bayonets could always carry trenches manned by somewhat less disciplined enemies. Faith in musket fire was dwindling. Those wonderful horse guns were the thing! Give an army enough light artillery and the bayonet, and victory was assured.[36]

Grant had learned that military etiquette, decorum, full dress, really meant nothing. Taylor and Duncan scorned it; Scott and Worth loved it; all had been successful.

A soldier need not pay too much attention to the old rules of war. Taylor hadn't worried about protecting his rear. Scott, for all his formalism, had cut loose from his base of supplies. Both had won.

And that old rule about never attacking a fortified enemy unless you had three or four times his number of men? Taylor and Scott had repeatedly reversed it, attacking when the odds were against them three, four or five to one.

Grant had learned that raw Volunteers, for all their caprices and indulgences, "became soldiers . . . almost at once." Sometimes they would run away only to turn and come back like tigers. But most of all, he had learned that victory and glory did not make a general superhuman. Nations might bow down before a conquerer, his own soldiers might cheer him till they were hoarse, the bands might play for him and he might sweep past on parade like a god, but Sam Grant would know "that he was mortal." [37]

The Sam Grant who left Jalapa on July 11, went down to Vera Cruz, and on the sixteenth boarded the transport for home, had come a long way in the nine years that had passed since that plebe day when he had worshiped Old Fuss and Feathers at the review.[38] Beside him on the deck stood a Mexican country boy, living evidence of the friendships Grant had made in the conquered land: "a Mexican gentleman," to show his regard for Grant, had presented him with a body servant, Gregory by name. Gregory could speak no English but Grant knew enough Spanish to explain the new world to him. He was also taking home with him a fine gray horse that had won his admiration.[39]

At last the steamer coughed and moved. The Yankees saw Mexico fall away — the hot stench of the water front — red flowers on stained white walls — overhead the eternal buzzard patrol circling, circling, looking for death below — the silken ruffles of the Gulf widening between the ship and the shore — the true perfume of the country coming now on the west wind, that heavy, vanilla scent of the acacia, the spicy fragrance of multitudinous blossoms blending with a faint whiff of decomposition, half sweet, half sickening — the shore line slowly fading from green to blue, then gone completely — and all that remained of Mexico was the Starry Mountain, the white cap of Orizaba suspended there between the earth and the sky.

On another transport, James H. Lane, the imaginative and oratorical colonel of his second command, the Fifth Indiana Volunteers, was taking home with him that joke the *American Star* had told about the traveler and Mexico, taking it home to use on the political stump when he needed to set the coonskin boys laughing. Jim Lane would sharpen it up a bit:

"Mexico, the country for which God has done so much and Man so God-damned little."[40]

CHAPTER SEVENTEEN

The Son of Temperance

THE OFFICER who rode up to White Haven's stile in the summer of 1848 was no longer "pretty as a doll." Emmy, who was now twelve, noted that his face was bronzed and that he was "sturdier and more reserved in manner." The whole family rushed to welcome him, Julia radiant, Mrs. Dent insisting that he had saved Fred's life at Molino, and Colonel Dent reconciled to the match.

Mary Robinson, the mulatto slave, hearing him tell how his fleet mare, Nelly, had raced him through the bloody streets of Monterey, relayed the word that "he appeared to look upon Nelly's conduct as more courageous than his own." [1]

The Captain, as they called him, using his brevet rank, had left his red, ragged whiskers and his regiment at Pascagoula on the Mississippi Sound. He was home on two months' leave. Another officer had taken over his quartermaster's duties on July 23, the day the regiment had landed. Emmy saw the courtship on horseback resumed where it had been interrupted four years before. Grant was showing Julia "the most devoted yet quiet attention." It seemed to him that he had always been in love with Julia, and in time Emmy would hear him say that it had been "a case of love at first sight" and that he "had never had but one love affair, but the one sweetheart." [2]

Julia named the day for the wedding, August 22, the hour eight o'clock in the evening, and the place the family's winter home in St. Louis, a house at Fourth and Cerre Streets that Colonel Dent had taken in recent years so that his children might live at home while attending school. It was a two-story brick house, "unpretending" yet suitable for the proper entertainment of the family friends, "the best society of the city." On the front steps the Captain and Julia would sit side by side. Sometimes when Nellie and her beau, a medical student, Sylvester Nidelet, would join them, Grant would talk "with great interest" about the Mexican War, but usually he "volunteered but little conversation." Nidelet thought him "a handsome fellow." [3]

After a few days with Julia, Ulysses left for Bethel, where his mother's welcome was as undemonstrative as her farewell had been. None of the letters he had written her during the last six months in Mexico had arrived. Up in Detroit his friend, Dr. Tripler, was arriving home to find that his wife had also gone that long without word. Guerillas outside Mexico City had riddled communications. [4]

Jesse Grant was so exuberant that the neighbors said, "He would stop any time in the rain to talk about Ulysses." No clownish hostler burlesqued his boy's uniform now. The neighbors crowded around to ask Ulysses about the war, calling him "Captain," and wondering how they had ever thought he wouldn't make a soldier. The war had brought him out! The cat no longer had his tongue in a crowd! He talked right up — made you see the smoke, the Mexicans, the bullets — the whole thing. [5]

He had come home a captain with a body servant.

Whether he had taken Gregory with him to St. Louis before coming to Bethel, the neighbors could never recall, but here he was, almost as big a sight as the Captain himself! The Mexican boy had learned no English but would talk to the natives through his master, who knew considerable Spanish, and he needed no language to display his specialty — the lariat. With gusto he roped horses, dogs, calves, pigs, small boys, and was considered by Uncle Samuel Simpson to be a nine-days' wonder. [6]

Jesse had a good horse for Ulysses to ride on visits to relatives — a horse named Agua Nova, a word associated with the Battle of Buena Vista. Jesse's satisfaction was so vast that he waived objections to his son's marriage into a Democratic slaveholding family. No, he and Hannah wouldn't come on to the wedding! Hannah's bashfulness would not enable her to face the strain of the festivities with which the Southerners would surround the marriage.

When Ulysses returned to St. Louis, Gregory remained behind with Jesse, who planned to turn him into a tanner — if there should be time between exhibitions with the rope. [7]

In St. Louis began what Emmy would recall as "happy days for us all." The house was "filled with gay company; both my sister and the Captain were very popular . . . he frequently took Julia and me to the theatre." Cousin James Longstreet was there with the bride he had married on March 8. Louise Garland had waited for him despite the strenuous attempts of Lieutenant Gordon Granger to win her in the summer of 1845, when he had come to the Detroit army post after graduating from the Academy. Granger had animal magnetism, but as Detroit people said, was "the roughest specimen of a West Point graduate . . . any one . . . ever saw." [8]

St. Louis society had taken on a martial note since the officers had come back from the war. Belles fluttered around them, tormenting them with arch inquiries about the charms of those *señoritas*. Presumably Sam Grant was content that Judah was in camp at Pascagoula and not present to be reciting their adventures, however innocent, with the daughters of the Alcalde in Puebla.

The queenly Mrs. O'Fallon entertained for Julia, buying "my beautiful wedding gown," as the bride would later say. One of the O'Fallon daughters was among Julia's bridesmaids and Captain Longstreet, called "Major" as his brevet rank befitted, acted either as the groom's best man or as an usher — the guests later were uncertain which. [9]

"A sweet, old-fashioned wedding" Emmy thought it, as she watched the ceremony from a table beside Miss Amanda Shurlds, soon to marry Emmy's brother John. Captain Cadmus Wilcox, Grant's old messmate, said afterward that Emmy had been "a most pestiferous little nuisance during the whole wedding," getting under everybody's feet. One of the lady guests thought the bride had the smallest hands she ever saw and that the groom was "brown . . . dignified and quiet." The honeymoon was spent in Ohio, where Jesse and Hannah were soon so fond of Julia that they wanted her to live with them if the Army should send her husband away. In Julia the bridegroom was finding a warmth of affection he had never known. He grew uxorious and seemed to enjoy hearing his bride call him "Dudy." Where he had always shrunk from nicknames, he purred at "Dudy" from the warm lips of Julia — she of the beautiful skin and the amorous figure. [10]

The change from the armed camp to the love bed was so marked that Ulysses wrote his regiment on September 12, asking for a two months' extension of his leave. In due time it arrived; he was to report November 17, at the newly established headquarters in Detroit. Old Colonel Whistler had returned to active command now that the war was over and was taking his post with two companies, the other six units being scattered along the northern frontier all the way from Sault Ste. Marie in Michigan to Plattsburg and Sacketts Harbor in New York. The Canadian border would bear watching. Brother Jonathan eternally distrusted John Bull.[11]

Life in a civilized army post would be better for the newly married couple than in the West where so many regiments were going. Only 8000 men were being retained in the standing Army and trouble had flared, intermittently, with the Indians across the plains. Rumor had it that gold in dazzling quantities had been found in California, and if true the rush overland would soon commence. Many settlers also would be crowding onto the Indian lands if so much immigration from Europe continued. Word that the land of liberty had now enlarged its area by a third was agitating Europeans. In the United States, native American agitators were demanding that no immigrant become a naturalized voter until he had lived in the new country twenty-one years. Anti-Catholic, anti-foreigner riots might break out any moment.

According to the newspapers that Jesse and Ulysses Grant read, it was the day of the soldier all over the world. Austrians, Hungarians, Italians, Germans, Parisians, were in revolution, rebellion and war. Ireland was talking of rising against the English. Printed circulars in New Orleans were calling for discharged soldiers and adventurers to join in a gigantic filibustering expedition, "The Grand Buffalo Hunt" — 5000 men to cross the border and help rebellious Mexicans free the northern provinces, and, with St. Louis as capital, negotiate for an annexation like that of Texas. The Polk Administration was denying that it was conveniently leaving unwanted war material on the Rio Grande for the Buffalo Hunters to seize. Factions in and around Mexico City were said to be plotting to repudiate "the infamous peace" and renew the war against the *paganos* of the North. Disbanded Yankee soldiers were rumored to be organizing for the capture and annexation of Cuba.[12]

Here at home the question of slavery in the new lands acquired from Mexico and Great Britain was splitting both Democratic and

Whig parties. Perhaps slavery could not thrive in Oregon, nor in the mountains and deserts where the Mormons had settled during the past year, but what about all those regions on or below the latitude of the slave state Missouri? The fertile bottoms of the Kansas River, for example, were south of the line which marked Missouri's northern boundary. And California had the climate of Florida, where slavery prospered. So severely was the question shaking the nation that at one time it had seemed that seven presidential tickets would be competing in the campaign of 1848. But the race was finally narrowed down to three, Lewis Cass heading the Democrats, Martin Van Buren leading the Free-Soilers and General Zachary Taylor marching at the head of the Whigs.

Ulysses needed none of his father's Whig gospel to bring him to favor Old Zach as the candidate whose election would bring peace to the country, but he did not bother to vote on election day. To the general indifference army officers felt toward voting was added the fact that he felt, from his father's cocksure talk, that Ohio was safe for the Whigs and his vote unneeded. Still in the flood tide of honeymoon festivities, he was in Kentucky visiting relatives when the first Tuesday after the first Monday in November came around. His only remembered comment on the campaign came when Democratic politicians charged that Taylor, at Camargo, had called Ohio Volunteers "a set of damned thieves, who would run at the sight of an enemy." Ulysses told people he knew about that. He had heard Taylor tell a soldier, "Throw down that chicken! Any man who will steal is a damned coward and would run from the enemy." Ulysses said somebody ought to ask Taylor to tell what happened and he'd tell the truth "though it might defeat his election." [13]

It was to the echoes of Taylor's victory — but his loss of Ohio — that the bride and groom paid a farewell visit to St. Louis, then journeyed to Detroit. Disappointment met them. Grant's quartermaster post was not to be returned to him and he was to report, on November 21, at Madison Barracks in Sacketts Harbor, a bleak, cold village on Lake Ontario. Friends of Grant later declared that Whistler, for the "surly" reason that he preferred to retain a favorite officer as quartermaster, had shipped Grant away, and that when Grant, upon arrival at Sacketts Harbor, had complained, Major Francis Lee agreed with him, forwarding a protest to General Scott.

The General obliged by ordering Grant back to Detroit, but the orders arrived after ice had closed navigation and the move was postponed until spring.[14]

As the Grants settled into the cramped rooms which were supplied officers and their families at Madison Barracks, the whole Army was buzzing with the news of the great gold strike in California. President Polk's message to Congress on December 6 gave official proof that the incredible rumors of the past months were true. Jesse Grant's mentor, Horace Greeley, in November had believed them, printing the word, "We are on the brink of the age of gold." The nation was going crazy with avarice. Newspapers in December were declaring that at least $15,000,000 worth of gold pebbles had already been picked up in California. Someone from apparently every family was planning to go, fighting for bookings on steamships or studying maps for the overland journey. Some New England towns were reporting that 20 per cent of their populations would soon be gone. Midland farmers were saying that there would be so few farmhands by summer that they must buy those newfangled wheat reapers if the crop were to be saved. Jobless men disappeared from city streets as factories and merchants worked day and night to supply the demand for firearms, boots, clothing, kettles, rubber blankets, shovels, wagons, stoves, pickaxes, hard biscuits, bowie knives, all the paraphernalia which anticipation painted.

Army officers itched to join in the rush, wished their regiments would be ordered to the lawless land, and yet wondered how long their men would stay in uniform once they came near the mines.

Adventure of this kind was not in Ulysses' blood and, moreover, he had a greater romance here at home — Julia. For the first time in her life Julia was without slave labor, but she managed her cramped honeymoon quarters well and kept up her end of the entertaining expected in the post. When not with her or on duty, Ulysses raced horses with a young lawyer of the town, Charles W. Ford, or drove ten miles to Watertown to play chess and checkers with local experts. The citizens there remembered how obstinate he was when beaten, insisting upon more and more games until he tired his opponents out, and how, at the end of one prolonged sitting, he bet his adversary that he could beat him in a running race across the public square — and won.[15]

By early March Ulysses was in his Detroit post, taking rooms for himself and Julia at the National Hotel until he could rent a house. Social life was more to Julia's liking here. The trading post had grown until it now held 20,000 souls, many of them members of "old families" which had grown wealthy in commerce. On March 3 Ulysses ordered a new military frock coat and vest. He did so, however, with indifference, merely writing to a tailor patronized by Captain Gore, who was stationed at the post, to cut it to Gore's measurements "except for about ½ inch shorter in the waist." [16]

Julia and Mrs. Gore were soon entertaining other officers and their wives, and by July Ulysses had a house, a cottage at 253 Fort Street East — rental $250 per annum — a cottage in a neighborhood of working people, as distinct from Fort Street West where more fashionable folk lived. In September Grant's Regimental Quartermaster assignment was returned to him and soon a clerk named Friend Palmer, in the office of Major E. S. Sibley, Post Quartermaster, was puzzled how so silent and diffident a man could be given these executive duties. One day Palmer questioned Grant's sergeant on the subject.

"The Captain, I'll own, is not much good when you come to papers, accounts, returns and all that sort of thing," said the sergeant, "but when you get to the soldier part of it, drill, manual of arms and so on . . . he can handle the regiment as well, if not better, than any other fellow in it." [17]

To Grant the quartermaster work was a bore, now that it was unrelieved by marches or opportunity to gallop away when battle smoke rolled. Years later he would say with more humor than accuracy, "I was no clerk, nor had I any capacity to become one. The only place I ever found in my life to put a paper so as to find it again was either a side coat-pocket or the hands of a clerk . . . more careful than myself." [18]

Although he would declare in later years that Army life had never been agreeable to him, the Detroit days were happier than any he had known since he first put the uniform on. Delighted at home with Julia, he was with horsemen when away from it. Retired officers, lieutenants from the post and the sporting element of the city met at the whiskey barrel in the departmental sutler's store on Jefferson Avenue. "French ponies" which ran wild in meadows near town provided steeds for the races which were the chief amusement of the populace. Presumably Sam Grant drank moderately with the others, and certainly raced Nelly at breakneck speed along the streets.[19]

Seeing that trotting races in buggies were more popular than running matches, he raffled off Nelly and bought, for $250, a small coal-black harness mare from Jim Cicotte, the Democratic politician who, in 1835, had built the second frame building in Detroit. One citizen, H. C. Kibbee, never forgot the day when Grant bet fifty dollars that his "Cicotte mare" could take him and another passenger a mile down Jefferson Avenue in less than three minutes. Grant won, thundering along the street while bettors who lined it screamed *Marche donc!* Kibbee saw Grant pocket the fifty dollars, "bestow affectionate caresses upon his horse, and after seeing her well cared for" lead his friends to a tavern to celebrate. "No man was permitted to leave the party before refreshing himself at least a dozen times."

A brother officer noted that Grant read little, smoked a pipe incessantly, played loo, a card game resembling euchre, "was regarded as a restless, energetic man, who must have occupation, and plenty of it, for his own good" and was "sincere and true, an amiable good fellow." [20]

With winter, horse racing took on new fascination — rough-shod horses drawing cutters on the River Rouge along a course which ended at such taverns as Mother Weaver's, near the foot of Twelfth, or "Coon" Ten Eyck's near the hamlet of Dearborn.[21]

Drinking was common at the social affairs in homes of retired army officers and old French families, where post officers were entertained. Ulysses and Julia attended the weekly cotillions in the Michigan Exchange Hotel. She danced; he did not. The quartermaster clerk, Friend Palmer, saw Grant "stand around or hold down a seat all the evening," always "ready to join the boys when they went out 'to see a man.'" Palmer, however, "never saw him under the influence of liquor." [22]

Dr. Tripler, home from Mexico and assigned as surgeon at the post, said to his wife one day on the street, pointing to a man flying past in a buggy, "That's Grant. How he does drive that little rat of a horse!" Eunice Tripler saw Grant and Julia at large parties and at one given by the retired General Hugh Brady, veteran of the

War of 1812. She noted how he stood aloof, "with his hands behind his back . . . like a school-boy who had not learned his lesson." However, exchanging calls with Julia, Mrs. Tripler came to see that Grant "was always very devoted and tender to his wife." Mrs. Tripler's first cousin, Lieutenant Lewis Hunt, who had joined the regiment in 1847, told her, "There's more to Grant than you think," and she began to agree when she found Grant laughing heartily at her husband's story about the soldier who had died at Fort Yuma, California, that hottest of all posts. Doctor Tripler said that the dead soldier soon opened communications with the Army through spiritualists and reported himself "getting on pretty well, but he really wanted his heavy overcoat." When asked why, he had explained, "Well, after a man has been at Fort Yuma for a while, Hell is an awfully cold place."

Grant's diffidence, however, was always to be compared to the many attractive officers Mrs. Tripler saw coming and going — Captain Joseph E. Johnston, for instance, who charmed everybody.[23]

Julia and Mrs. Gore gave domino parties, small masquerades and suppers in their homes, illuminating the rooms with candles impaled on the prongs of deer antlers. One fancy-dress party given jointly by the hostesses, with the "elite of the city" attending in gay costumes, always stuck in Clerk Palmer's mind as the most brilliant affair of its kind seen in town for several years before or after.[24]

Julia began to drop out of the dances as the winter of 1849–1850 passed; she was pregnant, and with the spring she sat with Ulysses on the back piazza of their cottage, looking at the garden and presumably holding hands as they were so often seen to do later in their lives. As the expected arrival of the baby, late in May, drew near, Julia went home to St. Louis and Ulysses moved in with Gore, Mrs. Gore and their small son. Colonel Dent was eager to have Julia with him and had long before forgotten his objections to the marriage. He treated her husband as a son, and it was he and not Jesse Grant who signed Ulysses' bond as Regimental Quartermaster. "Frederick Dent Grant" was the name Julia and Ulysses gave the baby when, on May 30, 1850, it was born. Ulysses was contemplating his first-born in July when he read that President Taylor had died in the White House — one idol passing, another arriving. Eunice Tripler's opinion of Julia rose as she saw the young wife, back in Detroit, keeping house, managing well on a small income, doing her work "with a great lump of a baby in her arms." [25]

Six months after he became a father, Grant felt bold enough to hale into court the "big man of the town," rich, ruthless, powerful Zachariah Chandler. Ever since migrating from New Hampshire in 1833, Chandler had plowed through Detroit like a steamer through floating ice. Traveling the farm regions for great distances in summer heat and winter storms, he had drummed up his dry-goods-store and jobbing trade until he became the first businessman of the area to gross $50,000 a year. He had bought real estate shrewdly, weathered national panics by virtue of his reputation for rigid honesty, and soon was wealthy enough to turn his driving vitality into politics. Coarse and cunning, he was also fearless, contributing openly to the Underground Railroad, speaking vehemently against slavery, and organizing vigorously for the Whigs. In fights around polling booths on election days, Democrats learned to beware of Chandler's long, sinewy arms. In January 1851, he was preparing to run for Mayor, challenging the traditional Democratic rule. Then Lieutenant U. S. Grant on the tenth of March, brought him into court on the charge of disobeying the city ordinance requiring homeowners to clear the ice and snow off sidewalks. For the past twenty-five days the officers at the post had been suffering from Chandler's neglect as they passed his home on Jefferson Avenue; Grant slipped on the ice one night returning from headquarters and sprained a leg.

At the trial Chandler, acting as his own attorney, lavished vituperation of his own already famous brand upon the officers, denouncing them as idlers, loafers, sponges on the community. He denounced Grant, Gore and Major Sibley in particular, snarling at them:

"If you soldiers would keep sober, perhaps you would not fall on people's pavements and hurt your legs."

Although the evidence was against him, the jury let him off with a fine of six cents and costs — less than eight dollars all told. Five weeks later he was nominated for mayor by the Whigs. At the election which Chandler won, Grant, like many other officers, did not go to the polls. The new constitution of Michigan permitted all residents to become, automatically, citizens of the state, but Grant did not vote since he still wanted to be considered a citizen of Ohio.[26]

Chandler's feud with the officers vanished with the ice that spring of 1851, and would never be revived, for the War Department, abandoning the Detroit barracks, transferred the Fourth Regiment to Sacketts Harbor.

Back to the sparse life of Madison Barracks went the Grants in June — a letdown after the pleasures of Detroit. Also, the friendly hand of Major Lee was gone; he had been moved to another post. Colonel Whistler was commanding now in person. The Colonel's daughter Louise, a "sparkling and vivacious beauty" who moved to the new post with her father, was a great vexation to Sam Grant. She had shown an imperious character in Detroit, once whipping a dagger out of her decolletage at a party and forcing a harmless, free-and-easy beau of the town, Charles S. Adams, to apologize for what other guests considered to have been merely harmless "pleasantries." Now, at Madison Barracks, she insisted upon relieving the tedium of the post by having the regimental band serenade her every evening. To Grant this was torture, and at the first toot he would flee, leaving his home, wife and baby and seeking peace in chess and whist games behind closed doors down in the village a half mile away.[27]

He rode and drove with his lawyer friend Ford, and went to Watertown for chess games, but at twenty-eight fatherhood was settling him down. By December he knew that another baby would be coming next July. He attended the Sacketts Harbor Presbyterian Church with Julia, joined the Independent Order of Odd Fellows and attended the weekly meetings. He quit drinking and joined the Rising Sun Division, No. 210, local chapter of the national fraternal order, the Sons of Temperance, whose elaborate constitution had as its essence, Article 1: "No brother shall make, buy, sell, or use, as a beverage, any Spirituous or Malt Liquors, Wine, or Cider." Violators were tried and, if found guilty, expelled, although if the Division wished, it could reinstate them with a fine of $1 for the first offense, and $2 for the second. So strict were the bylaws that a Son could not down spirituous medicines prescribed by a physician, or sell liquor even if he were an auctioneer, and was fined one dollar if he failed to report to the lodge any brother who broke his pledge. With 2434 lodges functioning in 28 states — one in California, 27 in Canada, and 4 in England — the Sons had, in 1848, claimed some 148,000 members. No matter what his hard-drinking comrades at the Barracks might be saying, Sam Grant wore the regalia of the Sons, a red, white and blue ribbon in his lapel, and the emblem, a triangle surrounding the Star of Temperance. Townsfolk of Sacketts Harbor late remembered Grant as holding successive offices in the lodge which was "kept in a flourishing condition . . . mainly through his efforts" and which "after his departure . . . became disorganized, and was finally discontinued." [28]

This departure came in the spring of 1852, when orders took the regiment to the Pacific Coast. The first news of the move sent elation through the barracks, Delia Sheffield, wife of a sergeant in Company H, recalling later that she had been "wild to go." The regiment was to go at government expense to California, towards which gold seekers had been straining across the past two years, and to the rich Washington Territory, towards which covered wagons had been rolling for the past ten. Many a soldier planned to desert when he reached the golden shores and lose himself in the mines, and those who planned to stick to the colors saw excitement ahead in protecting the white men out there from each other and from the Indians, who were starting to fight for their ancient lands in the Columbia River Valley.

In the fevered preparation for departure, news came thick and fast. The regiment was not to go overland, but by sea, either around Cape Horn or to Panama and across the Isthmus to board a Pacific steamer. Old Colonel Whistler was to remain behind on leave of absence, shelved either because of age and whiskey or to permit the regiment to be led by its lieutenant colonel, the famous explorer, Benjamin Louis Eulalie Bonneville, whose adventures in the Rocky and Cascade Mountains, twenty years before, had been celebrated by the literary giant, Washington Irving. As a major in the Sixth Infantry, Bonneville had fought under Scott in the Valley of Mexico and, on May 7, 1849, had come to the Fourth when Lieutenant Colonel Garland had moved up to the colonelcy of the Eighth.

The rendezvous was to be at Governor's Island, New York City, and toward it the regimental majors, Gabriel Rains and George Wright, were moving with their companies from Detroit and Fort Ontario. In January 1848 Wright had joined the Fourth, his wounds healed from that massacre of the officers of the Third Infantry at Molino del Rey. It was a regiment led by battle-trained officers that the War Department was sending West, and Sam Grant was the senior first lieutenant, due for the next captaincy when a vacancy should occur.

Neither prospect of promotion nor of travel weighed with him now, however, against the realization that he could not take Julia and little Fred with him. Mrs. Gore and her child were going, and Mrs. Wallen and her seven-year-old son and four-year-old daughter. But Julia was in the "family way" and a year at least would pass before she and the two infants could make the long journey.

Grant's brother officers remembered in later years that he had talked of resigning from the Army. His obligation to Uncle Sam had ended the previous July when his eight-year enlistment had expired. But it was late to be taking up a new profession with three mouths to feed. He decided to go ahead and wait for Julia to come when she could. Meanwhile, she would go to Bethel and live with Jesse and Hannah until he could send for her.

Jesse's success schedule was still running on time. Within three years he would be sixty, the appointed age for retirement, and he would meet it with ample funds. In addition to the home tannery, he had one at Portsmouth, Ohio, and his branch leather stores now included Galena, Illinois, La Crosse, Wisconsin, and another less important one in neighboring Iowa. It was understood that he was worth at least $100,000, and Julia's father estimated the sum, a few years later, at $150,000.[29]

Jesse's other sons were helping with the business and showing signs of inheriting his energy and acumen. For the past year Jesse had been mayor of Bethel, the first to be chosen after the town's incorporation. In the absence of a town hall he heard breach-of-the-peace cases in his currying room, and the whole town laughed about the time a small boy, climbing high on rolled hides the better to see the mayor try two men for fist-fighting, slipped on the slick skin and came rolling down to land in a tub of dubbing — fish oil and tallow. Jesse, long before, had decided that Gregory's future lay more in the roping of steers than the tanning of hides, and had sent him back to Mexico. Although Jesse was regarded as tight-fisted, Ulysses knew how wide his arms would open to Julia and his first grandchild.[30]

Julia apparently was indifferent to the Southern Rights issue that separated so completely her father and her father-in-law. At White Haven, Colonel Dent was feuding with some wealthy neighbors, the Sigersons, who were so strongly anti-Southern that they worked their large nurseries entirely with white labor. The trouble came to a climax when Louis Dent, outraged at a canard reputedly made against his family by the Sigersons, went gunning for them and was beaten over the head so badly with a club that he hovered for weeks between life and death. Soon after recovering, Louis migrated to California, where he hoped to see Ulysses.[31]

On June 15 Ulysses said his last farewell to Julia and the baby and was off for Governor's Island. When he arrived on the seventeenth another blow fell. Lieutenant Colonel Bonneville was letting it be known that "he would object to have another officer for quartermaster." Young Second Lieutenant Henry C. Hodges understood that Bonneville was objecting to Grant because of "something that had occurred in Mexico." It was all very vague and was never brought into the open because the other officers showed such "strong opposition to the change" that the matter was dropped. Nevertheless, Sam Grant now had a commanding officer and a senior captain, Buchanan, who had shown signs of disliking him.[32]

The Bonneville incident could only have strengthened Grant with his brother officers, for the new Lieutenant Colonel was generally unpopular with the Army. A small man, very bald, crotchety, extremely excitable and vain, he scorned, among other regulations, the usual officer's headgear and wore instead a huge, stiff white beaver hat which prompted the common soldiers to howl at him from hiding places, "Where did you get that hat?"

Bonneville was precisely the kind of colonel to be making life hard for his quartermaster. In Detroit, Eunice Tripler was regretting that her husband-surgeon had to serve under Bonneville, who was "a very stupid man mentally," and officers in general regarded him as the product of favoritism rather than military ability. Whispers commonly had it that he had been sent to West Point, in 1813, because his mother had been the mistress of the famous American patriot, Tom Paine; that he owed his promotions in the Army to the Marquis de Lafayette and President Andrew Jackson, and that the author Washington Irving had given him undeserved fame. Even when persons who knew the truth disproved the scandal about

Bonneville's mother, the fact remained that he had from boyhood been treated as the heir of Paine, to whom the Republic owed so much.

Paine had been a friend of Bonneville's father in Paris during the French Revolution and, back in America after the Terror, when he heard that Monsieur Bonneville had been jailed by the new regime of Napoleon Bonaparte as a republican pamphleteer, had sent for Madame Bonneville and her three sons to cross the ocean and live with him. He had educated the boys, made them his heirs, and at his grave Madame had stood with thirteen-year-old Benjamin and cried, "Oh! Mr. Paine! My son stands here as testimony of the gratitude of America, and I, for France!" When Benjamin had reached seventeen, the sympathetic administration of President Madison had sent him to West Point and, twenty months later, commissioned him in the Army. He had been a first lieutenant in the Indian country where he always preferred to be when Lafayette, visiting America, asked that the son of his old friend be attached to his party. Lafayette had taken the young man back to France with him on a year's leave of absence and, as they sailed, the War Department had made Bonneville a captain.

Another leave of absence in the early 1830's, one given him to explore the Far West with civilian trappers, had dramatized him still more as the pet of the Republic. With courage and skill Bonneville had penetrated the wilderness, but had airily overstayed his leave by a whole year or more, and had been dropped from the army rolls. Moreover, he had brought back to civilization none of the scientific data on the Indians he had promised to secure, and appeared to have spent a great deal of the time investigating the fur trade with an eye to his future. But President Jackson, delighted with a map Bonneville had made, had ordered him reinstated no matter what the Army said, and when his journals of exploration had been rewritten and expanded by Washington Irving into a popular book, he had been made a major.

As a prima donna and a man who had spent almost his whole career in the reckless West handling small bodies of loosely disciplined soldiers, Bonneville was unsuited to the management of some 700 officers and men, together with some 100 of their wives, children and camp followers in the cramped confines of a steamer on a long voyage. Eight companies were to sail with him on the side-wheeler *Ohio* for Panama, while Major Wright was to take two on the longer trip around Cape Horn.

To harass Bonneville's temper still more, the War Department had bunglingly booked passage on the *Ohio* at the last moment, when its 250 first-class cabins and 80 steerage berths had been filled by civilians, California-bound.[33]

Upon Sam Grant, as Quartermaster, fell the work of finding room for the latecomers and their baggage. He built tiers of berths on deck for the men. As the voyage commenced, on July 5, the little wife of Sergeant Sheffield saw how Grant smoothed over the "unpleasantnesses" created by Bonneville's "testy temper." The captain of the *Ohio*, Lieutenant Finley Schenck of the Navy, soon noted that the "disagreements" caused by Bonneville's "hasty and uncertain" actions were referred "to Grant as arbitrator," and that the Quartermaster's rulings were "distinguished by particular good sense." A member of the Fourth said in after years that arguments among the officers were often taken to "long-headed Sam" for settlement.[34]

To add to Grant's worries was the fear that disease would ravage the crowded passengers when the *Ohio* reached the tropics. Dr. Tripler was warning the surgeon general's office that it was "murder" to ship the men at a time when cholera would be ravaging Panama's jungles. Down there white workmen imported to work on the railroad that was starting across the Isthmus died like flies — "An Irishman for every tie." But the surgeon general had assured Tripler that the Fourth would cross too rapidly for the epidemic to catch them.[35]

As the *Ohio* got under way, Lieutenant Hodges admired the kindly generosity with which the "thin, quiet, reticent" Quartermaster treated soldiers and civilians, and gave "close attention to his duties." But as the cruise shook down, little Mrs. Sheffield noticed Grant pacing the deck "every day and the early part of each night . . . smoking, silent and solitary" and often with "head bent, as if in deep thought." Once, mistaking her for a child, he stopped, calling her attention to some whales following the ship, then discovering that she was married, said "Why, you ought to be under your mother's care, sleeping in your trundle bed." [36]

Homesickness was on Grant. Officers later remembered him staring at the sad and lonely sea. sitting apart from the rest. Lieutenant

Schenck, watching over his ship, also discovered that Grant was pacing the deck late at night, all alone. After a time, as work eased up, Schenck walked with him. Sometimes they walked in silence, sometimes they talked, "discussing such matters as came up from time to time," as the sailor said. Schenck did not penetrate the soldier's thoughts but, as he later stated, saw him to be "a man of an uncommon order of intelligence" with "a good education, and what his mind took hold of it grasped strongly and thoroughly digested." [37]

Up ahead, past the flying-serpent figurehead on the prow, Ulysses watched the southern constellations rise. When last he had seen them they had been falling down the sky, behind the ship, settling lower each night as that other steamer had brought him home from Mexico to Julia. Now the churning, splashing paddles were carrying him away from her. He might never see her again. If he did, little Fred might not know him. Would he ever see the second baby? It must be born by now. Julia might be in the pangs this minute; sometime around the middle of July was the time. Why had he gone into the Army? He had never liked it. Yet if he had not, how could he ever have met Julia or known what it was to sit holding her hand — her beautiful hand, so warm, so small.

In the night there were lights on the black edge of the horizon — ships heading home. And at one time the perfume of the tropics floated on the breeze from Cuba, off there somewhere to the left. He had wanted to go back to the tropics — but not now. He had loved the sea from the first time he had seen it — but not this sea.

Though other officers and Mrs. Sheffield thought the weather fair for the entire journey, Grant grew seasick for what would probably be the only time in his life. Loneliness, longing were tugging at his nerves. But he was himself, and in fact moving with a new efficiency and executive power as the *Ohio*, anchoring off the town of Aspinwall on July 16, began sending its passengers and baggage ashore in yawls. Slab hotels, boardinghouses, saloons and gambling hells proclaimed the Americanization which had built the town in 1849, when the gold rush to California had prompted the financier, William Henry Aspinwall, to start a steamship line and project a railroad across the Isthmus. Negro and Indian porters carried trunks across planks above sidewalks that were eight inches under water. The stench of slops in the stagnant pools, the sight of groggeries filling men with rum to ward off malaria and quinine to cure it, made Grant wonder "how any person could live many months in Aspinwall, and . . . still more why anyone tried." Outside in the harbor stood the ruins of Fort San Lorenzo, which Sir Henry Morgan and his buccaneers had sacked in 1671, and in the town now vagabonds hardly less desperate stole valises. Everybody, even the swarms of naked children who followed Indian women, smoked cigars.[38]

Within twenty-four hours the Quartermaster had all but one company of the Fourth steaming away on the little railroad to its terminus, a point twenty miles inland, where transportation up the Chagres River had been arranged. With the company which was to aid him, Grant saw the regiment start up the river in dugouts, *bungos* the natives called them, thirty to forty persons to a load, each *bungo* poled upstream, a mile an hour, by nearly naked Negroes or Indians who walked planks at the boats' sides, pacing their strides with wild, monotonous songs. Since the treaty obliged all soldiers to carry no firearms while crossing, the Quartermaster must bring up the rifles, along with the ammunition chests, tents, band instruments, camp kettles and baggage, official and personal, of the regiment.[39]

Up and down the river he worked, pushing the fleet toward the head of navigation, the village of Cruces, from where the journey would be overland twenty-five miles down to Panama City and the California steamer. The boatloads of women and children were a worry. Mrs. Sheffield and the other wives lay shivering in their *bungos* when the fleet tied up at night along the banks, for their boatmen were howling like the "drunken barbarians" they were, in the nearby village. Once when one boat tried to pass another, the crews quarreled and, pulling knives, dived off, making for each other, and would have reddened the water if the Army officers had not drawn swords and made them return to their work. At another time, word came back to Grant that a *bungo* of the wives and children had capsized somewhere on ahead, and that all were drowned. While the officers milled frantically, Grant rushed to the scene with a company of men and Lieutenant Henry D. Wallen, whose wife and two small children were in the party. Wallen later told how "we had not proceeded far, however, before we ascertained that the boat which had turned over contained a number of citizen passengers, and . . . that none of our party were injured." He said they pushed on until they reached the ladies and Grant "immediately perfected arrangements for sending them across the Isthmus." [40]

Establishing himself at the dingy village of Cruces, Grant saw seven companies off on the march down muddy roads to Panama City and, as soon as he could round up porters, sent the women and children after them in hammocks slung between the stalwart carriers. He could find no mules in Cruces to haul the baggage. The contractor with whom the War Department had made arrangements had yielded to the temptation to rent his drove to the passengers from the *Ohio* who had swept through a day or two earlier. Their haste to get to the gold fields of California had been increased by the rumor that cholera was in Cruces, and they had given the contractor forty dollars a mule instead of the customary sixteen dollars. Grant discovered almost immediately that the rumors were true — cholera began knocking down his men, striking sound men suddenly on the street. Quickly he ordered the unstricken to march on to Panama City. He would remain behind with his sick until the mules contracted for appeared. When his drum major said that the trip was too much for his wife to be walking it, Grant gave him $25 from his own pocket and told him to secure a mule from the natives. None could be bought, so Grant found her a citizen's coat, her husband gave her a pair of pantaloons and they trudged off. In a shack, Grant discovered some Sisters of Charity whom he had known on the *Ohio* nursing one of their number, sick with cholera. He watched her closely and as soon as she could travel, brought up Indian porters who carried the nuns down the road in hammocks.[41]

Each morning the palavering contractor promised to have the mules tomorrow. Each day Grant worked in the town or with the marchers, ahead or behind the *bungo* loads in the last lap of the river trip. Mrs. Sheffield saw him come up to her party on the trail the first afternoon of its overland trip and warn everybody against drinking the fever-laden water. By chance she had been given a mule, and the native who led it was on the point of bringing it and her into his hut that night when her screams brought her husband to the rescue. Captain Wallen's seven-year-old son rode a porter's back and his four-year-old daughter Nannie, a hammock. One night Nannie and her bearers did not reach the camp and Mrs. Wallen had hys-

terics until next morning when the porters brought the baby in safe
and sound. They had stopped off at their own home, which was not
far from the road, to spend the night.[42]

On the river, Grant saw the sights which American travelers always remembered — the jungle banks afire with flowers and red
macaws — a heavy green slime on the Chagres — the towering palms
full of squealing monkeys — the native cooks at village stops along
the way chewing sugar cane and spitting into the coffeepot to
sweeten it — villages with strange names like Ahorca la Gata, Hang
the Cat — natives climbing into church belfries to hit tongueless
bells with rocks when signals must be given.

After three days of toil, in addition to nursing the sick, Grant
threw army regulations out the window, told the mouthing, whining contractor to forget about the mules, and going out in the open
market hired animals at double the authorized sum. Two days later
he was ready and with his baggage on packsaddles, his sick on mule-
back or in hammocks, he started the cavalcade. When men died he
buried them under tangled blossoms by the roadside. The rain came
down and the mud was so deep that when Surgeon Tripler rode
back along the column to pick up men who had been stricken with
the cholera, he sometimes could not find them — they had disappeared
in the mire.[43]

By the time Grant came into Panama City with his groaning, dying, vomiting men, his mud-spattered civilians, mules and muleteers
he found that "about one-third of the people" with him had "died,
either at Cruces or on the way to Panama." [44]

He found the San Francisco boat, the *Golden Gate*, anchored
almost two miles out in the harbor, quarantined by the cholera.
Bonneville had put the women and children on board with the in-
fected regiment, and Dr. Tripler was denouncing this "inhumanity."
An old hulk was eventually leased as a hospital ship, anchored a mile
away, and to it the Quartermaster brought the sick from the
Golden Gate. Mrs. Sheffield saw strong men walking the deck of
the *Golden Gate* suddenly begin writhing with cramps and carried
away to die.

In time, enlisted men assigned to act as stewards on the hospital
boat became frightened, neglected their duties and, when the chance
came, slipped over the side and swam ashore. Tripler, nearing ex-

haustion, asked officers to volunteer, one at a time, to come on board
with him, stand watch for twenty-four hours and force the stewards
to do their duty. He would always remember Grant and Gore especially for their aid. Mrs. Tripler understood that Bonneville had
become "greatly exercised" at the doctor for this excess of authority
and had "threatened to have him court-martialed." The excitable
Colonel had backed down, however, when Tripler had told him to
go ahead and "make his threat good." [45]

For more than two weeks, Grant took his turn on the "death-
ship," brought to it the sick from the *Golden Gate*, furnished the
sacking and cannon balls with which the dead were lowered into the
bay, and supplied food, water and medicine from the city. A tender
hand at nursing, he was said by one officer to "take a personal interest in each sick man" and "to be a man of iron, so far as endurance
went, seldom sleeping, and then only two or three hours at a time."
Yet "his work was always done, and his supplies always ample and
at hand. . . . He was like a ministering angel to us all." [46] Wallen
thought Sam "one of the coolest men in all these trying emergencies
I ever saw." Particularly did he recall, later on, Grant's poise one
day on the *Golden Gate* when a frightening thing happened. Wallen,
Grant and Gore had been playing euchre when Gore suddenly
dropped his hand, turned pale and gasped:

"My God, I've got the cholera!"

"No, Major, you've only eaten something that doesn't agree with
you," Grant said, trying to quiet his fears. But they summoned the
surgeon. Gore was right. He died within a few hours.

As Quartermaster and as the closest friend of Mrs. Gore among
the officers, Grant's duty was to send Mrs. Gore and her child home
to her father at Covington, Kentucky. With the youngest of the
second lieutenants, Robert McFeeley, as escort, he saw her off up the
road toward Aspinwall, she in one hammock, her child's nurse in
another, her baggage in five more, while her infant son rode the
shoulders of an Indian. When McFeeley caught up with the regiment
five months later, he reported that the Indians had stolen all Mrs.
Gore's silver, jewelry and most of her extra clothing. [47]

In a letter of August 9, 1852 aboard the *Golden Gate*, "Near
Acapulco," Grant wrote but spared Julia the worst of the harrow-
ing trip. In the same letter he told her of his destination.

MY DEAREST JULIA:

I wish I could only know that you, and our dear little ones were as well as I am. Although we have had terrible sickness among the troops, and have lost one hundred persons, counting men, women & children, yet I have enjoyed good health. It has been the province of my place as Quarter Master to be exposed to the weather and climate on the Isthmus while most of the others were quietly aboard ship, but to that very activity probably may be ascribed my good health. It no doubt will be relief to you to know that we have been out from Panama over four days and no sickness has broken out aboard. All are healthy and every minute brings us towards a better climate.

Among the deaths was that of poor Maj. Gore. The Maj. was taken before daylight in the morning and in the afternoon was dead. Mrs. Gore took his death very hard and then to think too of the trip she had to undergo crossing the Isthmus again! My Dearest you never could have crossed the Isthmus at this season, for the first time, let alone the second. The horrors of the road, in the rainy season, are beyond description. Mrs. Gore will be at home, if she is so fortunate as to stand the trip, before you get this. I hope father and Ginnie will go and see her soon. Lieut. McFeeley 2d Lt. of Maj. Gore's Compy. accompanied Mrs. Gore and may go to our house to see you. He promised me that he would. I gave him an order on the Q. Mr. in New York for $150.00 Mr. Hooker owes me which if he gets he will send you.

Mrs. Wallen and the other ladies along are tollerably well, but a goodeal reduced. Mrs. Wallen's weight when she got across the Isthmus was 84 lbs. Her children, Harry Nanny & Eddy look quite differently from what they did when they left New York. But thank fortune we are fast approaching a better climate. The Golden Gate takes us nearly 300 miles per day.

We have seen from a California paper our destination. All but one Company go to Oregon. Head Quarters (and of course I with it) go to Columbia Barracks, Fort Vancouver, Oregon. In consequence of one Company of the Regt., and all the sick being left at the Island Flamingo, near Panama, to follow on an other steamer, we will remain at Benecia, Cal. for probably a month. Benecia is within a day's time of where John is and of course I shall see him.

You must not give yourself any uneasiness about me now

Dearest for the time has passed for danger. I know you have borrowed a goodeal of trouble and from the exaggerated accounts which the papers will give you could not help it. From Mrs. Gore however you can get the facts which are terrible enough.

I have not given you any description of any part of our journey, and as I told you in all my letters Dearest, I will not until I hear of your being well. I will say however that there is a great accountability some where for the loss which we have sustained. Out of the troops at Sackets Harbor some twelve or fifteen are dead, none that you would recollect however except O'Maley, and Sgt. Knox, the one you thought looked so much like Maloney.

Elijah Camp is with us. He goes as Sutler, probably with Head Quarters.

Give my love to all at home Dearest and kiss our dear little ones for me. Fred, the little dog I know talks quite well by this time. Is he not a great pet? You must not let them spoil him Dearest. A thousand kisses for yourself dear Julia. Don't forget to write often and direct, Hd. Qrs. 4th Inf. Columbia Barracks, Fort Vancouver, Oregon.

Adieu dear wife,
Your affectionate husband,

ULYSSES

P.S. You may be anxious to hear from Maggy. She looks worse than ever. She has been sea-sick ever since she started. She regrets very much that she had not staid with you.

Mrs. Wallen was going to write to you from Panama but Maj. Gore's taking sick prevented.

Again adieu dear dear wife,

U.

With all the strain and woe, Grant found time to laugh at another of the young lieutenants, William A. Slaughter, who had been sea-sick every moment of the trip down from New York to Aspinwall, and who was, as Grant said, never more so than while lying at anchor in the harbor off Panama City. On the *Golden Gate* Slaughter sat head in hands, groaning out the story of how he had been sent to the Coast back in 1848, a seven months' trip around Cape Horn, suffering agonies all the way, and had been returned to New York a few months later, over the same long, hideous path, and now here he was on his way out again.

"I wish I had taken my father's advice," he moaned. "He wanted me to go into the navy; if I had done so, I should not have had to go to sea so much." Grant said later of Slaughter, "It almost made him sick to see the wave of a table-cloth when the servants were spreading it." [48]

There was also humor for Grant at the time Captain Patterson of the *Golden Gate* and Dr. Tripler persuaded Bonneville to move the entire regiment on rafts over to the sandhills of neighboring Flamingo Bay, and encamp it in tents so that the ship could be fumigated. As the rafts with the people and tents were being rowed ashore, a tugboat came steaming out from Panama City, ready for war. The authorities had seen the movement through spyglasses and had leaped to the conclusion that the *Americanos* were landing an army of filibusters. Comic though this was, Yankee civilians in the past three years had given Panama City cause for alarm, fighting with each other and the natives, shooting and roaring their drunken way among the saloons, desecrating Catholic churches upon occasion, and generally complaining that the belfry bells rang too loudly and too often. [49]

Tent life and fumigation on Flamingo's shores began to break the back of the cholera, but "Panama fever," suspected of being a kind of malaria, increased and it was August 5 before the regiment sailed. Behind it all, all the way to Cruces, more than one hundred men lay moldering in graves or turning lazily with the tides on the bottom of Panama Bay. [50]

So many were the sick that the regiment was not taken to San Francisco, but invalided to Benicia Barracks, a few hours' sail on through the Bay to the mouth of the Sacramento River, where it would recuperate for three weeks more, with officers hurrying down from headquarters of the Pacific Division to observe it. On August 31, Major Osborne Cross, of the Quartermaster's Staff, wrote his chief in Washington that the fate of the Fourth ought to warn the Army to send troops henceforth around the Horn. The Isthmus route not only meant double expense but the Fourth's "loss has been seriously great, while those who have arrived are broken down with diseases, the seeds of which were engendered on the Isthmus." [51]

Again Grant saw that disease, not gunpowder, was the greater killer of soldiers. As long as he would live he would talk more of Panama than of any of his battles, even of that murderous day in the leaden hell of San Cosme. The sick and dying men, the rain and the mud, the burdens thrown upon him by the incompetent Bonneville had, however, lifted him from his own homesickness and had revealed to him his unguessed powers at this business of managing a command of military men.

CHAPTER EIGHTEEN

Letters from Home

A S THE STEAMER anchored in San Francisco Bay near noon on September 15, 1852, all officers not on duty were given permission to go ashore for twenty-four hours to see the fabled city where the gold nuggets were assembled. Leave could not be longer, for the regiment was two months overdue at its destination to the north — one company on the upper Sacramento in California, the rest along the Columbia River in Washington Territory, with headquarters at Fort Vancouver where Bonneville would be stationed with four companies.

"Let's go on shore together," Sam Grant said to Henry Hodges, and soon they were on San Francisco's Long Wharf where runners for hotels, eating places, gambling parlors, waited for the miners who arrived by boat from Stockton and Sacramento. Brushing past this horde of what Grant called "impecunious adventurers of good manners and good presence" all eager to be "asked to take a meal at a restaurant," the two officers were quickly in the center of the strangest Babel probably existing at that moment on the face of the globe.

The autumn of 1852 found the Gold Rush at its height. California, which had held 20,000 persons exclusive of Indians in 1848, and 100,000 at the end of '49, now boasted 225,000. On board sidewalks which cracked here and there and spurted muddy water, pressed a torrent of polyglot humanity — bearded miners pulling sacks of gold dust from torn pants and buying drinks for New York dudes; French dandies waving canes and making their high heels pop as they argued about rooms in crowded hotels; South Americans gesticulating over claims in brokers' offices; Kanakas from the South Seas arguing with freed Negroes from Alabama over incoming trunks; Germans and Australians buying patented mining tools from shifty Yankee merchants; Cuban artists painting portraits of newly rich Irishmen; Southern gentlemen who had struck it big in the mountains explain-

ing to English gentlemen who hadn't, the glories of Scott's *Ivanhoe;*
Mexicans brandishing stilettoes at Texans who waved bowie knives;
Bowery toughs yanking Chinese by the queues and booting them up
the street amid universal laughter; Hoosier farmers buying gewgaws
from Hindu peddlers; dancing girls, insisting that they were Creole
belles from New Orleans, fingering the gold-dust pokes of Harvard
men at tables in grogshops; Indian girls tittering quietly as Yale men
escorted them to the arena where Mexican horned bulls fought
grizzly bears to the death — and over everything the chant floating
from open doors of gambling parlors wherein the lords of the town,
elegant men in beaver hats and elegant plush vests, waved their quick,
white, elegant hands as they called:

"Come down! Come down! Come down on the red! Why work?
The money's here. The money's yours. Get it while it lasts. Step up!
Step up! Come down on the red!"

At a faro house Sam Grant said to Hodges, "Let's go in and win
our dinner." Inside the door, Grant hailed an affable gambler as
"Captain!" and introduced him to Hodges as a former officer of the
Third Cavalry in Mexican War days. The Captain led Sam to a faro
table to start "the battle for the dinner." At first Sam lost, but with a
second stack of chips he quickly won back all he had lost and $40 to
boot. "Well, Hodges," he said, "I rather think this will get us a pretty
good dinner." [1]

The suave Captain saw them to the door. Evidently California
was receiving its share of the officers who were resigning now at a
rate almost as high as in the 1830's. At Benicia Barracks, firewood had
come in on contract from Captain Joseph Hooker, who had bought
Sonoma land in preparation for a life of ease, whiskey and gambling
when his two years' leave of absence would end in resignation sometime in 1853. [2]

Here in San Francisco, said army officers, the brilliant Henry W.
Halleck was practicing law, directing a quicksilver mine and invest-
ing in real estate as he prepared to resign from the Engineers. The
officers told Sam it was all right if you resigned, but on army pay
you couldn't support a family. His basic salary, $480 a year, had been
increased only $197, to meet the increased cost on the Coast. "A cook
could not be hired for the pay of a captain," Grant said later. "The
cook could do better." [3]

Family men like Wallen were worried as the regiment sailed north on September 14, and Sam Grant was wondering how he could ever bring Julia and the babies to such a country.

The Columbia River was a stirring sight as the steamer, ploughing upstream, arrived at Fort Vancouver on September 22. Spruce and fir towered over the river and Mount Hood towered over the spruce and fir. More stirring to Grant was the sight of Rufe Ingalls on the bank — the first time they had met in seven years. Rufe and Sam French had done well and were captains, one grade ahead of any others in the Class of '43. Rufe was honing for companionship, since his convivial spirit had been confined across most of the past three years to this tiny trading post where Indians and half-breed trappers occupied log cabins around the depot of the Hudson's Bay Company. On the bluffs, a scant half mile back from the river, Ingalls had built a fort, a long stockade with a tower pierced for cannon and rifles, and inside the wall, storehouses and barracks of hewn trees, and frame houses for officers.

Rufe showed Sam to the best of the houses, "Quartermaster's Ranch," a two-story frame building with a long piazza and balcony, where Sam as Regimental Quartermaster would live and entertain officers of the surveying parties which Uncle Sam was sending into the new country.[4]

Sam had Rufe live with him, and to cut expenses, they included Captain Thomas L. Brent, who had come up from San Francisco to relieve Ingalls as Post Quartermaster. For the winter Rufe was to remain where he was, waiting until the Department gave him his next assignment. Since the Indians of the region were quiet and no expeditions would be coming through Vancouver before spring, Sam's duties were light and Rufe's none at all. They took long horseback rides together and re-created their old West Point days — and nights — clearing the tables for euchre, brag and loo. The Ranch was the social center. Augur, Wallen and Hodges were especially welcome, and from outside the Fourth's group of sixteen officers, Captain John S. Hatheway, present with a battery of the Fourth Artillery, was welcomed.

With Commandant Bonneville aloof in his own quarters and Captains Buchanan and Alvord with their companies along the Columbia River and Oregon Trail to the east, Grant and Hatheway were the only officers who could describe to the Ranch gatherings the fighting in the Valley of Mexico. Ingalls told afterward how often Sam "astonished his brother officers by his clear, luminous descriptions." Another officer, coming away from one of those evenings when Grant had recalled small incidents from memory and delivered criticisms of his generals' strategy and tactics, was heard to say, "How clear-headed Sam Grant is in describing a battle! He seems to have the whole thing in his head."

However much Grant enjoyed comradeship with this small group of men, his role of host was still that of a bachelor and the realization grew poignant when a letter from Bethel informed him that on July 22 Julia had borne him a second son, Ulysses S. Grant, Jr. On October 26, 1852, hardly more than a month after his arrival at Fort Vancouver, he had begun to feel his isolation from his family and initiated steps which he hoped would bring them to him. He wrote in part:

MY DEAREST WIFE:

Another mail has arrived and not one word do I get from you either directly or indirectly. It makes me restless, Dearest, and much more so because I now know that I must wait over two weeks before I can possibly hear. I can write you nothing until I hear from you and learn that you and our dear little ones are well. Just think, our youngest is at this moment probably over three months of age, and yet I have never heard a word from it, or you, in that time. I have my health perfectly and could enjoy myself here as well as at any place that I have ever been stationed if only you were here. It is true that all my pay would not much more than pay the expenses of the table, yet I think, judging from what has taken place, that this expense could be borne here better than the ordinary expenses in the Atlantic States. I have made something dearest for us, (including our children,) already, and have got the plans laid, and being carried out, by which I hope to make much more. I have been up to the Dalles of the Columbia, where the Immigrants generally first stop upon their arrival in Oregon, coming by the overland route. I there made arrangements for the purchase of quite a number of oxen and cows, and for having them taken care of during the winter. If I should lose one-fourth of my cattle I would then clear at least one hundred per cent, if I should lose all I would have the consolation of knowing that I was still better off than when I first came to this country. I have, in addition to cattle, some hogs from which I expect a large increase, soon, and have also bought a horse upon which I have been offered an advance of more than one hundred dollars.

Here on the post grounds other officers spent evenings with their families. Wallen was building easy chairs out of barrels for his home, stuffing them with moss and covering them with calico.[5] But everything was keeping Grant away from the woman he wanted — the high cost of living, the Indians, who, while quiet at the moment, were certain to make trouble as the stream of covered wagons coming in by the Oregon Trail touched new valleys. Congress was cutting Washington Territory in two that winter, parting it at the Columbia River, and calling the lower half Oregon Territory. Surveys would start next spring for a railroad through the Cascade Mountains, connecting the banks of the Pacific with those of the Mississippi River. The Fourth Regiment might be stationed out here for years.

Ulysses must make extra money somehow and bring Julia and the babies to him. Other officers were trying it. Dr. Tripler, down in San Francisco, was eking out his salary by practicing medicine among civilians.

Someone said ice was selling at fabulous prices in San Francisco. Sam, Rufe and Wallen sent 100 tons cut in the neighborhood down the Columbia in a Pacific Mail sailing schooner, whose skipper, Captain Dall, was included as partner. Two months or more later Dall came back with sad news. The wind had turned just outside the Columbia's mouth, the trip had taken six weeks, and when he had reached Frisco the prices had fallen. Other ice ships had come in from Sitka, Alaska — and the officers' investment was gone.[6]

All around the disappointed Ulysses the officers drank regularly at their card games in the evening. As at all frontier posts, it was rare to find an officer who did not tip the demijohn on his right arm and pour all he wished into a tumbler. One of the stock jokes of garrison life was that of the soldier who answered, "Do you take me for a camel?" when asked if he wished water in his liquor. Stories were common of officers standing outside their quarters at noon and signaling with forefinger laid to nose for all passing friends to "come in and partake," and of one post commander who always had his officers in to drink with him one at a time instead of in a group, "because I want to get half of my own liquor." [7]

Living the life of a host in such an atmosphere, and honing, as he was, for Julia, the Son of Temperance gave up his fraternal vows. Sam "was not by any means a drunkard," said Henry Hodges in later years; he merely went on "two or three sprees a year . . . was always open to reason, and when spoken to on the subject would own up and promise to stop drinking, which he did." From the stories told by his comrades at Vancouver, it was likely that he did not slake his sex yearnings, as did so many other lonely white men on the frontier, by visits to Indian women. When, years later, the wife of Sergeant Sheffield heard Grant's enemies whisper the "story of the Indian daughter," she knew just how the "baseless and malicious" tale had started — at another fort in the Territory had lived one Richard Grant, an agent for the Hudson's Bay Company, who was a squaw man with several half-breed children.[8]

The Indians stirred Grant's pity rather than passion. In a letter to an officer in San Francisco he said that the red men were "easily controlled and altogether to (sic) insignificant in prowess & numbers to need much care or attention and even this poor remnant of a once powerful tribe is fast wasting away before those blessings of 'civilization,' whisky and small pox." It saddened him to see the Indians attempt to cure the "amazingly fatal" epidemics of unfamiliar measles and smallpox by their ancient method of thrusting sufferers into mud ovens and steaming them to the point of exhaustion. "This treatment," said Grant, "may have answered with the early ailments of the Indians. With the measles or small-pox it would kill every time." [9]

Across the past twenty years many stories of the Indians' reliance upon heat to cure disease had been taken back to the States by travelers. One of the best known was that of the white trapper who had so exhausted himself in the arms of young squaws of the Flathead tribe that he developed consumption. The red men had killed a horse, slit open its belly, thrust the naked white man "into the foaming mass of entrails" and kept him there till the carcass cooled. Putting him to bed, they repeated the process a few days later, apparently willing to keep it up as long as their horses held out. The second treatment, however, restored the patient to health — and the beds of the squaws.[10]

Where most white individuals exploited the red men, Grant saw the Hudson's Bay Company at Vancouver pay them fair wages, sell them supplies at a uniform rate, teach them to raise crops and cattle, and when the smallpox epidemic struck, move promptly to their aid. Within a stone's throw of the Quartermaster's Ranch, the fur company's resident doctor set up a hospital, and in it saved practically all the sufferers he could collect.[11]

In allaying Julia's fears about the redskins he had written:

> You charge me to be cautious about riding out alone lest the Indians should get me. Those about here are the most harmless people you ever saw. It is really my opinion that the whole race would be harmless and peaceable if they were not put upon by the whites.

It was a relief to Grant that the Indian outbreaks, when they occurred, were too far away to involve the Fourth Infantry. The fighting along the Rouge River in Oregon in the spring of 1853 was far away. Grant heard that it had ended before Captain Lyon had arrived with a detachment of the Second Infantry, which was just as well for the red men. Officers still talked about the swift, secret marches and the sudden attacks with which the fierce redhead had crushed the Clear Lake Indians back in 1850 — killing at least two huge braves with his sword.

News of the outside world came slowly to Vancouver. It was deep in the winter before Grant knew that Franklin Pierce, whom he had liked so well in Mexico, was now President, winning as a Democrat over General Scott, the Whig, last November. The American people wanted Generals in the White House — George Washington, Andy Jackson, Taylor, and now Pierce.

With the coming of spring, life grew lonelier. Ingalls was ordered to Fort Yuma, leaving the Ranch to Grant, Brent and Grant's clerk, Eastman. Grant rode alone now in the wilderness, no other hoofs thudding softly in the pine needles — no Julia to swing down from her saddle and pick wild flowers — no Julia to rein in beside him and look at this river as they had looked at the Mississippi and the

Ohio. He wanted a woman's hand in the house. He asked Sergeant and Mrs. Sheffield to move in, and when the Sergeant feared that his wife was too young and inexperienced, Grant spoke reassuringly:

"Oh, that can be easily managed. I'll detail one of the soldiers who is a good cook, to do the cooking; besides, I have an excellent cookbook and am a pretty good cook myself, and I'm sure we shall manage very well."

They came, and the wife was quickly drawn to the quiet Ulysses — eternally grateful for the kindness with which he showed her how to cook wild swan, geese and duck which the other men brought him, and how to prepare his own favorite dish, beef à la mode. She would never forget the day when he asked if she thought she could make him some sweet butter — the kind they had been buying from the Indians was tasteless. Innocent of the butter-making art, she used sugar instead of salt when she churned and, at the next meal, when she saw the officers grinning at each other, timidly asked Grant how he liked it. "Well, it's the sweetest butter I ever tasted" was all he said, but she caught "a twinkle in his eye" and did not rest until she had made him explain her mistake. Everything that she would remember about Grant at Vancouver was colored by sympathy for him in his homesickness:

> Oftentimes while reading letters from his wife, his eyes would fill with tears, he would look up with a start and say, "Mrs. Sheffield, I have the dearest little wife in the world, and I want to resign from the army and live with my family.[12]

Sergeant Eckerson of the garrison told, in after times, of the day when he had received through the mail notice that he was appointed agent of the Ordnance Department, a promotion that Grant had obtained for him. As he was reading it, Grant came in to congratulate him and just before leaving said, "Oh, I, too, had a letter last night." He opened it at the last page which contained a penciled outline of a baby's hand, showed it, but said nothing as he stood there trembling and teary-eyed. Then he went away.

"He seemed to be always sad," the Sergeant said.[13]

Ulysses' relatives declared later that "no ship sailed from the West," without a letter or two from the young officer to his loved ones.[14]

Mrs. Sheffield, working in the kitchen, would see Grant walking back and forth on the porch, "thinking and smoking, for hours at a time, or he would order his horse and ride for a half day in the woods or along the Columbia river." Discarding Army regulations as to the relations between commissioned and noncommissioned officers, the Lieutenant would sit with the Sergeant and the Sergeant's wife of evenings around the fire and, as Mrs. Sheffield would later say, "tell me of his wife and children and how he missed them." [15]

With the springtime, Ulysses made another attempt to earn extra money. With Wallen he tried the shipping of cattle and pigs to Frisco, Wallen sailing down to the city to market the animals, as fast as Sam rounded them up among the settlers and Indians and sent them down on schooners.

"We continued that business until both of us lost all the money we had," said Wallen, "and when I got back to Vancouver three or four hundred dollars were yet due him [Grant], for which I was obliged to give my note and afterwards pay it off in instalments." Their failure was all the more ironic because a sow which Grant gave to their drum major produced a dozen pigs which the noncom sold for forty dollars apiece.[16]

Grant doggedly clung to his plan to make money. Farming was a thing he knew and the land along the river was black. Potatoes were selling at eight dollars or nine dollars a bushel. Wallen was still game, and they leased a tract from the Hudson's Bay Company, financing the venture, as the story later ran in Army circles, on money borrowed from Commandant Bonneville at 2 per cent per month. They hired a sergeant to clear away the underbrush. They sent to Frisco for seed potatoes, and Grant bought a pair of thin horses from an immigrant who had limped in from the cruel overland trail. Under Grant's skilled care the horses fattened rapidly enough to break the ground, Grant at the plow handles while Wallen dropped potatoes in the furrows. Mrs. Sheffield saw them plant oats, too, Grant striding across the ploughed ground, trousers tucked in boots and the seed hanging in a sheet tied around his neck, his right hand broadcasting the grain.[17] In the words of the lonely captain to his wife:

> About pecuniary matters dear Julia I am better off than ever before . . . I have got a farm of about one hundred acres, all cleared and enclosed, about one mile from here which I am going to cultivate in company with Captains Brent, Wallen &

McConnell. I have leased it in my own name but there is four times as much of it as I could possibly buy seed for. We expect to raise some thirty acres of potatoes which may safely be put down at one dollar & fifty cents per bushel, and may be twice that, and the yield in this country is tremendous. The balance we will put oats in. In the labor we all expect to assist. It is necessary in this country that a person should help himself because it takes a great deal to live. I could not possibly keep house here for less than about one hundred & fifty dollars per month, aside from all expenses of clothing etc.

Hope began to rise when the clusters of tiny green broke through the earth, indicating that the potato crop would be enormous. And on May 1, with the departure of Captain Brent, Grant became Quartermaster of the post as well as his regiment. Later on he would laugh about the "amusing predicaments" into which this dual role thrust him, forcing him, as post executive, to pass upon papers which he had drawn up as regimental quartermaster or commissary.

During the last week of May, Bonneville gave him news of an important special assignment. The Adjutant General's office had ordered the post to give "all assistance" and "hearty co-operation" to a party of Engineers, under Brevet Captain George B. McClellan, which would soon arrive "to explore the passes of the Cascade Range" and "to prepare a report upon a railroad route from the East." The War Department, pressed by Congress and the public, was expected to find a route by which the railroads, which had already reached Chicago, could progress to the Pacific. Within a few years the railroad engines would be drinking from the Mississippi and Missouri Rivers. Wagon routes across the plains were too slow and expensive for the emigrants to tolerate them much longer. Grant must have everything possible in readiness for McClellan when he arrived. Little Mac had acquired prominence in the Army since the Mexican War, thanks to the skill of his surveys in Texas.[18]

Mrs. Sheffield watched Grant measure up to his new responsibilities. At private theatricals, in the improvised post theater, she saw him one night come quietly down the aisle, collar the purser of the steamer *Eagle*, who was drunk and maudlin in the audience, yank him from his seat and march him from the room. She saw him hold dances in the dining room of the Ranch with the regimental band playing waltzes, and with guests coming from afar — sometimes from the village of Portland, across the river. She never saw Grant dance. Sometimes he "would come in and look on for a-while, then go upstairs to his room and remain there all evening smoking," and, as she felt certain, thinking about his distant wife.[19]

As June neared its end a new series of disasters descended upon Grant. First, the potatoes! Grant, in later life, wrote about it with humor:

> Our crop was enormous. Luckily for us the Columbia River rose to a great height from the melting of the snow in the mountains in June, and overflowed and killed most of our crop. This saved digging it up, for everybody on the Pacific Coast seemed to have come to the conclusion at the same time that agriculture would be profitable. . . . The only potatoes we sold were to our own mess.

Wallen remembered the disaster with more seriousness, saying that "We finally had to pay some of the farmers to haul the potatoes away" from an ammunition magazine in which he had stored them with Bonneville's permission. Among Grant's officer friends the story was that Bonneville held the principal debt "onerously . . . over him [Grant]" and that, to repay him, Grant had to borrow the amount from a sergeant.[20]

But at the time the failure of the crops had a more dismal aspect:

> I have been quite unfortunate lately. The Columbia is now far over its banks, and has destroyed all the grain, onions, corn and about half the potatoes upon which I had expended so much money and labor. The wood which I had on the bank of the river had all to be removed, at an expense, and will all have to be put back again at an expense.

On March 19, 1853, he had written to Julia in a hopeful and optimistic vein about his farming and woodcutting ventures which he hoped would produce the needed money to bring his family West perhaps:

> I have in the ground a field of barley every grain of which I sewed with my own hands. The ground is already broken for twenty acres of potatoes, and a five acres for onions and other

vegetables. I shall do all the ploughing myself all summer. You know besides my farming operation I have a large quantity of Steamboat wood cut for which I get $2.50 per cord more than it cost me to get it cut. It has to be hauled but a short distance and that is done with my own private horses and wagon. Besides these speculations Capts. Wallen, McConnell and myself are starting two drays which we think will bring in from $10 to 15 dollars per day each. If I am at all fortunate next fall will bring me in a good return which will make me easy for the future, for then I will never permit myself to get the least in debt.

Mrs. Sheffield saw Grant grow more restless after the potato failure and, with Wallen, arrange for her husband to "act as agent for them, and buy up all the chickens within twenty miles of Vancouver." They shipped them on a chartered vessel to Frisco, but "nearly all the chickens died on the voyage and they lost the money . . . put into the enterprise." [21]

On top of these two disasters, came the strain and stress of outfitting the all-important party of exploring Engineers. When McClellan arrived on June 27, Grant housed him at the Ranch and toiled with him night and day — a task indeed, for Little Mac was a perfectionist and consumed almost thirty days with preparations. On July 25, the day after McClellan's departure into the wilds, Grant wrote the division quartermaster at San Francisco that he had been prevented from making out and forwarding his annual report because of the "constant and unremiting [sic] calls upon the time of both myself and Clerk, consequent upon the fiting [sic] out of the expedition [sic] connected with the Northern Pacific R.R. survey." His report which followed was clear, and its description of the geography and resources of the region vivid, yet he wrote with a carelessness in spelling that was unusual even for him. "Yield" was yieald "occasional" was occational and at one point "fiscal" would be correctly spelled and at another appear as fical.[22]

Another possible evidence of the strain upon him was visible to Lieutenant Hodges, who was departing with McClellan as quartermaster. Years later Hodges wrote: "When the expedition was being fitted out, Grant got on one of his little sprees, which annoyed and offended McClellan exceedingly, and in my opinion he never quite forgave Grant for it, notwithstanding the necessary transportation was soon in readiness." [23]

The "expidition" gone, life at the post droned on until September 20, when Grant opened a letter from the Secretary of War, dated August 9, 1853, announcing that he had been promoted to a captaincy, filling the place of William W. S. Bliss, who had died August 5. He must leave as soon as possible to take command of Company F at Fort Humboldt, which Captain Buchanan and two companies had built in January on Humboldt Bay, the center of the new redwood lumber industry of northern California. Grant had learned of his promotion sometime before June 15 of that year, for one of his letters to Julia of that date which acknowledged a lock of young Ulys's hair spoke of having written about the promotion "in my letter from San Francisco."

> I shall go to California. It is not probable however that I shall leave here before October. . . . I am very busy now being both Depot Q. Master and Depot Commissary and having two expeditions to fit out for the great Pacific Railroad Surveying party under Governor Stevens. They require a large number of pack animals and many articles besides that have to be purchased, all of which has to be done by me.
>
> I am very well dear Julia but to write more about myself, as you so often request me to do, I do not know how.
>
> Give my love to all at your house and kiss our dear little boys for me. Does Ulys. walk yet? From the progress he appears to be making I suppose he must. Continue dear Julia to write me as you do about the boys. I like to hear of Fred's sayings. If he talks as he used to try to do he must be very interesting.
>
> People are waiting for me with a drove of horses so I must close. A thousand kisses for you dear dear Julia.
>
> Adieu from your affectionate husband.   ULYS.

Hiring an accountant from outside the Army to help him close his accounts and be off on time, he gave the man $200 for copying 266⅔ folios of public papers, and hoped the War Department would approve.[24]

For Grant's sake, Mrs. Sheffield welcomed his promotion and thought Fort Humboldt, a mere 250 miles from San Francisco, "a more desirable station." But she discovered that he wanted to resign as badly as ever. He was talking of going into the lumber business.[25]

The small increase in pay which the promotion brought him would not allow him to support Julia and the babies in this land of wild prices. If only he could find a business, he might resign and have them with him. Was luck against him? Had he been wrong all his life to believe that everything would turn out all right so long as a man did his duty? He had never been shiftless like Grandfather Grant, and had worked with the energy of his own father's generation. Yet where all of Old Captain Noah's children had grown wealthy in the toilsome midlands, Captain Noah's grandson could only lose money in the greatest field of lush, easy profits that the world had ever seen. Even farming, which Ulysses had done so well as a boy, had failed him here. Maybe he should quit the uniform and try farming — the sixty acres which Julia's father had given her when they were married?

His very promotion, coming as it did ten years to the month after he had been made a first lieutenant, was a reminder of the dismal slowness of advancement in the Army. With nine captains in the regiment now ranking him in seniority, it might be ten, twenty years — perhaps forever — before he could become a major. The nine appeared healthy and showed a peculiar reluctance to resign as so many in other regiments were doing. With the Army so small, transfers were few.

It was not battle but seniority rule that made Death the only real friend of a young officer. A man might win brevets galore for bravery and skill in the red smoke of battle and still find himself at his old grade when the smoke blew away — a dismal man rotting in the dull round of the years, waiting like a ghoul for some other officer up ahead of him on the register to die in bed.

Take Tom Jackson! His brevets had dazzled the Army in Mexico, yet six years later he was still a first lieutenant with ten other first lieutenants ahead of him in his regiment. So, in February 1852, he had resigned and gone to teaching philosophy and artillery at Virginia Military Institute.

Sherman had resigned from the Third Artillery on September 6 of this year, 1853, to become a banker in San Francisco. Burnside was resigning from the same regiment in October, to manufacture firearms. Three of Grant's classmates, Hamilton, Ripley and Peck had resigned earlier in the year. Ripley and Peck had been, for six years, majors by brevet, but still first lieutenants in the line. The brilliant Rosey Rosecrans, entrusted with important harbor improvements, had remained a second lieutenant for nine years before his promotion to first lieutenant last March. He was preparing to resign in the spring of 1854, and practice civil engineering in Cincinnati.

The case of Captain Bliss, the man whose death had elevated Sam Grant, redramatized for Grant the situation which had discouraged him back in 1844, the absence of so many regimental officers on staff duty that injustice was done officers of the line. For nineteen years, Bliss had been carried on the rolls of the regiment without coming near it. He had, in fact, never served with the Fourth beyond a few months after graduation from the Academy in 1834. Teaching for years at West Point and serving on the staffs of various generals, he had not even surrendered his position in the regiment when he had gone into the White House in 1849, as private secretary to President Taylor.

With rivalry so singularly absent from Grant's nature, it meant little to him that he now stood in the first five of his class — all captains, Ingalls, French, Augur, Van Bokkelen and himself. Of the eighteen others still in the Army, all were first lieutenants. Eight were dead, one had been cashiered and seven had resigned. Among the last were two of Grant's best friends, Quinby who had quit in 1852 and Deshon in 1851. The Dragoon who had, like Rosecrans, become a convert to Roman Catholicism, had changed the uniform for the cassock in 1851 and was studying to become a priest. Rumor said that Deshon had turned to religion because of the death of a lady three days before she was to have married him.[26]

Grant's talk of resigning had brought him to no decision when the hour came on September 24 for him to say good-by to his friends at Vancouver. "He gave me his famous cook-book, his feather pillows and a number of other small articles," Mrs. Sheffield said. "He gained the friendship and good-will of his men by a constant and watchful care of their interests," she added, and "had not made an enemy . . . and was kind and considerate to all." Sam Grant was leaving without being able to collect the money he had loaned the sutler — an amount rumored to be $1600 — or to pay the sergeant what was still due on the potato debt. Wallen saw him go down the Columbia on a timber schooner toward San Francisco, and thought he had never known "a stronger, better or truer man." [27]

San Francisco, where Grant must change ships for Humboldt Bay, amazed him as he came to it. Where steamers, a year ago, had tied up at the Long Wharf, there now stood houses and streets standing on piles. Coming ashore, Grant saw holes yawning in these board streets, which were lined by wild faro dens and saloons. It occurred to him that many of the gold hunters who had disappeared without a trace had been murdered and dropped into the water that lapped at the piles below.

"Besides the gambling in cards there was gambling on a larger scale in city lots," he later recalled. Speculators put up margins with brokers at 2 or 3 per cent interest a month, as they bought and sold lots on sand hills, some of which were "almost inaccessible to foot-passengers."

All through the streets, saloons and eating places white men were denouncing the Chinese laborers who poured off Oriental steamers. Grant said later that he too objected to the immigration but "not to the Chinaman coming to the United States, but to his coming in a condition of slavery." Under the contract terms upon which the timid, patient coolies arrived, Grant thought them "in practical bondage, the slaves of companies which owned them." [20] First the swarthy Mexican peons, then the redskins along the Columbia, and now the yellow man touched his heart as he had seen them mistreated by the conquering whites.

Fort Humboldt, when he came to it, was a group of log barracks and officers' cabins surrounded by a low earthwork on a bluff high above the harbor. A few log houses of the redwoods lumbermen and their sawmills straggled along the water front. Behind rose the dark, gigantic forest. Two companies which had totaled 126 men when they had arrived on the Coast, but which were now shrunk from desertions, made up the garrison. Of the six officers on hand none were old-time friends of Grant — and the commanding officer, Old Buch, was, as Lieutenant Hodges said, "a very good soldier but a martinet." Also, there was the possibility that neither Grant not

Buchanan had forgotten the incident of the wine bottle at Jefferson Barracks ten years before.

Lonelier now than ever, Grant took long rides when off duty and increased his drinking, but with his peculiar organization a little did the fatal work of a great deal. A contractor who supplied the garrison with beef saw what was happening to Grant and, in after years, sent a friend a passage that was, he declared, a true statement of the lonely officer's predicament:

> The line captain's duties were fewer and less onerous than the quartermaster's had been and the discipline was far more rigid and irksome. No greater misfortune could have happened to him [Grant] than this enforced idleness. He had little work, no family with him, took no pleasure in the amusements of his brother officers — dancing, billiards, hunting, fishing, and the like — and riding alone, however inspiring, may grow monotonous after several months of it! The result was a common one — he took to liquor. Not by any means in enormous quantities, for he drank far less than other officers, whose reputation for temperance was unsullied. Like Cassio, he had a poor brain for drinking. The weakness did not legitimately belong to his character, for in all other respects he was a man of unusual self-control, and thoroughly master of his appetites.[29]

No friends like Hodges, Wallen, Ingalls and Augur were here to speak to him now when he drank too much and remind him to go slow. Grant drank more and more. Captain Haller, though not at Fort Humboldt, learned from brother officers who were there that "the habit had become confirmed with Grant." Haller was with Grant enough, however, to know that he was a "four-finger drinker":

> He was in the habit of drinking in a peculiar way. He held the little finger just even with the . . . heavy glass bottom of the tumber, then lying his three fingers above the little one, filled in whiskey to the top of his first finger and drank it off without mixing water with it. This he would do more or less frequently each day, according to his mingling more or less with boon companions.[30]

On February 6, 1854 he wrote in desperation to Julia:

> A mail came in this evening but brought me no news from you nor nothing in reply to my application for orders to

go home. I cannot conceive what is the cause of the delay. The state of suspense that I am in is scarsely bearable. I think I have been from my family quite long enough and sometimes I feel as though I could almost go home "nolens volens". I presume, under ordinary circumstances, Humboldt would be a good enough place but the suspense I am in would make paradise form a bad picture. There is but one thing to console; misery loves company and there are a number in just the same fix with myself, and, with other Regiments, some who have been separated much longer from their families than I have been.

The method of consolation for the misery of the company of officers away from wives and family was of course not mentioned.

When Grant rode to the nearest town, Eureka, the lumber port three miles south of the Bay, he stopped at the home of the beef contractor's brother-in-law, the sawmill magnate, James T. Ryan, who owned Eclipse — the finest horse of the region — and kept a barrel of whiskey always on tap for the officers. Although Eureka hummed with Ryan's sawmills, and the redwood lumber trade was mounting day by day, Grant apparently gave up his thoughts of entering it. Instead he once proposed to the beef contractor that he join him in the beef-contracting business. The man thought Grant "a striking example of rigid honesty and steadfastness of purpose" but the partnership was never formed.[31]

A partnership that Grant did form during a visit to Frisco was as disastrous as the projects in ice, potatoes, pigs and chickens. With three other officers he leased, at five hundred dollars a month, the Union Hotel on Kearny Street, and left it with an agent to operate as "a sort of club billiard-room." According to the legend in the town, the agent proved "derelict or dishonest, and the rents did not come in." After a heavy loss the four officers threw up the lease. Mrs. Tripler, in later years, thought she had heard that Grant "had a coal yard in San Francisco" too, and that Wallen, at Vancouver, "had a milk route."[32]

Living at Fort Humboldt was somewhat cheaper than at Vancouver, and Grant was able to increase the amount of money he sent home, but it was little enough. His sight-seeing trips to points within horseback range of Vancouver and San Francisco were not expensive, for he could usually manage to stop at Army posts, or with ex-soldier friends. One trip took him one hundred miles east of Frisco to Knight's Ferry, where Julia's brother, Lewis Dent, was running a ferryboat on the Stanislaus River. Residents of the village would later describe the day when the Captain "in a peculiarly jovial mood" appeared in a buggy, driving three horses single file ahead of him, pulling two more empty buggies behind him — a long procession that came spanking down the street "to the amazement of the villagers."

Jimmy Sanderson was not there to be wondering if his friend could be groping back across the years to recapture those happiest of his days when all Georgetown had stood back as he thundered down the street.

To Grant at Knight's Ferry came an invitation from Captain P. E. Connor, a veteran of the Mexican War, to come to Stockton and be the guest of honor at a dress parade and "target excursion" that was to be held by the Stockton Blues. Grant attended, showing up, as the editor of the Virginia, Nevada *Enterprise* later said, in plain clothes and joining in the gusty consumption of "collations." At the completion of the marksmanship contest on the range, Grant was called upon to present a leather medal to the man who had made the worst shots. "Grant's eyes were brimful of mischief" as he said, "Your companions in arms have delegated me to present you with this neat and expressive token of their esteem. Take it and wear it with honor, sir, and may your future be as brilliant as your past." [33]

Once, in his tours, Grant spent some days with a lawyer from Ohio whom he had known in the war, and who, for two years, had been working on a sluice mine with a pair of partners. The freedom and independence of the three men "living pure lives, in the midst of the purity, grandeur and sublimity of nature" was a thing Grant would talk about later on. He said that when he rode through the great mountains, he would quote to himself, "Only man is vile." It disgusted him to see the low dens in every "diggings" where miners were robbed by "sharpers and cut-throats." Once he attended a miners' court and heard a stealer of gold dust sentenced to be hanged. After the trial he asked the judge why the penalty was so drastic, and was answered, "Here our property is acquired at great sacrifice. It has been purloined; we have no jails or prisons . . . no constitutional court within a hundred miles." If the guilty man were let off with whipping, he probably would kill the judge and witnesses in revenge.

The incident that impressed him most during those solitary trips into the mountains concerned a miner who, after sharing his hard, scanty fare with the visitor, grew confidential and took out a packet of letters that had been accumulating since 1849. The miner felt sad and wanted to talk to someone about them. They were from his sweetheart back in New York, pleading with him to return and marry her. The miner said he had been answering that he would come back as soon as he found gold, but whenever he got it, he would somehow lose it. Now he had several thousand dollars worth of dust in his poke, but he was afraid to face her. He knew he had, in four years, lost refinement, forgotten how to dress and talk, while she had grown more genteel. He shrank from having her and her family see him.

Breaking into tears he asked Grant what to do. The two men, each without his woman, talked by the campfire that threw shadows on the mountains. Grant advised him to turn his dust into cash, wash up, buy new clothes and go back. "All the rough corners in speech and manners would soon disappear; and in fact they would not in the least prejudice the true woman." The miner promised he would take the next steamer, but a few days later Grant met him on the streets of San Francisco "in utter despair" because he had lost the money in a gambling parlor. Two days later, Grant heard that the poor fellow's body had been fished from the bay, the coroner guessing suicide.[34]

Fond as he was of card games, Grant could not bring himself to take the long chances which gold mining itself demanded. That his trips, from the Fort to San Francisco, might have been "sprees" was later hinted by Mrs. Tripler, who said that "Grant was in my husband's care and Dr. Tripler was entirely frank and open in dealing with his case." She was more guarded in speaking of Grant than of Hooker, whom her husband knew at the same time, and who "was a gambler and drunkard." Another woman, Mrs. Emma Davis, whose husband was superintendent of a sawmill at Humboldt, recalled in after years seeing Captain Grant tumble tipsily off a boardwalk that ran along the waterfront above the tidelands. Arriving from

Canada, she was more afraid of the soldiers than of the Indians.[35]

With the springtime of 1854, all the forces were crowding Grant out of the Army — crowding toward crisis. His money, beyond that which he had sent home, was spent, lost or badly loaned. He could never support his family in California on his pay, and his experiments had convinced him that he could make nothing extra in sideline endeavors here where everything was at the mercy of chance or speculation. It would soon be two years since he had seen Julia and Freddy. He hungered to see Ulysses Grant, Junior. Hopelessness and loneliness combined were too much. Eighteen of the men he had known at West Point had quit the uniform in the past year and a half, and twelve more were preparing to follow within the next seventeen months.

Sam Grant's letters to Julia were now increasingly gloomy and filled with foreboding and with concern and poignant yearnings for his wife and his children, one of whom he had never seen. "Write me a great deal about our little boys. Tell me all their pranks. I suppose Ulys. speaks a great many words distinctly. Kiss both of them for me."

In February he gave unusual vent to his loneliness. "You do not know how forsaken I feel here," he wrote to Julia:

> The place is good enough but I have interests at others which I cannot help thinking about day and night; then too it is a long time since I made application for orders to go to Washington to settle my accounts but not a word in reply do I get. Then I feel again as if I had been separated from you and Fred long enough and as to Ulys I have never seen him. He must by this time be talking about as Fred did when I saw him last. How very much I want to see all of you. I have made up my mind what Ulys looks like and I am anxious to see if my presentiment is correct. Does he advance rapidly? Tell me a great deal about him and Fred and Fred's pranks with his Grandpa.

On April 11, he acted. Why it should have been that particular day, he never, in later years, revealed. Perhaps it was the arrival in the mail from San Francisco of his commission as Captain. The paper had no bearing upon his rank, which had been established by the War Department seven months before. It frequently took that long for commissions to be sent by the President to the Senate and for the Senate to pass them in routine form and return them to the War Department. Perhaps the sight of his commission, symbol of the profession he had never liked and now wished to escape, made up his mind for him. No one outside his family ever learned what was in his mind that day. All that was known was that on April 11 he wrote two letters to *Colonel S. Cooper, Adjutant General, U.S.A., Washington,* — one reading:

> Col. I have the honor to acknowledge the receipt of my commission as Captain in the 4th Infantry and my acceptance of the same.
>
> I am, Col.
> Very Respectfully,
> Yr. Obt. Svt.
> U. S. Grant, *Captain 4th Inf.*

And the other:

> Col. I very respectfully tender my resignation of my commission as an officer of the Army, and request that it may take effect from the 31st of July next.
>
> I am, Col.
> Very Respectfully
> Yr. Obt. Svt.
> U. S. Grant, *Capt., 4th Inf.*[36]

His friends, hurrying when they heard the news to discover why he had resigned, failed to see any significance in the arrival of the commission on the day of decision. They gathered a wholly different explanation of Grant's move — he had been forced out by his commanding officer, Buchanan — forced out because of his drinking! Henry Hodges, collecting stories from the other officers at Fort Humboldt, summed them up in a letter:

> It seems that one day while his company was being paid off, Captain Grant was at the pay table, slightly under the influence of liquor. This came to the knowledge of Colonel Buchanan; he gave Grant his option of resigning or having charges preferred against him. Grant resigned at once. In my opinion the regiment always thought Col. Buchanan was unnecessarily harsh and severe. . . . He knew that Grant was liked and highly respected in the regiment and it seemed as though he might have overlooked this first small offense at his [Buchanan's] post.[37]

A contractor selling beef to Fort Humboldt — a brother-in-law of Ryan, the sawmill proprietor — said in later years that as he got the story, Old Buch had been angered at seeing Grant tipsy at the paymaster's table and had told his Adjutant, Lewis C. Hunt:

"Mr. Hunt, I see that Captain Grant has been drinking again; place him in arrest."

Grant had been lying down when Hunt came in, and had asked:

"Well, is Old Buch going to let up on me?"

When Hunt told him that Buch was "going to push it," Grant said that "he had decided to resign and go to farming." [38]

Lieutenant Haller, who was with the regiment on the Coast, said that Buchanan, after arresting the Captain, showed leniency because of "Grant's very creditable services in Mexico" and, in the hope of reforming him, offered to withdraw the charge on certain conditions. Grant was to promise not "to offend again." He was to write out his resignation, "omitting the date," and Buchanan would hold it "and if Grant forgot his pledge . . . it was an explicit understanding" that the resignation would be dated and forwarded to the War Department and thus "save Grant the odium of being cashiered by a general court martial." Haller's understanding was that Grant did offend again and that Buchanan had, therefore, sent in the resignation.[39]

When Hodges heard for the first time, years later, the statement that Grant had given Buchanan the teetotaler's vow, he doubted it: "I never heard that Grant gave a pledge to Old Buch at all — indeed I always understood one of the chief grievances against Old Buch was that he, Buch, would not give him another chance, and that he demanded his resignation or stand on charges already prepared."

Rufe Ingalls, who was not only closer to Grant than any of the other officers, but far more distinguished by capacity, summed it up in later years:

> Grant, finding himself in dreary surroundings, without his family, and with but little to occupy his attention, fell into dissipated habits, and was found, one day, too much under the influence of liquor to properly perform his duties. For this offense Colonel Buchanan demanded that he should resign, or stand trial. Grant's friends at the time urged him to stand trial,

and were confident of his acquittal; but, actuated by a noble spirit, he said he would not for all the world have his wife know that he had been tried on such a charge. He therefore resigned his commission, and returned to civil life.[40]

With both Buchanan and Grant remaining silent on what had passed between them, it was wondered if Old Buch could have seized upon the arrival of Grant's commission for a lesson in discipline, or as a dramatic reason for forcing his resignation.

A few things in the case were certain: Buchanan had accepted the resignation. No reason for it was recorded. No mention of any arrest was on the books. Grant was leaving soon for the East. Buchanan gave him a leave of sixty days, to date from May 9, and Grant followed it with a formal request to Division Headquarters at San Francisco, not only for this leave, but for permission to apply for a four months' extension when he should arrive at New York.[41]

If for any reason his resignation was not accepted by the War Department, or should be delayed, he would thus have time to see his family.

Captain U. S. Grant was relieved of his command on May 1. The next day he wrote what was probably his last letter from Fort Humboldt. It contained nine sentences. Its brevity was perhaps accounted for by the rush of last-minute preparations to leave. The reference to the "leave of absence" was perhaps an irony which only Sam Grant fully understood.

DEAR WIFE:

I do not propose writing you but a few lines. I have not yet received a letter from you and as I have a "leave of absence" and will be away from here in a few days do not expect to. After receiving this you may discontinue writing because before I could get a reply I shall be on my way home. You might write directing to the City of New York.

It will require my presence in California for some four or six weeks to make all my arrangements, public & private, before starting. I may have to go to Oregon before leaving; I will not go however unless I get an order to cover my transportation. On my way I shall spend a week or ten days with John Dent.

My love to all at home. Kiss our little boys for their Pa. Love to you dear Julia.

Your affectionate husbd.   ULYS.

He put in shape all the vouchers for his years as a regimental quartermaster — vouchers running back through the Mexican War — accounting for the stores and for $2,906.47 that had been in the subsistence fund when he had left Fort Vancouver. Dispatching these papers in a trunk by steamer to the proper authorities, he wound up his personal affairs, told his friends at the Fort and at Eureka good-by and, on May 6, took a ship for San Francisco, saying, according to a legend, "Whoever hears of me in ten years, will hear of a well-to-do old Missouri farmer." [42]

Ahead of him his "Respectfully tendered" resignation was passing from office to office, acquiring signatures. Already it bore upon its back:

Respectfully forwarded with the recommendation that it be accepted.

BVT. COL. ROBERT C. BUCHANAN, April 11, 1854.
Approved and respectfully forwarded,
MAJOR GENERAL JOHN E. WOOL,
HD. QRS. DEPT. OF THE PACIFIC,
April 22, 1854.

It was speeding East.

"Respectfully forwarded by the command of General Scott, May 26, 1854." would be inscribed upon it by Assistant Adjutant General Irwin McDowell at the Army Headquarters in New York.

"Respectfully recommended that Captain Grant's resignation be accepted" would be written upon it May 30, by Adjutant General Samuel Cooper in Washington, followed by notice from the ordnance, pay and auditing officers to the effect that they had no charges against Captain Grant. Only his subsistence accounts were missing, and by custom they would arrive later.

And with that the "respectfullys" would stop, for the paper had come to the end of its travels, and on June 2 it would receive the last endorsement —

Accepted as tendered.

JEFFERSON DAVIS
Secretary of War.[43]

CHAPTER NINETEEN

Army Overcoat of Fading Blue

U P TO early June, the year 1854 had been one of vast satisfaction to Jesse Grant. On January 23, he had celebrated his sixtieth birthday, and with it had begun preparing for his long-scheduled retirement. The two goals he had marked out for himself, almost forty years before, had been reached — a good wife at twenty-six, and enough money at sixty to keep him and his family in comfort.

His retirement, however, would be "measurable." He would turn over his business to his sons, Simpson, who was now twenty-eight, and Orvil, eighteen. Both had shown themselves competent, but he would keep an eye on them, merely giving up what he said to be "direct personal supervision." To clear the decks, he and E. A. Collins had broken up their thirteen-year partnership amicably enough, Collins keeping the old retail stand at Galena, and Jesse the tannery in Ohio. Jesse, however, retained the privilege of launching another store in the Illinois trading center, and planned for Simpson and Orvil to spend most of their time there. To serve as clerks and learn the business, Orlando Ross and W. T. Burke, the son and son-in-law of Hannah's recently widowed sister, Ann, were also going to Galena.[1]

Jesse's prize son, Ulysses, was a Captain in the Army and although a very lonely man, to judge from his letters, such things must be expected in military service.

Jesse was planning to move, this year or next, to Covington, directly across the Ohio River from Cincinnati. Life close to the metropolis would be pleasanter for the girls now that Clara was twenty-five, Virginia, twenty-two and Mary Frances, fifteen. When Julia, who had returned to her own father's home, brought the grandchildren down to see him again, she would have a quicker trip — by fast steamer from St. Louis to Cincinnati.

Everything was lovely for Jesse, and the goose hung high. He wrote a humorous poem for the Galena newspaper, announcing the new arrangement, and wishing Collins well. The invoice of the business showed that he and Collins were dividing $100,000, which meant that with his other property and investments he was on easy street, as his descendants later said, "a rich man, for the country in those days, worth $150,000.00." [2]

Then in the first days of June there came a staggering blow — it had been announced in Washington that Ulysses had resigned from the Army. The news came, probably by telegraph, from Jesse's Congressman, Andrew Ellison, who was in the capital when the routine announcement had been released to the Army and newspapers on June 2.

Jesse was wounded that Ulysses should have made such a step without first conferring with him. He suspected what was wrong, however — loneliness for his wife and children had led Ulysses into rashness. There must be some way to prevent the resignation from going through. If only he could bring Ulysses back for a visit and a long talk, it could be straightened out. Ulysses must be held in the Army. He was too old to drop out.

What Hannah thought is unrecorded, unless it was at this time she told her cousin, Elizabeth Hare, what Elizabeth, years later, remembered was once said: that "she was sorry Ulysses ever had anything to do with this army business."

Evidently under Jesse's prompting by telegraph, Ellison on June 5 wrote Secretary of War Davis a request that Captain U. S. Grant be placed on recruiting service or granted a leave of absence. Two days later Davis acknowledged the note but said that Ellison was too late, Captain Grant's resignation had been accepted on the second. Ellison forwarded the tragic note to Jesse who, after debating for several days, sat down on June 21 and wrote Davis a personal plea:

> If it is consistent with your powers and the good of the servis [sic] I would be much gratified if you would reconsider & withdraw the acceptance of his resignation and grant him a six months leave, that he may come home & see his family.
>
> I never wished him to leave the servis [sic]. I think after spending so much time to qualify himself for the Army & spending so many years in the servis, he will be poorly qualified for the pursuits of private life.

He has been eleven years an officer, was in all the battles of Gens. Taylor and Scotts except Buena Vista, never absent from his post during the Mexican War & has never had a leave of six months. Would it then be asking too much for him to have such a leave that he may come home & make arrangements for taking his family with him to his post.

I will remark that he has not seen his family for over two years & has a son nearly two years old he has never seen. I suppose in his great anxiety to see his family he has been induced to quit the servis.

Please write me & let me know the results of this request.

For a week and more Jesse waited impatiently. Then came the answer:

WASHINGTON, June 28, 1854

SIR. In reply to your letter of the 21st inst. asking that the acceptance of the resignation of your son, Captain U. S. Grant may be withdrawn and he be allowed six months leave of absence, I have to inform you that Captain Grant tendered his resignation but assigned no reasons why he desired to quit the service and the motives which influenced him are not known to the Department. He only asked that his resignation should take affect [sic] on the 31st July next and it was accepted accordingly on the 2nd instant and the same day announced to the army. The acceptance is therefore complete and cannot be reconsidered.

Very Respectfully,
Yr. Obt Svt.

JEFFN DAVIS
Secretary of War[3]

It was not a time for the Secretary of War to be begging captains to give up thoughts of resigning. Davis himself had resigned from the Regulars nineteen years ago and when the War Department, after the Mexican War, had asked him to return as a Brigadier General after his Volunteers had disbanded, he had declined. Anyway, the resignations of more promising officers than this man Grant were coming across Davis's desk in the summer of 1854 — Halleck, Rosecrans, Gustavus W. Smith, Mansfield Lovell and a brilliant youngster, William Sooy Smith, who was quitting a year after graduation from the Academy to go to Chicago to become Assistant Chief Engineer of the sensational new railroad, the Illinois Central.

Jesse gave up, and forever after explained Ulysses' resignation as merely the act of an officer who, "seeing no prospect of having his family with him in the army, resigned and came home." Ulysses' public explanation was that he had resigned because he saw no chance of supporting his wife and two children "on the Pacific coast out of his pay as an army officer." However, in time to come, a distinguished and conscientious educator, John Eaton, would say that Grant had told him that "the vice of intemperance," which had been so common among officers on the Pacific coast, "had not a little to do with his decision to resign." Liquor was having a "deleterious effect upon the army," and with low pay making it impossible for him to support his family, and with the prospect of advancement so small, he had "determined to cut loose from a life which was so full of temptation, without many compensating advantages, and return to his family." [4]

Grant's friends got the story of his departure from the Coast in fragments, a detail here, a rumor there, anecdotes told after years of long remembrance. Brevet Major Robert Allen, Chief Quartermaster of the Pacific Division, was said to have heard that his friend was in San Francisco, down and out, and had discovered him in a cheap hotel room, sitting dejectedly at a table.

"Why, Grant, what are you doing here?"

"Nothing, I've resigned from the army. I'm out of money, and I have no means of getting home."

Bob Allen had quickly raised money and obtained from the Pacific Mail Steamship Company a free ticket to New York — a common courtesy. Allen's clerk, Richard L. Ogden, would later insist that it had been he who had helped Grant. Ogden maintained that as he was preparing to go home one afternoon "a shabbily dressed person" had entered, inquiring for Allen. Explaining that Allen had left for the day, Ogden asked if he could do anything. The stranger produced a certificate for $40.00 due Captain U. S. Grant for per diem service on a court-martial where he had been recently sitting as a judge. Ogden said the certificate was incorrectly drawn and could not be cashed, whereupon Grant's "countenance fell and a look of utter despair came over it." He turned to go, then hesitated and asked if he could spend the night on an old lounge in Allen's office, because, as he said, "I haven't a cent to my name."

Ogden told him he needn't do that, here was a dollar for a hotel bed! Grant took the dollar with thanks and said that if Ogden wouldn't mind, he'd spend it on dinner and breakfast and still sleep on the lounge. Early next morning Ogden, opening the office, found Grant arising from the rickety old sofa and declaring, "I slept well and saved my dollar." To the clerk Grant explained that he had been depending upon the forty dollars to pay his steerage passage East, and as he talked his face became so "dejected" that Ogden melted, cashed the certificate from his own pocket and said he would take a chance on getting it properly drawn up by the authorities who had issued it. Then he took Grant to the steamship company and obtained for him a free ticket good for the entire journey except for the leg across the Isthmus of Panama, which the company did not control. Ogden gathered that Grant would have fifteen dollars left when he reached New York.

A St. Louis friend of Grant's, Colonel John Emerson, later told a different story, telling it as he remembered it from Grant's lips five years after the voyage home:

On arriving at San Francisco from Vancouver, Grant collected two hundred and fifty dollars in accumulated back pay and allowances, a sum given him in twenty-dollar gold pieces, and since the steamer was not to leave for a few days, he had run out to spend the time with another officer at the mines. When he returned, Major Allen had introduced him to the steamship agent, with the assurance, technically correct, that he was on leave and entitled to the customary free pass.

Emerson understood Grant to say, "My trip to the mines, hotel bill and ticket across to Panama took about fifty dollars" — leaving him just ten of the gold pieces when he boarded the steamer. By the time the boat had reached Panama, Grant's sympathies had been touched by a sick man, a former soldier named Babcock, whose rheumatism, caused by working in cold water at the mines, had returned with a vengeance. Babcock confessed to Grant that he had no money to pay his way beyond Panama. "He appealed to me," said Grant, "to take him along to New York. I couldn't leave an old soldier to die, so I gave him two of my coins." Babcock signed a note for the amount, and when Grant was slow to take it, "pressed it into my hand." Discovering that two other returning miners, friends of Babcock, were sick in the steerage, Grant cut another gold piece in two and divided it between them. This left him seven coins, one hundred and forty dollars in gold, when he arrived in New York.

Although Grant's friends agreed that Bob Allen had obtained the free passage for Grant, and that it was utterly characteristic of the Captain to have given away money on the voyage home, they understood he arrived in New York low in funds, went to Sacketts Harbor to collect the $1600 debt from the regimental sutler who had returned shortly before from Vancouver and when that was refused, returned to the city to live on loans from officers at Governor's Island, while awaiting a check from his father.

Grant's old friend of West Point and Mexican days, Simon Bolivar Buckner, who was on commissary duty in New York, told later how Sam had asked him for money to pay his hotel bill until funds could arrive from Ohio. The hotel manager had reached the end of his patience. Perhaps fearful that Sam would spend cash on liquor, Buckner guaranteed his bills at the hotel and "took charge" of him. Within a few days, Sam came around, paid all debtors in full — he had heard from his father and was off for Bethel. One rumor had it that Jesse had sent Simpson to rescue Ulysses.[5]

With personal gossip so large a part of the officers' lives, Sam Grant was leaving under a heavy cloud. It was said that considering the amount of drinking that was condoned in the Army, Sam's case must have been a bad one indeed!

Humiliation was striking Jesse in the year that was to have crowned his whole life. He, in his hour of success, face to face with a penniless son! All that those small, envious neighbors had said about the boy not making a soldier would be repeated snickeringly. People would recall that the Army also had turned Jesse's father into a bibulous failure.

It was enough to hasten Jesse's removal to Covington, where he need not be suspecting every minute that people, behind his back, were mimicking his old boasts about "My Ulysses."

The family scene when Ulysses reached Bethel late that summer was a thing none of the Grants ever revealed, although the neighbors understood that Jesse had grimly said, "West Point spoiled one of my boys for business," and that Ulysses replied, "I guess that's about so." [6]

However, Jesse afterwards declared that when Ulysses went on to St. Louis to start life over again cultivating Julia's sixty acres, "I stocked the farm." Ulysses always said he had been "a happy man" as he hurried home to Julia and the farm life which he now expected to enjoy even more than when he had been a boy. [7]

At White Haven, Julia was waiting, not knowing the moment when he would arrive. But the moment came, and, as Emmy remembered it, a slave girl, in the house, heard sounds of alarm on the long front porch where four-year-old Freddie and his two-year-old brother "Buck" were playing. (The slaves had given this nickname to Ulysses Jr. because he had been born in Ohio, the Buckeye State.) The infants had taken fright at a dark-bearded man throwing the lap robe over the dashboard of a buggy at the front gate and climbing down.

One look at the stranger, and the slave girl burst out through the door, past the whimpering children, and raced down the walk waving her arms and shrieking, "Fo' de Lawd's sake! Hyar are Mars Grant!"

In Julia's arms Grant was at peace. The Army which he thought he had always hated was behind him now for good and all.

For the time being they could live at White Haven, or move, if they preferred, into the house, "Wish-ton-wish" (Indian for "Whippoorwill"), which Julia's brother Louis had built on a part of the farm his father had given him. Meanwhile, Ulysses could prepare to farm the acres and build a house on them.

With Louis in California, John, George and Nellie married, and only Emmy with her parents at White Haven, Mr. Dent was anxious to anchor Julia and Ulysses nearby. He promised to advance money for the flooring, window sash, doorways, etc., when the new house was ready for them.

As the first quiet raptures of his second honeymoon passed, Ulysses looked upon the farm and the neighborhood with new interest. The community centered at Sappington Post Office, named for a prominent family of farmers and physicians, a crossroads cluster of houses to which the mail was brought from St. Louis.

A region of farms ranging from large 900-acre ones, like Dent's, to small "forties," it held a few houses like White Haven, several of more modest proportions and many straggling log cabins. Farming and the sale of cordwood in St. Louis were the occupations. Oak and elm forests still covered much of the neighborhood and were thick on Julia's "sixty." [8]

Facing the springtime of 1855, Ulysses saw that he must rely upon the wood business to support his family. A new baby was due in July. He had no cash with which to buy the seed and farming implements that would properly operate Julia's cleared acres. He was able to buy a team of good horses on easy terms from the United Express Company in the city because Charley Ford, his friend from Sacketts Harbor, was now managing the company's St. Louis office. Planting oats, corn and vegetables as best he could, Ulysses worked hardest at cutting and hauling down the Gravois Road to the city the cordwood which he sold, in the beginning, to friends of the Dents, expanding later to other customers. He was as quick to introduce economies for his father-in-law as when he had set up bakeries to help his regimental fund in Mexico. Noting that the fireplaces at White Haven kept one slave cutting wood constantly, he proposed to Colonel Dent "a new idea," as one of his friends later expressed it. "Near by was a colliery, the owners of which were paying fifty cents apiece for stout saplings with which to shore up the roof of their mine. Grant suggested that he could cut and haul poles enough in one day to buy coal for an entire month, and in two more to pay for a grate or stove in every room." In a few days he had the innovation established. It paid to have a quartermaster in the family.[9]

Between the crops, the cordwood and the poles, Ulysses cut and squared off logs which, when seasoned for a year, would go into his house. Alone in the woods with his horses Tom and Bill was like being with Dave in the oak forests of Ohio. And the same lament from the whippoorwills throbbed in the dusk as he drove home.

Only trifling help could come from Colonel Dent's slaves, most of whom were women and children who, with such men as there were, had Dent's work to do. Julia's three slaves were, as Emmy described them, the cook "Colored Julia," the housemaid "Eliza," "a little ginger," and the houseman young Dan, "the most polished specimen of human ebony you ever saw." The irony of a farmer owning three house servants yet having to do all his own work in the field was a thing to be laughed about when neighbors met at the Sappington Post Office. They said that when the Captain did try to get the slaves to work they imposed on him, and, worse than that, when he hired free Negroes to help with the cordwood he spoiled them by paying them ten to fifteen cents a cord above the general scale. One of the freedmen, Uncle Jason, recalled in after years, "Some of the white men cussed about it, but Cap'n he jis' kep' right on a-payin' for er work jis' er same." [10]

Mary Robinson, at White Haven, thought that Mr. Grant, in addition to being "the kindest husband and the most indulgent father I ever saw" was "a very kind man to those who worked for him and he always said he wanted to give his wife's slaves their freedom as soon as he was able." Charley Weber, a young cabinet-maker who came to know Grant well, said in later times that one of the reasons the Captain was so anxious to build a house of his own was that he differed with his father-in-law on the slave question — "it got so that it was not very pleasant living under the same roof with Col. Dent." [11]

The country doctor who practiced in the neighborhood, William Taussig, heard much private talk among the wealthier families, such as the Sappingtons, Longs and Paddlefords, about Grant chafing at the "dependent position he occupied in the house of his father-in-law." Dr. Taussig was unable to learn more at firsthand because, as an ardent antislavery man, he was hated by choleric old Colonel Dent. [12]

To Mrs. Dent it was a joy to have Julia's husband living in the house and explaining politics, even if his version differed somewhat from the Colonel's. But to the Colonel himself, it was unquestionably irksome to find, as the months went by, that he, the lord of the manor, was no longer the central figure in the lives of his favorite daughter and his endearing grandchildren as he had been for the past two years. Julia and her husband were so affectionate toward each other and the Captain was always spoiling the babies!

Julia had certainly not done as well in marriage as her brothers and sisters. Nellie's husband was a promising physician. All four boys had won wives who could uphold the social traditions of the Maryland Dents; two of them had married daughters of Edward Shurlds, cashier of the Bank of the State of Missouri in St. Louis. Fred was a captain now, in the Fifth Infantry — doing well at Fort Vancouver, of all places! [13]

Julia's husband certainly worked hard enough, although he did humor himself by getting up late in the morning when he planned to drive wood to the city. The Captain could be stubborn at times, and said that it never disturbed him when the neighbors gave him superior stares as they met on the road at midday, they returning from town with empty wagons, he just starting out.

"The fact that their labors were over, never bothered me at all," he later declared. "I lost nothing and gained considerable. It was only possible to make one trip a day, so that by taking my morning nap I yet had plenty of time to reach the city, dispose of my wood and return before dark. They lost their sleep and gained nothing in the price of their wood; I gained my sleep and lost nothing in the price of the wood." [14]

Mary Robinson said in her old age that she had watched many farmers and none that worked harder than Mr. Grant. Seeing him pore over newspapers and books in the evenings, she pronounced him "a great reader." It pleased her to see him so fond of domestic animals, particularly of a large dog, Leo, whose chief talent lay in helping her catch chickens for the frying pan:

> All I would have to do, would be to point out the chicken I wanted, to Leo, and he would grab it for me. Mr. Grant sat and watched us one day. After I secured all I needed, Leo continued to catch them. This amused Mr. Grant very much and, turning to me, he said, "Mamie, that dog has gone into business on his own hook since you and he dissolved partnership." [15]

Whatever small pleasures like this White Haven afforded, it was probably a relief both to Ulysses and his father-in-law when, in the summer of 1855, Julia and her husband moved over to Wish-ton-wish to remain until the new house was erected. They were installed in time for the third baby to be born there on July 4. It was a girl, named Ellen after Grandmother Dent and, like its aunt, called "Nellie." Its father pushed hard to hurry their own house, cutting logs, squaring them with an adz and putting them on blocks to season. He split shingles, dug a cellar, hauled up stone for foundations and chimneys, and had Charley Weber plane the frames for windows and doors; but it was not until the summer of 1856 that everything was ready for the house-raising. Then the neighbors came with their slaves, the women at White Haven cooked monstrous amounts of food, and the logs, properly notched, were fitted one on top of another mid grunts, shouts, laughter, perspiration and the flitting of whiskey jugs from hand to hand.

A house of two stories it was, "built after a plan conceived by Julia" — Emmy declared later when she was emphasizing family pride — "fashioned and furnished with an eye to the artistic; and to the end that it was both homelike and cozy. Through the middle of the house ran a hall, on either side of which were the sitting room and dining room. Above these were three small bedrooms, two of good size, and a small front room over a portion of the hall-way below. The kitchen and servant's quarters were in cabins at the rear." The window frames, she remembered, "gave a pleasing effect since they opened outward from the middle." Emmy came to believe in after years that Julia had wanted "an old-fashioned house built in the old-fashioned way — log laid upon log by friendly hands." In the Sappington neighborhood it was believed that the house was of logs because that was all that the Captain could afford to build.[16]

With the chinks between the logs smoothed with plaster, and the interior decorated by Julia's hand, it inspired Mrs. Henry T. Blow of St. Louis to say of it, " 'Cabin' is a misnomer!" After a visit to it, Mrs. Blow wrote a friend that Julia was fortunate: "I quite envy her. No grand city home can compare with that log building. It's warm in winter and cool in summer; and oh, the happy life in the very heart of nature!" It was spotless, had "engravings on the walls . . . bits of delicate color in furnishings . . . books, reviews and magazines lying about." Mrs. Blow's pen gushed ecstasy, as she concluded, "It is a castle if we are allowed to estimate the structure by the happiness, the thought and the culture within it." [17]

Grant himself named it "Hardscrabble." The neighbors smiled, wondering if he were slyly satirizing the high-sounding names the Dents had given their homes.

Silent, home-loving, shy, he was for a time a puzzle to the neighbors. But his courage soon was apparent. They heard how he sat on a stump one moonlight night in his forest to catch a suspected thief at a woodpile, sat there humorously, allowing the fellow to load the loot before he stepped up to order it delivered to his own house. And when the thief objected to a demand that he also pay half the value of the wood previously stolen, Grant collared him so quickly that he commenced whining, "Hold on! I'll do it; but don't say a word to anybody."

At a neighborhood dance he kicked a truculent troublemaker through the door, down the path "and clear out the gate." For a small man he had astonishing strength when aroused.[18]

The neighbors learned that the Captain had a military man's strictness about obeying the law, yet a stubborn resistance to the law when pettifoggers attempted to enforce it. He refused to let anyone shoot deer out of season on his land, even though "everybody did it," but he took firm action to prevent a poor man losing a mule in a case involving unjust enforcement of a law. The man with the mule told about it later, saying that when a constable had taken his old work animal for debt, he sought help from the Captain, who bought it in at the legal sale for $20, part of which he had borrowed himself. Grant told the farmer to keep the mule. He'd send for it when he needed it. A few days later the constable, backed by a lawyer, seized the mule again, claiming that the execution of the law had been somehow faulty. Once more Grant bought the animal at auction, this time for $5, since no one would bid against him, and again he returned it to the farmer.

Sitting in the shade at his home a few days thereafter, he looked up to see the same constable leading the same mule down the road, and explaining that the lawyers still held that there hadn't been "a continued change of possession" or something like that. At the third auction Grant bought it for one dollar and as he led it away told the farmer: "I'm going to have that old mule if I have to buy it once a week all summer."

Two days later, Grant equipped the farmer with "a letter of authority" and told him to take the mule twenty-five miles into a neighboring county and trade it for another. Then he formally leased the substitute animal to the poor man for one cent a month, but as the grateful fellow said in time to come, "Captain Grant never asked me for either rent or mule . . . and every time I saw Grant for two or three years after that he would ask me if that constable had been around." [19]

Slowly the community filled with stories of the Captain's generosity — stories that fitted into a pattern: Grant would be returning from St. Louis with five dollars in his pocket, receipts from the sale of one cord of wood. Someone would tell him of a house that had burned down or a widow's cow that had died. Grant would hand over the five dollars, saying that he was sorry — it was "all he had," but the sufferers were certainly welcome to it. "I am very glad to," he was reported as saying when asked to contribute for the building of a new church. "I don't attend as much as I should, but Julia and the children do. We ought also to have a Sabbath-school in the neighborhood." [20]

Persons in predicaments discovered that the Captain could soothe human beings as well as horses. One morning the wife of an ex-soldier living nearby came running to Grant's home, her sunbonnet gone, her hair streaming and her tongue clanging hysterically. Later she said that when Grant had "sort o' quieted my excitables" she had explained that her husband, James, was drunk and had told her "he was going to sell the cow, saddle up Old Clay and go to Texas."

With her in tow, Grant sauntered up to James, and while she went into her home, began talking horse trade. He'd like to swap one of his own animals for Old Clay, who was at the hitching post, all prepared for Texas. James grew interested and soon the two men were talking and whittling, whittling and talking, while the forenoon slipped away. When the wife blew the dinner horn, she saw that James's "excitables" had been quieted too. He put Old Clay back in the stall, came into the house, sat down at the table and began to weep, quietly explaining that Captain Grant had given him "some new ideas," one of which was to swear off drinking. She said James never touched the stuff again. [21]

Stoically Grant endured the ordeal of meeting, on the streets of St. Louis, Army officers whose eyes betrayed their curiosity or their sympathy. News of his whereabouts since his pitiable resignation had spread among his acquaintances in their scattered army posts. The first word had come from Jefferson Barracks where he sold cordwood, and it increased throughout 1855 and 1856, as officers passing through St. Louis toward the troubled plains saw him sitting on his wagon, wearing old army clothing from which the insignia had been removed.

Did the liquor habit — "Old Gentleman Tipsy" — still have him?

Henry Coppée, visiting the city, thought not. Coppée, Buell, Major William Chapman and Joseph J. Reynolds, holding an impromptu reunion at a hotel, sent for Grant to join them, and as he arrived they started for the bar. Coppée heard Grant say:

"I'll go in and look at you, for I never drink anything."

As the group stood at the bar, comparisons were inevitable. Buell was a high-ranking assistant adjutant general, Chapman was a brevet lieutenant colonel. Both Coppée and Reynolds were resigning to take up the life Grant had once thought ideal — Coppée to become Professor of English at the University of Pennsylvania, Reynolds to take the chair of Engineering at George Washington University here in St. Louis. After Grant had gone, Buell and Reynolds told Coppée that what Grant had said was true; they saw him frequently and "he drank nothing but water." [22]

Brevet Brigadier General William S. Harney, preparing to march against the Sioux in 1858, was riding down a St. Louis street, "resplendent in a new uniform with gold trimmings," when he stopped a wagon and called to the driver, who sat between an ax and a whipstock:

"Why Grant, what in blazes are you doing here?"

Shifting one muddy boot across the other, the driver slowly answered, "Well, General, I'm hauling wood," which, as Emmy Dent understood, set Harney and his staff roaring with laughter. "They shook his hand and carried him off to dine at the Planters." [23]

One officer who had not seen him since Mexico took time off on a journey to Fort Leavenworth in 1857 to drive out and see Grant. As he neared the Gravois neighborhood he halted a farmer on a wagon and asked where Grant lived.

"Well, I am he," said the farmer.

Shocked at his run-down appearance, the officer asked him, "Great God, Grant, what are you doing?"

"I am solving the problem of poverty." [24]

Lieutenant William W. Averell, two years out of West Point,

was starting with an expedition for New Mexico in 1857 and had progressed fourteen miles west of St. Louis when he saw "a horseman in a blue overcoat, a hat broken and worn, and a stubby, sandy beard" overtake the column and engage the Commissary, Lieutenant William Craig, in conversation. After a time the man rode away and Craig, who had recently served as aide to Colonel Garland, said, "That's old Ulysses S. Grant of the Fourth Infantry. He wanted to be employed as commissary clerk to drive beef cattle and issue rations while we were crossing the plains. I couldn't employ him."

Brigadier General Edward F. Beale won Grant's undying loyalty one day when, arriving from California where he had known the Captain slightly, he stopped him outside the Planters and asked him to dinner.

"I'm not dressed for company," said Grant, whip in hand.

"Oh, that doesn't matter, come in!"

Grant talked easily with officers, but his conversation, they noted, was about old friends, where they were now. He asked especially for news of Alf Sully and Fred Steele.

One day in 1857 Grant met on the street a tall, red-haired man whose thin face, lined with worry like his own, was familiar. It was Sherman, whom he had not seen in seventeen years and then only from afar at West Point. They talked casually, neither revealing private affairs which would have shown parallels. Grant was running downhill, Sherman was calling himself "a dead cock in the Pit." The banking business had collapsed under Sherman in the panic. First the St. Louis firm for which he worked had closed its branch in California, then when he had come back to the New York branch, it too had closed, and a few days ago he had returned to St. Louis with his records, to help the firm wind up the venture. His accounts were in order, but he was out of a job and, moreover, haunted by the fact that on his advice brother officers had made investments which now had been wiped out by the panic. Although not legally or morally bound, he had written them that he would make good their loss, with interest, as soon as he could earn it. Proud and sensitive to a painful point, Sherman was shamefully preparing to return to Ohio and go to work for his father-in-law.

Two ex-soldiers come home to their wives' families to start over again, Sherman and Grant talked, then passed on, Sherman saying to himself, "West Point and the Regular Army were not good schools for farmers, [and] bankers." [25]

From other officers Grant heard scornful comments on "Bleeding Kansas." Joe Johnston, Lieutenant Colonel of the First Cavalry, had come back to Jefferson Barracks from the embattled Territory in 1856 to tell tales of the anarchy, assassination, arson and vote frauds that raged out there as "Border Ruffians" from Missouri, and "Nigger-Thieves," emigrants from free-soil states, fought for control. Johnston's second in command, Major John Sedgwick, rode his dragoons hard to prevent open warfare in May, 1856, when hundreds of armed Missourians came over the boundary, hunting the abolitionist who had massacred five proslavery settlers — John Brown of Osawatomie.

John Brown?

In Covington, Kentucky, Jesse Grant read the name in the newspapers, day after day. Could it be — yes, it was — that boy with whom he had worked and lived for more than a year back in Hudson Township — Owen Brown's boy — those gentle people spawning so bloody a son — the one who had been brooding over slavery forty years ago! If Jesse had heard of John Brown since that early day it had been as an Ohio wool buyer and grower in the 1840's, agitating against the strangle hold the Boston worsted mills kept on the farmers' throats. John Brown, fighting wool monopolists then, cotton monopolists now!

The same issue that had led John Brown into open warfare against the Slave Barons — the passage of the Kansas-Nebraska Bill in 1854 — was killing Jesse Grant's beloved Whig party. This new law had set aside the Missouri Compromise which had held since 1829 as a truce between the free-soil and proslave forces in the nation.

After admitting Missouri as a slave state, the Compromise had stipulated that any more states to be carved out of the Louisiana Purchase should be free if situated above Missouri's southern boundary, slave if below it. Since the new law threw open all such territories to the vote of the residents, all the old hostilities between North and South had broken out with increased violence. "Anti-Nebraska" factions were splitting off from the Democrats, from the Whigs and from the Order of United Americans, that ancient group which had always campaigned against foreigners and now, as a secret order, rose to new strength under the name of "Know-Nothings." Many Whigs were joining the Know-Nothings in the hope that if sufficient excitement were created over the danger of Roman Catholicism forcing a union of Church and State upon the Republic, the Free-Soilers and slave staters would compose their own quarrel before it wrecked the Union.

All around Jesse Grant the splintering of old party platforms grew louder in 1855. The abolitionists themselves were breaking up into factions. His friend, Thomas Morris, who had run for Vice-President on the Liberty party ticket in 1844, was dead, but Morris's disciple Salmon P. Chase had brought together in 1855 enough Free-Soil partisans from the Democrats, Whigs and Know-Nothings to get himself elected Governor of Ohio. Jesse had clung to the Whig Party as long as it lasted in his state, had written the platform at its expiring state convention in Columbus, but had then turned to work like a Trojan for Chase in the gubernatorial campaign that was only a step in the movement which produced the Republican Party in 1856. What Jesse thought of the Know-Nothings who had absorbed practically all the other places on the state ticket, Jesse never publically revealed.[26]

Ulysses joined the order and, in later years, gave his reasons. Many of his neighbors, like himself men of "Whig proclivities," had turned to the Know-Nothings when their own party died. "There was a lodge near my new home, and I was invited to join it. I accepted the invitation; was initiated; attended a meeting just one week later, and never went to another afterwards." [27]

Around St. Louis, the appeal of the American party was not so much to haters of Roman Catholicism as to opponents of foreigners. The tradition of St. Louis had always been friendly toward the pioneer French Catholic aristocrats of the place, and the German immigrants had included a strong proportion of anticlericals. But these Germans, particularly those who had come after the 1848 collapse of their democratic rebellion in the Fatherland, were violent agitators against slavery, and their radicalism appalled conservative Democrats, Whigs and Know-Nothings alike. Many Anglo-Saxons of colonial stock were outraged at the promptness with which the newly arrived Germans sought political power — Germans who still spoke their own tongue, read their own language newspapers, kept clannishly to their own social clubs and sang their own songs as if German music were something superior.

"I have no apologies to make for having been one week a member of the American party," Grant explained in later years, "for I still think native-born citizens of the United States should have as much protection, as many privileges in their native country, as those who voluntarily select it for a home." He was perhaps giving a hint as to his reasons for abandoning the party so suddenly when he said, "All secret, oath-bound political parties are dangerous to any nation." . . . "No political party can or ought to exist when one of its corner-stones is opposition to freedom of thought and to the right to worship God. . . . Nevertheless, if a sect sets up its laws as binding above the State laws, wherever the two come in conflict this claim must be resisted and suppressed at whatever cost." [28]

As the campaign began, Grant was undecided. To his orderly mind everything seemed at sixes and sevens. In the White House, Franklin Pierce thought so, even more, and took to drink. In St. Louis the political spearhead of the anti-Nebraska forces, Frank Blair, was drinking hard as he welded an organization which he would, at the proper moment, bring into the newly organized Republican party. That party was loosely drawing together anti-Southern sentiment in the North, and adding to it the discontented and fanatical elements of that section.

With the approach of November, Grant decided that, as a private citizen, he should vote. It would be his first. But how to vote?

Not for Millard Fillmore, who was the nominee of both the "pro-slavery section of the American party and the ghastly remnant of the Whigs."

Not for the Republican nominee, John C. Frémont, the dazzling "Pathfinder" of exploring fame. Frémont's own father-in-law, the statesman Thomas Hart Benton, was opposing him on the ground that the Republican party was so opposed to slavery that its victory would probably provoke the slave states to secede. Army officers as a class thought Frémont a shallow, vain adventurer, far too erratic to be entrusted with the Presidency. Army officers were by training conservative wherever change was concerned.

Should Grant vote with Colonel Dent and Benton for the Democratic nominee, Buchanan? Nothing about Buchanan stirred enthusiasm, yet he had had large experience in government, had a level head, was conservative to the point of timidity and was running on a platform that denounced antislavery agitation and swore to uphold "the Union as it was, the Union as it is, and the Union as it shall be." But could Grant now support the Democratic party which had surrendered to the "pro-slavery conspiracy" of the South on the Texas and Mexican issues?

In the end, that is what he did, although he scratched his ticket to vote for at least one non-Democrat who was a candidate for the state legislature.

One story had it that he had not intended to vote at all and was indeed only awakened to the fact that it was election day by noting a crowd at a polling booth as he passed with a load of corn. He stopped the team, saying, "I'll go back and vote against Frémont." [29]

In later years it was widely published, as an epigram, that he said, "I voted for Buchanan because I didn't know him and voted against Frémont because I did know him." [30]

His own explanation of his vote, made in the retrospect of many years, was that it had been determined by his chronic dread of war. He became convinced that the success of the Republican Frémont would mean the rebellion of the slave states.

Under the circumstances I preferred the success of a candidate whose election would prevent or postpone secession, to seeing the country plunged into a war the end of which no man could foretell. With a Democrat elected by the unanimous vote of the Slave States, there could be no pretext for secession for four years. I very much hoped that the passions of the people would subside in that time, and the catastrophe be averted altogether; if it was not, I believed that the country would be better prepared to receive the shock and to resist it. [31]

On December 28, 1856, as the South, now that Buchanan was elected, settled back to compose itself and the Republicans rejoiced over their capture of almost all the Northern states, Grant wrote his father about matters of more immediate interest.

He wanted five hundred dollars with which to buy the implements and the seed that he so badly needed for the 1857 crop. He would gladly pay 10 per cent for a loan:

This last year my place was not half tended because I had but one span of horses, and one hand, and we had to do all the work of the place, living at a distance, too — all the hauling for my building and take wood to the city for the support of the family. Since the 1st of April my team has earned me about fifty dollars a month, independent of my own work. This next year I presume I shall be compelled to neglect my farm some to make a living but by next year (1858) I hope to be independent.

Bravely, as if to encourage his father to make him that loan of five hundred dollars, he said:

Every day I like farming better and I do not doubt that money is to be made at it. So far I have been laboring under great disadvantage, but now that I am on my own place, and shall not have to build next summer, I think I shall be able to do much better. This year if I could have bought seed I should have made out still better than I did. I wanted to plant sixty or seventy bushels of potatoes but I had not the money to buy them. I planted twenty however and sold 225 bushels and have about 125 on hand besides all that I have used.

His twenty-five acres of winter wheat looked promising and he would add to it next spring Irish potatoes, on twenty acres of "new ground" that he had cleared, and five or six acres of cabbage, beets, cucumbers for pickles and melons which he hoped to peddle in St. Louis, keeping "a wagon going to market every day."

Wistfully he concluded:

Some three weeks since I went into the Planters House and saw registered 'J. R. Grant, Ky' on the book. Making inquiry I found that J. R. G. had just taken the Pacific R. R. Cars. I made shure [sic] it was you and that I should find you when I got home.

Was it you? [32]

The money was not forthcoming from Jesse, who apparently was leaving it to his daughters Virginia, nicknamed now "Jenny," and Mary to do most of the corresponding with Ulysses. As the days grew longer, Ulysses made a more direct approach. On February 7, 1857, he sent from the Sappington Post Office a letter:

DEAR FATHER, Spring is now approaching when farmers require not only to till the soil, but to have the wherewith to till it and seed it. For two years I have been compelled to farm without either of these facilities, confining my attention therefore principally to oats and corn; two crops which can never pay off; for if they bear a high price it is because the farmer has raised scarsely [sic] enough for his own use. If abundant they will scarsely [sic] bear transportation. I want to vary the crop a little and also to have implements to cultivate with.

To this end I am going to make the last appeal to you. I do this because when I was in Ky. you voluntarily offered to give me a thousand dollars to commence with and because there is no one els [sic] to whom I could with the same propriety, apply.

It is usual for parents to give their children assistance in begining [sic] life (and I am only begining, though thirty-five years of age, nearly) and what I ask is not too much. I do not ask you to give me anything. But what I do ask is that you lend me or borrow for me, $500 for two years, with interest at 10 per cent payable annually if you choose and with this if I do not go on prosperously I shall ask no more of you.

He was clearing ten or twelve additional acres this winter and was cutting three hundred cords of wood, "but the chopping has to be paid for now."

The fact is that, without means, it is useless for me to go on farming, and I will have to do what Mr. Dent has given me permission to do, sell the farm and invest elswhere [sic]. For two years now I have been compelled to neglect my farm to go off and make a few dollars to buy any little necessaries, sugar, coffee, etc, or to pay hired men.

Now do not understand from this, that if I had what I ask for, my exertions would sease [sic]: but that they would [be] directed to a more profitable end. . . . My expenses for my family have been nothing scarsely [sic] for the last two years. Fifty dollars, I believe, would pay all that I have laid out for their clothing. I have worked hard and got but little and expect to go on in the same way until I am perfectly independent; and then too most likely.

At the very end of the letter he told his father, who was cool toward the Dents, "Mrs. Dent died on the 4th of January, after an illness of about a month. This leaves Mr. Dent and one daughter alone." [33]

Ulysses' friends never knew whether Jesse responded to this "last appeal." Emmy Dent understood old Mr. Dent had given his son-in-law $1000 but that it had arrived at the time Hardscrabble was built. Others heard that Jesse's advances totalled $2000 in four years. There was no question that Jesse tried to help collect Ulysses' bad debt at Sacketts Harbor, but by March 1857 alarms about another financial panic were dimming hopes of creditors everywhere. [34]

Help or no help, Ulysses went on farming and hauling wood and vegetables to St. Louis. By midsummer he knew that his wheat, which had been expected to yield 400 or 500 bushels would produce a scant 75. And his corn and oats, while good, were not worth hauling to town because the panic had prostrated the country. Through the autumn banks suspended specie payments; bankrupt businessmen, here and there, were reported as firing derringers into their breasts, and mobs rattled big city windows with the cry, "Bread or Death." [35]

A day or two before Christmas Grant walked through the streets lined with the pinched faces of the jobless until he came to the pawnshop of J. S. Freligh where he exchanged his "gold hunting detached lever watch" and gold chain for twenty-two dollars, signing an agreement to return the money or make a new loan by January 23, 1858. His family must have presents on Christmas morning and Julia must have a happy holiday, for she was due to have another baby within a few weeks. The future looked tragic. The *New York Tribune* of December 25 (when it reached town), published Horace Greeley's report of a tour: "The West is very poor. I think a larger proportion of the people of Michigan, Indiana, Illinois, Wisconsin and Iowa are under the harrow now than at any former period." [36]

The fourth child, when it came on February 6, 1858, was named Jesse Root Grant, Jr., the grandfather, within a few years, pronouncing him "the most promising of the family." Colonel Dent was less buoyant. Since the death of his wife he had been thinking of his house in town. He was sixty-two. In the spring of 1858 he rented his farm and White Haven to Ulysses and Julia and with Emmy moved to St. Louis; Ulysses leased Julia's sixty to another farmer. In the big house and with 200 acres of plowed land, 250 more of pasture and the rest in woodland Grant saw bright prospects ahead: [37]

"I have now three negro men, two hired by the year and one of Mr. Dent's, which, with my own help, I think, will enable me to do my farming pretty well with assistance in harvest," he wrote his sister Mary. It was probably during this general change that he became what his father had refused to become, a slaveowner. From Colonel Dent he acquired in his own name, not Julia's, a mulatto slave named William Jones — a man in his early thirties "about five feet seven inches in height." [38]

Ulysses must pay a note at the bank — the last day of grace April 17 — he hinted to the family at Covington, but the new season was starting well. The hard times caused by the panic seemed to be passing. He enjoyed teaching eight-year-old Freddy to read. With the school a mile and a half away, the boy had as yet no education, but would start attending when weather permitted.

"I do not leave the farm except in cases of urgent necessity," he wrote as the vernal equinox sent farmers out to do their ploughing.[39]

But by June cold weather had crippled the crops even if the sensational freeze of June 5 had not killed the wheat, corn and potatoes in Missouri as it had done across so much of the West. And by midsummer sickness began striking White Haven — striking again and again. Little Fred went down with bilious fever which passed into typhoid, with Ulysses and Julia despairing of his life for days. Julia's sister Nellie, wife of Dr. Alexander Sharp, visiting the house with her children, fell ill. So did one of her youngsters. Seven of the slaves were sickened, and both Julia and Ulysses developed chills and fever.

By September 7 Ulysses was able to write his sister Mary that Freddy was now out of danger although his hearing was affected, but the others were still dragging along. "Not being able to even attend to my hands, much less work myself, I am getting behind hand. Cannot some of you come and pay us a visit?" [40]

The most discouraging thing about himself was that the ague, which he had thought buried on the heights at West Point, had returned. And that other threat, consumption, which he had considered lost in Texas, was it back too? His brother Simpson, over at Galena, was showing signs of developing the family weakness.

The ague was still burning and chilling Ulysses and Julia when, on October 1, he wrote Jesse that Freddy's hearing would be all right:

"Mr. Dent and myself will make a sale this fall and get clear of all the stock on the place, and then rent out the cleared land and sell about four hundred acres of the north end of the place." His own farm would be sold, too. He planned to go to Covington towards spring, and hoped his father would have a place for him — even in the hated tanning business. He was not asking for a job with any stipulated pay, merely the prospect of winning independence some day. If his father would open something for him in Kentucky, he would bring along Julia's "smart, active" slave boy "and let him learn the farrier's business." However, if Jesse, in his opposition to slavery, preferred, the boy could be left in Missouri where Ulysses could "get about three dollars per month for him now, and more as he gets older." [41]

Jesse discouraged the move to Covington of either Ulysses or the slave boy.

Repelled, Ulysses kept on hauling wood when able to sit his wagon, and wondered what he would do after the auction sale. His insufficiently tended crops were disappointing. Through the neighborhood went the whisper that Captain Grant was drinking. Sam Brown, who would in time become sergeant on the St. Louis police force, said that the Captain "Invariably stopped before a certain resort on the Gravois road, watered his team and took a little something stronger himself." Tales were told about sprees that Grant shared with W. D. W. Barnard, a socially popular druggist of St. Louis who married Eliza Shurlds, sister of John and Captain Fred Dent's wives. J. E. Barron, a bitter enemy of Barnard's in St. Louis, twelve years later swore on the Bible: "There is no doubt they got drunk together very often when Grant was a poor man." [42]

John F. Long, one of the neighbors closest to Grant and the Dents, declared in later years, when he was a highly respected judge and businessman in St. Louis, that he knew exactly how the stories of Grant's drunkenness got started, and that they were entirely untrue. He and Grant had been driving their respective loads of cordwood

to the city one day when he noticed that the Captain was shaking
with chills and fever:

We unloaded our wagons and started home at once. He grew
so much worse that I feared it would develop into a congestive
chill and I urged him to take something hot. I suggested a hot
toddy, but he was stubborn and refused. As we were passing
the last drugstore on our road homeward, I stopped the teams,
went in and got a dose of capsicum and sugar, brought it out
to Grant and made him take it. This diminished the severity of
the chill, but it made him so deathly sick that he was obliged
to lie down before we reached home. He had not tasted a drop
of liquor on the trip. He had not been out of my presence a
moment.

Next day, I met a neighbor who had seen us returning home
the previous day, and he said, "Oh, ho! So your friend, Grant,
came home drunk, — flat on his back — yesterday! Ho, ho!
That's great for Captain Grant!" The story, thus started, found
such swift wing that my denials and explanation never overtook
the lie. . . . Grant not only did not drink to excess, but seldom
drank at all.[43]

One day in 1858, Captain Longstreet, who had been at Texas
posts since the end of the war, chanced to be in St. Louis, and met
officer friends at the Planter's Hotel, where, as he later told it, "it
was soon proposed to have an old-time game of brag." Finding themselves one short of making a full hand, Captain Edmunds N. Holloway, also in from Texas, said he would go out and find someone. "In
a few minutes he returned with a man poorly dressed in citizen's
clothes and in whom we recognized our old friend Grant." It was a
happy reunion for both Longstreet and for Holloway, since the
latter had been in Grant's class at West Point.

Longstreet was depressed at their parting, for he saw that "Grant
had been unfortunate, and he was really in needy circumstances."
Next day, as Longstreet narrated it:

I was walking in front of the Planters', when I found myself
face to face again with Grant who, placing in the palm of my
hand a five dollar gold piece, insisted that I should take it in
payment of a debt of honor over 15 years old. I peremptorily

declined to take it, alleging that he was out of the service and more in need of it than I.

"You must take it," said he, "I cannot live with anything in my possession which is not mine." Seeing the determination in the man's face, and in order to save him mortification, I took the money, and shaking hands we parted." [44]

Other men noted that Grant's face was showing signs of pain and age, his body thin and his hands bent. A neighbor noted that "he was like a man thinking on an abstract subject all the time." [45]

When he stood on the streets of St. Louis talking to officers, his old slouch hat was in formless outline, their caps trim, neat and sharp. His shoulders drooped, theirs were straight and square. His beard was shaggy and vague of shape, theirs combed, crisp and flaring. The army blue in his old overcoat was fading into a misty gray; theirs were bright and brave.

Sam Grant was becoming the ghost of a soldier.

CHAPTER TWENTY

"I Set Free William Forever"

W E WILL not always be in this condition."
Mary Robinson heard Miss Julia say it when things
seemed to be at their worst. Miss Julia was sitting in a
large rocking chair, talking to other members of the Dent family
about "financial embarrassments." She told them Dudie would come
out all right. This was an old story to the slave woman — Miss Julia's
confidence in Dudie never let up one minute, come what might.[1]

Now that her husband was no longer able to stand the strain of
the farm, Julia pressed her father to find suitable work for him. The
Colonel thought of his sister's son, Harry Boggs, who had a small
real estate and rent-collection business in St. Louis. Everybody said
real estate would be a craze in the spring. Real-estate men were advertising houses and lots all over town right now and would be
launching exuberant subdivision campaigns within a few months.
New firms were being organized. Now was the time to get in.

Despite the panic, the assessed valuation of real estate in the city
had leaped from $60,000,000 in 1856 to $82,000,000 in 1858, and
population had climbed from 77,760 in 1850, to an estimated 180,000
in 1859. Civic prophets were crying the limitless future of the city
which had the most magnificent steamboat lines in the world, and
would soon have railroad pre-eminence as well — five railroads already had, or would quickly have, terminals in town, furnishing
express service in "patent ventilated sleeping cars" everywhere East
and many places South. Steamboats were advertised in newspapers
"For Upper Mississippi River," "For Lower Mississippi River," "For
Ohio River," "For Osage River," "For Cumberland River," "For
Illinois River," and some thirty boats a day for points on the Missouri
River.[2]

With Colonel Dent pressing him, Ulysses one day climbed down
off a load of wood and told Boggs, "The old gentleman . . . thinks

I could soon learn the details, and that my large acquaintance among army officers would bring enough additional customers to make it support both our families." [3] After talking it over with his wife Louisa Boggs agreed. Louisa felt sure Uncle Fred would drum up clients if his favorite daughter were to benefit. Colonel Dent went to 35 Pine Street, where Harry had desk space in the law firm of McClellan, Hillyer & Moody on the ground floor of an old French dwelling. Josiah G. McClellan always remembered the day "Colonel Dent came in and asked us to allow Grant to come in there, too. We did so, and he and Boggs had a sort of partnership in the collection of rents, etc." [4]

With no money to put into the business, Grant had to content himself with what amounted to little more than a clerkship, although the business cards read: "Boggs & Grant, General Agents, Collect Rents, Negotiate Loans, Buy and Sell Real Estate, etc."

The arrangements made, Ulysses spent the autumn of 1858 winding up his sad farm experiment. He auctioned off his horses, grain and implements and helped Colonel Dent rent the fields for next year. He would trade Hardscrabble for a house and lot in St. Louis as soon as possible. [5]

Julia wanted to take the four children to visit their grandparents in Covington, but since she could not make the journey without a slave woman to help her, she hesitated. The route would, as Ulysses wrote Jesse, touch "Free Soil" at several points, and Julia "was afraid she might have some trouble." [6]

For the past eighteen months, abolitionists in Illinois had been increasingly aggressive in helping slaves escape, prompted by a celebrated law case in which the Grants' friends, the Blow family, had become involved back in 1846. In that year, Henry T. Blow and his brother Taylor had gone to court to secure freedom for a former slave of their father's, a certain Negro who had been "Sam" when he lived with them, but who, while living with his new master at army posts in Illinois and Minnesota, during the 1830's, had acquired the name of Dred Scott. Some persons concluded that the name had been bestowed upon him by the soldiers who heard him babbling praise of "Great Scott" — General Winfield Scott — and that Negro dialect had supposedly twisted "Great" into "Dret," which had become "Dred."

Eventually abandoned by his owners, Dred had drifted home to the Blow brothers who, as thrifty drug and paint merchants, saw no reason to support him. Also they disliked slavery. The title to Dred was so cloudy that they could not free him out of hand, as they had done with some of their own slaves. Henry had signed his bond in November 1846, when he asked the Circuit Court of St. Louis to declare him free on the ground that he had already become so by residence in territory where slavery was illegal. The case, which had soon passed out of the Blows' hands, wound its way across various benches until the United States Supreme Court, on March 6, 1857, denied Dred freedom, declaring that Congress never should have prohibited slavery in the territories.

This revolutionary finding had set the whole nation in turmoil once more, interpreted as it was by Free-Soilers as giving the slave power the right to expand anywhere it wished, and establishing the rule that the Negro had no rights which a white man was bound to respect. By May 26, 1857, when Taylor Blow, with title to Dred established, gave him his freedom, the nation was shaking under the impact of politicians, editors, clergymen, arguing the new question pro and con, and rocking still more on September 17 when Blow buried Dred. The Negro had been slowly dying of consumption while the Justices had been pondering his, and the nation's fate.[7]

To Grant it was tragic that the long truce, for which he had voted so hopefully in November 1857, should have gone to smash within four months' time. The Dred Scott decision had been a brand to rekindle the Republicans' fire which had been dying down ever since the Free-Soilers' capture of Kansas, in 1857, had struck that fuel from their hands. Under the torchlights, Republican orators had promptly started to cry that the decision proved how the slave barons had perverted the highest court to their ruthless purposes. Armed with it, the domineering Southerners could now spread their "accursed institution" over the territories and add enough slave states to give them control of national legislation.

Through the summer and autumn, Grant saw Missouri and Illinois become the cockpit of the wild Republican assault upon the Democrats. In his own congressional district, the firebrand, Frank Blair, campaigned violently for election against "Missouri Dick" Barrett, a moderate Democrat who accused him of being a "Black Republican" extremist. Grant voted against Blair although he admired the courage with which the magnetic fellow excoriated the slave oligarchy and dared its "cowardly minions" to carry out their threats to assassinate him.[8]

Illinois dramatized the cleavage in a series of debates between its strongest Republican, Abraham Lincoln, and its famous Senator, Stephen A. Douglas, who was also the Democrat's most powerful national leader. Two years later Grant would tell how he had read those speeches between the rivals for the United States Senate, and how he thought "it was a nice question to say who got the best of the argument." [9] Douglas scored when he charged that Lincoln had fanned the danger of sectional warfare by saying, "A house divided against itself cannot stand. I believe this government cannot endure permanently half slave and half free." Lincoln outmaneuvered Douglas when he asked him how, in the light of the Dred Scott decision, the citizens of a territory could lawfully exclude slavery. Douglas, answering that the voters had a right to vote slave or free and enforce their vote no matter what the Supreme Court might have said, antagonized the South and widened the sectional split in the Democratic party. While Grant told friends that "he had a great admiration for Lincoln," he was not won to the Republicans.[10] Douglas's oratory had been convincing in picturing them as aiding abolitionists, no matter how much they insisted they only opposed the spread of slavery, not its existence in the Old South. He was persuasive when he declared that he stood for peace, harmony and good will among the states, and that Republican success would only aid and abet the abolitionists who openly preferred disunion to brotherhood, under the Constitution, with slaveowners.

It was, however, small comfort to men of Grant's pacific hopes when, in November, Douglas won — for he had lost in the popular vote, and only won the Senatorship because the State Legislators, who chose that officer, were, by gerrymander, narrowly Democratic. And although Barrett triumphed over Blair, the vote was so suspiciously close that the Republicans, crying fraud, were contesting the election. The Republicans emerged resurgent and if they should win in 1860, would establish something new in national politics, a wholly sectional party. And when that happened, said many extremist Southerners, the slave states would secede.

To fan the danger still more, Grant heard, soon after he moved into St. Louis in January 1859, the newspapers shrieking the news that his father's boyhood friend, John Brown, had led an abolitionist raid into Missouri, returned to Kansas with a party of kidnaped slaves and led them 600 miles up through Iowa and across Illinois to Chicago, whence the Underground Railway spirited them to the permanent safety of Canada.

Leaving the family at White Haven, Ulysses took the empty back room in the home of Harry and Louisa Boggs at 209 South Fifteenth Street — a stoveless room. He took his meals with the Boggses, and sat with them on cold evenings. On Saturdays, he walked the twelve miles to White Haven, and on Sundays, the twelve miles back.[11]

At the office, twenty-seven-year-old Hillyer was the partner he came to know best, although the thirty-six-year-old McClellan also became, in time, a warm friend. Hillyer, a voluble, intelligent, fat Kentuckian who had come to St. Louis in 1855, after college in Indiana, was a Know-Nothing, edging rapidly toward Republicanism. McClellan was a proslavery Democrat from Virginia. With politics so hot an issue, Hillyer thought Grant anything but silent, once he had come to feel at home with the two partners.

"We considered him more than commonly talkative," he said in after years. "He was entertaining, and I was attracted towards him." If it was not the state of the nation which the partners discussed with Grant, it was the state of the French and Italian war, which the newspapers reported lavishly. Hillyer and McClellan thought Grant liked best to talk about his Mexican battles and heard him compare them critically with what was happening in Italy.

But he was always sad in varying degrees. Something was depressing him. It might be a growing realization that he was not a real-estate salesman.

"He doesn't seem to be just calculated for business of that sort," McClellan said. "But an honester, more generous man never lived. I don't believe that he knows what dishonesty is." Hillyer, in time, figured it out that Grant's silence in certain situations was "partly discrimination and partly the form of an old bashfulness he had when a boy."[12]

Boggs, who shared his uncle's belligerent proslavery views, was understood to differ with Ulysses on politics. He and Louisa thought their boarder depressed; "he seldom smiled, and was never heard to laugh aloud." He came home on the horse cars some days shaking with ague, having been helped from the office to the cars by McClellan and Hillyer.[13]

Boggs was discovering that while Grant was useful at figuring discounts and other financial matters, and tried to collect rents conscientiously, he was apt to talk of old days rather than of new payments when trying to collect from army friends. Once he trustingly leased a house to a woman who turned out to be what her neighbors called one of "The Fancy." [14]

Nor did matters improve when, in early March, Ulysses moved Julia and the children into a small cottage he had rented at Seventh and Lynch streets. Situated in what he described as "the lower part of the city" and two miles from the office, Grant was occasionally late in coming to work, the story being around town that Boggs scolded him when this happened. Sometimes he would arrive as late as ten or eleven o'clock, meekly explaining that his wife, with all the little children to care for, had been delayed getting breakfast.[15]

Grant often dropped into the nearby office of the commission merchants, Moffett & Schroeter, for a chat. The senior partner, William A. Moffett, had stories himself to tell about people who slept late in the morning. His wife's red-haired brother, who was twenty-four that year of 1859, made his home with the Moffetts when his work as a steamboat pilot returned him to town, and would sit at the piano and sing a song satirizing his fondness for oversleeping:

> Samuel Clemens! The gray dawn is breaking,
> The cow from the back gate her exit is making, —
> The howl of the housemaid is heard in the hall;
> What, Samuel Clemens? Slumbering still!

Moffett never brought Grant and his brother-in-law together. He thought Grant not anxious to meet new people and noted how "very quiet" he was.[16]

Small though his cottage was, Ulysses kept urging his family to visit him. It was useless to expect his mother; she never left home. But the rest of them could stop off as they came and went between home and Galena, where Orvil, who was now married, had gone that summer to take some of the burden from Simpson's slowly weakening hands.[17]

Living expenses continued to outstrip income from the partnership. Nevertheless Grant appeared in court on March 29, 1859 and filed a signed document which read:

> Know all persons by these presents, that I Ulysses S. Grant of the City & County of St. Louis in the State of Missouri, for divers good and valuable considerations . . . do hereby emancipate and set free from Slavery my Negro man, William, sometimes called William Jones, of mullato complexion, aged about thirty-five years, and about five feet seven inches in height and being the same slave purchased by me of Frederick Dent. And I do hereby manumit, emancipate and set free said William from slavery forever.[18]

Grant was never known, outside of the family, to explain his reasons for the act. In August 1858 he had been ready to let Julia's slave boy be hired out for three dollars a month, but by March he was not only discarding such a plan for his own man, William, but was freeing him, even though the one thousand dollars which a slave usually brought at auction would have solved many of his financial problems. Nor was it likely that for all his growing resentment against "ultra-radicals" North and South, he was protesting in his obscure way against the vote of a convention of representative Southerners at Vicksburg that month — a vote demanding the restoration of the horror of horrors — the African slave trade.

Colonel John W. Emerson, a lawyer friend of Grant's from Ironton, Missouri, saw one day how a windfall of fifty dollars pleased him, but how the sentiment behind it delighted him still more. Emerson delivered the money (two twenty-dollar gold pieces and ten dollars), saying they came from an Ironton carpenter — name of Babcock — who, on learning Captain Grant's whereabouts, wanted to repay, with interest, the forty dollars which the Captain had loaned him at Panama in 1854. "It saved my life."

Grant managed to find the stained note which Babcock had forced upon him, sent it to Ironton, then, weighing the coins in his hand, mused: "It seems odd to get fifty dollars for forty dollars loaned! I believe this is the first interest I ever received in my life, and I didn't know I was a capitalist before."[19]

He saw no way to reduce expenses until next October, when he would move into a house of his own. Luckily he had been able to trade Hardscrabble for a house surrounded by fruit trees at Ninth and Barton Streets. In the transaction he had received to boot a note for $3000, due in five years, also a deed of trust on Hardscrabble to protect him against a $1500 mortgage on the Barton Street property, which its owner had been unable to pay.[20]

As the humid summer of St. Louis crept toward the dog days of August, Ulysses realized that in all fairness he must quit the association with Boggs. The income did not justify anything approaching a partnership. His father wrote him, urging that he seek a mathematics professorship said to be open at Washington University. Ulysses answered that the place had been filled and even if it had not, he would have no chance, since Quinby, who had been a better mathematician than he at West Point, and who since 1852, had been teaching the subject at the University of Rochester, had tried without success to secure it.[21]

More nearly possible was the job of County Engineer which would soon be open in St. Louis County. It paid $1500 a year and he would be required to oversee the public wagon roads and bridges. Ulysses spent the first two weeks in August collecting letters of recommendation. Henry T. Blow threw his strong influence into the campaign, and Taylor Blow signed a letter of recommendation, as did thirty-four other citizens of high standing, among them the revered aristocrats John O'Fallon and John F. Darby, L. A. Benoist, of an old banking family, Charles A. Pope, a prominent physician, G. W. Fishback, editor of Frank Blair's Republican newspaper, the *Democrat*, Hillyer, McClellan, Moody and Charley Ford. Three men with unmistakable Teutonic names signed. From his faculty desk at Washington University, Joe Reynolds wrote a letter to help his classmate, describing how Grant, at the Academy, had "always maintained a high standing, and graduated with great credit" and how his "strict integrity and unremitting industry" fitted him "in an eminent degree" for the post. Dan Frost, Class of '44, wrote under Reynolds's signature his own full endorsement of what the professor had said; Dan had known Grant intimately in West Point, and for eight or nine years in the Army.[22]

Frost's endorsement would count highly with the two Commissioners who were Democrats, but not with the three who were either Republicans or Free-Soilers, for Dan was strongly opposed to Blair and, as Brigadier General of the State Militia, was prepared to stop the abolitionists if they should try to coerce Missouri as he and his fiery friends believed they had coerced Kansas.

It was an impressive petition which, with its sheaf of accompanying letters, Grant sent to the Commissioners on August 16, explaining in his formal application: "I have made no effort to get a large number of names, nor the names of persons with whom I am not personally acquainted. . . . Should your honorable body see proper to give me the appointment I pledge myself to give the office my entire attention and shall hope to give general satisfaction." [23]

No reckless spelling in this letter.

Mary Robinson, in town helping Miss Julia, saw how earnestly Mr. Grant wanted the appointment, even if he were always so outwardly composed. He walked into the room one day while Mary and Miss Julia were laying a carpet and, after watching them for a few minutes, said "in a careless way" that he believed he'd go to see a popular French fortuneteller "and get her to tell me whether I will be elected." With that he walked out, and when he returned said "in an unconcerned way" that he had learned he was to come within an ace of winning, but would be beaten, and would soon thereafter leave the city to engage in a mercantile business.

The slave woman, describing the scene some twenty-five years later, said that Miss Julia had burst out:

"Nonsense! You will be elected, Dudie! Everyone says you cannot be beaten. The fortuneteller told you what was not true."

Although Mary Robinson admitted that this was "one of the most extraordinary events" she ever knew in Mr. Grant's life, she insisted stoutly that it was true. Grant himself based his doubt of election on grounds less occult. Realistic inquiry had revealed what he wrote his father; namely that "although friends who are recommending me are the very first citizens of this place, and members of all parties, I fear they will make strictly party nominations." [24]

Dr. Taussig, who was one of the three Free-Soilers, said later that although such powerful "Union men" as Henry T. Blow personally pressed him to vote for Grant, he could not do it because he felt it imperative to surround the County Commissioners with employees "whose loyalty to the Union was unquestioned." He knew that Grant was said to have voted Democratic on national issues, and assumed that he had been contaminated by Colonel Dent's loud pro-slavery views. Taussig and his two fellow Unionists, John H. Lightner and Benjamin Farrar, admitted Grant's technical fitness for the post, but it was no greater than that of his opponent, a German, F. Salomon, who was "an excellent civil engineer" and, moreover, a Republican whose selection would please the Teutonic population.

The three Republicans felt that with St. Louis dividing into two violent camps and with pro-Southern "Minute Men" and anti-Southern "Wide Awakes" drilling in semimilitary organizations, blood might start flowing any minute down the city's gutters.

Grant felt sure of the votes of the two Democratic members, Colonel Alton R. Easton, whom he had known in Mexico as Colonel of Missouri Volunteers, and Judge Peregrine Tibbets, whom even the Republicans admitted to be "a most estimable gentleman." [25]

Rodney H. Wells, when he was later Postmaster of St. Louis, would declare that Grant had waited on the courthouse steps for the result, and that when a friend had emerged saying, "You're beaten," Grant had said, "Yes, and by a Dutchman." [26]

"The Free Soil party felt themselves bound to provide for one of their own party," Ulysses wrote his father next day, "a German who came to the West as an assistant surveyor upon the public lands, and who has held an office ever since." This meant that now there was only "one paying office in the county held by an American, unless you except the office of Sheriff which is held by a Frenchman who speaks broken English, but was born here." The grievance was a deep one. Grant said years afterward, "My opponent had the advantage of birth over me (he was a citizen by adoption) and carried off the prize." But, as he remembered these late months of 1859 one thing had grieved him even more:

> It made my blood run cold to hear friends of mine, Southern men — as many of my friends were — deliberately discuss the dissolution of the Union as though it were a tariff bill. I could not endure it. The very thought of it was a pain. I wanted to leave the country if disunion was accomplished.[27]

What had driven his Southern friends closer to an outright demand for dissolution of the Union was a shattering thing that had happened in the third week in October — John Brown had raided, not Missouri this time, but Virginia, storming the United States Arsenal at Harpers Ferry with armed abolitionists in an attempt to free the adjacent slaves. Although Brown had been quickly captured, and no slaves had risen, newspapers carried the outcry of the whole South against the imminence of "servile insurrection" and its accompanying horrors of arson, murder and rape. Democratic politicians were charging that the Republicans had encouraged, abetted and financed Brown's raid. The Republicans were answering with denials and with charges that Brown was a lunatic.

Colonel Emerson, in from Ironton, often saw Grant in his blue coat, his hat low on his forehead, "a newspaper hanging listlessly by his side," sitting and staring into space. At first Emerson thought it mere "studiousness" but soon learned from remarks Grant would drop that all these "extravagant and vicious sentiments or proceedings" reported in the newspapers were giving him deep pain, "and it was this apprehension of evil which was menacing his country that produced in him a personal grief and sadness." Emerson concluded that "when he pulled his hat over his eyes, it was not so much for the purpose of shutting *out* the world, as it was to shut *in* his own thoughts." [28]

To a man who hated war first and foremost as he did, there were each day fewer and fewer persons with whom to be confidential. According to the later legend in St. Louis, Democratic criticism forced him to halt his visits to the office of the Radical *Democrat* where he talked to Fishback. Whispers said that Colonel Dent in conversation ridiculed his Yankee son-in-law who was such a failure at business. Still other whispers said that Harry and Louisa Boggs thought him so Northern that they refused to speak to him at one period. Yet to Republicans like his father and brothers Ulysses was a Democrat.[29]

He had become a man without a party and feared he would soon be without a country, too. Also, since his departure from the Boggs office in August or September, he was a man without an income.

"I don't want to fly from one thing to another," he wrote his father, "nor would I, but I am compelled to make a living from the start for which I am willing to give all my time and all my energy." [30]

Cash grew so scarce that when he moved from the rented house into his own, that October, he had to ask his landlady, Mrs. Lynch, to wait for several months' payments that were due. She trusted him. Her son Henry, preparing to join the new gold rush to recently discovered mines in the Rocky Mountains, near Denver City, was approached by Grant with a suggestion that he go along and open a hardware store in the Rockies. Lynch said Ulysses "Wrote his father in Ohio requesting pecuniary aid" but, after waiting a month received a letter which "threw a damper on his expectation and he abandoned the idea." [31]

Grant's friends started a movement to place him in either of the two posts that were expected to be filled at the United States Custom-house on November 1 by the Democratic Federal Administration, one job, that of Superintendent, would be worth $1500 to $1800 a year, the other, a minor one, paying $1200. The campaign was successful enough to land Grant, temporarily at least, in the second job, but in a few weeks the Collector of Customs died, and a new broom swept Grant out with less than two months' salary. [32]

His hat brim hung lower as he turned from the newspapers in late November and early December. Blood! Blood! Blood! "The slaves ought to wade to liberty through the blood of their masters knee deep," the Reverend Slossar was reported as telling abolitionists who met in Chicago to protest the hanging of John Brown. "The crimes of this guilty land will never be purged away but with blood," Old Brown was saying before they led him to the gallows on December 2. In the North, some poets and orators were speaking of Brown's blood in terms of Christ's crucifixion. In the South, fire-eaters were denouncing the North for not silencing such supporters of treason, and were declaring that in the quiet sympathy so many Free-Soilers were showing Brown's memory lay the proof that all political ties between the two sections must eventually be broken if blood should flow.

Grant saw that the four years' breathing spell for which he had voted was wasted. Buchanan had failed and the nation was drifting like a captainless ship toward the rocks, while the crew quarreled among themselves.

Although he kept looking for a position, Grant was drifting, too. On money borrowed probably from friends, his family ate well, and the children wore good clothes to school. Sometimes Ulysses and Julia attended the theater — he liked especially the British melodrama, *The Relief of Lucknow.* Ulysses' pride was low, and when he heard that Salomon might be ousted as County Engineer, he renewed his application, on February 13, 1860. The rumor was idle; Salomon held on.[33]

Soon it would be spring again. No horseback rides for a young lieutenant and the planter's daughter along the high banks of the Mississippi, as there had been seventeen years ago. No stopping of the slow, thudding hoofs by beds of wild flowers in the woods. Not even a saddle horse now.

Seventeen years! The older he got the more rapidly failure seemed to strike. Eleven years in the Army; four years farming; two years collecting rents and hunting jobs. In April he would be thirty-eight, with no prospects at all.

As if to signal his complete failure came the news that the one real-estate deal with which he had been satisfied — the trade of Hard-scrabble for the St. Louis house — had been a bad one. The former owner of the house could not pay the $1500 mortgage when it fell due, and Grant was having to sue. It might take years before he could clear the property or, if necessary, recover Hardscrabble.[34]

Slowly he came to the inevitable decision. He must go back to his father and make a second "last appeal" for help.

After a quick trip to Covington, he hunted up his antislavery friend Editor Fishback, and asked him to hire or buy one of Julia's women servants, since he couldn't take her North.

Surprised, Fishback asked, "So you're going North?"

"Yes, I can't make a success of it here and I'm going to Galena. My father has offered me a place in the leather business with my brothers, and I have accepted."[35]

Since he could not transfer the slave to a friend who would treat her well, or possibly set her free, Grant turned all of Julia's slaves back to Colonel Dent and, loading his family on a steamer, went up the river for a new start in life — but a return to the hated avocation of his father.

Up the river the echoes of his own voice, twenty years ago, came back to him above the splashing of the paddle wheels in the Mississippi:

"Father, this tanning is not the kind of work I like. I'll work at it though, if you wish me, until I am one and twenty; but you may depend upon it, I'll never work a day at it after that."

CHAPTER TWENTY-ONE

"The Awful Leap"

AFTER Ulysses' farming and real estate experiments failed to be self-supporting, he came to me at this place for advice and assistance. I referred him to Simpson, my next oldest son, who had charge of my Galena business, and who was staying with me at that time on account of poor health. Simpson sent him to the Galena store to stay until something better should turn up in his favor, and told him he would allow him a salary of eight hundred dollars per annum." [1]

Jesse remembered it so when, sitting in his home at Covington in after years, he was asked to explain the arrangement that had been made with Ulysses in 1860.

Ulysses' memory of the agreement varied in some respects. He said that while it sent him to Galena as "nominally only a clerk supporting myself and family on a stipulated salary, in reality my position was different." His father, who was sixty-six at the time, had concluded "to give up all connection with the business himself, and to establish his three sons in it." But Simpson, "who had really built up the business was sinking with consumption and it was not thought best to make any change while he was in this condition." [2]

Ulysses had come off better than he had feared. He was not being sent to the stinking tanyards. No tanning was done at Galena, and the worst that could happen would be the handling of green hides as they were brought in from the farms preparatory to shipment down to the tanneries in Ohio. The Galena store dealt in finished leather and hardware, retail and wholesale, and Ulysses with his quartermaster training was expected to keep the accounts and make the collections.

The Captain's son, Freddy, grew up believing that Grandfather Grant "who wasn't very liberal" had concluded that this was a good time to arrange for the eventual distribution of his property. Ulysses "and his two brothers should manage the tanneries and stores, each to be paid $600 a year for his services and place the profits of the business in a trust fund for their three sisters," and, "when the accumulated profits amounted to the value of the tanneries and store, the brothers were to have the physical property and the sisters the income from the money in trust." [3]

Jesse's nephew-in-law, W. T. Burke, who was in the Galena store, recalled later that although he, Simpson, Orvil and Ulysses were each guaranteed only $600 a year, "we were all working for a common fund, and we had what we needed." None of them, he said "were . . . really upon salaries, in the ordinary sense, at all." Captain Grant was being welcomed on even terms. "There was no bossing by Simpson or Orvil . . . no looking down on Ulysses as a failure. We all looked up to him as an older man and a soldier. He knew much more than we in matters of the world, and we recognized it." [4]

Whatever the precise details might be, the agreement was made on the sad assumption that Simpson might not have long to live, and that in the event he and his old father should both be taken off, Orvil was too young to be entrusted with the entire management.

The people of Galena were sorry about Simpson's bad health. They had liked him ever since he had started paying visits to his father's partner, Collins, at the age of fifteen. "He was a pleasant sort," they said and much admired for the way, as a grown man, he had conducted the store. Many of them disliked Orvil, one of them calling him "an uninhibited sharper, and rather arrogant and conceited as well." [5]

The firm of J. R. Grant was one of the most active in Galena, and its location, 145 Main Street, was in what many citizens regarded as the best business building in town, the Milwaukee Block; but an addition to its clerks was of no special moment in the life of a city of 14,000 people — especially when that newcomer arrived dressed like one of the hundreds of farmers who streamed into the city from the fields of northwestern Illinois, southwestern Wisconsin and northeastern Iowa.

From the steamboat as it edged in among other craft to the wharf Ulysses' family, seeing Galena for the first time, beheld a city strangely like a Mississippi Delta town set in an Alpine crevasse:

The little city . . . has a curious Swiss look [one traveler wrote]. The river cuts it in twain, and the narrow and crowded main street threads the valley, while on the north [west] side a bluff rises like a roof for two hundred feet. Upon the summit, and in terraces along the side, perch most of the residences. One ascends to them by wooden steps, leaving the top of the tallest spire far below.[6]

Most of the thirty-five hundred houses which rose shelf by shelf were of frame or brick, but enough mansions reared high pillars to make steamboat pilots think of Vicksburg and Natchez. As one of Ulysses' friends remembered it, the Captain was carrying some chairs as he led his family down the gangplank. Their home was near the summit of West, or, as it was sometimes called, Cemetery Hill, a small two-story brick house at 121 High Street, with the graveyard stretching away to the rear — headstones close to the back door. So little note was taken of the family's arrival that the townsfolk in later years could not recall whether Ulysses had rented the house himself or whether he took it over from Simpson. Some Galenians remembered that it had been rented from a man named Robinson for one hundred dollars a year and that Simpson lived with Ulysses and Julia when not in Covington. Orvil and his wife had a home of their own.[7]

From the front windows Ulysses could see the town below, the steamers in the river, the mansions on the opposite and lower bank, and hills rolling away across farmlands to the east and south. How long he expected to enjoy this view was never clear. The neighbors, noting how little was his interest in meeting them or in making inquiries about the life of the city, concluded that "the Grants were temporarily sojourning in Galena, and were looking forward to better days."[8]

John M. Shaw, whose law office was opposite the Grant store, saw that there was little curiosity in town about Ulysses, despite the fact that "it was generally understood . . . [he] had been a regular army officer, who had become somewhat broken down in health and reduced in fortune; and his misfortunes were quite commonly attributed in some degree to supposed habits of dissipation, to which the temptations of army life had subjected him, and which he had resigned to escape."[9]

Galenians, when asked in later years to describe Ulysses at the time of his arrival, had trouble in remembering anything beyond the fact that he had seemed depressed, perhaps haggard, and dressed poorly in an old slouch hat and faded blue overcoat. One man thought he recalled hearing the Captain say that he intended to make the army coat last ten years, which would have meant 1864. Augustus L. Chetlain, a brisk, long-nosed wholesale grocer and son of French Huguenot immigrants, saw Grant, "a night or two after his arrival in Galena," come quietly into a tavern where the lawyers of the city liked to loaf and where, this chilly evening, they were sitting in a tight circle around the stove. Grant stood outside the group listening as they discussed an important law case. Eventually tiring of the topic, one of them noticed the newcomer and asked, condescendingly:

"Stranger here?"

"Yes."

"Traveled far?"

"Far enough."

Waxing humorous, the lawyer went on, "Looks as though you might have traveled through hell."

"I have."

"Well, how did you find things down there?"

"Oh, much the same as in Galena — lawyers nearest the fire." [10]

L. M. Lebron, whose jewelry shop was across Main Street from the Grant store, had a son who stood inside the front window at a later date and told how the Captain had melted into Galena's crowd in 1860:

> If he was to walk up, right now, with these Saturday shoppers, you'd never see him. I'd have to point him out to you. That's the kind of a fellow he was.[11]

With no army friend to talk to, no horses to ride or drive, the Captain led a subdued life, keeping by day to the back of the deep storeroom bent over his ledger, and to his home by night. Conscious of his own failures amid all the hustle, bustle and prosperity of younger men on the streets, he found comfort in Julia and in children — his own and those of other people. Through the windows of his cottage passers-by saw him reading and smoking his pipe, or in the cool of the evening sitting in his yard with his children playing around and over him "by the hour," neither they nor he speaking a word. Each time he climbed the long wooden steps coming home from the store he knew that the baby, three-year-old Jesse, would be waiting at the door with a set challenge:

"Mister, do you want to fight?"

And he would always reply, "I'm a man of peace, but I'll not be hectored by a person of your size." And then they would wrestle until the father would fall in defeated exhaustion upon the sofa, leaving the infant to caper around the room exulting at another conquest over the "best battler in the world." When Buck, discovering — probably from his uncles — that his father had been made a captain for leading a charge at Mexico City, asked "Wasn't that courageous?" Grant replied that a lot of other soldiers had volunteered to go with him and explained that courage was the commonest thing you could find in men.[12]

A head carpenter of the town, John Corson Smith, saw Grant whittle sloops from shingles for town boys when flood waters came up into Main Street and crouch there as wrapt in enjoyment as any of the youngsters, as he rigged the boats with paper sails. The neighbor children on Cemetery Hill thought the Captain kindly and his wife "loveable," — much less strict than their own mothers. Mrs. Grant let them rampage in and out of the house with Freddy, Buck, Nellie and little Jesse, demanding cookies. At times she read children's stories to the whole pack, and they noted that she read a great many paper-backed romantic novels to herself. Some of them, observing that her husband often read to her, thought her eyes were weak.[13]

Freddy was chagrined that his mother should always dress him better than the neighbors' boys. When they went barefoot, he had to wear shoes and stockings; where their uniform was a hickory shirt and a one-suspendered pair of pants, he had to appear in a waist that buttoned, shamefully, to his trousers. Freddy understood that the money for this finery, and for such other conveniences as Maggie Cavanaugh, the hired girl, came in part from Grandfather Dent, who sent Julia sums now and then — once as much as one hundred dollars.[14]

Living in Galena was not cheap, since the style set by the mines and the steamboats still ruled. However, Ulysses' father declared that eight hundred dollars a year would have been ample if the Captain had not insisted upon immediately paying up old debts in St. Louis, personal loans, back rent, and various small grocery bills. By the time this was done Ulysses had received an additional seven hundred from the firm. Jesse was, however, satisfied with Ulysses' progress in the business; at least he was boasting, a few years later, that the Captain had taken "right hold of the business with his accustomed industry and was a very good salesman . . . but he never would take any pains to extend his acquaintance in Galena." [15]

John E. Smith, a Swiss immigrant who between hours at his jewelry shop dropped in to talk Republicanism to Simpson and Orvil, did not agree with Jesse. He said:

> Grant was a very poor businessman, and never liked to wait on customers. If a customer called in the absence of the clerks, he would tell him to wait a few minutes till one of the clerks returned, and if he couldn't wait, [Grant] would go behind the counter, very reluctantly, and drag down whatever was wanted; but hardly ever knew the price of it, and, in nine cases out of ten, he charged either too much or too little. [16]

Ulysses found the business, if not his ideal, promising him a good income for the future. The Grants shared the common optimism of Galena's merchants. Even if the price of lead continued to decline as it had since 1856, and even if the railroads made Chicago, at the other edge of Illinois, a greater wholesale center, Galena would still prosper. It might not be the metropolis of the upper Mississippi Valley as it had been in 1840, having remained wedded to the river traffic when it could have hitched its wagon to the rising star of the railroads, but to Jesse Grant it would still remain the trading center for at least a half dozen neighboring counties in Illinois, Wisconsin and Iowa, where the farm population was increasing so rapidly. Farmers would always need leather. Dubuque, twelve miles away as the crow flew, had become a lively center on the railroad, while Galena was only a stop on a branch line, but Galena still had forty wholesale houses. Few Galenians saw any threat in the way other towns were starting factories. Like citizens of many Mississippi River cities below St. Louis, Galena felt that the destiny of the railroads was to feed steamboats.

Simpson, whom Ulysses had pronounced as honorable a man as ever did business, had built up a large list of loyal customers across a wide expanse of the Northwest. From merchants in towns and at crossroads he bought green hides and, in return, sold Grant tannery leather which they resold to harness makers, cobblers and farmers who repaired their own shoes. Also, as a jobber, he sold them harness, trace chains, bridle bits, whips, saddles, stirrups, awls, show pegs, axes, wedges, saws, augers and a wide variety of articles classed as hardware. Now that Simpson was no longer able to travel the territory, Ulysses was expected to step into his shoes as soon as the details had become familiar.

Of these cities which Ulysses had seen, only San Francisco had held a stranger mixture of humanity. Here were Southern lawyers, Yankee merchants, steamboat gamblers at the bar of the four-story, two-hundred-room DeSoto Hotel which was the pride of the Northwest. Wives of wealthy commission men ate Creole cooking in the hotel dining room and stole chastely curious glances at famous steamboat pilots who called for the Negro waiters to bring more imported French wine.

Cornish and Welsh miners drank ale beside Irish deck hands who drank whiskey in some fifty lighthouses, as saloons were called. The blackened faces of Swiss, Scandinavians, Germans and New York Staters who burned charcoal for the lead smelters, peered over their wives' shoulders at Parisian gowns in shop windows.

Ulysses shrank from these crowds, and, moreover, found refuge in the shadows from the political talk which raged in the front part of the store, where Orvil and his violent Republican friends sat around the stove riddling the Democrats, the Secessionists and the Slavocrats. It was almost as bad as St. Louis for a man who craved peace, composure, reason and mathematical logic.

A group of Galena Republicans, including the merchants C. R. Perkins and L. S. Felt, and the lawyer-politicians R. H. McClellan and Elihu B. Washburne, were at the stove one day when, as so often happened in discussions, up popped the Mexican War, that so-called mother of the present chaos over slavery and state rights.

"By the way," said Felt, "there's a man we can leave it to," and he jerked a thumb at Ulysses in the rear.

"Who's he?" asked Washburne who, as Congressman from the

District for the past seven years, had been much of the time in Washington.

"Captain Grant," said Felt. "He was all through the Mexican War."

Called up, Ulysses listened to the question, answered "briefly and modestly," as Perkins said, then returned to his books.

But his personality was so repressed that Washburne, notoriously avid to line up new voters, promptly forgot that such a man existed. Perkins did not wonder at this too much, since "very few of our people knew the Captain personally or even by sight." [17] John Shaw, even though a next-door neighbor to the store, did not become ac- quainted with Ulysses in a whole year. Shaw saw that his intimate friend, the lawyer John A. Rawlins, was one of the first to break through Ulysses' shell of reticence — but Rawlins "had a knack of knowing everybody." Rawlins did whatever legal business the Grant firm required, but he had a more romantic reason for talking with Ulysses. Across recent years Rawlins had been hearing about the member of the Grant family who had been an officer in the Mexican War, and Rawlins had been excited about that conflict ever since he as a farm boy near town had been refused permission to enlist. He had been "almost crazy" as the Illinois volunteers had marched off to fight the "greasers" and had, as he said, grown up with "a great idea of a Mexican war soldier, the extent of our heroes being private soldiers of that war." [18]

Rawlins was a born enthusiast and, in addition, probably the best trial attorney in town, as well as a successful politician, known in the region as "the Jo Daviess County coal boy."

Artfully Rawlins drew Ulysses into conversation on the "beauty and resources" of Mexico. While Ulysses sat on the counter discours- ing, Rawlins listened, his eyes, black as night, glowing in his sallow face. Rawlins's eyes were what people always remembered. Shaw said, "When they looked at you, [they] looked through you." Look- ing into Grant's face, Rawlins was attracted, although, like Hillyer, he could not at first tell why. Eventually he concluded that it was "the marks of power . . . under his simplicity." But Rawlins, at twenty-nine years of age, felt some profound reserve in the thirty- eight-year-old Captain and could see no signs that Grant had "any special liking" for him. [19]

Where Grant was composed, Rawlins was ardent, emotional, aggressive. Where Grant was silently, doggedly trying to master his appetite for liquor, Rawlins was openly, almost fanatically, denouncing the Demon Rum. Rawlins had never been cursed with the habit, most Galenians believing that he had never touched it in his life, yet, as he admitted to the most intimate of confidants, "the blighting shadow of intemperance" hung over his pathway like a pall "all his life" and that wherever he went or wherever he was, he feared "to ask himself the question, 'Am I to die a drunkard?' " [20]

The trouble was his father. Everybody knew that James D. Rawlins was an improvident farmer who had never made money nor ever would. Everybody knew he would rather go hunting and roaming the woods than till his acres or stick to his secondary business, burning charcoal for the lead smelters. He loved his bottle as he did his gun, but few people thought him a sodden drunkard. At least the old man, in 1860, possessed such rugged health that he was apparently heading for a ripe old age unless a bee tree fell on him. Ignorant of books, he was wonderful company for children who liked to hear about red-eyed bears coming out of hibernation in the spring.

Some people, studying John, the son, suspected he unconsciously blamed liquor for what laziness had done to the father. There was no doubt that poverty had been a blighting shadow on the son. The father had never got down to hard work after he, a Scotch-Irish youth of twenty-six, had arrived from Kentucky in 1827, to claim 320 acres of woodland near Galena. He had gone off the next year to Missouri to marry Lovisa J. Collier, had installed her on the farm in October 1828, and promptly begun producing babies at a rate which numbered them at six in ten years, then two more — one in 1844 and one in 1846: — seven sons and one daughter.

Their second son, John Aaron, had been fifteen in 1846, old enough with his energy and ambition to take over the management of the farm. Marshaling those of his brothers who were big enough, he led them in a new attack upon the fields and the forest. He drew especially close to his mother, a puritanical Methodist, and began to dream of a career as a preacher. When, at eighteen, he saw his father set off merrily for the California gold fields, he was firmly installed as the man of the house, and there was no appreciable change when the father returned with no dust but some entertaining tales of adventure.

John A. had snatched what schooling he could in brief terms and had read books by torchlight at the charcoal pits in the woods. At twenty-one he had been ready to start preparing for the ministry and had attended for one term the Rock River Seminary at nearby Mount Morris.

With no money to carry him further — and too proud to borrow — he had been driving a load of charcoal to Galena one hot afternoon in September 1853, when his oxen had stalled on a steep hill and he had slept that night beside his load. Next morning he had barely got his team going when they stalled on another hill. Always decisive, he had promptly sold the oxen, the wagon, the charcoal at a nearby railroad construction camp for $250, and instead of walking home, had plunged straight on into town to ask a prominent lawyer, Isaac P. Stevens, to let him study in his office.

The pulpit abandoned, he had embraced the law so fiercely that by October 1854 he had passed the bar, become Stevens's partner, and was established in a surging career, with an amazingly eloquent command of profanity — probably the legacy of the stubborn oxen — on his rough, loud tongue. The next year, on Stevens's retirement, he had taken over the firm's large practice although he was too poor a collector of bills to grow wealthy.

In 1857, he had been elected City Attorney and became a fiery orator on political and patriotic occasions. His law partner in 1860 was David Sheean, newly elected City Attorney, one of the most brilliant attorneys of the region, and as cool as Rawlins was hot. Both were Democrats, but it was Rawlins who preached the nation-saving gospel of Stephen A. Douglas, and who was, as Grant first met him, running for Presidential Elector on the Democratic ticket.

Another fear was beginning to haunt Rawlins in 1860. His young wife, who had been Emily Smith of Goshen, New York, was showing signs of consumption and, since the birth of their third child in April, was failing rapidly. His family on the farm could help with the other children, aged four and two, but the vision of his youngsters, motherless, was before him as he spoke to crowds on the grievous state of the Union.[21]

Politically, Grant had more in common with Rawlins than with

Orvil, or with three Republicans whom he came to know, County Treasurer John E. Smith, Chetlain, and Circuit Court Clerk William Reuben Rowley. Two men who became friendly with Grant, his father's former partner, Collins, and M. J. Johnson, a Kentucky-born lawyer, were Democrats considerably more sympathetic than Rawlins with "Southern Rights." Chetlain regarded Grant as a "Free-Soil Democrat" and Rawlins said later, "We counted on him as a Douglas Democrat," which in the terminology of the time was the same thing. Chetlain understood that Grant's disappointment over Buchanan's weak Administration had turned him toward the dynamic Douglas.[22]

Under Buchanan, the Democratic party had split along the Mason and Dixon Line, the Northern wing supporting Senator Stephen A. Douglas's popular sovereignty, the right of the people in a territory to prohibit or admit slavery by their votes at the polls, while a powerful faction of the Southern wing, called "Ultras," insisted that, as a partisan but shrewd Republican put it, a "territorial legislature might protect slavery, but could not prohibit it; and that even the Congress of the United States could only intervene on the side of bondage, and never on the side of freedom." In other words, Congress must protect any citizen, Northern or Southern, in taking into a territory his property, even if it be a slave.[23]

When representative Southern men, meeting in ostensibly nonpolitical convention at Vicksburg, in 1859, voted 40 to 19 for the revival of the long-outlawed slave trade with Africa, the sectional split in the party widened, and when the Democratic national convention met at Charleston in April 1860, so many Southerners bolted, rather than nominate Douglas, that the assemblage adjourned to meet again in June at Baltimore.

"In less than twelve months we shall be in a war," said the Georgia conservative Democrat leader, Alexander H. Stephens, "and that the bloodiest in history." [24]

In May some quavering old Whigs and Know-Nothings convened hopelessly, murmured vaguely about compromise, took the name Constitutional Union Party and nominated sixty-three-year-old John Bell of Tennessee for President. That same month the rampaging Republicans met at Chicago, chose Abraham Lincoln as their nominee and adopted a platform which branded as "revoluntionary and heretical" the extreme Southern view that the Constitution carried slavery into the territories and boldly declared that "the normal condition of all the territory of the United States is that of freedom." On June 18, the regular Democrats reconvened, naming Douglas to run on a platform that clung to his popular sovereignty principles.

Ten days later the Southerners, who had bolted the regular convention, held one of their own, named John C. Breckinridge of Kentucky their candidate and drew up a platform that called for the full program of the Ultras.

As between Douglas and Lincoln, Grant was a Douglas man; at least years later he said, "My pledges would have compelled me to vote for him." As between Breckinridge and Lincoln, "I wanted . . . to see Mr. Lincoln elected." But he could vote for none of the candidates since he had not lived in Illinois long enough to qualify. Among the Republicans of Galena, it was said in later years that as the campaign progressed Grant's sympathies tended toward Republicanism, and that he told some of them after hearing Douglas speak in Iowa, "He is a very able, at least a very smart man, but I can't say I like his ideas. If I had the legal right to vote I should be more undecided than ever." His listeners imagined that he resented some "demagoguery" in Douglas, and Rowley, striking while he thought the iron was hot, began trying to persuade Grant that he was rightfully a legal voter. Rowley argued that Grant's preliminary visit to Galena in October 1859 had established his residence rather than his arrival in May 1860. According to the story, Orvil had broken in on Rowley's argument to say:

"Now you had better let Ulysses alone. If he were to vote he wouldn't vote our ticket."

"I don't know about that," Grant said. "I don't quite like the position of either party," and went on to say that the only time he had voted had been against a candidate, Frémont. "I thought it would be a misfortune for the country if he should be elected. Otherwise I have never meddled with politics." [25]

His years in the Army, where officers as a class distrusted politicians, were influencing him now. "He was not an arguer on politics," said Rawlins, who was himself scarcely off the stump during the campaign. But there came a time when Rawlins in excitement attempted to break through the Captain's shell and drag him into the Douglas ranks.

The excitement came on the evening of August 1, when, as Rawlins described it, "John E. Smith, a soldier of the Mexican war, burst upon the town with a magnificent display of Wide-Awakes, whom he had drilled secretly."

A blast of brass music and thunder of drums brought Galena running to the DeSoto House. Drawn up in military formation, up and down the street, were 242 Republican men wearing soldier caps, oilcloth capes and shouldering thin fence rails from which swung coaloil lanterns. Above their ranks swayed signs and transparencies celebrating their Presidential candidate, "Old Abe the Rail Splitter," "All Wide Awakes for Lincoln," "Old Abe the Giant Killer," and their candidates for Governor and Congress, Richard Yates and Elihu B. Washburne. A huge American flag, marked "Presented by the Republican Ladies of Galena," stood beside Gus Chetlain, chairman of the company. An orator presented to him a chair "made of rails split by Old Abe in days of yore."

Ulysses saw in the ranks his brother Orvil, his cousin Burke, and most of the Republicans who gathered so often in the front of the store. Some of the wild young spirits from the levee were in uniform, but businessmen dominated. The banker brothers, John and N. H. Corwith, were in the column as, at the end of the ceremonies, it paraded the town.[26]

It was Galena's first view of the Wide Awakes, who the newspapers said were spreading so rapidly across the North that they would soon number 400,000.

"This mortified our side a good deal," said Rawlins, "and we resolved to get up a similar organization." To help him came Jasper A. Maltby, who had been a soldier in the Mexican War, and was now proprietor of the town's leading "Sporting Establishment" at 184 Main Street, which advertised "shot guns, rifles, Colt's pistols, Bowie knives, shot pouches, etc. Guns made or imported to order."

"The Douglas Guards" was the name of the Democratic marching club and, said Rawlins, "We thought we would elect Captain Grant the marshal of it. . . . I was one of the committee to call on Grant. He said that he was beginning business, and should have to decline entering into politics. We therefore, chose Maltby."

John C. Smith, who was gravitating toward the Republicans, understood that Grant's answer to the committee, after thanking them for the honor, was "Having held a commission as Captain in the Army of the United States, I do not think it becoming for me now to serve a citizen body, though semi-military, as its Orderly Sergeant." [27]

In the days that followed, Ulysses buried his head in the ledgers by day and clung to his home by night, but he couldn't shut out the sound of marching feet. Through the front door of the store every so often would come the tramp, tramp, tramp of shoes crashing in unison, and if he stepped out of his house in the evening to stand at the edge of the cemetery for a moment under the stars, there would come up from the streets below the blare of the band and the rhythm of the drums. Bonfires down there would be throwing a faint glow on the wan old headstones as he turned to re-enter the house.

Before long, Grant was casually dropping into the Wide Awakes' warehouse-clubroom to help them with their drilling, although he declared in later years that this had been only occasional and that he had never paraded with either party." [28]

As the campaign swept toward its climax, hope for Douglas died. Pennsylvania and Indiana, holding their state elections in early October, forecast a Republican sweep in the North. Douglas told his private secretary, "Mr. Lincoln is the next President. We must try to save the Union," and struck off to stump the South, pleading with the Ultras not to secede, and warning them that the next President would stamp out secession as resolutely as Jackson had squelched nullification thirty years before. But the threats of secession grew louder as election day arrived, with Lincoln's election assured.

Two serious men, Grant and Rawlins, stood on the streets of Galena on the night of November 8 watching the Republican celebration rise higher and higher as returns came in — Lincoln had carried eighteen states and was the next President. Douglas had carried but two, Bell three, Breckinridge eleven.

In and out of the DeSoto bar and the forty lighthouses men rushed, slapping backs, crying that the South's bluff had been called. Torches blazed along the levee in one continuous row. Every house seemed to have a lamp and a little flag in the front window. Boys and men strung lanterns covered with colored paper in the trees. Behind two brass bands the Wide Awakes marched up the hill, drawing a cannon after them, stringing their column along Prospect Avenue. At the summit they began their prolonged ecstasy.

The night was inky black, and to the crowds looking up from Main Street, the celebration on the hill seemed to be hanging in the heavens. The houses and the trees had vanished in the dark and the little squares of lamp-lit yellow and the balls of red and blue were scattered stars. The cannon blasts were lightning and thunder. The hoarse cheers of the Wide Awakes and the shrill cries of innumerable small boys came floating down through the dark to remind exulting Republicans of avenging archangels and militant cherubim.

At times, red fire rose, and all along the brow of the hill were seen a row of uniformed men holding aloft Roman candles, aiming their shots at the sky. As the fireworks died, brass trumpets began "The Star Spangled Banner" in the dark, and the whole town sang. Then the cannon boomed and the cheering throngs danced in the streets below.

It was a night of endless rejoicing. A special "jollification" raged in the Grant store, with Orvil spreading raw oysters and liquor before the faithful who swarmed in. Ulysses helped his brother serve, but without elation.[29]

All around him tipsy voices were declaring that the "Chivs" (short for "the Chivalry") would never fight. The North had spoken! The North had the power now. All those states that had gone either for Lincoln or for Douglas had voted against the extension of slavery. And even the three that had gone for Bell — Virginia, Kentucky and Tennessee — had spoken against secession. More important than that, the Ultras had carried only the Deep South. Douglas had won Missouri. The big border states had refused to join the other eleven slave states in voting for the Ultras. Look at the popular vote! Lincoln was going to come out with around 40 per cent, Douglas 30, Bell 12. A lot of them would be against "coercing" any state to remain in the Union, but surely the Ultras would not continue their threats in the face of so overwhelming a verdict!

The general viewpoint in Galena solaced Rawlins in his sorrow over the defeat of Douglas. He spoke of his new hopes to Grant. Ulysses answered grimly:

"The South will fight."

"I could not bring my mind to contemplate this," said Rawlins, remembering the scene in later years, "but . . . from that day, [Grant] began to speak oftener of his military education, his debt therefor to his country, and talk with me upon the capacities of the North to raise troops." [30]

The news from the South in the first weeks after the election was dismaying to Northerners like Rawlins. Down there, the Ultras were encouraged, not discouraged, by the very size of the North's verdict against them. It only proved how impossible it would ever be for the Deep South to get justice! More than ever, now, secession — a separate nation — was their only hope.

The universal talk of war — would it come? — would it be averted? — brought Grant out of the shadows. Men who had never noticed him before came up to get the opinion of a veteran and an Army man on the situation. He was understood to be a "moderate Republican" now that Douglas was down and the issue drawn between Lincoln and the Ultras. He expected President Buchanan to do nothing to curb secession, and seemed to have but one hope — the bulk of the Southern states might "think well before they took the awful leap which they had so vehemently threatened." [31]

Wherever Grant went across Illinois, Wisconsin and Iowa, people came to him on steamers, in taverns and stores, asking questions, listening to him late into the night. To optimists who declared that the Chivs were merely gasconading now as they had in the past, Grant replied, "There *is* a good deal of bluster; that's the result of their education; but if they once get at it they'll make a strong fight. You're a good deal like them in one respect — each side underestimates the other and over-estimates itself." [32]

He wrote a friend in St. Louis:

It is hard to realize that a State or States should commit so suicidal an act as to secede from the Union, though from all the reports, I have no doubt that at least five of them will do it. And then, with the present granny of an executive, some foolish policy will doubtless be pursued which will give the seceding States the support and sympathy of the Southern States that don't go out. [33]

From his father came letters attacking secession, and from Julia's father letters applauding it.

In Grant's mind were developing the theories which he would later write out in detail:

Secession was wrong on two counts. First, whatever rights the original states might have had to leave the Union had been forfeited when, after forming the Constitution, they had added new states and adopted amendments to the Constitution. And there certainly remained no shadow of legal justification for any of those new states to withdraw since they "were purchased by the treasury of the entire nation." Texas had been annexed, it was true, but had "been permitted to retain as state property all the public lands within its borders" and "it would have been ingratitude and injustice of the most flagrant sort for this State to withdraw from the Union after all that had been spent and done to introduce her." To him "Secession was illogical as well as impracticable; it was revolution."

On the second count, secession was wrong because it was too late, in 1860, for political revolution — another and greater revolution had been won, the industrial revolution, which justified the present expanse and form of the Union. It was, in all logic, idle for the South to be insisting that under the Constitution no one had the right to prevent secession.

To Grant it did not matter that the Constitution was silent on the question. The Founding Fathers, in 1787, had "never dreamed of such a contingency occurring." They had lived in a different world, one where "the only physical forces that had been subdued and made to serve man and do his labor, were the currents in the streams and in the air we breathe." In 1787, "rude machinery, propelled by water power, had been invented; sails to propel ships upon the waters had been set to catch the passing breeze." Since then the steam engine had come "to propel vessels against both wind and current," to lace the lands with railroads and to drive machinery which completely changed man's work — and life. Since then, too, the telegraph had arrived to begin stitching together the far-flung reaches of the nation.

But if it were true, as Southerners said, that the Founding Fathers would have sanctioned secession, in 1787, rather than see brother fight brother, the real question was, "Would they do so if they were here today?" And Grant was sure they would not. They would, he claimed, "have been the first to declare that their prerogatives were not irrevocable. . . . We . . . ought not to be rigidly bound," said

Grant, "by the rules laid down under circumstances so different for emergencies so utterly unanticipated." [34]

Grant's dissatisfied years in the hide-bound Army had shaped his mind to distrust the dead hand of the Past, and to look realistically upon the Present. Uneducated in the classics, fond only of mathematics as a study, because he could master it by what he regarded as "intuition," he had grown up with the native Westerner's trust in his ability to improvise. Forms and precedents must always give way to common sense and adaptability.

Grant's new confidence in himself was rising rapidly as 1861 began. "In my new employment I have become pretty conversant," he wrote a friend in St. Louis, "and am much pleased with it. I hope to be a partner soon, and am sanguine that a competency at least can be made out of the business." The talk of secession had paralyzed many businesses, but not his. "With us the only difference experienced as yet is the difficulty of obtaining Southern exchange." And Galenians later said it was he who took steps to better the firm's position in the matter. Since exchange ran as high as 10 per cent, he shipped dressed pork to Cincinnati, loading the white carcasses on steamers himself. [35]

In the light of Simpson's steady decline, Jesse Grant took double pleasure in Ulysses' attitude toward the work. Now that occupation was constant, security more certain with each day, and his family at hand, Ulysses found no need for liquor. Rawlins, who made it his business to know about such matters, endorsed the statement that while Grant smoked a clay pipe to excess, "he was temperate in every thing else, for he had totally abstained from drink for several years," and had not touched a drop even while passing drinks around the store the night of the great Republican "jollification." And the lawyer, Shaw, declared in after years that he had not heard it hinted, while Grant lived in Galena, that "there was the slightest lapse from perfect sobriety."

A bartender of the town always remembered that, when Eastern salesmen "treated" Captain Grant, he took a cigar, not a drink. A tavern keeper in Wisconsin insisted that whenever Grant stopped with him, he usually took one drink after the evening meal, but none at other times. The son of Lebron, the jeweler, summed it up in later days:

Oh, you know lots of men that, after supper, will come downtown, sit around some store front and visit awhile. Maybe before going home they'll take a drink, maybe not. That's all Grant's drinking ever amounted to, and anyone who knew him in Galena will tell you the same thing. I never saw him drunk nor anyone else with whom I've talked. His circle of friends here was not large at the time and we are all in agreement on that matter.[36]

Whispers that Grant had been seen staggering tipsily up the long steps to his home could never be traced to an eyewitness.

Ulysses' fondness for card games had been limited at first to evenings at Burke's home, where a boarder, O. B. Upson, a watchmaker of the town, was a regular player. Upson was much impressed by a joke Grant made about being the only person in the city who ever played "old sledge" with a man who subsequently became a President of the United States — General Franklin Pierce, in Mexico City.[37] But as more people came to know the veteran of the Mexican War, in the winter of 1860–1861, Ulysses played cards with friends in an unused room above the store. Julia's social life, which had begun by exchanging dinners with the wives of Burke and Orvil, enlarged as she found friends of her Southern friends. Her son Fred, who would grow up remembering with optimism the family's social life in Galena, said in later years, "We had dinner parties, and my parents, in turn, were guests of the principal families." [38]

The citizens of Prairie du Chien, a town on the Mississippi, knew Grant as a decisive man as well as an adviser on prospective wars. They saw him arrive one day to collect payment for a stock of goods which one of the firm's customers had fraudulently transferred to a third party. Discovering that the merchandise was locked in a large stone building, Grant hired a lawyer, O. B. Thomas, secured a writ of replevin from the local court and summoned the sheriff. That official being absent, his deputy, a burly and reputedly bold fellow known as Boss Brunson, accompanied them to the building where, behind a barred door, sat the pretended owner who, having heard that one of the Grants was in town, was waiting inside with a loaded shotgun. On being told not to force the door on pain of being killed, Grant and Thomas urged the deputy to break it down. Boss quailed, whereupon Grant said, "If you're afraid to go in the building yourself, why don't you deputize someone to go in for you?"

"Very well," blustered the fellow, "I'll deputize you."

Grant stepped back ten or twelve feet, then came with a rush, smashing his heel strategically near the lock, and, as the door flew open, pounced on the defender, wrested the gun away, ordered him to box the goods, and within a short time had his property on the steamboat, Galena bound.[39]

One cold morning in Dubuque, Grant was standing at the stove in the hotel lobby when he noticed standing next him the new pastor of Galena's Methodist Church, the Reverend John H. Vincent. Grant had heard him preach a few times but had never met him. He introduced himself. Vincent asked if he were the son of Jesse Grant of Covington. Vincent knew Jesse and had corresponded with him, some time before, concerning a pastorate in Kentucky. The two men talked. Vincent said that he had come across the river last night in a skiff through floating ice and wanted to get word back to his worrying wife that he was safe. Grant said that he was returning today and would tell her.

They talked about the secession crisis and soon the preacher, as he later described the scene, found himself the listener while the leather salesman, "standing by the fire in his old blue army overcoat, his hands clasped behind him," spoke with an "intelligence . . . a knowledge of men and measures, a discrimination, animation and earnestness that both surprised and interested me. . . . After that morning I often watched, during the public services in my church at Galena, the calm, firm face of my interesting hearer."

Cultivating Grant, the pastor saw that it was no use to urge him to become a church member. "His religious life was the inner life," Vincent perceived. "He naturally disliked the over-emphasis of ceremony, and excessive religious volubility. He once said 'I often pray to God in the night silently.'" Vincent concluded, "There was much of the Quaker in Grant."[40]

While Grant traveled the Northwest the war drew nearer. The newspapers told how President Buchanan was treating with South Carolina on the subject of two Federal forts in Charleston Harbor. South Carolina wanted assurance that he would not reinforce Forts Sumter and Moultrie, when it seceded as it was sure to do when the state convention met. Northern Republicans and Democrats, who held to the old faith of the supremacy of the Federal Government, sighed, "Oh, for one hour of Andy Jackson." John A. McClernand, horse-faced, aggressive Congressman from the Springfield, Illinois district, was declaring "God's grace could scarcely save Buchanan from endless and infinite damnation."

Douglas was declaring that the Northwest would never consent to have its trade route to the Gulf of Mexico cut off by secession guns along the bluffs of the Mississippi. Horace Greeley, who had for years baited the slaveholders without mercy, was turning soft and urging that the South be allowed to depart in peace. Others among the Republicans were willing to abandon the Chicago platform and restore the Missouri Compromise. Still others cried that any such retreat would be a shameful surrender to treason.

Congress set up committees to search for a peaceful compromise, but all broke down before the demand from President-Elect Lincoln that his incoming party must "hold firm as a chain of steel against propositions for compromise of any sort of slavery extension." To him it was clear that the instant there was any weakening, the Southern Ultras would "have us under again. . . . The tug has to come, and better now than later."

On December 20, South Carolina made "the awful leap" and on January 9, Mississippi plunged after it, followed by Florida on the tenth, Alabama on the eleventh, Georgia on the nineteenth, Louisiana on the twenty-sixth, and Texas on February 1.

Everywhere, men were crying war and peace, peace and war, but Grant was still certain that it would be war and that the fighting would be over in ninety days. His mathematician's brain could see no more than a three months' stand by the secessionists against the overpowering weight of materials which the businessman's North could throw against them.[41]

Grant was standing on a counter in the store sometime during the second week in February, stowing away goods on the top shelf, when his friend M. J. Johnson burst in with the news hot off the telegraph — delegates from the seceding states, meeting at Montgomery, Alabama, had set up The Confederate States of America, and had chosen Jefferson Davis President!

"What's that you say?" asked Grant, over his shoulder.

Johnson said it again, probably with exultation, since his sympathy with the secessionist was keen.

Grant turned around, looked down, and grimly sliced out the words:

"Davis and the whole gang of them ought to be hung!" [42]

CHAPTER TWENTY-TWO

Washburne and War

WHEN men came rushing from the telegraph office on April 15, 1861, crying that Fort Sumter had fallen, Galena was stunned. For weeks people had argued that South Carolina would not start the shooting, or that South Carolina would start shooting, but now that the thing had been done, realization came slowly.

All the reasons for the shocking turn of events were not clear, but one fact struck home — the Rebels had fired on the nation's flag. They had bombarded the Federal troops in the fort until the Stars and Stripes had come fluttering down in surrender. No lives had been lost — but the flag had been insulted!

The flag was down? Then, up with the flag!

Galena rushed indoors, dragged out flags and waved them, hung them, nailed them to posts, to fences, to steamboat railings. Storekeepers and lawyers, closing their offices for the day, saw to it that flags were hanging over the front door before they turned the key and were caught up in the milling, shouting crowds along Main Street. The men who came from printing offices to tack up notices calling for a mass meeting in the Court House the next evening, stuck little flags alongside the placards.

Galena, Illinois, was answering Charleston, South Carolina — flag for flag.

And the great banner of the Wide Awakes was cheered wildly as, with two brass bands, it went through the streets at sundown, heading for the Court House.

The cheers were coming from the Republicans and some of the Democrats — cheers for war, for vengeance. President Lincoln was calling for 75,000 militiamen to volunteer for ninety days.

The people must crush this rebellion. The Regular Army could not do it, having only some 16,000 men and 1100 officers scattered widely across the country.

Some Democrats like Postmaster Bushrod B. Howard, who only last autumn had worked for Breckenridge and the Southern Ultra ticket, were now asking for a whack at the traitors; others like Collins, Jesse Grant's former partner, were arguing quietly for delay, for sober thought, for peace — their party should keep aloof from this blood lust of the abolitionists, work for compromise. The President's call was unconstitutional! Congress alone could declare war, and Congress was not in session! The Federal Government had no legal right to coerce a sovereign state!

Most Democrats stood perplexed and stricken, torn this way and that, waiting for word from their idol, Steve Douglas in Washington. The telegraph declared that Douglas had pronounced for the Union and the flag, but his followers wanted fuller assurance. With so many wild rumors flying, they needed to hear from him direct.

In the meantime where was Rawlins? Which way would he go? His law partner, David Sheean, was against war — that much was known.

Congressman Washburne and his friends, Chetlain, Rowley, Felt, John E. Smith, watched these silent, undecided Democrats narrowly. What these Democrats decided to do tonight was undoubtedly what the Democrats of the entire North would be deciding — and upon this decision hung the fate of the Union. Most of the Northern Democrats were Douglasites, and relatively few had voted for Breckenridge, but grouped together they represented about 40 per cent of the Free-State voters — and here in the Central States 45 per cent.

In the upper Mississippi Valley the tug would come, for if Ohio, Indiana, Illinois and Iowa did not leap promptly to support Lincoln, the bordering slave states of Missouri and Kentucky would be almost certain to secede. Tennessee, Arkansas and North Carolina were preparing to join the seven cotton states of the Confederacy. Virginia's western counties, bordering on Ohio, were leaning toward the Union, differing from the pro-Confederate eastern counties, yet they might be swept into secession, too, unless Ohio called overwhelmingly now for war.

Ulysses S. Grant came to the Court House that evening certain that logic would win — the North would stand firm, the nearby border states would not secede and the war would end in three months' time. As Galenians remembered it later, he had said on Monday, when the stunning news arrived:

> I thought I had done with soldiering. I never expected to be in military life again. But I was educated by the Government; and if my knowledge and experience can be of any service, I think I ought to offer them.[1]

The courtroom on the second floor filled and buzzed as town notables arrived, Postmaster Howard breathing fire, Mayor Robert Brand breathing peace. Congressman Washburne and his law partner, Charles S. Hempstead, were said to be behind the posting of the call for this meeting.

This was to be the first time Grant had seen Washburne in action. "A broad-shouldered, good-bellied, large, and yet a thin man," a newspaper writer described the politician whose influence in the state had suddenly swelled since the Republican victory in November. Long service in the House of Representatives at Washington had brought him important committee posts, now that the Democrats were down. President Lincoln was seeing to it that he had liberal patronage. Smooth-shaven, plainly dressed, he had, as an observer wrote, "a very impulsive manner, accompanied with a look almost of fanaticism out of large lightish-gray eyes . . . his face in repose is rendered almost untranslatable by his intense industry, which, being of a nervous sort, keeps him screwed up to a headlong gait all the while." [2]

Notoriously impatient in normal times when forced to listen to voices other than his own, even those of his two brothers, Israel, who had been a Representative from Maine since 1851, and Cadwallader, a Representative from Wisconsin since 1855, he could be expected to erupt all over the courtroom if any speeches ran counter to his views. All three brothers had been antislavery Whigs until joining the new Republican party. For the coming session, Elihu would be alone, since Israel was moving into the Governorship of Maine, and "Cad" had retired to handle his rich law practice, banking business and lands around Mineral Point and LaCrosse, Wisconsin.

The three headstrong, aggressive brothers had sprung from poverty in Maine, and Elihu, starting as a printer's devil, had wrested a law degree from Harvard and come west in 1840, settling in Galena on the recommendation of Cad, who was already making money in nearby Wisconsin. The town, was, as Elihu wrote home upon arrival, "a horrid rough place," offensive to a Yankee Puritan like himself who had vowed never to drink, smoke, play cards or attend the "devilish" theater. But lawyer's fees were high in Galena and the people, he saw, were "a litigious set." [3] Within a month he had been sending money home to the family in Maine, and within five months he was assistant to the busiest attorney of the region, Hempstead, living in his employer's home. A little later he was a partner, and married to Hempstead's niece, a brunette belle related to the famous Chouteaus of St. Louis. Since her family spoke French, Washburne had mastered that language, too.

At forty-five years of age, he was now throwing all his driving energy to promoting the war which he believed was righteously unavoidable, and into the political party which he believed to be the child of destiny. His own political future, like that of the Administration, was hanging in the balance tonight.

A hint of how the evening might go came as two of the staunchest pro-war Republicans, Rowley and John C. Smith, arrived outside the Court House, practically arm-in-arm with the two leaders of the recent "Douglas Guards — Maltby and Rawlins."

As Rawlins started into the building, a hand caught his sleeve: "John, you don't want to go up there and talk to that crowd; it's a God-damned Black Republican meeting!"

John C. Smith saw Rawlins turn and with "face aglow with the intense fire of patriotism" answer:

"I'm going up to the courtroom and I intend to make a speech. We're going to have a great war, and in time of war there are no Democrats or Republicans. There can be but two parties now, one of patriots and one of traitors!"

He strode up the stairs with that final epithet searing the air behind him.

Lawyer Hempstead, calling the meeting to order, suggested that Mayor Brand preside. The Mayor spoke for peace:

"I am in favor of any honorable compromise that will again unite the country. I am in favor of sustaining the President so long as his efforts are for the peace and harmony of our whole country. I am in favor of a convention of the people that an adjustment might be made, sustaining alike the honor, interest and safety of both sections of our country. I am in favor of sustaining our flag, our constitution and our laws, right or wrong. Yet I am opposed to warring on any portion of our beloved country, if a compromise can be effected."

As he spoke, a murmur began in the crowd ranging from "Pay no attention to him; he's a Southerner anyway" to "He's talking treason." [4]

The murmur turned to shouts and the stamping of hobnailed boots. The Republicans were taking charge. Silent, wondering, puzzled, the bulk of the Democrats sat and listened.

Brand pleaded to be heard and when quiet was restored explained that he had come thinking that the situation was to be discussed. He had expected to have all viewpoints rationally considered. He had given his opinions. These were apparently not the views of the majority, so he would vacate the chair. He sat down, leaving the impression that all this was typical of the way Republicans everywhere in the North were stampeding the nation into war.

Chetlain, who was a henchman of Washburne, said later that "after some discussion, it was agreed that he [Brand] continue to preside." Other Galenians recalled, in after times, that tactful persons had placated the meeting and arranged for the Mayor to resume the chair. But the commonest legend in town, later on, was that Washburne had leaped to his feet as Brand's opening speech ended, and denounced him as either a "traitor" or at least so far out of step with the patriotic feeling of the assemblage that he be ousted. Washburne nominated a new chairman. Brand "courteously" put it to a vote, and Washburne lost amid a bedlam of voices. [5]

Brand agreed to remain the chairman and Washburne then offered resolutions — "that we will support the Government . . . maintain the integrity of the American flag . . . recommend the immediate formation of two military companies in this city . . . and having lived under the Stars and Stripes by the blessing of God, we propose to die under them!"

Chetlain remembered years later that the resolutions had been carried "unanimously." One of Rawlins's close friends understood that the bulk of the Democrats were still in "hesitation and doubt." [6]

Certain it was that soon thereafter calls came for Rawlins to speak. Applause from both Republicans and Democrats accompanied "The Jo Daviess County Coal Boy" as his black head was seen moving to the platform. He turned on the audience eyes which, in his white face, were as black and hot as the charcoal pits on the long nights of his boyhood. The fires were being fed now by patriotism and also, in all probability, by the subconscious memory of the days when he had been "crazy" to get into the Mexican War.

He was facing a new jury tonight — his fellow Democrats who up to last November had always ruled Galena's politics and who had lost that election by a mere fifty-seven votes. [7]

Rawlins spoke, and his deep, rich voice "would have filled a hall ten times as large." For forty-five minutes it was the one sound that was heard. He told what the slaveholders believed about the wrongs that the North had done them. He spoke of how often the Free-Soil people had gone down to defeat in the disputes over slavery and how they had, as a minority, submitted when they lost on the Missouri Compromise, the Mexican War, the Compromise of 1850. The will of the majority was the law of the land. Americans had always trusted to the ballot since the signing of the Constitution. He was addressing men who had known him as a boy, known him all his life, known what he stood for, what he believed. He had no secrets from them.

Then he brought the crowd to the climax and the edge of their chairs:

"I have been a Democrat all my life; but this is no longer a question of politics. It is simply country or no country. I have favored every honorable compromise; but the day for compromise is passed. Only one course is left for us."

Grant with all the rest bent forward as Rawlins tossed his black hair and gathered all eyes into his own as he cried:

"We will stand by the flag of our country, and appeal to the God of battles!" [8]

The crowd rose as his sentence neared its end, and as that final "battles!" cracked, a tremendous cry picked it up and carried it on, out through the open windows, over the heads of the throng outside, up the hill and beyond. For a long time the courtroom was bedlam. Cheers followed cheers for President Lincoln, for the Union, for the flag!

Rawlins's Democrats were with him now, cheering like the rest, saying that they would be there when, as was announced, another meeting to accept volunteers would be held on the night of the eighteenth.

Other orators spoke briefly and were half heard, and in time, came adjournment. Along the sidewalks and dirt streets in the dark, up the long steps to the hill, across the bridge to the east side, back into steamer cabins along the levee, out from town in buggies jogging toward farm homes, men went that night talking of Rawlins's speech.

Ulysses and Orvil walked away together. Behind Ulysses' grave face his blood was pounding. No need for Rawlins ever to think again that Grant had "no special liking for him." Ulysses was thinking that Rawlins had said just what he would have liked to say. All his life he would remember how Rawlins had said it. Ulysses had never heard a speech like this one.

But all that he said to Orvil was, "I think I ought to go into the service."

In the darkness Orvil answered, "I think so, too. I'll stay home and attend to the store." [9]

Across the next two days every word that came in over the telegraph, every newspaper that came in from Chicago, Springfield, Quincy, St. Louis whipped excitement higher. There was no doubt now that those first reports of Steve Douglas's support of Lincoln were correct. Douglas expected his friends to join in defending the Union to the last. Rumor had it Lincoln was going to make him a Brigadier General. Except for southern counties in Illinois and Indiana, where secession sympathy was strong, the Northwest was rising as one man. Governor Yates was announcing that Illinois's quota of the nation's militia force would be 4458 men and 225 officers, 6 regiments. Except for a few companies in the large cities such as Chicago, the regular militia was as good as defunct — "the cornstalk militia" it had been called for years. And the small companies in the cities were independent organizations, made up of young men who met for amusement and acrobatic rather than military drill. [10]

The six regiments would be almost wholly new, with officers to be elected. Here were political jobs to be filled, as well as a nation to be saved. In the minds of Republican leaders like Washburne, patronage and patriotism blended. It had been the Republicans who had borne the heat and burden of the long fight against the Fire-Eaters, but Northern Democrats who were rising above party must be given important posts. Washburne corresponded rapidly and often with Governor Yates.

On the afternoon of Thursday, April 18, Washburne suggested to Chetlain that Captain Grant be made chairman of the meeting at which recruits were to be raised that night. Chetlain agreed. Grant had been a professional soldier — and a Democrat — just the man to give the call a nonpartisan color.[11] Washburne's men were in charge as the courtroom filled to overflowing. John E. Smith was in the chair. He would not be able to volunteer since he, as an aide on the staff of Governor Yates, must leave soon for the state capital. Chetlain was near the speaker's platform, primed to start the ball rolling when the volunteering began. First to his feet, he would put himself in line for captaincy of the company.

Smith rapped for order. A voice called, "I nominate for chairman, Captain Ulysses S. Grant." Chetlain said afterward that the voice had been Washburne's.[12] Rawlins later approved the statement that it had been Smith's.[13]

Grant was so overcome with bashfulness that he could not tell who had made the motion. All he heard was a chorus of "Ayes," then found himself on the platform. "With much embarrassment and some prompting," he later recalled, "I made out to announce the object of the meeting." So confused was he that he later believed and repeated, as a comic illustration of his own lack of prominence, the legend that Washburne had come into the back of the hall, after the meeting was on, had stared at him on the rostrum, "and expressed a little surprise that Galena could not furnish a presiding officer for such an occasion without taking a stranger." Innocent of politics, Grant would always believe that "the sole reason" for his selection that night had been the knowledge that he had once served in the Army.[14] He did remember out of his dazed bashfulness that Washburne had been among others who came up during the meeting to make patriotic speeches.

Rawlins, sitting in the audience, asked to be excused this time and when admirers tried to drag him up, he explained that he could not volunteer; his wife was dying of consumption and he couldn't leave her. He said that if things were otherwise, "I wouldn't say, 'Go, boys!; I'd say, 'Come boys!' " [15]

Grant was, himself, not ready to enlist. He must first make arrangements with his father, who would have enough trouble as it was, what with the paralysis of business. Also it would be his duty as a trained officer to serve in a higher rank than company commander — a colonelcy or a post on some central staff where organizational experience was needed. The governors of states would need expert help to suddenly convert their amateur militia system into a professional war machine. Grant had never asked for promotion in the Army and could not start now pulling wires for a colonelcy. Army men had always jeered at the militia system of electing officers. Such posts were for huckstering politicians, not West Point graduates. If advancement came it should be by the way of a call from above, not below. [16]

The Southerners were awarding increased rank to officers who gave up United States Army commissions and joined the Confederacy. Beauregard, for example, had been only a Captain when he resigned as Superintendent at West Point on February 20, but was now a Brigadier General of the forces which had captured Fort Sumter.

But Ulysses, as he heard the call for volunteers on April 18, was certain that it would be only a matter of time before he was in uniform too.

Chetlain was the first to respond. Twenty others followed — enough to show that within a few days one hundred men could be enrolled. A telegram was sent to Yates offering the company. Washburne, Chetlain, Grant, Rawlins, Rowley and others agreed to split up in twos and threes tomorrow and scour the surrounding country. Washburne walked home with Grant after the meeting. He heard the Captain say, "I am going into this thing. . . . I'm acquainted with the Governor of Ohio, and I'm going to write to him to-night and ask him to give me a commission."

Washburne asked why he didn't apply to Governor Yates. Grant answered that he didn't know Yates and did know William Dennison, the Governor of Ohio. Dennison had been the hotel manager's son with whom he had become friendly in days when he, a small boy, had waited in the lobby of Cincinnati's Dennison House for passengers to be hauled back to Georgetown. Washburne urged Grant to serve Illinois and said that he would urge Governor Yates to commission him.[17]

Next day, April 19, Ulysses wrote his father-in-law a letter revealing how willing he was to try to correct the old gentleman's "Rebel" views — a letter which also revealed how strongly Rawlins's oratory was, for the moment, influencing Grant's expressions:

> The times are indeed startling; but now is the time, particularly in the border slave states for men to prove their love of country. I know it is hard for men to apparently work with the Republican party but now all party distinctions should be lost sight of, and every true patriot be for maintaining the integrity of the glorious old Stars and Stripes, the Constitution and the Union.
>
> The North is responding to the President's call in such a manner that the Confederates may truly quake. I tell you there is no mistaking the feelings of the people. The Government can call into the field 75,000 troops, and ten or twenty times 75,000 if it should be necessary.

Knowing that the old aristocrat was hearing, if not indeed repeating, the current secession jeer that the money-grubbing civilization of the North would never endorse actual warfare, Ulysses warned him:

> It is all a mistake about the Northern pocket being so sensitive. In times like the present no people are more ready to give their own time or of their abundant means. No impartial man can conceal from himself the fact that in all these troubles the Southerners have been the aggressors, — and the administration has stood . . . more on the defensive than she would dare to have done, but for her consciousness of strength and the certainty of right prevailing in the end.
>
> The news to-day is that Virginia has gone out of the Union. But for the influence she will have on the other border states, this is not much to be regretted. Her position, or rather that of Eastern Virginia, has been more reprehensible from the beginning than that of South Carolina. She should be made to bear a heavy portion of the burden of the war for her guilt.

In all this I cannot but see the doom of slavery. The Northerners do not want, nor will they want, to interfere with the institution. . . . They will refuse for all time to give it protection
unless the Southerners shall return soon to their allegiance; and
then, too, this disturbance will give such an impetus to the
production of their staple — cotton — in other parts of the
world that they can never recover the control of the market
again for that commodity. This will reduce the value of the
negroes so much that they will never be worth fighting over
again.

I have just received a letter from Fred [Dent]. He breathes
forth the most patriotic sentiments. He is for the old flag as
long as there is a union of two States fighting under its banner,
and when they dissolve he will go it alone.

This is not his exact language, but it is his idea not so well expressed as he expresses it.

Julia and the children are all well and join me in love to you
all. I forgot to mention that Fred has another heir, with some
novel name that I have forgotten. Yours truly,

U. S. GRANT [18]

That night he, Rawlins and Rowley raised a dozen or so recruits
at Hanover, fourteen miles south of Galena and next day,[19] when
eighty-odd assembled in town, it was time to elect officers. Rawlins,
Rowley [20] and Chetlain all urged Grant to accept command. He was
the first choice of the Volunteers.

Grant said to Chetlain, "I don't know as I ought to take that
company; I've been captain in the regular army, and I don't know
as I ought to take a captaincy of Volunteers." [21] He suggested that
Chetlain take it.[22] Jesse Grant always believed his son had done this
because Chetlain had "frankly confessed" to him his ambition to
secure the post "as a stepping-stone to a higher military position." [23]
Ulysses said, "I declined the captaincy before the balloting, but
announced that I would aid the company in every way I could
and would be found in the service in some position."

It might have been before the election on Saturday, which went
to Chetlain, that Washburne told Grant, "The Legislature meets
next Tuesday [April 23]; several of us are going to Springfield;
come along — you'll surely be wanted." [24] As word arrived from
Yates accepting the company, Washburne and his friends increased

their pressure to place Grant in the state's new war machine. Both Washburne and McClellan gave him letters to be presented to the Governor.[25] And John E. Smith, departing from Springfield, carried with him Grant's promise to help organize the new regiments at the capital if the Governor should send for him.

The recruiting work brought Grant another friendship, that of Dr. Edward Kittoe, whose large practice in the region made him effective when he came up in horse and buggy calling the young men out. Kittoe said he himself was going soon, in spite of the need for him to stay, and in spite of the fact that he was forty-seven and must leave a wife and six children. He said he owed it to the land of his adoption. Born in England, the scion of a long line of naval officers, he had come to America at sixteen, graduated from Jefferson Medical College at Philadelphia in 1841, won honors in his profession, yet had migrated in 1851 to the new Eldorado, Galena, in far-off Illinois. He had quickly become a personality in the region, since he was a physician, surgeon, and upon occasion a dentist, a lay reader in the Episcopal Church and "somewhat given to eccentricity." [26]

The telegram from Governor Yates accepting Galena's company had contained a specification which sent the City Fathers to Grant with such demands that he found it impossible to give any attention whatever to the store. Yates had specified that the company must be uniformed at home. The state had no uniforms on hand and worse than that, only 600 decrepit muskets and rifles and 297 horse pistols. The militia companies which Yates was sending on Sunday, April 21, from Chicago to occupy Cairo, at the southern tip of the state, were amateurishly armed — four old cannon, no shell, no canister, merely some lead slugs which blacksmiths had sliced, and shotguns and sporting rifles hastily commandeered in hardware stores.[27]

L. S. Felt, the rich dry-goods merchant, supplying the cloth for Galena's uniforms, had Grant select the material. The Corwith Brothers, who owned a tailorshop as well as a bank, supplied the money for the uniforms and the tailors to fashion them in styles and sizes prescribed by Captain Grant — blue frock coats for the privates, dark-gray pantaloons with blue cords. Chetlain, following Grant's directions, drilled the men with laths in lieu of muskets.

Postmaster Howard advised with Grant on the organization of a second company, "The Anti-Beauregard Guards." "Handsome Ben" Campbell, wholesale grocery and steamship packet-line magnate, had Grant draw up for his daughter Annie the dimensions for a flag which she and other patriotic ladies were making for Chetlain's men.[28] Campbell's partner and brother-in-law, the politically powerful J. Russell Jones, began to find in Grant qualities not previously noted. Jones had recently resigned the office of State Representative to which he had been elected in November, and had as Washburne's henchman accepted the political plum of United States Marshal of the Northern District of Illinois, with offices in Chicago. Jones had known Lincoln on visits to Springfield during the late months of 1860, but it was apparent that the President had appointed him to please Washburne.

It was the grinding of Washburne's political machine that had brought Jones back to Galena now, for on the day that Grant started the recruits drilling with laths, the Republicans were deciding that the Illinois Central Railroad's local lawyer, Robert H. McClellan, should run for Jones's vacated seat in the Legislature at a coming special election.

Of all the new Washburne men whom Grant was meeting, Russ Jones attracted him most, for Jones had two qualities of especial appeal, a genius for business success and for saying witty things. Small, sandy-haired, merry Jones was in personality far different from Washburne, yet his rise in Galena had been strangely like his sponsor's. With only one dollar in his pocket, Jones had arrived in Galena in 1838, a seventeen-year-old dry-goods clerk from Ohio. He knew not one soul in town and yet within six months was clerking in the city's foremost wholesale dry-goods establishment, that of Ben Campbell. A little later he had married the boss's sister and became not only a partner in the store, but manager of Campbell's Galena and Minnesota Packet Company with lucrative contracts for steaming the United States mail between Galena, Dubuque and St. Paul.

Jones told Grant that he was going to Springfield and would use his influence with the Governor to have the Captain given a suitable position.

In Springfield John E. Smith, sporting now the title of Colonel and toiling in the Adjutant General's office close to the Governor's, was keeping his word with Grant. The chance came when Yates, never an even-tempered man, burst in with angry denunciations of the chaos that was on the capital. Through the city, companies were marching to Camp Yates on the outskirts — companies without organization, without discipline and with insubordination rampant. As a patriot and as Governor of President Lincoln's home state, Yates wanted desperately to lead in the crusade. Since his boyhood in Kentucky he had hated slavery and the slave barons and had carried this zeal through his career in Springfield as a lawyer, State Legislator, Congressman and now Governor. The trouble, Dick Yates growled to Smith, was that nobody knew how to organize a regiment. "Do you?"

"No, I never saw a full regiment in my life," replied John E.

"Do you know anyone else?"

"Yes — Captain Grant, who was a Regular in the Mexican War and wants to come."

Yates said to have Grant come right away, then turned back to face the mass of paper on his desk and the hordes of politicians who rivaled each other in demands that their particular home-town companies be accepted.[29]

By Sunday, April 21, Ulysses knew his program, and between conferences with the tailors, he snatched time to write his father: "We are now in the midst of trying times when every one must be for or against his country, and show his colors too, by his every act." Since there were more than enough to fill the first call, he had not yet enlisted, but he had promised the members of the Galena company and Mr. Washburne "to go with them to the State capital" and if he could aid "the Governor in organizing his state troops to do so. What I ask now is your approval of the course I am taking, or advice in the matter." [30]

He could do no less. "Having been educated for such an emergency, at the expense of the Government, I feel that it has upon me superior claims, such claims as no ordinary motives of self-interest can surmount." [31]

He feared that his absence from the store would put his father "in an awkward position, and a dangerous one pecuniarily, but costs cannot now be counted."

Ulysses worried about his father's safety. The sharp-tongued old man of sixty-seven would be no one to take back talk from the sprigs of Kentucky Chivalry — not if in his increasing deafness he heard it. The bulk of Kentucky's people were opposing secession but her Governor had refused to furnish troops "for the wicked purpose of subduing her sister Southern States."

"My advice would be to leave where you are," wrote Ulysses, "if you are not safe with the views you entertain. I would never stultify my opinion for the sake of a little security." [32]

On the Monday morning that started his letter to Covington, the company had filled and the tailors were saying their uniforms would be ready Wednesday noon.[33] Belated recruits looked for other companies. Rawlins, hoping that his domestic situation would permit, talked of joining with John E. Smith to raise a regiment. John C. Smith was arranging to enlist in a matter of weeks and his employer, Ely S. Parker, the chief civil engineer of the new Federal buildings at Dubuque, was saying that he would switch from the Treasury Department to the War Department as soon as he could.

Acquaintance between the thirty-three-year-old Parker and Grant turned into friendship as they found a common interest in horses and silence. Also Parker was the one man in Galena who had had an engineering education comparable to Grant's.

As a full-blooded Seneca Indian, born on the reservation in Genesee County, New York, and named "The Wolf," he had as a boy refused to remain there and inherit the position due him as the son of a Seneca chieftain father, an Iroquois mother, herself the daughter of an Iroquois chief, and a grandson, by clan descent, not blood, of the celebrated Red Jacket, headman of the Six Nations, in which the Senecas and Iroquois were members. Pushing his way through the Baptist Missionary school, and two neighboring private academies, he had studied law, and when New York State refused him a license because he was not a citizen of the United States, had turned to civil engineering, studying at Rensselaer Polytechnic Institute. In this profession he had worked for the Government for many years and had been stationed in Galena since 1857, superintending Federal constructions in that city and Dubuque. Honored by his tribe in 1852 with an election to the post of Sachem, he was proud of his new name, "Do-ne-ho-geh-weh," which in English meant "Keeper of the Western Door of the Long House of the Iroquois." Fond of ceremonials, he had risen to the highest chairs in the Galena chapter of Masonry, where he worked with Rawlins, Rowley and the two Smiths. The 200-pound, flat-faced, swarthy Parker was a figure of picturesque dignity in Galena, and sometimes during long hours over the billiard table — his favorite game — he would reveal bits of information about his past — information that showed his great self-confidence. As a young man he had spent some time in Washington, urging his people's rights on Senators Webster, Clay and Calhoun and occasionally upon the Great White Father himself, President Polk. His own experience with Southerners had not prepared him to believe their current boasts as published in the newspapers that each of them could whip five Northerners. One time while employed at Fortress Monroe, Virginia, he and a friend had been denied admission to a ball at Norfolk. Perhaps he had been mistaken for a Negro. The Wolf hadn't inquired, he had merely taken the chairman of the floor managers by the collar and the seat of the pants and dropped him over a banister to the floor below.[34]

Grant's new associations and prominence did not affect his modesty and when the city and surrounding country turned out on Thursday, April 25, to give the Jo Daviess Guards a great send-off, he was not in the parade but in his home on Cemetery Hill, packing a carpetbag and telling his family farewell. It was not a dramatic farewell. He didn't expect to be gone long, three months at the most, a few days at the least. It all depended on what the Governor might want.

He came down the long stairs as the parade — soldiers, fire engines, civic bodies, lodges, brass bands — wound through the streets. Mayor Brand, atoning for his pacific words of a week ago, presented the company color bearer with a pistol. So huge was the throng that the Reverend Vincent had to mount a boxcar for his farewell address and prayer. The ladies presented the flag. Captain Chetlain accepted it, and as he finished, the procession started for the passenger cars. Chetlain looked back at his marching men. They were keeping step badly to the crashing of the cymbals, and were grinning and waving at familiar faces in the walls of humanity on either side. Could he ever turn them into soldiers?

Then as the last file passed Greene Street, Chetlain saw a small man in an old slouch hat and overcoat of fading blue quietly step out of the crowd, carpetbag in hand, and fall in — "left and rear of the company!"

CHAPTER TWENTY-THREE

"Men, Go to Your Quarters!"

IT WAS RAINING on Friday, April 26, as Grant and Chetlain herded the Jo Daviess Guards off the train at Springfield and out through the city to Camp Yates in the suburbs. Earlier in the day Grant had drilled the men for an hour during a wait for a change of cars at Decatur, Illinois, and he was anxious to give them more practice now, but the meadows around the capital were ankle-deep in mud.

At the camp the mustering officer turned out to be Captain John Pope, on leave from Army Departmental Headquarters at St. Louis. Not without reason was Pope hoping to be made brigadier general of the Illinois militia as soon as a brigade was formed. The son of one of the state's most famous pioneers and himself "elegant in deportment, [and] charming in manners" he was regarded by many influential politicians as the "favorite son of Illinois, destined for a grand career." [1]

Pope was the first of his old Army acquaintances Grant had seen since the fall of Sumter. They had scant words, as yet, on their friends. George B. McClellan had dropped his railroad superintendency to become Major General of Ohio's militia and Volunteers. Captain Nathaniel Lyon was commanding a handful of Regulars inside the Arsenal in St. Louis, where fighting might break out any moment. Over him was Brigadier General Harney, whom Frank Blair and the violent pro-Union citizens suspected of softness towards the "Rebels." Blair had raised five regiments of loyal Guards. Dan Frost, commanding the anti-Lincoln militia of the state, was assembling his men on the outskirts of St. Louis.

The worst news to West Pointers of Grant's and Pope's vintage was the resignation of Joseph E. Johnston, Quartermaster General, whom they regarded as the ablest man in the service. He had handed in his commission as brigadier general and joined the Virginia state forces. Of the other brigadier generals, Twiggs had been dishonorably dismissed for surrendering his troops and stores to Texas secessionists. Wool and Totten, while loyal, were respectively seventy-seven and seventy-three. Colonel Samuel Cooper, although Northern born, was Southern wed and had resigned as adjutant general in March to accept the same post with the Confederates.

Of the Army's seven departments only one, that of the Corps of Engineers where Totten held on stoutly, was not immediately due for a new chief. Age, sickness, incapacity were sweeping out heads of the Departments of Subsistence, Medicine, Pay, Ordnance and Topographical Engineers. General Scott, weighed down with obesity, crippled joints and seventy-five years, must soon be replaced. He had persuaded President Lincoln to offer the post to Robert E. Lee, who had, since Mexico, been the favorite of Old Fuss and Feathers. Although Lee had accepted promotion to a colonelcy on March 16, he had not only refused a high command but had resigned on April 20, when Virginia seceded. He was said to be accepting charge of Virginia's Volunteers. No one had yet heard from Scott's other favorite, Albert Sidney Johnston, who had re-entered the Army in 1849, and was now in command of the Second Cavalry on the Pacific Coast. Would he remain loyal, join the Confederacy, or merely resign again as he had twice before?

Replacements in the staff and field would be coming fast from the War Department. Grant's old Fourth Regiment must have a real colonel now, since Whistler, at eighty-one, could no longer hold the post in his armchair as he had during the Mexican War. It was, however, in the temporary volunteer militia that Grant hoped for a place. He would not, however, enter into the political scramble, and when Pope offered to use his influence among the chief politicians of Illinois, Grant shrank away. "I declined," he afterward said, "to receive endorsement for permission to fight for my country."

The political shambles at Springfield offended him. Most companies had arrived with from ten to sixty members above the prescribed limit and these Volunteers, refusing to go home, were weeping, cursing and beseeching their representatives and governor for permission to stay. Other companies over the state were boiling with anger at being told not to entrain for the capital.

Under this pressure, the Legislature was authorizing ten additional regiments of thirty-day men on the expectation that President Lincoln would soon call out more Volunteers. There were ten colonelcies to be filled. Ulysses wrote his father that he was "perfectly sickened at the political wire-pulling for all these commissions, and would not engage in it." [2]

With the spring rains keeping the troops in their tents, Grant took a room in a private residence downtown and invited Chetlain to stay with him. During the day he met by chance the great Stephen A. Douglas, who had come to town the day before to address the Legislature, and who had remained over for a day to whip up pro-war enthusiasm among his Democratic followers.[3]

Half a century later Douglas's descendants would be declaring in fantastic fashion that, according to the legend in the family, Douglas had found Grant "about . . . to accept a Confederate commission" and had "dissuaded" him from the step.[4]

To Grant's intimates it was apparent that while Grant might have become depressed as early as his first day in Springfield over his chances of securing a proper place immediately in the Union forces, neither his loyalty to the cause nor his belief in the quick suppression of the "rebellion" were in question.

His feeling against secessionists in the border states was mounting, although he was amused at hearing from Covington that his Aunt Rachel Tomkins in Virginia was carrying on a spirited dispute, by mail, with his sister Clara. Aunt Rachel, who had several sons and slaves endangered by the approaching war, had ended the correspondence with, "If you are with the accursed Lincolnites, the ties of consanguinity shall be forever severed." [5] Ulysses wrote Mary to get him a copy of that final letter — it fitted into his opinion of Virginia secessionists. Bad as South Carolina's course had been, he told Mary that more allowances should be made for its people than for the Virginians. The South Carolinians "for the last generation have been educated, from their infancy, to look upon their [national] Government as oppressive and tyrannical and only to be endured till such time as they might have sufficient strength to strike it down. Virginia, and other border states, have no such excuse and are therefore traitors at heart as well as in act." The news from Kentucky and Missouri was disturbing and he renewed his pleas that the family quit Covington and come north "until the present excitement subsides." If his father were younger and Simpson stronger he would advise them to stay in Kentucky, since it was necessary, just now, for "every Union man in the border slave states to remain firm at his post. Every such man is equal to an armed volunteer at this time in defence of his country." [6]

The news was worse from Missouri, where a clash between Grant's friends Lyon and Frost drew nearer, day by day. On Friday the latest word had come by the special train on which muskets had arrived in Springfield from Lyon's stores in the St. Louis Arsenal. Springfield was resounding with praise for the cleverness with which Illinois had thus been armed.

The story had begun when Yates, on the heels of Sumter's fall, had sent a militia captain, James H. Stokes of Chicago, to Washington to ask for guns. Stokes, returning with an order on the St. Louis Arsenal, had been hurried to that city and arriving Wednesday, April 24, had found the Arsenal besieged by a secession mob clamoring to get guns for Dan Frost's militia which were soon to come to town. By pretending to be a secessionist, Stokes had worked his way through the crowd and presented his requisition to Lyon. The little red-haired Lyon to whom the smashing of Fire-Eaters was a holy cause, approved the order, but saw no way to get the guns out through the mob. However, he would try. On Thursday, April 25, one of Lyon's spies wormed his way in to say that Governor Jackson had decided to storm the Arsenal. Stokes telegraphed friends at Alton, Illinois, a few miles up the river, to have a steamer drop down to the Arsenal at midnight. Then he and Lyon, as if in a great rush to get their guns to safety, sent out soldiers, in full view of the mob, to load 500 deficient old flintlocks on the boat in the river. Fooled completely, the secession mob swarmed over the boat and carried the precious guns through the streets amid triumphant cheers.

By that time Lyon and Stokes were having the soldiers pile the useable munitions in boxes at Arsenal windows so that when the Alton steamer glided up at 11 P.M. the real prizes were quickly slid on planks to the deck. When 10,000 muskets had been counted off, Stokes urged Lyon to let him take 10,000 more, so the Rebels would never have them, should they overpower the Arsenal. Lyon agreed, retaining only 7000 for himself and the loyal militia which he proposed to arm for the decisive fight that was to come.

Out on the black river at 2 A.M., Stokes told the ship's captain to head for Alton and to sink the craft if enemies overtook them. But the loading and departure had been unobserved and at five o'clock in the morning the steamer wharfed safe and sound. Stokes was taking no chance, however, and raced through the town bringing men, women and children from their beds to rush the munitions from the deck to a railroad train that was waiting. By that night, the rifles and cartridges were in Springfield and the secessionists of St. Louis, having discovered the ruse, were in utter consternation.[7]

Excitement over this event was agitating Governor Yates when Washburne brought Grant into the executive offices to apply for a state position. Yates also had on his mind another particular matter. He had ordered the militia companies which he had sent to Cairo to seize the steamboats suspected of spiriting munitions south. They had confiscated two boats and trouble might ensue, for the War Department in Washington had not yet sanctioned any such step against private parties.

Yates was not in his office when Washburne and Grant appeared. His volunteer assistant, Gustave Koerner, received the callers in an anteroom. A German lawyer who had come to Belleville, Illinois, in 1835, Koerner had served in the State Legislature, in Congress and as Lieutenant Governor of the State. Shrewd, energetic and well educated, Koerner was not impressed by the man whom Washburne introduced as a former army quartermaster who should now be useful in those departments of the state militia organization. "Hardly of medium height, broad-shouldered and rather short necked," said Koerner in later years, "his features did not indicate any very high grade of intellectuality. He was very indifferently dressed, and did not at all look like a military man."

As they talked, Koerner heard Yates come into his office and quickly managed to bring the two callers to him. The door shut. After a time they emerged, Washburne looking rather dissatisfied and saying that the Governor had told him there was no place for Grant "as there were now sufficient assistants in the military offices, but he would consider the matter and let him know the result."

Washburne attributed the trouble to an ancient brush he had had with Yates when they had served together in Congress. Koerner said that he would "talk plainly to Yates" and did so, securing an appointment for Grant for the next day.[8]

Chetlain, back in the rooming house, had been worried because Grant had gone to make the call so "plainly if not poorly clad in citizen's clothes," and understood when Grant returned that the Governor had "looked at him critically, and with apparent indifference said that he didn't know of anything he could give him then, but that the Adjutant General (Colonel Mather) might have some employment for him in his office, and that he might call again." [9]

Jesse Grant understood at the time that "Mr. Yates did not appear to take much notice" of Ulysses when introduced by Washburne, but that the Governer had sent for him a day or two later.[10]

Chetlain stated that when Grant called on the Governor next day, he was introduced to Mather, "who after some conversation said he knew of no employment he could give him unless it was some clerical work in his office, such as arranging and copying orders, ruling blanks for reports, etc." Grant had replied that since "for the present he was willing to make himself useful in any way, he would begin at once." [11]

On Monday, April 29, Ulysses, writing his sister Mary, indicated that his interview with Yates had taken place on Sunday, April 28. "It was my intention to have returned to Galena last evening," he said, "but the Governor detained me, and I presume will want me to remain with him until all the troops are called into service, or those to be so called, are fully mustered in and completely organized." [12]

Years later when he had quarreled with Washburne, Grant gave an account of his meeting with the Governor which eliminated his Congressman entirely and made Koerner wonder how Grant could have fallen into other errors of time and place. Grant's memory was that he had concluded to go home, after seeing the Jo Daviess Guards established in camp, and to wait in Galena for any call that might come. Having supper in the Chenery Hotel, he noticed the Governor eating at his accustomed table, but did not speak to him since, as he recalled, they had never been introduced. After supper he had walked out to the front door of the hotel and was standing there killing time till the nine-o'clock train left for Galena, when Yates came out, halted and said: "Captain, I understand you are about to leave the city." Grant said that he was. The Governor asked him to remain overnight and call at the executive office next morning, which Grant did and, on being asked to help out, accepted.

Friends of Rawlins and Rowley understood that Washburne, upon discovering that Grant was intending to go home, had said to him: "Hold on a little, Captain. Every thing can't be done in a moment. Have patience." These men said, "Grant's Galena friends kept him in Springfield with the greatest difficulty." [13]

Yates's private secretary, John Moses, always remembered that Washburne had arranged for the meeting with the Governor, and J. Russell Jones's friends insisted that "Russ" along with "other Galena friends" had been responsible. Galenians in general supported the statement of one of them: "John E. Smith did it, seconded by R. H. McClellan. What they didn't do, Washburne did." [14]

Two years later Yates himself gave the impression, without actually saying so, that he had hired Grant at their first meeting. Impressed, he said, by Grant's "modesty and earnestness" and "plain straightforward demeanor" in describing his wish to repay his debt to a nation which had educated him, Yates had found himself "at once" awaking to "a lively interest in Grant and had assigned him a desk in the Executive office to give counsel on the organizing of volunteer regiments." Grant was, said Yates, "an invaluable assistant in my own and the office of the Adjutant-General." [15] His salary was two dollars a day and kept him in civilian uniform. Chetlain always remembered that four days after their arrival in Springfield, he looked in on Grant's new employment and found him in an anteroom of the Adjutant General's office, "a small, poorly lighted and scantily furnished room," writing at a small table. When Chetlain asked him how he was getting along, Grant "looked up with an expression of disgust, and said, 'I'm going back to the store tonight. I'm of no use here. You have boys in your company who can do this work.'" Chetlain begged him not to be hasty and, that evening, renewed his advice, "something better would undoubtedly turn up." Grant finally "decided to remain a few days longer." [16]

To Chetlain it was apparent that many politicians around the capital "looked upon Grant as a sort of a 'dead beat.'" Other friends of Grant's suspected that Captain Pope had spread the old army gossip about the reasons for Grant's resignation from the Army. John M. Palmer, a leading Republican politician and lawyer who was helping organize the new regiments, said later that as he passed through the Adjutant General's office one day he asked who Grant was and was told "He's a dead-beat military man — a discharged officer of the regular army." [17]

On Thursday, May 2, Ulysses wrote his father that he would not apply for any of the colonelcies since it would put him under obligations to politicians, "and I do not care to be under such persons." He expected to be in Springfield all next week, "but suppose I shall not be here long." He urged his father not to have Orvil and Burke press for collection of debts at this time, nor to try and sell goods "in the present distracted state of our currency. The money will not buy Eastern exchange and is liable to become worse; I think that thirty days from this we shall have specie, and the bills of good foreign banks to do business on, and then will be the time to collect." [18]

Next day John Pope came inadvertently to Grant's aid. Having finished mustering in the six regiments of ninety-day men, Pope expected the officers of the brigade to name him Brigadier General at the election. Instead they chose Colonel Benjamin M. Prentiss who had led the first companies to Cairo and won applause by seizing contraband munitions on steamboats. Pope, in a huff, departed for headquarters at St. Louis. A regular officer stood small chance of election when opposed by a popular Volunteer, particularly a "windy," dynamic politician like Prentiss. The new brigadier was a Virginian who in 1841, at the age of twenty-two, had come to Quincy, Illinois, as a ropemaker, then had become a commission man, a lawyer and office seeker. Joining the militia he had helped expel the Mormons from Illinois and had been elected captain of a company that had fought well at Buena Vista. Striding about with great vigor and heartiness, he had been voted colonel of the fourth regiment to be organized under Yates — a regiment named the Tenth, since numbers given the new organizations began with Seven out of deference to the six "sucker" regiments that had served in the Mexican War.

On May 4, the day that Pope departed, the Jo Daviess Guards with eight other companies were incorporated in the Twelfth Regiment, with John McArthur, Captain of a Chicago company of independent militia, the Highland Guards, chosen as Colonel. A boilermaker who had emigrated to Chicago from Scotland in 1841, this "tall, brawny,

tight-lipped, zealous and efficient Scot" wore the cap of his clan and
won friendships, including that of Grant, around Springfield before
being ordered to Caseyville, in the southern part of the state, near
St. Louis. Blair and Lyon were expecting the crises to come momen-
tarily and wanted supports near at hand.

With Pope gone, Governor Yates was confounded to learn, from
the Illinois Central and Chicago & Alton railroads, that they had insufficient cars and locomotives to take the Twelfth and other regiments to the border of Missouri. Yates was complaining about this
to State Auditor Jesse K. Dubois, when the latter urged him to send
for Grant in the next office. Putting the question to Grant, Yates was
told to march the men down. Yates was astounded. All that he had
heard so far was that distances like that must be covered by rail, not
marching.[19] Yates now had three office advisors, Smith, Dubois and
Koerner, not to speak of Washburne, McClellan and Jones, who kept
bringing Grant to his attention. Koerner had formed the habit of
talking to Grant in the office, sitting with him, each smoking cane-
stemmed pipes. When they were alone Grant talked freely and Koerner "thought he was quite a good fellow for a West Pointer." [20]

On May 4 Yates named Grant to succeed Captain Pope as commander of Camp Yates and four days later appointed him Mustering
Officer to handle the incoming regiments of thirty-day men at $4.20
a day, more than double his former salary. Still a civilian appointee
and wearing his seedy clothes, Grant was nevertheless called "Colonel" and took the responsibilities of the rank. He still expected to
return to Galena when the mustering was completed, for no offers
of genuine colonelcies came his way. He heard men say he should
have one, and what a shame he did not receive one, but he would not
budge unless the thing came as a call wholly unsolicited and uncon-
trived.

"I feel that I have done more now than I could do serving as a
captain under a green colonel," he wrote his father on May 6, "and
if this thing continues they will want more men at a later day." He
could go back to Galena and drill the three or four companies which
were gathered there. Lincoln's call for more Volunteers for three
years — 22,000 for the regular Army and 18,000 sailors — was precisely right. The Volunteers would never have to serve three years.
It would be a short war.

Grant approved the sagacity with which the Lincoln Administration was moving, holding back until it had an army. "When they do strike," he wrote his father, "our thoroughly loyal states will be fully protected, and a few decisive victories in some of the southern ports will send the secession army howling, and the leaders in the rebellion will flee the country. All the states will then be loyal for a generation to come." More clearly than ever, he now saw that "the negro will never disturb this nation again." Once the Confederacy fell, slaves would be worth nothing and the only thing to fear was that the Negro "may revolt and cause more destruction than any Northern man, except it be the ultra-abolitionist. . . . A Northern army may be required in the next ninety days to go South to suppress a negro insurrection."

It made him laugh to read about the Confederacy sending "the *valiant* Pillow" to attack Cairo, and he felt sure the hero of Camargo would find the ditches here on the outside, not the inside of the breastworks. With memories of Pillow's comic performances at Cerro Gordo and Chapultepec in mind, he wrote his father that since the great man "would find it necessary to receive a wound . . . he would not be a formidable enemy. I do not say he would shoot himself, ah no! I am not so uncharitable as many who served under him in Mexico." But he felt sure Pillow would irritate any slight scratch "until he convinced himself that he had been wounded by the enemy." [21]

Camp Yates, under Captain Grant was, as his home newspaper, the *North Western Gazette* proudly told Galenians, "under strict military law. The horse-play and insubordination of the past was gone. The men had plenty of fresh hay for bedding. Guards who watched day and night inside and outside the camp were changed every two hours." [22]

Five days after taking command of the camp, Grant was ordered by Yates to take charge of the mustering of the thirty-day men at various points in the state. The important thing now was to fill these troops with zeal to re-enlist quickly as three-year men. To some points Grant sent lieutenants but took three for himself in southern counties where pro-secession sentiment was strongest. At Mattoon and Belleville he found the regiments not yet assembled, and crossed the Mississippi into St. Louis to see if

Lyon could have a place for him in the volunteer force that was burgeoning in Missouri.[23]

As he approached the Arsenal on the morning of May 10, he saw flags flying and a large force under arms. Hurrying up, he learned from Lyon that this was the moment when all the nonsense about Missouri and secession was to end. The Southern Rights party had railed and stormed for months now about the sinfulness of any Lincolnite proposing to coerce Missouri. Its people, he felt sure, were predominantly pro-Union, but Governor Jackson was intriguing with the Confederacy to deliver the state into the secession ranks. Since Lyon had armed Illinois he had distributed the rest of his guns to the loyal Home Guards, his little band of Regulars, and to many of the Germans, who swore to follow Frank Blair to the death. Posting his men on the hills around the Arsenal, Lyon had waited, while General Frost on May 6 moved his brigade of volunteer state militiamen to Camp Jackson, across town from the Arsenal. On May 8 guns which Alabama secessionists had seized in the Federal Arsenal at Montgomery were smuggled through to Frost in boxes labeled "marble." What Frost intended to do next was never clear. With only 635 men he had no dream of attacking the 7000 whom Lyon could assemble around the Arsenal. Lyon and Blair, however, had decided to capture Frost's men and break the back of secession in Missouri. Through spies they learned that Frost would break camp on May 11, and on May 9 Lyon, disguised in a dress and shawl borrowed from Blair's mother-in-law, and with a veiled sunbonnet covering his red beard and hot blue eyes, had himself driven in an open carriage all through Camp Jackson noting the impromptu street names "Beauregard," "Jeff Davis" and the like. On his arm, as he sat in the barouche, was an egg basket which contained no eggs but several loaded revolvers. If apprehended Lyon proposed to shoot his way out of the rebel camp unassisted. Returning undetected, he had called the Union leaders of the city together and announced his plan — Camp Jackson would fall tomorrow.

It was at this point in the morning that Grant arrived, and as the column formed he introduced himself to Frank Blair, who was on horseback giving orders. Although he had disapproved of this Black Republican six months before, he now told Blair that he was in "sympathy with his purpose" and wished the expedition success.

The column marched westward through the town, followed by panting crowds. Grant remained behind. He saw "the rebel flag" flaunting from the headquarters of the secessionists at Fifth and Pine Streets, symbol of the defiance which had seemed to dominate the city. Hours passed, then runners came in crying that riots had broken out and the Germans were shooting citizens. Fuller reports made it clear that after Lyon and Blair had surrounded the camp, received Frost's surrender and were marching the prisoners back toward town, a mob had begun waving clubs and knives and screaming "Down with the damned Dutch!" Next, stones had begun to fly. A pistol had been fired at the German Home Guards, who answered with a volley that cut swaths in the throng.

With twenty-eight civilians dead and no one knew how many wounded, Grant saw a great change come over the downtown section and the secession leaders. "They had been playing the bully," said Grant. When Union men strode up boldly to the clubrooms and, in what Grant heard as "tones of authority," ordered the rebel flag to come down at once — it came.

Rejoicing at Lyon's and Blair's success, Grant took a horsecar for the Arsenal, seeing as he went knots of secessionists muttering to each other in suppressed rage. On the car "a dapper little fellow" began denouncing the day's events:

"Things have come to a damn pretty pass when a free people can't choose their own flag. Where I came from if a man dares to say a word in favor of the Union we hang him to a limb of the first tree we come to."

Grant answered, "After all, we aren't so intolerant in St. Louis as we might be; I've not seen a single rebel hung yet, nor heard of one; there are plenty of them who ought to be, however." The dapper little fellow subsided.[24]

Congratulating Blair and Lyon as they rode up to the Arsenal with their prisoners, who would be paroled tomorrow, Grant asked about a position in the new war machine that was to be constructed. With so pure a militarist as Lyon in charge and protected by Blair from political influences, it seemed that Missouri might be a good place to serve. But Grant received no encouragement and next day after equally vain conferences with Union friends in town, Grant went to Belleville to examine the accounts of contractors who had been clothing and feeding a regiment. His new friend from the Adjutant General's office, Koerner, was at home and to him Grant explained that he must proceed to Caseyville, a few miles distant, and that he had no money with which to hire a horse and buggy. Yates had equipped him with railroad passes but no trains ran to Caseyville. Quickly Koerner secured a citizen to furnish transportation free.[25]

Into Chetlain's headquarters at Caseyville Grant came "depressed in spirits." He wanted to serve and yet could find no chance. "I don't think I'm conceited," he said, "but I feel confident I could command a regiment well; at least, I would like to try it." He thought he would go to Cincinnati and see if George B. McClellan could use him; he considered Little Mac one of the brightest of the Regulars now entering Volunteer service. "I think he is sure to make his mark in this war." [26]

In the week that followed he mustered in the Seventh District Regiment at Mattoon on May 15 and the Eighteenth on May 19. The boys of the Seventh liked him in their brief view of him, heard him called "Colonel" and some among them began wishing they could have a leader like him.

Their own Colonel, Simon S. Goode, from Decatur, was thrilling to behold. Tall, booted to the hips, shirted in handsome gray, wide-hatted, with three revolvers and a bowie knife, he talked stirringly of his days as an adventurer with Captain Walker's famous filibustering expedition to Nicaragua. Goode's speeches were rousers, but his knowledge of army organization was nothing at all, and discipline was growing worse.

The boys watched the small, silent Grant in his rusty civilian clothes going about military matters with quiet efficiency, and as he left they named their camp for him.[27]

Grant had hardly settled in his room in Springfield after his tour when First Lieutenant Joseph W. Vance came in from Mattoon to see him. The boy wanted to tell how things were in the regiment. He had been two years at West Point himself and there was a lot Grant should know. Goode was impossible, drank too much, quoted Napoleon all the time, and went around at night in a cloak like Bonaparte's, telling sentries "I never sleep." Vance didn't know how much longer the regiment would hold together under such a fool. Seeing that Grant was listening in utter silence, the young Lieutenant realized that he shouldn't be talking out of school and went away. But within a few days he discovered himself promoted to drillmaster and learned that Grant was responsible.[28]

On May 22 Grant's mustering work was done and Yates gave him leave to visit his home. The $130 due him would be issued in a couple of days. Grant took the train for Galena where, on May 24, he wrote Colonel Lorenzo Thomas, who was now taking Joe Johnston's place as Adjutant General in Washington and as a member of the Fourth Regiment would know him and should be able to help him:

> SIR:
>
> Having served for fifteen years in the regular army including four years at West Point and feeling it the duty of evry [sic] one who has been educated at the government's expense to offer their services for the support of that Government, I have the honor, very respectfylly [sic] to tender my services, until the close of the war in such capacity as may be offered. I would say that in view of my present age, and length of service, I feel myself competent to command a Regiment if the President in his judgement should see fit to entrust one to me.
>
> Since the first call of the President I have been serving on the staff of the Governer [sic] of this State rendering such aid as I could in the organization of our State Militia, and am still engaged in that capacity. A letter addressed to me at Springfield, Ill, will reach me.
>
> I am very
respectfully,
Y. Obt svt.
U. S. GRANT [29]

Six days later he wrote his father that he had tendered his services to the National Government and was today returning to Springfield. Somehow he hoped to make himself useful "until all our National difficulties are ended." Ever since he had come home on leave he had been restless: "I have felt all the time as if a duty were being neglected that was paramount to any other duty I ever owed. I have every reason to be well satisfied with myself for the services already rendered, but to stop now would not do." [30]

In Springfield he found nothing to do. Charles Lamphier, editor of the *Springfield Register*, thought he looked lonesome as he stood in the Chenery House and when he asked him what he was doing, Grant merely replied, "Nothing — waiting." [31]

The newspapers were reciting the feats of General McClellan in organizing Ohio. Across the river in Kentucky, Grant's old friend Buckner was heading the state militia and from what Grant had heard — or perhaps hoped — would in the final analysis be loyal. Buckner was, in Grant's mind, one of the soldiers who, along with McClellan, would be most successful in crushing the Rebellion. The others were Buell, Rosecrans, McDowell and Charles P. Stone. The more he thought about it the clearer he saw that McClellan was "the man who was to pilot us through, and I wanted to be on his staff." He had helped McClellan outfit the expedition at Fort Vancouver, had known him in Mexico. Surely Little Mac would make him a major or perhaps a lieutenant colonel. "I wanted to be with him," Grant recalled in later years.

This was his real purpose when, receiving no answer from Lorenzo Thomas, the first week in June he asked Yates for a week's leave in which to visit his parents in Covington. From his father's home he quickly crossed into Cincinnati and entered McClellan's headquarters where he found several old friends among the staff officers in an anteroom — Seth Williams for one. Grant asked for the General. The result was something he liked to describe with dry humor later on:

> I was told he had just gone out, and was asked to take a seat. Everybody was so busy that they could not say a word. I waited a couple of hours. I never saw such a busy crowd — so many men at an army head-quarters with quills behind their ears. But I supposed it was all right, and was much encouraged by their industry. It was a great comfort to see the men so busy with the quills.
>
> Finally after a long wait, I told an officer that I would come in again next day, and requested him to tell McClellan that I had called. Next day I came in. The same story. The General had just gone out, might be in at any moment.
>
> Would I wait? I sat and waited for two hours, watching the officers with their quills, and left.

This is the whole story. McClellan never acknowledged my call, and, of course, after he knew I had been at his headquarters I was bound to await his acknowledgment. I was older, had ranked him in the army, and could not hang around his headquarters watching the men with the quills behind their ears. . . . Still I should like to have joined McClellan.[32]

He visited Georgetown and Batavia, talked about trying to get a contract to supply bread for the Ohio volunteers who were assembling in Camp Dennison at Columbus, and said to Chilton White, "You remember my success at bread-making in Mexico." [33]

At the end of the week he left, depressed, for Springfield, telling his father that he would stop for a day or two in Indiana to visit "a favorite classmate," Joe Reynolds. Joe had resigned from Washington University's faculty in 1860 to become a grocer at Lafayette, Indiana and was now colonel at the rendezvous of Indiana's Volunteers at Camp Morton in Indianapolis, expecting to be made a brigadier general soon. Ulysses, having failed in Illinois, Missouri and Ohio, was apparently now to try Indiana.

He had no more than departed from Covington when a telegram came to him in care of his father. Jesse read it. It was from Yates, offering him the colonelcy of the Seventh District Regiment. Jesse forwarded it, as he remembered in after times, to Ulysses in care of Reynolds at Terre Haute where Reynolds was at the moment. When it arrived, Grant had gone, probably further dismayed at finding Indiana's regiment in need of no colonels.[34]

Jesse learned from Burke in Galena that he had helped obtain the offer from Yates. Burke said that he had been in Springfield during Ulysses' absence and that in the course of a conversation the Governor had asked:

"What kind of a man is this Grant? He has been educated at West Point and says he wants to go into the Army; several regiments have offered to elect him colonel, but he says, No, and declines to be a candidate. What does he want?"

"You see, Governor," said Burke, "Grant has only served in the regular Army, where they have no elections, but officers are promoted according to seniority. Whatever place you want him for, just appoint him without consulting him at all beforehand, and you will find he will accept whatever he is appointed to." [35]

Yates needed a colonel for the Seventh District Regiment, whose officers had told him that men would not re-enlist on June 15 for the three-year term unless Colonel Goode was replaced. Farm boys unused to restraint, they took a fiendish delight in plaguing their tipsy peacock of a commander, had mutinied over bad bread and had burned the guardhouse. Discipline had vanished entirely. Ununiformed as yet and undrilled, the men robbed hen roosts for miles around and stayed out all night in the saloons of Mattoon. "Governor Yates's Hellions," they were called — another reason for the Executive to act. Polling the regimental officers as to a successor, Yates found them voting for Grant and when Secretary of State Dubois and John S. Loomis, an assistant in the Adjutant General's office, both urged this choice upon Yates, he sent the telegram to Covington. Ordering the regiment brought to Camp Yates, the Governor was now, the second week in June, waiting to hear Grant's response.[36]

Grant arrived and on June 15 accepted Yates's offer and, as Galenians afterward said, "within a short time" received a telegram forwarded from Orvil containing another offer, a colonelcy in an Ohio regiment, which Governor Dennison had sent to Galena.[37]

Committed, however, to Illinois, Grant boarded a Springfield horsecar on June 16 and with John E. Smith beside him rode out to his regiment at Camp Yates. Smith later described Grant's arrival:

"He was dressed very clumsily, in citizens' clothes — an old coat, worn out at the elbows, and a badly dinged plug hat. His men, though ragged and barefooted themselves, had formed a high estimate of what a Colonel ought to be, and when Grant walked in among them they began making fun of him.

" 'What a Colonel! Damn such a Colonel!'

"A few of them, to show off to the others, got behind his back and commenced sparring at him and while one was doing this, another gave him such a push that made him hit Grant a terrible blow between the shoulders" knocking off his hat. Grant quietly stooped down, picked it up, dusted it, then placed it upon his head without saying a word. He turned around and looked at the men, however, for an instant, and in that look the latter saw they had a soldier and a man of nerve to deal with.

Smith said the boys began to feel "very much mortified" and one of them came up to explain "it was all in fun, and hoped the new Colonel wouldn't get mad about it."

"But he did," said Smith. "Grant went to work immediately, and in a very short time had his men clothed and fixed up in good style." [38]

Lieutenant J. W. Wham saw Grant walk into the Adjutant's tent, saying "he guessed he'd take command," then sit down to write orders and eventually stroll over the camp to look around. "The first thing that caught his eye was the camp guard . . . which Colonel Goode had created to keep the men from climbing the fence and going in to the city to see the girls." Grant told the guard, which consisted of eighty men with clubs, to disband. There would be no more guards, he told the gaping soldiers; each man must be present at the roll calls of which there would be several a day. He gave the times of the calls. "The effect of that order was wonderful," said Lieutenant Wham. "There was no more climbing the fence after that." [39]

"We could not exactly understand the man," remembered Private Aaron Elliott in later years. "He was very soon called 'the quiet man' . . . and in a few days reduced matters in camp to perfect order." [40]

With his new commission to take effect on June 17, Ulysses made a flying trip to Galena to raise money for a uniform, a horse and what had been called in the Mexican War "horse furniture." His home town was astir over him. Both Illinois and Ohio had wanted him. Probably for reasons of pride, Ulysses borrowed money — two or three hundred dollars — not from the firm but from E. A. Collins who, while known as "one of the leaders of the rebel element," had always had a soft spot in his heart for his former partner's son. Years later, Galenians would say that Collins had always felt Jesse was stingy with Ulysses. [41]

The congratulations of his fellow townsmen were sweet, but a great doubt lay on Grant. Within another week he might not be needing the uniform. On June 28 his regiment was to decide whether to go home or to re-enlist for three years. Already it had shrunk from the 1250 whom he had mustered in May 15 to scarcely more than 600 on June 16, the day he had taken command. And he knew that many of the 600 who had remained to consider the new enrollment were growing tired.

As the day of decision neared, friends of Grant tried to help him with his problem. They introduced him to two Democratic Congressmen who might exhort his regiment — John A. McClernand and John A. Logan. Grant hesitated, for while McClernand was being widely praised by Republicans for his violent pro-Unionism, Logan was receiving vilification for his silence on the subject. Gossip had it that Logan had renounced his idol Stephen Douglas for "selling out the Democratic party." Logan had denied the right of secession on the floor of Congress in February, but in his home district in southern Illinois, had compared the secessionists to the heroes of 1776! His wife's brother had gone across the Ohio to join the Rebels, and Logan himself was accused of discouraging Union enlistments in his home county, Williamson.

Grant was turning the question in his mind as he faced the two politicians, McClernand with a beak of a nose and a headlong, testy, irascible manner, Logan, swarthy, black-mustached and with eyes so piercingly dark that the iris was invisible.

Logan, thirty-five, had been a leader since boyhood, Lieutenant in the First Illinois during the Mexican War, a State Legislator, Prosecuting Attorney, and now Congressman since 1858 — magnetic, oratorical, holding the loyalty of his constituents as probably no other Illinois Congressman of his time.

Grant was afraid of what Logan might say, yet so long as he would be coupled with McClernand it was worth the chance. He gave his assent.

June 28 came. McClernand spoke first, patriotic as had been expected. Then Logan rose and did to Grant all that Rawlins in the Court House had done. Years later Grant still thrilled to the memory of "the loyalty and devotion to the Union" which came from the orator with such "force and eloquence." Logan said later of the regiment, "I was acquainted with nearly every man in it. . . . I made a speech ridiculing the idea of soldiers going out of service in a time of war without having seen what war is and without having left the peaceful borders of their own state." Listeners told long afterward how Logan, after painting the glories of defending the flag, dramatically changed his tone:

"You can't fall out now. If you go home now to Mary, she will say, 'Why, Tom, are you home from the war so soon?'"

" 'Yes.'

" 'How far did you get?'

" 'Mattoon.' "

In the roar of laughter and cheers that went up Grant knew that his worries were over. The whoops of the men carried the promise of what they would do later in the day when 603 volunteered — "almost," as Grant said, "to a man."

As the applause died, Grant heard Logan present "your new commander, Colonel U. S. Grant," and cries of "Speech! Speech!" come up from the men. Grant stepped forward and said, in that low yet curiously penetrating and arresting tone which his voice at times possessed:

"Men, go to your quarters!" [42]

The men looked at him, then at each other

They were in the Army now.

Notes

CHAPTER ONE

1. Albert Deane Richardson, *A personal history of Ulysses S. Grant*, Hartford, Conn., 1868, p. 45 (cited hereafter as "Richardson").
2. Richardson, p. 45.
3. Richardson, p. 42; Jesse Root Grant in *New York Ledger*, March 7, 1868 (cited hereafter as "*Ledger*").
4. Edward Chauncey Marshall, *The ancestry of General Grant, and their contemporaries*, New York, 1869, p. 63 (cited hereafter as "Marshall"); Richardson, pp. 29, 40–41.
5. Marshall, p. 164.
6. Richardson, p. 41.
7. Letter, Jesse Grant to Lawson Grant, April 15, 1869; *Ledger*, March 7, 1868; Marshall, pp. 170–172; Jesse Grant to J. S. Buell, *St. Louis Republican*, July 28, 1885.
8. *History of Portage County, Ohio*, Chicago, 1885, p. 421; Richardson, p. 41.
9. Richardson, pp. 31–33.
10. Deed Book H, Court records, Mason County, Kentucky, p. 256; Marshall, p. 171.
11. Ulysses Simpson Grant, *Personal memoirs of U. S. Grant*, 2v. in 1, New York, 1894, p. 16 (cited hereafter as "*Memoirs*"); Marshall, pp. 171–172.
12. *Memoirs*, p. 17; on David Tod, *Chicago Times*, December 10, 1868. p. 7.
13. Richardson, p. 42; *Chicago Times*, December 10, 1868, p. 7.
14. Richardson, p. 43.
15. Richardson, p. 44.
16. Deed Book M, court records, Mason County, Kentucky, p. 273; Richardson, p. 44; *Memoirs*, p. 17; *Ledger*, March 7, 1868.
17. *Ledger*, March 7, 1868.
18. Oswald Garrison Villard, *John Brown, 1800–1859*, Boston and New York, 1910, p. 4.
19. *Ledger*, March 7, 1868; *History of Portage County, Ohio*, p. 526.
20. Richardson, p. 46.
21. Marshall, pp. 171–172; *Ledger*, March 7, 1868.
22. Jesse Grant to J. S. Buell, *St. Louis Republican*, July 28, 1885; Louis H. Everts, *History of Clermont County, Ohio*, Philadelphia, 1880, pp. 383–389 (cited hereafter as "Everts").

23. Richardson, p. 47.
24. Everts, p. 383.
25. Sources on the Simpson family: *Memoirs,* pp. 18–19; Charles S. Mann, "The Bucks and Montgomery County kindred of General U. S. Grant," *Historical Sketches,* Historical Society of Montgomery County, Pennsylvania, Norristown, 1925, vol. 5, pp. 218–236; Everts, pp. 317, 383; Helen Augusta Simpson, *Early records of Simpson families in Scotland, North Ireland, and eastern United States,* Philadelphia, 1927, pp. 134, 144–147; interview with Elizabeth Hare, *Philadelphia Times,* July 26, 1885.
26. Sources on Hannah Simpson courtship by and marriage to Jesse Grant: *Ledger,* March 7, 1868; Phineas Camp Headley, *The life and campaigns of Lieut.-Gen. U. S. Grant, from his boyhood to the surrender of Lee,* New York, 1868, p. 19 (cited hereafter as "Headley"); Daniel Ammen, "Recollections and letters of Grant," *North American Review,* 141(July–December 1885)361; Isaac N. Morris in *National Intelligencer,* March 22, 1864; Elizabeth Hare, *Philadelphia Times,* July 26, 1885; "General Grant as his son saw him," interview with Frederick Dent Grant by A. E. Watrous, magazine article bound in special edition Grant's *Personal memoirs,* vol. 3, possession author; Henry Howe, *Historical collections of Ohio,* 3v. in 2, Columbus, 1889–1891, vol. 1, pp. 419–420; Everts, p. 153.
27. Sources on the first home of Jesse and Hannah Grant: Everts, p. 380; Howe, previous citation; Richardson, p. 48; C. B. Galbreath, "Centennial anniversary of the birth of Ulysses S. Grant," *Ohio Archaeological and Historical Quarterly,* 31(1922)234–235 (cited hereafter as "Galbreath").

CHAPTER TWO

1. Jesse Grant in *Ledger,* March 7, 1868.
2. Richardson, p. 49.
3. Richardson, pp. 49–50; *Ledger,* March 7, 1868; March 14, 1868; Hamlin Garland, *Ulysses S. Grant; his life and character,* New York, 1898, p. 6 (cited hereafter as "Garland"). Jesse Grant quoted in Headley, p. 19; Jesse Grant quoted by a relative by marriage, W. Lee White, *Washington Post,* April 29, 1892.
4. Everts, p. 141; Marshall, p. 69.
5. *Ledger,* March 7, 1868; Richardson, p. 50.
6. Richardson, p. 51.
7. Purchase of lot by Jesse Grant, and description of Thomas L. Hamer, W. H. Beers & Co., *The history of Brown County, Ohio,* Chicago, 1883, pp. 343–344, 351, 393, 395 (cited hereafter as "Beers").
8. *Memoirs,* p. 19; Beers, p. 393.
9. Richardson, p. 52. Staff officers and messengers with U. S. Grant, during battles in 1864, remarked his unique faculty of never showing

"the quiver of an eyelid" when missiles "zipped" or roared past his head. General Horace Porter, quoted in John Bach McMaster, *The life, memoirs, military career, and death of General U. S. Grant*, Philadelphia, 1885, p. 42; Colonel W. J. White interview, *Cincinnati Gazette*, August 9, 1885.

10. Anecdote baby and pistol: Richardson, p. 52; U. S. Grant quoted in *St. Louis Globe Democrat*, July 28, 1885; John Luther Ringwalt, *Anecdotes of General Ulysses S. Grant, illustrating his military and political career and his personal traits*, Philadelphia, 1886, p. 5 (cited hereafter as "Ringwalt"). Anecdote baby and powder: Richardson, p. 52.

11. Baby plays under horses' feet: Nellie Grant Jones, quoted in Frank Hatch Jones, *An address delivered by Frank H. Jones before the Chicago Historical Society at the celebration of the 100th anniversary of the birth of General Ulysses S. Grant, Thursday, April 27th, 1922*, Chicago, 1922, pp. 7–8; Garland, p. 6. Baby holds horses: James S. Sanderson quoted in *New York Times*, July 30, 1885, p. 3 (cited hereafter as "Sanderson"). Neighbor quoted on Hannah's trust in the Lord, Garland, p. 7.

12. U. S. Grant stands on trotting horses: *Ledger*, March 7, 1868; Jesse Grant pays debt on house: Marshall, p. 67; Jesse Grant's library: Sanderson.

13. U. S. Grant starts to school: Richardson, p. 68; *Memoirs*, p. 19; *Ledger*, March 14, 1868. Description subscription school: Beers, p. 583; *Memoirs*, p. 19; *Ledger*, March 14, 1868. U. S. Grant on switchings: *Memoirs*, p. 23.

14. Schoolmates on U. S. Grant in school: [Frank Harrison], *Anecdotes and reminiscences of Gen'l U. S. Grant*, New York, 1885, p. 14; Beers, pt. 5, "Biographical Sketches," p. 28.

15. Anecdote frozen feet: Richardson, p. 58. U. S. Grant studious in school: Jesse Grant quoted in Whitelaw Reid, *Ohio in the war: her statesmen, her generals, and soldiers*, 2v., Cincinnati and New York, 1868, vol. 1, p. 352; *Memoirs*, p. 20.

16. Richardson, p. 52; *Memoirs*, p. 20.

17. Reverend John Newman quoted in *New York Times*, July 24, 1885, p. 6.

18. Jesse Grant and Hamer as Masons: Beers, p. 404; *Ledger*, March 7, 1868. Mrs. George B. Bailey quoted: Richardson, pp. 56–57.

19. Death of Bailey's son: Richardson, p. 56; *Ledger*, March 7, 1868.

20. Daniel Ammen quoted on U. S. Grant, Hannah Grant, and Grant home: Daniel Ammen, "Recollections and letters of Grant," *North American Review*, 141(July–December 1885)361; Daniel Ammen, *The old navy and the new . . . with an appendix of personal letters from General Grant*, Philadelphia, 1891, pp. 16–19. Anecdotes David Ammen, Jacob Ammen, and Reverend John Rankin: Whitelaw Reid, *Ohio in the war: her statesmen, her generals, and soldiers*, 2v.,

Cincinnati and New York, 1868, vol. 1, p. 901; John Beatty, *Memoirs of a volunteer, 1861–1863*, edited by Harvey S. Ford, New York, 1946, pp. 120–123; Beers, pp. 423, 425, 449; Henry Howe, *Historical collections of Ohio*, 3v. in 2, Columbus, 1889–1891, vol. 1, pp. 337–339. Jesse Grant in *Castigator* office: Reverend E. Cox interview, *Cincinnati Gazette*, August 9, 1885. Anecdote of Colonel Higgins: Beers, pt. 5, "Biographical Sketches," p. 21.

21. Anecdote Ralston horse trade: *Memoirs*, pp. 22–23; Captain Walker quoted *New York Tribune*, August 2, 1885.
22. *Ledger*, March 7, 1868; [Frank Harrison], *Anecdotes and reminiscences of Gen'l U. S. Grant*, New York, 1885, p. 14; Garland, p. 15.
23. Sanderson; *Memoirs*, p. 126.
24. Grant's horsemanship: *Ledger*, March 7, 1868; Whitelaw Reid, *Ohio in the war: her statesmen, her generals, and soldiers*, 2v., Cincinnati and New York, 1868, vol. 1, p. 352; Richardson, pp. 56–57; Chicago Home Visitor quoted in *Chicago Tribune*, May 25, 1865; Sanderson.
25. Richardson, pp. 68–69; *Memoirs*, p. 21; *Ledger*, March 7, 1868.
26. U. S. Grant and tannery: Richardson, p. 63; *Ledger*, March 14, 1868; *Memoirs*, p. 20.
27. Garland, p. 14.
28. Reverend John Newman in *New York Times*, July 24, 1885, p. 6.
29. *Memoirs*, p. 35.
30. Richardson, p. 67.
31. U. S. Grant and circus ponies: *Ledger*, March 7, 1868; Garland, pp. 13–14.
32. U. S. Grant's first cousins: Marshall, pp. 171–172; Helen Augusta Simpson, *Early records of Simpson families in Scotland, North Ireland, and eastern United States*, Philadelphia, 1927, p. 147; *Memoirs*, p. 18. Jesse Grant on Southern nephews and nieces: "War memories" [by a Surgeon of the 16th Iowa Infantry], *Iowa Historical Record*, 7–9(1891–1893)378.
33. Marshall, pp. 171–172; *Memoirs*, pp. 30, 126.
34. *Memoirs*, p. 25.
35. Richardson, p. 69.
36. Sanderson.
37. Anecdotes of U. S. Grant and Marshall cousins: Richardson, pp. 60–62; Garland, p. 13; *Ledger*, March 14, 1868; Everts, pp. 28–29 (biographical section).
38. Richardson, p. 59.
39. *Memoirs*, p. 20.

CHAPTER THREE

1. *Ledger*, March 14, 1868.
2. "Dave and I" anecdote: *Ledger*, March 7, 1868; "General U. S. Grant by one who has known him from his boyhood" [Isaac N. Morris],

National Intelligencer, March 22, 1864; U. S. Grant to Isaac N. Morris, August 10, 1864, in Frank Hatch Jones, *An address delivered by Frank H. Jones before the Chicago Historical Society at the celebration of the 100th anniversay of the birth of General Ulysses S. Grant, Thursday, April 27th, 1922*, Chicago, 1922, p. 21. Anecdote Jesse Grant and bag of meal: Richardson, p. 40.

3. *Ledger*, March 7, 1868.
4. Anecdote phrenologist: *Ledger*, March 14, 1868; Garland, pp. 10–11.
5. Sanderson.
6. Horace Porter, *Campaigning with Grant*, New York, 1897, p. 251.
7. Georgetown boys: Garland, p. 12. U. S. Grant sensitive to pain: John Russell Young, *Men and memories; personal reminiscences*, ed. by his wife, May D. Russell Young, 2v., New York, 1901, vol. 2, p. 482. Grant's aversions in food: Horace Porter, *Campaigning with Grant*, New York, 1897, pp. 213–214.
8. Sanderson.
9. Garland, p. 22.
10. Sanderson.
11. Break between Jesse Grant and Hamer: *Memoirs*, pp. 24–25, 126; Beers, p. 352; Richardson, p. 68; John Russell Young, *Around the world with General Grant: a narrative of the visit of General U. S. Grant, ex-president of the United States, to various countries in Europe, Asia, and Africa, in 1877, 1878, 1879*, 2v., New York, 1879, vol. 2, p. 278 (cited hereafter as "*Around the world*"). Morris influence on Salmon P. Chase: Henry Howe, *Historical collections of Ohio*, 3v. in 2, Columbus, 1889–1891, vol. 1, pp. 413–414.
12. *Ledger*, March 7, 1868; Garland, p. 12.
13. Richardson, pp. 66–67.
14. Robert Allen reference: Jesse Grant Cramer, ed., *Letters of Ulysses S. Grant to his father and his youngest sister, 1857–18*, New York and London, 1912, p. 63 (cited hereafter as "Cramer"). Ammen references: Daniel Ammen, *The old navy and the new . . . with an appendix of personal letters from General Grant*, Philadelphia, 1891, pp. 19–21. Jesse Grant quoted: W. Lee White letter, *Washington Chronicle*, April 29, 1892.
15. Marshall, p. 172; Richardson, p. 71.
16. Richardson, p. 70.
17. A. H. Markland quoted in *New York Times*, August 4, 1885; U. S. Grant on Richeson and Rand's: *Memoirs*, pp. 19–20.
18. Bailey appointment: United States Military Academy Papers, 1838, National Archives. Carr B. White in *National Republican*, August 9, 1885. Jesse Grant appeal to Morris, *Ledger*, March 14, 1868.
19. Beers, pp. 393, 395, 401. Revival orgies: Simon Ansley O'Ferrall, *A ramble of six thousand miles through the United States of America*, London, 1832, pp. 74–76; Mrs. Frances [Milton] Trollope, *Domestic manners of the Americans*, 2v. in 1, London, 1832, pp. 236–246.

Grant family and religion: Garland, p. 20; Reverend John Newman quoted in *New York Times,* July 24, 1885, p. 6; *New York Tribune,* July 26, 1885.

20. U. S. Grant and music: Benjamin Perley Poore and O. H. Tiffany, *Life of U. S. Grant,* Philadelphia, 1885, p. 492; Frederick D. Dent quoted in *New York Herald,* July 25, 1885; W. W. Belknap in *Proceedings of Crocker's Iowa Brigade, at the third reunion, held at Iowa City, Iowa, September 23d and 24th, 1885,* Iowa City, 1885, pamphlet, pp. 103–104.

21. Reverend E. Cox quoted in *Cincinnati Gazette,* August 9, 1885.

22. *Memoirs,* pp. 21–22. Robert E. Lee letter to Talcott, February 2, 1837, quoted in Douglas Southall Freeman, *R. E. Lee, a biography,* 4v., New York and London, 1934–1935, vol. 1, pp. 135–136.

23. *Ledger,* March 14, 1868.

24. *Memoirs,* pp. 23–24; Henry Howe, *Historical collections of Ohio,* 3v. in 2, Columbus, 1889–1891, vol. 1, 1889, p. 337; Beers, pp. 314–315.

25. Garland, pp. 27–29.

26. Beers, pp. 303–304, 430.

27. Jesse Grant to Thomas L. Hamer, *Cincinnati Gazette,* August 9, 1885.

28. *Ledger,* March 14, 1868; Post orders, battalion orders and military academy orders, 1837, United States Military Academy Library, West Point, New York.

29. *Memoirs,* pp. 23–24.

30. Garland, p. 26.

31. *Ledger,* March 14, 1868; Daniel Ammen, *The old navy and the new . . . with an appendix of personal letters from General Grant,* Philadelphia, 1891, p. 21; Richardson, p. 75.

32. *Memoirs,* p. 25; Richardson, p. 75.

33. Richardson, pp. 70, 75–76.

34. Beers, pt. 5, "Biographical Sketches," p. 47.

35. Richardson, p. 74.

36. *Memoirs,* p. 27; James Grant Wilson, *The life and public services of Ulysses Simpson Grant, general of the United States army, and twice president of the United States,* rev. ed., New York, 1885, p. 109 (cited hereafter as "James Grant Wilson"); Richardson, p. 76.

37. *Memoirs,* pp. 30, 126; Headley, p. 19.

38. Garland, pp. 30–31.

39. Richardson, p. 76.

CHAPTER FOUR

1. *Memoirs,* p. 25.

2. *Memoirs,* pp. 26–27.

3. Horace Porter, *Campaigning with Grant,* New York, 1897, p. 108.

4. *Memoirs,* p. 27.

5. Elizabeth Hare quoted *Philadelphia Times,* July 26, 1885.

6. W. T. Sherman quoted *New York Tribune*, August 2, 1885.
7. Garland, pp. 31–32.
8. United States Military Academy, West Point, *Register of graduates and former cadets, United States Military Academy*, New York, 1946, p. 136.
9. Richardson, p. 75.
10. *Memoirs*, p. 7.
11. Frank A. Burr, *A new, original and authentic record of the life and deeds of General U. S. Grant*, Boston, 1885, p. 82 (cited hereafter as "Burr").
12. W. T. Sherman quoted *New York Tribune*, August 2, 1885.
13. W. T. Sherman to Allen Thorndike Rice, "Sherman on Grant," *North American Review*, 142(January–June 1886)112.
14. *Ibid.*
15. Letter by "P" in "Jackson at West Point," Annals of war scrapbook, clippings from *Philadelphia Times*, 1877, possession author.
16. George Rippey Stewart, *John Phoenix, Esq., the veritable Squibob, a life of Captain George H. Derby, U. S. A.*, New York, 1937, p. 27.
17. Letter by "P," previous reference.
18. Horace Porter, *Campaigning with Grant*, New York, 1897, p. 15.
19. "Grants at West Point," in *New York Tribune*, quoted *Army and Navy Journal*, June 13, 1903, p. 1038.
20. *Ledger*, March 14, 1868.
21. Burr, pp. 84–87; Richardson, p. 90; *New York Herald*, December 30, 1863; Headley, p. 31; Horace Porter, *Campaigning with Grant*, New York, 1897, p. 342.
22. Elizabeth Hare, *Philadelphia Times*, July 26, 1885.
23. *Memoirs*, p. 27.
24. Dabney Herndon Maury, *Recollections of a Virginian in the Mexican, Indian, and Civil Wars*, 3d ed., New York, 1894, p. 22, gives number of applicants at 164 (cited hereafter as "Maury"); United States Military Academy, West Point, *Register of graduates and former cadets, United States Military Academy*, New York, 1946, number admissions, class of 1846, as 111.
25. Ellsworth Eliot, Jr., *West Point in the Confederacy*, New York, 1941, p. 2.
26. Lloyd Lewis, *Sherman, fighting prophet*, New York, 1932, p. 117, quoting Braxton Bragg.
27. Biographical sketch of Henry Wager Halleck, by William E. Marsh, MS.
28. George Rippey Stewart, *John Phoenix, Esq., the veritable Squibob, a life of Captain George H. Derby, U. S. A.*, New York, 1937, p. 25; Samuel Gibbs French, *Two wars: an autobiography of Samuel G. French*, Nashville, Tenn., 1901, p. 13 (cited hereafter as "French").
29. Henry Coppée, *Life and services of Gen. U. S. Grant*, New York, 1868, pp. 21–22 (cited hereafter as "Coppée"). Monthly consolidated

reports of weekly class reports, including conduct roll, United States Military Academy Papers, War Department Records, National Archives.

30. U. S. Grant Account Book, 1839–1843, Huntington Library; French, p. 10; Garland, p. 41.

31. *Memoirs*, p. 27; Morris Schaff, *The spirit of old West Point, 1858–1862*, Boston and New York, 1907, pp. 46–47.

32. *Memoirs*, p. 29.

33. Details of Thomas's life: Thomas Budd Van Horne, *The life of Major-General George H. Thomas*, New York, 1882, p. 2; Oliver Otis Howard, "General George H. Thomas," in *Personal recollections of the war of the rebellion*, ed. by James Grant Wilson and Titus Munson Coan, New York, 1891, pp. 285–302; Rosecrans quoted, *Society of the Army of the Cumberland, fourth re-union, Cleveland, 1870*, Cincinnati, 1870, p. 88; *Around the world*, vol. 2, p. 296. Sources on Ewell: G. Moxley Sorrel, *Recollections of a Confederate staff officer*, New York and Washington, 1905, p. 53.

34. Penciled note by Edward C. Boynton in U. S. Grant Account Book, 1839–1843, Huntington Library; Morris Schaff, *The spirit of old West Point, 1858–1862*, Boston and New York, 1907, p. 37.

35. French, p. 17.

36. Frank Abial Flower, *Life of Matthew Hale Carpenter. A view of the honor and achievements that, in the American republic, are the fruits of well-directed ambition and persistent industry*, Madison, Wis., 1884, p. 44.

37. U. S. Grant to McKinistry Griffith, quoted in Garland, pp. 40–42.

38. Marks on conduct roll: Monthly consolidated reports of weekly class reports, including conduct roll, United States Military Academy Papers, War Department Records, National Archives. Sketch of Steele: Major John F. Lacey, "Major-General Frederick Steele," *Annals of Iowa*, 3rd s., 3(1897–1899)424–438. Nicknames of cadets: Richardson, p. 91; Fred Dent in *Sedgwick Memorial association; 6th army corps, Spottsylvania court house, Va., May 11, 12 and 13, 1887*, Philadelphia, 1887, pp. 13–14, pamphlet. Quinby's intellect: French, p. 15.

39. Oliver Ellsworth Wood, *The West Point scrap book: a collection of stories, songs, and legends of the United States Military Academy*, New York, 1871, pp. 261–262.

40. *Memoirs*, p. 28.

41. Richard Stoddert Ewell, *The making of a soldier; letters of General R. S. Ewell*, arranged and edited by Captain Percy Gatling Hamlin, Richmond, Va., 1935, p. 32 (cited hereafter as "Ewell"); John Eaton, *Grant, Lincoln and the freedmen; reminiscences of the Civil War with special reference to the work for the contrabands and freedmen of the Mississipi Valley*, in collaboration with Ethel Osgood Mason, New York, 1907, pp. 255–256.

42. Correspondence of Superintendent of United States Military Academy, War Department Records, National Archives, Joseph I. Totten to Jesse R. Grant, March 19, 1840, and Jesse R. Grant to Joseph I. Totten, August 15, 1840; *Memoirs*, p. 27; Horace Porter, *Campaigning with Grant*, New York, 1897, p. 342.
43. *Memoirs*, p. 27; *Around the world*, vol. 2, p. 291; Ingalls interview, *New York Herald*, April 7, 1885.
44. Horace Porter, *Campaigning with Grant*, New York, 1897, p. 342.
45. *Around the world*, vol. 2, p. 450.
46. Oliver Ellsworth Wood, *The West Point scrap book: a collection of stories, songs, and legends of the United States Military Academy*, New York, 1871, pp. 258–262.
47. Ewell, p. 27.
48. Garland, p. 50.

CHAPTER FIVE

1. James Grant Wilson, p. 109.
2. Ewell, p. 32.
3. James Grant Wilson, p. 109.
4. W. R. Marshall, "Reminiscences of General U. S. Grant," in *Glimpses of the nation's struggle*, 1st series, St. Paul, 1887, pp. 97–98.
5. French, p. 11.
6. U. S. Grant and sophomore mathematics, descriptive geometry anecdote: U. S. Grant III to author; Horace Porter, *Campaigning with Grant*, New York, 1897, p. 342.
7. Sully and Grant: Major John F. Lacey, "Major-General Frederick Steele," *Annals of Iowa*, 3rd s., 3(1897–1899)424–438; M. R. Morgan, "Types and traditions of the old army," in *Glimpses of the nation's struggle*, 6th series, Minneapolis, 1909.
8. McLaws and U. S. Grant: McLaws interview, *New York Times*, July 24, 1885, p. 6. Longstreet and U. S. Grant: Longstreet interview, *New York Times*, July 24, 1885, p. 6.
9. Longstreet interview, *New York Times*, July 24, 1885, p. 6; Garland, p. 45.
10. Frank Abial Flower, *Life of Matthew Hale Carpenter. A view of the honor and achievements that, in the American republic, are the fruits of well-directed ambition and persistent industry*, Madison, Wis., 1884, p. 44.
11. Maury, p. 208.
12. Sketch of D. H. Hill, *New York Herald*, October 27, 1862.
13. Post Order Books, United States Military Academy Library.
14. Cadets on "personal beauty": Erasmus Darwin Keyes, *Fifty years' observation of men and events, civil and military*, New York, 1885, p. 154. Grant on Lyon: *Around the world*, vol. 2, p. 468; James Grant Wilson, p. 109.

15. Truman Seymour, "Politics and West Point," *Army and Navy Journal*, September 24, 1864, p. 70.

16. Post Order Books, United States Military Academy Library, Order No. 2, February 23, 1843.

17. Fred Dent Grant quoted on U. S. Grant smoking: *Army and Navy Journal*, November 14, 1908, p. 280; Garland, p. 46; Richardson, p. 92.

18. Garland, p. 45; Richardson, p. 90; Coppée, p. 22.

19. *Memoirs*, p. 28.

20. Jesse Grant in *Shoe and Leather Reporter*, September, 1868, quoted in Marshall, p. 68. Description Bethel Tannery: Galbreath, p. 242.

21. Galbreath, p. 241; *Memoirs*, p. 28.

22. Monthly consolidated reports of weekly class reports, including conduct roll, United States Military Academy Papers, June 4, 1839, to September 30, 1849, War Department Records, National Archives; U. S. Grant Account Book, 1839–1843, Huntington Library.

23. Garland, pp. 47–48.

24. Richardson, p. 91.

25. Garland, p. 48; Galbreath, p. 243.

26. William Conant Church, *Ulysses S. Grant and the period of national preservation and reconstruction*, New York, 1897, p. 19 (cited hereafter as "Church, *Grant*").

27. Garland, p. 48; Church, *Grant*, p. 19.

28. *Memoirs*, p. 28.

29. *Memoirs*, p. 29.

30. *Around the world*, vol. 2, p. 289; Obituary McDowell, *New York Herald*, May 6, 1885; John Mead Gould, *History of the First–Tenth–Twenty-ninth Maine regiment. In service of the United States from May 3, 1861, to June 21, 1866*, Portland, 1871, p. 211.

31. Notebook of James Edward Kelly, MS.

32. "Brevet Major-General Gordon Granger," *Society of the Army of the Cumberland, fifteenth reunion, Cincinnati, Ohio, 1883*, Cincinnati, 1884 (obituary), pp. 209–225.

33. W. T. Sherman interview, *New York Tribune*, August 2, 1885.

34. Elizabeth Hare interview, *Philadelphia Times*, July 26, 1885.

35. U. S. Grant punishments: Monthly consolidated reports of weekly class reports, including conduct roll, United States Military Academy Papers, War Department Records, National Archives; Grant's textbooks, etc.: U. S. Grant Account Book, 1839–1843, Huntington Library.

36. Maury, p. 22.

37. Maury, p. 59.

38. Anecdote of Jackson: Maury, pp. 22–23; Henry Alexander White, *Stonewall Jackson*, Philadelphia, 1909, pp. 27–32; letter by "P" in "Jackson at West Point," Annals of war scrapbook, clipping from *Philadelphia Times* [1887–1888?], possession author.

39. *Around the world,* vol. 2, p. 210.

40. Horace H. Thomas, "What I saw under a flag of truce," *Military essays and recollections,* papers read before the commandery of the state of Illinois, Military order of the loyal legion of the United States, Chicago, 1891, vol. 1, p. 143.

41. Erasmus Darwin Keyes, *Fifty years' observation of men and events, civil and military,* New York, 1885, p. 198; *Mark Twain's autobiography,* with an introduction by Albert Bigelow Paine, 2v., New York and London, 1924, vol. 1, pp. 25–26.

42. Maury, p. 39.

43. Frank Abial Flower, *Life of Matthew Hale Carpenter. A view of the honor and achievements that, in the American republic, are the fruits of well-directed ambition and persistent industry.* Madison, Wis., 1884, pp. 40–43. Benjamin Perley Poore, *Perley's reminiscences of sixty years in the national metropolis,* 2v., Philadelphia, 1886, vol. 2, p. 310.

44. George Edward Pickett, *The heart of a soldier as revealed in the intimate letters of Genl. George E. Pickett,* New York, 1913, p. 3; La Salle Corbell Pickett (Mrs. General G. E. Pickett), "General George E. Pickett," *Southern Historical Society papers,* vol. 24, Richmond, 1896, p. 151.

45. *Memoirs,* p. 32; "Grant at West Point," *Army and Navy Journal,* June 13, 1903, p. 1038.

46. W. T. Sherman in *Society of the Army of the Cumberland, ninth reunion, Utica, N. Y., 1868–1875,* Cincinnati, 1876, p. 56.

47. French, pp. 14–15.

48. "Professor D. H. Mahan" (obituary), *Army and Navy Journal,* October 7, 1871, pp. 119–120; "The cadet life of Grant and Sherman" (Letter of D. H. Mahan, March 8, 1866), *Army and Navy Journal,* March 31, 1866, p. 507.

49. Richardson, p. 93; Garland, p. 46; Burr, p. 185.

50. Ringwalt, pp. 12–13.

51. Horace Porter, *Campaigning with Grant,* New York, 1897, pp. 341–342.

52. Post Order Books, United States Military Academy Library.

53. Hamilton quoted in Richardson, pp. 92–93.

54. James B. Fry, "An acquaintance with Grant," *North American Review* 141(July–December 1885)540. Height of Grant's jump with York: Garland, p. 51; Richardson, p. 92.

55. Benjamin Perley Poore, *The life and public services of Ambrose E. Burnside, — soldier, — citizen, — statesman,* Providence, 1882, pp. 26–27.

56. W. T. Sherman interview, *New York Tribune,* August 2, 1885.

57. U. H. Grant to Messrs. Carey and Hart, April 8, 1843, ALS, Illinois State Historical Library.

58. Ingalls interview, *New York Herald,* April 7, 1885.

59. *Memoirs*, pp. 29, 35–36.
60. U. S. Grant Account Book, 1839–1843, Huntington Library; Richardson, p. 86.
61. *Memoirs*, p. 30.

CHAPTER SIX

1. Adjutant General's Correspondence, War Department Records, National Archives.
2. *Memoirs*, p. 30.
3. *Memoirs*, p. 65.
4. *Around the world*, vol. 2, p. 278; Horace Greeley, *The American conflict: a history of the great rebellion in the United States of America, 1860–[65]*, 2v., Hartford, 1864–1866, vol. 1, pp. 158–159.
5. Anecdote uniform and sword: *Memoirs*, pp. 30–31; James Grant Wilson, p. 106.
6. Date Grant's arrival: Regimental Reports, War Department Records, National Archives. Anecdote Buell, temperance: Ethan Allen Hitchcock, *Fifty years in camp and field; diary of Major-General Ethan Allen Hitchcock*, ed. by W. A. Croffut, New York and London, 1909, pp. 180–184 (cited hereafter as "Hitchcock").
7. Anecdotes of Buchanan: Burr, p. 91; Emma Dent Casey quoted in "Grant in civil life before war," *Army and Navy Journal*, May 2, 1908, p. 938. U. S. Grant's assignment: Regimental Reports, War Department Records, National Archives. Ewell quoted: Ewell, pp. 40–41, 48, 52–53.
8. *Memoirs*, p. 36.
9. Emma Dent Casey, "When Grant went a courtin'," typewritten MS.
10. Description of Dent family: Emma Dent Casey, "When Grant went a courtin'," typewritten MS; Emma Dent Casey, "When Grant wooed and won Julia Dent," *Sunday Magazine*, clippings; *Memoirs*, p. 33; Richardson, pp. 95–96. The Grant-Dent families: from Professor Gustave Anjou's compilation, privately printed, no date, Missouri Historical Society; John Thomas Scharf, *History of Saint Louis city and county, from the earliest periods to the present day*, 2v., Philadelphia, 1883, vol. 1, p. 351; Mary Robinson quoted in *St. Louis Republican*, July 24, 1885.
11. Anecdotes O'Fallon family: John Fletcher Darby, *Personal recollections of many prominent people whom I have known, and of events — especially of those relating to the history of St. Louis — during the first half of the present century*, St. Louis, 1880, pp. 146–148; William Hyde and Howard L. Conard, eds., *Encyclopedia of the history of St. Louis, a compendium of history and biography for ready reference*, 4v., New York, 1899, vol. 3, pp. 1661–1665.
12. Emma Dent Casey, "When Grant went a courtin'," typewritten MS.; *Memoirs*, p. 33; Longstreet interview in *New York Times*, July 24.

1885, p. 6; slave quoted in John W. Emerson, "Grant's life in the West and his Mississippi Valley campaigns," *Midland Monthly Magazine,* November 1896, p. 388 (cited hereafter as "Emerson, *Midland Monthly*").

13. Emma Dent Casey, "When Grant went a courtin'," typewritten MS.
14. Longstreet interview in *New York Times,* July 24, 1885, p. 6.
15. Emma Dent Casey, "When Grant went a courtin'," typewritten MS.
16. Burr, pp. 91–92.
17. Emerson, *Midland Monthly,* November 1896, pp. 392–394.
18. *Memoirs,* p. 37; Hitchcock, p. 185; Ashbel Woodward, *Life of General Nathaniel Lyon,* Hartford, Conn., 1862, p. 63 (cited hereafter as "Woodward, *Lyon*").
19. Mrs. Dent quoted by U. S. Grant, Jr., in Galbreath, p. 286. U. S. Grant's leave: *Memoirs,* p. 34; Post Reports, Jefferson Barracks, and Camp Salubrity, 1844, War Department Records, National Archives.
20. U. S. Grant's courtship: *Memoirs,* pp. 34–35; Emma Dent Casey, "When Grant wooed and won Julia Dent," *Sunday Magazine,* clipping; Emma Dent Casey, "When Grant went a courtin'," typewritten MS.; Julia Dent Grant quoted in Foster Coates, "The courtship of General Grant," *Ladies' Home Journal,* October, 1890, p. 4; Mary Robinson quoted in *St. Louis Republican,* July 24, 1885.
21. Emma Dent Casey, "When Grant went a courtin'," typewritten MS.; Jeremiah Chaplin, ed., *Words of our hero, Ulysses Grant,* with personal reminiscences by Jessie Benton Frémont, Boston, 1886, p. 65.
22. William Taussig, *Personal recollections of General Grant,* St. Louis, 1903 (Missouri Historical Society, Publications, vol. 2, no. 3), p. 2.
23. *Memoirs,* p. 35.
24. Although Grant in his *Memoirs,* p. 34, says he returned at the end of his leave, his letter to Mrs. Bailey (Burr, p. 94) and Ewell's Post Reports at Jefferson Barracks for May, 1844 (War Department Records, National Archives) indicate he must have arrived on May 15 or 16.

CHAPTER SEVEN

1. Burr, pp. 93–99.
2. Henry Edward Chambers, *Mississippi Valley beginnings; an outline of the early history of the earlier West,* New York and London, 1922, pp. 359–361 (cited hereafter as "Chambers").
3. Burr, p. 100.
4. Holman Hamilton, *Zachary Taylor, soldier of the republic,* Indianapolis, 1941, p. 101; Charles S. Hamilton, "Memoirs of the Mexican war," *Wisconsin Magazine of History* 14(1930–1931)66 (cited hereafter as "Charles S. Hamilton, 'Mexican war'").
5. Henry W. Webb, "The story of Jefferson Barracks," *New Mexico Historical Review,* 21(1946)197–198; [George Ballentine], *Adven-*

tures of an English soldier in the Mexican war, New York, 1860, pp. 28–29, 34–35 (cited hereafter as *"English soldier"*).

6. Burr, pp. 100–101; Maury, p. 29; Regimental Reports, Post Records, Camp Salubrity, War Department Records, National Archives.
7. *Memoirs*, p. 39.
8. Longstreet interview, *New York Times*, July 24, 1885, p. 6.
9. Chambers, p. 358.
10. Ingalls quoted, Burr, p. 101.
11. Chambers, p. 357.
12. Hitchcock, p. 187.
13. Chambers, pp. 357–358.
14. Grant's statement (*Memoirs*, p. 35) that his leave was for twenty days in May 1845 was erroneous if Regimental Records, Camp Salubrity Post Reports, in National Archives, were correct in marking him absent on leave from April 1 to May 6, 1845.
15. Foster Coates, "The courtship of General Grant," *Ladies' Home Journal*, October 1890, p. 4.
16. Emma Dent Casey, "When Grant went a courtin'," typewritten MS. Ulysses' news: U. S. Grant to Julia Dent, ALS, June 5, 1846, and September 6, 1846.
17. *Memoirs*, pp. 40–41.
18. *Memoirs*, p. 41.
19. Anecdote of Whistler and Indian: James Grant Wilson in Milo Milton Quaife, comp., *The development of Chicago, 1674–1914, shown in a series of contemporary original narratives*, Chicago, 1916, p. 67. Anecdote of Whistler in police court: Richardson, pp. 99–100.
20. Ephraim Kirby Smith, *To Mexico with Scott; letters of Captain E. Kirby Smith to his wife*, prepared for the press by his daughter, Emma Jerome Blackwood, Cambridge, Mass., 1917, pp. 17–18 (cited hereafter as "E. K. Smith"); *Memoirs*, p. 41.
21. *Memoirs*, p. 42.
22. E. K. Smith, p. 23; *Memoirs*, p. 49.
23. *Memoirs*, p. 50.
24. McLaws interview, *New York Times*, July 24, 1885, p. 6.
25. *Memoirs*, pp. 37, 45.
26. *Around the world*, vol. 2, pp. 447–448.
27. Hitchcock, pp. 198, 203.
28. *Memoirs*, p. 47.
29. Longstreet in *New York Times*, July 24, 1885, p. 6; Helen Dortch Longstreet, *Lee and Longstreet at high tide; Gettysburg in the light of the official records*, Gainesville, Ga., 1904, pp. 140–141.
30. John Russell Young, *Men and memories; personal reminiscences*, ed. by his wife, May D. Russell Young, 2v., New York, 1901, vol. 2, p. 479.

31. Diary of Henry M. Judah, MS., Library of Congress (cited here-after as "Judah diary").

32. *Memoirs*, pp. 50–51.

33. Helen Dortch Longstreet, *Lee and Longstreet at high tide . . .*, Gainesville, Ga., 1904, p. 144; Grant to Lowe, *Chicago Tribune*, August 14, 1885, p. 10 (cited hereafter as "Grant to Lowe").

34. George Gordon Meade, ed., *The life and letters of George Gordon Meade, major-general United States army*, 2v., New York, 1913, vol. 1, pp. 43–44 (cited hereafter as "Meade").

CHAPTER EIGHT

1. *Memoirs*, p. 53.

2. *Memoirs*, p. 55.

3. Cadmus Marcellus Wilcox, *History of the Mexican war*, ed. by his niece, Mary Rachel Wilcox, Washington, 1892, p. 33 (cited here-after as "Wilcox").

4. *Memoirs*, p. 54.

5. [Luther Giddings], *Sketches of the campaign in Northern Mexico, in eighteen hundred forty-six and seven. By an officer of the First regiment of Ohio volunteers.* New York, 1853, pp. 71–72, 78 (cited hereafter as "Giddings"). Zachary Taylor, *Letters of Zachary Taylor from the battle-fields of the Mexican war; reprinted from the originals in the collection of Mr. William K. Bixby, of St. Louis, Mo.*, Rochester, N. Y., 1908, p. 6 (cited hereafter as "*Taylor Letters*"); Charles S. Hamilton, "Mexican war," p. 90.

6. *American Star*, Mexico City, May 2, 1848.

7. Charles S. Hamilton, "Mexican war," p. 79 ff.; William W. Belknap, "The obedience and courage of the private soldier, and the fortitude of officers and men in field, in hospital, and in prison, with some inci-dents of the war," *War sketches and incidents*, as related by com-panions of the Iowa commandery, Military order of the loyal legion of the United States, Des Moines, 1893, vol. 1, p. 163.

8. *Memoirs*, p. 101; John Sedgwick, *Correspondence of John Sedgwick, major-general*, 2v., New York, 1902–1903, vol. 1, p. 18 (cited here-after as "Sedgwick"). Sketch of Samuel Ringgold: *Appleton's cyclo-paedia of American biography*, ed. by James Grant Wilson and John Fiske, vol. 5., New York, 1888, p. 257. Description of uniforms: George Deas, "Reminiscences of the campaign of the Rio Grande," *Historical Magazine*, January 1870, p. 20.

9. *Memoirs*, p. 55.

10. Wilcox, p. 118; Giddings, p. 76.

11. Bragg as disciplinarian, testimony Lovell H. Rousseau: *The war of the rebellion: a compilation of the official records of the Union and Confederate Armies*, ser. 1, vol. 16, pt. 1, Washington, 1886, p. 348.

Bragg on The Great Western: "The heroine of Fort Brown," *Spirit of the Times,* New York, July 25, 1846, quoting *New Orleans Picayune.*

12. Painful march: N. S. Jarvis, "An army surgeon's notes of frontier service — Mexican war. Extracts from the diary of his father, contributed by Captain N. S. Jarvis," *Journal of the Military Service Institution of the United States,* 40(1907)p. 441. (Cited hereafter as "Jarvis, 'Army surgeon's notes'"). Grant quoted: Grant to Lowe.

13. Grant on wild mustangs: *Memoirs,* pp. 55–56. Mejía and diplomatic negotiations: Wilcox, pp. 35–36; James Daniel Richardson, comp., *A compilation of the messages and papers of the presidents, 1789–1897,* 10v., Washington, 1900, vol. 4, p. 439.

14. Hitchcock, p. 211; "The heroine of Fort Brown," *Spirit of the Times,* New York, July 25, 1846, quoting *New Orleans Picayune.*

15. *Memoirs,* p. 56; Thomas Bangs Thorpe, *Our army on the Rio Grande. Being a short account of the important events transpiring from the time of the removal of the "Army of occupation" from Corpus Christi, to the surrender of Matamoros.* . . . Philadelphia, 1846, pp. 13–14 (cited hereafter as "Thorpe").

16. E. K. Smith, Hitchcock, p. 212; George Deas, "Reminiscences of the campaign of the Rio Grande," *Historical Magazine,* January 1870, p. 22.

17. Hitchcock, p. 216.

18. E. K. Smith, pp. 33–34.

19. [John Blount Robertson], *Reminiscences of a campaign in Mexico; by a member of the "Bloody-First." Preceded by a short sketch of the history and condition of Mexico from her revolution down to the war with the United States.* Nashville, Tenn., 1849, p. 116 (cited hereafter as "Robertson").

20. Jarvis, "Army surgeon's notes," 40(1907)445; Hitchcock, p. 217.

21. Meade, vol. 1, p. 53.

22. Philip Norbourne Barbour, *Journals of the late Brevet Major Philip Norbourne Barbour . . . and his wife, Martha Isabella Hopkins Barbour, written during the war with Mexico — 1846,* ed. with foreword by Rhoda van Bibber Tanner Doubleday, New York and London, 1936, pp. 27–28 (cited hereafter as "Barbour").

23. House documents, vol. 7, 30th Congress, 1st session, 1847–1848, Executive document 60, pp. 303–304; Thorpe, p. 25.

24. Meade, vol. 1, p. 53; Jarvis, "Army surgeon's notes," 40(1907)447.

25. Jarvis, "Army surgeon's notes," 40(1907)448, 450.

26. George Archibald McCall, *Letters from the frontiers. Written during a period of thirty years' service in the army of the United States,* Philadelphia, 1868, pp. 441–442; Jarvis, "Army surgeon's notes," 40(1907)450–451.

27. Anecdotes Thornton: *Niles' National Register,* October 2, 1847, p. 73, quoting *Richmond Republican.*

28. Giddings, p. 15; Wilcox, pp. 47–48; Jarvis, "Army surgeon's notes," 41(1907)90–92.
29. Grant to Lowe.
30. Explanation of "greaser": *Army and Navy Journal*, January 24, 1891, p. 372; Giddings, p. 59; *Niles' National Register*, September 26, 1846, p. 54.
31. *Memoirs*, p. 58.
32. James Grant Wilson in Milo Milton Quaife, compiler, *The development of Chicago, 1674–1914, shown in a series of contemporary original narratives*, Chicago, 1916, pp. 66–67.
33. Taylor on bayonet: Wilcox, p. 51.
34. Grant to Lowe.
35. George Archibald McCall, *Letters from the frontiers. Written during a period of thirty years' service in the army of the United States*. Philadelphia, 1868, pp. 449–450; *Memoirs*, p. 59.
36. *Memoirs*, p. 59.
37. *Ibid.*
38. Ulysses to Julia: ALS, May 11, 1846; Grant to Lowe.
39. Grant to Lowe.
40. *Memoirs*, p. 60.
41. Thorpe, p. 81.
42. Grant to Lowe.

CHAPTER NINE

1. Sedgwick, vol. 1, p. 16.
2. Grant to Lowe.
3. Thorpe, pp. 108–109.
4. E. K. Smith, p. 53.
5. Ulysses to Julia: ALS, May 11, 1846.
6. *Memoirs*, pp. 61–62.
7. Thorpe, p. 127.
8. George Archibald McCall, *Letters from the frontiers. Written during a period of thirty years' service in the army of the United States*. Philadelphia, 1868, p. 448. *Around the world*, vol. 2, p. 162; *Niles' National Register*, September 26, 1846, p. 58; George Deas, "Reminiscences of the campaign of the Rio Grande," *Historical Magazine*, January 1870, p. 20, February 1870, p. 103.
9. Ulysses to Julia: June 5, 1846.
10. Donn Piatt, *General George H. Thomas, a critical biography*, with concluding chapters by Henry V. Boynton, Cincinnati, 1893, p. 67.
11. *Memoirs*, p. 64; Major John F. Lacey, "Major-General Frederick Steele," *Annals of Iowa*, 3d. s., 3(1897–1899)437–438.
12. *Memoirs*, p. 62; *Around the world*, vol. 2, pp. 162–163.
13. *Taylor Letters*, p. 53; Charles S. Hamilton, "Mexican war," p. 75; Barbour, p. 70.

14. "Rough and Ready" nickname: Daniel H. Hill, "The real Stonewall Jackson," *Century Magazine*, 47(November 1893–April 1894)623. Taylor quoted: *Taylor Letters*, p. 4.
15. George Deas, "Reminiscences of the campaign of the Rio Grande," *Historical Magazine*, April 1870, p. 237; Barbour, pp. 66–67.
16. Richardson, p. 103; Barbour, pp. 88–89.
17. *Memoirs*, p. 64.
18. Grant to Lowe.
19. Robertson, p. 166.
20. Description of Mexican women: *Niles' National Register*, September 26, 1846, p. 55; Giddings, p. 58; Diary of Joshua E. Jackson, MS., Illinois State Historical Library; Richard McSherry, *El Puchero; or, a mixed dish from Mexico, embracing General Scott's campaign, with sketches of military life, in field and camp, of the character of the country, manners and ways of the people, etc.*, Philadelphia, 1850, p. 157 (cited hereafter as "McSherry, *El Puchero*"); [Benjamin F. Scribner], *Camp life of a volunteer. A campaign in Mexico, or a glimpse at life in camp.* By "one who has seen the elephant," Philadelphia, 1847, p. 29; Gomez quoted: *Niles' National Register*, April 10, 1847, pp. 87–88.
21. Foster Coates, "The courtship of General Grant," *Ladies' Home Journal*, October 1890, p. 4; Emma Dent Casey, "When Grant went a courtin'," typewritten MS.
22. Ulysses to Julia: June 5, 1846.
23. John Russell Young, *Men and memories; personal reminiscences*, ed. by his wife, May D. Russell Young, 2v., New York, 1901, vol. 2, p. 475; Grant to Lowe; Sedgwick, vol. 1, p. 37.
24. Albert Gallatin Brackett, *General Lane's brigade in Central Mexico*, Cincinnati, 1854, pp. 152–153 (cited hereafter as "Brackett").
25. *Around the world*, vol. 2, p. 448; *Memoirs*, p. 64.
26. "Mexican war letters of Col. William Bowen Campbell, of Tennessee, written to Governor David Campbell, of Virginia, 1846–1847," *Tennessee Historical Magazine*, 1(1915)139, 142 (cited hereafter as "Campbell").
27. *Taylor Letters*, p. 24; Meade, vol. 1, pp. 161–162.
28. *The "high private," with a full and exciting history of the New York volunteers . . . including the mysteries and miseries of the Mexican war*, by "Corporal of the guard," New York, 1848, p. 8.
29. *Taylor Letters*, p. 8.
30. John Reese Kenly, *Memoirs of a Maryland volunteer. War with Mexico, in the years 1846-7-8*. Philadelphia, 1873, pp. 47–48 (cited hereafter as "Kenly"). *Niles' National Register*, September 19, 1846, p. 40; October 10, 1846, p. 88.
31. *Niles' National Register*, August 22, 1846, p. 386, November 6, 1847, p. 152; Brackett, p. 35.
32. George C. Furber, *The twelve months volunteer; or, Journal of a*

private, in the Tennessee regiment of cavalry, in the campaign, in Mexico, 1846–7; etc., Cincinnati, 1848, pp. 428–432 (cited hereafter as "Furber"); Robertson, pp. 71–72.

33. Meade, vol. 1, p. 94: *Niles' National Register*, October 2, 1847, pp. 73–74; Robertson, p. 96; Giddings, p. 81.

34. Taylor quoted: *Niles' National Register*, October 3, 1846, p. 67. Eastman quoted: *Niles' National Register*, October 24, 1846, p. 119.

35. Sedgwick, vol. 1, pp. 30–37; Diary of Joshua E. Jackson, MS., Illinois State Historical Library; Campbell, pp. 140–141; Giddings, p. 83.

36. *Niles' National Register*, October 3, 1846, p. 67, December 26, 1846, p. 266.

37. Carl Sandburg, *Abraham Lincoln, the prairie years*, 2v., New York, 1926, vol. 1, p. 285.

38. Campbell, p. 142; Wilcox, pp. 113–114; Brackett, p. 24.

39. John Francis Hamtramck Claiborne, *Life and correspondence of John A. Quitman, major-general, U. S. A., and governor of the state of Mississippi*, 2v., New York, 1860, vol. 1, pp. 235, 241, 271 (cited hereafter as "Claiborne").

40. Sketches of Hamer: *Biographical directory of the American Congress 1774–1927*, Government Printing Office, 1928, p. 1051 (House document, 783, 69th Congress, 2nd session); Beers, p. 350; and pt. 5, "Biographical sketches," pp. 47–48. Data on Hamer: Daniel Ammen, *The old navy and the new . . . with an appendix of personal letters from General Grant*, Philadelphia, 1891, p. 22; *Niles' National Register*, July 25, 1846, p. 326; Giddings, p. 23; William Seaton Henry, *Campaign sketches of the war with Mexico*, New York, 1847, p. 128; Campbell, p. 142.

41. Emerson, *Midland Monthly*, January 1897, p. 34.

CHAPTER TEN

1. Taylor's equipment: House documents, vol. 7, 30th Congress, 1st session, 1847–1848, Executive document 60, pp. 557–558, 674, 679–684. Creation of post of Regimental Quartermaster: U. S. Grant to Major F. A. Winship, February 10, 1849, Adjutant General's Papers, War Department Records, National Archives.

2. Coppée, p. 25.

3. Coal imports: Campbell, p. 136.

4. Emerson, *Midland Monthly*, January 1897, p. 36.

5. William H. Powell, History of the organization and movement of the Fourth Regiment of Infantry, 1871, MS. (cited hereafter as "Powell, Fourth Regiment); *Memoirs*, pp. 62–63.

6. Grant quoted: *Memoirs*, p. 66. Hays quoted: Emerson, *Midland Monthly*, May 1897, p. 432. Ailments of mules: House documents, vol. 7, 30th Congress, 1st session, 1847–1848, Executive document 60, p. 737.

7. Giddings, pp. 143–144.
8. *Taylor Letters*, pp. 59, 62.
9. Sedgwick, vol. 1, p. 16.
10. Giddings, pp. 152–159.
11. *Memoirs*, p. 68.
12. Grant and Hoskins: *Memoirs*, p. 69. Anecdote of Twiggs: Kenly, p. 119.
13. *Memoirs*, p. 69; Campbell, p. 144; Claiborne, vol. 1, pp. 245–246; Robert McNutt McElroy, *Jefferson Davis; the unreal and the real*, 2v., New York and London, 1937, vol. 1, p. 83.
14. Kenly, p. 119.
15. French, p. 62; Giddings, pp. 168–169.
16. Giddings, p. 186; Robertson, pp. 145–147; Kenly, p. 120.
17. Giddings, p. 184; Emerson, *Midland Monthly*, January 1897, p. 40; Robertson, p. 146.
18. Claiborne, vol. 1, pp. 246–247; *Niles' National Register*, October 17, 1846, p. 103; Meade, vol. 1, pp. 165–166.
19. Sedgwick, vol. 1, p. 33.
20. *Memoirs*, pp. 72–73; House documents, vol. 3, 30th Congress, 1st session, 1847–1848, Executive document 17, p. 5.
21. Meade, vol. 1, p. 151; *Taylor Letters*, pp. 61–62; Roswell Sabine Ripley, *The war with Mexico*, 2v., New York, 1849, vol. 1, pp. 240–242.
22. Richardson, p. 112.
23. *Niles' National Register*, October 9, 1847, p. 88, quoting *New York Courier*; Brackett, p. 207.
24. George Deas, "Reminiscences of the campaign of the Rio Grande," *Historical Magazine*, May 1870, p. 315; *Memoirs*, p. 73.

CHAPTER ELEVEN

1. Wilcox, pp. 110–117; Donn Piatt, *General George H. Thomas, a critical biography*, with concluding chapters by Henry V. Boynton, Cincinnati, 1893, p. 67.
2. John Clifford Pemberton, *Pemberton, defender of Vicksburg*, Chapel Hill, 1942, p. 14.
3. Wilcox, pp. 119–121.
4. Wilcox, pp. 118–119; Maury, p. 29.
5. Diary of Joshua E. Jackson, MS., Illinois State Historical Library.
6. Claiborne, vol. 1, p. 274.
7. Anecdotes of Hamer: Henry Howe, *Historical collections of Ohio*, 3v. in 2, Columbus, 1889–1891, vol. 1, p. 331; Emerson, *Midland Monthly*, January, 1897, pp. 34–35; Giddings, pp. 243–246; *Memoirs*, pp. 64–65.
8. Emerson, *Midland Monthly*, February, 1897, p. 139.

9. House documents, vol. 7, 30th Congress, 1st session, 1847–1848, Executive document 60, p. 570.
10. Emerson, *Midland Monthly*, February, 1897, pp. 138–139.
11. *Memoirs*, p. 108.
12. *Diario del Gobierno*, quoted in *Niles' National Register*, October 16, 1847, pp. 103–104; *El Monitor Republicana*, January 22, 1847.
13. *Niles National Register*, June 19, 1847, p. 251.
14. *Diario del Gobierno*, quoted in *Niles' National Register*, October 16, 1847, p. 104.
15. Giddings, pp. 275–277; Sedgwick, vol. 1, p. 37.
16. J. Jacobs Oswandel, *Notes of the Mexican war 1846–47–48. Comprising incidents, adventures and everyday proceedings and letters while with the United States army in the Mexican war.* Philadelphia, 1885, p. 230 (cited hereafter as "Oswandel"). *English soldier*, p. 255.
17. Gustavus W. Smith, *Company "A," corps of engineers, U. S. A., 1846–'48, in the Mexican war*, The Battalion Press, 1896, pp. 10–12, 13–15.
18. *Army and Navy Journal*, September 5, 1863, p. 23; *Niles' National Register*, October 9, 1847, p. 88.
19. Robertson, p. 205; Furber, p. 145.
20. *Memoirs*, pp. 76–77.
21. Wilcox, p. 193.
22. *Memoirs*, p. 77; Judah diary.
23. *Memoirs*, p. 75.
24. Robert Anderson, *An artillery officer in the Mexican war, 1846–7; letters of Robert Anderson, captain 3rd artillery, U. S. A.*, New York and London, 1911, p. 49.
25. Maury, p. 29; Diary of Joshua E. Jackson, MS., Illinois State Historical Library.
26. Claiborne, vol. 1, p. 288.
27. Scott quoted in Charles Winslow Elliott, *Winfield Scott, the soldier and the man*, New York, 1937, p. 448 (cited hereafter as "Elliott, *Scott*").
28. Ewell, pp. 63–64.
29. Daniel H. Hill, "The real Stonewall Jackson," *Century Magazine*, 47(November 1893–April 1894)624.
30. *Memoirs*, pp. 77–78.
31. Loyall Farragut, *The Life of David Glasgow Farragut, first admiral of the United States navy, embodying his journal and letters*, New York, 1879, pp. 156–164.
32. Robertson, p. 235.
33. Winfield Scott, *Memoirs of Lieut.-General Scott, LL.D.*, 2v., New York, 1864, vol. 2, p. 419 (cited hereafter as "Scott's *Memoirs*"). Address by Meade in *Report of the Proceedings of the fifth annual meeting of the Society of the Army of the Tennessee, held at Cincinnati, Ohio, April 6th and 7th, 1871*, Cincinnati, 1872, p. 55.

34. Maury, p. 32; Gustavus W. Smith, *Company "A," corps of engineers, U. S. A., 1846–'48, in the Mexican war,* The Battalion Press, 1896, pp. 19–20.

CHAPTER TWELVE

1. Hamilton Basso, *Beauregard, the great Creole,* New York, 1933, pp. 5–6, 17–18.
2. Raphael Semmes, *Service afloat and ashore during the Mexican war,* Cincinnati, 1851, p. 140 (cited hereafter as "Semmes, *Service afloat and ashore*").
3. Emerson, *Midland Monthly,* March, 1897, p. 221.
4. "Brevet Major-General Gordon Granger," *Society of the Army of the Cumberland, fifteenth reunion, Cincinnati, Ohio, 1883,* Cincinnati, 1884 (obituary), p. 211.
5. *Spirit of the Times,* New York, March 27, 1847, p. 49.
6. Wilcox, p. 262; *English soldier,* pp. 162–163.
7. Wilcox, p. 262; Scott's *Memoirs,* vol. 2, pp. 422–423.
8. *Congressional Globe,* February 11, 1847 (Appendix, p. 217).
9. *Niles' National Register,* April 24, 1847, p. 128, quoting *Baltimore Clipper.*
10. *Niles' National Register,* April 17, 1847, p. 107 ff.; Semmes, *Service afloat and ashore,* pp. 137–138; Wilcox, p. 256.
11. E. Parker Scammon, "A chapter of the Mexican war," *Magazine of American History,* 14(July–December 1885)569–570.
12. *Niles' National Register,* May 8, 1847, p. 150.
13. Oswandel, pp. 97–99.
14. *Memoirs,* p. 85.
15. Scott's orders for invasion, and his proclamation to the Mexican people: House documents, vol. 7, 30th Congress, 1st session, 1847–1848, Executive document 60, pp. 912, 921, 935, 937.
16. *American Star,* Mexico City, May 28, 1848.
17. Armistead Lindsay Long, *Memoirs of Robert E. Lee; his military and personal history . . . Together with incidents relating to his private life,* collected and edited with the assistance of Marcus J. Wright, London, 1886, pp. 69–70.
18. E. Parker Scammon, "A chapter of the Mexican war," *Magazine of American History,* 14(July–December, 1885)573–574.
19. Wilcox, p. 318.
20. E. K. Smith, pp. 133–134; *Niles' National Register,* July 10, 1847, p. 298, quoting *New Orleans Picayune.*
21. Judah diary.
22. Johnston's wound: *Niles' National Register,* May 22, 1847, p. 183.
23. Garland, p. 87.
24. Scott's *Memoirs,* vol. 2, pp. 445–448, 450–451; Garland, p. 87.
25. Robertson, pp. 252–253.

26. Wilcox, p. 296; Maury, pp. 38–39.
27. Ezra M. Prince, "The fourth Illinois Infantry in the war with Mexico," *Transactions of the Illinois State Historical Society . . . 1906* (Publication no. 11, Illinois State Historical Library), Springfield, 1906, pp. 183–184; Oswandel, pp. 223–224.
28. *Niles' National Register*, May 15, 1847, p. 164, quoting correspondent of *Vera Cruz Eagle* writing April 20, 1847.
29. William Starr Myers, ed., *The Mexican war diary of George B. McClellan*, Princeton, 1917, p. 91; Robertson, p. 255; Oswandel, p. 145; Judah diary.
30. Garland, p. 88.
31. Wilcox, p. 298.
32. Judah diary.
33. Roswell Sabine Ripley, *The war with Mexico*, 2v., New York, 1849, vol. 2, p. 85.
34. Garland, pp. 87–88.
35. *Memoirs*, pp. 75–76.
36. Oswandel, p. 157.
37. *English soldier*, pp. 212–213; Oswandel, pp. 154–155.
38. Robertson, pp. 261, 263–264; Brackett, p. 141.
39. *Memoirs*, pp. 83–84; Wilcox, p. 307.
40. *English soldier*, p. 221.
41. Garland, pp. 91–92; *Memoirs*, pp. 100–101.
42. Wilcox, pp. 307–308; Scott's *Memoirs*, vol. 2, p. 455.
43. Wilcox, pp. 310–312.

CHAPTER THIRTEEN

1. Wilcox, p. 311; Judah diary.
2. Judah diary.
3. Judah diary; *Memoirs*, pp. 83–84; Hitchcock, p. 258.
4. Hitchcock, pp. 258–259.
5. *Memoirs*, p. 84.
6. *Ibid.*
7. Wilcox, p. 336.
8. *Niles' National Register*, October 2, 1847, pp. 65, 77; Wilcox, pp. 320–325.
9. Richardson, p. 126; A. E. Watrous, "Grant as his son saw him," magazine clipping, possession author.
10. Semmes, *Service afloat and ashore*, pp. 266–271; McSherry, *El Puchero*, pp. 92–94, 98; Brackett, pp. 138, 143.
11. Judah diary.
12. *Ibid.*
13. Wilcox, p. 312.
14. Emerson, *Midland Monthly*, April 1897, pp. 317–318.
15. Scott's *Memoirs*, vol. 2, p. 460; Oswandel, p. 331.

16. Scott's *Memoirs*, vol. 2, p. 466, note.
17. Wilcox, pp. 338–339; Scott's *Memoirs*, vol. 2, p. 460.
18. Scott's *Memoirs*, vol. 2, p. 530; Wilcox, p. 339.
19. Semmes, *Service afloat and ashore*, p. 321.
20. Wilcox, p. 341; Semmes, *Service afloat and ashore*, pp. 323, 325.
21. Scott's *Memoirs*, vol. 2, p. 467.
22. Semmes, *Service afloat and ashore*, pp. 348–349, 353.
23. Emerson, *Midland Monthly*, April 1897, pp. 318–319.
24. Emerson, *Midland Monthly*, May 1897, p. 433; *Memoirs*, p. 100.
25. Semmes, *Service afloat and ashore*, p. 350.
26. Hitchcock, p. 276.
27. *Niles' National Register*, October 2, 1847, p. 73; Judah diary.
28. Emerson, *Midland Monthly*, April 1897, pp. 320–321.
29. Douglas Southall Freeman, *R. E. Lee, a biography*, 4v., New York and London, 1934–1935, vol. 1, p. 272; Semmes, *Service afloat and ashore*, p. 379.
30. Charles S. Hamilton, "Reminiscences of the old army forty years ago," in Military order of the loyal legion of the United States — Wisconsin commandery, *War papers read before the commandery of the state of Wisconsin*, Milwaukee, Wis., 1891, p. 35; *American Star*, Mexico City, April 29, 1848.
31. Maury, p. 43.
32. Maury, pp. 40–41; Douglas Southall Freeman, *R. E. Lee, a biography*, 4v., New York and London, 1934–1935, vol. 1, p. 266.
33. Notebook of James Edward Kelly, MS.
34. Roy Franklin Nichols, *Franklin Pierce, Young Hickory of the Granite Hills*, Philadelphia and London, 1931, p. 161 (cited hereafter as "Nichols, *Pierce*").
35. Scott's *Memoirs*, vol. 2, pp. 481–482.

CHAPTER FOURTEEN

1. E. K. Smith, pp. 201–203.
2. Ewell, p. 72; Woodward, *Lyon*, pp. 117–118.
3. Hitchcock, pp. 282–283; Nichols, *Pierce*, p. 163; Woodward, *Lyon*, p. 117.
4. Hitchcock, p. 282; Nichols, *Pierce*, p. 163.
5. Worth report, House documents, vol. 2, 30th Congress, 1st session, 1847–1848, Executive document 8, p. 319; Oswandel, p. 472.
6. Wilcox, pp. 394–395; Oswandel, pp. 471–472.
7. Thomas Kearny, *General Philip Kearny, battle soldier of five wars, including the conquest of the West by General Stephen Watts Kearny*, New York, 1937, pp. 96–110; Ewell, p. 72.
8. Emerson, *Midland Monthly*, May 1897, p. 433.
9. Lee report, House documents, vol. 2, 30th Congress, 1st session, 1847–1848, Executive document 8, Appendix, p. 52.

10. Claiborne, vol. 1, p. 394.
11. *Memoirs,* p. 92.
12. Hitchcock, p. 297; Sedgwick, vol. 1, p. 131.
13. House documents, vol. 7, 30th Congress, 1st session, 1847–1848, Executive document 60, pp. 1074–1075.
14. Richardson, p. 121; *Memoirs,* p. 93.
15. Ringwalt, p. 59; *Philadelphia North American* quoted in *New York Tribune,* November 28, 1868.
16. Charles S. Hamilton, "Mexican war," p. 81; Hitchcock, pp. 297–298; Sedgwick, vol. 1, pp. 113, 138; Woodward, *Lyon,* p. 123.
17. Charles S. Hamilton, "Mexican war," pp. 79–80; biographical sketch of Martin Scott, *Appleton's cyclopaedia of American biography,* ed. by James Grant Wilson and John Fiske, vol. 5, New York, 1888, p. 438.
18. *American Star,* Mexico City, September 25, 1847.
19. *Diario del Gobierno,* quoted in *Niles' National Register,* October 16, 1847, pp. 103–104; McSherry, *El Puchero,* p. 92.
20. Oswandel, pp. 424–426; Elliott, *Scott,* pp. 528–529; Charles S. Hamilton, "Mexican war," p. 82.
21. *Niles' National Register,* October 16, 1847, pp. 103–104; Oswandel, pp. 427–428.
22. Charles S. Hamilton, "Mexican war," pp. 82–83.
23. Semmes, *Service afloat and ashore,* pp. 442–444.
24. *American Star,* Mexico City, April 12, 1848; Claiborne, vol. 1, pp. 353–355.
25. Mary Anna Jackson, *Life and letters of General Thomas J. Jackson (Stonewall Jackson),* New York, 1892, pp. 42–43; Worth's report, House documents, vol. 2, 30th Congress, 1st session, 1847–1848, Executive document 8, p. 391.
26. Pillow quoted: House documents, vol. 2, 30th Congress, 1st session, 1847–1848, Executive document 8, pp. 406–407; McSherry, *El Puchero,* p. 110.
27. *New York Courier,* quoted in *Niles' National Register,* October 30, 1847, p. 137; Elliott, *Scott,* p. 546. From portraits of the six cadets in National Museum of Mexico City, their names and ages were: Agustin Melgar, 18; Fernando Montes de Oca, 17; Francisco Excutia, 17; Francisco Marquez, 15; Vincente Suarez, 13; Juan Barrera and Teniente, 19.
28. "General Harney," *Journal of the United States Cavalry Association,* Fort Leavenworth, Kansas, March, 1890, pp. 1–8. Details of hanging: James Reilly, "An artilleryman's story," *Journal of the Military Service Institution of the United States,* 33(July–November 1903) 443–444.

CHAPTER FIFTEEN

1. *Memoirs*, p. 94.
2. Justin Harvey Smith, *The war with Mexico*, 2v., New York, 1919, vol. 2, pp. 408–409.
3. Grant quoted on emotions in battle: *Around the world*, vol. 2, p. 451. Sources for description of the fighting, unless otherwise specified in this chapter, are: House documents, vol. 2, 30th Congress, 1st session, 1847–1848, Executive document 8, W. R. Montgomery, appendix, pp. 182–183; Francis Lee, appendix, pp. 175–177; William J. Worth, pp. 391–395; Horace Brooks, appendix, pp. 174–175. House documents, vol. 7, 30th Congress, 1st session, 1847–1848, Executive document 60, John H. Gore, pp. 1071–1073. Senate documents, vol. 1, 30th Congress, 1st session, 1847–1848, Executive document 1, Thomas S. Jesup, pp. 543–551; John Garland, appendix, pp. 169–171; Gustavus W. Smith, appendix, pp. 167–169; John A. Quitman, pp. 409–420.
4. *Memoirs*, p. 95.
5. Sedgwick, vol. 1, pp. 129–130.
6. Worth, Garland, Pemberton and Grant in belfry incident: *Memoirs*, pp. 96–97; Emerson, *Midland Monthly*, April 1897, pp. 327–328.
7. *Memoirs*, p. 97.
8. Wilcox, p. 475; James Reilly, "An artilleryman's story," *Journal of the Military Service Institution of the United States*, 33 (July–November 1903) 444.
9. Captain Edwin E. Woodman, "Death and dishonor," *Glimpses of the nation's struggle*, 5th series, St. Paul, Minn., 1903, p. 306.
10. *Memoirs*, p. 97.
11. Scott in House documents, vol. 2, 30th Congress, 1st session, 1847–1848, Executive document 8, p. 383.
12. Semmes, *Service afloat and ashore*, p. 464.
13. Emerson, *Midland Monthly*, April 1897, p. 323.
14. Wilcox, p. 483.
15. *Memoirs*, pp. 100–101.
16. Wilcox, pp. 483–484.
17. Gustavus W. Smith, *Company "A," corps of engineers, U. S. A., 1846–'48, in the Mexican war*, The Battalion Press, 1896, pp. 54–56.
18. Emerson, *Midland Monthly*, April 1897, pp. 328–329.
19. Lee faints: Scott's *Memoirs*, vol. 2, pp. 533–534. Beauregard's fall: Hamilton Basso, *Beauregard, the great Creole*, New York, 1933, pp. 44–45.
20. *American Star*, Mexico City, December 9, 1847.
21. Kenly, p. 393; *North American*, Mexico City, October 15, 1847.
22. *Memoirs*, p. 99.
23. Theodore Lyman, *Meade's headquarters, 1863–1865; letters of Colo-*

nel Theodore Lyman from the wilderness to Appomattox, selected
and ed. by George R. Agassiz, Boston, 1922, p. 313.

24. Grant quoted, "I never asked for any position or any rank," evidently
referring to his whole military career: John H. Vincent, "The inner
life of Ulysses S. Grant," *The Chautauquan; a weekly newsmagazine,*
30(October 1899–March 1900)636. Longstreet quoted in Galbreath,
p. 268.

25. A. C. Avery, "Life and character of Lieutenant-General D. H. Hill,"
Southern Historical Society Papers, vol. 21, Richmond, Va., 1893,
p. 115.

26. Hooker address: *Society of the army of the Cumberland, fifth reunion, Detroit, 1871,* Cincinnati, 1872, p. 16. Sherman on Buell: *War
of the rebellion: a compilation of the official records of the Union
and Confederate armies,* 1st series, vol. 30, pt. 4, Washington, 1890,
p. 358.

CHAPTER SIXTEEN

1. Burr, pp. 107–108; Coppée, p. 25.
2. *Memoirs,* pp. 103–105; Hitchcock, p. 307.
3. Helen Dortch Longstreet, *Lee and Longstreet at high tide; Gettysburg in the light of the official records,* Gainesville, Ga., 1904, pp.
159–160; *Around the world,* vol. 2, p. 212; Mary Anna Jackson,
Life and letters of General Thomas J. Jackson (Stonewall Jackson),
New York, 1892, pp. 45–47.
4. McSherry, *El Puchero,* pp. 157–158, 161–162; *American Star,* Mexico
City, February 11, 1848.
5. *Niles' National Register,* January 1, 1848, p. 276.
6. Benjamin Perley Poore, *The life and public services of Ambrose E.
Burnside, — soldier, — citizen, — statesman,* Providence, 1882, pp. 26–
41.
7. McSherry, *El Puchero,* pp. 127–128; *Aztec Club of 1847; report of
a committee appointed by resolution adopted at the annual meeting,
October, 1887, and continued in 1888, to October, 1889,* Washington,
1890, pamphlet; Eunice Tripler, *Eunice Tripler: some notes of her
personal recollections,* New York, 1910, pp. 99–100 (cited hereafter
as "Tripler").
8. *Memoirs,* p. 89; Nichols, *Pierce,* p. 156; Galena correspondent in
St. Louis Globe Democrat, July 24, 1885.
9. Scott's *Memoirs,* vol. 2, p. 532.
10. *Memoirs,* p. 108.
11. *Niles' National Register,* December 25, 1847, p. 257, and December 4,
1847, pp. 214, 218.
12. *Niles' National Register,* December 25, 1847, pp. 261, 272.
13. Quotations from *American Star,* Mexico City, October 22, 1847 to
May 30, 1848; *North American,* Mexico City, September 29, 1847

to March 31, 1848; *Niles' National Register*, October 23, December 25, 1847, and January 22, 29, 1848.

14. *English soldier*, p. 274; McSherry, *El Puchero*, p. 160.
15. Scott to J. M. Clayton, March 4, 1852, quoted in Elliott, *Scott*, pp. 579–580.
16. Emerson, *Midland Monthly*, May 1897, p. 435.
17. Sedgwick, vol. 1, p. 166.
18. Hitchcock, p. 320.
19. *Memoirs*, pp. 104–105; Sedgwick, vol. 1, pp. 166, 175.
20. *Memoirs*, p. 105.
21. Burr, p. 110.
22. *Memoirs*, pp. 108–114; Horace Porter, *Campaigning with Grant*, New York, 1897, p. 489; Emerson, *Midland Monthly*, May 1897, pp. 435–437.
23. Ringwalt, p. 16.
24. *Memoirs*, pp. 105–107.
25. U. S. Grant to General R. Jones, May 19, 1848, Adjutant General's correspondence, War department records, National Archives; Hitchcock, p. 329; *American Star*, Mexico City, April 8, 1848.
26. *American Star*, Mexico City, May 25, 1848.
27. *Niles' National Register*, January 8, 1848, p. 304; Logan Uriah Reavis, *The life and military services of Gen. William Selby Harney*, St. Louis, 1878, p. 245.
28. *Niles' National Register*, August 2, 1848.
29. Church, *Grant*, p. 42.
30. Wilcox, pp. 551–552.
31. *Niles' National Register*, July 12, 1848.
32. Church, *Grant*, p. 42.
33. Church, *Grant*, p. 47; Major General U. S. Grant, III, "General Grant, Pater Familias," MS.
34. *Niles' National Register*, November 15, 1848.
35. Justin Harvey Smith, *The war with Mexico*, 2v., New York, 1919, vol. 2, pp. 318–319; [Assistant Surgeon J. J. Woodward], "Sickness and mortality of the army," *Army and Navy Journal*, October 10, 1863, p. 102.
36. Charles S. Hamilton, "Mexican war," p. 88; Roswell Sabine Ripley, *The war with Mexico*, 2v., New York, 1849, vol. 2, p. 78.
37. *Memoirs*, pp. 102, 116.
38. Powell, Fourth regiment; *Niles' National Register*, August 2, 1848.
39. Richardson, p. 128; Garland, pp. 109–110; Galbreath, p. 244.
40. Thomas Bailey, "Diary of the Mexican war," *Indiana Magazine of History*, 14(1918)145–147. Anecdote of Lane told author by Victor Murdock of Wichita, Kansas, and William Allen White of Emporia, Kansas.

CHAPTER SEVENTEEN

1. Emma Dent Casey, "When Grant went a courtin'," typewritten MS.; Mary Robinson in *St. Louis Republican*, July 24, 1885.
2. Emma Dent Casey, "When Grant went a courtin'," typewritten MS.; Powell, Fourth regiment.
3. Nidelet in *St. Louis Republican*, July 24, 1885.
4. Richardson, p. 128; Tripler, p. 95.
5. Garland, pp. 109–110.
6. *Ibid.*
7. Galbreath, p. 243.
8. Friend Palmer, *Early days in Detroit; papers written by General Friend Palmer, of Detroit, being his personal reminiscences of important events and descriptions of the city for over eighty years*, Detroit, 1906, pp. 408–409 (cited hereafter as "Palmer").
9. William Hyde and Howard L. Conard, eds., *Encyclopedia of the history of St. Louis, a compendium of history and biography for ready reference*, 4v., New York, 1899, vol. 3, p. 1666; G. Moxley Sorrel, *Recollections of a Confederate staff officer*, New York and Washington, 1905, p. 24.
10. Emma Dent Casey, "When Grant went a courtin'," typewritten MS.; Emerson, *Midland Monthly*, June 1897, pp. 497–498.
11. MS. letter, U. S. Grant to "Captain," September 12, 1848, Illinois State Historical Library.
12. *Niles' National Register*, September 20, 1848.
13. Richardson, p. 128.
14. Garland, p. 110; Richardson, p. 129.
15. Emma Dent Casey, "When Grant went a courtin'," typewritten MS.; Garland, pp. 111–112.
16. MS. letter, U. S. Grant to William Earl, March 3, 1849, Huntington Library; Silas Farmer, *The history of Detroit and Michigan; or, the metropolis illustrated; a chronological cyclopaedia of the past and present, including a full record of territorial days in Michigan, and the annals of Wayne County*, Detroit, 1884, p. 104.
17. Silas Farmer, *The history of Detroit and Michigan . . .*, Detroit, 1884, p. 104; Richardson, pp. 130–131; Palmer, pp. 225–226.
18. *Memoirs*, pp. 139–140.
19. Richardson, pp. 130, 132–133.
20. Ringwalt, pp. 90–91; Palmer, p. 633; Richardson, p. 138.
21. Palmer, p. 669.
22. Palmer, p. 225.
23. Tripler, pp. 103–104, 165–166.
24. Richardson, p. 133; Frederick Dent to General Jesup, May 7, 1850, Consolidated File, Office Quartermaster General, War Department Records, National Archives; Palmer, p. 552.

25. Richardson, pp. 131, 133; Tripler, p. 103.
26. Chandler anecdotes: *Memoirs*, p. 116; Richardson, pp. 134–135; *Zachariah Chandler: an outline sketch of his life and public services*, by Staff, *Detroit Post and Tribune*, Detroit, 1880, pp. 80–82.
27. Louise Garland anecdotes, Palmer, pp. 535–536; *History of Jefferson County, New York, with illustrations and biographical sketches of some of its prominent men and pioneers*, Philadelphia, 1878, p. 416.
28. U. S. Grant in Sons of Temperance: Richardson, p. 137; *History of Jefferson County . . .*, Philadelphia, 1878, pp. 403–404. Description of Sons of Temperance: *Constitution of the national, grand and subordinate divisions of the Sons of Temperance, of the United States: together with the by-laws and rules of order of the Grand division, of the state of New York . . .*, New York, 1848, pp. 18, 24, 28, 69, 89–90, 102 and back cover.
29. Garland, pp. 115–116; Walter Barlow Stevens, *Grant in St. Louis, from letters in the manuscript collection of William K. Bixby*, St. Louis, 1916, p. 60 (cited hereafter as "Stevens"); William S. Lewis, "Reminiscences of Delia B. Sheffield," *Washington Historical Quarterly* 15(1924)50 (cited hereafter as "Lewis, 'Sheffield' ").
30. *Ledger*, March 14, 1868; Galbreath, pp. 242–243.
31. William Taussig, *Personal recollections of General Grant*, St. Louis, 1903 (Missouri Historical Society, Publications, vol. 2, no. 3), pp. 2–3.
32. H. C. Hodges to William C. Church, January 7, 1897, Church Papers (cited hereafter as "Hodges (Church Papers)").
33. B. L. E. Bonneville anecdote: Moncure Daniel Conway, *The life of Thomas Paine; with a history of his literary, political and religious career in America, France, and England*, 2v., New York and London, 1892, vol. 2, pp. 278, 357, 393, 399, 403; Frank Smith, *Thomas Paine, liberator*, New York, 1938, p. 335; Hiram Martin Chittenden, *The American fur trade of the far West; a history of the pioneer trading posts and early fur companies of the Missouri Valley and the Rocky Mountains and of the overland commerce with Santa Fe*, 3v., New York, 1902, vol. 1, pp. 397–399, 428–432; Tripler, p. 108; Lewis, "Sheffield," p. 51.
34. Lewis, "Sheffield," pp. 51–52; Schenck quoted in Garland, p. 117; Church, *Grant*, p. 50.
35. Tripler, pp. 106–108.
36. Hodges (Church Papers); Lewis, "Sheffield," p. 52.
37. Garland, p. 117.
38. Church, *Grant*, p. 48; *Memoirs*, p. 117; Chauncey D. Griswold, *The Isthmus of Panama, and what I saw there*, New York, 1852, pp. 45–46, 132; Powell, Fourth regiment; Lewis, "Sheffield," p. 51.
39. *Memoirs*, pp. 117–118; Richardson, p. 140; John Haskell Kemble, *The Panama route, 1848–1869*, Berkeley and Los Angeles, 1943, p. 167.
40. Lewis, "Sheffield," p. 53; Burr, p. 113.

41. *Memoirs,* pp. 118–119; Church, *Grant,* p. 49; Richardson, p. 141.
42. Lewis, "Sheffield," pp. 54–55.
43. *Memoirs,* pp. 118–119; Tripler, p. 107; Lewis, "Sheffield," p. 53; Chauncey D. Griswold, *The Isthmus of Panama, and what I saw there,* New York, 1852, pp. 77, 80, 164.
44. *Memoirs,* p. 119.
45. Tripler, pp. 108–109; *Memoirs,* p. 119; Lewis, "Sheffield," p. 56.
46. Garland, p. 119.
47. Burr, p. 114; Richardson, p. 143.
48. *Memoirs,* pp. 119–120.
49. Richardson, p. 143; John Haskell Kemble, *The Panama route, 1848–1869,* Berkeley and Los Angeles, 1943, pp. 176–177.
50. Burr, p. 114; *Memoirs,* p. 119; Powell, Fourth regiment.
51. House documents, vol. 1, pt. 2, 32nd Congress, 2nd session, 1852–1853, Executive document 1, p. 89.

CHAPTER EIGHTEEN

1. Chants of gamblers: Evelyn Wells and Harry C. Peterson, *The '49ers,* Garden City, N. Y., 1949, p. 169; Hodges (Church Papers).
2. Walter H. Hebert, *Fighting Joe Hooker,* Indianapolis and New York, 1944, p. 39.
3. Biographical sketch of Henry Wager Halleck, by William E. Marsh, MS.; *Memoirs,* p. 121.
4. Richardson, pp. 144–145; Powell, Fourth regiment.
5. Richardson, p. 146; Ingalls interview, *New York Herald,* April 7, 1885; Lewis, "Sheffield," p. 59.
6. Burr, pp. 115–116.
7. General Michael R. Morgan, "Types and traditions of the old army," *Glimpses of the nation's struggle,* 6th series, Minneapolis, 1909.
8. Hodges (Church Papers); Lewis, "Sheffield," p. 62.
9. Grant to Osborne Cross, July 25, 1853, ALS; *Memoirs,* p. 123.
10. Ross Cox, *Adventures on the Columbia River, including the narrative of a residence of six years on the western side of the Rocky Mountains, among various tribes of Indians hitherto unknown; together with a journey across the American continent,* New York, 1832, p. 209.
11. *Memoirs,* pp. 122–124.
12. Lewis, "Sheffield," pp. 59–61.
13. Garland, p. 122.
14. Major General U. S. Grant, III, "General Grant, Pater Familias," MS.
15. Lewis, "Sheffield," p. 61.
16. Burr, p. 116; Richardson, p. 145.
17. Burr, p. 115; Lewis, "Sheffield," p. 59.
18. Grant quoted on predicaments: John Eaton, *Grant, Lincoln and the*

freedmen; reminiscences of the Civil war with special reference to the work for the contrabands and freedmen of the Mississippi Valley . . . in collaboration with Ethel Osgood Mason, New York, 1907, p. 99. McClellan's approach: E. D. Townsend to Col. Bonneville, May 23, 1853, Adjutant General's Correspondence, War Department Records, National Archives.

19. Lewis, "Sheffield," pp. 60–61.
20. *Memoirs*, p. 122; Burr, p. 115; article on Grant, *New York Tribune*, July 26, 1885, p. 10.
21. Chicken venture: Lewis, "Sheffield," p. 61.
22. Grant and McClellan incident: Hodges (Church Papers); Lewis, "Sheffield," p. 59; I. I. Stevens's report, House documents, vol. 18, pt. 1, 33rd Congress, 1st session, 1853–1854, Executive document 129, pp. 137–138; Grant to Osborne Cross, ALS, July 25, 1853.
23. Hodges (Church Papers).
24. Jefferson Davis to U. S. Grant, August 9, 1853, War Department Records, National Archives; Quartermaster General Consolidated Reports, November 26, 1853, War Department Records, National Archives.
25. Lewis, "Sheffield," p. 61.
26. Deshon rumor: *St. Louis Globe Democrat*, August 3, 1885.
27. Lewis, "Sheffield," p. 62; Richardson, pp. 146, 149–150; Burr, p. 116.
28. *Memoirs*, pp. 124–125; Grant quoted: *Cincinnati Commercial*, May 21, 1879.
29. W. I. Reed to William C. Church, ALS, August 25, 1909, Church Papers.
30. Granville O. Haller to William C. Church, ALS, March 17, 1897, Church Papers.
31. W. I. Reed to William C. Church, ALS, August 25, 1909, Church Papers.
32. Richardson, p. 146; Tripler, p. 109.
33. Grant sends home money: Emerson, *Midland Monthly*, September, 1897, p. 209. Visit to Knight's Ferry and Stockton: Richardson, p. 148; *Virginia Enterprise*, Nevada, July 12, 1868, quoted *Chicago Tribune*, August 6, 1868.
34. Emerson, *Midland Monthly*, August 1897, pp. 140–143.
35. Tripler, p. 111; Statement to author by Dr. Amos Christy, grandson of Mrs. Emma Davis.
36. Grant's communications with Cooper: Adjutant General's Papers, War Department Records, National Archives.
37. Hodges (Church Papers).
38. W. I. Reed to William C. Church, ALS, August 25, 1909, Church Papers.
39. Granville O. Haller to William C. Church, ALS, March 17, 1897, Church Papers.
40. Garland, p. 127.

41. U. S. Grant to E. D. Townsend, May 7, 1854, Adjutant General's Papers, War Department Records, National Archives. Notations by "A. A. G.," on letter U. S. Grant to Colonel S. Cooper, April 11, 1854, Consolidated File, Office Quartermaster General, War Department Records, National Archives.

42. Grant relieved of command: Notations by "A. A. G.," previous citation. Grant sends home accounts in trunk: N. E. Dawson interview, *New York Herald*, August 17, 1885, p. 6. Grant quoted on future: Richardson, p. 149.

43. Recommendations of Grant's superiors on resignation: Reverse side of letter Grant to Colonel S. Cooper, previous citation; Adjutant General's Papers, War Department Records, National Archives; Garland, pp. 125–126.

CHAPTER NINETEEN

1. Jesse Grant in *Shoe and Leather Reporter*, September, 1868, quoted in Marshall, pp. 72–73; *Ledger*, March 7, 1868; Helen Augusta Simpson, *Early records of Simpson families in Scotland, North Ireland, and eastern United States*, Philadelphia, 1927, p. 147.

2. Fred D. Grant, quoted in *Army and Navy Journal*, May 23, 1908, p. 1029.

3. Jesse Grant's reactions to U. S. Grant's resignation: Jefferson Davis to Hon. A. Ellison, June 7, 1854, and J. R. Grant to Hon. Jefferson Davis, June 21, 1845, with notations from William G. Freeman and "J. D." on back, War Department Records, National Archives. Hannah Grant quoted: interview Elizabeth Hare, *Philadelphia Times*, July 26, 1885. Jefferson Davis to J. R. Grant, June 28, 1864, War Department Records, National Archives.

4. Jesse Grant on son's resignation: *Ledger*, March 21, 1868. U. S. Grant on own resignation: *Memoirs*, p. 125; John Eaton, *Grant, Lincoln and the freedmen; reminiscences of the Civil war with special reference to the work for the contrabands and freedmen of the Mississippi Valley* . . . in collaboration with Ethel Osgood Mason, New York, 1907, p. 100.

5. Grant in San Francisco: Robert Allen quoted in Garland, pp. 128–129; Richard L. Ogden quoted "Grant" by William H. L. Barnes, *War Papers*, no. 19, read December 22, 1896, before the commandery of the state of California, military order of the loyal legion of the United States; Emerson, *Midland Monthly*, September 1897, pp. 210–211; Richardson, pp. 149–150.

6. Garland, p. 129.

7. Jesse stocks farm: *Ledger*, March 21, 1868. Grant as "happy man": *Around the world*, vol. 2, p. 451; Grant in conversation with Duke of Cambridge, William C. King and W. P. Derby, comp., *Camp-fire*

sketches and battle-field echoes of the rebellion, Springfield, Mass., 1887, p. 230.

8. Emma Dent Casey, "When Grant went a courtin'," typewritten MS.; Fred D. Grant quoted: Stevens, p. 33.

9. Ford and horses: Garland, p. 134. Grant and colliery: Charles Anderson Dana and James Harrison Wilson, *Life of Ulysses S. Grant, general of the armies of the United States,* Springfield, Mass., 1868, p. 38.

10. Emerson, *Midland Monthly,* September 1897, p. 213.

11. Mary Robinson quoted in *St. Louis Republican,* July 24, 1885; letter: "The U. S. Grant Cabin," from Mr. F. A. Weber to Mrs. Eugene Marsh, *Missouri Historical Review,* 15(1920–1921)414.

12. William Taussig, *Personal recollections of General Grant,* St. Louis, 1903 (Missouri Historical Society, Publications, vol. 2, no. 3) pp. 4–5.

13. J. B. Gazzam to M. L. Dalton, ALS, November 17, 1906, Missouri Historical Society.

14. Isaac H. Sturgeon in *St. Louis Republican,* July 24, 1885.

15. Mary Robinson quoted in *St. Louis Republican,* July 24, 1885.

16. Emma Dent Casey, "When Grant wooed and won Julia Dent," *Sunday Magazine,* clipping; letter: "The U. S. Grant Cabin," from Mr. F. A. Weber to Mrs. Eugene Marsh, *Missouri Historical Review,* 15(1920–1921)413.

17. Emerson, *Midland Monthly,* September 1897, pp. 212–213.

18. Richardson, pp. 156–157.

19. Emerson, *Midland Monthly,* September 1897, pp. 214–215.

20. Richardson, p. 156; page of anecdotes on Grant, *St. Louis Republican,* July 24, 1885.

21. Emerson, *Midland Monthly,* September 1897, pp. 216–217.

22. Church, *Grant,* p. 57.

23. Emma Dent Casey, "When Grant went a courtin'," typewritten MS.

24. *Washington Post,* July 24, 1885.

25. Beale quoted, Garland, pp. 137–138. Grant asks for Sully and Steele: Major John F. Lacey, "Major-General Frederick Steele," *Annals of Iowa,* 3rd s., 3(1897–1899)428. Sherman quoted, Church, *Grant,* p. 57.

26. *Ledger,* March 7, 1896.

27. *Memoirs,* p. 127.

28. *Ibid.*

29. Richardson, pp. 155–156.

30. Grant and the Frémonts, *St. Louis Republican,* August 24, 1885.

31. *Memoirs,* p. 128.

32. U. S. Grant to Jesse R. Grant, ALS, December 28, 1856, Rutgers College Library.

33. U. S. Grant to Jesse R. Grant, ALS, February 7, 1857, Rutgers College Library.

34. Emma Dent Casey, "When Grant went a courtin'," typewritten MS.; Richardson, p. 157; Cramer, pp. 4–5.

35. Cramer, pp. 3–4.
36. L. H. Freligh to W. R. Benjamin, March 19, 1910, Illinois Historical Library.
37. Marshall, p. 174; Cramer, p. 7.
38. Manumission paper of William Jones, given by U. S. Grant, March 29, 1859, Missouri Historical Society.
39. Cramer, pp. 5–6, 8.
40. Cramer, pp. 9–10.
41. Cramer, pp. 11–12.
42. Barron testimony, Belknap committee, quoted *Chicago Times*, March 30, 1876.
43. Emerson, *Midland Monthly*, October, 1897, pp. 317–318.
44. Longstreet interview, *New York Times*, July 24, 1885, p. 6.
45. Garland, p. 139.

CHAPTER TWENTY

1. Mary Robinson quoted in *St. Louis Republican*, July 24, 1885.
2. *St. Louis Republican*, 1858–1859.
3. Richardson, pp. 157–158.
4. *St. Louis Republican*, July 24, 1885.
5. *Memoirs*, p. 126; Richardson, p. 159.
6. Cramer, p. 14.
7. John A. Bryan, "The Blow family and their slave Dred Scott," Missouri Historical Society *Bulletin*, 4, no. 4(July 1948)223–231, and 5, no. 1(October 1948)19–33.
8. A. R. Corbin quoted, *Cincinnati Gazette*, August 8, 1885.
9. John A. Rawlins interview, *Hartford Post* in *Army and Navy Journal*, September 12, 1868, p. 53 (cited hereafter as "Rawlins interview").
10. Rawlins interview.
11. Richardson, pp. 159–160; Garland, p. 141.
12. Richardson, p. 163; *St. Louis Republican*, July 24, 1885; Marshall, p. 77; Garland, p. 142.
13. Richardson, p. 161; Garland, pp. 141–142.
14. Richardson, p. 161.
15. *St. Louis Republican*, July 30, 1885; Richardson, pp. 160–162.
16. Samuel Charles Webster, ed., *Mark Twain, business man*, Boston, 1946, p. 39.
17. Cramer, pp. 16–17.
18. Manumission paper of William Jones, given by U. S. Grant, March 29, 1859, Missouri Historical Society.
19. Emerson, *Midland Monthly*, September 1897, pp. 210–211.
20. Cramer, p. 20; Richardson, p. 162.
21. Cramer, pp. 17–18.
22. Garland, p. 143; Richardson, p. 166.

23. Richardson, pp. 164–165.
24. Mary Robinson quoted in *St. Louis Republican,* July 24, 1885; Cramer, p. 17.
25. William Taussig, *Personal recollections of General Grant,* St. Louis, 1903 (Missouri Historical Society, Publications, vol. 2, no. 3), pp. 5–7.
26 *St. Louis Republican,* July 24, 1885.
27. Cramer, p. 21; *Memoirs,* p. 126; *Around the world,* vol. 2, p. 446.
28. Emerson, *Midland Monthly,* October 1897, p. 323.
29. Garland, pp. 144–145.
30. Cramer, p. 18.
31. *St. Louis Republican,* July 24, 1885.
32. Cramer, p. 23.
33. Grant and theater: *New York Times,* July 26, 1885, p. 3. Grant renews County Engineer application: William Taussig, *Personal recollections of General Grant,* St. Louis, 1903 (Missouri Historical Society, Publications, vol. 2, no. 3), p. 7.
34. Richardson, p. 162.
35. Garland, p. 145.

CHAPTER TWENTY-ONE

1. James Grant Wilson, p. 18.
2. *Memoirs,* pp. 128–129.
3. Stevens, p. 60.
4. Garland, p. 149.
5. Galena correspondent in *St. Louis Globe Democrat,* July 24, 1885; Lawrence E. Blair, collector of interviews with Galenians, in letter to author, May 27, 1945 (cited hereafter as "Blair").
6. Richardson, p. 171.
7. Garland, p. 149; S. W. McMaster to Missouri Historical Society, October 20, 1903.
8. Blair.
9. Captain John M. Shaw, "The life and services of General John A. Rawlins," in *Glimpses of the nation's struggle,* 3rd series, St. Paul, 1893, p. 392 (cited hereafter as "Shaw").
10. Thomas L. Stitt, "Who put down the rebellion" in Military order of the loyal legion of the United States, *War papers read before the Indiana Commandery,* Indianapolis, 1898, p. 274.
11. Blair.
12. Anecdotes Jesse R. Grant, Jr.: Jesse Root Grant, *In the days of my father, General Grant,* in collaboration with Henry Francis Granger, New York and London, 1925, pp. 10–11. Anecdote "Buck" Grant: Frank Hatch Jones, *An address delivered by Frank H. Jones before the Chicago Historical Society at the celebration of the 100th anniversary of the birth of General Ulysses S. Grant, Thursday, April 27th, 1922,* Chicago, 1922, p. 17.

13. John Corson Smith, *Grant; an address delivered at the 23d annual reunion of the old soldiers' and sailors' association of Jo Daviess County, Turner hall, Galena, Ill. August 15, 1905, General John C. Smith, Commander, Department of Illinois, Grand army of the republic*, Chicago, 1905, pamphlet, p. 13. Julia Grant and children: Blair.

14. Fred Grant quoted: Stevens, p. 61. Name of hired girl: Julia Dent Grant to E. B. Washburne, from Burlington, New Jersey, 1864, Washburne Papers.

15. James Grant Wilson, p. 18.

16. Captain George Whitfield Pepper, *Personal recollections of Sherman's campaigns in Georgia and the Carolinas*, Zanesville, Ohio, 1866, pp. 391–392.

17. Ringwalt, pp. 23–24.

18. Shaw, p. 392; Rawlins interview.

19. Rawlins interview; Shaw, pp. 383, 385.

20. Rawlins quoted: John A. Rawlins to Emma (Miss Mary E. Hurlburt) ALS, November 16, 1863, Chicago Historical Society.

21. Rawlins anecdotes and biographical data: Rawlins interview; Rawlins family genealogy, MS, possession Louis A. Nack, Galena; Edward A. Rawlins interview with author, 1947; James Harrison Wilson, *The life of John A. Rawlins, lawyer, assistant adjutant-general, chief of staff, major general of volunteers, and secretary of war*, New York, 1916, pp. 30–38; Obituaries of Rawlins in *Chicago Tribune*, September 17, 1869, and *New York Sun*, September 8, 1869.

22. Rawlins interview; Augustus Louis Chetlain, *Recollections of seventy years*, Galena, 1899, p. 66 (cited hereafter as "Chetlain, *Seventy years*"); Galena correspondent in *St. Louis Globe Democrat*, July 21, 1885.

23. James Gillespie Blaine, *Twenty years of congress: from Lincoln to Garfield. With a review of the events which led to the political revolution of 1860*, 2v., Norwich, Conn., 1884, vol. 1, p. 151.

24. Rudolph Radama Von Abele, *Alexander H. Stephens, a biography*, New York, 1946, p. 181.

25. Grant quoted: *Memoirs*, p. 129; Richardson, pp. 174–175. Grant's Republican sympathies: Leigh Leslie, "Grant and Galena," *Midland Monthly*, September 1895, p. 199.

26. Rawlins interview. Description of Wide Awakes: *Weekly Northwestern Gazette*, August 6, 1860.

27. References to Maltby: *Weekly Northwestern Gazette*, February 13, 1860; Rawlins interview. Grant to committee: Rawlins interview; John Corson Smith, *Personal recollections of General Ulysses S. Grant; before U. S. Grant post, no. 28, G. A. R. Department of Illinois, Grand army of the republic, U. S. A. February 11, 1904*, Chicago, 1904, pamphlet.

28. *Memoirs*, p. 129.

29. Wide Awakes celebration: *Weekly Northwestern Gazette*, November 9, 1860. Grant at "jollification": Richardson, p. 175.
30. Rawlins interview.
31. Grant as "moderate Republican": Richardson, p. 175. Grant quoted: *Memoirs*, p. 129.
32. Richardson, p. 176.
33. Richardson, p. 175.
34. *Memoirs*, pp. 130–132.
35. Richardson, p. 175; Garland, p. 149; S. W. McMaster, *60 years on the upper Mississippi, my life and experiences*, Galena, Ill., 1895, pp. 193–194.
36. Shaw, p. 392; Richardson, pp. 172, 175; Blair. (Richardson's quotation from Rawlins must be evaluated in the light of the statement, in James Harrison Wilson, *The Life of John A. Rawlins* . . . , p. 50, that Richardson's biography of Grant "was corrected by Rawlins" before publication.)
37. Blair.
38. Galena correspondent: *St. Louis Globe Democrat*, July 24, 1885, Blair; Frederick D. Grant quoted in *Army and Navy Journal*, May 23, 1908, p. 1029.
39. *Janesville Gazette* (Wisconsin) quoted in *New York Tribune*, August 7, 1885, p. 5.
40. John H. Vincent, "The inner life of Ulysses S. Grant," *The Chautauquan; a weekly newsmagazine*, 30(October 1899–March 1900)634.
41. *Memoirs*, p. 132.
42. Galena correspondent in *St. Louis Globe Democrat*, July 24, 1885.

CHAPTER TWENTY-TWO

1. Richardson, p. 177.
2. "Gossip about General Grant," by "Swede," *Cincinnati Commercial*, November 16, 1868; Gaillard Hunt, comp., *Israel, Elihu and Cadwallader Washburn; a chapter in American biography*, New York, 1925, pp. 191–192.
3. Gaillard Hunt, comp., *Israel, Elihu and Cadwallader Washburn* . . . , New York, 1925, p. 172.
4. Jeanne Lebron in *Rockford Morning Star*, January 19, 1940.
5. Garland, p. 155; Richardson, p. 178; Jeanne Lebron in *Rockford Morning Star*, January 19, 1940; Chetlain, *Seventy years*, p. 69.
6. James Harrison Wilson, *The life of John A. Rawlins* . . . , New York, 1916, p. 48; Chetlain, *Seventy years*, p. 70.
7. *Weekly Northwestern Gazette*, November 13, 1860.
8. Richardson, pp. 178–179.
9. Richardson, p. 179.
10. *Report of the Adjutant General of the state of Illinois*, Revised by

Brigadier General J. W. Vance, Adjutant General, Vol. I (Containing reports for . . . 1861–1866), Springfield, 1886, p. 6.

11. Augustus Louis Chetlain, "Recollections of General U. S. Grant," *Military essays and recollections; War Papers* read before the commandery of the state of Illinois, military order of the loyal legion of the United States, Chicago, 1891, vol. 1, pp. 11–12 (cited hereafter as "Chetlain, 'Grant' ").
12. *Ibid.*
13. Richardson, p. 179.
14. *Memoirs*, p. 138.
15. Garland, p. 158.
16. *Ledger*, March 21, 1868.
17. William C. King and W. P. Derby, comp., *Camp-fire sketches and battle-field echoes of the rebellion*, Springfield, Mass., 1887, p. 119.
18. Burr, pp. 130–132.
19. Chetlain, "Grant," p. 12.
20. Richardson, p. 181.
21. Chetlain in *Society of the Army of the Cumberland, nineteenth reunion, Chicago, Illinois, 1888*, Cincinnati, 1889, p. 143.
22. Chetlain, *Seventy years*, p. 71.
23. *Ledger*, March 21, 1868.
24. *Memoirs*, p. 138; Richardson, p. 182.
25. John Moses, private secretary to Governor Yates, *Chicago Tribune*, March 20, 1886, p. 12.
26. Lucy Kittoe Chamberlain, "A short history of my family," MS.
27. *Report of the Adjutant General of the state of Illinois*, Revised by Brigadier General J. W. Vance, Adjutant General, Vol. I (Containing reports for . . . 1861–1866), Springfield, 1886, pp. 6–7.
28. Chetlain, *Seventy years*, pp. 72–73.
29. John Corson Smith, *Personal recollections of General Ulysses S. Grant . . .* , Chicago, 1904, pamphlet, p. 8.
30. Cramer, pp. 24–25.
31. Cramer, p. 24.
32. Cramer, p. 25.
33. *The history of Jo Daviess County, Illinois, containing a history of the county, its cities, towns, etc. A biographical directory of its citizens, war record of its volunteers in the late rebellion, etc.*, Chicago, 1878, pp. 376–378.
34. "Marking the grave of Do-Ne-Ho-Geh-Weh," *Buffalo Historical Society, Publications*, vol. 8, Buffalo, 1905, pp. 511–536; *The history of Jo Daviess County . . .* , Chicago, 1878, p. 515.

CHAPTER TWENTY-THREE

1. Clark Ezra Carr, *The Illini, a story of the prairies*, Chicago, 1905, p. 364.

2. *Memoirs*, p. 143; Cramer, p. 35.
3. *Memoirs*, p. 143.
4. George Fort Milton, *The eve of conflict; Stephen A. Douglas and the needless war*, Boston and New York, 1934, pp. 566–567.
5. Cramer, p. 27.
6. Cramer, pp. 29–30.
7. *Report of the Adjutant General of the state of Illinois*, Revised by Brigadier General J. W. Vance, Adjutant General, Vol. I (containing reports for . . . 1861–1866), Springfield, 1886, pp. 241–242; Thomas Mears Eddy, *The patriotism of Illinois. A record of the civil and military history of the state in the war for the Union, with a history of the campaigns in which Illinois soldiers have been conspicuous, sketches of distinguished officers, the roll of the illustrious dead, movements of the sanitary and Christian commissions*, 2v., Chicago, 1865–1866, vol. 1, pp. 103–105.
8. Gustave Philip Koerner, *Memoirs of Gustave Koerner, 1809–1896, life sketches written at the suggestion of his children*, ed., by Thomas J. McCormack, 2v., Cedar Rapids, Iowa, 1909, vol. 2, pp. 126–127 (cited hereafter as "Koerner").
9. Chetlain, "Grant," p. 13.
10. *Ledger*, March 21, 1868.
11. Chetlain, "Grant," pp. 13–14.
12. Cramer, pp. 27–28.
13. *Memoirs*, p. 139; Richardson, pp. 182–183.
14. John Moses, private secretary to Governor Yates, in *Chicago Tribune*, March 20, 1886, p. 12; James Harrison Wilson, *The life of John A. Rawlins* . . . , New York, 1916, p. 50; Galena correspondent in *Chicago Tribune*, April 6, and November 8, 1885.
15. Headley, p. 49.
16. Chetlain, "Grant," p. 14.
17. Garland, p. 164.
18. Cramer, pp. 32–33.
19. John Corson Smith, *Personal recollections of General Ulysses S. Grant* . . . , Chicago, 1904, pamphlet; Chetlain, "Grant," p. 15.
20. Koerner, vol. 2, p. 127.
21. Cramer, pp. 35–37.
22. *Weekly Northwestern Gazette*, May 10, 1861, dispatch from Camp Yates, May 4.
23. Chetlain, "Grant," p. 15.
24. *Memoirs*, pp. 140–142; Woodward, *Lyon*, pp. 248–254.
25. Koerner, vol. 2, pp. 145–146.
26. Chetlain, *Seventy years*, pp. 76–77.
27. Garland, p. 165; J. W. Wham interviewed, *New York Tribune*, September 27, 1885, p. 3.
28. Garland, p. 166.

29. Adjutant General's Papers, War Department Records, National Archives.

30. Cramer, pp. 38–39.

31. Garland, p. 167.

32. *Around the world,* vol. 2, pp. 214–215.

33. Garland, pp. 168–169; Ringwalt, p. 25.

34. *Ledger,* March 21, 1868.

35. *Ibid.*

36. Yates quoted in Headley, p. 50; Aaron Elliott in *St. Louis Republican,* August 22, 1885; J. W. Wham in *New York Tribune,* September 27, 1885, p. 3; Garland, pp. 169–170.

37. C. R. Perkins quoted in dispatch from Galena, November 7, 1885, *Chicago Tribune,* November 8; Chilton White quoted Garland, p. 169 as saying Dennison offered Grant command of the 12th Ohio Volunteers.

38. Captain George Whitfield Pepper, *Personal recollections of Sherman's campaigns in Georgia and the Carolinas,* Zanesville, Ohio, 1866, pp. 392–393.

39. J. W. Wham interviewed, *New York Tribune,* September 27, 1885, p. 3.

40. *St. Louis Republican,* August 22, 1885.

41. S. W. McMaster, *60 years on the upper Mississippi, my life and experiences . . . ,* Galena, Ill., 1895, pp. 194–195; Richardson, p. 186.

42. J. W. Wham interviewed, *New York Tribune,* September 27, 1885, p. 3; Garland, p. 172; Captain George Whitfield Pepper, *Personal recollections of Sherman's campaigns . . . ,* Zanesville, Ohio, 1866, p. 393. NOTE: Garland, p. 175, says, "On the 28th of June the Seventh District Regiment was mustered in and became the Twenty-first Illinois Volunteers."

Bibliography

BOOKS AND ARTICLES

Ammen, Daniel. *The old navy and the new . . . with an appendix of personal letters from General Grant*, Philadelphia, 1891.

—— "Recollections and letters of Grant," *North American Review*, 141(July–December 1885)361–373.

Anderson, Robert. *An artillery officer in the Mexican war, 1846-7; letters of Robert Anderson, captain 3rd artillery, U. S. A.*, New York and London, 1911.

Anjou, Gustave. *The Grant-Dent family*, privately printed, n.p., 1906.

Army and Navy Journal. September 5, 1863; September 12, 1868; January 24, 1891; June 13, 1903; May 2, 1908; May 23, 1908; November 14, 1908.

Around the world. See Young, John Russell.

Avery, A. C. "Life and character of Lieutenant-General D. H. Hill," *Southern Historical Society Papers*, vol. 21, Richmond, Va., 1893, pp. 110–150.

Aztec Club of 1847; report of a committee appointed by resolution adopted at the annual meeting, October, 1887, and continued in 1888, to October, 1889, Washington, 1890. Pamphlet.

Bailey, Thomas. "Diary of the Mexican war," *Indiana Magazine of History*, 14(1918)134–147.

[Ballentine, George]. *Adventures of an English soldier in the Mexican war*, New York, 1860.

Barbour, Philip Norbourne. *Journals of the late Brevet Major Philip Norbourne Barbour . . . and his wife, Martha Isabella Hopkins Barbour, written during the war with Mexico — 1846;* edited with foreword by Rhoda van Bibber Tanner Doubleday, New York and London, 1936.

Barnes, William Henry Linow. "Grant," *War Papers*, no. 19, read December 22, 1896, before Commandery of California, Military Order of the Loyal Legion of the United States.

Basso, Hamilton. *Beauregard, the great Creole*, New York, 1933.

Beatty, John. *Memoirs of a volunteer, 1861–1863*, ed. by Harvey S. Ford, New York, 1946.

Beers, W. H., and Co. *The history of Brown County, Ohio*, Chicago, 1883.

Belknap, William W. "The obedience and courage of the private soldier, and the fortitude of officers and men in field, in hospital, and in prison, with some incidents of the war," *War sketches and incidents,* as related by companions of the Iowa Commandery, Military Order of the Loyal Legion of the United States, vol. 1, Des Moines, 1893, pp. 157–171.

Blaine, James Gillespie. *Twenty years of congress: from Lincoln to Garfield. With a review of the events which led to the political revolution of 1860,* 2v., Norwich, Conn., 1884.

Brackett, Albert Gallatin. *General Lane's brigade in Central Mexico,* Cincinnati, 1854.

Bryan, John A. "The Blow family and their slave Dred Scott," Missouri Historical Society *Bulletin,* 4, no. 4(July 1948)223–231, and 5, no. 1 (October 1948)19–33.

Burr, Frank A. *A new, original and authentic record of the life and deeds of General U. S. Grant,* Boston, Mass., 1885.

Campbell, William Bowen. "Mexican war letters of Col. William Bowen Campbell, of Tennessee, written to Governor David Campbell, of Virginia, 1846–1847," *Tennessee Historical Magazine* 1(1915)129–167.

Carr, Clark Ezra. *The Illini, a story of the prairies,* Chicago, 1905.

Casey, Emma Dent. "When Grant wooed and won Julia Dent," *Sunday Magazine,* clipping.

Chamberlain, Lucy Kittoe. "A short history of my family," in Galena Correspondent, *Chicago Tribune,* January 27, 1877.

Chambers, Henry Edward. *Mississippi Valley beginnings; an outline of the early history of the earlier West,* New York and London, 1922.

Chandler, Zachariah. Staff, *Detroit Post and Tribune. Zachariah Chandler: an outline sketch of his life and public services,* Detroit, 1880.

Chaplin, Jeremiah, ed. *Words of our hero, Ulysses Grant,* with personal reminiscences by Jessie Benton Frémont, Boston, 1886.

Chetlain, Augustus Louis. "Recollections of General U. S. Grant," *Military essays and recollections;* papers read before the Commandery of the state of Illinois, Military Order of the Loyal Legion of the United States, vol. 1, Chicago, 1891, pp. 9–31.

—— *Recollections of seventy years,* Galena, Ill., 1899.

Chittenden, Hiram Martin. *The American fur trade of the far West; a history of the pioneer trading posts and early fur companies of the Missouri Valley and the Rocky Mountains and of the overland commerce with Santa Fe,* 3v., New York, 1902.

Church, William Conant. *Ulysses S. Grant and the period of national preservation and reconstruction,* New York, 1897.

Claiborne, John Francis Hamtramck. *Life and correspondence of John A. Quitman, major-general, U. S. A., and governor of the state of Mississippi,* 2v., New York, 1860.

Coates, Foster. "The courtship of General Grant," *Ladies' Home Journal,* October, 1890, p. 4.

Conrad, Bryan. *See* Eckenrode.

Conway, Moncure Daniel. *The life of Thomas Paine; with a history of his literary, political and religious career in America, France, and England,* 2v., New York and London, 1892.

Coppée, Henry. *Life and services of Gen. U. S. Grant,* New York, 1868.

Cox, Ross. *Adventures on the Columbia River, including the narrative of a residence of six years on the western side of the Rocky Mountains, among various tribes of Indians hitherto unknown: together with a journey across the American continent,* New York, 1832.

Cramer, Jesse Grant, ed. *Letters of Ulysses S. Grant to his father and his youngest sister, 1857–78,* New York and London, 1912.

Dana, Charles Anderson, and Wilson, James Harrison. *Life of Ulysses S. Grant, general of the armies of the United States,* Springfield, Mass., 1868.

Darby, John Fletcher. *Personal recollections of many prominent people whom I have known, and of events — especially of those relating to the history of St. Louis — during the first half of the present century,* St. Louis, 1880.

Deas, George. "Reminiscences of the campaign of the Rio Grande," *Historical Magazine,* January 1870, pp. 19–22, February 1870, pp. 99–103; April, 1870, pp. 236–238; May 1870, pp. 311–316.

Derby, W. P. *See* King.

Do-Ne-Ho-Geh-Weh. "Marking the grave of Do-Ne-Ho-Geh-Weh," Buffalo Historical Society, *Publications,* vol. 8, Buffalo, 1905, pp. 511–536.

Eaton, John. *Grant, Lincoln and the freedmen; reminiscences of the Civil war with special reference to the work of the contrabands and freedmen of the Mississippi Valley* . . . in collaboration with Ethel Osgood Mason, New York, 1907.

Eckenrode, Hamilton James, and Conrad, Bryan. *James Longstreet, Lee's war horse,* Chapel Hill, 1936.

Eddy, Thomas Mears. *The patriotism of Illinois. A record of the civil and military history of the state in the war for the Union, with a history of the campaigns in which Illinois soldiers have been conspicuous, sketches of distinguished officers, the roll of the illustrious dead, movements of the sanitary and Christian commissions,* 2v., Chicago, 1865–1866.

Eliot, Ellsworth. *West Point in the Confederacy,* New York, 1941.

Elliott, Charles Winslow. *Winfield Scott, the soldier and the man,* New York, 1937.

Emerson, John W. "Grant's life in the West and his Mississippi Valley campaigns," *Midland Monthly Magazine,* 6(July–December 1896)291–303, 387–399, 488–499; 7(January–June 1897)30–41, 138–147, 218–226, 316–329, 430–438, 497–501; 8(July–December 1897)3–9, 138–143, 206–220, 316–325, 451–460, 494–504.

English soldier. See Ballentine.

Everts, Louis H. *History of Clermont County, Ohio,* Philadelphia, 1880.

Ewell, Richard Stoddert. *The making of a soldier; letters of General*

R. S. Ewell, arranged and edited by Captain Percy Gatling Hamlin, Richmond, Va., 1935.

Farmer, Silas. *The history of Detroit and Michigan; or, the metropolis illustrated; a chronological cyclopaedia of the past and present, including a full record of territorial days in Michigan, and the annals of Wayne County,* Detroit, 1884.

Farragut, Loyall. *The life of David Glasgow Farragut, first admiral of the United States navy, embodying his journal and letters,* New York, 1879.

Flower, Frank Abial. *Life of Matthew Hale Carpenter. A view of the honor and achievements that, in the American republic, are the fruits of well-directed ambition and persistent industry,* Madison, Wis., 1884.

Freeman, Douglas Southall. *R. E. Lee, a biography,* New York and London, 4v., 1934–1935.

French, Samuel Gibbs. *Two wars: an autobiography of Gen. Samuel G. French,* Nashville, Tenn., 1901.

Fry, James B. "An acquaintance with Grant," *North American Review,* 141(July–December 1885)540–552.

Furber, George C. *The twelve months volunteer; or, journal of a private, in the Tennessee regiment of cavalry, in the campaign, in Mexico, 1846–7,* Cincinnati, 1848.

Galbreath, C. B. "Centennial anniversary of the birth of Ulysses S. Grant," *Ohio Archaeological and Historical Quarterly,* 31(1922)221–288.

Garland, Hamlin. *Ulysses S. Grant; his life and character,* New York, 1898.

[Giddings, Luther]. *Sketches of the campaign in northern Mexico, in eighteen hundred forty-six and seven.* By an officer of the First regiment of Ohio volunteers, New York, 1853.

Gould, John Mead. *History of the First–Tenth–Twenty-ninth Maine regiment. In service of the United States from May 3, 1861, to June 21, 1866,* Portland, 1871.

Government Documents.

   Congressional Globe, appendix, February 11, 1847.

   House documents, vol. 2, 30th Congress, 1st session, 1847–1848, Executive document 8.

   House documents, vol. 3, 30th Congress, 1st session, 1847–1848, Executive document 17.

   House documents, vol. 7, 30th Congress, 1st session, 1847–1848, Executive document 60.

   Senate documents, vol. 1, 30th Congress, 1st session, 1847–1848, Executive document 1.

   House documents, vol. 1, pt. 2, 32nd Congress, 2nd session, 1852–1853, Executive document 1.

   I. I. Stevens's report, House documents, vol. 18, pt. 1, 33rd Congress, 1st session, 1853–1854, Document 129.

Grant, Jesse Root. *In the days of my father, General Grant,* in collaboration with Henry Francis Granger, New York and London, 1925.

Grant, Ulysses Simpson. *Personal memoirs of U. S. Grant,* 2v. in 1, New York, 1894.

Grant to Lowe, see *Chicago Tribune.*

Greeley, Horace. *The American conflict: a history of the great rebellion in the United States of America, 1860–['65],* 2v., Hartford, 1864–1866.

Griswold, Chauncey D. *The Isthmus of Panama, and what I saw there,* New York, 1852.

Halleck, Henry W. Recollections of Gen. Henry W. Halleck in 1847–49, *Overland,* 9(July 1872)94. *See also* Marsh MS.

—— U. S. Army telegrams received by Maj. Gen. Halleck, Washington, War Department Printing Office, 1877, 5v. in 6.

—— Telegrams sent by Maj. Gen. Halleck, Washington, War Department Printing Office, 1877, 4v.

—— The character of Gen. Halleck's Administration, S. M. Quincy, Military Historical Society of Massachusetts Papers, vol. 2.

Hamilton, Charles S. "Memoirs of the Mexican war," *Wisconsin Magazine of History,* 14(1930–1931)63–92.

—— "Reminiscences of the old army forty years ago," *War papers read before the Commandery of the state of Wisconsin, Military Order of the Loyal Legion of the United States — Wisconsin Commandery,* Milwaukee, 1891, pp. 31–46.

Hamilton, Holman. *Zachary Taylor, soldier of the republic,* Indianapolis, 1941.

Harney, General. "General Harney," *Journal of the United States Cavalry Association,* March 1890, Fort Leavenworth, Kansas, pp. 1–8.

[Harrison, Frank]. *Anecdotes and reminiscences of Gen'l U. S. Grant,* comp. by an old soldier, New York, 1885.

Headley, Phineas Camp. *The life and campaigns of Lieut.-Gen. U. S. Grant, from his boyhood to the surrender of Lee,* New York, 1868.

Hebert, Walter H. *Fighting Joe Hooker,* Indianapolis and New York, 1944.

Henry, William Seaton. *Campaign sketches of the war with Mexico,* New York, 1847.

The "high private," with a full and exciting history of the New York volunteers . . . including the mysteries and miseries of the Mexican war, by "Corporal of the guard," New York, 1848.

Hill, Daniel H. "The real Stonewall Jackson," *Century Magazine,* 47 (November 1893–April 1894)623–628.

Historical sketches. Historical Society of Montgomery County, Pennsylvania, vol. 5, Norristown, 1925.

History of Jefferson County, New York, with illustrations and biographical sketches of some of its prominent men and pioneers, Philadelphia. 1878.

History of Jo Daviess County, Illinois, containing a history of the county, its cities, towns, etc. A biographical directory of its citizens, war records of its volunteers in the late rebellion, etc., Chicago, 1878.

History of Portage County, Ohio, Chicago, 1885.

Hitchcock, Ethan Allen. *Fifty years in camp and field; diary of Major-General Ethan Allen Hitchcock*, ed. by W. A. Croffut, New York and London, 1909.

Howard, Oliver Otis. "General George H. Thomas," *Personal recollections of the war of the rebellion*, ed. by James Grant Wilson and Titus Munson Coan, New York, 1891, pp. 285–302.

Howe, Henry. *Historical collections of Ohio*, 3v. in 2, Columbus, 1889–1891.

Hunt, Gaillard, comp. *Israel, Elihu and Cadwallader Washburn; a chapter in American biography*, New York, 1925.

Hyde, William, and Conard, Howard L., eds. *Encyclopedia of the history of St. Louis, a compendium of history and biography for ready reference*, 4v., New York, 1899.

Jackson, Mary Anna. *Life and letters of General Thomas J. Jackson (Stonewall Jackson)*, New York, 1892.

Jarvis, N. S. "An army surgeon's notes of frontier service — Mexican war. Extracts from the diary of his father, contributed by Captain N. S. Jarvis," *Journal of the Military Service Institution of the United States*, 40(1907)435–452; 41(1907)90–105.

Jones, Frank Hatch. *An address delivered by Frank H. Jones before the Chicago Historical Society at the celebration of the 100th anniversary of the birth of General Ulysses S. Grant, Thursday, April 27th, 1922*, Chicago, 1922.

Kearny, Thomas. *General Philip Kearny, battle soldier of five wars, including the conquest of the West by General Stephen Watts Kearny*, preface by Frank Monaghan, New York, 1937.

Kemble, John Haskell. *The Panama route, 1848–1869*, Berkeley and Los Angeles, 1943.

Kenly, John Reese. *Memoirs of a Maryland volunteer. War with Mexico, in the years 1846–7–8*, Philadelphia 1873.

Keyes, Erasmus Darwin. *Fifty years' observation of men and events, civil and military*, New York, 1885.

King, William C., and Derby, W. P. *Camp-fire sketches and battle-field echoes of the rebellion*, Springfield, Mass., 1887.

Koerner, Gustave Philip. *Memoirs of Gustave Koerner, 1809–1896, life-sketches written at the suggestion of his children*, ed. by Thomas J. McCormack, 2v., Cedar Rapids, Ia., 1909.

Lacey, John F. "Major-General Frederick Steele," *Annals of Iowa*, 3rd s., 3(1897–1899)424–438.

Leslie, Leigh, "Grant and Galena," *Midland Monthly Magazine*, 4(July–December, 1895)195–215.

Lewis, Lloyd. *Sherman, fighting prophet*, New York, 1932.

Lewis, William S. "Reminiscences of Delia B. Sheffield," *Washington Historical Quarterly*, 15(1924)49–62.

Long, Armistead Lindsay. *Memoirs of Robert E. Lee; his military and personal history . . . Together with incidents relating to his private life*, collected and ed. with the assistance of Marcus J. Wright, London, 1886.

Longstreet, Helen Dortch. *Lee and Longstreet at high tide; Gettysburg in the light of the official records*, Gainesville, Ga., 1904.

Lyman, Theodore. *Meade's headquarters, 1863–1865; letters of Colonel Theodore Lyman from the wilderness to Appomattox*, selected and ed. by George R. Agassiz, Boston, 1922.

McCall, George Archibald. *Letters from the frontiers, written during a period of thirty years' service in the army of the United States*, Philadelphia, 1868.

McClellan, George Brinton. *The Mexican war diary of George B. McClellan*, ed. by William Starr Myers, Princeton, 1917.

McElroy, Robert McNutt. *Jefferson Davis; the unreal and the real*, 2v., New York and London, 1937.

[McMaster, John Bach]. *The life, memoirs, military career and death of General U. S. Grant*, Philadelphia, 1885.

McMaster, S. W. *60 years on the upper Mississippi, my life and experiences*, Galena, Ill., 1895.

McSherry, Richard. *El Puchero; or, a mixed dish from Mexico, embracing General Scott's campaign, with sketches of military life, in field and camp, of the character of the country, manners and ways of the people, etc.*, Philadelphia, 1850.

Mahan, D. H. "The cadet life of Grant and Sherman" (letter, March 8, 1866), *Army and Navy Journal*, March 31, 1866, p. 507.

Mahan, D. H. "Professor D. H. Mahan" (Obituary), *Army and Navy Journal*, October 7, 1871, pp. 119 120.

Marshall, Edward Chauncey. *The ancestry of General Grant, and their contemporaries*, New York, 1869.

Marshall, W. R. "Reminiscences of General U. S. Grant," *Glimpses of the nation's struggle*, 1st series, St. Paul, 1887, pp. 89–106.

Maury, Dabney Herndon. *Recollections of a Virginian in the Mexican, Indian, and Civil wars*, New York, 1894.

Meade, George Gordon, ed. *The life and letters of George Gordon Meade, major-general United States army*, 2v., New York, 1913.

Memoirs. See Grant.

Milton, George Fort. *The eve of conflict; Stephen A. Douglas and the needless war*, Boston and New York, 1934.

Morgan, Michael R. "Types and traditions of the old army," *Glimpses of the nation's struggle*, 6th series, Minneapolis, 1909.

Nichols, Roy Franklin. *Franklin Pierce, Young Hickory of the Granite Hills*, Philadelphia and London, 1931.

Niles' National Register, 1846–1848.

O'Ferrall, Simon Ansley. *A ramble of six thousand miles through the United States of America*, London, 1832.

Oswandel, J. Jacob. *Notes of the Mexican war 1846–47–48.* Comprising incidents, adventures and everyday proceedings and letters while with the United States army in the Mexican war. Philadelphia, 1885.

Palmer, Friend. *Early days in Detroit; papers written by General Friend Palmer, of Detroit, being his personal reminiscences of important events and descriptions of the city for over eighty years*, Detroit, 1906.

Pemberton, John Clifford. *Pemberton, defender of Vicksburg*, with a foreword by Douglas Southall Freeman, Chapel Hill, 1942.

Pepper, George Whitfield. *Personal recollections of Sherman's campaigns in Georgia and the Carolinas*, Zanesville, Ohio, 1866.

Peterson, Harry C. *See* Wells.

Piatt, Donn. *General George H. Thomas, a critical biography;* with concluding chapters by Henry V. Boynton, Cincinnati, 1893.

Pickett, George Edward. *The heart of a soldier as revealed in the intimate letters of Genl. George E. Pickett*, New York, 1913.

Pickett, La Salle Corbell. "General George E. Pickett," *Southern Historical Society Papers*, vol. 24, Richmond, 1896, pp. 151–154.

Poore, Benjamin Perley. *The life and public services of Ambrose E. Burnside — soldier, — citizen, — statesman*, Providence, 1882.

—— *Perley's reminiscences of sixty years in the national metropolis*, 2v., Philadelphia, 1886.

—— and Tiffany, O. H. *Life of U. S. Grant*, Philadelphia, 1885.

Porter, Horace. *Campaigning with Grant*, New York, 1897.

Prince, Ezra M. "The Fourth Illinois Infantry in the war with Mexico," *Transactions of the Illinois State Historical Society . . . 1906* (Publication no. 11, Illinois State Historical Library), Springfield, 1906, pp. 172–187.

Proceedings of Crocker's Iowa Brigade, at the third reunion, held at Iowa City, Iowa, September 23d and 24th, 1885, Iowa City, 1885.

Quaife, Milo Milton, comp. and ed. *The development of Chicago, 1674–1914, shown in a series of contemporary original narratives*, Chicago, 1916.

Rawlins, John A. Interview of Rawlins from the *Hartford Post. Army and Navy Journal*, September 12, 1868, p. 53. *See also* Shaw, Wilson.

Reavis, Logan Uriah. *The life and military services of Gen. William Selby Harney*, St. Louis, 1878.

Reid, Whitelaw. *Ohio in the war: her statesmen, her generals, and soldiers*, 2v., Cincinnati and New York, 1868.

Reilly James. "An artilleryman's story," *Journal of the Military Service Institution of the United States*, 33 (July–November, 1903) 438–446.

Report of the Adjutant General of the state of Illinois, revised by Brigadier General J. W. Vance, adjutant general, vol. 1, Springfield, 1886.

[Rice, Allen Thorndike]. "Sherman on Grant," *North American Review*, 142 (January–June 1886) 111–113.

Richardson, Albert Deane. *A Personal history of Ulysses S. Grant*, Hartford, Conn., 1868.

Richardson, James Daniel, comp. *A compilation of the messages and papers of the presidents, 1789–1897*, 10v., Washington, 1900.

Ringwalt, John Luther. *Anecdotes of General Ulysses S. Grant, illustrating his military and political career and his personal traits*, Philadelphia, 1886.

Ripley, Roswell Sabine. *The war with Mexico*, 2v., New York, 1849.

[Robertson, John Blount]. *Reminiscences of a campaign in Mexico; by a member of the "Bloody-First." Preceded by a short sketch of the history and condition of Mexico from her revolution down to the war with the United States*, Nashville, 1849.

Sandburg, Carl. *Abraham Lincoln, the prairie years*, 2v., New York, 1926.

Sanderson, see *New York Times*.

Scammon, E. Parker. "A chapter of the Mexican war," *Magazine of American History*, 14(July–December 1885)562–576.

Schaff, Morris. *The spirit of old West Point, 1858–1862*, Boston and New York, 1907.

Scharf, John Thomas. *History of Saint Louis city and county, from the earliest periods to the present day*, 2v., Philadelphia, 1883.

Scott, Winfield. *Memoirs of Lieut.-General Scott, LL.D.*, 2v., New York, 1864.

[Scribner, Benjamin F.]. *Camp life of a volunteer. A campaign in Mexico, or a glimpse at life in camp*, by "One who has seen the elephant," Philadelphia, 1847.

Sedgwick, John. *Correspondence of John Sedgwick, major-general*, 2v., New York, 1902–1903.

Sedgwick Memorial Association; 6th army corps, Spottsylvania Court House, Va., May 11, 12 and 13, 1887, Philadelphia, 1887.

Semmes, Raphael. *Service afloat and ashore during the Mexican war*, Cincinnati, 1851.

Seymour, Truman. "Politics and West Point," *Army and Navy Journal*, September 24, 1864, p. 70.

Shaw, John M. "The life and services of General John A. Rawlins," *Glimpses of the nation's struggle*, 3rd series, St. Paul, 1893, pp. 381–403.

Simpson, Helen Augusta. *Early records of Simpson families in Scotland, North Ireland, and eastern United States*, Philadelphia, 1927.

Smith, Ephraim Kirby. *To Mexico with Scott; letters of Captain E. Kirby Smith to his wife*, prepared for the press by his daughter, Emma Jerome Blackwood, Cambridge, Mass., 1917.

Smith, Frank. *Thomas Paine, liberator*, New York, 1938.

Smith, Gustavus W. *Company "A," corps of engineers, U. S. A., 1846–'48, In the Mexican war*, Battalion Press, 1896.

Smith, John Corson. *Grant; an address delivered at the 23d annual reunion of the Old Soldiers' and Sailors' Association of Jo Daviess County, Turner Hall, Galena, Ill., August 15, 1905*, Chicago, 1905.

Smith, John Corson. *Personal recollections of General Ulysses S. Grant; before U. S. Grant post, no. 28, G. A. R., Department of Illinois, Grand Army of the Republic,* . . . *February 11, 1904,* Chicago, 1904.

Smith, Justin Harvey. *The war with Mexico,* 2v., New York, 1919.

Society of the Army of the Cumberland, *fourth re-union, Cleveland, 1870,* Cincinnati, 1870.

―― *fifth reunion, Detroit, 1871,* Cincinnati, 1872.

―― *ninth reunion, Utica, New York, 1868–1875,* Cincinnati, 1876.

―― *fifteenth reunion, Cincinnati, Ohio, 1883,* Cincinnati, 1884.

―― *nineteenth reunion, Chicago, Illinois, 1888,* Cincinnati, 1889.

Society of the Army of the Tennessee. *Report of the Proceedings of the fifth annual meeting of the Society of the Army of the Tennessee, held at Cincinnati, Ohio, April 6th and 7th, 1871,* Cincinnati, 1872.

Sons of Temperance. *Constitution of the national, grand and subordinate divisions of the Sons of Temperance, of the United States: together with the by-laws and rules of order of the Grand division, of the state of New York,* New York, 1848.

Sorrel, G. Moxley. *Recollections of a Confederate staff officer,* New York and Washington, 1905.

Stevens, Walter Barlow. *Grant in St. Louis, from letters in the manuscript collection of William K. Bixby,* St. Louis, 1916.

Stewart, George Rippey. *John Phoenix, Esq., the veritable Squibob, a life of Captain George H. Derby, U. S. A.,* New York, 1937.

Stitt, Thomas L. "Who put down the rebellion?" *War papers* read before the Indiana Commandery, Military Order of the Loyal Legion of the United States, Indianapolis, 1898, pp. 273–277.

Taussig, William. *Personal recollections of General Grant,* St. Louis, 1903. (Missouri Historical Society, Publications, vol. 2, no. 3.)

Taylor, Zachary. *Letters of Zachary Taylor, from the battle-fields of the Mexican war; reprinted from the originals in the collection of Mr. William K. Bixby, of St. Louis, Mo.,* Rochester, N. Y., 1908.

Thomas, Horace H. "What I saw under a flag of truce," *Military essays and recollections,* papers read before the Commandery of the state of Illinois, Military Order of the Loyal Legion of the United States, vol. 1, Chicago, 1891, pp. 135–146.

Thorpe, Thomas Bangs. *Our army on the Rio Grande. Being a short account of the important events transpiring from the time of the removal of the "Army of occupation" from Corpus Christi, to the surrender of Matamoros,* Philadelphia, 1846.

Tripler, Eunice. *Eunice Tripler: some notes of her personal recollections,* New York, 1910.

U. S. Military Academy, West Point. *Register of graduates and former cadets, United States Military Academy,* New York, 1946.

Van Horne, Thomas Budd. *The life of Major-General George H. Thomas,* New York, 1882.

Villard, Oswald Garrison. *John Brown, 1800–1859*, Boston and New York, 1910.

Vincent, John H. "The inner life of Ulysses S. Grant," *The Chautauquan; a weekly newsmagazine*, 30(October 1899–March 1900)634–638.

Von Abele, Rudolph Radama. *Alexander H. Stephens, a biography*, New York, 1946.

"War memories" [by a Surgeon of the 16th Iowa Infantry], *Iowa Historical Record*, 7–9(1891–1893)375–382.

Webb, Henry W. "The story of Jefferson Barracks," *New Mexico Historical Review*, 21(1946)185–208.

Weber, F. A. "The U. S. Grant cabin (letter), *Missouri Historical Review*, 15(1920–1921)413–415.

Wells, Evelyn, and Peterson, Harry C. *The '49ers*, Garden City, N. Y., 1949.

White, Henry Alexander. *Stonewall Jackson*, Philadelphia, 1909.

Wilcox, Cadmus Marcellus. *History of the Mexican war*, ed. by his niece, Mary Rachel Wilcox, Washington, 1892.

Wilson, James Grant. *The life and public services of Ulysses Simpson Grant, general of the United States army, and twice president of the United States*, New York, 1885.

Wilson, James Harrison. *The life of John A. Rawlins, lawyer, assistant adjutant-general, chief of staff, major general of volunteers, and secretary of war*, New York, 1916.

Wood, Oliver Ellsworth. *The West Point scrap book: a collection of stories, songs, and legends of the United States Military Academy*, New York, 1871.

Woodman, Edwin E. "Death and dishonor," *Glimpses of the nation's struggle*, 5th series, St. Paul, 1903, pp. 301–313.

Woodward, Ashbel. *Life of General Nathaniel Lyon*, Hartford, 1862.

[Woodward, J. J.]. "Sickness and mortality of the army," *Army and Navy Journal*, October 10, 1863, pp. 102–103.

Young, John Russell. *Around the world with General Grant: a narrative of the visit of General U. S. Grant, ex-president of the United States, to various countries in Europe, Asia, and Africa, in 1877, 1878, 1879*, 2v., New York, 1879.

—— *Men and memories; personal reminiscences*, ed. by his wife, May D. Russell Young, 2v., New York, 1901.

MANUSCRIPTS

Among the War Department Records in the National Archives, the Papers and Correspondence of the Adjutant General, the Consolidated File of the Quartermaster, Post and Regimental Reports, and the Papers of the United States Military Academy provided most information. The Post Order Books of the Academy are preserved at West Point.

Of many scattered manuscripts consulted, a few need specific mention here: Emma Dent Casey's typescript, "When Grant went a courtin'," in the Missouri Historical Society; the U. S. Grant Account Book, 1839–1843, in the Huntington Library; the Diary of Joshua E. Jackson, in the Illinois State Historical Library; the Diary of Henry M. Judah, in the Library of Congress; William H. Powell's "History of the organization and movements of the Fourth Regiment of Infantry, 1871," in the National Archives; for family history: Major General U. S. Grant III, "General Grant, Pater Familias," MS. in possession of General Grant, Washington, D. C., and the Rawlins family genealogy in the possession of Louis A. Nack, Galena; MSS. by James E. Kelly, "the Notebook of James Edward Kelly," and by William E. Marsh, "Biographical Sketch of Henry Wager Halleck."

NEWSPAPERS

The most important of the newspaper articles are those in the files of the *American Star*, Mexico City, and the *North American*, Mexico City, for the years 1847–1848; the "Grant to Lowe" letter, August 14, 1885, and the John Moses interview, March 20, 1886, in the *Chicago Tribune*; Lucy Kittoe Chamberlain, "A Short History of My Family," Galena Correspondent in *Chicago Tribune*, January 27, 1877; the series of articles on "The early life of Gen. Grant" by his father, March 7, 14, and 21, 1868, in the *New York Ledger*; the Longstreet, McLaws, and Newman interviews, all July 24, 1885, and the James S. Sanderson article, July 30, 1885, in the *New York Times*; the interviews of W. T. Sherman, August 2, 1885, and J. W. Wham, September 27, 1885, in the *New York Tribune*; "Jackson at West Point," by "P" (clippings, 1877–1878), and the Elizabeth Hare interview (July 26, 1885), *Philadelphia Times*; and the articles in the *St. Louis Globe Democrat* and the *St. Louis Republican* on Grant at the time of his death, especially the July 24, 1885, issue of the *St. Louis Republican*.

Index

Index

can people, 203–204; advances on Mexico City, 204–206; report of Battle of Cerro Gordo, 212; quarrel with Polk, 212–213; at Jalapa, 231; quoted on Mexican people, 215; at Puebla, 217, 223–224; squabbles with Trist, 218; advances from Puebla, 224, 225; on Valley of Mexico, 225; plans assault on Mexico City, 226–227, 237, 244, 245, 249; on Lee at Contreras, 229; on victory at Contreras, 231; at Battle of Churubusco, 232, 233, 234; negotiates armistice with Santa Anna, 236, 237; on fighting at Molino del Rey, 242; enters Mexico City, 255–257; Mexican campaign summarized, 256; sends Santa Anna's wife to Guadalupe, 259; treatment of prisoners, 265; circumvents Buchanan at Aztec Club, 268; urged as Presidential nominee, 270, 274; on annexation of Mexico, 272; removed from command by Polk, 273–274; defeated by Pierce for Presidency, 314

Secession, of South from Union, 391–392, 395; Grant's views on, 388–389

Second Artillery, moves to Rio Grande, 133; in attack on Mexico City, 250, 252

Second Dragoons, at Battle of Palo Alto, 144; in advance on Mexico City, 226

Second Infantry, at Madison Barracks, 109; at siege of Vera Cruz, 199; at Contreras, 229

Secretary, steamer at Vera Cruz, 194–195

Sedgwick, John, quoted on Taylor's forces, 133; on Mexican Catholicism, 157–158; joins Second Artillery, 173; in action at Churubusco, 233; on desertions after Molino del Rey, 241; in attack on Mexico City, 251; in Mexico City, 266; on peace with Mexico, 273; on Pillow's court of inquiry, 273; in Kansas agitation, 348

Semmes, Lieutenant Raphael, quoted on siege of Vera Cruz, 201; on departure of troops from Puebla, 225;

on Mexican women at Lake Chalco, 226; on Scott's approach to Mexico City, 227; on Lee, 229; at Churubusco, 233; at capture of Mexico City, 250, 253, 255

Seventh Infantry, Grant transferred to, 128; at Rio Grande, 141; at Contreras, 229

Seymour, Thomas, at West Point with Grant, 82

Sharp, Dr. Alexander, 355

Sharp, Ellen Dent, sister of Julia Dent Grant, 103, 104, 108, 171, 283, 339, 355; rides with Grant, 104–105, 106; marriage, 341

Shaw, John M., 379; on Grant at Galena, 374, 389

Sheean, David, law partner of Rawlins at Galena, 381, 395

Sheffield, Delia, 294, 299, 300, 301, 302, 313; quoted on Grant, 298, 317–318, 322; keeps house with husband for Grant at Vancouver, 315–316

Sheffield, Sergeant, 315

Sherman, William Tecumseh, at West Point, 62, 69, 76, 86, 91, 92; sails for California, 183; quoted on Buell, 263; resigns from Army, 321; meeting with Grant, 347–348

Shields, General James, joins Scott's Mexican expedition, 163–164, 192; at Tampico, 194; in action at Churubusco, 233; wounded at Chapultepec, 245; announces senatorial candidacy, 270

Shurlds, Amanda. *See* Dent, Amanda Shurlds

Shurlds, Edward, 342

Shurlds, Eliza. *See* Barnard, Eliza Shurlds

Sibley, Major E. S., post quartermaster at Detroit, 289

Sickness, in American forces in Mexican War, 162–163, 170, 223, 280; cholera epidemic at Panama, 301–303, 306

Sigersons, neighbors of Dents at White Haven, 296

Simons, James, assistant regimental surgeon, 222